323.3

4²⁵

PROBLEMS OF CITY LIFE

PROBLEMS OF CITY LIFE

A Study in Urban Sociology

BY

MAURICE R. DAVIE

Associate Professor of the Science of Society
in Yale University

NEW YORK
JOHN WILEY & SONS, Inc.
London: CHAPMAN & HALL, Limited
1932

Copyright, 1932
By Maurice R. Davie

Printed in the U. S. A.

THE HADDON CRAFTSMEN
CAMDEN, N. J.

ACKNOWLEDGMENTS

I AM deeply indebted to Professor James Elbert Cutler, head of the department of Sociology at Western Reserve University, who, more than ten years ago, when I had the privilege of serving on his faculty, first awakened and guided my interest in the modern city and its problems. This volume, both in its approach to the subject and in its interpretation of the data, testifies to his influence. To Professor Henry Pratt Fairchild, former teacher and long-standing friend, I am indebted for many helpful suggestions. For criticism of the manuscript in the raw state I have had the invaluable assistance of my former graduate students, Professor Harold E. Adams of Western Reserve University and Professor Victor A. Rapport of the Connecticut Agricultural College, both of whom gave generously of their time and thought to this enterprise.

NEW HAVEN, CONN.   MAURICE R. DAVIE
September 19, 1931

CONTENTS

PART I. INTRODUCTORY: THE MODERN CITY

PART II. HOUSING

PART III. HEALTH

PART IV. EDUCATION

PART V. RECREATION

CONTENTS

Part I. INTRODUCTORY: THE MODERN CITY

Part II. HOUSING

Part III. HEALTH

Part IV. EDUCATION

Part V. RECREATION

PART I

INTRODUCTORY: THE MODERN CITY

CHAPTER I

THE MODERN SOCIAL ENVIRONMENT

THE most striking characteristics of present-day civilization are industrialization and urbanization. They present the environment, both natural and human, to which an increasing majority of people must adapt.[1] Both phenomena represent recent, radical changes calling forth new types of adjustment. "Suppose a man," writes Walter Lippmann,[2] "who knew nothing of the history of the nineteenth century were shown the tables compiled in the *Statistical Abstract of the United States* for the period from 1800 to 1918: He would note that the population of the world had multiplied 2½ times; its total commerce 42 times; its shipping tonnage more than 7 times; its railways 3664 times; its telegraphs 317 times; its cotton production 17 times; its coal 113 times; its pig iron 77 times. Could he doubt that in a century of such uneven changes men had faced revolutionary social problems? Could he not infer from these figures alone that there had been great movements of population, vast changes in men's occupation, in the character of their labor, their wants, their standards of living, their ambitions? Would he not fairly infer that the political system which had existed in 1800 must have altered vastly with these new relationships, that customs, manners and morals appropriate to the settled, small and more or less self-contained communities of 1800 had been subjected to new strains and had probably been thoroughly revised? As he imagined the realities behind the tables, would he not infer that as men lived through the changes which these cold figures summarize they had been in conflict with their old habits and ideals, that the process of making new habits and adjustments must have gone on subject to trial and error with hopefulness over material progress and yet much disorder and confusion of soul?" It is with the history of this great problem of adjustment—the successes and failures which societies have had in attempting to meet their great group needs—that this book will deal.[3] We will be concerned not with

[1] Henry P. Fairchild, *Foundations of Social Life*, 1927, pp. 133-134, and especially ch. VI, "The Challenge of the Human Environment." Reference is made to this volume as the groundwork for the present study.

[2] *The Phantom Public*, 1925, pp. 84-85.

[3] Henry P. Fairchild, *Foundations of Social Life*, 1927, p. 189.

3

the abnormal and pathological, but with the methods of gratifying the common needs of the great mass of the people—of what O. Henry called "The Four Million."

What is a City?—A comprehensive definition of the modern city must indicate that it is a legal, political, economic, and social unit all rolled into one. "It is a large body of people, possessing some striking social characteristics, massed in a small area, chartered as a municipal corporation, having its own local government, carrying on various economic enterprises, and busily engaged in trying to solve the multifarious problems which its own crowded life puts upon it." Professor Munro,[4] who thus defines the city, explains the different phases of municipal organization and life as follows.

1. *Legal.*—First of all, the city is a corporation at law, a municipal corporation as we call it. It is endowed with an artificial personality. It may sue and be sued, hold property, make contracts, and do in its corporate capacity most of the things that a natural person or individual may do. It employs officials or agents, and in some cases assumes legal liability for what these employees do. In other cases it is immune from such liability. The city, as a municipal corporation, may levy taxes, and the power to tax is the most far-reaching power that a corporation can possess. It has power to borrow money, and to give in pledge the private property of its citizens. The bonded indebtedness of a city constitutes in effect a first mortgage on every piece of property within its boundaries, no matter by whomsoever owned. It has the right of eminent domain, the right to take private property for public use, against the will of the owner, on payment of just compensation. All these things the city can do, and does, in its capacity as a municipal corporation at law. A study of such legal powers and their exercise is what chiefly interests the lawyer.

2. *Political.*—Secondly, the city is a unit of government. It is an agency which the state uses, as a matter of convenience, for the better government of its people. A city may be older than the state in which it is located, but it is the creature of the state nevertheless. New York City is nearly a hundred years older than New York State, yet the subordination of the metropolis to the larger entity is beyond dispute. The state endows the city with a charter, which is its warrant for existence. It may permit the people of the city to frame their own charter, as some states do; but the state retains the ultimate power, control, and responsibility. No city in the United States has a charter which the higher authorities cannot revoke or take away. The city is the agent of the state, holding a delegated authority to perform certain governmental functions on the state's behalf, and for the sole reason that these functions can be more conveniently performed by the municipality than by the state itself.

[4] William B. Munro, *Government of American Cities*, 1926, pp. 13-16.

In order to carry on the work thus delegated to it by the state, the city is provided with a frame of government. It has a mayor and council, or an elective commission, or a council and city manager. It has a variety of administrative boards and appointive officials, likewise a large number of subordinate municipal employees. The duties of these various authorities are prescribed by the city charter, or by the general statutes of the state, or by municipal ordinances. There is a city electorate which nominates and elects the higher officials, and these in turn appoint the lower ones. This mechanism, which is sometimes very elaborate, constitutes the city government. A study of these powers, functions, relations, and personalities is what chiefly interests political scientists.

3. *Economic.*—The modern city is an agency of economic enterprise, engaged in work which is by no means strictly governmental in its nature. It is a purveyor of water (and sometimes of gas, electricity, and transportation), an employer of labor, a purchaser of supplies and materials, a seller of service. Much of what the modern city does is business, not government. It consists in providing services which would be furnished by private enterprise were it not that the municipality, for one reason or another, has seen fit to assume the task. . . .

Nor is this all. The city government comes into contact with many economic organizations and enterprises which it does not directly control. It deals not only with its own municipal water service but with privately owned gas and electric plants, street railways, bus lines, and telephone companies. It has dealings with banks and other financial institutions, for it is a large collector, depositor, spender, and borrower of money. It enters into relations with contractors and others for all sorts of work or service. It regulates, by licensing or otherwise, a long category of trades and vocations. These things give the city, as a unit of government, a considerable rôle in the economic life of the community, and the student of economics finds interests in this phase of its activity.

4. *Social.*—Finally the city is an agency for the promotion of the social welfare. Its officials are engaged not only in governmental and economic enterprises but in work of social amelioration as well. They provide from the public taxes free education, health protection, poor relief, and public recreation. More than one-third of the average city's annual expenditures is now devoted to these social welfare undertakings, including the public schools. . . .

There is everywhere an insatiable demand that the city shall do more for its people along lines of education, philanthropy, health protection, recreation, and amusement. We are steadily transferring responsibilities from the home to the school, to the public playground, to the neighborhood house, or to the civic center. You will find on the payroll of some municipalities today a "city mother," whose duty it is to look after the welfare of youngsters whose parents are not properly attending to it! Thus have we passed the stage of paternalism and are moving to maternalism in the work which the city is being asked to perform. There is no forecasting where this absorption of new welfare activities will ultimately lead the municipality. Certain it is, in any event, that we must look for an uninterrupted expansion of the city's work in this field, for the crowding of people into great centers is bound to bring social responsibilities which cannot be evaded. A great throbbing wen of human beings, in which common needs demand satisfaction by means of social effort and control—that is the city as the sociologist sees it.

The Inordinate Growth of Modern Cities.—The following table from the United States Census Report of 1930 indicates in a graphic manner the remarkable growth of cities in continental United States.[5]

POPULATION IN PLACES OF 8,000 INHABITANTS OR MORE: 1790–1930

Census year	Total population	Places of 8,000 inhabitants or more		
		Population	Number of places	Per cent of total population
1790	3,929,214	131,472	6	3.3
1800	5,308,483	210,873	6	4.0
1810	7,239,881	356,920	11	4.9
1820	9,638,453	475,135	13	4.9
1830	12,866,020	864,509	26	6.7
1840	17,069,453	1,453,994	44	8.5
1850	23,191,876	2,897,586	85	12.5
1860	31,443,321	5,072,256	141	16.1
1870	38,558,371	8,071,875	226	20.9
1880	50,155,783	11,365,698	285	22.7
1890	62,947,714	18,244,239	445	29.0
1900	75,994,575	25,018,335	547	32.9
1910	91,972,266	35,570,334	768	38.7
1920	105,710,620	46,307,640	924	43.8
1930	122,775,046	60,333,452	1,208	49.1

Urban territory was defined in the early census reports as places of 8,000 or more inhabitants. The Census Bureau today classifies as urban population that residing in cities and other incorporated places having 2,500 inhabitants or more. There are slight modifications of this rule to meet special conditions found in a few states where certain densely populated areas are not incorporated separately as municipalities. On the present basis of classification comparable figures are available only for the last six censuses. The obvious effect is to make the tendency toward city growth even more conspicuous.

The movement of the population to the cities, which was first perceptible in the twenties, became marked after 1840. In this year there

[5] *Fifteenth Census of the United States*, 1930, I, 9.

URBAN POPULATION OF THE UNITED STATES: 1880–1930
(Basis: 2,500 population)

Census	Per Cent Urban
1880	28.6
1890	35.4
1900	40.0
1910	45.8
1920	51.4
1930	56.2

were 44 cities in the United States with a population of 8,000 or more, but by 1860 the number had grown to 141. The percentage of the population living under urban conditions increased from 8.5 in 1840 to 16.1 in 1860. "Then, as now, the chief causes of this urban concen-

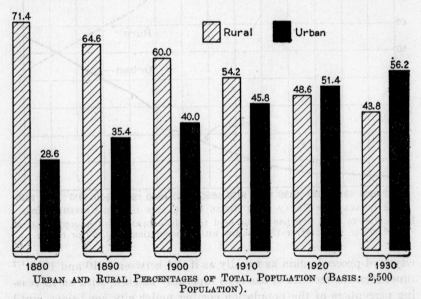

URBAN AND RURAL PERCENTAGES OF TOTAL POPULATION (BASIS: 2,500 POPULATION).

tration were the improvements in the means of transportation and the increasing use of machinery. Population was massed in the growing factory towns in order to supply the needed labor for the expanding manufactures, while the western prairie and southern cotton-fields furnished the necessary food and raw material. The manufacturing towns of New England grew the fastest, and places like Lowell,[6]

[6] Cf. George F. Kenngott, *The Record of a City. A Social Survey of Lowell, Massachusetts*, 1912. This study portrays vividly the social consequences of the growth of an industrial city.

which were unheard of in 1830, had grown to be flourishing cities in 1860. New York City grew during the twenty-year period 1840-60 from 300,000 to 800,000. Most of this industrial development took place in the North, where there were four times as many towns of over 8,000 inhabitants as in the South. . . . In the decade 1850-60 the movement to the cities slackened perceptibly, owing to the gold discoveries and the rush to the far West. Not until 1880 did the drift

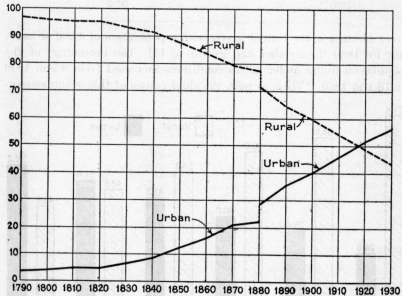

THE INCREASE OF URBAN OVER RURAL POPULATION IN THE UNITED STATES
From 1790 to 1880, ''urban'' was held to include towns with a population of 8,000 or more; after 1880, towns with a population of 2,500 or more.

cityward proceed again as rapidly as it did between 1840 and 1850.''[7] Since then the movement has been especially marked, with an increasing percentage of the population coming under city conditions, until by the last census over half of the total population of the United States is urban. Certain sections of the country have become urbanized more rapidly and completely than others. The height of this development is represented by such states as Rhode Island and Massachusetts which are over 90 per cent urban. Rhode Island today has almost no rural population.

[7] Ernest L. Bogart, *Economic History of the United States*, 1914, pp. 256-257 (quoted). Adna F. Weber, *Growth of Cities*, 1899, pp. 20-40.

URBAN POPULATION BY DIVISIONS AND STATES: 1930[8]

Per Cent Urban

New England	77.3	*South Atlantic*	36.1
Maine	40.3	Delaware	51.7
New Hampshire	58.7	Maryland	59.8
Vermont	33.0	District of Columbia	100.0
Massachusetts	90.2	Virginia	32.4
Rhode Island	92.4	West Virginia	28.4
Connecticut	70.4	North Carolina	25.5
		South Carolina	21.3
Middle Atlantic	77.7	Georgia	30.8
New York	83.6	Florida	51.7
New Jersey	82.6		
Pennsylvania	67.8	*East South Central*	28.1
		Kentucky	30.6
East North Central	66.4	Tennessee	34.3
Ohio	67.8	Alabama	28.1
Indiana	55.5	Mississippi	16.9
Illinois	73.9		
Michigan	68.2	*West South Central*	36.4
Wisconsin	52.9	Arkansas	20.6
		Louisiana	39.7
West North Central	41.8	Oklahoma	34.3
Minnesota	49.0	Texas	41.0
Iowa	39.6		
Missouri	51.2	*Mountain*	39.4
North Dakota	16.6	Montana	33.7
South Dakota	18.9	Idaho	29.1
Nebraska	35.3	Wyoming	31.1
Kansas	38.8	Colorado	50.2
		New Mexico	25.2
Pacific	67.5	Arizona	34.4
Washington	56.6	Utah	52.4
Oregon	51.3	Nevada	37.8
California	73.3		

The growth and importance of cities may be seen in an even more startling manner by considering the following facts brought out by the Fifteenth Census. Nearly one-fourth of the population of the United States is now located in the 37 cities having each 250,000 or more inhabitants. Approximately 30 per cent of all Americans live in the 93 cities of 100,000 or more inhabitants each. The combined population of the 3 largest cities in the United States is something over 12,000,000, or about one-tenth of the total population. Their combined area is roughly 620 square miles. This means that in contrast to an average density of 41.3 persons per square mile in the United States as a whole, in New York, Chicago, and Philadelphia there are over 18,000 persons to the square mile. Ten per cent of the people of the United States living on two-hundredths of one per cent of the

[8] *Fifteenth Census of the United States*, 1930, I, 15. If the 1930 census had followed the same ruling as that of the 1920 census with reference to unincorporated areas of dense population, the percentage of the urban population in Massachusetts would have been 95.3 instead of 90.2, and in Rhode Island 97.5 instead of 92.4. See above, note to p. 8.

area! If the metropolitan districts are included, the concentration of population in urban areas is still more striking. Considering the giant city itself, there are only three states in the Union, including the State of New York itself, where the population exceeds that of New York City.[9]

The same trend is characteristic of Western Europe. In Germany the growth of cities has been especially marked since the industrial expansion following the wars with Austria and France. Today more than half of the population is urban and large cities are numerous.[10]

URBAN CONCENTRATION IN GERMANY: 1925

Number of Towns	Inhabitants
154	Between 20,000 and 50,000
45	Between 50,000 and 100,000
25	Between 100,000 and 250,000
21	Between 250,000 and 1,000,000
2	Over 1,000,000

France is almost 50 per cent urban. It has seventeen cities of over 100,000 population. One-seventh of the total population of France lives in the metropolitan district of Paris. Belgium has become a highly industrialized country with a density of population in 1929 of 686 per square mile. The urban population of Scotland is 77 per cent of the total. In England approximately four-fifths of the people live in an urban environment. Here, too, is to be noted the giant city. Over a fifth of the whole population of England and Wales lives in London. Its population, nearly seven and a half million in 1921 and estimated to be nearly eight million in 1930, is four-fifths as large as that of the Dominion of Canada, while it exceeds by more than a million the total population of the Australian Commonwealth.[11] "A spreading man-reef," Patrick Geddes[12] calls it, who says with Shelley: "Hell is a city much like London." The inordinate growth of modern cities is to be observed even in new and rather sparsely settled countries. Sydney, the capital of New South Wales, has nearly half the population of that state. The city of Melbourne, inclusive of the suburbs, has considerably more than half of the population of Victoria. The city of Buenos Aires, standing in an enormous country, has about one-fifth of the population of the whole of Argentina. The city of Montevideo has almost one-fourth of the population of Uruguay.[13]

[9] *Fifteenth Census of the United States*, 1930, I, 10, 14.
[10] William B. Munro, *Government of European Cities*, 1909, pp. 110, 210. *Statesman's Year Book*, 1931, p. 919.
[11] *Statesman's Year Book*, 1931, pp. 16, 17, 282, 348, 674, 842, 843.
[12] *Cities in Evolution*, 1915, pp. 26, 30, 88.
[13] *Statesman's Year Book*, 1931, pp. 363, 373, 652, 1338. James Bryce, "The Menace of Great Cities," in *National Housing Association Publication*, No. 20, June, 1913, p. 10.

Imagine the problem of adjustment presented by such concentration of population. Geddes[14] thinks some name is wanted for these city-regions. "Constellations we cannot call them; conglomerations is, alas! nearer the mark at present, but it may sound unappreciative; what of 'conurbations'? That perhaps may serve as the necessary word, as an expression of this new form of population-grouping, which is already, as it were subconsciously, developing new forms of social grouping and of definite government and administration."

American cities differ in at least one important respect from the cities of other countries: they are more cosmopolitan.[15] Here, of course, is to be seen the effect of immigration, which has brought to the United States over thirty-five million persons from practically every country in the world. Most of the recent immigrants have settled in cities, establishing foreign colonies. Whereas only 2 per cent of the population of Vienna is foreign-born, 3 per cent of London and Berlin, and 6 per cent of Paris, American cities show very high percentages, as, for example, Detroit 29.3, Chicago 29.9, Cleveland 30.1, Boston 32.4, and New York 36.1. To these figures of foreign-born in American cities should be added in each case the almost equal percentages of native born of foreign parentage.[16] A social item in a small-town newspaper in Indiana was recently quoted by a humorous magazine as follows: "Mr. and Mrs. Arthur W. Brady and sons Arthur Jr. and George left yesterday for New York, where they remain abroad for a month." As a matter of fact, it is quite easy to be abroad in New York. There are more Italians in New York City than there are in Rome; more than in Milan or Naples or any other Italian city; more than in Florence, Venice, and Genoa combined. There are more Germans in New York than in any city in Germany except Hamburg and Berlin. There are twice as many sons of Ireland in New York as in Dublin. There are more Bohemians than there are in Prague. More Jews than there ever were in Palestine; in fact, New York City has the largest community of Jews in the world. And to add to its racial diversity New York has now become the largest Negro center in the world.[17] It has been said, with some truth, that New York City is owned by the Jews, run by the Irish, and enjoyed by the Negroes.

Can Cities Be Too Big?—These few facts may be taken as indicative of a revolutionary environmental change. "The growth of cities,

---

[14] *Cities in Evolution*, 1915, p. 34.
[15] Adna F. Weber, *Growth of Cities*, 1899, pp. 304-314.
[16] *Fourteenth Census of the United States*, 1920, II, 49.
[17] *Ibid.*, II, 55, 941. Frederic C. Howe, *The Modern City*, 1915, p. 46.

the world over," says Munro,[18] "has been the most conspicuous social phenomenon of the past hundred years." The world has never before known such huge cities nor so many of them.[19] Can cities be too big? Are our giant cities, like the dinosaur, disproportionately large and in danger of breaking down of their own weight? There is plenty of evidence that they have at least grown well out of hand.[20]

Witness the case of New York City. Historically, the first great maladjustment, if not breakdown, of the metropolis came in housing. "Today half the population of Manhattan are living in quarters which are below the standard fixed as safe and sanitary by the tenement house law of 1901"—the basic housing law of New York City. "The new tenements meet a minimum standard of sanitation and ventilation; but they do this at a price beyond the reach of two-thirds of the population; while their bleak courts, their white-washed walls, their dull streets, their occasional glimpse of the sun are still a long way from being the kind of environment in which mothers and children can flourish. . . . In the great city there are not enough decent quarters to go round; and even the decent quarters are not good enough."[21] We will discuss the housing problem in some detail later on; here we may merely make passing reference to the problem of satisfying this common elemental need and wonder what conditions will be like when New York City has a population of ten millions, and the metropolitan area one of twenty millions, as the regional planning commission predicts will occur within fifty years. Are we destined in the future to have our cities composed of apartment houses running up hundreds of stories and buildings without windows, lighted by electric light and ventilated by some artificial system?[22]

The second tremendous problem of the big city occurred in its water system and its sewers. New York City has been forced to build one new system after another. "This process must come to an end either when the existing areas have been drained dry, or when the cost per capita for water-mains reaches a point at which water will become a luxury—supplied at an *uneconomic rate* for the same reason that bread and shows and baths were provided in ancient Rome, namely, to keep the population contented." The difficulties that Chicago has

[18] *Municipal Government and Administration*, 1923, I, 110.
[19] Frederic C. Howe, *The Modern City*, 1915, ch. II, "The Ancient City"; ch. III, "The Mediaeval Town." William B. Munro, *Municipal Government and Administration*, 1923, I, chs. I-IV.
[20] James Bryce, "The Menace of Great Cities," in *National Housing Association Publications*, No. 20, June, 1913, pp. 11-17.
[21] Clarence S. Stein, "Dinosaur Cities," *The Survey*, May 1, 1925, 54:3:135.
[22] *Housing Betterment*, Dec., 1926, 15:4:295. *Housing*, March, 1931, 20:1:23-24.

experienced in getting rid of its sewage are notorious. In New York "the spread of sewage in the Hudson, the East River, and the Harbor has not merely destroyed the opportunities for bathing and caused the practical disappearance of North River shad; it has also, according to the latest report of the Joint Legislative Committee at Albany, cut the city off from 80 per cent of its shellfish, increased the dangers of typhoid (as nearly a thousand cases in the past winter testify) and now threatens the bathing beaches of Coney Island and Brighton."[23] So far the sanitary engineers have been able to solve these problems, but the expense of engineering schemes is becoming unbearable. The "overhead" of the city may increase to a point at which it will outmeasure any of its tangible or intangible benefits. The history of the attempts to meet these common sanitary needs is already one of marvelous accomplishment, as we shall later see. Still greater feats will be required.

The third breakdown concerns the street system and the inability of the overground and underground ways to carry the load of traffic. The automobile has added the proverbial last straw, for each car, with its two or three occupants, occupies several times the amount of space that an equal number of pedestrians would need. According to one estimate, a man walking in the street requires about 10 square feet of its surface. A standing automobile occupies 100 square feet; moving slowly it needs 200 square feet and moving between 15 and 20 miles an hour it needs 300 to 400 square feet. It is further estimated that each person in a loaded five-passenger automobile is using seventeen times as much street space as each person in a completely filled street car.[24] So great has street congestion become that the automobile is no longer a means of rapid transportation. Late afternoon rush-hour travel in Fifth Avenue, between 34th and 42nd Streets, had been reduced to 5 miles an hour in 1924, according to the Regional Plan of New York and Its Environs. This dragging pace has now been still further slackened down to 2½ to 3 miles per hour, according to Harold M. Lewis, its executive engineer.[25] "Our city officials and engineers are now hinting that the 'solution' lies in building overhead streets. But even if it were conceivable that a complete system of aerial streets could be built for the population, this could be done *only at a cost which would fall*

[23] Clarence S. Stein, "Dinosaur Cities," *The Survey*, May 1, 1925, 54:3:135-136.
[24] Harvey W. Corbett, "Up with the Skyscraper," *National Municipal Review*, Feb., 1927, 16:2:100. Miller McClintock, *Street Traffic Control*, 1925, p. 6.
[25] Waldo Walker, "Great Express Highways for New York Zone," New York *Times*, Nov. 21, 1926.

back upon the land in the shape of taxes—and in turn this· would make it necessary to build higher buildings and more streets!"[26]

New York City has been forced to extraordinary ends in the attempt to solve its traffic problem. One of the mightiest of engineering feats in the New York district is the recently constructed Holland Tunnel under the Hudson River, which provides a double roadway between New York and New Jersey. The tunnel, which is named after its first chief engineer, took seven years to build; it was opened to traffic in the fall of 1927. Each tube accommodates an average of 1,900 motor vehicles per hour. The problem of ventilating the tunnels was unprecedented. In tubes nearly 2 miles in length life could not be sustained by natural ventilation. Even if the tunnels were used only by pedestrians, the problem of supplying sufficient fresh air would be complicated. Through these tubes pass thousands of automobiles every hour, and the carbon monoxide gas given off by them would quickly prove deadly if it were left to accumulate. It was obviously impossible to force air into the middle of the tunnel since the tubes pass directly under a busy river that is crowded with shipping. A tunnel shaft built anywhere in the channels of the river would be a menace to navigation. The problem has been solved by placing ventilating plants on either shore and again on both sides of the river at the extreme ends of the pierheads. The distance between these river shafts is 3,354 feet. The new tunnels are the only ones in the world ventilated artificially from both ends.

The method of ventilating the Holland Tunnel and the design of the ventilating equipment were based upon an exhaustive series of original tests and investigations carried on for several years. Experiments were conducted under the direction of the United States Bureau of Mines in an "experimental mine" near Pittsburgh, as to the nature and quantity of gases emitted by motor vehicles under usual road operation conditions. The physiological effects of the gases, particularly carbon monoxide, were investigated in the laboratories of Yale University under the direction of Professor Yandell Henderson, who determined that more than 4 parts of carbon monoxide to 10,000 parts of fresh air would be dangerous. From these two experiments it was possible to calculate how much fresh air would be required to make the tunnel safe. A third series of experiments was conducted at the Engineering Experiment Station, University of Illinois, as to the method of admitting and exhausting the air and the factors for power determination. The air in the tunnel can be completely changed

[26] Clarence S. Stein, "Dinosaur Cities," *The Survey*, May 1, 1925, 54:3:136.

in a little less than 1½ minutes, or 42 times per hour. Every minute nearly 4,000,000 cubic feet of fresh air is pumped down to the motorists speeding under the Hudson tides.[27]

In the attempt to solve the traffic problem, it would seem that one elaborate device merely leads to another. To handle the immense traffic that has arisen with the opening of the Holland vehicular tunnel, New Jersey and Manhattan are now building elevated express highways. The Manhattan elevated boulevard, to cost $13,500,000, will run along the west-side waterfront. This route will float an automobile overhead all the way to or from the Canal Street mouth of the Holland Tunnel and the 72nd Street end of Riverside Drive at 30 to 35 miles an hour and without a stop. New Jersey announces plans to spend $40,000,000 on an even greater ''express highway'' of its own, the opening sections of which are already under construction. This route now ascends from the Jersey Avenue mouth of the tunnel into upper Jersey City and has tunneled part way through the Palisades. Once through, the highway is planned to hurdle the Jersey meadows and Hackensack River, gradually descend to grade in the outskirts of Newark, and, by passing that city, sweep down to Elizabeth—a complete distance over all of some 13 miles. ''These highways, taken with the similar 'super-highways' projected by Detroit, promise to be the first of their kind in America. Furthermore, they are features, but only features, in a general picture of traffic reorganization now under way in the metropolitan district.'' This wider panorama includes, in addition to the Holland Tunnel, three bridges to connect New Jersey and Staten Island, at a cost of around $33,000,000, the George Washington Bridge across the Hudson River, completed in 1931 at a cost of $60,000,000, and various minor developments attendant upon the whole.[28] New tunnels and bridges, and then new highways to meet the demands of tunnel-and-bridge-fed traffic—and still the traffic problem is unsolved!

A fourth evidence that our great cities have grown well out of hand is the breakdown of the mechanical means of transportation fol-

[27] Waldemar Kaempffert, ''The Holland Tunnel,'' in New York *Times*, Oct. 9, 1927. Waldo Walker, ''Holland Tube Roadways,'' in New York *Times*, Aug. 21, 1927. Ole Singstad, ''Relation of Tunnels and Bridges to Traffic Congestion,'' in *Annals of the American Academy of Political and Social Science* (referred to below simply as *Annals*), Sept., 1927, 133:222:67.

[28] Waldo Walker, ''Great Express Highways for New York Zone,'' in New York *Times*, Nov. 21, 1926. L. H. Robbins, ''New Jersey Weaves a Vast Fabric of Super-Highways,'' New York *Times*, Oct. 19, 1930. Arthur Warner, ''World's Greatest Bridge Links Two States,'' New York *Times*, Oct. 18, 1931; ''Bridge Across Kill van Kull Another Link in Port Unity,'' New York *Times*, Nov. 8, 1931.

lowing hard upon the collapse of the street system. The same causes are at work. "As the city increases in height it increases also in area; for the railroad and subway must be introduced to carry the main load of passengers from the central district of skyscraper offices and lofts to the outlying areas. When the vacant land on the outskirts is filled up, the net result is congestion at both ends. This causes a demand for additional means of transportation. Beyond a point which big cities reach at a very early point in their career, more transportation routes mean more congestion. The only way this could be avoided is by duplicating the existing transportation lines; but this method would reduce the earnings of the existing lines by distributing the load, and it is never even considered except when an equal degree of congestion can be secured to the new line." The truth seems to be that transportation companies thrive on congestion.

"The cost of all these facilities increases steadily as the lines are lengthened into more remote area so that in one way or another a subsidy must be introduced to support them at a price per ride the ordinary commuter can afford. At the present time New York, with its five-cent fare, is losing more than $12,000,000 annually on the money it paid for constructing subways, and it will lose even more on the new lines, which the transit engineers estimate will be three times as costly."[29] Business men in the city are urging higher subway fare as an aid to the taxpayer. According to a report of the Chamber of Commerce of the State of New York, "the City has had for some time $324,000,000 invested in subways from which no income is received, except on the $58,000,000 invested in the original subway, known as Contract No. 1. It is now working on a program calling for the investment of about $750,000,000 additional by 1931, upon which also no income will be received according to present plans. The total investment in subways, therefore, will soon be around $1,000,-000,000. This huge sum will absorb all the debt-incurring power of the City. The interest and amortization charges will, therefore, make serious inroads on the City's annual income. The emergency cannot be met by increasing the tax rate or by raising assessments. . . . All this financial predicament has been imposed upon the City by making a political issue of a five-cent fare. . . . The maintenance of a five-cent fare is not so serious for the private companies operating our transit facilities as for the City of New York, which is supplying the money to build the subways. Present fares may or may not bring

[29] Clarence S. Stein, "Dinosaur Cities," *The Survey*, May 1, 1925, 54:3:137. George McAneny, "The City of the Future," *National Housing Conference*, 1923, IX, 261-280.

bankruptcy to the operating companies, but the five-cent policy is certainly bringing disaster to the City's finances. Any advance in fare that could be granted, under conditions which would allow the larger part of the increase above five cents to go into the Treasury of the City of New York, would eliminate the charging to taxation of operating deficits."[30]

It would seem as if the present methods of transit development merely increase congestion. Certainly they have done little if anything to lessen it. Says a newspaper editor:[31] "Give a New Yorker an inch and he'll take the 'L' and ride to work. Six days in the week, from the reaches of the Bronx and Brooklyn, will he come sweltering through the subway under this island to his job. Then, on the seventh, he sits down and writes to the editor demanding more subways. What, in the name of common sense, does the man want more subways for? Give him one and he goes out a little farther to cheaper rents and painted bungalows to crowd up a new district until the traffic again becomes insufferable when he starts moving and howling for another line. To our obtuse economic way of thinking, this seems rather silly. The more subways, the more suburbs, the more population." Anyway, it is certain that rapid transit construction cannot keep up with the demand. The first subway, built in 1900, was congested immediately. Mr. D. L. Turner,[32] consulting engineer of the New York Transit Commission, has suggested a way to break the vicious circle of transit development and city congestion by building decentralizing lines or by limiting building operations and the extent to which land can be used. After pointing out how both business and residential development follows each new subway line, he states: "Either we must restrict or limit the building operations in such areas thus balancing the land use with the transit facilities available, and thereby relieve congestion; or we must change our transit construction policy, and build new rapid transit facilities through outlying unpopulated areas and route them through unbuilt business sections—in other words, construct decentralizing rapid transit lines, thus inducing the use of undeveloped sections for both home and business purposes, thereby

[30] Chamber of Commerce of the State of New York, *Monthly Bulletin*, Oct., 1926, 18:3:22-23. *Cf.* Ole Olmsted, "Rapid Transit and Social Values," in *City Planning*, Jan., 1927, 2:1:19-23; John Bauer, "Transit Programs Proposed for New York City," in *National Municipal Review*, Dec., 1927, 16:12:745. New York *Times*, Aug. 28, 1931.

[31] L. Weitzenkorn, quoted in *The Survey*, May 1, 1925, 54:3:178.

[32] "Is There a Vicious Circle of Transit Development and City Congestion?" in *National Municipal Review*, June, 1926, 15:6:320-326. The same conclusion is reached with reference to Los Angeles by C. A. Dykstra, "Congestion De Luxe—Do We Want It?" in *National Municipal Review*, July, 1926, 15:7:394-398.

attracting the population away from the congested districts and in this way relieve the congestion.''

To a certain extent residential congestion on Manhattan Island has been replaced by traffic congestion. People are moving from the heart of the city to the outlying boroughs and then riding in to work. For instance, twenty-five years ago probably a majority of the garment workers in Manhattan walked to their work, from the lower east side to the lower west side. Today they ride in from the Bronx and Brooklyn. While the population of the other boroughs was increasing rapidly, that of Manhattan declined 17.3 per cent in the period 1910 to 1920 and 18.2 per cent in the following decade. As evidence of the tremendous size of the problem of transportation, it is stated by J. R. Bibbins,[33] consulting engineer, Washington, D. C., that ''the modern transit system must transport every day an entire city's population once or more times and 20 per cent of the day's traffic during the rush.'' In New York City that means that millions of people (the estimate is at least 2,800,000) must be moved into lower Manhattan every morning and out every night. In 1922 two and one-half billions of passengers were carried. Here the commuter problem is especially serious. In the same year there were no less than 428,000 daily commuters to New York City—a large city population traveling back and forth to their work every day.[34]

A further difficulty arises from the fact that these people all want to arrive and depart at about the same time. This, coupled with skyscrapers, each housing hundreds, even thousands of persons, presents a general problem of congestion. The Equitable Building alone houses more than 10,000 persons. ''These great masses of buildings,'' asserts Mr. Curran,[35] who is supported by other investigators, ''are a direct cause of overcrowding in subways, upon the sidewalks and the streets. They have made motor traffic almost impossible in congested centres and wherever a skyscraper rises congestion follows. Each skyscraper requires tons of material every day, conveyed through streets taxed beyond capacity. Many skyscrapers in turn produce still other tons of manufactured articles to be moved through the same streets. Meanwhile we have a host of people struggling to enter the buildings.

[33] ''Rapid Transit Development,'' Annals, Sept., 1927, 133:222:197.
[34] Thomas Adams, ''The City of the Future,'' National Housing Conference, 1923, IX, 288; Planning the New York Region, pp. 21, 119.
[35] ''Against the Skyscraper,'' New York Times, Dec. 5, 1926; also ''The Skyscraper Does Cause Congestion,'' National Municipal Review, April, 1927, 16:4:-231-232. Frederic A. Delano, ''Skyscrapers,'' American City, Jan., 1926, 34:1:8. Lawson Purdy, ''Zoning,'' National Housing Conference, 1923, IX, 218-220. Ernest P. Goodrich, ''Zoning and its Relation to Traffic Congestion,'' Annals, Sept., 1927, 133:222:227-229. Miller McClintock, Street Traffic Control, 1925, p. 3.

Regularly at 9 o'clock and again at 5 the host goes through a nerve-fraying conflict to enter and depart. Every subway platform within reach, every elevated station and corner stopping place becomes a football field. And, worst of all, every rush hour has its tragic accidents, a product of this haste and crowding that arises from the grouping of skyscrapers.'' As someone has said in rhyme:

The
s k y -
scraper
t a l l
i s   a
wonder
to all,
a thing
to admire
b e y o n d
question,
Butoh!downbelowwherepedestriansgo
itcertainlyaddstocongestion.

On the other hand, it may be noted that the skyscraper lessens congestion during some parts of the day. At 9 o'clock in the morning it absorbs a host of people and keeps them off the street as a rule until 5 o'clock. Mr. Harvey W. Corbett,[36] a skyscraper architect, points out how ''in downtown New York, a business man consults his broker, eats his lunch, sees his lawyer, buys his wife a box of candy, gets a shave, all in the same building. At most he walks a few blocks. Most of the time he travels up and down instead of to and fro.'' True enough, but when he came to work in the morning he added to the congestion of street and subway and when he leaves the skyscraper at the end of the day to go home he will do so again. The principal need, as Mr. Corbett admits, is to find relief for the two hours before and after. An answer to this is the so-called stagger plan.

A study of transit conditions and travel habits in New York shows three peaks of congestion with reference to time of arriving at work: at 8, 8:30, and 9 o'clock. As someone has facetiously remarked, this involves, in turn, the workers, the clerkers, and the shirkers (the last peak is highest). In the evening, it would seem, they all leave together. Now if the time of opening and closing business establishments could be ''staggered,'' that is, distributed over a longer period of time, subway congestion and also congestion at skyscrapers and other buildings would be reduced. Relief would come through distributing traffic more evenly. A Transit Census Committee estimates that a stagger system would reduce morning and evening rush-hour traffic

[36] ''Up with the Skyscraper,'' *National Municipal Review*, Feb., 1927, 16:2:98, 99; also, ''For the Skyscraper,'' in New York *Times*, Dec. 5, 1926.

on the rapid transit systems from 30 to 50 per cent. The Metropolitan Life Insurance Company has already put the plan into operation by regulating the time of arrival and departure of its 10,000 employees. They are divided into four groups, one of which arrives at 8:30, another at 8:45, another at 9, and the last group at 9:15 A.M. The first group quits work at 4 P.M. and the others at fifteen-minute intervals thereafter. Under this plan only 2,500 of the company's employees have to use the subway at the highest peaks of the morning and afternoon rush hours. Other benefits of the plan are the elimination of danger from overcrowded elevators in the building and, since the luncheon hours have also been changed, less congestion in the company's restaurant. A widespread adoption of the plan will undoubtedly involve either a zone system or special schedules for different industries and business groups, or both. The scheme may also be applied to other groups, as for instance, shoppers and theatre crowds. Consider the theatre rush in the *roaring forties*: Within a distance of a few blocks from 42nd Street and Broadway there are 78 theatres having a total seating capacity of 95,294. "When it is realized that practically all of the performances begin at the same hour and that there is a certain amount of uniformity in the completion of the performances an idea of the concentrated street burden can be obtained." This situation has recently been relieved by varying the time for "curtain up" and "curtain down" in certain theatres.[37] The stagger plan is an excellent adjustment to the ebb and flow of the life of the city.

All the above relief measures, however, fail to offer any fundamental solution because they do not touch the root difficulty of centralized urban growth. If New York City, for example, is to increase in size, and especially if industrial centralization in Manhattan is to continue, it is doubtful whether the most elaborate schemes of transit extension will bring relief. Subways under every longitudinal avenue, subways under the two rivers every ten blocks of latitude, may only supply the incentive for forty-story lofts and multiple-acre office buildings. The process seems to go on in an endless circle: more buildings, more streets and subways, and again more buildings, and again more streets and subways. The central districts go up and the periphery pushes outward. The planning engineer, Jacob L. Crane,[38] says: "Apparently the process goes on until the actual rate of diminishing return in public economy and in the amenities has long been passed." If there is, as Mr. Crane suggests, a law of diminishing ad-

[37] New York *Times*, Oct. 17, 1926; Jan. 24, 1928; Jan. 15, 1929. Miller McClintock, *Street Traffic Control*, 1925, p. 27 (quoted).

[38] "Decentralization," *Annals*, Sept., 1927, 133:222:235.

vantages in cities in proportion to cost, like the law of diminishing returns in agriculture, it will sooner or later fix a limitation to the size of existing cities and compel new populations to establish settlements elsewhere.[39] The facts would indicate that this is so. Industries in New York City, according to Clarence S. Stein,[40] who is chairman of the New York State Commission of Housing and Regional Planning, are finding the disadvantages of centralized location to be mounting. "In most industries it actually costs more to carry on manufacturing on the congested island of Manhattan than it does in smaller industrial centers. The reasons are plain. The transportation of goods through the streets and on railways is the very life-blood of industry; and in all our big centers these arteries are clogged. Lacking streets to keep pace with the multiple-city, the trucks in New York City spend less time in active hauling than in unproductive work —locked in congested streets, or waiting at the crowded loading stations and stores. . . . The periodic congestion of freight terminals and docks—with the spoiling and rotting of perishable goods—presents another facet of the same difficulty. At the pier, in the railway yard, at the factory, congestion obstructs the normal processes of industry." It has been estimated on good authority that the cost of vehicular congestion on Manhattan Island reaches $500,000 per day, and in the entire New York region amounts to as much as $1,000,000 per day.[41] Furthermore, the crowded conditions of the city have increased the overhead within the factory, involving higher cost of land and structure.

Here are strong economic reasons for decentralization. As a matter of fact, decentralization of factories is taking place, under the lash of the competition for space, as Professor Haig[42] has demonstrated in his excellent study, though there is considerable variability in the degree of persistence with which the different industries cling to choice central locations, printing being an outstanding example. In fact, it is the only industrial group that showed a consistent record of gain in the central zone (Manhattan south of 59th Street) in the period studied, 1900 to 1922. Both the men's and women's clothing groups, which employ the largest number of workers, have grown

[39] John Nolen, *New Towns for Old*, 1927, pp. 139 ff. He is convinced that this is so and predicts phenomenal suburban movement, which calls for extensive planning of new communities.

[40] "Dinosaur Cities," *The Survey*, May 1, 1925, 54:3:137-138.

[41] Harold M. Lewis, "Routing Through Traffic," *Annals*, Sept., 1927, 133:-222:23. See ch. IV, below.

[42] "Toward an Understanding of the Metropolis," *Quarterly Journal of Economics*, May, 1926, XL, 408-414.

more rapidly outside the central zone than in it. The economic and industrial survey which he directed for the Regional Plan of New York furnishes grounds for the belief that "the peak of manufacturing in the center of the city was reached about ten years ago, and that a process of decentralization is already under way."

This situation is general; every large city offers many examples which indicate decentralization tendencies of various types: retail business, industry, residences, etc. With respect to residential decentralization, the federal census reports that the metropolitan population outside the political boundaries of the twenty-nine largest cities of the nation (New York included) is growing faster than that within the cities. In his significant study of *Satellite Cities*, Graham Taylor gives many illustrations of the industrial exodus from city center to suburb. "Congestion," he says, "with all that it means in choked streets, dark work rooms and high taxes, has been forcing factories to our city limits and beyond."[43] Factors which have accelerated the movement outward of industry, business, and residence are belt line railroads giving switching access to many trunk lines, high-tension power lines making cheap, flexible power available to areas formerly unsuitable for industrial works, the automobile, new highways and transit lines, the telephone and radio for communication.[44] Yet these very factors tend to bind the new communities as satellites to the mother city and to lead to further central growth. "The decentralization tendency so far," asserts Mr. Crane,[45] "is only a forced driving out of industry, business and residence to areas destined to become part of the centralized city or part of secondary uncontrolled decentralizations." City planners are convinced that decentralization will not solve any problem unless it is accompanied by regulation and planning.

In a city of the decentralized pattern, as they conceive of it, only such central administrative and cultural activities as pertain to the whole community would be placed in the downtown district—clearing-houses, general industrial management and sales offices, and central hotels, museums, theatres, etc. "All else—manufacturing, most retail business, local banking, branch libraries, and nearly all residence, would be distributed in secondary foci, laid out and controlled in a designed relation to street capacity. And as each local area reaches

[43] Graham Taylor, *Satellite Cities*, 1915, pp. 129-130. *Cf.* Warren S. Thompson, "On Living in Cities," *American Mercury*, June, 1930, 20:78:192-201.
[44] Howard Strong, "Regional Planning," *Annals*, Sept., 1927, 133:222:216. Jacob L. Crane, "Decentralization," *Annals*, Sept., 1927, 133:222:238.
[45] "Decentralization," *Annals*, Sept., 1927, 133:222:238. Graham Taylor, *Satellite Cities*, 1915, p. 6.

its reasonable complete development new ones, separated from the others, would be opened up. A central area would readily be reserved large enough to accommodate the central uses for a decentralized city of any size (area or population) within reason. The 'loop' in Chicago takes up only about 0.10 per cent of the area of the city, less than a quarter of a square mile, and that is partly occupied by manufacturing and storage buildings. The basic idea of decentralization, then, is the controlled and *limited* development of an indefinite number of interrelated cities, each for special or for mixed uses, with a 'hub' of limited purpose, in contrast to the unlimited growth outward and practically unlimited growth upward of a single huge city area."[46]

This sort of decentralization involves the new science of regional planning, which is proposed as a real solution of the problems of the large city. Like city planning it is a method of giving intelligent guidance to future growth of the city; but it differs from city planning in extent and general character of area to be dealt with and in the degree of elasticity of the planning proposals. Under modern conditions of urban growth it is impossible to give effective guidance with sole regard to areas within the arbitrary boundaries fixed for purposes of local government. Industrial, economic, and social factors, and not political boundaries, control the selection of a regional area. Consider, for example, the New York Region, which is being studied by the Committee on the Regional Plan of New York and Its Environs, of which Thomas Adams is director. It comprises 5,528 square miles, chiefly in the states of New York and New Jersey but including also a few hundred square miles in Connecticut. There are 277 cities, towns, villages, and boroughs in that area, and 144 separate unincorporated units. This metropolitan region may be roughly defined as the area within commuting distance of the central or mother city; it includes all the suburban growth extending from or related to the city.[47] It is planned to treat this region as a unit, but in such a way as to bring about decentralization without the usual pyramiding fea-

[46] Jacob L. Crane, "Decentralization," *Annals*, Sept., 1927, 133:222:235-236.
[47] *Plan of New York and Its Environs*, maps and diagrams. Thomas Adams, *Planning the New York Region*, 1927, pp. 17 ff. John Ihlder, "Housing and the Regional Plan," in *City Planning*, Jan., 1927, 3:1:1-16; and the following articles by Thomas Adams: "The Technical Approach to the Study and Planning of Regions," in *City Planning*, April, 1927, 3:2:87-95 (87 quoted); "Regional Planning in Relation to Public Administration," in *National Municipal Review*, Jan., 1926, 15:1:35-42; "A Forecast of the Regional Community of the Future," in *American City*, Nov., 1926, 35:5:617-619; "The Social Objective in Regional Planning," in *National Municipal Review*, Feb., 1926, 15:2:79-80; "The City of the Future," in *National Housing Conference*, 1923, IX, 281-299.

tures. As Lewis Mumford[48] expresses it, "Regional planning asks not how wide an area can be brought under the aegis of the metropolis, but how the population and civic facilities can be distributed so as to promote and stimulate a vivid, creative life throughout a whole region. . . . The regionalist attempts to plan such an area so that all its sites and resources, from forest to city, from highland to water level, may be soundly developed, and so that the population will be distributed so as to utilize, rather than to nullify or destroy, its natural advantages. It sees people, industry, and the land as a single unit. Instead of trying, by one desperate dodge or another, to make life a little more tolerable in congested centers, it attempts to determine what sort of equipment will be needed for the new centers."

This is the city of the future, as the regional planners conceive of it. Will their plan be followed? To the extent that it is in line with economic and social forces, the idea is sound. There are a number of indisputable advantages of centralized location, and so long as they exist concentration will go on; but when there is too much crowding together to obtain these advantages, decentralization will automatically occur, and it may be controlled and guided. As for the city of the present—inadequate housing facilities, inadequate water supplies, inadequate sewerage, inadequate streets, and inadequate transportation —these are but the larger and more obvious evils that derive from the congestion of population. They are enough, however, to show that the great city, as a place in which to live and work, breaks down and will continue to do so as long as the pressure of population within a limited area remains. To answer the question with which we started—can cities be too big?—there does seem to be a point when the further growth of a city is a detriment and not a benefit. "The history of all the great cities that have gone in for limitless growth and expansion is monotonously the same. Once they pass the limits of functional size and use, their further history can be summed up, as Professor Patrick Geddes has done, in four stages: Megalopolis, Parasitopolis, Patholopolis, Necropolis. The sequence of deterioration is fairly plain."[49]

Cities, however, seem not to be aware of the folly of mere size, and continue to plan on continuous increase in population. They even advertise, expressing their aspirations in city slogans.[50] The city that has a hundred thousand inhabitants fixes twice that number as its

[48] "Regions—To Live In," *The Survey*, May 1, 1925, 54:3:151.
[49] Lewis Mumford, "The Next Twenty Years in City Planning," in *National Conference on City Planning*, 1927, XIX, 48.
[50] Robert M. Brown, "City Growth and City Advertising," *Scientific Monthly*, Jan., 1923, 16:1:85.

goal for 1950. "The more congested a city already is, the more bright are its expectations for making matters a little worse."[51]

Large as New York City is today, it will probably continue to grow. To what size and how fast? This is a question of special import to the men who must plan the water, the lighting, telephone, and transportation systems, the public works, and the parks to meet the needs of the people several decades hence.[52] City planners are estimating a population of ten millions for New York City within fifty years. What will the city be like then; what of living conditions, and working conditions? Mr. Phillips,[53] columnist in the New York *Sun*, imagines the following "City News Items in 1975":

Rosenhoff & McGinty, real estate operators, have purchased the 200-story synthetic-steel apartment house at 356 Park Avenue. They intend to remodel the structure, adding another half mile of stories and putting in individual high-speed rapid-fire elevators. The old flying field on top of the present structure will be torn off and a new airdrome erected. There will be no plumbing in the building, all water being supplied by radio.

* * * * *

Wilbur Waffle, the six-year-old son of Otis H. Waffle, the well-known parachute magnate, was badly injured while playing in a kiddie-plane in the air above his home yesterday. The child swerved suddenly and was struck by the last car of an aerial excursion train. The chief of police again warned parents of the danger of children playing near congested air lanes.

* * * * *

X. Hemingway Glitz, who is erecting the city's newest apartment house (it will be three miles high and cover twenty-four acres of land) announces many innovations that will appeal to tenants. Among other things it will have kitchenettes equipped with the new Masconi-Frischetta apparatus for extracting fresh vegetables and staple meats from the air.

* * * * *

Jeffrey D. Weasel is building a new home at Wistaria Manor. It will be of the new cast-in-bloc type with folding porches and interchangeable lawns. There will be a broadcasting station in every room and a novel feature will be a radio-movie auditorium with connections with all baseball fields, football stadiums, etc. It will be heated entirely by telephone. There will be two

[51] Lewis Mumford, "The Next Twenty Years in City Planning," *National Conference on City Planning*, 1927, XIX, 47.

[52] H. L. Badger and N. S. Hill, "Public Services which Require Regional Planning and Control," *National Conference on City Planning*, 1927, XIX, 111-115, 116-125.

[53] New York *Sun*, April 30, 1925; quoted in *Housing Betterment*, Aug., 1925, 14:3:228-229.

airplane hangars in the yard, with room for six planes and sleeping apartments for twelve visiting airmen.

* * * * *

The Department of Public Works is advertising for 100 able balloonists for aerial street cleaners.

* * * * *

The city administration is to issue bonds to provide more underground golf links and submarine baseball parks.

* * * * *

Work is progressing rapidly on the new $10,000,000 Municipal Weather Control Station, by which any kind of weather the taxpayers desire may be instantly provided at a small cost.

* * * * *

COMMUTERS PROTEST

Citizens are complaining again of the poor service given by the Compressed Air Transportation Company. While the company claims to shoot passengers through its tubes at 150 miles an hour, indignant commuters say they seldom make better than 135. Something went wrong with the air valves last evening and over 6,000 commuters had nearly reached home when the air current suddenly reversed, blowing them all back to town again!

A week ago something went wrong with the compressed air in the rush hour and thousands were left stranded inside the tubes. It was necessary finally to extract them by means of high-pressure suction pumps.

Chapter II

CAUSES AND CONSEQUENCES OF THE GROWTH OF CITIES

Forces Creating Cities.—Both causes and consequences of city growth may be considered briefly under the subheadings of economic, social, and political. Our modern cities are largely the result of economic forces. They are very directly a consequence of the industrial and commercial revolutions; their growth has proceeded *pari passu* with the expansion of industry and commerce. At the same time, improvement of agricultural methods and the application of labor-saving machinery to agriculture have released population from the soil and brought about a large surplus of farm products for the maintenance of urban populations. The growth of cities has been made possible by the invention and use of machinery and by improvement in the means of transportation.

Commerce, or the distribution of commodities, involves their storage and transfer, and requires warehouses, docks, and freight depots; the population engaged in this business requires residences, shops, and public buildings. Where the transfer of goods is accompanied by a breaking of bulk or by change of ownership, there wealth is accumulated and localized, and population grows rapidly. Modern means of manufacturing have also had a highly concentrating effect upon population. The factory system is characterized by the grouping of workers under a single management, with the use of machinery and division of labor. Some modern cities have been created solely by manufactures, as, for instance, Essen, Germany; Pullman, Illinois; Gary and South Bend, Indiana. The growth of other cities has been greatly furthered owing to the development of the factory system and the advantages of labor supply, transportation, and markets.[1]

There are three ways in which city population can grow: by natural increase, by immigration, and by migration from rural districts. Our cities owe their growth mainly to the last two. The effect of industry and of city life has been largely repellent with respect to natural

[1] Adna F. Weber, *Growth of Cities*, 1899, pp. 160-218. Richard M. Hurd, *Principles of City Land Values*, 1905, ch. II; William B. Munro, *Municipal Government and Administration*, 1923, I, 111-120. Robert M. Brown, ''City Growth,'' *Scientific Monthly*, Jan., 1923, 16:1:80-81.

increase, or the excess of births over deaths. The declining birth-rate has been especially marked in urban environments, while—until the public health movement made it possible to survive in crowds—the death-rate in cities was higher than in rural communities.[2] Our cities have grown mainly by accretion. The economic and other advantages of cities have attracted immigrants here from abroad and Americans from the farms and villages.

Eugenists tend to believe, with Professor East,[3] that "the good germ-plasm in the country has been and is rising to the top, going to the cities, and there being sterilised." Huntington[4] thinks that the sifting power of cities makes them self-destructive. On the other hand, Munro[5] maintains that "history affords no ground for the belief that a nation is weakened by the urbanization of its people."

Some cities owe their growth, and in a few cases their founding, to the fact that they are political centers.[6] Political forces operate to create a city when it is the seat of national, state, or county government, either legislative, executive, or judicial, or all combined. As a single factor, political forces have created but few cities, of which may be mentioned Leningrad, Moscow, Washington, Columbus, Indianapolis, and Lincoln.

Social forces have played a more important part in the growth of cities, which have always been centers of culture and have furnished education, art, fashion, intellectual stimulus, and amusements to their contributing country.[7] Writing, art, science, architecture, literature, the theatre—the list is endless—have received their highest development in the city. One need merely mention the superior educational and recreational advantages of the city, the higher standard of living, the fuller, more diversified life, to recall its attractiveness. Idealization of city life has also been effective in attracting people from rural districts. These social factors operate in direct ratio to the size of the city. A few cities, such as Atlantic City and Newport, seem to be consuming points only.

Historically, cities have been the greatest tools of civilization; they have furnished in the extreme the conditioning factors of numbers and the contact of numbers.[8] They have been in the vanguard at all

[2] Adna F. Weber, *Growth of Cities*, 1899, pp. 155-156, ch. IV.
[3] *Heredity and Human Affairs*, 1927, pp. 261-262.
[4] *The Pulse of Progress*, 1926, ch. IV.
[5] *Municipal Government and Administration*, 1923, I, 4.
[6] Adna F. Weber, *Growth of Cities*, 1899, pp. 172, 174.
[7] Adna F. Weber, *Growth of Cities*, 1899, pp. 218-222. Ellsworth Huntington, *The Pulse of Progress*, 1926, pp. 52, 62.
[8] Albert G. Keller, *Societal Evolution*, 1915, pp. 21, 310.

stages in the history of civilization. Whenever large numbers of people are crowded into a limited area they must inevitably raise their plane of life above that of the surrounding territory. This is a condition of their existence, as Munro[9] has pointed out. "If a large city, for example, had no better sanitation than the average rural district it would soon be overwhelmed by epidemics. If it had no better protection against fire it would soon be in ashes. If it had no better facilities for transporting goods its people would starve. The great city, in short, cannot rest content with those simple measures for the care of the public health, for fire and police protection, for recreation, for the handling of traffic, for water supply, and for education which satisfy the countryside. It must make more and better provision for all these things as the price of its existence and progress. The city population is driven to a different plane of life by reason of the exigencies which arise from the massing of people together."

This has always been so. All great cultures have been city-born. "The development of the arts and sciences, the prosecution of industry, and political activity—all the social forces going to make up civilization—were phenomena of the great capitals like Memphis, Thebes, Nineveh, Babylon. In classic antiquity, indeed, the identification of city and civilization becomes complete; the Greek republics were city states, and when Aristotle wishes to characterize man as a social or gregarious animal he says man is by nature a citizen of the city (*politikon zoön*). The essential identification of the city with all the higher interests of humanity by the Greeks and Romans is to be observed at the present day in the English words 'city' and 'civilization,' both of which are derived from the Latin 'civis.' The tremendous influence of the classic city on the life of society has since been equaled by the mediaeval city republics in Italy (Venice, Florence, Genoa) and Germany (the Hansa towns and free imperial cities). Society then entered upon a new phase of development, and it is only with the prodigious growth of the great centres of population and industry in the last half of the nineteenth century that the city has come once more to have something like the dominating influence that it exercised in antiquity."[10]

Economic Consequences.—One striking result of the change from rural to urban conditions has been the change from economic independence to dependence. This may be illustrated in the matters of food, shelter, and employment. Before 1880, which roughly marks the

[9] *The Government of American Cities*, 1926, pp. 1-2.
[10] Adna F. Weber, *Growth of Cities*, 1899, pp. 5-6. *Cf.* Oswald Spengler, *The Decline of the West*, translated by C. F. Atkinson, 1928, II, 90.

real development of industrialization and urbanization in this country, we were largely a nation of small, independent farm-owners, each family was self-sufficient, and all were more or less on a plane of economic equality.[11] Now, instead of having one's own farm and farm-house and providing directly for one's own needs, in the majority of cases one rents from a landlord, buys food from others, and works for someone else. The wage-earning class is typically a city class; most city-dwellers are tenants; and the city naturally depends upon the rural districts for its sustenance. No city is self-sufficient nor could it be, unless some such revolutionary changes occur as Haldane[12] in a speculative mood imagines. ''Within the next century,'' he writes, ''sugar and starch will be about as cheap as sawdust. Many of our foodstuffs, including the proteins, we shall probably build up from simpler sources such as coal and atmospheric nitrogen. I should be inclined to allow 120 years, but not much more, before a completely satisfactory diet can be produced in this way on a commercial scale. This will mean that agriculture will become a luxury, and that man-kind will be completely urbanized. Personally I do not regret the prob-able disappearance of the agricultural labourer in favour of the fac-tory worker, who seems to me a higher type of person from most points of view. Human progress in historical times has been the prog-ress of the cities dragging a reluctant countryside in their wake. Synthetic food will substitute the flower garden and the factory for the dunghill and the slaughterhouse, and make the city at last self-sufficient.''

Other economic characteristics of the city are the greater division of labor and the consequent monotony. Whereas the farmer is the proverbial jack-of-all-trades, the city wage-earner is a mere cog in the industrial machine. Lemontey once complained that as a result of the factory system a man may spend his whole life in doing noth-ing more important than performing the eighteenth operation in the making of a pin.[13] Modern industry furnishes more extreme examples. In a modern factory it takes one hundred and fifty men to make an ordinary suit of clothes. It takes about two hundred men today to make a pair of shoes formerly made, under the handicraft system, by one man. There are one thousand and eighty-eight different workmen employed in the making of a watch. There are over four hundred operations in the packing industry, over five thousand in the making

[11] Malcolm Keir, *Industrial Organization*, 1923, pp. 39-42, 207. W. G. Sumner, *Challenge of Facts and Other Essays*, 1914, pp. 290 ff.
[12] *Daedalus*, 1924, pp. 38-39.
[13] Charles Gide, *Principles of Political Economy*, 1903, p. 179.

of a Ford. The monotony produced by such minute division of labor has its effect, among other things, on leisure-time activities, as will be later seen.[14]

Further economic consequences are evident in the labor movement, which has always been a city movement, as have socialism and radicalism; the tendency toward a higher standard of expenditure; the increased opportunity for speculative profits, as in real estate, franchises, and other socially created values; and in the accentuated economic competition which draws the social scale out into extremes of poverty and of wealth, the large city being at once the wealthiest and the most poverty-stricken of any community.[15]

Political Consequences.—One striking political effect of the growth of cities is the hugeness of the problem of administration. More people respond to the authority of the mayor of New York than did to the first President of the United States. The employes of the city (about 120,000) constitute an army larger than marched with Sherman to the sea. The annual budget of the city is larger than any budget of the Federal Government down to a period about twenty years ago. New York City takes over $900,000,000 a year from its citizens, the bulk of it in taxes, and spends as much for services in their behalf. It is a two-billion-dollar concern.[16] In this connection it is of interest to recall that Aristotle saw the difficulty of governing a vast agglomeration of people and limited the population of his ideal city state to 10,000. Today this figure is the minimum rather than the maximum of cityhood.[17]

The growth of cities has everywhere enhanced the difficulties of government. Our modern cities are faced with two stern facts: First, the governing problems are becoming more technical, more difficult, and require a scientific handling; in the second place, the electorate is constantly growing larger and more cosmopolitan in character and is less able to decide upon specific issues.[18] Viscount Bryce[19] once said

[14] George B. Cutten, *The Threat of Leisure*, 1926, pp. 52. See also ch. XVIII, below.

[15] Adna F. Weber, *Growth of Cities*, 1899, pp. 410-425. William B. Munro, *Government of American Cities*, 1926, pp. 67-68; *Municipal Government and Administration*, 1923, I, 143-144.

[16] Stuart Chase, ''New York: A Two-Billion Dollar Concern,'' in New York *Times*, May 22, 1927. *Cf.* New York *Times*, October 11, 1930, for 1930 budget and requests for 1931.

[17] Aristotle, *De Republica*, line 7. Adna F. Weber, *Growth of Cities*, 1899, p. 428.

[18] Adna F. Weber, *Growth of Cities*, 1899, pp. 425-431. William B. Munro, *Government of American Cities*, 1926, pp. 49-54; *Municipal Government and Administration*, 1923, I, 144-148.

[19] *American Commonwealth*, 1917, I, 642 ff.; II, 165, 389.

that "the government of cities is the one conspicuous failure of the United States"; that municipal affairs had been marked by inefficiency, corruption, "politics," lack of concentration of authority, and disinterestedness on the part of the people. The indictment must be admitted, especially when we contrast our cities with those of England and Germany where trained officials and experts carry on the administrative work and where high traditions of public office exist.[20] Our lack of trained administrative officials may be charged in part to the "democratic" idea that anyone can satisfactorily fill any public office and that everyone should have a chance; to the spoils system by which offices are used to pay political debts; and to the short tenure of office, which makes it impossible to attract and hold competent officials. Among our chief needs are undivided responsibility and the continued employment of experts.

With respect to the electorate, it is a matter of common knowledge that the average citizen gives but a little of his time to public affairs, has but a casual interest in facts and but a poor appetite for theory. "There is nothing particularly new," comments Walter Lippmann,[21] "in the disenchantment which the private citizen expresses by not voting at all, by voting only for the head of the ticket, by staying away from the primaries, by not reading speeches and documents, by the whole list of sins of omission for which he is denounced. I shall not denounce him further. My sympathies are with him, for I believe that he has been saddled with an impossible task and that he is asked to practice an unattainable ideal. I find it so myself for, although public business is my main interest and I give most of my time to watching it, I cannot find time to do what is expected of me in the theory of democracy; that is, to know what is going on and to have an opinion worth expressing on every question which confronts a self-governing community. And I have not happened to meet anybody, from a President of the United States to a professor of political science, who came anywhere near to embodying the accepted ideal of the sovereign and omnicompetent citizen." The same author has summarized so well the field of activity of the public that he should be quoted in full:

1. Executive action is not for the public. The public acts only by aligning itself as the partisan of some one in a position to act executively.

2. The intrinsic merits of a question are not for the public. The public intervenes from the outside upon the work of the insiders.

3. The anticipation, the analysis and the solution of a question are not

[20] Frederic C. Howe, *The Modern City*, 1915, chs. X, XI. William B. Munro, *Government of European Cities*, 1909.

[21] *The Phantom Public*, 1925, pp. 20-21, 24-25, 144-145.

for the public. The public's judgment rests on a small sample of the facts at issue.

4. The specific, technical, intimate criteria required in the handling of a question are not for the public. The public's criteria are generalized for many problems; they turn essentially on procedure and the overt, external forms of behavior.

5. What is left for the public is a judgment as to whether the actors in the controversy are following a settled rule of behavior or their own arbitrary desires. This judgment must be made by sampling an external aspect of the behavior of the insiders.

6. In order that this sampling shall be pertinent, it is necessary to discover criteria, suitable to the ¡nature of public opinion, which can be relied upon to distinguish between reasonable and arbitrary behavior.

7. For the purposes of social action, reasonable behavior is conduct which follows a settled course whether in making a rule, in enforcing it or in amending it.

It is the task of the political scientist to devise the methods of sampling and to define the criteria of judgment. It is the task of civic education in a democracy to train the public in the use of these methods. It is the task of those who build institutions to take them into account.

Some adjustment has already been secured in municipal government. The Dark Ages of American municipal history—when Lincoln Steffens wrote on *The Shame of Our Cities* (1904), with chapters on graft and corruption, and on *The Struggle for Self-Government* (1906), in an attempt to trace American political corruption to its sources—have passed.[22] New charters have provided for the mayor-and-council form of city government, in which the chief executive has more responsibility and power; for the commission form of government, in which a small executive committee is elected to run the city; and for the city-manager plan, in which a non-political central executive is given full and responsible charge of the administration. As a consequence many striking improvements in city administration have been effected. In addition, city government in the United States has been considerably improved during the past twenty-five years by simplifying it, by reducing the number of elective officials, by defining more exactly the powers of the various officers, and by shortening the ballot.[23]

A great difficulty still remains, however, owing to the fact that the

[22] William B. Munro, *Government of American Cities*, 1926, pp. 32, 36, puts the "Dark Ages" in the period 1870 to 1900.
[23] Frederic C. Howe, *The Modern City*, 1915, ch. IX. Leonard D. White, *The City Manager*, 1927. Clinton R. Woodruff, "The City-Manager Plan," *American Journal of Sociology*, Jan., 1928, 33:4:599-613. William B. Munro, *Government of American Cities*, 1926, p. 19, chs. XVI, XVII.

city as a municipal corporation is the creature of the state legislature
and possesses only such powers as are expressly enumerated or clearly
implied in the city charter. Most cities suffer from control by the
state legislature and are sorely in need of home rule.[24] An acute type
of maladjustment exists in some states where, because of the rotten
borough system, the state legislature is controlled by the rural districts
and the rural members neither understand nor are in sympathy with
the needs and problems of cities. Rhode Island, for example, is over
90 per cent urban, yet the few farming communities virtually control
the state. Under the constitution of 1842, still in force, each city and
town is entitled to one member of the Senate and one only. Thus the
great industrial cities of Providence, with 250,000 population, Paw-
tucket, with over 75,000, and Woonsocket, with almost 50,000, are
forever outvoted by men from tiny fishing villages and rural hamlets
such as West Greenwich with 402 souls; Foster, with 946; Charles-
town, with 1,118; and Narragansett, with 1,258. It is possible for
9 per cent of the population to elect twenty senators, or a majority.
The rural districts are Republican, the cities Democratic. Bitter
partisan wrangles have marked the legislative sessions, and city-led
attempts at reform have been frustrated. In Connecticut each town
has two representatives in the General Assembly. As a result, the
town of Union, with 196 persons, has equal voice in the lower house
of the legislature with the cities of Hartford, Bridgeport, and New
Haven, the population of which in each case is well over 140,000.
"The most spectacular effect of this system recently has been the
passage of a strong anti-daylight-saving law to which the cities
strenuously but vainly objected." At a recent session, three of the
most important educational measures were killed because the farmers
who dominated the committee on appropriations could not see the
need of them for the more congested districts. These bills applied to
special education for backward children, to Americanization of the
foreign-born, and to night schools—peculiarly city problems. In New
York no county is permitted to have more than one-third of the members of the state Senate, and no two counties adjoining or separated
only by public waters more than one-half. This restriction was obviously aimed at New York City. Each county is given one member
of the Assembly regardless of population, and this provision has
enabled rural up-state New York to maintain its grip on the lower
chamber of the legislature. Social legislation affecting cities is

[24] Delos F. Wilcox, *The American City*, 1904, p. 314, ch. XI. William B. Munro,
Municipal Government and Administration, 1923, I, 168-176, ch. IX.

slaughtered by the rural representatives. The New Jersey state constitution provides one senator and one only for each of the twenty-
one counties. Thus Essex, with 833,000 population, has the same vote
in the Senate as Cape May County, with hardly 30,000. Hudson, with
690,000 roughly, is balanced by Sussex with 27,000. "Herein lies the
key to the retention of the state's bluest of the blue laws, the enforcement of which is attempted now and then." Wilmington, the only
large city in Delaware, has almost exactly 50 per cent of the voting
population of the state. Yet it has only 13.5 per cent of the representation in the General Assembly. "Of the thirty-five members of the
House, Wilmington gets only five. Of seventeen state senators, Wilmington gets but two. In the party conventions also the city is grossly
misrepresented." This city wants to get a city manager; the farmers
will not let her. Wilmington would like to have daylight-saving time;
the farmers passed a law forbidding it. A similar situation exists in
Maryland, where one-half of the population lives in the city of Baltimore. Baltimore has a voting representation of 28.5 per cent on joint
ballot in the Legislature. "The effect of this rural control has been
particularly controversial in the levying and distribution of taxes.
The city pays the larger portion of both direct and indirect taxes, but
receives only two-fifths of the road fund and about the same proportion of the school fund. The city is wet and the rest of the state is
dry: the Eighteenth Amendment was ratified, but all state enforcement bills have been defeated." Pennsylvania is between 65 and 70
per cent urban, yet is under rural control, for each of the 76 counties
has one member of the legislature regardless of population. In 1923
the rural members forced through a bill prohibiting daylight-saving
time. The state is another stronghold for puritanical (rural) observance of the Sabbath. In Ohio, too, each county has at least one member of the House regardless of population. As a result of rural control, cities cannot raise taxes and must skimp on schools and hospitals,
and even suspend a number of municipal functions. Other examples
could be cited, but these are sufficient to indicate the handicap of the
city under "government by yokel" and the crying need for home
rule.[25]

A little-appreciated effect of city growth has been the eclipse of
county government. "In New England it is almost non-existent. In
the central and western states it performs a series of routine func-

[25] Orville A. Welsh, "American Rotten Boroughs," *The Survey*, Aug. 1, 1924,
52:9:509-513; "Government by Yokel," *American Mercury*, Oct. 1924, 3:10:199-
205. Frederic C. Howe, *The Modern City*, 1915, chs. VI, VII. Population figures
from the 1930 census report.

tions which comprise the minimum which a government must perform in a simple neighborhood. . . . In some southern states the early traditions of the county survive simply because cities have not grown up nor industrial life developed to disturb them." But where people have concentrated within limited areas, the new and striking tasks arising from the complexity of urban life have been delegated to the city government, and the county remains as little more than a geographical expression. In fact, many of us are men without a county.[26] In a number of instances the city has grown until it has swallowed up the county; yet there are many of these counties still carrying on governmental activities, with inefficient rural methods and much wasteful duplication. "There are still five separate county governments within the single city of New York. This is an unnecessary luxury. The county governments cost the city almost twelve million dollars a year. A considerable part of this sum may be saved by abolishing the five counties and transferring the remaining county functions to the city. This is not a novel or radical proposal. It has already been put into operation in San Francisco, Denver, Washington (D.C.), Baltimore, St. Louis, and all of the cities of Virginia, and is partially in effect in Philadelphia, Boston, and a number of other cities."[27]

American judicial organization has been seriously affected by the growth of cities and there is much maladjustment. Our judicial organization and the great body of American common law are the work of the last quarter of the eighteenth century and the first half of the nineteenth century. On the other hand, our great cities and the legal and social problems to which they give rise are of the last half of the nineteenth century, and indeed the pressing problems do not become acute until the last quarter of that century. "These changed conditions, to which our rigid court organization with inflexible machinery was unable to adapt itself, are mainly due to immigration, the rise of the wage-earning class, and above all, to the startling growth of urban population with all that it entails. With the great cities came the infinite complexity of modern life, of business, and of affairs in general which breeds litigation. The law itself became highly complicated. With thirteen thousand decisions of courts of last resort being made each year and twelve thousand laws annually enacted by the

[26] Harold Dodds, "A County Manager Charter in Maryland," *National Municipal Review*, Aug., 1920, 9:8:512.
[27] R. F. Cutting, "New York City's Expanding Government," *National Municipal Review*, Sept., 1926, 15:9:507. William B. Munro, *Government of American Cities*, 1926, pp. 447-448.

legislatures, no man could determine his rights without employing attorneys. The legislative attempt to fix the machinery of justice in all its details made of procedure a maze which precluded litigation unless the suitor could engage counsel to guide his case through all the technicalities.'' In brief, the task which the bar faces is literally that of making over a judicial machine that was organized to suit the needs of a simple, homogeneous, agricultural population living in sparsely settled communities so that it may be adapted to the needs of a complex, heterogeneous, urban population crowded together in a modern industrial society. In particular has the maladjustment been marked in the criminal branch, which is one explanation of the highly unenviable crime record of our cities.

As an illustration from the judicial field of the principle that, when social conditions change, our institutions must change accordingly, there may be cited the way in which small claims have been handled. ''In our judicial history small cases were first entrusted to justices of the peace. This plan for a while gave simplicity and despatch, but when applied to cities it failed utterly. The justices, being subject to no supervision, and depending so much on their fees that J. P. came to mean 'Judgment for the Plaintiff,' formed unholy alliances with collection agencies, instalment houses, and the like, and very generally became actually corrupt. They were so strongly entrenched in local politics that the process of ousting them, which is not yet completed, has been long and difficult. They have aptly been called 'those barnacles of jurisprudence' because they have clung on long after their usefulness expired.''[28] They have been succeeded in many places by the organized municipal court, the modern type of adjustment.

Transition from rural to city life on the part of so large a proportion of the population has had the further result of profoundly affecting our political ideals. In the early history of this country the people adopted that negative attitude toward government which they inherited from the English struggle with the Crown. The protection of property rights was regarded as the real and usually the only legitimate field of governmental action. For the government to do anything more than that was looked upon as state interference—an encroachment upon the liberty of the individual. That view was in perfect harmony with the character of the early settlers and the conditions under which they lived. ''In any new country the pioneers

---

[28] Reginald Heber Smith, *Justice and the Poor*, 1919, pp. 7, 42-43 (quoted); ''Social Work and the Law,'' *The Survey*, July 15, 1922, 48:12:504.

are, by a process of natural selection, the most energetic and independent. They constitute a population trained to depend upon themselves and with little sympathy for schemes involving governmental co-operation.'' They are intense individualists. They prefer to take care of themselves rather than have the government exercise a kind of paternal care over them. Those principles and that attitude are adapted to rural conditions. The adaption is lost, however, when such political and social ideals are introduced into urban communities.[29]

Whether we like it or not, with increasing density of population and growth of urban communities new standards of governmental action are forced upon the community. They are adopted out of necessity, and not because of any acceptance of socialistic principles or any other scheme. Students of government have noticed that it is in the cities that the reconstruction of political practice and of social institutions goes on most rapidly. This is the reason why municipal government is of so much interest to the political scientist. Here is to be found the most extensive and natural encroachment of government on the field of private initiative. ''It is more than likely,'' comments Wilcox,[30] ''that if socialism ever comes, it will come by way of the city; that is, the way will lead up to general socialism by the steady enlargement of municipal functions.'' One might go farther and say that if it comes that way it will come because it is an adjustment. The process is not one of socialism, however, but of socialization. City conditions have made it imperative that many functions formerly performed by the individual under rural conditions be transferred to the community in its organized capacity. Abundant illustration will be given in succeeding chapters; here let us simply focus the contrast.

''In the country,'' writes Hayes,[31] ''the farmer's own lamp in the house and the lantern on the road furnish light; his own well and cistern supply water; his own care defends him and his family against fire, tramps, and microbes, and his own conveyance transports them.'' In urban communities the individuals and households depend largely upon communal activities and not upon their own resources. ''Light, air, fuel, and water, the products of Nature,'' writes Anderson[32] of the city-dweller, ''are fed to him through tubes. The municipality of

---

[29] L. S. Rowe, ''Political Consequences of City Growth,'' in *Yale Review*, May, 1900, IX, 21.

[30] *City Government*, 1897, p. 235.

[31] *Introduction to the Study of Sociology*, p. 64, quoted by William C. Smith, ''The Rural Mind,'' in *American Journal of Sociology*, March, 1927, 32:5:783.

[32] *The Farmer of Tomorrow*, p. 9, quoted in the above.

which he is a member in good standing, disposes of his waste paper and potato peelings; regulates noise and smell; inspects his food; guarantees him so many cubic feet of air to sleep in, a minimum bacterial count of 50,000 to the c.c. in his morning's milk, and a ladder in case of fire; assumes the supervision of the eyes, teeth, and intellect of his children; polices him; sweeps his streets; counts him at birth, marriage, and death and at the polls; fumigates him; makes music for him in the parks, and keeps him off the grass.''

Yes, all this the city does for him, and much more. It does so because it has to, and the citizen pays for it. In 1856 there were 19 activities carried on by the city government of Detroit at a per capita cost to the taxpayer of $3.85. In 1921 that number had been increased to 184 at a per capita tax of $42.62. From 1851 to 1921 the per capita debt in Detroit rose from $18.71 to $93.06. Someone has recently estimated that the indebtedness of all cities of more than 100,000 population is $135.38 per capita.[33] In 1914 the budget of New York City was $190,000,000, or $37 for every man, woman, and child in the city; in 1927 the budget called for expenditures of $475,000,000, or $81 per capita. In 1930 it was over $550,000,000. In 1898 the net funded debt of the city stood at $228,000,000. By 1910 it had jumped to $688,000,000; in 1920 it stood at $1,031,000,000; in 1927 it was $1,367,000,000.[34] Such extension of governmental functions is as necessary as it is costly and unprecedented. It exists because of the basic reason that under modern urban conditions common needs demand satisfaction by means of social effort and control. The process is that of socialization or social adjustment.

Social Consequences.—A striking contrast between the city and the country is the greater complexity of social relations and the higher degree of interdependence in the former case. No community shows more highly organized social life than the city. It presents an exceedingly complex social environment to which one finds difficulty in adapting, as evidenced by the trials of persons from the country as well as those of recently arrived immigrants. Cities must evolve elaborate means to meet elemental needs which rural communities handle in a simple way. Illustrations that come readily to mind are roads and other means of transportation, schools, and protection of life, property, and health. A further distinction is that in the city common needs must be met by group action, which involves munic-

[33] William J. Norton, ''The Philanthropic Taxpayer,'' *The Survey*, April 15, 1924, 52:2:87.
[34] Stuart Chase, ''New York: A Two-Billion-Dollar Concern,'' in New York *Times*, May 22, 1927. New York *Times*, Oct. 11, 1930.

ipal control or operation. Take, for example, the elemental need of a water-supply. The city-dweller cannot have a well nor can he arrange himself to bring water from a lake or river or from a watershed that may be a hundred miles away, nor can he purify it. Here is a necessary and proper field for community action, and it is illustrative of the new attitude toward government that city-dwellers must take.

A second social result of the change from rural to urban conditions has been the disintegration of old traditions and former standards of conduct. A new environment always has this effect; it is one of the laws of social change. The drift of the population from country to city and the transition from rural to urban conditions have acted as a destructive agency upon our early traditions of government and social action. Many thinkers, noticing this disintegrating action, have called city life wholly destructive in its tendencies, in no sense constructive. They have pointed out that it destroys all accepted ideas, traditions, and beliefs. This was a hasty and premature generalization. But it had its justification and explanation in the fact that up to recent years "the conspicuous function of city life has been to break down the social and political standards developed under rural conditions."[35] The old rural religious and ethical notions do not seem to be adapted to the city. Observe the contrast with respect to notions concerning the observance of the Sabbath. City mores are more cosmopolitan, less traditional, less stable; there is more toleration.[36] To rural people the city appears God-less. There is unquestionably more vice, crime, and dissipation in cities; there is a greater problem of control presented in the use of leisure time, as will be discussed in a subsequent chapter. Moreover, we have lost the social control that sprang from neighborhood opinion. "I suppose," writes Newton D. Baker,[37] "most of the human race grew up under the correcting tutelage of such opinion until our day. Now there is no such thing. There were people in the village in which I lived as a boy before whom I had to behave most circumspectly. If I did anything of which they disapproved, it would have been reported to others, who in turn would have carried it back to my parents, with results which I did not care to bring about. That is all gone. We have not enough neighborhood association to make for correction and control of opinion."

[35] L. S. Rowe, "Political Consequences of City Growth," *Yale Review*, May, 1900, IX, 21.
[36] Albert G. Keller, *Societal Evolution*, 1915, pp. 313-320. William B. Munro, *Municipal Government and Administration*, 1923, I, 139-140.
[37] "Citizens in Transit," *The Survey*, April 1, 1928, 60:1:44.

Among the psychological effects of urban growth are the radicalism of the city as contrasted with the conservatism of the country, the great rôle of suggestibility, and various aspects of mob psychology. Further consequences are the intensified nervous strain and excitability. "Life in the great city," says Viscount Bryce,[38] "tends to stimulate and increase beyond measure that which is the menace of the American city—intensification of nervous strain and nervous excitability. Cities are the homes—especially in the United States—of every kind of noise, and nothing in the long run puts a greater strain on the nervous system than incessant noise. People live in crowds, under the ceaseless stimulus of always seeing one another in crowds, always moving to and fro in street cars and railroads and automobiles, backwards and forwards at an increasing rate of speed. They are always under that exciting influence which the mere sense of living in a crowd of people and of trying to pack so many things in the twenty-four hours, including the reading of numerous newspapers, produces. It tells injuriously upon the nervous system. All these things tend to increase the nervous excitability and the consequent neurasthenia from which we are told most of us are suffering. Some people think this is going to be the real danger in the future of the human race, and that unless the right means are found for the protection of our nervous system, its undue stimulation and consequent exhaustion may become a source of weakness for mankind." The increasing tendency of mental and nervous disorders, especially noticeable in cities, would seem to bear this out.

Noise has always been a characteristic of cities. There is evidence that definite steps to abate noise were taken by the Greeks several centuries before the Christian era. The Roman poet Juvenal complained that "the passing of wagons in the narrow curves of the streets, and the mutual revilings of the team-drivers brought to a standstill, would banish sleep even from Drusus and sea-calves." But this situation could have been nothing compared to the machine-made noises of the modern city. The reader can compile his own list of horrid noises, but from the thousands of complaints that have been made it is safe to assume that it will contain excavation blasts, the stabbing roar of pneumatic drills, riveting, hammering, steelwork, shrieking brakes, repeated blowing of automobile horns, the booming of airplanes, trolley cars, radio loud-speakers, the clattering of dishes in restaurants, the resounding of garbage and ash cans, barking dogs,

[38] "The Menace of Great Cities," *National Housing Association Publication*, No. 20, June, 1913, 12-13. *Cf.* William B. Munro, *Government of American Cities*, 1926, pp. 66-67.

unseasonable piano playing, and the sound of revelry by night. A tabulation of complaints sent to the New York City Noise Abatement Commission shows that traffic, transportation, and radio noises head the list. This Commission was appointed in 1929 to study the complex noise situation in the city with a view of finding means of eliminating unnecessary noise and of determining the effect of noise in general on the inhabitants of a metropolitan center. Its report is, incidentally, the first book ever printed on the subject of city noises. One of its committees which studied the effect of noise on human beings summed up its preliminary findings as follows:

1. Hearing is apt to be impaired in those exposed to constant loud noises.

2. Noise interferes seriously with the efficiency of the worker. It lessens attention and makes concentration upon any task difficult.

3. In the attempt to overcome the effect of noise, great strain is put upon the nervous system, leading to neurasthenic and psychasthenic states, and necessitating frequent recuperation in the country to maintain mental efficiency and alertness.

4. Noise interferes seriously with sleep, even though in some cases it appears that the system is able to adjust itself so that wakefulness does not result.

5. It is well established that, in addition to these other evil effects, the normal development of infants and young children is seriously interfered with by constant loud noises.

The committee and the Commission believe that the work already done proves sufficiently what every worker in New York City already knows if he has thought about the matter—that the constant racket of traffic, construction, industry, and innumerable unnecessary noises added to it produces a profound depression upon the nervous system, reduces mental efficiency and makes for dullness and ill health, matters which may well concern the city in its efforts toward greater alertness and health among its citizens. Not only in New York but everywhere the protest against the noises of modern civilization is arising, as if, after a century of our more and more raucous machine age, human ears and human nerves could endure it no longer.[39]

The formation and separation of social classes are more sharply marked in cities than in rural districts. In addition to the economic lines of cleavage mentioned earlier, there are social, racial, and religious lines, produced by competition and the cosmopolitan character

[39] Noise Abatement Commission, Department of Health, City of New York, *City Noise*, 1930, pp. 23-24 (quoted). Shirley W. Wynne, "Noises that Assail the New York Ear," *The New York Times Magazine*, Nov. 3, 1929. Eunice F. Barnard, "Cities Begin to Wage War on Their Own Noise," New York *Times*, Nov. 4, 1928.

of the population. In its extreme form this situation leads to class struggle.[40] A further characteristic of the population is its mobility, which not only forms a point of sharp contrast of the city with the country but also of the United States with Europe. Three types of mobility may be noted: inter-community, intra-community, and mobility without change of residence.

The leading causes of inter-community mobility, or migration from one city to another, are given by McKenzie[41] as follows: "The sudden change from a predominantly agricultural to a predominantly industrial society has occasioned a mobility of life unknown before. As long as the soil furnished the chief basis of economic income man was obliged to live a comparatively stable life in a fixed and definite locality. With the development of the modern capitalistic régime, the presence of the individual is no longer necessary to insure the productivity and security of his property. He may now, if he chooses, invest his savings in interest-bearing securities which require neither his personal presence nor his attention to insure an income. He is thus left free to live, if he so desires, a nomad life. Of course all classes in society are not equally free to move about. The middle-class tradesman and many of the professional groups are more or less tied to definite localities by the very nature of their work. On the other hand, the well-to-do and the day-laborer are free to move almost at will. Our modern factory system is the chief cause of the present migratory tendencies of the wage-earning class. In an open labor market with employers competing with one another in their demands for labor, the wage-earner is fast becoming a sort of tourist who spends but a short period in each community during his trip around the country." Rapid community turnover of this sort plays havoc with local standards and neighborhood mores. It is impossible to have an efficient local opinion in a neighborhood where the people are in constant move.

Intra-community mobility, or change of residence from one section to another within the community, is quite as disturbing to neighborhood association as is movement from one community to another. This type of mobility is especially characteristic of American cities because of their rapid growth. With the growth of a city appears the

[40] See Harvey W. Zorbaugh, *The Gold Coast and the Slum*, 1929, for a vivid portrayal of the different classes and kinds of people to be found in an urban community, the barriers of social distance, and the effect of this situation upon the political system.

[41] "The Neighborhood," in *American Journal of Sociology*, Sept., 1921, 27:2:-158, 161 (quoted), 162, 167. Aryness Joy, "Note on the Changes of Residence of Families of American Business and Professional Men," in *American Journal of Sociology*, Jan., 1928, 33:4:614-621. R. E. Park and E. W. Burgess, *The City*, 1925, pp. 17-20, 58-62.

phenomenon of the changing neighborhood, in which one social, and often racial, class succeeds another in a given district as housing and other conditions deteriorate. The most mobile class is that living in boarding and rooming houses and cheap hotels near the business center of the city. Tenantry is also a contributing factor, along with the turnover of labor, so that when a man takes a job in another section of the city he is both anxious and free to move.

The third type of mobility is one which is not indicated by change of residence but is measured by the ability of the individual, because of modern methods of communication, to utilize the larger social environment afforded by the community as a whole. The automobile, street car, telephone, and press, together with increased leisure time, have all contributed greatly to the breakdown of neighborhood ties. A city-dweller may have his friends and interests scattered all over town and keep in close communication or touch with them and at the same time not know his neighbors in the apartment house where he lives.

Mobility of population, and especially the existence of a large floating population, greatly increase the difficulties of city government. "The thousands of new residents are strangers to the city's history and traditions, have no local attachments, and do not readily acquire any civic pride. The vast majority are non-taxpayers and feel little concern in the city's government."[42] It is almost impossible to create interest in municipal affairs among citizens in transit. "Stability of residence, as a rule, implies home ownership, which in turn gives rise to local sentiment and interest in neighborhood surroundings. In a region where the population is continually shifting there is little opportunity for the development of neighborhood sentiment, and as a result local concerns are usually left to take care of themselves. It is hard to develop interest in neighborhood affairs among families who are the while conscious of the temporary nature of their domicile within the district." The fact that there is usually a residence qualification for voting leaves every year an increasingly large number of disfranchised citizens. The problems which the mobility of population presents to political reformers are likewise common to social workers in other fields. "Organizations dealing with delinquency and dependency are hampered in their efforts by the frequent movements of their 'cases.' Similarly the church, trade union, and other voluntary forms of association lose in their efficiency through the rapid turn-

[42] Adna F. Weber, *Growth of Cities*, 1899, pp. 429-430.

over of their local membership lists.''[43] Our distinguished critic,
James Bryce,[44] drew attention years ago to our excessive mobility
and its effects: ''In no State of the Union is the bulk of the population
so fixed in its residence as everywhere in Europe; in some it is almost
nomadic. Except in the more stagnant parts of the South, nobody
feels rooted to the soil. Here to-day and gone to-morrow, he cannot
readily contract habits of trustful dependence on his neighbours.''

A final social consequence of the growth of cities that calls for
special mention is the disintegrating effect on the family. The type
of family organization as we know it was evolved under rural conditions; it has been seriously affected by the economic and environmental changes that have produced the modern industrial city. ''The
fact that agriculture is still a family industry where the work and
the home life are not divorced, and where all members of the family
participate in the common toil for the support of the home, gives a
natural basis for a type of family life which it is very difficult to
maintain in the city.''[45] Under earlier agricultural conditions the
family, it is generally conceded, had worked out a fairly satisfactory
adjustment, as Ogburn[46] has clearly brought out. ''The family was an
economic institution as well as an affectional and biological one. In
fact, under agricultural conditions, it was a most significant unit
in society possessing in addition to biological and economic functions,
many other functions such as recreational, educational, protective
and religious. Woman's economic function was most important, and
a woman of ability was of great economic value to the farm. Marriage
was, in part, the taking of a business partner, and early marriage
was of economic advantage because it was entering business early.
The wife's duties, spinning, weaving, sewing, preparing foods, the
manufacture of different articles, and various other tasks around the
farm, were quite comparable, in economic return, with the husband's
work. The education that was necessary for life and business success
was acquired in large part in the home, with the exception of such
elementary book education as the three R's. It was an excellent institution for supervising the activities of children because the child's
future life as an adult was to be spent on the farm. Divorce was a
particularly serious event because it meant a rupture to so many
economic and social activities. The agricultural family was also in a

[43] R. D. McKenzie, ''The Neighborhood,'' in *American Journal of Sociology,*
Sept., 1921, 27:2:158, 159.
[44] *American Commonwealth,* 1917, II, 293.
[45] Thomas N. Carver, *Rural Economics,* 1911, pp. 21 (quoted), 22-25.
[46] *Social Change,* 1923, pp. 241-242.

fortunate position to render protection to the dependent kin. The functioning of the family under these conditions indicates an excellent adjustment between the family as a social organization and the material culture, though no doubt there were tyrannies, repressions of instincts and resistances to new ideas.''

Then came the economic changes produced by the Industrial Revolution, epitomized in the advent of the factory, and as a result the impairment of the old-time unity of the family group. The immediate effect of the growth of large-scale production was to take from the home an increasing number of economic functions and place them in factories. This was particularly true of the work which was formerly woman's share. As Professor Cutler[47] has said, ''The domestic arts are now largely factory processes. There is almost no sex division of labor in the household, for there are left to it none but the 'sweated trades.' To contribute to the support of the family it is necessary for both sexes to work away from home and become wage-earners. No longer is the household a self-sufficient unit, either socially or economically.'' The changed conditions have made the woman who has remained in the home more dependent economically. ''Her services are narrowed to the biological function of bearing children and the social function of rearing them. If she leaves the home in order to contribute to the support of the family (fulfilling again her primordial economic duty), under the new conditions her functions as bearer and rearer of children are sadly interfered with.''[48] The services performed by the family living in a modern city apartment illustrate what a great change has taken place in the economic functions of the family. It is said that as a result of the factory system and the delicatessen store the only equipment for keeping house the modern city woman needs are a can-opener and a corkscrew.

''Such profound changes in the economic functions of the family and the creation of new forms of economic activity,'' comments Professor Ogburn,[49] ''meant that new adjustments would have to be made by the family, since it was hardly possible to stop or change significantly the march of material progress. The educational function, for instance, can not now be performed as satisfactorily by the family as was once possible. The diversification and the specialized technique of industry and the transfer of occupations from the home to the factory have meant the necessity of special vocational and trade education

[47] ''Durable Monogamous Wedlock,'' in *American Journal of Sociology*, 22:-2:229.
[48] F. W. Blackmar and J. L. Gillin, *Outlines of Sociology*, 1923, pp. 126 ff.
[49] *Social Change*, 1923, p. 242.

outside the home. Manual training which was formerly quite readily learned at home must now be taught in city schools. The technical efficiency demanded by modern industrial life has necessitated changes in the curricula of the schools.[50] These are all special adjustments of education to the changed material conditions. The juvenile court has arisen as an adjustment agency to the changed material conditions through the failure of the family to make the proper adaptation. With the industrial revolution came the great growth of cities, little adapted to child life. The congestion of cities was accompanied almost nowhere with adequate development of play space for children.[51] Coupled with these conditions was the breaking up of homes and the drawing of mothers into industry.

"The factory immediately brought children to work within its walls, with unsatisfactory results, and a better adjustment was made through child labor laws and compulsory school laws, with inspectors and attendance officers. Such special laws were unnecessary under the old material conditions. Special forms of State insurance and various types of pensions seem a desirable form of adjustment to the new conditions which face the family. The agricultural family with a relatively more stable abode was very well suited for caring for widows, the aged, and dependent kin. There were rooms and food, and light tasks to be done. But with the scattered and more migratory family living in congested centres, such care of dependents can be effected in fewer families and with more difficulty. Women have not become satisfactorily adjusted to these new material conditions of the factory system. Their work as producers has largely been taken away, so that many are idle, or do work which is only slightly productive of substantial economic values; or else they go into industry under such chance conditions as they may find. The introduction of women into industry may call for special adaptations in regard to such matters as sanitary conditions, hours of labor, and maternity insurance. A somewhat wider life for women outside the home seems desirable, since so many of the home occupations are now found outside the family. The extension of the franchise to women is only a minor step in that direction. Finally, the reduction of the economic function of the family together with other functions has rendered the marriage union of man and woman less stable.

"It is thus seen that the change from agriculture to the modern factory system has necessitated changes in the family organization.

[50] See ch. XV below.
[51] See ch. XXI below.

There is abundant evidence to show that the old agricultural family organization is no longer adapted to industrial life as seen in modern cities. Many functions which were performed reasonably satisfactorily by the family in farm life have been or are being taken over by the State, by industry, by special organizations. Special organizations have been developed to perform functions affecting women, children, education, dependency, recreation, etc. In these cases, it is no doubt difficult to measure the delay in each case in developing the new forms for performing these functions. But it seems quite clear that there has been a delay. Few would maintain that child labor laws, compulsory education, vocational and industrial education, playgrounds, and social insurance, for instance, have been developed as promptly as they should. The material culture has gone forward, while the adaptive culture has lagged behind.''

It would seem as if the family-institution in the city is in a transitional stage. Eventually it will work out a fairly complete and satisfactory adjustment. Meantime there is much evidence of disintegration and maladaptation. The apartment house, the employment of women in industry, the high cost of home space, commercialized recreation, all are antagonists of domesticity that subtly weaken home ties. Effects approaching the pathological may be seen in the high and increasing divorce-rate, limitation of the birth-rate, juvenile delinquency, evils of leisure-time activities, and in other respects many of which will be discussed in later connections. Although it is evident that the modern family is suffering from unsatisfactory living conditions, it is also plain that the Colonial type of home is an anachronism today. As Professor Cutler[52] has pointed out in a penetrating article, ''We must concern ourselves with a new type, or types, and we must consider a larger unit. We must put into the meaning of *home* something of its old Teutonic sense when in the form *Heim* it meant a village, or a community. . . . In a number of ways the conception of a larger domestic unit is already finding expression and taking tangible form. There was a time when the provision of a water supply was an individual household matter. For an ever-increasing number of households it is no longer an individual or private matter at all. If the homes are to have an adequate, pure, and safe supply of water, it must come through intelligent and far-sighted community action.'' The development of community agencies to take care of sanitation, food supply, and other essentials are further ex-

[52] ''Durable Monogamous Wedlock,'' *American Journal of Sociology*, 22:2:229 (quoted), 230, 234 (quoted), 250-251 (quoted).

amples. ''The family is no longer an isolated societal unit; it has become a constituent part of a complex and intricate community life. The cross-currents of this community life, if it be poorly organized and its potency misdirected, tear the family asunder. Those who would conserve the family need to concern themselves with the disordered social and industrial conditions which impinge upon a normal and wholesome life for husbands, wives, and children.'' The author concludes that ''the growing conception of the modern home as a domestic unit much larger and more inclusive than that cherished in our traditions, together with the fact that women in increasing numbers are entering wage-earning occupations and effecting a new sex division of labor which is rapidly gaining general recognition, may reasonably be expected to contribute to the durability and the permanence of monogamous wedlock. Such symptoms of instability in the institution of marriage as are now current are to be regarded as characterizing a notable transition period, the culmination of which will be a more perfect adaptation to the new life conditions and a new status for the women.''

One thought we should take with us from this discussion of the transition from rural to urban life and its effects, viz., that conditions of life in the city are capable of indefinite modification through the action of individuals or through the concerted action of the community.[53] This situation derives from the fact that the urban environment is artificialized, man-made. In the development of cities there has come to be a diminishing degree of dependence on purely physical conditions: an artificial environment has gradually been developed to replace natural physical conditions.[54] The platting, grading, and paving of streets, construction of wharves, public water-supply, sewage and drainage systems—all these public works are carried on to meet certain needs which natural conditions fail to meet. ''The whole structure of the modern city is artificial and can be corrected by the same human intelligence that created it.'' Thus the inhabitants of an urban community have a power over environment which carries with it the most far-reaching consequences. Since conditions of life can be modified, a large share of the responsibility for social welfare is placed upon the members of the community. There are limits, of course, to what societies can do; there are great economic, social, and natural forces at work which determine the lines of adjustment; but within

[53] Henry P. Fairchild, *Foundations of Social Life*, 1927, ch. VI, ''The Challenge of the Human Environment.''

[54] Albert G. Keller, *Societal Evolution*, 1915, ch. X.

the restrictions imposed there remains an extensive domain for the play of human ingenuity. The history of every large city bears testimony to the possibility of radical changes in environmental conditions, changes which have profoundly affected the health, morals, and welfare of the community.[55]

[55] L. S. Rowe, "Political Consequences of City Growth," *Yale Review*, May, 1900, IX, 23. Lewis, Heydecker, and O'Hara, *Land Values*, 1927, p. 22.

CHAPTER III

CITY PLANNING

AMERICAN cities have been inadequately planned; most of them, like Topsy, have "just growed." The process of growth, in the majority of cases, has been by agglutination, and as Geddes Smith[1] remarks, "Agglutination sometimes has unfortunate results. It produces, for instance, such words as the Mohawk term for stove-polish: Deyeknonhsedehrihadasterasterahetakwa. That may be natural, but it looks absurd. Agglutination works much the same way in the growth of cities. One subdivision is added to another, and you have a suburb. One straight line is added to another, usually at right angles, and you have a street system. But God save us from the consequences." With the exception of Washington, there has been no realization of the permanence of the city, of the importance of streets and open spaces, of building regulations, transportation, waterfronts, and the physical foundations which underlie the city's life. Private builders have been permitted to do as they wished with their property. There has been little control of the amount of land that might be built upon, of the height of buildings, of the style of tenements, of the materials used in construction. Nor has there been much attempt to determine the uses to which property may be put. Factories have located everywhere, stores and apartment houses have been erected in good residential neighborhoods. American cities have neglected to retain possession of their waterfronts, which have been privately exploited by railroads and industries instead of being utilized for beauty and recreation as in Europe, where they have been retained in public hands and developed as civic centers. Nor have our cities provided for the proper location of public buildings. There are few great civic centers here as compared with Europe—centers about which public buildings are grouped. All these agencies are closely related to the life of the community, and their control and correlation under a definite plan are involved in the art of city planning.

There are a number of reasons for the failure of American cities in this respect.[2] Our cities have been helpless; they have been unable

[1] "Planning for Permanency," *The Survey*, Dec. 15, 1927, 59:6:381-382.
[2] Adapted from Frederic C. Howe, *The Modern City*, 1915, ch. XV.

to control the public-service corporations or to compel the speculator to plat his land as the city decreed. Only within limits has the city been able to control the height of buildings or restrict the amount of land that they may cover. It has lacked power to locate factories. There has been statutory limitation on the city's borrowing powers, and the city has been unable to carry through needed improvements. Besides these restrictions on the powers of the city, due to lack of home rule, there has been little understanding of these matters on the part of the people, little community sense, few traditions of beauty. Public opinion, as well as the law, has been very solicitous of the rights of private property.

History of City Planning.—The first great city to be planned in the modern sense of the idea was Paris. Louis XIV, ambitious for his capital, intrusted its planning to the Academy of Architects, which prepared designs in which the Madeleine, Place de la Concorde, Hôtel des Invalides, and the wide avenues about the Tuileries existed years before they were realized. The work was continued by Napoleon I and Napoleon III. Modern city planning as an organized art has reached its highest development in Germany. When the beauty of the old towns was threatened by the growth of industry, city planning was taken up, as a protest against the social abuses of private property. The German city said to the landowner, the factory- and home-builder: "You must so use your property that it will conform with the general plan which our architects have designed; you must plat your streets, locate your structures and use your property so that it will not injure the health and well-being of the community." Today every large city in Germany has an official plan. Experts go from city to city to advise on these matters. Town planning is developed as a science and is taught in the universities. Zoning has there received its first and fullest development. German cities and towns are unique in that they own so much common land. The city is free to buy and speculate in land; the unearned increment goes to the benefit of the people. There are said to be 1,500 towns and villages which own so much common land that their inhabitants pay no taxes. Ownership of land enables the city to plan for its development in a generous way. By acquiring land in advance of its growth, a city can anticipate its needs. This has been of considerable aid in housing, and it has, more broadly, fostered a sense of the unity and permanence of the city. The underlying idea is the subordination of the individual to the common good.

France was the first country in the world to pass a compulsory city-planning law; this was in 1909, and it applied to cities of 10,000 or more population. In the same year city planning was made optional in England; in 1919 it was made compulsory for all cities of 20,000 or more inhabitants.[3] In the United States, the World's Fair in Chicago in 1893 marked the beginning of popular interest in city planning, although some appreciation of the possibilities and advantages of the planning of cities has been current from early Colonial times.[4] In one sense, ever since cities have been built there has been city planning. But beyond a superficial and arbitrary plan of streets most of our cities have not been planned in any adequate sort of way. "They have met each problem as it arose, separately, and as well as they could, considering the situation in which they found themselves at the time."[5] About the beginning of the twentieth century several movements met in a unified effort to produce city planning. The most dramatic of these movements, as stated above, was inaugurated at the World's Fair in Chicago. The "white city," created by the genius of the late Daniel H. Burnham and an able group of associates for the international exposition in Chicago, made a profound impression upon all who saw it. "It is safe to say," comments Nelson P. Lewis,[6] a noted city planner, "that such effective grouping of a series of monumental buildings of harmonious design had never before been accomplished or even attempted and, while the buildings themselves were temporary, the effect which they produced has been permanent, and the influence of the general plan is quite evident in most of the ambitious projects for the creation of civic centers which have since been put forward." Visitors left the Fair with this thought: "Why cannot cities be built like a world's fair; why should we not employ architects and artists in their designing; why should we not live in cities as beautiful as this fugitive play city, that will disappear at the end of the summer?" And the men who designed the Fair became interested in the grouping of public buildings, in the control of streets and open spaces, in the idea of building cities with a vision of the future.[7] The World's Fair at Chicago may thus be said to have constituted the threshold of the architectural approach to city planning. It revived interest in architecture and led to coöperation of architects,

[3] *Housing Betterment*, June, 1919, 8:2:15; Feb., 1925, 14:1:15-16.
[4] Frederick L. Olmsted, "The Town-Planning Movement in America," *Annals*, Jan., 1914, 51:140:172-181. Harlean James, *Land Planning in the United States*, 1926, ch. III. William B. Munro, *Municipal Government and Administration*, 1923, II, 72-77.
[5] Harlean James, *Land Planning in the United States*, 1926, p. 44.
[6] *The Planning of the Modern City*, 1923, p. 17.
[7] Frederic C. Howe, *The Modern City*, 1915, pp. 200-201.

landscape architects, and engineers.[8] Then it was discovered that America possessed in its capital one of the most completely planned cities in the world. Washington was designed over a century ago. It might have grown up as other American cities in a haphazard way had it not been for the imagination of the first President, who called to his aid a French military engineer, Peter Charles L'Enfant, who had been with him during the Revolutionary War. Major L'Enfant devised a plan for the city which has been followed in the main ever since.[9] At the end of 1930, city planning commissions had been established in 786 different municipalities, located in 46 states and the District of Columbia. The city planning movement has thus become nation wide.[10]

Definition.—The planning of cities involves the adjustment of the physical resources of the city to meet the needs of its population, present and future. As Lewis[11] phrases it, ''City planning is simply the exercise of such foresight as will promote the orderly and sightly development of a city and its environs along rational lines with due regard for health, amenity and convenience and for its commercial and industrial advancement.'' It means the forecasting of city growth, and the guiding and directing of natural development along prearranged lines. Orderly development, or the attainment of unity in city construction, is its objective. ''It brings the city government and its citizens together in preparing for their own future needs and for the probable requirements of their commerce and industries. A city or town is a place in which to live, to work, and to play, and should be planned systematically with these ends in mind, just as the location of buildings on a factory site is carefully determined.''[12]

Types of City Planning.—The function of city planning may be considered conveniently under two headings: First, the remodeling of the old city; and second, the determination of the future type of development of the city and especially of new sections. Of these, the first program is largely remedial in character and is usually very

[8] Harlean James, *Land Planning in the United States*, 1926, chs. II, III.

[9] U. S. Grant, 3d, ''The Development of the Plan of the City of Washington,'' *National Conference on City Planning*, 1927, XIX, 206-212. Charles W. Eliot, 2d, ''Bringing the L'Enfant Plan up to Date,'' *National Conference on City Planning*, 1927, XIX, 213-219.

[10] *Housing*, October, 1931, 20:3:234-235. United States Department of Commerce, *A Tabulation of City Planning Commissions in the United States*, 1931.

[11] *The Planning of the Modern City*, 1923, p. 11. See also S. D. Adshead, *Town Planning*, 1923, p. 36. Frank B. Williams, *The Law of City Planning and Zoning*, 1922, pp. 1, 4. John Nolen, *City Planning*, 1916, p. 1. Edward M. Bassett, ''What is City Planning?'' *City Planning*, Oct., 1925, 1:3:196.

[12] Advisory Committee on Zoning, Department of Commerce, *A City Planning Primer*, 1928, p. 1.

costly. Planning of this sort on an extensive scale is possible where a
city or part of it has been destroyed. Urban disasters offer an opportunity for a city to rectify its mistakes of the past. Sir Christopher
Wren made a plan of reconstruction for London after the great fire
in 1668, "to remedy the deformity and inconveniences of the old
town." His suggestions were not followed. "The missing of that great
opportunity more than 200 years ago has cost Londoners collectively
untold health and wealth and time."[13] Nor did San Francisco take
advantage of its opportunity following the earthquake, or rather fire,
in 1906. But there are several notable American examples of planning
following a disaster, such as the rebuilding of Salem, Massachusetts,
after the conflagration which occurred on June 25, 1914; the rehous-
ing and redistricting of Halifax after the explosion of December,
1917; and the rebuilding of Santa Barbara, California, after the
earthquake of June 29, 1925.[14] Under French law, every city, town,
and village devastated in the World War—and there were some 2,600
of them—must make plans not only for the improvement of the older
part of the town, but for extensions into newer areas. "When these
towns are rebuilt, they will have wider streets, the housing will be
more open, they will have planted spaces, a better setting or grouping
for the public buildings, they will have better sanitation and better
water supply; and in general, these towns will be more livable, more
comfortable, more sanitary, more the types of places that they have
a right to live in as good citizens of France."[15]

Another example of the remedial type of city planning is the
widening and straightening of narrow, crooked streets. The voters of
Detroit have recently approved of a plan of street remodeling which
calls for the expenditure of more than $100,000,000. The major
project, which includes the condemnation of property adjacent to
Woodward Avenue, the city's main artery, involves demolition of a
score of skyscrapers, at an estimated cost of $73,000,000. This will
create an avenue 8 miles in length and 120 feet in width, leading
from the center of the city. Other important streets, affecting the
downtown section, are to be widened at a cost of $40,000,000.[16] Tear-
ing down old buildings to make way for parks or playgrounds is another illustration of corrective city planning; a more common ex-

[13] J. S. Nettlefold, *Practical Housing*, 1910, p. 99.
[14] James Ford, "The Rebuilding of Cities after Disaster," *City Planning*, Jan.,
1927, 3:1:38-54; *Housing Betterment*, Sept., 1919, 8:3:35 ff.
[15] George B. Ford, "Housing in France," *National Housing Conference*, 1920,
VIII, 147.
[16] New York *Times*, July 31, 1926.

ample, and one more closely related to housing reform, is the destruction of unsanitary areas—what the English call "slum-clearance." This will be discussed fully in later chapters on housing conditions. Instances of the destruction of unsanitary areas by the government are not wanting in this country, though perhaps more has been effected automatically through the expansion of industry. Remedial city planning may be even more comprehensive in scope; Nolen[17] cites six typical examples of small cities that have been replanned or remodeled as a unit to meet new requirements.

Less costly is the second type of city planning, which looks to the future and is fundamentally preventive and constructive in character. This involves the exercise of foresight in the development of new sections of a city or the laying out and construction of new communities—either what are known as satellites of existing cities, or complete and separate new towns in new locations, like the English "Garden Cities."[18] A city plan should not stop short at the city limits but should include the whole urban region—the city and the surrounding territory. Most of the preventive work can be done in the developing areas outside the political boundaries of the city. Regional planning has the same objective as city planning; it is concerned merely with a larger unit. The regional plan of New York City and its environs, cited in the first chapter, is a case in point. The smaller cities around New York are affected by it in many ways. It is stated, for example, that Yonkers cannot properly analyze its own traffic congestion, White Plains its housing problem, Passaic its sewage problem, or Stamford its paving program without recognizing the existence of the problems created by the whole metropolitan district.[19]

Essential Elements in a City Plan.—"City planning includes in its scope the planning not only of the public features of the community, such as streets and parks, but of the land devoted to private uses, such as residence, business and industry, in the effort to direct, so far as may be deemed wise, the development of the community as a whole. For the most part, at present, the private features of the town, city or region, in so far as they are controlled by the public in

[17] *Replanning Small Cities*, 1912; *cf.* his *New Towns for Old*, 1927, discussing the achievements in civic improvement in some American small towns and neighborhoods.

[18] John Nolen, "New Communities Planned to Meet New Conditions," *National Conference on City Planning*, 1926, XVIII, 5. Garden Cities are discussed in ch. VIII, below. An excellent example of a completely planned city is Radburn, New Jersey, a diagram of which is presented in the following chapter.

[19] *The American City*, 1922, 26:533-534.

the effort to create a unified and coördinated community, are regulated by zoning laws and ordinances."[20]

The most basic concern of city planning is with the location of the means of circulation—streets, rail and water transportation, transit, traffic, etc. "Facility of communication is the very basis for the existence of cities; improved methods of general transportation are at the root of the modern phenomenon of rapid city growth; and the success of a city is more dependent upon good means of circulation than upon any other physical factor under its control."[21] Under modern conditions, a community may be approached by highway, by railroad, by watercourse, by airway, or by a combination of these four methods. A publication by the Department of Commerce considers these methods of transportation in the light of city planning as follows. "Highway approaches are of enormous importance in these days of the automobile, and thought should be given as to whether roads shall lead only through the heart of the town or shall avoid congested districts by appropriate by-passes. Railroads are usually the basic means of contact between the city and the outside world. Their freight terminals, spurs, and sidings should be located and arranged for economical handling and trucking of the city's outgoing products, and of incoming food, merchandise, building materials, and raw products for industry. Passenger stations, or a single union station, if considered practicable, should be convenient and well served by local transit facilities. Property bordering the tracks should be well maintained and give a creditable impression of the community to passengers entering and leaving. Water approaches may be made effective in serving commerce, and where that is not practicable, may be made invaluable in serving the health and pride of the community. The air approach involves landing fields, which, if properly provided and located, may be of great advantage."[22]

Under the street system are to be considered questions of layout, width, and arrangement, and relation to traffic and transit. In general, a system of wide, well-arranged thoroughfares is basic to good city planning. They should lead from the central part of the city to outlying territory, and there should be belt streets affording direct travel between one section and another without passage through the central business district. The actual street systems to be found are of four types: irregular or meandering; concentric; diagonal or

[20] Frank B. Williams, "Legal Notes," *City Planning*, April, 1925, 1:1:52.
[21] John Nolen, *City Planning*, 1916, p. 5.
[22] Advisory Committee on Zoning, Department of Commerce, *A City Planning Primer*, 1928, p. 5.

radial; and perpendicular. Where streets have been platted, the latter
is the most common type. Rectangular street platting—the gridiron
plan—probably goes back to the dawn of history. William Penn used
it in 1682 when he made a checkerboard plan for Philadelphia, perhaps the earliest example in America. New York City was laid out
in blocks 200 by 800 feet, with the narrow dimension on the avenues.
This was the system of land surveying adopted by the Federal Government. It tends to produce standardization, but breaks down under
modern conditions. Rectangular street platting has been unthinkingly
applied to cities regardless of topography, the disposal of buildings
of varying size and importance, strategic lines of communication,
uses or needs. As such it is wasteful and inelastic. It is like trying
to make one suit of clothes fit all sizes of men. Though superior to
irregular or meandering streets, it does not permit the freest movement to the outlying sections of the city. This purpose is best served
by diagonal or radial streets. Moreover, streets are differently used
and should be adapted to the different utilities. Streets of the traffic
group constitute the framework of the city and should be wide and
well paved. Streets for business and industrial use call for paving
of different width and material from that of minor residence streets.
It is wasteful to have a single street pattern. Where the street patterns in single-family residence neighborhoods are the same as those
in apartment-house neighborhoods and business districts, as is often
the case, the result is burdensome to residence districts, discouraging
to business districts, costly for the city and wasteful of its potentialities.[23]

Adequate recreation space, although often overlooked, is of great
importance to a community, and provision for it rightly belongs in a
city plan. Parks, playgrounds, and other open spaces, essential to the
recreational life of the community, should be conveniently located.
The need of more public open spaces of all kinds is one of the consequences of living in multi-family dwellings in congested cities.[24]
The dignity and attractiveness of a community and the convenience

    [23] Charles M. Robinson, *City Planning, with special reference to the planning
of streets and lots*, 1916, pp. 16-19, 86 ff. Nelson P. Lewis, *The Planning of the
Modern City*, 1923, ch. VI. Lewis, Heydecker, and O'Hara, *Land Values*, 1927,
p. 50. Frederick N. Evans, *Town Improvement*, 1919, pp. 30-40. J. C. Nichols,
"Financial Effect of Good Planning in Land Subdivision," *National Conference
on City Planning*, 1916, VIII, 96-98. Harlean James, *Land Planning in the
United States*, 1926, chs. VI-IX.
    [24] Nelson P. Lewis, *The Planning of the Modern City*, 1923, ch. VIII. Harlean
James, *Land Planning in the United States*, 1926, ch. XI. Frederick N. Evans,
Town Improvement, 1919, chs. VII-XII. John Nolen, *City Planning*, 1916, chs.
VII, VIII.

of its citizens may also be served by thoughtful location of public and semi-public buildings. These will ordinarily include the city hall, courthouse, public library, art museum, churches, public schools, and, perhaps, university buildings. "Each building of this type becomes more impressive when part of a well-arranged group, especially when it can be seen from long street approaches. But in such an arrangement special care should be taken to preserve a practicable street plan. In smaller communities the principal public buildings may form a single group, while in larger cities there may be a principal civic center, a principal educational and art center, and a number of outlying community centers."[25]

Zoning.—An essential feature of city planning is zoning, which may be defined as the establishment of districts in a city in which the height of buildings, the area of the lot that they may cover, and the uses to which they may be put are regulated in accordance with a predetermined city-wide scheme of development.[26] Although French in origin, zoning was first developed in Germany, where it has also been most widely employed. Use-zoning was the first to appear; then bulk-zoning, that is, rules fixing the maxima which structures shall not exceed. The districts thus established are in accordance with the three main utilities of city land: residential, business, and industrial. The residential districts are generally divided into different grades, as Class 1, limited to single-family dwellings; Class 2, permitting two-family dwellings and apartment houses; and Class 3, any kind of dwelling. The business district is further divided into zones for retail stores and offices and for wholesale establishments. Industrial districting often provides for a separation of ordinary, non-offensive industries and the odor-, dust-, and smoke-producing plants. Sometimes there is a separate district for public and semi-public buildings and parks.

In planning for the future it is necessary to understand completely the mechanism of cities in order to be intimately acquainted with every tendency of use and growth. City planning on a large scale, and particularly zoning, are practicable only when they are an adjustment to the laws which govern the growth and physical structure

[25] Advisory Committee on Zoning, Department of Commerce, *A City Planning Primer*, 1928, p. 7.

[26] Advisory Committee on Zoning, Department of Commerce, *A Zoning Primer*, 1926; *A City Planning Primer*, 1928, 12-13. Lawson Purdy, "The Zoning of Cities," *National Housing Conference*, 1917, VI, 214-228. Frank B. Williams, *The Law of City Planning and Zoning*, 1922, p. 210. Harlean James, *Land Planning in the United States*, 1926, p. 85.

of cities and the distribution of utilities. It is essential to a scientific
understanding to know what these laws are.

At first glance, land utilization in an urban area appears, as Professor Haig[27] remarks, to be without rhyme or reason, a confused and
baffling welter of anomalies and paradoxes. He cites the case of New
York City and its environs. "The land is being used, most of it,
very intensively indeed. Nine million people eat and sleep, work and
play in the area. But the assignment of the land to the various uses
seems to the superficial observer to have been made by the Mad
Hatter at Alice's tea party. Some of the poorest people live in conveniently located slums on high-priced land. On patrician Fifth Avenue, Tiffany and Woolworth, cheek by jowl, offer jewels and jimcracks
from substantially identical sites. Childs restaurants thrive and multiply where Delmonico's withered and died. A stone's throw from the
stock exchange, the air is filled with the aroma of roasting coffee;
a few hundred feet from Times Square, with the stench of slaughter-
houses. In the very heart of this 'commercial' city, on Manhattan
Island south of 59th Street, the inspectors in 1922 found nearly
420,000 workers employed in factories. Such a situation outrages
one's sense of order. Everything seems misplaced. One yearns to re-
arrange the hodge-podge and to put things where they belong. The
confusion, of course, is more apparent than real. The deeper one
delves into the reasons underlying the present layout, the more dis-
trustful he becomes of sweeping indictments of its soundness and
efficiency. Most of the apparent anomalies and paradoxes dissolve
into commonplaces when subjected to serious study and detailed examination." Thus an analysis of the organic structure of cities shows
that they conform more or less rigidly to certain principles of growth.

Laws of City Growth.[28]—A study of the origin and development
of cities reveals that their starting-points are the most convenient
points of contact with the outer world. These are a wharf, if transportation is by water; the intersection of turnpikes or highways, if
transportation is by wagon; a railroad depot, if transportation is by
rail. Where at the inception of a city the first settlers lay out a plat,
the central point may be determined arbitrarily, with a public square

---

[27] "Toward an Understanding of the Metropolis," *Quarterly Journal of Economics*, May, 1926, XL, 403-404.

[28] The following is adapted from that excellent study by Richard M. Hurd,
Principles of City Land Values, 1905. His work has been brought up to date
in a few respects by Lewis, Heydecker, and O'Hara, *Land Values*, 1927. The
reader of this section will find that reference to a city map, especially that of
his own city, will make the discussion both clearer and more interesting.

or public building as the nucleus. The ground plan of cities is determined by several factors, chief of which is topography. Topographical faults normally control the shape of cities by interfering with their free growth in all directions from the point of origin. These are of two kinds: (a) water surfaces, such as harbors, lakes, rivers, creeks, and swamps; and (b) sharp variations from the normal city level, such as steep hills, deep hollows, and ravines. The influence of topography may be summarized by saying that level land attracts business, moderate elevations attract residences, and land below the normal level attracts transportation lines and industry. The main direction of city growth is usually determined by topography.

As to their lay-out, cities may be divided into two classes: those which have grown up without any definite ground plan; and those whose ground plans have been defined in advance of growth. Cities which have grown up haphazardly exhibit a tangle of narrow and crooked streets of varying and irregular size, evolved from cow paths or old trails whose directions were originally influenced by trifling obstacles such as hillocks, rocks, or clumps of trees. These first streets left large tracts between them, which were later pierced by irregular streets or lanes laid out for the convenience of the owner of the tract and without consideration for the general interests of the city. Where a plat has been laid out in advance, there are usually found long, straight streets of even width and at right angles to each other, leaving rectangular blocks for building sites. Older cities with marked modern growth show an old center of crooked streets surrounded by modern rectangular plats, although some cities have never changed to rectangular platting. In waterfront cities with rectangular plats the waterfront is normally used as a base, whether straight, curving, or broken and irregular; in inland cities the turnpikes are used as a base. The general effect of irregular arrangement is to strengthen central growth as opposed to radial growth, quick access to or from the business center being afforded only by turnpikes. This leads to congested housing conditions, congested traffic, and other problems. As already pointed out, it is expensive if remodeling is necessary. The effect of rectangular platting is to permit free movement throughout the city, which is further promoted by the addition of long diagonal streets. The need for diagonal streets depends largely on the shape of the city's site: there is less demand for them in narrow cities like New York and Boston than in cities that are spread out like Chicago and Detroit.

All city growth is central or radial. Central growth consists in the clustering of utilities around any point of attraction and is based on proximity, whereas radial growth is the result of transportation facilities and is based on accessibility. A continual contest exists between radial growth pushing out from the center along transportation lines, and central growth constantly following and obliterating it, while new projections are being made farther out the various radii. The normal result of radial and central growth combined is a star-shaped city, the growth extending first along the main thoroughfares radiating from the center and later filling in the parts lying between. The modifications of the shape of cities come chiefly from topography; lesser influences are an uneven development of some one factor of growth or individual ownership of land.

Radial Growth.—The framework of a city is laid down by its watercourses, main highways, and railroads. Waterfronts, if navigable, invite commerce, resulting in docks and warehouses; those away from the city center attract factories. If not navigable, and not bordered by railroads, and if the land is not low, they attract residences. In older cities, turnpikes, as the original highways were called, have been of chief importance. Broadway in New York City was part of the old Albany turnpike, Washington Street in Boston was part of the turnpike to New York which, in passing through Providence, was known as Westminister Street; and Main Street in Hartford was the New Haven turnpike. Turnpikes or highways are the natural outlets for residences forced away from the business center. Growth along highways continues to a point where the inconvenience of living so far out of town more than offsets the attractions of the highway, when back streets are laid out. Steam railroads affect city land in three ways, (*a*) by their terminals; (*b*) by their lines as barriers to growth or communication; and (*c*) by their lines as influencing land immediately adjacent. In the first case, the central effect of the passenger depot in a small city is to attract cheap hotels and shops, in larger cities high-class hotels. The radial effect of depots is of great importance in smaller towns, where they attract traffic within the city. In the second place, the restraining effect of the railroad varies according to the territory traversed. Where a railroad runs through a business section at grade, it limits communication between the divided sections and tends to concentrate business on one side of the line; where it is carried below or above grade, the effect is minimized. In a poor residential section a railroad has little or no restrictive effect upon growth, but in a high-class residence section it forms a nuisance which good residences shun. Consider, for example, the

Grand Central Terminal district in New York. A vast area here was formerly blighted by smoke and noise. It has since been reclaimed for intensive business and residential purposes. The improvement was made possible by the substitution of electric for steam power on the railroad lines entering the terminal, which are below grade and covered. One result of the transformation was the creation of a great new apartment district along Park Avenue, with enormously increased values. In the final instance, the effect of the railroad is to make the adjacent frontage of little value for shops or residences; a notable exception is the case of Syracuse.

Central Growth.—There are two aspects of central growth: (*a*) the main general growth in all directions centering about the point of origin; and (*b*) the growth about various subcenters within the city, such as transportation intersections and termini, public buildings, exchanges, and factories. The first and simplest form of central growth is that of the aggregation or adding of buildings one after another along the streets in the center of the city. The first dwellings in a village are located near the business buildings so that the merchants can walk to and from their business, and so great is the power of inertia that even in the smallest villages the few stores find it advantageous to be close together. The influence of public buildings on the structure of a commercial city is small unless such a city is also a national capital (London, Paris). In a wholly political city, as Washington, the public buildings largely determine the structure of the city. The smaller public buildings found in all cities, like the post office and city hall, have considerable influence in determining the line of early growth, but are of constantly diminishing importance as the other factors of a city's life become stronger, so that not infrequently the public building which created a street may in time be a detriment to it. Public buildings, if located at or near the old business center, tend to maintain central strength in their first location (Boston, New York, Philadelphia, and Chicago furnish noteworthy examples); this is the normal case. Exceptions occur either where public buildings are located at a moderate distance from the center, in which case the tendency is to draw business in their direction, or where they have been so misplaced that they fail to have any influence. Exchanges arise later in the life of a city, but in time acquire more central influence than any other factor. The New York Stock Exchange maintains the financial district. Factories create subcenters, most distinct when on the outskirts of the city, by causing the erection of working-class dwellings nearby, which in turn attract small shops and public and semi-public buildings. When located within the built-up sections of a city they attract tenements near at hand. In all growth the vital feature is continuity, the universal tendency being to add on buildings one by one, buildings of the same general character as those which preceded them.

The forces that create urban growth also create urban land values. These forces consist of the topographical advantages and transportation facilities that lead to the development of commerce and industry and to the demand for land areas for residence, business, and other social needs. "The adaptability of land for the most profitable use is the basis of its value. As a rule, land in cities is profitably used for business, industry or residence—all involving the erection of buildings." The highest values of land occur where there is the greatest concentration of population and wealth; yet in the final analysis it is the purchasing power and demands of the population more than their numbers that make or raise values. In all great cities, the highest grade of values is to be found in the principal financial and business centers. The next grade is that of the high-class apartment-house districts adjacent to these centers.[29]

As a city evolves, a continual specialization in business and a differentiation in social grades take place. There arise the three main classes of city land utilization mentioned above: business, industry, and residence. As to business land, retail stores either cluster at the business center or follow out the traffic streets. They find most business where the largest number of people pass. Wholesale establishments dealing in objects of great weight or bulk but relatively small value seek locations near transportation lines or termini for economy of handling; the selling is done by traveling salesmen or by selling agencies located in the business center. Companies wholesaling articles of small bulk but high value (e.g., jewelry) seek locations near their chief customers, the retail stores. Here the ability to supply quickly a small order of mixed goods is the inducement. In the larger cities a separate district evolves devoted to office buildings, whose ground floors are utilized by banks, trust companies, and the like, and whose offices are rented to brokers, lawyers, architects, and others. The location of such an administrative district is usually the result of slow growth around old institutions. With respect to industrial utility, the manufacturing of articles of great weight or bulk and small value seeks the waterfronts or railroads away from the center of the city, both for economy in handling the product and because the re-

[29] Lewis, Heydecker and O'Hara, *Land Values*, 1927, pp. 13, 31.

quirement of a large area for low utilization necessitates cheap land. The manufacturing of light articles of high value or that which consists of the final combination or finishing of products seeks the wholesale or retail stores which constitute their customers. In such manufacturing the seller usually seeks the buyer and sells by sample; the requirement of constant visits to customers, and the ability to supply small articles quickly, cause these manufacturers to pay considerable rents. Finally, as to residence land, where the basis of value is social as well as economic, the rich take locations that suit them— sections near parks, with good approach to the business center, elevation, and absence of nuisances; the less rich live as near as possible, and the poorest take the least desirable spots. Hotels of various classes seek locations similar to the retail stores of the same classes on convenient traffic streets. The highest-class apartment hotels seek locations on or near such main thoroughfares as run through or near the fashionable districts; the rents are dependent both upon fashion and on the character and service of the building. Below this grade the various classes of apartments seek locations for the convenience of their tenants, tending to draw nearer and nearer to their tenants' places of business, and finally come tenements crowded among the factories where their occupants work.

As a city grows there occurs a movement away from the center. This is promoted by the fact that land is cheaper farther out. There exists an unstable equilibrium between the centripetal force of economy in the transaction of business and the centrifugal force of cheap land. The uniform tendency as a city grows is toward greater concentration in the business center and greater dispersion in the residence sections. The outward pressure of one zone upon another involves the slow advance of the banking and office section (slow because it can largely solve the problem of more space by building higher in the air) into the older retail or wholesale districts, the continual following along of the lighter wholesale houses into buildings vacated by the retail shops, the close pursuit of the best residence sections by the best retail shops, with normally a mixed zone of institutions acting as a buffer between them, and the steady march of residences into the outlying country first utilized for gardens or cottages.

The Need of Guiding City Growth.—City planning and in particular zoning are based on these principles and are therefore scientifically sound. They represent an attempt to give more order and direction to city growth and the distribution of utilities—to substitute rational for natural selection—and to avoid the waste and maladjustment resulting from the encroachment of one utility upon another. As an English planning expert says, ''The town of natural growth embodies and displays the uncertainties and erratic tendencies of undisciplined growth.''[30] The forces of competition do tend to approximate the ideal layout, and the trends actually in operation are the surest indication as to what is economically sound, but, as Professor Haig[31] points out, ''the trends are the result of the individual decisions of persons in search of a dollar of profit. It so happens that unless social control is exercised, unless zoning is fully and skillfully applied, it is entirely possible for an individual to make for himself a dollar of profit but at the same time cause a loss of many dollars to his neighbors and to the community as a whole, so that the social result is a net loss. A glue factory on the corner of Park Avenue and 50th Street [a high-class residential district in New York] might show a net profit, considered by itself and ignoring the losses of its neighbors. The truth is that an individual simply by buying title to a single lot should not be given the right to use it as he chooses, whenever by merely buying a lot he does not meet his full site costs. Zoning finds its economic justification in that it is a useful device for ensuring an approximately just distribution of costs, of forcing each individual to bear his own expenses.'' Again, stores, factories, and garages may invade residential districts; apartment houses, covering a high percentage of the lot area, may be erected amid the most select homes. Not only are housing conditions detrimentally affected by such encroachment, but property values depreciate. In a decision by the United States Supreme Court (Village of Euclid v. Ambler Realty Co., November, 1926), sustaining the right of municipalities to enforce the zoning of business and residence property, it is recognized that general welfare is a proper basis for a regulatory law of this kind. Zoning is a legitimate exercise of the police power in the interests of public safety, health, and general welfare.[32]

The matter of zoning has received much attention at the hands of commissions and experts, and the results of their investigations have been set forth in comprehensive reports. These reports, which bear every evidence of painstaking consideration, concur in the view that the segregation of residential, business and industrial buildings will make it easier to provide fire apparatus suitable for the character and intensity of the development in each section; that it will increase the safety and security of home life;

[30] S. D. Adshead, *Town Planning and Town Development*, 1923, p. 36.
[31] ''Toward an Understanding of the Metropolis,'' *Quarterly Journal of Economics*, May, 1926, XL, 433-434.
[32] *Housing Betterment*, Dec., 1926, 15:4:279-283.

greatly tend to prevent street accidents, especially to children, by reducing the traffic and resulting confusion in residential sections; decrease noise and other conditions which produce or intensify nervous disorder, preserve a more favorable environment in which to rear children, etc.

Referring to the advance of apartment houses into districts that might be reserved for individual dwellings, Justice Sutherland, who wrote the decision, said: "Under these circumstances, apartment houses, which in a different environment would be not only not objectionable but highly desirable, come very near to being nuisances." He justified the zoning system as analogous to regulations governing traffic on city highways.

Regulations, the wisdom, necessity and validity of which, as applied to existing conditions are so apparent that they are now uniformly sustained, a century ago, or even half a century ago, probably would have been rejected as arbitrary and oppressive. Such regulations are sustained, under the complex conditions of our day, for reasons analogous to those which justify traffic regulations, which, before the advent of automobiles and rapid transit street railways, would have been condemned as fatally arbitrary and unreasonable.

Benefits of City Planning and Zoning.—The benefits of city planning, according to Robinson,[33] are "an improvement in those circulatory conditions created by indirect streets and congested traffic, the betterment of social conditions in many directions—notably in that of housing, and an increase in the visible beauty and splendour of cities. Under these headings, gains are anticipated in economy, efficiency, health, comfort, and looks." Through the exercise of foresight such as is involved in city planning, a community can avoid large future expenditures. "By anticipating the probable needs of the city for streets, parks, playgrounds, schools, and police and fire stations the city can save large sums through securing its rights and purchasing land before it is built up. Small investments in park lands have proved profitable to many municipalities through the enhanced taxable values of the adjoining neighborhoods. The early setting-aside of land for playgrounds and for other public purposes may prevent the high subsequent expense of removing buildings to obtain such locations. A city may often save much of the cost of widening streets, where the need is plainly indicated, by requiring or encouraging all new structures to be set back a given distance from the street line. Thus, when the abutting structures are rebuilt, the city is able to obtain the land needed for widening without un-

[33] *City Planning*, 1916, p. 3.

necessarily paying for expensive buildings. Most real estate men, land development companies, persons proposing to erect large buildings, and the like, welcome a city plan, for it enables them to proceed with greater confidence and assurance that their investments in improvements will be of a more permanent and desirable character. Large sums of money have been wasted and are still being wasted in many cities where piecemeal street opening and other projects are undertaken without relation to a comprehensive city plan."[34] Through good planning of street intersections and of transit facilities a city plan helps to reduce traffic accidents. Similarly, it is frequently able to insure that the streets adjacent to schools will not carry heavy traffic. "Research has disclosed an intimate relationship between building use and bulk, and street traffic. Office buildings, loft buildings, department stores, theatres and apartment houses obviously may be said to create vehicular and pedestrian street traffic, each to a different degree and of a different kind."[35] Zoning makes it possible to provide adequately for each type.

Zoning prevents depreciation of land values such as occurs when an apartment house is erected in a district of private dwellings, manufacturing plants move into districts occupied by stores, a public garage is built in a business section or, worse, in a residential district. Under an adequate zoning plan the purchaser of property obtains security against changes that would injuriously affect his prospective use. "He obtains the advantages of control of the surroundings and character of the development and therefore a better income-producing property. While zoning is often applied to promote or stabilize the values of private property, its primary object is the promotion of health, safety and general welfare in connection with its development. . . . It is not sufficiently recognized that those things that promote the health and safety of the community are the things that give permanence and real stability to values of land."[36]

The advantages of zoning are manifold. If the following list is not complete enough, Mr. Rolland S. Wallis[37] can probably add to it.

[34] Advisory Committee on Zoning, Department of Commerce, *A City Planning Primer*, 1928, p. 13.
[35] Ernest P. Goodrich, "Zoning and its Relation to Traffic Congestion," *Annals of the American Academy of Political and Social Science*, Sept., 1927, 133:222: 222.
[36] Lewis, Heydecker and O'Hara, *Land Values*, 1927, p. 18.
[37] "Advantages of Zoning," *Housing Betterment*, March, 1926, 15:1:33-35. See also Lawson Purdy, "The Districting of Cities," *National Housing Conference*, 1916, V, 111 ff., "The Zoning of Cities," *National Housing Conference*, 1917, VI, 222-224; Advisory Committee on Zoning, Department of Commerce, *A Standard State Zoning Enabling Act*, 1926, *A Zoning Primer*, 1926; and the following articles in *National Housing Conference*, 1923, IX: George S. Edie, "What

1. Zoning stabilizes real-estate values. "To the owner of neighboring property the invasion of an injurious use often spells financial ruin."

2. Zoning promotes the peace and quiet of residential districts. Noisy industries are kept out.

3. Zoning protects residential districts from offensive odors and reduces the amount of smoke, dust and dirt.

4. Zoning promotes the public health. Less dirt, less noise, less impure air, and more sunlight mean an increase in physical efficiency.

5. Zoning makes a city a better place in which to live and to work—not only more healthful, but more pleasant in many ways.

6. Zoning results in orderly community growth. The chaos resulting from the haphazard mixing of conflicting interests is avoided.

7. Zoning permits the efficient platting of land to suit the needs of its intended use, uninfluenced by the requirements of other districts as to the arrangement and development of streets or the sizes and proportions of lots and blocks.

8. Zoning permits the planning of a functional street system in which each street is designed to serve a specific purpose.

9. Zoning places the design of street paving on an economic and scientific basis. Better results are secured at a financial saving. Each street can be paved as best suits the district and its traffic, the needs of which can be foreseen for a long period.

10. Zoning permits large economies in the construction of sewers and water-mains. Where definite knowledge of the future character of a district is available, comparatively little allowance need be made for increased demands due to possible changes in the character of a district.

11. Zoning reduces street congestion, not only by preventing "skyscraper" districts, but also by tending to segregate the different kinds of street traffic. The mixing of fast and slow traffic makes traffic regulation difficult.

12. Zoning reduces street accidents. Segregation of traffic makes streets safer for vehicles and pedestrians.

13. Zoning simplifies the problem of street cleaning.

14. Zoning simplifies city transit problems. The distribution of residential, business, and industrial districts determines the arrangement of transit lines. The permanency of zoning districts permits the development of a satisfactory system.

15. Zoning reduces the fire hazard. Much of the menace of high buildings is avoided, and the segregation of each of the various types and uses of buildings in suitable districts permits the effective location of the type of fire-fighting equipment needed by each district.

16. Zoning facilitates the efficient location of new parks and playgrounds.

the Banker Thinks of Zoning,'' 225-232; Ernest P. Goodrich, ''What the City Engineer Thinks of Zoning,'' 233-237; Harvey W. Corbett, ''What the Architect Thinks of Zoning,'' 238-252; J. W. Cree, ''What one Realtor Thinks of Zoning,'' 253-257; Bernard J. Newman, ''What the Banker Thinks of Zoning,'' 341-349.

With less shifting of residential areas the future needs of any district may be more accurately predicted.

17. Zoning facilitates the efficient location of public-school buildings, just as in the case of parks and playgrounds.

18. Zoning protects the public schools from noisy industries and other nuisances.

19. Zoning promotes home ownership, and thus tends to stabilize labor conditions.

20. Zoning fosters a wholesome neighborhood spirit and greater civic pride.

21. Zoning affords a better basis for the assessment of property for taxation.

22. Zoning results in greater total tax values. Though it tends to check sudden increases in land values (especially in business districts), this results in spreading out these values over a much greater area.

No city in the United States had adopted a comprehensive zoning law in 1915. By the end of 1930, according to a report of the United States Department of Commerce, zoning laws had been enacted by 45 states and the District of Columbia. The number of zoned municipalities in the United States at the close of 1930, was 981, with a combined population in excess of 46,000,000. Fully two-thirds of the urban population is represented in these 981 places. Eighty-two of the 93 largest cities, which in 1930 had each more than 100,000 population, now have zoning ordinances in effect, and zoning activities in the remaining 11 unzoned cities of that group are in various stages of development. At the other end of the list with respect to size, there are 44 municipalities of less than 1,000 population which are now zoned.[38] "Bankers in zoned cities say they would not wish to return to the unzoned state. Big insurance companies making mortgage loans give preference to applications from zoned places. Merchants in New York promoted it. Real estate men in Chicago recognized it as a selling point in moving new developments. Home owners everywhere want it."[39]

In short, city planning, including zoning, constitutes a fundamental approach to the solution of urban problems. It is not just a fanciful idea; it has met the test of experience. Nor is it merely an aesthetic measure. As will be pointed out in more detail in later chapters, it underlies the methods of dealing with various problems of our common life, such as traffic, housing, sanitation, and recreation. It further illustrates the major thesis of this volume, that science is the most highly developed instrument of adjustment.

[38] *Housing*, October, 1931, 20:3:235-236. United States Department of Commerce, *Zoned Municipalities in the United States*, 1931. John Nolen, "Twenty Years of City Planning," *National Conference on City Planning*, 1927, XIX, 20.
[39] *Housing Betterment*, June, 1926, 15:2:137. *Cf.* John Ihlder, "The Chamber of Commerce and City Planning," *City Planning*, April, 1925, 1:43-46.

CHAPTER IV

THE TRAFFIC PROBLEM

AN EXCELLENT illustration of the problem of adaptation to the modern city environment is furnished by the ubiquitous question of traffic control. This subject also illustrates the general principle that the most hopeful approach to the solution of modern social problems lies in science and engineering. The following discussion of the traffic problem indicates, largely in their own words, what the traffic engineers and city planners have so far contributed.

Street traffic in American cities has reached a state of congestion and danger which now holds national attention. Hardly a city in the country fails to report confusion, injury, and discord. Concentration of skyscrapers and shopping centers is one reason for the problem, but more important is the increase of automobiles.

MOTOR VEHICLE PRODUCTION AND REGISTRATION IN THE UNITED STATES

Year	Passenger cars		Trucks	
	Produced	Registered	Produced	Registered
1895............	4	4	...	...
1900............	4,192	8,000	...	...
1905............	24,550	77,400	450	600
1910............	181,000	458,500	6,000	10,000
1915............	895,930	2,309,666	74,000	136,000
1920............	1,905,560	8,225,859	321,789	1,006,082
1925............	3,870,744	17,496,420	557,056	2,440,854
1930............	2,910,187	23,042,840	559,991	3,480,939

In 1930 there were over twenty-six million motor trucks and passenger cars registered in the United States, giving a ratio of 4.63 population per motor vehicle. There was one passenger car to every five persons. The total of new cars since 1923 has been approximating four million a year.[1] This yearly output of automobiles aggravates a condition almost beyond control. Every new automobile does not mean another one added to street congestion, but the ratio is about three new cars to one retired. The average life of motor cars is seven years. So great

[1] National Automobile Chamber of Commerce, *Facts and Figures*, 1931 edition, pp. 4, 15, 16.

has the production of automobiles become, and so difficult the problem of street regulation, that the motor car in large measure defeats its prime purpose of speed. In the early days of its introduction it afforded a quick and sure means of transportation. The fact of its success has brought other millions of cars into use until they clutter every street.

This condition of affairs is most pronounced in America, where cars are more numerous (the United States has three-fourths of all the motor vehicles in the world) and the psychology of the people reflects more vividly the motor age. The Englishman, Douglas Woodruff, in his *Plato's American Republic*, has Socrates say:[2]

"But for the ordinary Americans, I think, there is no solution except the abolition of offices and the transaction of all business in cars. They will equip their cars as offices and drive from their homes to the market-place. These car-offices will enjoy all the space that is at present filled with buildings. When their cars are so fitted as to take all the papers of their business, they can work freely on the journeys out and home, dictating to their clerks as they go. Nor will it much surprise me if the private home is abolished to give place to the residential car so that the American soul may find a final happiness, and men may be born in cars and live and wed and die in them, and be cremated in the engine, without ever having to put a foot on the ground. And so will arise a new race to take the place of the centaurs of old. For, as the centaurs were half men and half horses, so will these be half men and half motor-cars. And it would seem that of such a race the natural sustenance would be alcohol. So, at least, the future appears to me, or do you not think so, Agathon?"

"No," he said.

"Well," I replied, "you may be right. It may happen that everybody will be run over in the next few years, which will disprove all our prophecies and speculations."

"Yes," he said, "that is much more likely."

While automobiles have been increasing at a rate measured only by the American pocketbook, streets and highways have increased but slowly, at least by comparison. The pressure for room is greatest in the streets. The truth of the matter seems to be that American cities reached maturity too soon. They were designed—when there was any designing—for the day of the horse-car and the horse and buggy. Then came rapid transit in the form of the street car, the elevated road and subway. Old streets were made to serve the new purpose as best they might. Next came the motor-car in rising millions and a stalemate that urgently presses for solution.

[2] 1926, pp. 11-12.

The problem presents an obstacle in the path of the city, especially the super-city. It has been diagnosed as a condition of urban arteriosclerosis.[3] The effects of congestion may be seen in the slowing down of traffic, the increased cost of transportation, and the mounting number of accidents. The cost of the time lost on account of congestion has been variously estimated, but the rate of one cent a car-minute appears to be a conservative figure. Some authorities say two or three cents a minute for passenger cars and up to five cents a minute for motor-trucks.[4] On this basis, the cost of vehicular congestion in a large city reaches hundreds of thousands of dollars a day.

Traffic Accidents.—Automobile fatalities in the United States have been increasing since 1920 at an average rate of 10 per cent per annum. The total for the year 1930 was approximately 30,500; the record of injuries looks like a war report. A hopeful aspect of the situation is the fact that up to 1927 the ratio of automobile fatalities to motor-vehicle registration steadily declined, which meant that although automobiles were becoming more numerous they were also becoming less dangerous instruments of transportation. Since that time, however, the ratio has been increasing, though it is still below the earlier rate. The rate of motor fatalities per 100,000 registration was 240.0 in 1915, 119.8 in 1920, 98.3 in 1925, and 114.2 in 1930. Nevertheless, the problem is serious, and the motor-car is at present the greatest public destroyer of human life. According to an analysis made by the Metropolitan Life Insurance Company, the streets have become the most hazardous of all places. Approximately 90,000 persons were killed by accidents in the United States in 1926, the year of their study. About 48,000 of these deaths occurred upon the streets and in public places, 23,000 in homes, and 19,000 in industry.[5]

A high percentage (at least 40) of automobile accidents occur at street or highway intersections, which points invariably are centers of confusion.[6] The peak appears to be during the evening rush hour.

[3] Russell Black, ''The Spectacular in City Building,'' *Annals of the American Academy of Political and Social Science*, Sept., 1927, 133:222:50. This special number of the *Annals* on traffic control will be referred to below simply as *Annals*.

[4] Harold M. Lewis, ''Routing Through Traffic,'' *Annals*, 133:222:23. Fred Lavis, ''Grade Crossings, The Money Value of a Car-Minute,'' *Annals*, 133:222:-172-177.

[5] Metropolitan Life Insurance Company, *Promoting Community Safety*, 1927, p. 3. National Automobile Chamber of Commerce, *Facts and Figures*, 1931 edition, p. 67. Miller McClintock, *Street Traffic Control*, 1925, pp. 7-8. A. B. Barber, ''Making Our Traffic Laws Uniform,'' *Annals*, 133:222:128.

[6] David Beecroft, ''Equipment and Control of the Motor Vehicle,'' *Annals*, 133:222:140. Guy Kelcey, ''Traffic Regulations to Prevent Accidents,'' *Annals*, 133:222:161. R. S. Kirby, *Motor Vehicle Accidents in Connecticut*, 1926, p. 16. Miller McClintock, *Street Traffic Control*, 1925, p. 113.

"In the cities of Chicago and Grand Rapids data are available show-ing the percentages of traffic flow and of traffic accidents that take place during each hour of the day. The curves for the two cities show a striking similarity. In both, the accident curve crosses above the traffic curve at 4 P.M.—that is, before 4 o'clock the number of ac-cidents is smaller in proportion to the volume of traffic, but after 4 o'clock the number of accidents is greater in proportion to the vol-ume of traffic. In Chicago especially there is a peak of traffic at the morning rush hours, 8 to 10 o'clock, but relatively few accidents occur. The traffic in the evening rush hour, 5 to 6, is only slightly greater than in the morning, but the accidents are more than three times as many."[7] The conclusion is drawn that fatigue is a major cause and that extra caution is needed by drivers as the day con-tinues.

Many of the victims are children. A careful statistical study of automobile accidents in Connecticut discloses that nearly half of the pedestrians struck are children. The motor-vehicle death-rate in that state for 1923, 1924, and 1925 shows that "school children under ten and persons past middle life are being killed at a more rapid rate than the rest of the population. . . . Of the total persons killed, one-third were children and young people under twenty and nearly one-fifth were children under ten years old."[8] In New York State during 1926 out of nearly 36,000 pedestrians injured or killed, more than one-third were children playing or otherwise occupied in the street between intersections. The next largest classification, more than one-fourth of the total, was adults in the streets between intersections—commonly termed "jay-walkers." In a certain large city where over a hundred children are killed annually in traffic, a study of the records reveals that nearly half of the fatal and serious accidents occurred in the block where the child was living and more than two-thirds no farther away than the next block; also that by far the greatest num-ber occurred between 4 and 8 P.M. "These figures," comments Sidney J. Williams,[9] of the National Safety Council, "proved beyond ques-tion that the problem of traffic accidents to children in that city was a problem of the child playing in the immediate vicinity of his home, especially during the evening rush hour, and not a problem of trans-porting the child to and from school."

[7] S. J. Williams, "Finding the Causes of Accidents," *Annals*, 133:222:159. National Automobile Chamber of Commerce, *Facts and Figures*, 1928 edition, p. 73.

[8] R. S. Kirby, *Motor Vehicle Accidents in Connecticut*, 1926, pp. 12, 18.

[9] S. J. Williams, "Finding the Causes of Accidents," *Annals*, 133:222:157, 159, 160.

The Connecticut study, made by Professor Kirby of the Department of Engineering, Yale University, discloses that two-thirds of the motor-vehicle accidents in that state are collisions between cars. A pedestrian is struck in one accident in six, and a trolley car or train in one accident in twenty. These proportions were practically the same for the two years studied (1924 and 1925).[10] A significant movement indicative of awakened public consciousness was inaugurated on January 1, 1927, when the Massachusetts compulsory automobile-liability insurance act went into effect. This law was the result of the fact that a large number of persons injured by automobiles were unable to secure compensation because of the financial irresponsibility of drivers. Under this act no one can get an automobile license in Massachusetts who has not guaranteed his liability for damages on account of personal injury or death of others to the extent of $5,000 and $10,000—$5,000 as security in the event one person is injured by the motorist; $10,000 if two or more persons are injured in a single accident. The act does not provide for security for property-damage claims. Despite the fear expressed by some insurance companies opposed to the plan, that drivers would become more reckless, universal automobile insurance will probably make the roads safer. The insurance companies will be stimulated to work for more careful licensing of drivers; and automobile-owners, fearful lest their premiums mount, will have an added interest in supporting such a campaign.[11]

As to the specific factors contributing to traffic accidents, the following may be listed: haste or too great speed under a given set of conditions, discourtesy, carelessness in drivers and pedestrians, inadequate traffic regulation, obstruction of operator's vision, poor marking of street crossing, too narrow streets, obscured corners, inadequate street lighting, defective equipment, and other factors.[12] According to the study published by the Metropolitan Life Insurance Company,[13] "Accidents result from the failure of the average citizen to adapt previously formed habits to the rapidly changing conditions of life brought about by recent scientific, engineering and commercial

[10] R. S. Kirby, *Motor Vehicle Accidents in Connecticut*, 1926, p. 16.
[11] *The Nation*, Oct. 20, 1926, 123:392. *Literary Digest*, Jan. 8, 1927, 92:68-70.
[12] H. S. Buttenheim, "Have Our Cities Fallen Down on their Traffic Job?" in *National Municipal Review*, Dec., 1927, 16:12:755-761. R. S. Kirby, *Motor Vehicle Accidents in Connecticut*, 1926, pp. 22-29. David Beecroft, "Equipment and Control of the Motor Vehicle," *Annals*, 133:222:140. Miller McClintock, *Street Traffic Control*, 1925, p. 86.
[13] *Promoting Community Safety*, 1927, p. 4.

developments. Carelessness, recklessness and ignorance are the outward indications of this failure. Habits which were entirely safe on the streets and highways a few years ago have become dangerous practices today due to the revolutionary changes in transportation methods. This is particularly true in the case of the present widespread use of the motor vehicle." It follows that "the prevention of accidents in a community is dependent upon the proper adjustment of the habits of the public to modern living conditions. This adjustment can best be made through intensive educational activities."

The establishment of playgrounds adequately distributed over the city would do much to reduce the number of accidents to children. "The playground may be said to have two functions in relation to street safety. First of all, it is a safety zone; secondly, it is a medium for safety education."[14] A further safety precaution, and also an aid to traffic movement, is the subway to carry pedestrians under busy streets. Several cities (Boston, Chicago, Detroit, Pasadena) have a few such pedestrian subways either at street intersections or at mid-block; Los Angeles has plans for about forty under-the-street passages. These subways are to be for the most part near schools to furnish the proper safe means of street crossing for school children. Overhead street crossings for pedestrians would probably be preferred to subways; they would also be less expensive to construct. Fences to direct pedestrians to designated crosswalks and to make it difficult or impossible for them to cross the roadway at other places will also help to reduce the number of street accidents by a physical separation of the warring elements—vehicles and pedestrians. Professor McClintock says: "Eventually it is to be anticipated that physical barriers will be erected which will make it as difficult for pedestrians to enter the roadway as the curbing now makes it for vehicles to enter the sidewalk space." Some such adaptation is bound to come, if cities are to increase in size and the volume of traffic to become greater. A leading architect, Mr. Harvey Corbett, has predicted that the city of the future will have three levels of streets, with heavy traffic and auto-trucks at one level, swift-moving and lighter-weight vehicles on the second level, and pedestrians on the third and highest level.[15]

[14] W. W. Pangburn, "Playgrounds a Factor in Street Safety," *Annals*, 133:-222:185.
[15] J. H. Bell, "The Pedestrian and the City Plan," *Annals*, 133:222:210. Miller McClintock, *Street Traffic Control*, 1925, pp. 77-80, 160 (quoted). Harvey W. Corbett, "Up with the Skyscraper," *National Municipal Review*, Feb., 1927, 16:2:99; see H. H. Curran's comments, *ibid.*, April, 1927, 16:4:234.

The Radburn Plan.—Another possible line of development is suggested by the new town of Radburn, New Jersey, which the City Housing Corporation of New York, a limited-dividend company, is

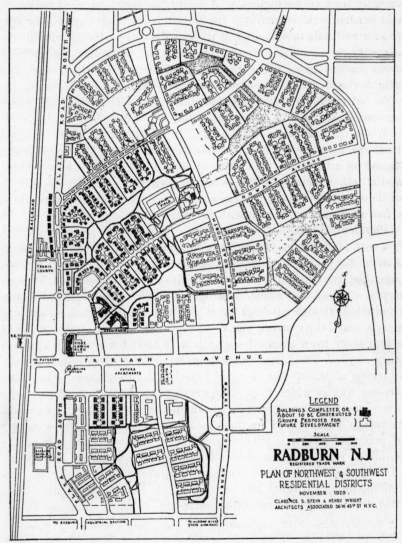

(Courtesy of the City Housing Corporation)

building. This is a town for the motor age, a town in which children never need dodge motor-trucks on their way to school. The most unique feature in this experiment is the attempt to develop a street system which will make for greater safety from traffic accidents than the average residence area affords. A unit has been built for from 400 to 600 families in houses grouped about a series of closed-end streets opening from traffic highways. A complementary system of parkways and garden paths is provided for pedestrians. "Children will be able to go a half mile to school along these paths and parkways without the necessity for crossing a street; there will be playgrounds in the park areas reached by garden paths leading directly from the houses; and neighborhood shopping centers will be equally accessible with the same safety. Should the experimental unit built on this plan prove successful, succeeding units will follow the same general scheme."[16]

Work on this community project was started in 1928. In 1931 Radburn numbered about a thousand inhabitants. The town is designed for an ultimate population of 25,000 with homes, stores, schools, and all other facilities which make for pleasant living. In the opinion of the sponsors of Radburn, the achievement of real community life is a fact of equal importance with the physical lay-out of the town.

Physical Causes of Congestion.—The above proposals suggest how city planning may contribute to a solution of the traffic problem. Among the physical causes of traffic congestion are steep grades, jogs, bad curves and points where vision is obscured, rough pavements, and railroad grade crossings, most of which could be readily eliminated, though often at great expense. More serious are narrow streets and faulty street plans. "The street space designed to serve a four-story town cannot be stretched to meet the needs of a thirty-story city."[17] The use of one-way streets affords some relief, but the widening of streets now used as principal thoroughfares is the most obvious way in which to provide greater capacity for traffic, and the means most commonly employed. In districts where land values are extremely high, one of the first methods considered in the widening of principal streets is that of arcading or cutting back part of the buildings to provide for sidewalk space and then giving the greater part of the former street width to roadway and vehicular use. In Philadelphia, Fifteenth Street and South Penn Square were widened by setting the sidewalk under the abutting building in an

[16] *Housing*, June, 1928, 17:2:145-146 (quoted). Geddes Smith, "A Town for the Motor Age," *The Survey*, March 1, 1928, 59:11:695-8. Stuart Chase, "A Suburban Garden City for the Motor Age," New York *Times*, June 24, 1928. *The Survey*, April 15, 1931, 66:2:99-100. City Housing Corporation, *Radburn Garden Homes*, 1930.

[17] John P. Hallihan, "Transit Facilities of Cities," *Annals*, Sept., 1927, 133:-222:59 (quoted). L. V. Sheridan, "Planning and Replanning the Street System," *Annals*, Sept., 1927, 133:222:30 ff. Miller McClintock, *Street Traffic Control*, 1925, pp. 42-64.

attractive arcade; the New York Telephone Company building is arcaded on the Vesey Street side; there is an arcade through the Louvre Department Store at Palais Royal and Rue de Rivoli, Paris; other examples are Arlington Street at Piccadilly, London; "The Rows," Chester, England; and smaller ones in Zurich, Switzerland. "While we think of arcades that widen the street, there is another form of arcading that relieves sidewalk congestion, facilitates pedestrian movements, protects shoppers from weather, and furnishes splendid opportunity for shop display windows. This is the arcading through buildings or city blocks. Probably one of the best examples of this traffic innovation is in Milan, Italy, where a spacious, glass-covered arcade passes through a popular shopping block. Single buildings may be designed to provide such mid-block ways because of economic advantages as well as a relief to thoroughfare traffic. This has been done in St. Louis and Atlanta."[18]

Other relief measures, often involving the spectacular such as elevated sidewalks, double-decked streets, automobile subways and tunnels, have been proposed or adopted by some cities. Some traffic engineers, however, believe that it is not so much the lack of street room that has brought about our traffic knots as the poor distribution of this street room and unintelligent use of the space we have. In addition to a program of correction of the physical defects of the street system, there is need of a street plan that will afford means of segregating traffic: of separating the movement of through, semi-through, and local traffic, and separating the movement of heavy freight and truck traffic and rapidly moving light passenger traffic.[19] The express highway and the by-pass system represent attempts in that direction.

The Express Highway and Segregation of Traffic.—A brief résumé of the development of traffic communication in this country will make clearer the theory of the express highway. Traffic communication, according to the treatment by Waldo Walker,[20] has gone through three major phases. First there was the original highway, known variously as post road, turnpike, state highway, and so forth. "This set out to go from given point to given point, and tried to touch as many intermediate points en route as possible—often wander-

---

[18] J. H. Bell, "The Pedestrian and the City Plan," *Annals*, Sept., 1927, 133:-222:209. Miller McClintock, *Street Traffic Control*, 1925, p. 53.

[19] Russell Black, "The Spectacular in City Building" *Annals*, 133:222:50. L. V. Sheridan, "Planning and Replanning the Street System," *Annals*, 133:-222:33.

[20] "Great Express Highways for New York Zone," New York *Times*, Nov. 21, 1926.

ing at will in doing so. The points thus tended to determine where the route should be. Then came the railroad. Its very rails imposed new and more rigid conditions. 'Through' (or 'express') and 'local' service still followed one and the same track, but to the exclusion of intermediate points which did not lie precisely along that track. The route began to determine where the points should be. Then came the automobile. Its extreme mobility emancipated hosts of 'intermediates' from the hard and fast thrall of the rails. It offered perhaps a half-score of routes superior (in point of personal convenience) to the railroad trunkline between major points. This mobile machine stole overnight into thousands of American communities, and by morning had stirred up revolution. Lifting old embargoes upon communication, it deftly unlocked each and every lane the country over, and declared it a potential trunkline. Once again the points determined the route—embarrassed only by the plethora of choices. But though, like some Pied Piper, the automobile soon had the entire country on the go, this very popularity became, if not a hazard, a problem. It began to appear that there were not roads enough to accommodate the swelling travel; that some more favored roads had ceased to be large enough. Under the country's new will to go its roads were bogging down. The spectre of congestion arose in increasing proportions; often from cumulative jams starting at crossings. The emergency soon made it apparent that higher travel speed was one solution; that when the motor mass lagged or was retarded it became unmanageable; when speeded up it tended to clear its own entanglement.''[21]

Then it was realized that different cars are operated with different purposes. ''The heavy touring car, thundering along on sonorous balloon tires in obvious determination to complete a 300-mile day's schedule before sundown, and the domestic town car going just a few blocks, or maybe only around the corner, clearly did not make good road-fellows.'' Traffic experts became convinced that it is the miscellany of traffic as much as its volume that congests the roadways. Says Ihlder:[22] ''Street cars, trucks, passenger automobiles, long distance and short distance, all using the same traffic lane, present one of the most striking instances of inefficiency to be found in America.'' Since it is a basic principle of the movement of traffic that converging

[21] Studies of traffic speed in its relation to roadway capacity within the city seem to indicate that a larger number of vehicles can be moved at a relatively low uniform speed than at a high one. This factor is determined by a calculation of the necessary headway between cars on the basis of the number of feet covered in stopping at various speeds. A practical test made on a number of principal streets in Los Angeles indicated that the most efficient speed was about 22 miles per hour.—Miller McClintock, *Street Traffic Control*, 1925, pp. 46-47.

[22] ''Coördination of Traffic Facilities,'' *Annals*, 133:222:4.

lines produce congestion—and each intersection is a point of convergence—it is obvious that "the principal source of traffic congestion is the convergence upon a city of masses of through traffic and the convergence within the city of both local and long distance traffic upon the central business district and important commercial and industrial subcenters."[23] Differentiation of traffic, especially between through or express and local traffic, is imperative. To divorce the two kinds of cars and give them separate trackage, to keep them out of each other's way, is becoming increasingly necessary. Through traffic is that traffic which originates beyond the city and is destined for points outside the city. Almost anyone would admit that through traffic should be routed so as to avoid the most congested points where delays would be unavoidable.

The express highway is the result. It is designed to route "through" cars at maximum speed (within sensible limits) over lanes kept free from cross-traffic. Unlike conventional highways, it seeks not to "make" intermediate points, but to miss them. The secret of its success is the best possible use of the so-called "by-pass," and this shrewd detouring around crowded centers offers what engineers count one of the latest contributions to traffic technique. The by-pass thoroughfare would leave the main highway near one edge of the city and connect with it again beyond the developed districts on the other side. Mr. Harold M. Lewis, executive engineer, Regional Plan of New York and Its Environs, mentions three ways in which such a route can avoid the congested center: (1) It can be carried on one side of the business center. (2) It can traverse the business district on a relatively direct line over a viaduct or embankment, which would be free of any interference from cross traffic. (3) It can be depressed below the normal street level and carried in open cut or tunnel directly beneath the business center.[24] The first method is the one that would be most generally used. Under the last two methods, which lead to the super-highway, no vehicle or pedestrian would ever have occasion to cross the express highway. This feature will permit with safety a high rate of speed and thus go far toward solving the traffic problem, for it is not speed but the lack of it that causes most of the trouble. Examples of express highways are New York's partly completed elevated road from Canal Street to Riverside Drive and Chicago's great double-decked river road, Wacker Way, which cost $30,000,000 a

[23] L. V. Sheridan, "Planning and Replanning the Street System," *Annals*, 133:222:29. Miller McClintock, *Street Traffic Control*, 1925, p. 113.
[24] Harold M. Lewis, "Routing Through Traffic," *Annals*, 133:222:23 ff.

mile; also Woodward Avenue in Detroit and Michigan Avenue in Chicago are to be developed into super-highways.[25]

Parking.—A more important cause of congestion than actual traffic volume, it would seem, is the clogging of the traffic flow by parked cars and the loading and unloading of commercial vehicles. The demand for parking space is greater than the supply, which leads to further congestion. "Street storage not only produces an artificial shortage of curb space, but adds unnecessary street traffic by owner-driven vehicles cruising in search of a place to stop, and by chauffeur-driven vehicles which find it convenient and sometimes necessary to 'cruise' in the neighborhood in which the owner is transacting business. A sort of 'mobile' parking thus arises in that portion of the street which should be devoted to moving traffic." Taxicabs are notorious offenders; either because they have no fixed stands or because more business is desired, they cruise through the streets looking for fares. A count in New York City in 1923 showed some 15,000 licensed taxicabs, while the hack stands available provided accommodations for only 1,500. Some restriction of parking is obviously necessary. Parking under any conditions infringes on the rights of everybody and should never be permitted for more than a few minutes. One standing vehicle, during the period that it is stationary, renders useless the lane behind it for such distance as it can be observed by approaching drivers. Double parking reduces available traffic area by two lanes. Street storage of vehicles, benefiting only the individual at the expense of the municipality, is not efficiency. Most cities have come to limit parking in the congested area and many to prohibit it entirely in the downtown district during the busiest hours. Loading zones for the loading and unloading of commercial vehicles have provided relief in some instances.[26]

The most active and determined opposition to restricted parking is apt to come from the merchants, who in the long run would be most benefited by it. "Many retailers have an exaggerated idea of the business they would lose—and underestimate greatly the business they would gain—if unrestricted parking were abolished." According to a study of traffic congestion and retail business published by the United States Department of Commerce, "the majority of all recorded

[25] S. D. Waldon, "Superhighways and City Planning," *National Conference on City Planning*, 1927, XIX, 163. J. R. Bibbins, "Rapid Transit Development," *Annals*, 133:222:198. A. J. Brosseau, "New Speed Laws for a New Area," *Annals*, 133:222:138.

[26] Hawley S. Simpson, "Downtown Storage Garages," *Annals*, 133:222:82 (quoted). Russell Black, "The Spectacular in City Building," *Annals*, 133:222:-55. Miller McClintock, *Street Traffic Control*, 1925, pp. 37-38, 141-142.

stores reported the average shopping period to be less than one-half hour and that this is true to a greater extent as cities decrease in size. The longer shopping periods of one hour or more are found to occur in the largest cities and are almost negligible in cities of less than 50,000 in population. It is evident that the shopping period is longest where there is more traffic congestion and at the same time less opportunity for a long parking time privilege."[27]

Although streets are primarily for moving traffic, terminal or parking facilities at or near destination must be provided, else there is no purpose in moving. "An automobile is useful chiefly because it takes people *from* somewhere *to* somewhere; if it merely takes them *through* somewhere it has fulfilled but half its function. To keep traffic moving is a laudable aim; but motor cars must stop occasionally, else there is no point in their moving." Forbidden the use of the streets without restriction for storage purposes, what is the average urban automobilist to do? Several alternatives are suggested by Prof. Austin F. Macdonald,[28] of the University of Pennsylvania:

"First, he may leave his car at home and find some other, less pleasant way of reaching his destination. This solution of the problem is receiving increasingly widespread acceptance. It has the indisputable advantage of reducing the number of vehicles on the road, but it has also the marked disadvantage of making large numbers of automobiles virtually useless to their owners most of the time." The problem of finding a place to park has become almost insoluble. A foreign observer remarks: "As among many peoples a youth is not granted the dignity of manhood until he has slain an enemy, so among the Americans must he first prove himself by parking a car."[29]

The second alternative of the city motorist is to find a suitable storage place near his destination, *e.g.*, the downtown garage. Private initiative has provided many such places, but it has been pointed out by Hawley S. Simpson,[30] a traffic engineer who has made a special study of this subject, that with but few exceptions existing storage garages even in centers of extreme congestion are not being used to capacity; "not because the public does not desire the service, but rather because the service available is beyond reach of their purse. Increased use will result with lowered charges, and lower charges are dependent upon lower cost of construction and lower land value.

[27] H. S. Buttenheim, "The Problem of the Standing Vehicle," *Annals*, 133:-222:148; quoting *Vehicular Traffic Congestion and Retail Business,* published by the Domestic Commerce Division of the United States Department of Commerce.
[28] "Parking Facilities Outside the Traffic Zone," *Annals*, 133:222:78-79.
[29] Douglas Woodruff, *Plato's American Republic,* 1926, p. 10.
[30] "Downtown Storage Garages," *Annals*, 133:222:89.

Means to secure lower costs are available and encouragement should be offered to private capital to increase the storage capacity available to persons of moderate income. Probably the most fertile, but by no means the only field, is in construction of sub-surface garages under public property. Free storage offered to shoppers by merchandising interests is an economic error and acts as a boomerang not only to the merchant, but to regular storage garage enterprises.''

The city automobilist has still a third choice. ''In all probability he lives a considerable distance from the downtown area, and he may therefore drive his car to the rim of traffic congestion, park it in a convenient space, and make use of some other conveyance, probably the trolley, to complete his journey. Such an arrangement results in a minimum of wasted time and a maximum of comfort for the motorist; it also brings about a reduction of traffic congestion. Whether it will be used to any considerable extent in the future depends largely on the nature of the facilities provided at the outskirts of the traffic zone. As yet very little has been done to encourage automobile drivers to park outside the central business district. Most cities have directed their efforts instead to the negative task of discouraging motorists from entering the district.'' A few municipalities, however, of which Pittsburgh, Akron, and Michigan City may be cited as examples, have established parking spaces on city-owned property, some of these spaces being within the downtown area and some at its border. A small charge is made, although some cities provide free parking spaces. ''Usually no attempt is made to establish these parking facilities at points where they will be of greatest value to motorists and will serve best to relieve congestion. Their sites are determined instead by the chance location of vacant city land.'' More significant is the experience of a number of street railway companies which have hit upon the plan of providing ample parking space at their suburban terminals, making it an easy matter to transfer from the private to the public conveyance. ''Park With Us and Ride With Us'' is the slogan of the Philadelphia Rapid Transit Company; the parking charge is ten cents. In most cities, however, parking space outside the traffic zone is provided by private initiative. Nowhere has the plan been given a fair trial. Macdonald mentions the following as essentials for its success: there should be little or no charge; the plan should be operated primarily for the purpose of reducing congestion and not of producing revenue, else the motorist will park in town; the areas should be in the hands of the city or the street railway company, should be conveniently located, and should be covered to protect against the elements; attendants should be on duty; service facilities should be provided; and publicity should be ample.

Traffic Control.—A turning-point in the historical development of traffic control came at the beginning of the century. Up to that time the police had given attention to traffic only when there were parades, disputes between drivers, vehicles blocking the highway, or children and the infirm to be assisted across the street. Officers were probably first assigned to traffic duty in 1903, in New York City. "At first the officers were mounted and did not have duty at a single fixed post. Attention was soon directed to intersections, however, as most troubles occurred there. Officers stationed at important intersections developed crude hand motions to slow up, stop, or move traffic, as was necessary. As traffic grew, it became necessary for the officer to stop traffic on each street in turn to give traffic on the other street the opportunity to move. Thus began what is now popularly called 'stop-and-go' traffic control. Arm signals, body positions, and whistle signals were gradually developed and to some extent standardized in each city. Then came the well-known hand semaphore to aid the traffic officer. The semaphore had the advantage of giving a positive, unmistakable signal visible over other vehicles. Stands and even towers were developed in connection with semaphores, mainly to give the officer a clearer view in all directions."[31] As the problem became greater, traffic officers became more skilled in their work.

Control by traffic officers has a number of advantages, which are reducible largely to flexibility and intelligent adjustment to the conditions that exist at a given place at a given time. Also the officer can control any unusual condition or emergency. The disadvantages, on the other hand, are numerous. The traffic officer must at times be the law enforcement officer, and while engaged in such duties, as also in case of fire, accident, or other emergency, he must frequently leave his post uncontrolled for considerable periods of time. His attention is diverted by his serving as a general information bureau as well as by the necessity of answering lengthy greetings, though some officers initiate conversations themselves. But the chief disadvantage of control by traffic officers is the lack of coördination. "It is impossible for an officer to coördinate his work with the efforts of officers on all four sides of him one block away. This limitation can be quickly grasped if one will imagine all four officers at intersections surround-

---

[31] The following is largely adapted from the excellent article, "Traffic Control," in the *Annals*, 133:222:90-113, by Burton W. Marsh, Traffic Engineer, Department of Public Safety, Pittsburgh.

ing the one in question, releasing a stream of traffic at such a time
that all four streams arrive at the corner in question at the same time.
The importance of this inability to coördinate officers' efforts throughout a business district or along an artery, is tremendous. Impossibility
of coördination is the main reason why a proper electrical traffic
control *system* can, if conditions are favorable, usually handle traffic
in an important business district more expeditiously and efficiently
than can even first-class officers working as isolated individuals.''

After ''stop-and-go'' traffic control by cornermen came to be seen
as an important field and one which was bound to develop, ''experi-
mentive and inventive individuals and various companies saw the
possibilities of traffic control by electric signalling devices. The development and success of railroad signals doubtless played a part in
the early efforts toward development of traffic control signals. About
1910 the development of electric traffic control signals commenced.
A new field was then started, the importance of which to traffic control of the future is not fully appreciated by many persons today.
The earliest installations of which record has been found were naturally for the control of one particular corner. They were designed for
manual control by an officer stationed at the corner.'' One of the
earliest of these signals was erected in Cleveland at the intersection
of Euclid Avenue and East 105th Street in 1914; San Francisco and
Salt Lake City installed signals in 1915 and 1916, respectively. New
York City had a kind of electric traffic signal installed on the original
wooden towers on Fifth Avenue in 1918, and Detroit and Philadelphia are also known to have been pioneers in this respect. The real
commercial development and sale of electric traffic signals began in a
small way about 1921. The development was slow until 1923 or 1924.
By 1926 signals had been installed at approximately 8,000 intersections in different cities of the United States. The earliest signals
were for the control of one intersection. The control was at first
manual; later, automatic timers or controllers were used. Municipalities quickly became interested in automatic control as a means of
taking care of intersections where officers could not possibly be provided. As contrasted with the officer, the automatic signal has the advantage of costing less, having greater attention-compelling value,
and being always on the job. It is an aid to pedestrians, especially at
points where officers are not stationed. On the other hand, being a
mechanical device it controls traffic with machine-like regularity and
constancy: conditions must be such that this sort of control is satisfactory for the corner in question. The relative proportions of traffic

on the intersecting streets should not greatly vary while the signal
is in use. Also, the fewer left turns, the more satisfactorily will signal
control handle the situation. The invention by Henry A. Haugh, Jr.,
of a full-automatic, traffic-control system, which adjusts to the varying volume of traffic on the intersecting streets, is an attempt to offset
the limitation of the common automatic signal. It was first given a
successful try-out in New Haven.

The next development was what is known as automatic synchronized control, in which on a given highway a number of intersection
signals show red or green at the same time. A pioneer case in which
lights were used in the attempt to synchronize traffic movement was
the relay of signals by the manual method in the towers on Fifth
Avenue, New York, in 1918. But the first electrically interlocked
traffic signal system was installed at nine adjacent intersections in
Houston, Texas, in 1922. In this case, as in most of the early installations, the changing of the lights was done manually by an officer at
the most important or "key" intersection. Then came the use of the
automatic controller to bring about the changing of the signal colors.
"The idea that traffic would cross the main artery at all side streets
at one time seemed to mean a greater efficiency of traffic movement
on the main artery." The controller was set to give a long period for
movement on the main street. During this period traffic moved considerable distances, instead of having to stop at a large number of
intersections as when it was controlled individually. But drivers soon
found that under synchronized control the thing to do is to see how
many intersections can be passed before the lights change, so as to be
stopped the fewest possible number of times in passing through the
system. Such a system, therefore, encourages speeding. The accident
hazard is naturally increased, pedestrians being those who suffer
most. This system has the further disadvantage that it does not permit continuous movement, except in very short systems where the
driver races all the way through before the "stop" light appears.
The long period given to main-artery traffic penalizes the waiting
driver on the side street. With a synchronized system the cycle is
generally split so as best to take care of the most troublesome intersection; naturally traffic, especially on cross streets, must suffer at
all other intersections. The high speed of traffic while in motion often
gives a false impression as to the average or over-all speed (stops
included). For example, the casual observer would say that the
speed of synchronized movement on Michigan Boulevard in Chicago
is high because vehicles seen in motion move so rapidly. Because of

the rather long stops, however, checks indicate that the average speed is only about eleven miles per hour.

These difficulties have been largely overcome by the progressive or continuous movement system. In general, "a progressive or continuous movement system is one in which, if a driver starts at the first signal at the beginning of the green 'go' period and proceeds at the proper speed [the system can be set for any predetermined speed], the signal lights at succeeding corners change to green in his favor as he approaches them." In 1918 Salt Lake City installed a system employing this principle. About 1923 Los Angeles installed a partially progressive system, and in 1924 Lancaster, Pennsylvania, adopted the plan. These were the pioneers. The system may be either limited or flexible. "The Flexible Progressive Control System reduces the serious handicap of the Limited Progressive System in that the percentage of the total cycle apportioned to movement on each street at any intersection may be varied to take account of the time demands of traffic on each street. This system also removes another serious limitation of the Limited Progressive System. Although the total cycle is constant over the entire controlled area, the time when the green light appears may be selected at will—an important advantage. For example, assume a vehicle starting at the first corner just as the green light appears. If, at a desired speed of twenty-two miles an hour, it would take twenty seconds to traverse the first block, the signal at the second intersection would appear at the end of this twenty-second period. Now, suppose that the next block were considerably longer so that it required thirty-two seconds for this constant-speed-vehicle to traverse it. This *flexible* progressive system would permit this signal at the third intersection to have its 'go' period start thirty-two seconds after that at the second intersection." This is the best system so far devised for giving continuous movement of traffic at a relatively high rate of speed. According to the experience of Chicago in the Loop district, it also appears to reduce accidents. In addition to two installations in Chicago, notable examples of the flexible progressive system are to be found in Cleveland, East Cleveland, Detroit, and Des Moines. "The Carnegie Avenue installation in Cleveland is four miles in length, probably the longest stretch of one street under flexible progressive control in the world."[32]

Connected with any signal system are technical questions of equip-

[32] Burton W. Marsh, "Traffic Control," *Annals*, 133:222:105 (quoted). Edward J. Donahue, "Traffic Signalling in Cleveland," in *American City*, Sept., 1927, 37:3:304-308.

ment and maintenance. The pendant type of signal, for example, which is suspended from a wire spanning the street, has disadvantages in that it often cannot be seen under the sun visor, and the accident hazard is thereby increased; it is also often difficult for both pedestrians and motorists to distinguish in bright sunlight which light is burning. Other systems are being tried out; a limiting factor is that of expense.

The need of standardizing the meaning of signals is urgent. Some cities permit a left turn on green, others do not; some cities permit a right turn on red. The yellow or amber signal when displayed between the green and red has been used for a variety of purposes, such as a warning of change, to clear the intersection, as a signal for left-hand turns, as a signal for pedestrian traffic to move in all directions while vehicular traffic is stopped. Much confusion is also caused where the speed regulations of cities vary. Then there is the vexatious practice of some small communities of establishing unreasonably low speed limits and enforcing them rigorously for the sake of the fines which they are able to collect.

Traffic may be speeded up and at the same time be rendered safer by extensive use of road signs, pavement markings, and other means of guiding the traffic flow.[33] If "stop" signs are to be used instead of electric signals, a regulation will be needed to compel all vehicles on the cross streets to come to a full stop upon arriving at the main artery. The latter then becomes a through-traffic road with complete right of way. In Cleveland, Detroit, Chicago, and other large cities, in order to expedite traffic and to lessen the danger of collision at crossings, the authorities have designated certain boulevards or thoroughfares as right-of-way streets and all traffic before entering those streets is warned to come to a full stop. This system has many advantages provided the "boulevard stop" regulation is strictly enforced. "The through street traffic has a right to believe itself protected at each intersection from cross traffic, and, therefore, cross traffic must come to a complete stop and remain standing until the main highway can be crossed or entered without interfering with through traffic."[34] This plan is better adjusted to city conditions than that of giving the right of way at an intersection to the vehicle entering from a side-street on the right.

The technique for traffic control has been largely drawn from

[33] M. G. Lloyd, "Uniform Traffic Signs, Signals, and Markings," *Annals*, 133:-222:122. Irving C. Moller, "Guiding the Traffic Flow," *Annals*, 133:222:118. Miller McClintock, *Street Traffic Control*, 1925, p. 91.

[34] Irving C. Moller, "Guiding the Traffic Flow," *Annals*, 133:222:117.

allied fields of engineering, transportation and electrical, and from public administration. The question of street traffic is being subjected to scientific study.[35] Significant of its importance in modern urban life is the establishment in Harvard University of the Albert Russel Erskine Bureau for Street Traffic Research.

Decentralization as a Solution.—More fundamental to a solution of the traffic problem than any of the above measures, in the opinion of many city planners, is the process of decentralization. This is an attempt to cure the more serious defects in the physical growth of cities. The basic idea of decentralization, as explained in the first chapter, is the controlled and limited development of an indefinite number of interrelated cities, each for special or mixed uses, with a "hub" of limited purpose, in contrast to the unlimited growth outward and practically unlimited growth upward of a single huge city area. As related specifically to the problems of traffic congestion the proponents of this theory submit three propositions: "First, they maintain that the usual process of city growth by building upward at the center and by continued accretive growth at the outer periphery, with remedy for the increasing traffic congestion by street widenings and openings, is an endless circle, where the relief measures fail to eliminate the cause of congestion and may even create more congestion, requiring in turn additional relief. Second, they claim that since this type of city-building must fail of a genuine final solution of the traffic problem, a fundamentally different theory must be applied, and the decentralized city development, in contrast to accretive growth, supplies that theory by removing the cause of the continued multiplication of traffic congestion and curing the disease at its source. Third, they believe that decentralization has or will set in in the larger cities, and that it may be hastened and guided by intelligent *regional* planning."[36] Conditions in the large cities would indicate that the city planners are justified in seeking a new theory for solving the traffic problem.

[35] Miller McClintock, "The Traffic Survey," *Annals*, 133:222:8-18; *Street Traffic Control*, 1925, ch. II.
[36] Jacob L. Crane, "Decentralization—Eventually but Not Now," *Annals*, 133:222:234.

PART II

HOUSING

CHAPTER V

THE HOUSING PROBLEM

THE housing problem is primarily a city problem. The only exception to this rule is the congestion and unsanitary housing conditions found in lumber camps, collieries, and on construction jobs where the workmen live in company shacks. Such inadequate housing is due either to the factor of remoteness, as in the case of the mining camp, or to the temporary nature of the provisions, as in construction jobs, harvesting, and lumbering. Such conditions in the Far West have occasioned some of the grievances of the I.W.W. and other migratory workers. California, through its Commission on Housing and Immigration, has done much to improve conditions.

Causes.—With this exception, the housing problem is a city problem, and its acuteness varies directly with the size of the city. Fundamentally it is due to congestion of population. Think of the physical difficulties of housing New York City's nearly seven million inhabitants on what remains of 299 square miles after providing for business and industrial sites, for streets and other necessary appurtenances. Density of population may be relieved somewhat by adequate and cheap transportation facilities, but these are usually lacking. Transportation facilities generally lag behind the growth of population.[1] It is to the interest of transportation companies to restrain population within narrow limits, for the short haul is more profitable than the long one. The large number of people creates a great demand for land, which in turn creates high land values. This involves intensive use of the land by the owner in order to secure a commercial return on the investment. This means land overcrowding, high buildings, multiple dwellings, high rents, and congestion.[2] Expressed more simply, the housing problem is due to high land values on the one hand and inadequate transportation facilities on the other.

These are the fundamental reasons. Immigration, land speculation, poor planning and construction of buildings, defective sanitation, lax laws and enforcement, the greed of landlords, the ignorance and care-

[1] Henry C. Wright, "Transit and Housing," *National Housing Conference*, 1913, III, 68-74.
[2] Frederic C. Howe, *The Modern City*, 1915, p. 276.

lessness of tenants, public indifference, and other conditions are merely contributing factors.[3] These reasons also set the conditions to which we must adapt. Because of high land values and inadequate transportation facilities the single-family dwelling must give way to the multiple as the prevailing city type. The detached one-family house may be ideal, but it is impossible in the large city. Manhattan for fifty years has been a city of multiple dwellings. Today it is almost exclusively so. "A new private dwelling in Manhattan is as much an object of curiosity as a horse-drawn vehicle in its streets; only five new private dwellings were erected there last year [1927]." In New York City only the rich can afford to live by themselves and only the very rich can afford a private yard. Nowhere in the world, it is claimed, is the possession of a front yard or a garden so expensive a luxury as on Manhattan Island. Every foot of space on the streets of the city has a definite if exaggerated value. A flower bed or a grass plot, however small, represents a considerable investment. There are said to be several side or front yards in New York which would readily bring a million dollars.[4] It would seem to be almost a vulgar display of wealth to have a lawn.

With urban population in the United States, according to the latest findings of the Census Bureau, showing a rate of increase five times as great as that of rural population, what is happening to the nation's housing habits? Are urban Americans tending to become typically apartment-dwellers? Is the American home of the traditional type vanishing? An answer to these questions is given in the analysis of new building permits made by the United States Bureau of Labor Statistics in cities of over 25,000 population. These figures clearly

PER CENT OF FAMILIES PROVIDED FOR IN DIFFERENT KINDS OF DWELLINGS IN 257 IDENTICAL CITIES IN 1921, 1929, AND 1930

Year	Total number of families provided for	Per cent of families provided for in		
		one-family houses	two-family houses	multi-family houses
1921	224,545	58.3	17.3	24.4
1929	244,394	40.2	11.4	48.5
1930	125,322	45.7	12.1	42.2

[3] Elmer S. Forbes, "Causes of Bad Housing," *National Housing Conference*, 1915, IV, 65-74. James Ford, "Fundamentals of Housing Reform," *American City*, May, 1913, 8:5:473.

[4] *Housing*, June, 1928, 17:2:84. New York *Times*, Nov. 16, 1924. Lewis, Heydecker and O'Hara, *Land Values*, 1927, p. 26.

show a decreasing percentage of new residential construction in one-
and two-family houses and a rapidly increasing percentage in some
form of multiple dwelling. Especially is this trend noticeable if 1929
is considered instead of 1930, when the amount of new construction
appreciably fell off owing to the business depression. Analysis of the
figures by population groups shows that the larger the city the higher
the percentage of families for whom provision is made in multi-family
houses.[5]

Definition.—What is meant by the term "housing problem"? To
some people it means the scarcity of houses, which of course is one
phase of the matter, but only one. During the past decade this has
been an important factor owing to the lack of construction during the
Great War when men and materials were needed for other purposes
and to the check on building operations since the Armistice because
of the high cost of labor and material. To others the problem is one
of high rentals, a vital question because most city-dwellers are tenants.[6] Recognition of this factor has led both in this country and
abroad to attempts at rent control through legislation.[7] Tenantry is
the characteristic type of house occupancy in the city because of high
land values on the one hand and the small income and mobility of the
wage-earners, who make up the majority of city-dwellers, on the other
hand. Fundamentally related to housing, as will be brought out further in the immediately following chapters, are the questions of wages
and standards of living. According to the best available estimate of
the distribution of family income in New York City, 69 per cent of
all families have a family income of less than $2,500 a year, 23 per
cent have an income of from $2,500 to $5,000 a year, and only 8 per
cent have incomes above $5,000. All the evidence collected by the
housing committees of the State Legislature indicated a condition of
acute shortage of dwellings in New York City, especially for the great
mass of the population with the smaller incomes. The item of housing
represents about one-fifth of the cost of living in all the great cities
of the United States. In the adjustment of the family budget this is
about the maximum proportion that may be devoted to housing unless
other essential items are to be curtailed. Investigations in New York
have disclosed that increased rents cause downward pressure of the

[5] *Monthly Labor Review*, May, 1931, 32:5:133.
[6] *Fourteenth Census of the United States*, 1920, II, 1284 ff.
[7] *Report of the Joint Legislative Committee on Housing*, New York Legislative
Document No. 60, 1922, ch. III. Harold G. Aron, "What is a Fair Rent?"
National Housing Conference, 1920, VIII, 153-164. *Housing Betterment*, current
numbers. Herbert B. Dorau and Albert G. Hinman, *Urban Land Economics*, 1928,
pp. 337-347.

population into apartments at lower rent levels. "Families, unable to meet the demand for increased rents, have found their only recourse in economy of space. Wherever possible they have moved into a smaller apartment. For this smaller apartment they are now compelled to pay approximately the same rent which they had heretofore paid for the larger apartment. This downward pressure has fixed the highest demand for apartments at the lower rentals and has resulted in restoring to use old-law tenements which had been abandoned years ago as unfit for human habitation."[8] An almost insoluble aspect of the housing question, as we shall see later, is the adequate housing of the lowest-paid workers.

More basic than the scarcity and cost of dwellings, though intimately related to those matters, is the question of standards. "The fundamental trouble," says Mrs. Wood,[9] "is the scarcity of wholesome houses of an acceptable standard at a low enough rental for the rank and file of unskilled wage-earners." This question of acceptable standards is and has been the most serious aspect of the housing situation. It involves questions of health, of safety, of sanitation, of morality, and of nearly every phase of social life. It includes technical and financial questions of construction, legislative and administrative questions of building codes and their enforcement, and social and political questions of government intervention.[10] It is this aspect of the problem that Lawrence Veiller,[11] an outstanding American authority on housing, emphasizes. "The housing problem," he writes, "is the problem of enabling the great mass of people who want to live in decent surroundings and bring up their children under proper conditions to have such opportunities. It is also to a very large extent the problem of preventing other people who either do not care for decent conditions or are unable to achieve them from maintaining conditions which are a menace to their neighbors, to the community and to civilization." To mention "decent surroundings" and "proper conditions" is to introduce the relative. A definition of such terms will vary from place to place and from time to time. But some definite measurement of them may be found in the minimum standards established by the housing law in any given case.

A housing problem, then, may be said to exist wherever any portion

---

[8] *Report of Commission of Housing and Regional Planning*, New York, Legislative Document No. 43, 1924, pp. 20 (quoted), 32 ff.

[9] *Housing of the Unskilled Wage Earner*, 1919, p. 133.

[10] Carol Aronovici, "Housing and the Housing Problem," *Annals*, Jan., 1914, 51:140:1-7.

[11] *Model Housing Law*, 1920, p. 4. *Cf.* Albion Bacon, *et al.*, "What is the Housing Problem?" *National Housing Conference*, 1913, III, 197-207.

of a population dwells under conditions dangerous to health, safety, or morality. The problem, thus defined, is present to some degree in every American city. The specific items of the problem have been summarized as follows: "Housing evils as we know them today are to be found in dangerous and disease-breeding privy vaults, in lack of water supply, in dark rooms, in filthy and foul alleys, in damp cellars, in basement living rooms, in conditions of filth, in inadequate methods of disposal of waste, in fly-borne disease, in cramped and crowded quarters, in promiscuity, in lack of privacy, in buildings of undue height, in inadequate fire protection, in the crowding of buildings too close to each other, in the too intensive use of land."[12]

Effects.—Nearly everybody familiar with the life of great cities regards the housing problem as the most pressing question of all. It has been said that the housing problem touches every other social question, and the statement, if not mathematically precise, at least serves the purpose of indicating some explanation of the difficulty experienced by reformers and administrators in their struggle to bring about better housing conditions.[13] The housing problem is fundamental because it directly affects the family and through it social relations. "The place in which a man or a woman dwells," says Bryce,[14] "is vital to the character of the man or woman. To begin with, there is the consideration of health and of all that follows from bad health. Depressed vitality is a most fruitful cause of intemperance. Bad housing is one of the direct causes of that evil. Cleanliness is not only a condition for health, it is a condition for self-respect. . . . and it is the basis of good manners. Overcrowding is almost as incompatible with good manners as with good morals. Cleanliness, health, self-respect, manners and morals, all are immensely depressed by bad housing and correspondingly raised when the environment is improved."

The bearing of bad housing conditions on health and physical development is so obvious that an elaborate argument need not be attempted. The correlation between death-rates, particularly infantile death-rates, and density of population is undoubted, though rough and inexact in detail; and, despite the fact that among people who live closely packed together other causes of a high death-rate inde-

[12] Lawrence Veiller, *Model Housing Law*, 1920, p. 5. James Ford, "Fundamentals of Housing Reform," *The American City*, May, 1913, 8:5:473.

[13] E. R. Dewsnup, *Housing Problem in England*, 1907, p. 211.

[14] "The Menace of Great Cities," *National Housing Association Publications* No. 20, June, 1913, p. 5. W. Thompson, *Housing Hand-Book*, 1903, p. 432. John J. Murphy, "Effects of Bad Housing," *National Housing Conference*, 1915, IV, 81-82.

pendent of overcrowding are usually operating, we may infer, in view
of the evidence at hand, that this correlation reflects a causal connection.[15] Nor is this all. Among the survivors, disease and a low
level of vitality become common when population is congested; and
it would seem not unlikely that physical conditions are affected also.
Anthropometric surveys of school children made in a number of
British cities show a close correlation of height and weight with
house-room, which arouses a suspicion that growth is retarded by
overcrowding, although other factors are undoubtedly present.[16] A
housing survey undertaken by the health authorities of American
cities of 200,000 or more population discloses that room overcrowding
results in an increase in the infant death rate and is an important
factor in the spread of communicable diseases.[17] Dr. Haven Emerson,
professor of public health at Columbia University, is quoted as saying
that room overcrowding is probably the most important factor in the
spread of the diseases of the respiratory tract.[18] Housing congestion
appears to be related to the spread of venereal diseases, especially
where lodgers are intermingled with the family. Room overcrowding,
lack of privacy, the presence of lodgers and prostitutes have all been
factors in the problem of immorality in tenement houses.[19]

Associated also with inadequate housing conditions is the problem
of crime and disorder. Thrasher[20] says "the characteristic habitat of
Chicago's numerous gangs is that broad twilight zone of railroads
and factories, of deteriorating neighborhoods and shifting populations, which borders the city's central business district. The gangs
dwell among the shadows of the slum." Again, "the beginnings of

[15] Robert W. DeForest and Lawrence Veiller, *The Tenement House Problem*,
1903, I, 445-470. Edward F. Hartman, "Sanitary Inspection of Tenements,"
National Housing Conference, 1911, I, 77-82. C. J. Hastings, "Public Health
Administration and Housing," *National Housing Conference*, 1913, III, 81-85.
Frank A. Craig, "Housing and Disease," *National Housing Conference*, 1916,
V, 366-369. W. W. Pangburn, "Housing and Disease," *National Housing Con-
ference*, 1916, V, 370-374. John Molitor, "Housing as a Part of the Work of a
local Health Department," *National Housing Conference*, 1916, V, 198-208. Regional Survey of New York and Its Environs, *Buildings: Their Uses and the
Spaces About Them*, 1931, VI, 208 ff.
[16] Sydney J. Chapman, *Work and Wages*, 1914, III, 24. E. R. Dewsnup, *Housing
Problem in England*, 1907, p. 24.
[17] Henry F. Vaughan, "Room Overcrowding and its Effect upon Health,"
National Housing Conference, 1920, VIII, 183-197.
[18] *Report of Commission on Housing and Regional Planning*, New York, Legislative Document No. 43, 1924, p. 41.
[19] Robert W. DeForest and Lawrence Veiller, *The Tenement House Problem*,
1903, I, 50-52; II, 17-23.
[20] *The Gang*, 1927, pp. 3, 26. *Cf.* Herbert Ashbury, "Old-Time Gangs in New
York," *American Mercury*, Aug., 1927, 11:44:478-486; Jacob Riis, *How the
Other Half Lives*, 1890, p. 15.

the gang can best be studied in the slums of the city where an inordinately large number of children are crowded into a limited area." Spot-maps of the distribution of cases of juvenile delinquency show a correlation with congested housing conditions, as studies in a number of cities have shown. Disrespect for law and for the community behind it may often go back to the earliest memories of the boy who has had only the street for a playground and a wretched tenement apartment for a home. Our crowded "east sides" are the home of radicals of every school. The well-known city planner, Thomas Adams, is quoted as saying: "Glasgow, with its model system of transit, sanitation and local government, is the center of Communism in Great Britain, chiefly because of its overcrowded housing conditions."[21] It may be questioned whether bad housing is a causative factor in these respects, but certainly it is closely associated with a number of economic and social problems. Perhaps the worst effect of bad housing in a city is the demoralization and consequent lowering in productive power of a great proportion of its inhabitants.[22]

The "Slums."—The housing problem is most serious in the most congested sections of the city popularly referred to as the "slums." Here the effects of inadequate housing are most marked. If it were not for the "slums," a lot of social workers would lose their jobs; the police force, the fire department, and the health department could all be cut down. Fire insurance would be cheaper, in many districts, and so would life insurance. Albion Bacon,[23] in discussing the relation of housing to social work, says: "I need not go into the details of sights, odors, inconveniences, that every one of you recall. When you went to wait on a sick mother, you had to go downstairs for water to wash the baby, go across the hall to get something to wash it in, and go upstairs to heat the water. You had to close the windows to keep out smells and flies, you had to put a chair against the door to keep out the fighting boys. When you found her husband had deserted her, you wondered how he had slept in that stuffy room so long, when a hobo life beckoned him to sweet air and the greenwood tree for shelter. When the pretty daughter went wrong, you remem-

---

[21] In New York *Times*, Feb. 7, 1926. *Cf.* Patrick Geddes, *Cities in Evolution*, 1915, pp. 134-137, on housing conditions in Glasgow and other Scottish cities.

[22] Massachusetts Homestead Commission, *3rd Annual Report*, 1915, Public Document No. 103, pp. 57-63. Lawrence Veiller, "Slumless America," *National Municipal Review*, Aug., 1920, 9:8:496. Jacob Riis, *How the Other Half Lives*, (1890) 1926, ch. XIX. Regional Survey of New York and Its Environs, *Buildings: Their Uses and the Spaces About Them*, 1931, VI, 211-214, 220.

[23] "Housing—Its Relation to Social Work," *National Housing Association Publication* No. 48, June, 1918, pp. 3, 7 (quoted).

bered that she would never bring her 'gentlemen friends' up those greasy stairs, to the room where the wash tub and the coal pile jostled the beds, and the family circle had to stand up and lock arms. When the little boy got into the juvenile court, you didn't wonder why he stayed out as long as he could keep awake, before he crept into the stifling room, and fell onto his pallet.'' All the conditions surrounding the "slum-dweller," writes Veiller,[24] make for discomfort of body and discontent of soul. "He has no peace and no privacy—he has not even elbow-room, night or day. He sees no beauty and has no repose. His neighbors' wash shuts out his small patch of sky and he must close such insufficient windows as his room may have if he would not hear his neighbors' quarrels. He works without inspiration and finishes his day without satisfaction or hope.''

Highly congested and inadequately housed areas, however, are not necessarily "slums." The word has no legal existence. As popularly used, there is a certain social stigma attached to it. The term "slum" makes an insidious social distinction. As Todd[25] remarks, it gives some people a chance to feel righteous. Its use should be tabooed as well for the reason that it is not an accurate term. The word itself is not American, but English, and was first applied in London to overcrowded and undersanitated sections, chiefly composed of one- and two-story houses. "The slums of cities, according to the dictionaries, are dirty back streets, especially such streets as are inhabited by a squalid and criminal population; they are low and dangerous neighborhoods.''[26] Such neighborhoods may be found in any large city, but the term in popular parlance is not so restricted. Many decent, honest workingmen and their families live in congested tenement districts, and it is these normal people and their needs that we are interested in. Housing conditions in New York City as we will describe them affect several million people—ordinary people, average persons, not "slum-dwellers," a term which they naturally resent. To give statistical weight to the assertion that the terms "slums" and "slum-dwellers" are incorrect as popularly used and defined, reference may be made to Booth's classification of the people of East London, which was compiled after careful and extensive study.[27] The

[24] "Slumless America," National Municipal Review, Aug., 1920, 9:8:495.
[25] "Sentimentality and Social Reform," American Journal of Sociology, Sept., 1916, 22:2:163, 172.
[26] Seventh Special Report of Commissioner of Labor, 1894, p. 13. Cf. "What is a Slum?" Housing, Sept., 1928, 17:3:164-166.
[27] Charles Booth, Life and Labour of the People in London, First Series; Poverty, I, East, Central and South London, 1902, pp. 28-72.

eight classes into which he divided the people, and the percentage of the population that each composed, are as follows:

Classification	Percentage
A. The lowest class of occasional labourers, loafers, and semi-criminals	1.25
B. Casual earnings—"very poor"	11.25
C. Intermittent earnings	8.00
D. Small regular earnings	14.50
E. Regular standard earnings—above the line of poverty	42.50
F. Higher-class labour	13.50
G. Lower middle class	4.00
H. Upper middle class	5.00

Class A represents the dregs of the population; it is a "squalid and criminal population." Class B is hardly much above it. Together they make up about 10 per cent of the population of London as a whole—the "submerged tenth." They live in a state of chronic want. Classes C and D, which are lumped together as "the poor," are defined as those whose means may be sufficient, but barely sufficient, for decent independent life. All the rest of the population is above the line of poverty, as so defined. To use Booth's words, "E, F, G, and H are the classes in comfort, or even in affluence." It is significant that Class E, typical wage-earners, is the largest single class and comprises almost one-half of the population of East London. Almost two-thirds (65 per cent) of the people are above the poverty class, and nearly 90 per cent of them—all except Classes A and B—are average, normal people. These people are not of the "slums."

Tenement House.—The housing problem is to be found in its most acute form in the tenement sections. What is a tenement house? Legally defined, it is "any house or building, or portion thereof, which is either rented, leased, let or hired out, to be occupied, or is occupied, in whole or in part, as the home or residence of three families or more living independently of each other, and doing their cooking upon the premises, and includes apartment houses, flat houses and all other houses so occupied."[28] This verbosity is not only due to the fact that legal writers were once paid by the word and the habit has persisted; it is also occasioned by necessity. It is the experience of New York, for instance, that if there be any loophole of escape left by unfortunate wording of the law, or by an omission, the intent of

[28] *New York Tenement House Law*, 1912, article I, § 2.

the law will not be realized.[29] The most important parts of the definition are the phrases "the home or residence of three families or more," which rules out single-family and two-family dwellings, and "living independently of each other and doing their cooking upon the premises," which rules out hotels. The last-mentioned section of the law has recently been called into action in New York to determine whether apartment hotels, in which the tenants were found to be cooking within their own apartments, are not thereby covered by the law relating to tenement houses. The point is important because the ordinary transient hotel is regulated only by the building code, in which there are practically no restrictions as to light and ventilation, whereas apartment houses must comply with the strict provisions of the tenement-house law. Because of this difference, "it is obvious that unscrupulous builders would find it very greatly to their financial advantage to erect their buildings in the guise of 'hotels,' rather than as 'apartment houses,' and evade the requirements of the tenement house law imposed for the protection, safety and health of the occupants."[30] The owners of such apartment hotels have protested against being included under the tenement-house act and have announced that some $300,000,000 investment was involved, affecting 150 buildings and 15,000 families.

So much for the legal aspects of the question. A descriptive definition of tenement houses is "the poorest class of apartment houses. They are generally poorly built, without sufficient accommodations for light and ventilation, and are overcrowded. The middle rooms often receive no daylight, and it is not uncommon in them for several families to be crowded into one of their dark and unwholesome rooms. Bad air, want of sunlight, and filthy surroundings work the physical ruin of the wretched tenants, while their mental and moral condition is equally lowered."[31] These aspects of the tenement-house problem will be discussed later on when considering the situation in New York City.

Location of the Tenement Section.—Generally speaking, the utility of land in the city falls into three classes: business, industrial, and residential. The areas devoted to these purposes are separated by more or less definite lines and are themselves subdivided according to the specific nature or class of use for each purpose.

"Business area for instance lies generally at the focus of local transportation routes or in other words at the point of intersection of the

[29] Lawrence Veiller, *Housing Reform*, 1910, ch. IX.
[30] *Housing Betterment*, May, 1927, 16:1:70, 74.
[31] *National Cyclopedia*.

strongest lines of local travel. This point is very often at the geographical center of the city which can be reached from all sections of the city with equal facility. The industrial area on the other hand has no one definite location, as has the business area. Depending largely on railroad facilities, it soon becomes scattered throughout all sections of the city, forcing its way from all directions in wedges almost to the business heart. There is generally no control and no concentration other than that offered by the railroad lines. To residential purposes is devoted the rest of the land in the city. This is generally of three classes: fine residential area; general residential area; and tenement area. The first of these preëmpts those sections of the city which have the greatest number of pleasing and natural advantages. The second, in general, lies along the thoroughfares and highways which have the best transportation facilities and also along such railroads as provide suburban transportation. The third class, the tenement areas, are generally found in the industrial regions and in the pockets or areas that lie between railroad lines and close to the center.''[32]

The most important factor in creating the first type of tenement area—in the industrial regions—is the factory. Factories create sub-centers, most distinct when on the outskirts of the city, by causing the erection of laborers' cottages nearby, which in turn attract small shops and public and semi-public buildings. When located within the built-up sections of the city they attract tenements near at hand, such multiple dwellings being called for by the relatively high value of the land. The centralizing effect of the factory is due in large measure to the desire or necessity of workmen to live nearby because of the convenience and the saving of time and money that are involved in transportation. According to the excellent statistical study made by Professor Pratt,[33] the longer the working day and the lower the wages, the greater is the tendency of workers to live near the factory. The second type of tenement section—close to the center of the city—is located in a deteriorating neighborhood. This situation arises as follows. The growth of a city leads normally to the ultimate conversion of residence land into business land. Most of our cities, by reason of their rapid growth, have districts that are going through a transition from residential districts to factory and business districts. This change

[32] E. H. Bennett, ''Planning for Distribution of Industries,'' *Annals*, Jan., 1914, 51:140:217-218.

[33] Edward E. Pratt, *Industrial Causes of Congestion of Population in New York City*, 1911, pp. 116-146. Richard M. Hurd, *Principles of City Land Values*, 1905, ch. V.

is accompanied by depreciating values from a residential standpoint. The good residences in the district, erected before the change occurred, become rooming and boarding houses. They are not kept in repair or improved because the owners argue that it would be a waste to put more money into the houses that will in themselves bring no return when the land is sold.[34] Rent from dwellings is decreasing, whereas land value is greatly increasing. Further deterioration occurs when the houses are divided into places of residence for several families. This is the "converted dwelling" or "hovel" type of tenement—a house that was once a single-family dwelling but is now the residence of three or more families living independently of one another and doing their cooking on the premises. Tenements are then erected in the rear or on vacant lots and in time the whole district becomes one of the lowest type of residential utility. As Professor Burgess[35] remarks, "In the zone of deterioration encircling the central business section are always to be found the so-called 'slums' and 'bad lands,' with their submerged regions of poverty, degradation, and disease, and their underworlds of crime and vice."

To illustrate: the rich in New York City formerly used to live around the Battery and on Bowling Green and lower Broadway. Battery Park was the promenade of fashion and the playground for wealthy children. Then business crept in, factories were established, immigrant workers arrived, and the district depreciated. The rich moved away. Their brownstone dwellings were converted finally into tenements. This was the origin of the tenement-house problem in New York.[36] Again, consider the North End of Boston, the oldest section of the city, originally the best residential quarter but now surrounded by trade and industry. "It is the landing place and the first living section for the immigrant, especially Italians and Greeks. It has remained a residential area since the founding of the city, and business encroachments on its boundaries have been negligible during 300 years. In the beginning there were the narrow, winding streets of the colonial town, large blocks with residences around the front street, each standing in its own ground with deep gardens behind. Little by little the intervening yard areas were built up with intruding tenements. Then the back gardens were made available, stables gave place

[34] Mildred Chadsey, "The Old House as a Social Problem," *Annals*, Jan., 1914, 51:140:87. John R. Richards, "The Problem of the Old House," *National Housing Conference*, 1913, III, 47-53.

[35] R. E. Park and E. W. Burgess, *The City*, 1925, pp. 54-56. Richard M. Hurd, *Principles of City Land Values*, 1905, ch. VI.

[36] *Report of Reconstruction Commission on Housing Conditions, New York*, 1920, p. 32. Jacob Riis, *How the Other Half Lives*, 1890, ch. I.

to more tenements crowded into the rear areas, until at last the whole territory was packed almost solid with tenement houses and small shops, great quantities of the former being packed in the middle of blocks with no street frontage, little light, less air, and frequently no means of approach except through covered tunnels sometimes not more than 4 ft. wide. Many of the houses are old wooden structures roughly made over for tenement house purposes from what once had been spacious residences.''[37]

Housing Index.—One point more before turning to the history of the development of the problem in a given case. What index or indices can be used for measuring the housing problem? The size of the tenement building, which appeals to the average person, is a poor index. According to this concept, only cities like New York have a tenement-house problem, whereas New York differs from other cities only in that it has more layers (it builds higher), and not necessarily more people per layer. Further, the converted dwelling or hovel type of tenement often presents the worst conditions. The density of population, or the number of people per acre, is a better index, though not a perfect one, for it does not take into consideration the number of stories and the local conditions. There may be a very high density of population in a given section, as for instance one composed of hotels and apartment houses, and yet quite satisfactory housing conditions. "The vital question," as Veiller[38] says, "is the distribution of such population, the actual close proximity in which people live." The degree of overcrowding, both of land and room, is also an important factor to consider. There is land-overcrowding— what the English call "overhousing"—when houses are packed together with excessive closeness so that sufficient ventilation, light, and sanitation are lacking and even impossible. This has been one of the main evils in New York City, and one of the chief accomplishments of housing reform there has been to lessen the amount of land-overcrowding. Room-overcrowding exists where an excessive number of people live in an apartment. The authorities in England make use of this index and regard a tenement as overcrowded when there are more than two persons per room.[39] A four-room apartment, then, is not overcrowded unless there are nine or more people living in it.

[37] Ralph A. Cram, "Scrapping the Slum," *National Housing Conference*, 1918, VII, 246-247.

[38] *Housing Reform*, 1910, p. 28. Lawrence Veiller, "A Safe Load of Population on Land," *National Housing Conference*, 1910, II, 75-76.

[39] E. R. Dewsnup, *Housing Problem in England*, 1907, pp. 45-46; see ch. II on overhousing and ch. III on overcrowding in rooms. Lawrence Veiller, *Housing Reform*, 1910, pp. 28-35. *Housing Betterment*, June, 1919, 8:2:36.

Where the index has been used in this country, it is usually one and a half persons per room, or not more than six persons to a four-room apartment. To be sure, there ought to be a standard room to make the index generally valuable, yet the rooms of tenement houses are usually about the same size. Real congestion or room-overcrowding is dependent not only on the number of occupants, but on their sex, age, and relationship. A man and wife and six young children would not be as overcrowded in a given apartment as a man and wife, a boarder, two working sons, and a married daughter, her husband and child.[40]

With respect to density of population, England has adopted as her standard for post-war housing a maximum of 12 families to the acre, although in extreme cases in her crowded cities sometimes as many as 16 families or 80 persons to the acre are permitted. Contrast this with Manhattan Island, where the average density of population is about 150 persons to the acre. There are even individual blocks in Manhattan, of a size 200 by 600 or 800 feet, which contain as many as 4,000 people each, or a larger population than many country towns. In fact, according to the Census Bureau definition of a city, as an incorporated place containing 2,500 or more population, each such block represents, in size, a city population by itself. New York is said to be the most densely populated city of ancient, medieval, or modern times.[41]

[40] *Report of Reconstruction Commission on Housing Conditions*, *New York*, 1920, p. 24.
[41] Thomas Adams, *Planning the New York Region*, 1927, pp. 17, 119. E. R. L. Gould, ''Housing of City Masses,'' *International Quarterly*, Jan. 1905, X, 361. *Housing*, June, 1928, 17:2:84.

CHAPTER VI

THE TENEMENT-HOUSE PROBLEM IN LONDON AND NEW YORK

THE tenement-house problem first appeared in the large cities and there received its first attention. Neglect may be said to have created the problem: when conditions became intolerable, intervention occurred. This happened at about the same time in London and New York, the first cities in their respective countries to be affected by housing legislation. They present an interesting contrast in that each represents the best example of two different, and the two most important, methods of dealing with housing conditions.

LONDON

It was about the middle of the nineteenth century when the public-spirited citizens in London became aroused by the degradation and sickness resulting from the conditions in which a large proportion of the common people lived. The leader in the agitation for improvement and reform was the noted philanthropist, the Earl of Shaftesbury. In presenting his famous bill for the regulation of lodging houses, in 1851, he referred to a parliamentary paper dated 1842, which gave the results of a house-to-house visitation in St. George's, Hanover Square, reported by the London Statistical Society. In this survey 1,465 families of the laboring classes were found to have for their residence only 2,174 rooms. Of these families, 929 had but one room for the whole family to reside in; 408 had two rooms; 94 had three; 17 had four, and but 17 over four. This was the condition in one of the better parishes of London. The greatest evil of that time was, obviously, room-overcrowding.

Among other sources of evidence, Lord Shaftesbury quoted from the report of the London Fever Hospital in 1845 the following statement in reference to one particular room: "It is filled to excess every night, but on particular occasions commonly 50, sometimes 90 to 100 men are crowded into a room 33 feet 9 inches long, 20 feet wide and 7 feet high. The whole of this dormitory does not allow more space, that is, does not admit of a larger bulk of air for respiration than is appropriated in the wards of the fever hospital for three patients. As a consequence more than one-fifth of the whole admissions into the fever hospital for that year—no less than 130 patients affected with fever—were received from that one room alone." He also quoted one of the city missionaries, or charitable workers, concerning a house similar to the "hovel" type. "In my district is a house containing 8 rooms, which are all let separately to individuals who furnish to re-let them. The parlor measures 18 feet by 10 feet. Beds are arranged on each side of the room. In this one room there slept, on the night previous to my inquiry, 27 male and female adults, 31 children, and 2 or 3 dogs, making up in all 58 human beings breathing the contaminated atmosphere of a close room. In the top of the same house, measuring 12 feet by 10 feet, there were 6 beds, and on the same night there slept in them 32 human beings [probably this should be referred to as bed-overcrowding], all breathing the pestiferous air of a hole not fit to keep swine in. The beds are so close together, that when let down on the floor there is no room to pass between them; and they who sleep in the beds furthest from the door can, consequently, only get into them by crawling over the beds which are nearer the door. [There is need of a stagger plan here.] In one district alone there are 270 such rooms. These houses are never cleaned or ventilated; they literally swarm with vermin. It is almost impossible to breathe. Missionaries are seized with vomiting or fainting upon entering them." The London Statistical Society examined in 1848 what was then known as the Church Lane District in Bloomsbury, one of the filthiest and unhealthiest in the metropolis. It is described as "a picture in detail, of human wretchedness, filth, and brutal degradation. In these wretched dwellings, all ages and both sexes, fathers and daughters, mothers and sons, grown-up brothers and sisters, the sick, dying, and dead, are herded together. Take an instance—House No. 2, size of room 14 feet long, 13 feet broad, 6 feet high, rent 8s. [$2.00] for two rooms per week; under-rent [sub-let] for 3d. [6 cents] a night for each adult. Number of families, 3; 8 males above 20, 5 females above 20, 4 males under 20, 5 females under 20; total, 22 souls. The landlady receives 18s. [$4.50] a week; thus a clear profit of 10s. [$2.50]. State of room filthy."[1]

Conditions like these were brought to the attention of Parliament in such vivid form that the government was forced to intervene. The bills were passed giving England the first housing laws of any coun-

[1] E. R. L. Gould, "Housing of City Masses," *International Quarterly*, Jan., 1905, X, 349-350. E. R. Dewsnup, *Housing Problem in England*, 1907, pp. 91-112.

try. The Common Lodging House Act of 1851 was intended to improve the quality of dwellings. It provided for inspection, the notification of infectious diseases, the keeping of such places in good sanitary condition and repair, and the separation of the sexes among the occupants. The Labouring Classes Lodging House Act of 1851 aimed at increasing the number of houses suitable for workingmen, by facilitating the establishment in populous districts of well-ordered lodging houses. The money expended was to come out of that part of local taxation denominated the "Poor Rate." It was a permissive, not a mandatory act. Its main purpose was to minimize the herding together of the poorest classes in the manner described above. Government policy was thus at first narrow and limited; only the worst and most dangerous forms of overcrowding were attacked. In course of time, however, this policy has been extended to the provision of model tenements for the people built under municipal supervision and supported by municipal taxes and credit, until England has today the most advanced housing legislation of any country.

A number of other housing acts were passed, which we may skip over because they were all superseded by the basic Housing of the Working Classes Act of 1890. This act applies to the United Kingdom and is still in force except as modified by subsequent legislation, notably in 1909 and 1919. Part I of this Act deals with "unhealthy areas" and is limited to cities and towns. Power is given to the local sanitary authority to declare a certain district an "unhealthy area" and forthwith to prepare some scheme for improvement. Such an area is one unfit for human habitation on account of the bad arrangement or condition of the houses, courts, alleys, or streets; the want of light, air, ventilation, and proper conveniences, or on account of any other sanitary defects; any one or more of such causes being dangerous or injurious to the health of the inhabitants. It must be clear that "the evils connected with such houses, courts, or alleys, and the sanitary defects in such area can not be effectually remedied otherwise than by an improvement scheme for the rearrangement and reconstruction of the streets and houses within such area, or of some such streets or houses." Under this Act compulsory purchase is provided for, but it need not be resorted to if the owner or owners will confer with the local authority and make the required changes under the latter's control and superintendence. Failing that, the local authority is to purchase the property—"no lease, settlement, entail or other private arrangements can deter a local authority from acquiring it"—at a fair market value and demolish it. This is popularly known as "slum clearance.'' If the local authority fails to make a scheme, the central authority (the Local Government Board) may make and enforce one. The local authority is further given power to provide accommodations for the tenants thus displaced either by using lands already owned or by purchasing suitable sites. Expenses for such improvement schemes are to be defrayed either from local taxation or from special loans. The principle underlying this whole plan is that expropriation and demolition of insanitary areas entail benefit to the entire community, and it is but fair that the community as a whole should bear a moderate portion of the cost.

Part II of this Act deals with unhealthy dwelling houses. The district health officer must report to the local authority any places which appear to be in so bad a condition as to be unfit for habitation. The initiative may also be taken by any four householders living in or near the same street where the property complained of is situated. Notice is given to the owner to put it in good condition. Whenever proper diligence is not exercised by the owner, the local authority may determine to abolish it. Procedure is then by purchase or by condemnation. The owner has certain rights of appeal to higher authority.

Part III relates to provision of lodging houses for working people by governmental authority, and is made applicable both to urban and rural districts. The expression lodging houses includes here separate houses or cottages, whether containing one or several apartments. Either land may be acquired and lodgings erected, or existing lodging houses may be purchased or leased, management and control of all being vested in the local authorities.[2]

The chief characteristic of this Act is the fixing of responsibility upon owners for the sanitary condition of their property. They are given the privilege of taking the initiative in the matter of improvement. Should they fail to satisfy the authorities, the latter must undertake the work. The law is not socialistic in character or intent. It is a sanitary measure, a public welfare measure. The purpose of the Act was not the encouragement of the erection of houses for working people by municipal authority; that was an incidental measure which was adopted out of justice to them when displaced while the improvement scheme was in progress. It later led, however, to a complete program of government housing.

[2] E. R. L. Gould, *Housing of the Working People*, 8th Special Report of the Commissioner of Labor, 1895, pp. 56-62. E. R. Dewsnup, *Housing Problem in England*, 1907, chs. V, VI. J. S. Nettlefold, *Practical Housing*, 1910, chs. III, IV. Edith Wood, *Housing of the Unskilled Wage Earner*, 1919, p. 143.

The Act was amended in 1909 by the Housing of the Working Classes and Town Planning Act, which added the new feature of a town or city plan designed to avoid such conditions as unhealthy areas in the future. This again was permissive. As amended again in 1919, it became mandatory. The last-mentioned Act added somewhat to the powers of the local governments in housing and town planning, and it increased very considerably the financial assistance and the direction and control of the central government (now the Ministry of Health instead of the old Local Government Board) in these matters. Financial assistance was now given by the treasury to meet any deficit resulting from a housing scheme beyond the product of a penny rate. Hitherto these local authorities were empowered to frame and carry out schemes for increased housing and the improvement of slum areas, subject to the direction of the state, and could be compelled to this course to any considerable extent only on complaint of local health officers or of citizens of the locality. Now it was made the duty of every local authority to survey the housing needs of its district, to prepare a plan to meet those needs and to submit it for approval; and when so approved it became their further duty to carry it out. In default of action by the local authorities, the central authority was to act. New powers were also given the local authorities to aid limited dividend corporations devoting themselves to housing—public utility societies, as they are called—by making grants or loans, subscribing to shares of capital, or guaranteeing the interest on money borrowed, on such terms as to rate of interest and repayment and on such security as they thought fit. In town planning, also, whereas it was formerly optional with the local authorities to prepare schemes, now all such authorities with a population of over 20,000 were required to formulate such schemes within a specified time and have them approved. Both in housing and town planning, there are provisions for compelling the local authorities to act, and for state action at their expense if they fail to take such action. In brief, it is accepted as a public responsibility in England to see that the working classes are adequately housed.

Subsequent acts have dealt primarily with government subsidy to private builders and on slum-clearance schemes, and have not altered the basic procedure. Much has been accomplished in the way of demolishing unsanitary areas and erecting suitable dwellings. Hundreds of thousands of houses have been built and millions of pounds have been spent by the central government and local authorities. The usual beneficial results of improved housing have followed.[3] Great Britain, however, is still wrestling with the housing problem, as will be discussed in more detail in a later chapter where consideration is given to the advantages and disadvantages of government aid.

NEW YORK

The genesis of New York City's tenement-house problem came in the years following the War of 1812, when trade, industry, and increased immigration changed the character of the lower and middle east side. In thirty-five years the city of about a hundred thousand came to harbor half a million souls, for whom homes had to be found. The process of neighborhood deterioration set in. "As the middle east side, for example, changed from an aristocratic residence section where fine old houses clustered along the banks of the river to a district given over to lumber and coal yards, to abattoirs and factories, the workers who were brought to the region sought residence there. The old three-story brown stone houses were hurriedly made over into apartments, with one family to a floor, or became rooming houses. Tenements sprang up to fill further demands. The low rents demanded by the lack of space inevitably led to the interior rooms—the cheap construction—the evil air shafts—the small rooms, which are the architectural characteristics of the New York tenement."[4]

The first written record of inadequate housing conditions in New York is contained in a pamphlet entitled "A Brief View of the Sanitary Condition of the City," published in 1842 by Dr. John H. Griscom, City Inspector of the Board of Health.[5] Among other facts he mentioned that 1,459 cellars or underground rooms were being used as places of residence by 7,196 persons and that there were as many as 6,618 different families living in courts or in rear buildings. In regard to the influence of these localities upon the health and lives of the occupants, Dr. Griscom said: "There are, there can be no dispute, but few who know of the dreadful extent of the disease and suffering to be found in them. In the damp, dark and chilly cellars, fevers, rheumatism, contagious and inflammatory disorders, affections

[3] Frank B. Williams, "England's Newest Housing and Town Planning Act," *Housing Betterment*, Feb., 1920, 9:1:1-3. S. D. Adshead, *Town Planning*, 1923, chs. XI, XII, XIII. Edith Wood, *Housing of the Unskilled Wage Earner*, 1919, pp. 140-164; *Housing Progress in Western Europe*, 1923, pp. 41-57. *Housing*, June, 1928, 17:2:107-108.

[4] *Report of the Reconstruction Commission on Housing Conditions*, New York, 1920, p. 32. Jacob Riis, *How the Other Half Lives*, 1890, p. 7 ff.

[5] Robert W. DeForest and Lawrence Veiller, *The Tenement House Problem*, 1903, I, 71-118, contains an excellent discussion of tenement-house reform in New York City, 1834 to 1900.

of lungs, skin and eyes, and numerous others, are rife and too often successfully combat the skill of the physician and the benevolence of strangers. . . . A due regard for the health of the citizens and residents would justify the city legislature in prohibiting cellars as dwellings; in requiring the owner or lessee to keep all the out and in-door premises clean and free from everything likely to prove injurious to public health; and an immediate stop should be put to the practice of crowding so many human beings in such limited spaces as we often see them. The wise prohibition to carry more than a graduated number of people on sea-going vessels should be extended to dwellings on land. If there is a propriety in the law regulating the construction of buildings in reference to fire, equally proper would be one respecting the protection of the inmates from the pernicious influences of badly arranged houses and apartments. The power given to a magistrate to pull down a building whose risk of falling endangers the lives of the inmates or passers-by, may, with equal reason, be extended to the correction of the interior condition of tenements when dangerous to health and life. The latter should be regarded by the legislator and executive with as much solicitude as the property of citizens.''

In 1853 the Association for Improving the Condition of the Poor appointed a special committee ''to inquire into the sanitary condition of the laboring classes, and the practicability of devising measures for improving the comfort and healthfulness of their habitations.'' The committee reported that there were ''thousands of poor persons, but comparatively few buildings suitable for their accommodation. Most of the houses are those that were formerly occupied by the wealthy who have removed up-town, and now in their dilapidated state many of them are tenanted by miserably poor Irish and German emigrants. Large rooms have been divided by rough partitions into dwellings for two or three families (each, perhaps, taking boarders), where they wash, cook, eat, sleep, and die—many of them prematurely, for the circumstances in which they live make fearful havoc of health and life; and in addition, night lodgers consisting of homeless men, women, and children are not unfrequent, who for a trifling sum are allowed temporary shelter. There, huddled together like cattle in pens, the inmates are subjected to the most debasing influences. Many of the dwellings, moreover, are out of repair, and the yards, from neglect of the sinks, in so vile a condition they can scarcely be stepped into, without contracting filth of the most offensive kind. Crazy old buildings—crowded rear tenements in filthy yards; dark, damp basements; leaky garrets, shops, outhouses, and stables converted into dwellings, though scarcely fit to shelter brutes —are the habitations of thousands of our fellow-beings in this wealthy city.'' The committee concluded: ''The dwellings of the industrial classes in New York are not adapted to the wants of human beings, nor compatible with the health or the social or moral improvement of the occupants.''[6]

In 1856 a legislative commission was appointed to investigate and report. It attributed the evil conditions to neglect and greed, and advocated reform on the ground that it would prevent crime and pauperism and improve the public health. It prepared a scheme for licensing tenement houses so as to bring them under strict sanitary control. Its recommendations were not adopted by the legislature. The Draft riots of 1863, which called attention to the character of some of the population living in these tenement conditions, and the dread of advancing cholera and other epidemics, coupled with a citizens' movement which resulted in an extensive survey of conditions, all led finally to the enactment of the Tenement House Law of 1867, the first such law to be passed in this country. At the time this law was enacted there were some 15,000 tenement houses in the city, all of which had been built without any legal regulations whatsoever and with little if any regard for the safety and health of the occupants.[7] There is no need to recite the provisions of this law nor those of subsequent acts until we come to the basic tenement-house law of 1901. It should be noted that these early laws did not accomplish much either because of looseness in the wording of the text, the granting of too much discretion to the Board of Health which was charged with their enforcement, or because the provisions did not strike at the real roots of the difficulty.

Another movement for reform was begun in 1877, incited by an experiment in model tenements by Mr. Alfred T. White of Brooklyn. He had been impressed by some model tenements he had seen in London, and upon similar plans he erected in Brooklyn his well-known ''Home Buildings.'' A year later he built an entire block of similar model tenements, the ''Tower Buildings,'' with a large park or courtyard in the center. Mr. White was probably the first one in America to realize the desirability of building houses around a hollow

[6] E. R. L. Gould, ''Housing of City Masses,'' *International Quarterly*, Jan., 1905, X, 351-353. Robert W. DeForest and Lawrence Veiller, *The Tenement House Problem*, 1903, I, 77.

[7] Robert W. DeForest, ''History of the Housing Movement in America,'' *Annals*, Jan., 1914, 51:140:9.

square. A building such as his, only two rooms deep, solves all problems of light and ventilation. He utilized only 50 per cent of the lot, at a time when commercial builders were regularly erecting tenements that covered 90 per cent of the lot, resulting in dark inner rooms and insufficient ventilation. His experiment was a success financially and had the effect of stimulating public interest in the housing problem. A result of the agitation which followed was the Tenement House Law of 1879, which restricted for the first time the percentage of lot to be occupied by a new tenement house.[8]

In 1879 the proprietor of a paper called the *Sanitary Engineer*, with four other men offered prizes of $500 for the best architectural designs for a tenement house on an ordinary city lot, 25 by 100 feet. The size of the unit lot in New York City is an important matter, closely related to housing conditions. Most of the housing difficulties in New York have arisen from it. The depth of 100 feet is occasioned by the fact that the streets are laid out 200 feet apart, which gives 100 feet depth to the lots facing on each of the two streets forming a block. The other dimensions are usually 600 or 800 feet, because the avenues are that far apart. On account of high land values the unit frontage became 25 feet, the smallest multiple of 600 or 800 upon which it is at all practicable to build. Tenements on a 25 by 100 foot lot were regularly built up to both side lot lines and back about 90 feet, leaving a 10-foot yard in the rear as the only open space. A row of tenement houses of this sort makes it impossible to have any direct access to light and air except in the front facing the street and in the rear facing the yard. The only exception is the corner building. As a consequence, in the typical tenement house having four apartments to a floor, two facing front and two facing rear, only the front rooms and the very rear rooms have windows. All the other rooms are either semi-dark or entirely dark. In many cases conditions were even worse because tenements were back-to-back. Over 500 such tenements were still in existence in 1930. In 1901, when the newly created Tenement House Department began its work of inspection, there were enumerated over 350,000 dark interior rooms in the tenement houses of New York.

The first prize in the architectural competition mentioned above was awarded to a plan which has since become known as the "double-decker dumb-bell tenement"—incorrectly referred to as "double-

[8] Robert W. DeForest, "History of the Housing Movement in America," *Annals*, Jan., 1914, 51:140:9-10. Robert W. DeForest and Lawrence Veiller, *The Tenement House Problem*, 1903, I, XVII, 97-100. *Housing Betterment*, Dec., 1927, 16:4:315-316.

decker,'' for they have usually been built four, five, or six stories high, but quite properly designated ''dumb-bell,'' not only because of the semblance of the structure to the well-known instrument of calisthenics but also because of the other, more vulgar connotation of the term. This type of tenement house soon came to be regarded by tene-

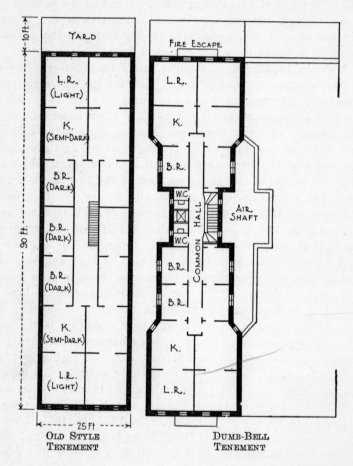

ment-house reformers in New York as the curse of the city. If buildings on this plan had been limited to two stories, some improvement in housing conditions would have been made, but with five- and six-story buildings the indentation, which gave the structure its chief characteristic, formed nothing but a narrow shaft inadequate to the task of providing light and air to the inner rooms. It is impossible for much light to penetrate five stories down a three-foot shaft; at most there was just light enough so that families living opposite each other had no privacy.[9] The tenants soon discovered that the air-shafts provided a much more convenient receptacle for banana skins, potato parings and more objectionable refuse than the garbage cans at the back of the building. This was especially so when disposing of garbage in the proper way meant carrying it down four, five, or even six flights of stairs.[10] As a result of this use of the airshaft, even though there were now windows in every room it was a distinct disadvantage to open them. "The chief function of the airshaft often seemed to be the interchange of smells, profanity and bacteria. 'Gigantic culture tubes,' some one called them."[11] There are about 10,000 dumb-bell tenements still standing.

Further investigation and further legislation followed, but without much change in conditions. In the "gay nineties" Jacob Riis performed a notable task by waging his "Battle with the Slum" and by advising the privileged class "How the Other Half Lives." Through his efforts, knowledge of housing conditions and concern over them became general. Two more architectural competitions were held, which deserve mention because they contributed to the reform brought about by the law of 1901. In 1896 the Association for Improving the Condition of the Poor called a series of conferences as a result of which the City and Suburban Homes Company was formed for the purpose of building model tenement houses in New York as a business investment. A special architectural competition was held, the prize going to Mr. Ernest Flagg for his plan which proved that the more nearly square the building the better the conditions. It is necessary, in other words, to get away from the 25-foot lot. In the competition of 1900, fostered by the Charity Organization Society, the first prize went to Mr. R. Thomas Short, who used Mr. Flagg's contribution that the square tenement was superior to the oblong. He added this new feature: the necessity of making proper provision for light and air on each lot on which a tenement house is built, without depending on what the owner of the adjoining lot will do or not do.

The stage is now set for the law of 1901. Governor Theodore Roosevelt in 1900 appointed a Tenement House Commission, of which the

---

[9] Mary K. Simkhovitch, *The City Worker's World*, 1917, p. 26. Robert W. DeForest and Lawrence Veiller, *The Tenement House Problem*, 1903, I, 100-102.

[10] *Report of the Reconstruction Commission on Housing Conditions, New York*, 1920, p. 28.

[11] Edith Wood, *Housing of the Unskilled Wage Earner*, 1919, p. 38.

late Robert W. DeForest, a noted philanthropist, was Chairman, and
the housing expert, Lawrence Veiller, was Secretary. This commission, after careful and extensive study, the results of which were embodied in an excellent two-volume publication,[12] summed up the evils
of New York's tenement houses as follows: "Insufficiency of light
and air due to narrow courts or air shafts, undue height, and to the
occupation by the building or by the adjacent buildings of too great
a proportion of the lot area; danger from fire; lack of separate water-
closets and washing facilities; overcrowding; foul cellars and courts
and other like evils, which may be classified as bad housekeeping."
The Commission undertook to solve this five-fold problem by three
definite lines of action: First, to provide proper types of new tenement houses for the future by means of adequate restrictive legislation, and to forbid the erection of any others. Second, to remedy the
errors of past years by altering and improving the old tenement
houses so as to make them fit for human habitation. Third, to maintain present and future tenement houses in sanitary condition by
adequate supervision.[13] Let use see how wisely they planned.

The first difficulty—insufficiency of light and air—was due fundamentally to land-overcrowding. To overcome this it was necessary to
limit the height of the buildings and the area of the lot that might
be built upon. With regard to the first, the law prescribes that "the
height of no tenement house hereafter erected shall by more than
one-half exceed the width of the widest street upon which it stands."
The value of this provision may be seen in the fact that the higher
the building with reference to the width of the street, the less sunlight will reach the lower stories. The percentage of a lot that might be
built upon is restricted in a number of ways. Behind each new tenement house there must be a yard extending across the entire width
of the lot and at every point open to the sky unobstructed, except that
fire escapes or unenclosed outside stairs may project not over 3 feet
from the rear line of the house. Except upon a corner lot the depth
of this yard behind every tenement house thereafter erected 60 feet
in height shall be not less than 12 feet in every part. The size of the
yard shall be increased in depth 1 foot for every additional 12 feet
of height of the building, and decreased 1 foot in depth for every
12 feet of height of building less than 60 feet, with the exception
that no yard shall be less than 10 feet in depth in any part. Instead

[12] Robert W. DeForest and Lawrence Veiller, *The Tenement House Problem*,
1903.
[13] *Ibid.*, I, xiv ff.; 6, 11. Lawrence Veiller, *Housing Reform*, 1910, ch. IV.
The Tenement House Law of the State of New York, 1912.

of the old narrow airshafts the law provides for inner and outer courts that shall not be less in area than certain minimum sizes, governed by the height of the building. For a four-story building, for example, the inner court must be at least 8 by 14 feet. All told, not more than 70 per cent of the lot, or 90 per cent if a corner lot, may be built upon. These provisions have made it commercially unprofitable to build on a lot 25 by 100 feet. They have thus driven that narrow lot, the root of most of the evils, out of existence. Tenements erected under the requirements of the law, although on larger plots of ground and covering but 70 per cent of the area, are profitable and in the long run, because better built, prove more satisfactory as investments. "If the tenement house law of 1901 had done nothing else it would have furnished the greatest boon to future generations ever given by American enactments of this sort in its restriction of overcrowding buildings upon lot space, thereby abolishing the iniquitous light shaft, and giving every room direct access to light and air."[14] Careful provisions are also made in regard to the lighting and ventilating of rooms, windows in rooms, size of rooms, etc. For instance, every room must have a window of one-tenth its floor area opening upon the street or upon a yard or court; at least one room in each apartment must have an area of 120 square feet and no room can be less than 70 square feet. No room shall be less than 9 feet high. With respect to old tenement houses, light was introduced into the dark inner rooms by cutting large windows in the partitions separating these rooms from the outer rooms; daylight was let into the public halls, and at night the owner of the building was obliged to keep a proper light burning from sunset to sunrise throughout the year.

The second evil mentioned by the Commission was the fire hazard. The law of 1901 requires two entirely independent means of escape in case of fire to be provided for each apartment. The halls and stairs of every new tenement house must be fireproof. If the building is six stories or under in height it shall be semi-fireproof, if over six stories entirely fireproof. Fire-escapes were ordered installed on old tenement houses. An authority on housing conditions states that "the height of the tenements and apartments is limited by the height at which the fire department can effectively fight a fire from the street, and the number of stories that children or the infirm can safely walk

[14] E. R. L. Gould, "Housing of City Masses," *International Quarterly*, Jan., 1905, X, 360, 361. *Cf.* Lawrence Veiller, *Light*, National Housing Association Publications No. 60, 1930, pp. 8-19.

down under panic conditions. Under normal conditions this would limit height to five or, at most six stories, although fireproof construction, fire towers and adequate elevators would make increased height practicable. In any case non-elevator apartments should not be over four stories high or, at most, five stories high, even in Manhattan.''[15] No better proof of the safety of ''new-law tenements'' is needed than to point out that not a single life has been lost because of conflagration in any tenement built under the provisions of this act, although hundreds of lives have been lost in ''old-law tenements,'' as the buildings previously erected are called. This point cannot be overemphasized. Nearly half of the fires in New York City occur in tenements. The annual report of the Fire Department for 1929 shows a total of 17,145 fires in buildings, 7,678 of which were in tenements. There were 119 deaths at fires during the year, 63 of them occurring in this type of building. In the old-law tenements, each family must supply its own heat, a practice that multiplies the dangers of conflagrations. Refuse, decay, and combustible building materials also greatly augment the hazards.[16]

The third evil was lack of separate water-closets and washing facilities. The law prescribes ''a separate water-closet in a separate compartment within each apartment.'' The toilet compartment must have a window of 3 square feet, must be floored with waterproof material and must be accessible from each bedroom without passing through another bedroom. With regard to old tenements, all school sinks and privy vaults were abolished and individual water-closets were ordered installed before January 1, 1903. This provision was contested by one Katie Moeschen, who owned some tenement property, but was upheld by a decision of the United States Supreme Court in 1906.[17] How necessary this provision was is indicated by the official report on housing conditions in 1920, which shows that there is still much left to be done with respect to old-law tenements. ''The lack of proper and sufficient toilet facilities is one of the greatest hardships of the tenements. It is a menace to the health of the com-

[15] George B. Ford, ''Standards for Improved Housing Laws,'' *National Municipal Review*, Oct., 1927, 16:10:636.
[16] Lawson Purdy, ''New York's New Dwellings Bill,'' *The Survey*, Feb. 15, 1928, 59:10:616. Robert W. DeForest and Lawrence Veiller, *The Tenement House Problem*, 1903, I, 261-274. Silas Bent, ''Housing Evils of City Shown by New Survey,'' New York *Times*, March 7, 1926. *Ibid.*, April 5, 1924. Fire Department of the City of New York, *Annual Report*, 1929, pp. 9, 10, 48, 60.
[17] 203 U. S. 583. Edith Wood, *Housing of the Unskilled Wage Earner*, 1919, pp. 79-80. John Ihlder, ''The Problem of the Old City House,'' *Annals*, Jan., 1914, 51:140:96.

munity. One of the first requisities of a decent house is the toilet for the exclusive use of each family, situated in its apartment. The best of the old houses have toilets in the halls, two to a floor. The worst of them have them in the cellars or yards. This means for people on the upper floors a trip of from eight to twelve flights of stairs. The toilet doors are supposed to be kept locked, but often the keys are lost. The little cubby holes are generally dark. They are ventilated, if at all, on small shafts. Some of them have no window. The air of the hallway is rank with the smell from the toilets." With regard to washing facilities, the kitchen sink was the only convenience that was found in every house in the investigation of 1920. Washtubs and bathtubs are rare, although in new-law tenements they are generally being installed voluntarily by the owner. About a million people living in tenements in New York City have no bathtubs. "Cleanliness is made difficult when the only source of water is the tea kettle." General lack of conveniences characterize the old-law tenements. "We have come to accept kitchen sinks, stationary laundry tubs, toilets and steam heat as adjuncts to modern life. Yet in these residences where the household work must be done in the shortest possible time, as all the adults of the family have outside jobs, and to mother is left also the care of young or dependent members of the group, these 'conveniences' are almost unheard of. Dumbwaiters, where they exist, are practically always nailed closed. Climbing even four flights of stairs, with provisions or fuel, is a fairly taxing task. There is, in most cases, no steam heat and therefore no hot water. This means that the tenants must have their own supplies of coal and wood, thereby materially increasing their rental. They must carry them up—and the ashes down, and water for cooking, washing and bathing must all be heated."[18]

The fourth point was room-overcrowding. In this respect the law has been less successful. It provides that "no room in any tenement house shall be so overcrowded that there shall be afforded less than 400 cubic feet of air to each adult, and 200 cubic feet of air to each child under twelve years of age occupying such room." The number of cubic feet of air is not as important as the temperature of the air, its relative humidity and its movement. As Professor Winslow[19] has demonstrated, "the effects of the atmosphere of an ill-ventilated room are primarily and fundamentally due to a high temperature

[18] *Report of the Reconstruction Commission on Housing Conditions, New York,* 1920, pp. 5-35, (pp. 27, 28, 29 quoted).
[19] *Fresh Air and Ventilation,* 1926, ch. II, (p. 48 quoted).

(combined with stagnation and sometimes with high humidity) and consequent interference with the processes of body temperature regulation." How can the law on room-overcrowding be enforced? In the days when the enforcement of the tenement-house laws was vested in the Health Department, that is up to 1901, policemen were sent in squads to make night inspections in those tenements in which the Board of Health expected that room-overcrowding would prevail. The practice of night inspection was abandoned by the Tenement House Department, "not because the evil of room overcrowding had ceased, but because it had been shown conclusively that the methods used had not proved successful."[20] When the inspector comes around, the tenants, especially the children, go out on the fire-escapes or climb on to the roofs or otherwise disappear. Intrusion of the inspector into private homes is resented. The roots of the difficulty of room-overcrowding are poverty, greed, racial solidarity, low standard of living, and high rents. Legislation cannot affect them.

The final difficulty to which the Commission referred was "bad housekeeping." The law makes strict provisions in regard to the care and cleanliness of the buildings. Experience has shown that the danger points in the tenement house from a sanitary point of view are the public parts of the building for which no one is responsible: the cellars, yards, roofs, halls, stairs, out-premises.[21] What is everybody's business is generally nobody's business. The law requires that a janitor be engaged if there are more than eight families to a building, and that receptacles be provided for ashes, garbage and refuse. But what janitor is going to put much enthusiasm into scrubbing the public halls of a six-story tenement for the sake of free rent of some wretched rooms? The law further states: "No horse, cow, calf, swine, sheep or goat shall be kept in a tenement house, or on the same lot or premises thereof, and no tenement house or the lot and premises thereof shall be used for a lodging house or stable, or for the storage or handling of rags." Every one of these things had previously been done. In cleaning up the old tenements the Tenement House Department removed tons of accumulated filth and rubbish. In coöperation with the police, fire, health, street cleaning, and water-supply departments of the city it is attempting to educate the tenants in sanitation and housekeeping.

The law of 1901 created a Tenement House Department, with the

[20] Lawrence Veiller, "Room Overcrowding and the Lodger Evil," *National Housing Association*, Publication No. 18, Feb., 1913, pp. 7-9.
[21] Lawrence Veiller, *Housing Reform*, 1910, p. 113.

dignity and powers of a regular branch of the city government. The previous system had left undefined spheres of authority between the Board of Health, the Building Department, and the Fire Department. The new plan provides centralization of authority and responsibility. It is an interesting example of the expansion of the powers of municipal government. In general this department is charged with the duty of sanitary inspection of tenement houses and the enforcement of all the provisions of the tenement-house act.[22]

This act in general offers the best example of restrictive housing legislation, the typically American method. Along with Veiller's *Model Tenement House Law* and his *Model Housing Law,* it has served as the basis for practically all the housing laws in the United States. The New York law of 1901 represents not ideal standards, but only those standards that were possible of adoption at the time of its enactment. Consider, for example, the provision limiting the height of non-fireproof tenements to six stories. ''Owing to high land values and the cost of building, a four-story tenement could not then have been erected on Manhattan Island and made to pay; nor indeed could a five-story one, without unduly raising rents and seriously increasing the cost of living.'' It would be unwise for other cities to copy arbitrarily such requirements and embody them in their statutes. A tenement-house law to be effective must be adapted to local needs.[23]

A little more than a quarter of a century has now elapsed since the basic New York tenement-house law was passed. What has it accomplished? To what extent has it justified the hopes of its sponsors? In the quarterly journal, *Housing Betterment*, edited by Lawrence Veiller, these questions are answered as follows :[24] ''The theory back of that legislation and of the work of the Tenement House Commission of that time, was that the way to get the right kind of tenement houses in New York City for the future, was to set certain minimum standards in the law below which such buildings could not fall, and to require as a matter of statute that every building erected thereafter should have proper sanitation, proper light and air, proper space, rooms of the proper size, reasonable fire protection and all the conveniences and decencies of living. It was believed that if such a law were formulated on a practical basis that would not interfere

[22] See Lawrence Veiller, *Housing Reform,* 1910, ch. XI, on the enforcement of housing laws. The law of 1901 was superseded in 1926 by the Multiple Dwellings Law, which attempted to consolidate all tenement-house legislation and to provide for increased protection of the health and safety of tenants.

[23] Lawrence Veiller, *Model Tenement House Law,* 1910, pp. 4-5, 8.

[24] *Housing Betterment,* Dec., 1926, 15:4:305-306. In 1928 the name of this journal was changed to *Housing.*

with the normal play of private enterprise, that the speculative builder, working for his own profit, would build sufficient tenement houses to house the population of New York City; and that, ultimately, the great mass of the people living in houses constructed under such a law would have light and air, sanitation, health protection, fire protection and the other conditions of living which they should have. . . . This hope and expectation of the Tenement House Commission of 1901 has been more than justified; for, as the figures show, new-law tenements have been built in the five boroughs of New York since the enactment of the Tenement House Law of 1901 to the number of 38,311 containing 563,465 separate apartments or accommodations for that number of families. As the total number of apartments in 'old-law' houses is given as 564,561, it becomes apparent that practically half the tenement house population of the city is now living in the new-law tenements, that is, with the light and air, the protection against fire, the modern sanitary conveniences, and the comforts and conveniences that a new-law tenement implies. This is an amazing justification of the hope and theories of the framers of the Tenement House Law of 1901. It is safe to say that not even the most ardent member of that Commission would have believed it possible that in the short period of 25 years they would see one-half the city's tenement house population housed in new-law tenement houses under the ordinary operation of the laws of supply and demand.''

New York City is still faced, however, with a serious tenement house problem which is largely in the nature of a ''hang-over'' from the past—the problem of the old-law tenements still standing. Being older, they are worse today than ever before. High rents have forced into use many thousands of these buildings that had previously been vacant. Their disappearance has been slow. In the twenty-year period ending in 1928 approximately 100,000 apartments in old-law tenements were destroyed. At this rate it would take almost a hundred years for the last of these buildings to disappear. In 1928 there were 69,432 old-law tenements in New York City (three-fifths of the total number) containing 544,684 apartments housing nearly half of the city's population.[25] The evils of these old houses, according to the findings of a state commission, fall into two categories: ''There are the conditions that can be remedied by painting, cleaning, repairing. There are the conditions that are beyond remedy, the foul toilet vents,

[25] Regional Survey of New York and Its Environs, *Buildings: Their Uses and the Spaces About Them*, 1931, VI, 237-238.

the narrow courts and shafts. For these, destruction of parts or all of the building is the only cure."[26] What New York City really needs is extensive "slum clearance" of the British type. Yet there are so many tenements that are below the minimum standard of the present tenement law that it is impracticable to attempt slum clearance on the vast scale that is necessary, if the same end can be attained by remodeling the old buildings. The latter view was the opinion of the Joint Legislative Committee on Housing and the Reconstruction Commission which arranged in 1920 for an architectural competition, under their joint auspices, related to the remodeling of the old buildings. The results of the competition indicated, however, that adequate rehabilitation would be impracticable. The demolition of obsolete structures and their replacement by new buildings is the only feasible plan. The cost would be tremendous. Merely to acquire these old-law tenements and raze them to the ground would cost the taxpayers about three billion dollars—to say nothing of the cost of building new ones in their place.

The tremendous size of the problem has not daunted the well-known philanthropist, Mr. August Heckscher, who in 1926 outlined a plan to spend $100,000,000 a year for five years in the task of rebuilding slum areas. He announced that he intended to seek $50,000,000 a year of private capital to be invested in the enterprise, and proposed that the other half of the cost be borne by the state. When other philanthropists failed to come forward, and when his plan was criticized because too altruistic and impracticable, he proposed that the city finance the entire project. Something may come of the latter proposal.

In May, 1926, the New York Legislature passed what is known as the State Housing Law, based on the findings of the New York State Commission of Housing and Regional Planning and its recommendations for permanent housing relief.[27] The Commission reported that more than two-thirds of the families of New York City have annual incomes of less than $2,500 and that this class, which includes almost the entire wage-earning population, cannot pay more than $12.50 per room per month. Analysis of rents in newly constructed apartments and dwellings in New York City revealed to the Commission that commercial enterprise fails to supply adequate housing to meet the needs of the great mass of the people, that it operates successfully

[26] *Report of the Reconstruction Commission on Housing Conditions, New York,* 1920, pp. 9, 33 (quoted). *Housing Betterment,* June, 1926, 15:2:93. *Housing,* June, 1931, 20:2:81-82.

[27] *New York State Commission of Housing and Regional Planning,* Legislative Document No. 66, 1926.

for only the upper third of the population. The problem, then, is how to promote the construction of adequate dwellings to replace the old-law tenements that can be rented at prices which the average wage-earner can afford. The second paragraph of the new law, giving the legislative finding, comes nearer to the English policy of "slum clearance" than any American enactment.

It is hereby declared that congested and unsanitary housing conditions which exist in certain areas of the state in low priced dwellings are a menace to the health, safety, morals, welfare and reasonable comfort of the citizens of the state. The correction of these conditions in such areas being now otherwise impossible, it is essential that provision be made for the investment of private funds at low interest rates, the acquisition at fair prices of adequate parcels of land, the gradual demolition of existing unsanitary and unsafe housing and the construction of new housing facilities under public supervision in accord with proper standards of sanitation and safety and at a cost which will permit monthly rentals which wage earners can afford to pay and not in excess of rates hereinafter provided. Therefore, there are created and authorized the agencies and instrumentalities hereinafter prescribed, which are declared to be the agencies and instrumentalities of the state for the purpose of attaining the ends herein recited, and their necessity in the public interest is hereby declared as a matter of legislative determination.

Under the law a State Board of Housing is created to select and to approve areas in which construction may be undertaken under the terms of the act. No project is to be approved unless it shall appear practicable to rent the accommodations to be constructed at a monthly rental not to exceed from $9.00 to $12.50 per room, varying as specified in the act in the different counties within the city of New York and in other cities of the state. So-called public limited-dividend housing companies or private limited-dividend companies may operate under the terms of the act and the direction of the Board. The act is designed primarily to stimulate housing construction by private enterprise operating through such companies. After a project is approved, a public limited-dividend company may exercise the power of eminent domain, under and pursuant to the condemnation law, to acquire the property needed for said project. Both kinds of companies are exempt from the payment of any and all taxes to the state. Any municipality in which the projects authorized are located is permitted to exempt the buildings and improvements created in connection with such projects from local taxation, such exemption not to extend to buildings erected after January 1, 1937. In short, all the resources of expert advice, the power of condemnation, the aid of tax exemption, will be at the service of these companies, so that by careful planning and the most rigorous economies they may erect, in these days of high prices, modern tenements which can be rented at a price that the present old-law tenement dweller can afford to pay.[28] In 1930 the total investment in low-cost housing under the jurisdiction of the State Housing Board was about $10,000,000. Meantime New York City, under the so-called Mayor Walker plan, proposes to effect "slum clearance" through exercising the power of excess condemnation in connection with street widening and similar public improvements. More property is to be taken than is needed in such improvements, and the land thus acquired is to be leased on long terms to private corporations for the purpose of erecting model tenements to be rented for not more than a specified amount per room per month which wage-earners can afford to pay.[29] If the city were to provide an adequate waterfront park and a number of small playgrounds and to make certain street changes on the lower east side, private enterprise would probably accomplish the needed improvement in building. With such public improvements, the lower east side would become a good residential district for white-collar workers, for it adjoins the downtown office section.[30] If neither the state nor the city plan should be productive of results, it is conceivable that New York may eventually go over entirely to the English method of direct government housing.

[28] *Laws of New York*, ch. 823. George Gove, "New York Housing Law to Aid Wage Earners," *National Municipal Review*, July, 1926, 15:7:381-385.
[29] *Housing*, June, 1928, 17:2:95 ff., Dec., 1930, 19:4:279-283.
[30] Loula D. Lasker, "Putting a White Collar on the East Side," *The Survey*, March 1, 1931, 65:11:584-589, 626-627. Regional Survey of New York and Its Environs, *Buildings: Their Uses and the Spaces About Them*, 1931, VI, 296-298.

CHAPTER VII

ROOMING AND LODGING HOUSES AND HOTELS

CLOSELY related to the tenement-house problem, and particularly to the matter of overcrowding, is the rooming- and lodging-house question. It is the problem of housing the homeless working people, who are obliged to live in the congested quarters of the city. They are people who have no family life and therefore constitute a very mobile group. The line between the two types of accommodation for these people is blurred, but in general, rooming houses accept persons by the week or month, deal with a less transient group, and are in the nature of private lodgings, whereas lodging houses receive persons for a single night or for less than a week at a time, provide for a more transient group, and are public accommodations.[1] Lodging houses are really cheap hotels.

The number of rooming and lodging houses per 1,000 population has been steadily increasing as a consequence of the growth of cities; they occupy a much larger place in city life today than they did, say, twenty-five years ago. The War accentuated conditions in many localities. The demand for such accommodations is furnished by the movement of population, especially young, single persons, from country to city, and by immigration, which is largely composed of single men. Intra- and inter-community mobility of population intensifies the situation.[2]

THE LODGING-HOUSE PROBLEM

Types of Lodgers.—Lodging houses or cheap hotels are of divers types and are patronized by a most heterogeneous group of men ranging from beggars, thieves, tramps, hoboes, casual laborers who work a week, rest a week (Booth's classes A and B), to young men attracted

[1] A legal definition of lodging houses is as follows: "A lodging house shall be taken to mean and include any house or building or portion thereof in which persons are harbored, or received, or lodged for hire, for a single night or for less than a week at one time, or any part of which is let for any person to sleep in for any term less than a week." This is the definition given in the original New York Tenement House Law of 1867. E. R. L. Gould, *The Housing of Working People*, 8th special report of the Commissioner of Labor, 1895, pp. 33-34. Lawrence Veiller, *Model Housing Law*, 1920, pp. 34-35. A. B. Wolfe, The Lodging House Problem in Boston, 1906, p. 1.
[2] See pp. 43-45 above.

to the city looking for work and adventure, men unemployed, those regularly employed but poorly paid, and clerks and mechanics who have no home of their own. Considered from a socio-economic standpoint, the cheap lodging-house population falls into four groups: (1) self-supporting; (2) temporarily dependent; (3) chronically dependent; and (4) parasitic. The first group is composed of able-bodied men of whatever trade or occupation who work all or most of the year and who expect to support themselves by their own exertions. In the second group are men capable of self-support but temporarily and in many cases quite accidentally dependent. Included among them are runaway boys, the unemployed, victims of accident or illness, convalescents, and other men without means who could again become self-supporting if tided past temporary difficulties. In the third group are men who, on account of age, chronic physical or mental disability, extreme ignorance and inefficiency, or other handicap have become continuously dependent upon the public for support. "Men of this class may sometimes again become at least partially self-supporting and are not parasitic in spirit." Finally, there are the parasites, men —whether able-bodied or defective—who make a business of living off the public and who apparently do so from choice rather than from necessity. "Some are thieves and criminals, some clever impostors and beggars who live by their wits; still others are only 'tramps,' not necessarily criminal, but nevertheless anti-social."[3] The lodgers comprise the majority of the floating population of the city.

Types of Lodging Houses.—The characteristic location of the lodging-house area is Hobohemia, the district of the homeless man Lodging houses may be classified as follows:

I. Private Charitable:
    (a) Religious.
    (b) Non-religious.
II. Municipal.
III. Commercial:
    (a) The "flop."
    (b) The degraded rooming house:
        (1) Respectable.
        (2) Disreputable.
    (c) The "cell" or "cubicle."

I*a*. As an example of the lodging house run by a religious charitable organization may be cited the mission, which dispenses charity in the

[3] Alice W. Solenberger, *One Thousand Homeless Men*, 1911, pp. 10-11. New York Department of Public Charities, *The Men We Lodge*, 1915, p. 10.

form of food, clothing, and beds for homeless men. Lodgings are usually free, but the men are required to attend the religious meeting held every night.

> We huddled in the mission
> Fer it was cold outside,
> An' listened to the preacher
> Tell of the Crucified;
>
> Without, a sleety drizzle
> Cut deep each ragged form,—
> An' so we stood the talkin'
> Fer shelter from the storm.
> —"*A Tramp's Confession,*" *by Harry Kemp.*

A premium is put on conversion. Many are converted again and again, the "professionals" always managing to get saved in missions where there is something to eat. "Every mission has its permanent, periodic, and temporary converts; its 'alumni.' Some of these linger about the mission doing odd jobs, others go to work or into business, only returning occasionally to bear testimony. Many of these have prospered both spiritually and materially, and assist the mission in its work. . . . Of course there are temporary converts who become victims of their old environment. For awhile they go straight, but eventually they yield to 'the world, the flesh, and the devil.' Some periodic converts kneel before the altar every year and each time go out with renewed determination to avoid sin, but they often succumb the first time they are subjected to temptation. The mission workers expect this periodicity of conversion with some of these men just as they expect the winter."[4] Of other lodging houses conducted by religious organizations the most important are the Salvation Army hotels for workingmen, usually charging from 25 to 50 cents, and conducting religious services at which attendance is voluntary. Accommodations are either small private rooms or dormitories.

I*b*. The wayfarers' lodge maintained by the organized charities is typical of the non-religious, privately supported charitable institution. Its purpose is to shelter temporarily the homeless and incapacitated men while an effort is made to reëstablish them in normal living. Baths, fumigation of clothes, and medical inspection are often compulsory. The first is so great a deterrent to some applicants that they decline the accommodations. Some charity organization societies also

[4] Nels Anderson, *The Hobo,* 1923, pp. 3, 27, 251, 253-254, 255-256 (quoted), 257 (quoted).

conduct a wood-yard in connection with the lodging house, requiring the men to saw so much wood for a lodging and meal; this operates as a further deterrent.[5] In a number of cities there are private semi-charitable lodging houses, like the Workingmen's Palace and the Rufus F. Dawes Hotel in Chicago, which probably belong in this class of welfare institutions. These buildings are generally large, clean, and modern, and attract a less shabby group of men; being semi-charitable they can force certain requirements upon their patrons. "Like all paternalistic, quasi-charitable institutions, however, they are not popular, although the charges for a room and bed are hardly sufficient to cover the operating expenses."[6]

II. Municipal lodging houses in America are a form of public charity for homeless men; they are also sometimes a substitute for the police station. The Chicago Municipal Lodging House, opened in 1901, provides free temporary shelter and food for destitute, homeless men. It has been operated in turn under the Department of Police, the Department of Health, and the Department of Public Welfare. It closed because of lack of applicants during the wartime prosperity.[7] The first real attempt to find out about the men who take refuge in a municipal lodging house was made in connection with the Municipal Lodging House of New York City in 1915, when a medical examination of 2,000 men was conducted by 15 medical examiners. "Of the 2,000 men who were given a medical examination, 1,774, approximately nine out of every ten, were, according to the adjudgments of the examining physicians, physically able to work. Twelve hundred and forty-seven, or 62 per cent of the total, were considered physically able to do regular hard manual labor; 354, or 18 per cent, to do medium hard work; and 173, or 9 per cent, to do light work only. Two hundred and twenty-six, one out of every ten, were adjudged physically unable to work."[8] During a period of widespread unemployment, the capacity of municipal lodging houses is taxed to the limit.

IIIa. The lowest type of commercial lodging house is the "flop." "Flophouses" are nearly all alike. Guests sleep on the floor or in bare, wooden bunks. The only privilege they buy is the privilege to lie down somewhere in a warm room—hence the name. The price is

[5] Amos G. Warner, *American Charities*, 1919, p. 237.
[6] Nels Anderson, *The Hobo*, 1923, pp. 27-28.
[7] *Ibid.*, pp. 260-261.
[8] New York Department of Public Charities, *The Men We Lodge*, 1915, p. 13. For the work of a municipal lodging house in a time of depression, see *Annual Report, Department of Public Welfare, the City of New York*, 1930, pp. 61-75.

usually a thin dime. Sanitary provisions are lacking and the places are in vile condition. Bugs are numerous, efficient, well organized, and enterprising. These places are patronized by the lowest type of lodgers, most of whom never work and do not care to work; they generally live by begging and pilfering.[9]

III*b*. The degraded rooming house is, as its name implies, an old rooming house which now takes in transients. Rooms may be obtained by the night as well as by the week. Sometimes the old rooms have been cut up into cubicles, in other cases they have been turned into dormitories. In the respectable houses one may secure a fairly good night's lodging at a reasonable price. The disreputable ones are simply houses of assignation.[10] Such places were formerly known in Chicago as "barrel-houses." "The barrel-house was a rooming-house, saloon, and house of prostitution, all in one. [Homeless] men with money usually spent it in the barrel-houses. There they found warmth and companionship. They would join the circle at the bar, buy drinks for the crowd, and have a good time. Men who were afraid of being robbed placed their money with the bartender and charged against it the drinks purchased. As soon as they were overcome by drink they would be taken upstairs to bed. The following day the program would be repeated. A three- or four-hundred-dollar stake at this rate usually lasted a week. Not infrequently the barrel-house added to its other attractions the opportunity for gambling."[11] Fortunately the barrel-house is now a thing of the past.

III*c*. The most common variety of commercial lodging house is the "cell" or "cubicle" house, charging usually twenty-five, thirty-five, forty, or fifty cents a night. The name is derived from the size and appearance of the rooms. "The term 'room' is a misnomer when applied to a sleeping apartment in a cheap hotel. These rooms have been aptly termed 'cubicles,' and among the patrons they are known as 'cages.' A cubicle is usually from 6 to 8 feet in width and from 8 to 12 feet in length. The thin walls, composed of steel or matched lumber, are usually about 8 feet in height. A wire netting over the top admits air and prevents the guests climbing from one cubicle to another. The furnishings are simple; sometimes only a bed, sometimes a bed and a chair, and in more expensive places a stand. They are not constructed either for comfort or convenience; lighting and ventilation are usually

---

[9] Nels Anderson, *The Hobo*, 1923, pp. 30-33. There are illustrations of "flops" in the appendix to Alice W. Solenberger, *One Thousand Homeless Men*.

[10] F. K. Fretz, *The Furnished Room Problem in Philadelphia*, 1911, pp. 129 ff. A. B. Wolfe, *The Lodging House Problem in Boston*, 1906, pp. 140-141, 171.

[11] Nels Anderson, *The Hobo*, 1923, p. 27.

bad. But they are all they were intended to be: places for men to sleep with a limited degree of privacy.'' Different types of hotels attract different types of men. The better class of workingmen who patronize the hotels where the prices range from forty to seventy cents, wear collars and creased trousers. The hotels provide stationery and desks. ''Hotels where the prices range from twenty-five cents to forty cents are patronized by a shabbier group of men. Few of them are shaven. Some of them read, but most of them sit alone with their thoughts. In some second-class places a man is employed to go the rounds and arouse the sleepers. In the twenty-five cent hotels, the patrons not only are content to sit unshaven, but they are often dirty. Many of them have the faces of beaten men; many of them are cripples and old men.'' The population is very mobile, the greatest turnover occurring in the cheapest hotels. Better-class places have a large proportion of permanent guests, who remain for two or three months or longer. Many of the older hotels have permanent patrons who are seasonal but regular; others never leave the city. Aside from the character of the patrons and the influence upon them—problems of vice, crime, and immorality—the lodging houses in general present a problem of congestion, inadequate ventilation and sanitation, and infectious disease control.[12]

Model Lodging Houses.—In addition to the licensing of lodging houses and their inspection and control by the city health department, conditions have been improved by the building of model lodging houses either as private or municipal enterprise. Examples of the latter may be found in various European countries; the municipal lodging houses in the United States are of a different character and serve a different purpose, as already mentioned. The experience of Glasgow, which took the initiative in providing model lodging houses, may be cited. This city, like many others in Great Britain, established lodging houses as a municipal enterprise following ''slum-clearance'' developments, to provide living quarters for the people displaced. The city now owns and operates several model lodging houses, one for women, one for families (that is, a widow or widower with children, the latter being cared for while the parent is away at work), and the rest for men. Each lodger has a private compartment with 400 cubic feet of air space. Other provisions include reading rooms, dining rooms, baths, and facilities for cooking and washing. The prices for lodgings charged by the town council are very small. Beneficial results

[12] Nels Anderson, *The Hobo*, 1923, pp. 28, 29, 30. A. B. Wolfe, *The Lodging House Problem in Boston*, 1906, chs. XIV, XV.

that have accrued are: (1) the competition has improved conditions in commercial lodging houses; (2) other model enterprises have been stimulated; (3) by barring out undesirable applicants and by placing a premium on sobriety, cleanliness, and industry, the character of the lodgers has been raised; (4) improved health and reduced hospital and dispensary expenses in congested districts have been especially noticeable; and (5) an annual dividend of 5 per cent even on the heavy cost of the condemned and new property has been earned.[13]

Rowton Houses.—The pioneers in the field of model lodging houses erected as private enterprises were Lord Rowton and Sir Richard Farrant. Lord Rowton, the prime mover, was at one time private secretary to the Earl of Beaconsfield. Impressed by the need of adequate provisions for housing the unmarried male population of London, and acting largely from motives of philanthropy, he built in 1892 Rowton House No. 1, where for sixpence a night a man could get a small bedroom and clean, wholesome surroundings. This experiment yielded an unexpected result: business showed a profit of 6 per cent on the investment. Lord Rowton then organized a stock company, which has since built many more. Two types of rooms are provided: the cubicle and the special bedroom, the charge for the latter being one shilling a night. There is a dining room where food can be purchased at exceptionally low prices; a smoking room with a plentiful supply of stationery, books and magazines; baths; lockers; parcel room; laundry; barber shop; shoemaker shop; tailor shop; etc. The house rules are strict:

Bedrooms must be vacated before 9 o'clock in the morning.

Admission to bedrooms: The stair-case gate is open every quarter of an hour after 7 p.m. Tickets must be shown at the gate.

Smoking in bedrooms is strictly forbidden.

Card-playing and gambling are prohibited.

Residents are not allowed upon any bedroom floor other than the floor upon which their own bedroom is situated.

The public rooms will be closed at night, and the light turned out at 12:30; on Sunday at 11:30.

Bed tickets are not transferable, and if transferred will be forfeited.

Residents must make good any damage done to the company's property.

An authority on housing conditions in England states with reference to the Rowton Houses: "There can be no question but what these

[13] E. R. L. Gould, *Housing of the Working People*, 8th Special Report of the Commissioner of Labor, 1895, pp. 404-407, 414-415.

lodging-houses have proved a boon to thousands of London working men.''[14]

Mills Hotels.—Influenced by the example set by Lord Rowton, the American capitalist, Darius Ogden Mills, erected in New York City a number of hotels where the patron has all the conveniences of a good hotel at much less than current prices. The Mills Hotels were not built to house the vagabond, but to help the self-respecting man of small means. The first of these hotels was opened in 1897. At that time it was a rather novel idea to give to single men or men away from home, who have but moderate means, more comfort for their money than could be obtained elsewhere. In opening the first Mills Hotel, Mr. Mills said in part:

My attention was called years ago to the difficulties of self-respecting men, either unmarried or compelled to live in great cities away from their families, who earned only small salaries or were hunting work, in trying to live decently within their means. For clerks, salesmen, mechanics, laborers and others thus situated there were three kinds of accommodations to be had:

First, respectable hotels, which charge prices practically prohibitory to the class I have in mind; secondly, small hall bedrooms in private houses or flats; thirdly, private lodgings in some family, which are apt to be in a tenement under unsanitary conditions.

It should be known at the outset that this enterprise is in no sense a charitable concern. It would be affectation on my part to deny a humanitarian impulse and a fervent desire to benefit my fellow men. But I do seek to do this in a strictly business way, without offending the pride or the praiseworthy independence of those whom I strive to serve. It is the intention from the very beginning to conduct the enterprise upon a business basis, and this implies not only self-support but a steady, perhaps small, but fair margin of profit.

To avoid any misapprehension, no patron of the Mills Hotels will receive more than he pays for, but in doing the work on so large a scale, and in securing the utmost economies in purchases and administration, I hope to give him a larger equivalent for his money than has hitherto been possible.

In 1898 a second hotel was opened, located like the first in the downtown district, and in 1907 a third, this time located uptown. There are in all four thousand rooms in the three Mills Hotels. In the two downtown hotels rooms are sold for fifty cents a day, in the uptown hotel for sixty cents a day. They are all operated on the same plan. Each guest's sleeping room is equipped with a rug, chair, and locker, besides the bed. In addition to this basic accommodation, the guest has the use of large reading and writing rooms, a free circulating

[14] E. R. Dewsnup, *The Housing Problem in England*, 1907, pp. 288-289.

library, modern shower facilities and a large baggage room where he may check his baggage. The bedrooms are solely sleeping chambers, comfortable in size, each with a window and sufficient heat. All bed linen is changed daily on each and every bed. The usual conveniences of good hotels are to be found. They are advertised as "hotels for respectable men," and are paying propositions. The standards set by the founder have been steadily maintained by the trustees. In more than thirty years of service, thousands of men have passed through the hotels; they include not merely men of the occupations Mr. Mills first had in mind as patrons, but also students and men getting a start in business and the professions.[15]

THE ROOMING-HOUSE PROBLEM

The rooming-house situation has not been investigated to a great extent, although the subject is one of increasing importance. Professor Wolfe's monograph on *The Lodging House Problem in Boston* (1906) —by "lodging house" he means "rooming house"—was probably the first important special study along this line. The supply of such accommodations ranges from the cheapest tenement to residential clubs, like those of the Y.M.C.A. and Y.W.C.A., and high-class residential districts, though the great majority of roomers live either in tenements or in the rooming-house district.

In the first case, where roomers are taken by a tenement-house family, there often results increased congestion, increased danger of the spread of communicable diseases, destruction of family privacy, quarrels, and immorality. As a result of over twenty years' observation of life among the poor, Veiller[16] states that "the lodger [roomer] evil is caused far more by greed than by need; by the desire to rapidly acquire money than by the necessity for increasing the income," although he admits that racial solidarity is also an important factor. Since a large percentage of recent immigrants are unattached males, the taking of roomers is especially characteristic of the foreign-born residents, and what is more natural than for an immigrant to find lodgings with a family of his own nationality? In some industrial communities this has led to cases of what amounts to actual polyandry.[17]

[15] Based on a statement furnished in August, 1928, by Mr. A. A. Hartmann, Secretary-General Manager, Mills Hotels Trust; and on a pamphlet entitled "Address of Mr. Mills at the opening of Mills Hotel No. 1, Oct. 27, 1897."

[16] "Room Overcrowding and the Lodger Evil," *National Housing Association*, Publication No. 18, Feb., 1913, 3-15. Lawrence Veiller, *Model Housing Law*, 1920, pp. 230-232.

[17] Graham Taylor, *Satellite Cities*, 1915, pp. 204-205.

The Rooming-House District.—Usually a higher income and occupational group lives in the rooming-house district, which forms a belt adjacent to the business section of the city, most of the district being within easy walking distance of downtown. It is a changing, deteriorating neighborhood in which practically all houses have been converted from private single-family dwellings into rooming houses.[18] As a typical illustration of such a district we may cite the excellent study made by Professor Zorbaugh[19] of the rooming-house area on the lower north side of Chicago. Ninety blocks in the better rooming area north of Chicago Avenue were studied intensively by means of a house-to-house census. This study revealed that 71 per cent of all the houses in the district take roomers, and that, of the people who live in these rooms, 52 per cent are single men, 10 per cent single women, and 38 per cent are couples, "married," supposedly with the benefit of clergy, though actually 60 per cent of these couples are living together unmarried. "The rooming-house population is typically what the labor leaders refer to as the 'white collar' group—men and women filling various clerical positions, accountants, stenographers, and the like. There are also students from the many music schools of the Lower North Side. Most of them are living on a narrow margin, and here they can live cheaply, near enough to the 'Loop' to walk to and from their work if they wish."

Mobility.—The constant comings and goings of its inhabitants is the most striking and significant characteristic of this world of furnished rooms. A population "restless, shifting, fugacious as time itself," as O. Henry says in his story *The Furnished Room*: "Homeless, they have a hundred homes. They flit from furnished room to furnished room, transients forever—transients in abode, transients in heart and mind." In the Chicago study, "this whole population turns over every four months. There are always cards in the windows, advertising the fact that rooms are vacant, but these cards rarely have to stay up over a day, as people are constantly walking the streets looking for rooms. The keepers of the rooming-houses change almost as rapidly as the roomers themselves. At least half of the keepers of these houses have been at their present addresses six months or less. This extreme mobility results in startling anonymity." A case is cited.

[18] A. B. Wolfe, *The Lodging House Problem in Boston*, 1906, ch. II. F. K. Fretz, *The Furnished Room Problem in Philadelphia*, 1911, pp. 5-18.

[19] "The Dweller in Furnished Rooms," *American Journal of Sociology*, July, 1926, 32:1:pt.2:84-87. *Cf.* Harvey W. Zorbaugh, *The Gold Coast and the Slum*, 1929, chap. IV.

I had occasion to inquire for a man living in a rooming house. He had roomed there about a week. There was no 'phone in the place, so I had to call at his address. I went there about 7:30. After I had rung the bell for some time, a woman about 45 answered the door. She wore a house apron and was evidently the landlady. I asked for Mr. X. She said "Who?" I repeated the name. She shook her head, and said that she didn't know anyone of that name. I looked at the address in my notebook, to see if I had the address correct. I told her that this was the address he had given, and went on to describe him. She knew of two men in the house who might answer to his description. I then told her that he did a lot of work on the typewriter in his room. Then she knew whom I meant. She told me to go to the third floor front and see if he was there. He was not in. I knocked at several other rooms, but no one knew anything about him. When I got downstairs the lady had disappeared, and I could not leave a message. I came back a week later, and the same woman came to the door. I asked if Mr. X. was in. She said he had moved yesterday. I asked if she knew where he went, but she did not know. She said he left when his week was up. He had left a note for her saying that he had to leave. I asked her if he might not have left a forwarding address for his mail. She said that he did not, that he never got any mail.

The rooming house is not to be confused with the old boarding house with its common dining room, the landlady's parlor with evenings of euchre and whist, and the piazza with summer evenings of gossip. The boarding house has largely passed out of existence in the modern city.[20] Not half a dozen were found in the lower north side district in Chicago. The rooming house which has replaced it is a very different sort of place in which to live. "It has no dining-room or parlor, no common meeting place. The roomers do not know one another. The keeper of the house has no personal contact with or interest in the roomers. People come and go without speaking or questioning. Anonymity is well nigh complete. In this situation of mobility and anonymity the person is isolated. His social contacts are more or less completely cut off. His wishes are thwarted. He finds in the rooming house neither response or recognition. His physical impulses are curbed. He is restless and he is lonely."[21]

The Landlady.—Any discussion of the rooming-house situation must consider the part played by the landlady. Interest attaches to her for two reasons: first, because she does much to make the rooming house what it is, and to determine its influence over the lodger; and

[20] A. B. Wolfe, *The Lodging House Problem in Boston*, 1906, ch. VI. F. K. Fretz, *The Furnished Room Problem in Philadelphia*, 1911, pp. 25 ff.
[21] Harvey W. Zorbaugh, "The Dweller in Furnished Rooms," *American Journal of Sociology*, July, 1926, 32:1:pt.2:86.

secondly, because her class is a large one and is beset with some difficult problems of its own. The landlady is a product of hard circumstances, one whose life is as isolated and monotonous as that of many of her roomers. "She is, moreover, often the prey of various sorts of sharpers, chief of whom is the 'real estate' agent who sells her lodging-house furniture and good-will at exorbitant rates and ensnares her in the toils of installment payments and mortgages." When the landlady is a widow or a single woman wholly dependent for her livelihood upon the keeping of roomers, she has difficulty in making ends meet. This is cited as a prominent cause for the existence of immoral tendencies. She must either keep her house full or cut down expenses. "Economic pressure makes many landladies—perhaps the majority—indifferent to questionable practices on the part of their lodgers. . . . This blunting of the moral standards of the landladies themselves is a sinister and dangerous aspect of lodging-house life. . . . It gives rise to two great classes of lodging-house keepers—those who care about what their lodgers do and are, and those who do not care."[22]

The Problem of Single Women.—The problem of housing single people in the city is especially serious in the case of single women, more and more of whom are coming to the city to make an independent living. Their lodging presents some factors differentiating it from that of men: they find it more difficult to get suitable accommodations at their rates of income, which are lower than corresponding rates for men; they often encounter a prejudice, particularly in the case of a family taking just one or two roomers, because, unlike men, they want cooking and laundering facilities and the privilege of entertaining friends; the need of seeking companionship and recreation outside the house is fraught with more danger to them; they are more in need of home life or some good substitute; and finally, attempts to house women in hotels have usually been met by the question of the existing public sentiment as to what is conventional for women, a problem which does not arise in the case of men. Because women are more surrounded by conventions they are mainly restricted to rooming houses, while men utilize both rooming and lodging houses.[23]

[22] A. B. Wolfe, *The Lodging House Problem in Boston*, 1906, pp. 64, 65, 168.
[23] A. B. Wolfe, *The Lodging House Problem in Boston*, 1906, pp. 1, 101, 112. O. Henry bases one of his short stories, *Brickdust Row*, on the lack of any place in the rooming house where girls may receive company, which forces them to seek companionship outside.

Dorothy Richardson[24] thinks that "what the working girl needs is a cheap hotel or a system of hotels—for she needs a great many of them—designed something after the Mills Hotels for workingmen. She also needs a system of well-regulated lodging-houses, such as are scattered all over the city for the benefit of men." She specifies as conditions for success that there should be no semblance of charity, no insistence upon "coercive morality"; they should be not only non-sectarian but non-religious; should provide good room and meals at a price which the working girl can pay; and should by all means have a parlor where men friends may be entertained. There are a few working-girls' hotels, but it has been hard to make them self-supporting. More success has been had with the club plan such as that developed by the Eleanor Association of Chicago, which maintains six clubs accommodating from 80 to 140 members; each has a superintendent or house-mother and the necessary employees, and is run on a strictly self-supporting basis. The rates ($6.50 to $8.50 per week) are within the means of girls receiving low wages. In addition to the resident clubs, the Association maintains a downtown club for social and recreational purposes. Organizations like the Y.W.C.A. have performed a notable service in providing a home for self-supporting young women and in conducting a room registry bureau which supplies lists of furnished rooms and boarding places known by investigation to meet an accepted moral and physical standard.[25]

BETTER-CLASS HOTELS AND PERMANENT GUESTS

Although hotels may be defined legally as buildings or dwellings which contain bedrooms to be rented out to transient guests, many are coming to house individuals and families more or less permanently. Those that have specialized in this respect are known as residential hotels, or as family-, apartment-, and club-hotels. Like the rooming house and the apartment house, though in some respects offering more advantages, they appear as modern urban adjustments to the needs of single persons primarily but also of families, especially broken families, that is, where one of the three parts of the natural triangle—husband, wife, child or children—is missing. Probably the first sociological study of hotel life is that made by Dr. Norman S.

[24] The Long Day, 1905, pp. 285-288.
[25] Social Service Directory, Chicago, 1926, pp. 80-81. Directory of Community Activities, Cleveland, 1921, pp. 114-116. A. B. Wolfe, The Lodging House Problem in Boston, 1906, pp. 176-177. City and Suburban Homes Company, Twentieth Annual Report of the President, May, 1916, p. 6. New York Times, April 8, 1906; Sept. 9, 1923. Social Work Year Book, 1929, pp. 212-214.

Hayner,[26] of the University of Washington, who conducted a survey in the month of November, 1927, of hotel dwellers in Seattle, in which data were gathered on the population in 220 of the 437 hotels listed in the state inspector's files. Eliminating from our consideration the aspects of hotels as business institutions catering to travelers and other transients, and restricting attention to the residential type of hotel and the permanent guests, we may note certain facts revealed by that survey which throw light on urban housing trends.

More than one-fourth of the hotel-dwellers enumerated were women. Since there was a much greater preponderance of men in the hotel population of the past, this finding may be an index to the growing freedom and independence of women. In one of Seattle's large downtown hotels, 60 per cent of the guests were women, of whom 14 per cent were teachers. As contrasted with the bachelor apartment and the rooming house, hotel residence offers many attractions, as the following two cases cited by women teachers indicate.

Previous to my moving here, I had lived for two years in an apartment with a stenographer when she decided to stay with friends. We had become tired of each other's company and I was more than tired of her beau.

In the hotel I can entertain my friends without feeling that they are not wanted, and I have no roommate to bother me with her friends when I should like to be alone. I do not take care of the room as I did in the apartment. I have four towels each day, fresh sheets several times a week, hot water any hour of the day or night, lots of light and heat and a private bathroom. Here in the hotel are a restaurant, laundry, dry-cleaning establishment, store, bootblack and many mail deliveries a day. The management does not object to the use of electrical appliances, so I have a grill, iron and percolator.

Another Seattle teacher, who has been for about five years a permanent guest in various apartment-hotels, explains why she moved to a hotel and also why she plans to stay there rather than in a private home or boarding house:

My last experience in a private family drove me to a hotel, and now I think it would be impossible to live in a home again. The family from whom I rented a room were inquisitive and prying. I'm sure they investigated my room during my absence. The bathroom was occupied for prolonged periods, and last but not least, they seemed to think I should remain with them for the rest of my life. My relief was great the day I left with bag and baggage and moved into a hotel.

[26] "People Who Live in Hotels," *The Survey*, May 15, 1928, 60:4:225-227; "Hotel Life and Personality," *American Journal of Sociology*, March, 1928, 33:5:784-795; "Hotel Homes," *Sociology and Social Research*, Nov.-Dec., 1927, 12:2:124-131.

No matter how secluded one keeps in a private family, if the members don't ask questions directly, they are conjecturing among themselves. They know exactly the time one returns home, of what one's personal effects consist, the status of one's friends. In a hotel all this is avoided. After a day of hard work it is a comfort to return home without having to meet inquisitive or talkative people in whom one is not especially interested. If one wishes to move furniture, change pictures, entertain guests, there is nothing to interfere. This gives a feeling of stability. This may sound laughable to a person who is living in his own family, but nevertheless my hotel apartment gives me that feeling. I can come home in the afternoon, make a cup of tea or have a nap before dinner.

A second fact of significance revealed by the Seattle survey is that most of the couples living in hotels are childless. It is suggested that the hotel is the natural habitat for the "companionate," which may be defined as "the state of lawful wedlock, entered into solely for companionship, and not contributing children to society." There appear to be many young couples who prefer to work for two salaries and live in a hotel free from household responsibilities rather than skimp along on one meager income. There are others to whom living in a hotel may be more convenient because of the type of occupation in which the husband is engaged.

There were also found in the hotel population many elderly couples whose children are grown and no longer live with them. They have retired to a hotel to live in comfort and ease for the remainder of their days. There are many such tag-ends or fragments of families— families broken by desertion, divorce or death, as well as by the departure of son or daughter from home. "In fact the hotel family is more commonly the beginning or ending of a family rather than the fully rounded, normal family." Some couples with children live permanently in hotels; they are adjusted to hotel life and prefer it to life in an individual house or apartment. There are more cases, it would seem, of families listed among the "permanent" guests in residential hotels who do not plan to live always in hotels, realizing that they are not the best place in which to rear children.

Life in a hotel is even more impersonal and anonymous than that in a rooming house. "The modern hotel dweller is characteristically detached in his interests from the place in which he sleeps. Although physically near the other guests, he is socially distant. He meets his neighbors, perhaps, but does not know them. 'One may be ill and die without producing a ripple on the surface of the common life. One loses his identity.'" Anonymity and impersonality make the hotel "the most lonely place in the world," but also the freest. So long as the guest preserves the conventions he may do as he pleases and no one will object. This situation may involve a moral let-down. "Released from the bonds of restraint operative in smaller and more intimate circles, the individual tends to act in accordance with his impulses rather than after the pattern of the ideals and standards of his group."

It would seem as if urban life in general is becoming more and more like life in a hotel—transient, detached, and free. "A very large part of the populations of great cities," writes Professor Park,[27] "including those who make their homes in tenements and apartment houses, live much as people do in some great hotel, meeting but not knowing one another. The effect of this is to substitute fortuitous and casual relationship for the more intimate and permanent associations of the smaller community."

[27] R. E. Park and E. W. Burgess, *The City*, 1925, p. 40.

CHAPTER VIII

METHODS OF DEALING WITH THE HOUSING PROBLEM

1. PHILANTHROPY AND MODEL TENEMENTS

SHALL wealthy persons who are philanthropically inclined build model tenements for the poor? Is this a possible or satisfactory solution? Experience has answered in the negative. Not that the philanthropic motive cannot be utilized in attacking the problem; it has its special field. But philanthropy alone cannot solve the housing question. Economic motives largely govern the everyday actions of men; the business and industrial world is controlled by economic forces. Philanthropy is governed by impulses, it is irregular and spasmodic and cannot be depended upon. "The business of housing the poor," said Riis,[1] "if it is to amount to anything, must be business. . . . As charity, pastime, or fad, it will miserably fail, always and everywhere." Veiller[2] has pointed out how insignificant, comparatively, have been the results secured by the construction of model tenements. He gives figures showing how few people have been provided for in them, during the same period that private initiative has been building tenements under a good tenement-house law. Philanthropy has provided 0.7 per cent of improved living conditions, whereas 99.3 per cent has been provided by speculative builders restrained and controlled by wise legislation. "At the outset, there is not over $10,-000,000 invested in model tenement property in Greater New York, nor more than 20,000 persons housed in this way, and this represents the developments of forty years."[3]

Moreover, the working people do not want philanthropy and will go out of their way to avoid it. They are willing to pay a fair price for fair accommodations. They demand this as a right, not as charity. "Upon any other plan than the assumption that the workman has a just claim to a decent home, and the right to demand it, any scheme for his relief fails. It must be a fair exchange of the man's money for what he can afford to buy at a reasonable price. Any charity

[1] *How the Other Half Lives*, 1890, p. 271.
[2] *Housing Reform*, 1910, pp. 63 ff.
[3] Edith Wood, *Housing of the Unskilled Wage Earner*, 1919, p. 101.

scheme merely turns him into a pauper, however it may be disguised, and drowns him hopelessly in the mire out of which it proposed to pull him.''[4] These are the reasons for saying that the housing problem must be attacked and solved, if ever it is completely solved, on economic rather than on philanthropic principles. Sentiment may prompt the effort, but then it must stand aside and let business make it.

Establishing Standards.—This does not mean, however, that philanthropy has no function to perform in relation to housing. It has a very proper and valuable, though limited, field; this is to experiment and demonstrate. Philanthropy in connection with model tenements is highly useful in demonstrating that a solution is possible on economic principles. In the social sciences as in the natural, there is need of experimentation to advance knowledge, discover new processes, and work out methods of adjustment. Philanthropy can do this in relation to housing, whereas commercial builders will not experiment because of possible loss. If a philanthropic housing scheme succeeds, that is, if it provides improved housing conditions and at the same time makes a fair return on the investment, it is thereby making a demonstration of great value, the results of which may be embodied in legislation. Legislators will not require higher standards in housing laws unless they are convinced that they are economically sound. Philanthropy of the kind that pays—''philanthropy and 5 per cent''—may render the service of making the demonstration. There are many examples.

In 1877, the philanthropist Alfred T. White experimented with model tenements in Brooklyn. Although his buildings covered not over 50 per cent of the lot—commercial builders were utilizing 90 per cent with the result that light and air were inadequate—the enterprise was successful financially, earning 7.5 per cent net the first year. This was a clear demonstration to the legislature that a restriction of the percentage of the lot that might be built upon was economically sound, as well as desirable from a residential standpoint, and in the Tenement House Law of 1879 this provision was included for the first time. The Association for Improving the Condition of the Poor took the initiative in 1896 in arranging for a series of conferences to consider the advisability of building improved tenement houses in New York. The result was the organization of the City and Suburban Homes Company for the purpose of building model tenements as a business investment. Its object has been to supply to wage-earners improved dwellings at market rates of rental. An architectural com-

[4] Jacob Riis, *How the Other Half Lives*, 1890, p. 271.

petition was held in order to get the best type of plan. As mentioned in an earlier chapter, the winner, Mr. Ernest Flagg, demonstrated that the secret of tenement-house planning lies in constructing a building more nearly the shape of a square than of a long parallelogram. This has been seen to have had great influence on the reform effected by the Tenement House Law of 1901. The first group of buildings erected by this company earned a profit of a little more than 5 per cent the first year. The company has had an unbroken dividend record since it began. Its whole history is a demonstration of the fact that improved housing is commercially profitable and that legislation requiring higher standards from commercial, speculative builders is entirely sound. This company owns several large model tenement properties and a working-girls' hotel on Manhattan Island and has developed a suburban property in Brooklyn. It has been a pioneer in providing model housing for Negroes, who usually suffer especially from inadequate housing conditions because of race prejudice and discrimination.[5] Other notable experiments by semi-philanthropic housing companies with the problem of Negro housing have been made by the Whittier Center Housing Company of Philadelphia, and by the philanthropist, Jacob G. Schmidlapp, in Cincinnati, in which latter case there has been developed the idea of a community plan rather than segregation. Outstanding examples of high-class dwellings for Negroes are the Paul Laurence Dunbar Apartments, erected by Mr. John D. Rockefeller, Jr., in New York City, and the Michigan Boulevard Garden Apartments built by Mr. Julius Rosenwald in Chicago.[6]

Other fields for experimentation have been entered by "philanthropy and 5 per cent." In the national capital, the experiment of the Sanitary Improvement Company "was successful in establishing standards, introducing a new type of domestic architecture in Washington, and proving that sound business management is not incompatible with humanitarian aims."[7] In New York, Mr. John D. Rockefeller, Jr., has recently engaged in a number of housing projects—in Manhattan, the Bronx, and Harlem—which tend to show that low-priced homes can be profitably erected on high-priced land and yet generous allowance be made for light and air. In one of his model

[5] *Annual Reports of the City and Suburban Homes Company.* Allan Robinson, "The Essentials of Good Management," *National Housing Conference,* 1916, V, 209 ff.

[6] *Housing Betterment,* Sept., 1917, 6:3:8-10. J. G. Schmidlapp, "Low Priced Housing for Wage Earners," *National Housing Association,* Publication No. 34, Oct., 1916. *Housing,* Mar., 1930, 19:1:15-21; Dec., 1930, 19:4:296-297.

[7] Edith Wood, *Housing of the Unskilled Wage Earner,* 1919, p. 102.

tenements located in the Bronx, a demonstration is being made of the English co-partnership plan. Under the conditions established in connection with this project, only stockholders may be tenants and only tenants may be stockholders. Furthermore, each tenant stockholder may lease only one apartment and that only for his own occupancy, and his stock ownership is limited to the cost value of the apartment he selects.[8] Another object lesson of good housing on a commercial basis is the experiment of the Metropolitan Life Insurance Company. It has built a number of blocks in the borough of Queens, the apartments to rent for $9.00 per room per month—"the best large-scale example of modern housing at low rents so far produced within the radius of a nickel fare from Times Square."[9] Each apartment has a bath, steam heat, hot-water supply, and electric light wiring and fixtures; more than ordinary protection against fire is structurally provided for; there are no dark rooms; each room is exceptionally well ventilated. Not only is this plan unique as to the equipment of each apartment for the price of rental; it also makes a distinct contribution from an architectural standpoint. The buildings are placed in units along two sides of a block, with a large interior area for a common garden from which courts open out. In addition there are passageways between the units which further aid in ventilation and make unsightly fire escapes unnecessary. Together these features embody what is called "block circulation," a principle violated in most apartment houses. Again legislation has been influenced. The State Housing Commission, for the purposes of Governor Smith's housing plan (State Housing Law, 1926), based its construction costs on the experience of the Metropolitan Life Insurance Company's large-scale buildings.[10]

To cite but one more experiment in city housing, attention may be called to the colony for wage-earners opened in 1924 at Sunnyside, Long Island City, by the City Housing Corporation, a limited-dividend company. The Sunnyside community is designed primarily for tenants with annual earnings of between $2,500 and $3,500. Although New Yorkers of all moderate incomes have lifted up their voices against rental values in the city, studies by housing experts have reached the conclusion that the people hardest hit by city rents are in this particular income class. Their living scale is above that of inhabitants of the tenement districts, and yet the increase of building

[8] *Housing Betterment*, July, 1927, 16:2:128-129; March, 1928, 17:1:44-46.

[9] *The Survey*, July 15, 1922, 48:12:527.

[10] *Reports of the Commission of Housing and Regional Planning*, Legislative Documents Nos. 43 and 78 (1924). New York *Times*, Feb. 28, 1925.

within recent years has scarcely touched their needs. Like the middle class in many other respects, they have not been thought of in community schemes. They recall Sumner's "Forgotten Man."[11] Most of the new living quarters provided by speculative builders have been apartments for people with higher incomes; for people of moderate means the only solution has been either the tenements or the outskirts, with long rides to and from work. The president of this corporation, Mr. Alexander M. Bing, has definitely stated the company's function of experimenting and demonstrating. "We are not antagonistic to the speculative builder," he writes. "We realize that upon him the city must rely for most of its houses, but, being a limited dividend company, we can do things which he cannot do. We can, to a certain extent, experiment with new types of houses and new methods of community layout. This we have already done in our first unit." The two main demonstrations of this undertaking are, first, that with quantity production of good houses, homes can be purchased for little if anything more than what is now being paid for rent. Houses and apartments in the Sunnyside colony are taken on the tenant-ownership plan, which calls for an initial payment of from $500 to $2,000 and the balance, together with operating expenses and interest, paid at the rate of about $10 a month per room. Secondly, what Mr. Bing considers the most important contribution that Sunnyside has made to the cause of housing reform, is the demonstration that its type of apartment, only two rooms deep and covering but 30 per cent of the land, with liberal provisions for gardens and playgrounds, is commercially profitable when built on inexpensive land. "When this is demonstrated—and we think," states Mr. Bing, "we have already proved its commercial soundness—it may be expected that commercial builders will engage in similar enterprises on a still wider scale."[12] Six per cent dividends have been paid regularly since the City Housing Corporation was formed, and in addition a surplus has been accumulated. As mentioned earlier, this company is now carrying on the interesting experiment of building Radburn, New Jersey, a town for the motor age.

It is now being suggested by some housing experts that the next great step to be taken in housing reform in New York is to require by law that no dwelling erected in the future shall exceed two rooms

[11] William G. Sumner, *The Forgotten Man and Other Essays*, 1919, pp. 465 ff.
[12] Alexander M. Bing, "Sunnyside Gardens," *National Municipal Review*, June, 1926, 15:6:330-336. "Housing for Wage Earners," New York *Times*, Nov. 16, 1924. *The Survey*, Nov. 15, 1924, 53:4:189. *Housing Betterment*, March, 1928, 17:1:36-42.

in depth. If such a measure should be passed, it would be due primarily to the demonstration in a number of examples in Manhattan in various classes of model tenements that this method of construction is entirely feasible and profitable, at least when a whole block is taken as a unit. "Under such a method of construction, there would be no courts, no airshafts, no inadequate lighting or ventilation; for every room in every dwelling would obtain its light either from the street or from a similar open space at the rear, equivalent to the street in width and area."[13] Mathematical studies, it is stated, indicate clearly that the only way in which one can be sure of having sunlight in every room, even on the shortest day in winter, is to make the tenement house only two rooms deep from outside wall to outside wall and to make most of the windows face in a general easterly or westerly direction.[14] Furthermore, through such a method of design of building, adequate "through ventilation" could be secured. Practically all the problems which now vex the city with regard to light and ventilation would be remedied by this one measure.

2. IMPROVING THE TENANTS

Among the bits of wisdom culled from *How the Other Half Lives* is the following: "Those who would fight for the poor must fight the poor to do it." In other words, efforts to improve housing conditions are often obstructed by the tenants themselves, especially the poorest and most ignorant. This is the personal factor in the housing problem and must not be overlooked in any program of reform. Riis[15] recalls the discomfiture of a certain well-known philanthropist, since deceased, "whose heart beat responsive to other suffering than that of human kind. He was a large owner of tenement property, and once undertook to fit out his houses with stationary tubs, sanitary plumbing, wood-closets, and all the latest improvements. He introduced his rough tenants to all this magnificence without taking the precaution of providing a competent housekeeper, to see that the new acquaintances got on together. He felt that his tenants ought to be grateful for the interest he took in them. They were. They found the boards in the wood-closets fine kindling wood, while the pipes and faucets were as good as cash at the junk shop. In three months the owner had to remove what was left of his improvements. The pipes were cut and the houses running full of water, the stationary tubs were put to all

[13] Lawrence Veiller, "Housing in New York," *Housing*, June, 1928, 17:2:85-86.
[14] George B. Ford, "Standards for Improved Housing Laws," *National Municipal Review*, Oct., 1927, 16:10:636.
[15] *How the Other Half Lives*, 1890, pp. 273-274.

sorts of uses except washing, and of the wood-closets not a trace was left. The philanthropist was ever after a firm believer in the total depravity of tenement-house people. Others have been led to like reasoning by as plausible arguments, without discovering that the shiftlessness and ignorance that offended them were the consistent crop of the tenement they were trying to reform, and had to be included in the effort.''

Landlords have generally urged as an excuse for not providing better housing conditions and keeping their property in better repair that the tenants are not of a class that requires anything very good, that they do not know how to take care of a house, and that through their carelessness and ignorance all attempts to improve conditions are undone. There is some justification for this complaint. Many cases can be cited where the tenants throw garbage out into the court and yard, spill slops about the sinks, drag pieces of wood and boxes for fuel through the halls, breaking the plaster and defacing the walls, and make no attempt to keep the children from whittling and scrawling with crayon and chalk over doors, the walls of the halls and courts, woodsheds and any other available surfaces. The amount of preventable wear and tear, breakage and general damage is enormous.[16] ''It may be accepted as axiomatic,'' writes the architectural engineer and adviser to the U. S. Steel Corporation, which houses many thousand employees, ''that the lower the cost of the house the higher the percentage of upkeep or maintenance charge. This is due less to the character of material employed than to the character of the tenant and the frequent changes in occupants.''[17] An official investigating committee in New York found that the tenants are careless and destructive partially because they are only temporary lodgers. They do not feel that their apartment is home and probably would not care to have it as a permanent abode.[18] There appears to be an absence among many tenants of what the English call house-pride. There is too much truth in the small boy's answer to his friend, who said, ''Hullo, Bill! where are you living now?'' ''Oh, we're still in the same house, but we shan't stay long. Father's used all the doors for firewood, and now he's starting on the stairs.'' A common complaint among property owners in England is that it is unfair to call

[16] Adolph Bloch, ''The Tenant's Responsibility,'' *National Housing Conference*, 1911, I, 152-159. Emily W. Dinwiddie, ''The Tenant's Responsibility,'' *National Housing Conference*, 1911, I, 52-60.
[17] Owen Brainard, ''Types of Construction for Low Cost Houses,'' *National Housing Conference*, 1916, V, 84.
[18] *Report of the Reconstruction Commission on Housing Conditions, New York*, 1920, p. 58.

upon them to repair their houses and not to punish the tenants for the wanton damage they commit.[19]

The problem of the careless, irresponsible tenant is perplexing to the health authorities even in the city of the one- and two-family house. But it is infinitely more acute in the city where predominates the house-of-many-families, and more acute still when there exists the combination of the multiple dwelling and the immigrant tenant. In some instances, the houses, wretched as they are, compare more than favorably with what the tenants, recent immigrants from southern and eastern Europe, have been accustomed to; they do not understand how to live in multiple dwellings and among sanitary surroundings; coming for the most part from a rural background they are unfamiliar with city conditions. Many are ignorant of modern plumbing and soon have it out of order. Garbage and rubbish are scattered everywhere; pigs are kept in the parlor; laws of hygiene and sanitation are blissfully ignored. The fire-escapes are cluttered with boxes and barrels, coal and wood, and anything else they want to get out of the way. There is no doubt that much of the unsanitary and inadequate housing conditions can be laid at the tenants' door.[20]

On the other hand, such conditions are sometimes due to the fact that the tenements are owned by absentee landlords who operate through incompetent agents and are entirely ignorant of the condition of their property. The list of real estate ownership on the Bowery today reads like a page from the Social Register. "A great part of the houses in which the working people of New York live have come into the hands of absentee landlords or lessors. The latter are holding the properties, very often only for a short time, with the idea of getting as much out of it as they can. They at present control the conditions of sanitation and upkeep of a large part of the homes of New York." The report of the state commission from which this statement was taken goes on to say that although the tenants are often dirty, careless and indifferent, they are not entirely responsible for the conditions that exist especially in the old-law tenements, many of which are rotten through and through.[21]

[19] J. S. Nettlefold, *Practical Housing*, 1910, p. 118.
[20] Bleecker Marquette, "Educating the Tenant," *National Housing Conference*, 1916, V, 217. E. W. Parker, "Workmen's Houses in the Anthracite Regions," *National Housing Conference*, 1916, V, 64-65. Graham Taylor, *Satellite Cities*, 1915, p. 192.
[21] *Report of the Reconstruction Commission on Housing Conditions, New York*, 1920, pp. 22, 31. See Joseph Platzker, "Who Owns the Lower East Side?" *East Side Chamber News*, July, 1929, 2:5:9-10.

From all parts of the city come tales of leaking roofs, lack of water or gas, leaking pipes, stairs that are rotten and shaky, lack of repairs, walls needing painting, plaster falling from walls, dirty halls, courts and yards, and unsanitary conditions brought about through lack of care of toilets. Similar conditions to a lesser degree have always existed in these houses. Many of them are rotten through and through. The landlord often blames the condition of upkeep on the tenants, and particularly the children. To an extent he is right. They are often dirty, careless, indifferent. They throw their garbage out the window, but they have no dumbwaiters. Their houses are sometimes dirty, but what chance is there for cleanliness when half of the rooms are in partial darkness throughout the day.

The responsibility of the cleaning of the house is often on the shoulder of the janitor, or more often the janitress. But what janitor is going to put much enthusiasm into scrubbing the public halls of a six-story tenement for the sake of free rent of the wretched rooms. Some of them, according to the reports of our investigator, get as high as $6.00 a month, but plenty get only a broom and in many apparently better grade tenements the janitor gets only a reduction of rent.

Moreover, the owners may be not merely ignorant of conditions but indifferent to them; they may believe that anything is good enough for the tenants who are a low class of people anyway. Trinity Church Corporation, which has long been an owner of tenement property, fought in the courts until 1895 the provisions of the New York Tenement House Act of 1887 requiring running water on each floor of a tenement house. There was obviously class bias in this case. Since then, be it said to the credit of Trinity Church, it has become a model landlord.[22] It might be said that "to reform the tenant one must begin with the landlord." Miss Ellen Collins, an owner of tenement property in New York City who some years ago set an example of what she called fair play between tenant and landlord, was of the opinion that the best way to rouse the tenant to a sense of responsibility was for the landlord to show responsibility. Many landlords themselves need education as much as the tenants.[23]

However, the greater part of the responsibility for the conditions described above falls on the tenants. From England's experience in re-housing insanitary areas the maxim may be deduced that to clear out a slum without regard to what happens to those who lived in it is to insure that another slum shall be created in the place of the one destroyed. "Left free of control, habitual slum-dwellers carry

[22] Edith Wood, *Housing of the Unskilled Wage Earner*, 1919, p. 9.
[23] Emily W. Dinwiddie, "The Tenant's Responsibility," *National Housing Conference*, 1911, I, 54-55. Jacob Riis, *How the Other Half Lives*, 1890, pp. 285-287. Lawrence Veiller, *Housing Reform*, 1910, pp. 186-188.

about in themselves the causes of slums.''[24] Another example concerning a different class and more illustrative of our main point is the experience of Mr. Henry Ford. Some years ago when he increased the wages of his employees he found that their homes and living conditions were not improved. He then put into operation a plan of investigation and supervision of living conditions and ordered that men who continued to live under squalid conditions would lose their jobs.[25] The lesson to be learned is that nothing is accomplished merely by raising wages; the standard of living must also be raised. Nothing is accomplished merely by putting improvements in tenement houses; the tenants themselves must be improved. How can this be done? Certainly they can not be legislated into habits of cleanliness nor out of habits of slovenliness; fines may frighten for a while the particular tenants punished, but it is impossible to reach all careless tenants by this means and there is nothing constructive in the method. Nor can they be inspected into proper regard for the principles of sanitation; ''no number of inspections could possibly clean up the dirt as fast as tenants can pile it up.''[26] The only possibility is in education.

The Octavia Hill Plan.—The first person to devise a plan of approaching the tenement problem in this way—improving the surroundings by improving the tenants—was Miss Octavia Hill (1838-1912), one of the most practical of English philanthropists and for years a leader in the efforts to improve housing and social conditions not only in London but throughout the United Kingdom.[27] With the aid of John Ruskin and others she purchased some tenements that were out of repair and filled with the lowest class of poor having settled habitation. She also undertook to manage similar property for other owners. She had the houses put in order, but not improved. New appliances, she said, would be installed only after the tenants had shown ability to use and not abuse them. A fixed sum out of the rent—and she was very strict about punctual payment of rent—was set aside for breakage and repairs; if any of it remained after breakage and damage had been paid for, each tenant in turn was

[24] Sydney J. Chapman, *Work and Wages*, 1914, III, 43, 44.

[25] Lawrence Veiller, ''Industrial Housing,'' *National Housing Conference*, 1916, V, 46-47.

[26] Bleecker Marquette, ''Educating the Tenant,'' *National Housing Conference*, 1916, V, 217-218.

[27] A good biography is that by C. Edmund Maurice, *Life of Octavia Hill*. Somewhat autobiographical is her book, *Homes of the London Poor* (1875, new ed. 1883).

permitted to decide in what way the surplus should be spent so as to add to the comfort of the home. The tenants were thus gradually brought to a higher level and by the time rebuilding was necessary they were capable of enjoying and properly using the better facilities that might be offered. The method, be it noted, was to begin with the improvement of the individual rather than of the surroundings, or rather to improve both together. As she herself expressed it, "You cannot deal with the people and their homes separately. The principle on which the whole work rests is, that the inhabitants and their surroundings must be improved together. It has never yet failed to succeed."[28]

The actual education of the tenants was accomplished through her plan of rent collection. Landlord and friendly visitor were combined in the rent collector, who entered into friendly intercourse and helpful relations with the tenants. Cleanliness, ventilation and good order, along with promptness and regularity in the payment of rent, were shown to depend largely upon the tenants themselves, and so amelioration was secured through self-help. The tenants were taught industry, frugality, thrift, carefulness, cleanliness, and good housekeeping. Their standard of living was raised. Miss Hill's work was especially successful with the lower element.[29] An American writer[30] thinks it would not work with any other group. "The Octavia Hill idea in housing is only one special application of the Charity Organization Society philosophy. This thought suggests at once its appropriate sphere of action and its appropriate limits. It has a most useful function to perform in subnormal or misfit groups, including under the latter [in America] such non-English-speaking immigrants as need a temporarily paternalistic treatment." In the opinion of Mr. J. S. Nettlefold,[31] an English housing expert, the Octavia Hill plan is "the only method for surmounting the difficulties between landlord and tenant and removing existing slums in a manner that will be permanently satisfactory and successful." Another English writer comments: "After the object-lesson of her long and successful labour in reforming slum-property, and its tenants at the same time, the community can have no excuse for overlooking the personal factor in the housing problem."[32]

[28] Octavia Hill, *Homes of the London Poor*, 1883, p. 51.
[29] E. R. L. Gould, *Housing of the Working People*, 8th Special Report of the Commissioner of Labor, 1895, pp. 161-164.
[30] Edith Wood, *Housing of the Unskilled Wage Earner*, 1919, p. 110.
[31] *Practical Housing*, 1910, pp. 119-125.
[32] Sydney J. Chapman, *Work and Wages*, 1914, III, 44.

Similar Experiments.—Her system has been adopted with uniform success in many large cities in Europe and to a smaller extent in this country. Notable examples of experiments conducted along similar lines in the United States are to be found in Boston, New York, and Philadelphia. In the latter city there was organized in 1896 the Octavia Hill Association, which operates along the lines followed by Miss Hill in London, buying up or securing the agency for old houses and by careful management making them safe, well-repaired and wholesome buildings. Trained women are employed in the collection of rents. "Their duties provide for a friendly contact with the tenant, quite often extending to that of counsellor in the family affairs, aid in obtaining employment, adviser in the proper care of sickness, and even provider for those dire needs which occasionally seem inevitable." The latest published annual report of the Association shows that it owns 221 properties and manages for other owners 140 properties, housing over 1,800 people. Notwithstanding its semi-philanthropic nature, its stock pays dividends of 4 per cent. The work has more recently been broadened to include agitation for more adequate housing legislation and enforcement, and the improvement of housing conditions throughout the entire city.[33]

The City and Suburban Homes Company of New York utilizes the Octavia Hill plan of rent collection. "All rents are collected weekly in advance; the collections being made by women workers. These women workers go into the various apartments, and in this way are brought in close touch with all the tenants. They are not only able to ascertain whether the tenants are desirable, and keep their apartments in a clean and healthful condition, but this close contact affords the tenants themselves an opportunity of asking advice when they need help or assistance. Whenever it can properly do so, the company is glad to assist its tenants, and our women collectors have frequently found employment for the wage earner in our buildings who may have lost his job. The success which the company has had in keeping its tenants satisfied is largely due to the character and continuity of its contact with the tenants."[34] It has been the experience of this and other companies that weekly collections of rent are best. Workmen

[33] *Annual Reports of the Octavia Hill Association of Philadelphia.* F. L. Waldo, *Good Housing That Pays, a study of the aims and accomplishments of the Philadelphia Octavia Hill Association,* 1896-1917. *Housing Betterment,* Sept., 1927, 16:3:217-218. *Housing,* Dec., 1930, 19:4:293-294.

[34] Allan Robinson, "Essentials of Good Management," *National Housing Conference,* 1916, V, 214. *Cf.* Lawrence Veiller, *Housing Reform,* 1910, pp. 177-180.

are in the habit of running their affairs on a weekly basis: they get paid weekly, they pay their insurance weekly, and handle their other financial affairs on a weekly basis; why not pay their rent weekly? It is easier and more certain than saving part of the weekly earnings until the end of the month.[35]

The Cincinnati Better Housing League has extended the plan of using friendly rent collectors: it employs visiting housekeepers, to each of whom is given a definite territory in which to work. The visiting housekeeper's duties are described as follows. "She first makes a survey of every house in her district, entering upon proper cards essential information with regard to each house. She makes the acquaintance of the tenants in her district as well as of the landlord. Where she finds tenants ignorant, careless or destructive it is her business to teach them to improve their housekeeping conditions. Where she finds defective conditions which should be remedied by the owner she personally interviews him explaining the work she is trying to do, the service she is rendering and asks in return that he make the repairs which she recommends. In eighty per cent of the cases so far handled it has been possible to get results through persuasion. Where obstinate landlords are encountered, the cases are referred to the proper city department for action."[36] This sort of activity might be developed by the city tenement-house department, or the department of public health, or the bureau of sanitary inspection. It can be both constructive and preventive.

The Woman's City Club of Cincinnati, through its Housing Committee, has established a model flat in what is probably the worst-housed section of the city. The purpose of the undertaking is to demonstrate to the mothers in the district how to secure the most desirable living conditions at the least expense. The flat is model only in the sense that it represents the best conditions obtainable within the means of the people living in the neighborhood. Classes are held there to give the women instruction in good housekeeping.[37] Social settlements in a number of cities have given similar instruction, while some of the public schools have model laundries, rooms, and flats which are utilized in connection with courses in domestic science. By these and other means some permanent improvement in housing

[35] Fred C. Feld, "Some Problems of Management," *National Housing Conference*, 1918, VII, 214 ff.

[36] *Housing Betterment*, May, 1920, 9:2:131. Bleecker Marquette, "Cincinnati," *National Housing Conference*, 1918, VII, 387. *Housing*, Mar., 1930, 19:1:64-67.

[37] *Housing Betterment*, Sept., 1919, 8:3:77.

conditions will result; their essence lies in raising the standard of living through education.[38]

3. INDUSTRIAL HOUSING

The housing of their employees by industrial concerns is not necessarily model housing nor is it philanthropic, though both factors have been present. It was developed at first out of necessity. Many companies located in out-of-the-way places were forced to provide houses for their employees because of the lack or scarcity of accommodations. In some instances, towns have been created anew by an industry, and housing provisions by the company were as necessary as factory establishments. The cotton and woolen mill towns North and South furnish examples, as do the many new towns of the U. S. Steel Corporation, which houses about 10,000 of its employees.

Early Mill Towns.—The earliest examples of industrial housing were of two types: the mill tenements and boarding houses, and the mining camps. The first were developed in the textile industry about the beginning of the nineteenth century, which makes company housing almost as old as the industrial history of the United States. The early mill sites were generally located at those points where water power was available. These were usually in undeveloped country, and force of necessity compelled the employer to provide housing accommodations for the labor which he brought to his establishment. This was the origin of the New England mill towns, some of which date back to 1791. Among the early New England company towns is Lowell, Massachusetts, founded in 1820. Like Robert Owen at New Lanark (1799) in Scotland, Francis Cabot Lowell in Massachusetts endeavored to improve conditions by constructing model mill tenements and boarding houses; "model," that is, for those days, though they would not compare favorably with the dwellings of modern industrial villages. Extensive real estate holdings by the company were not an unusual feature of the early industrial undertakings; and in several of the New England cotton-mill centers today the operating companies own much property in the form of land and dwellings.

There was a distinct development, if we may believe the early records, of autocratic control in these company towns. "Many colonial iron-masters ruled with almost feudal sway over a neighborhood settlement of their laborers and country people, and such enterprises

[38] Lawrence Veiller, *Housing Reform*, 1910, pp. 185-187. Emily W. Dinwiddie, "Educating the Tenant," *National Housing Conference*, 1916, V, 386-392. *Housing*, June, 1930, 19:2:149-150.

often became the nucleus of a permanent village.''[39] Among such single developments may be mentioned the building of Brady's Bend, Pennsylvania, in 1839, when the Great Western Iron Co. was formed and $500,000 invested in land and works in western Pennsylvania. Six years later the Brady Bend Iron Co. purchased the property from the original company, which had failed, and built a steel-manufacturing plant on this spot. It housed in its own tenements 538 laboring families.

Mining Towns.—This type of industrial housing is also prevalent in the mining industry, which is usually carried on in isolated, uninhabited localities where, just as on construction jobs, some type of shelter for the labor force must necessarily be provided. ''Under these conditions, and without the ideals that were back of the first mill tenements, the first mining villages (and many of the later ones) grew up as garish groups of shanties, without adequate sanitary facilities, and absolutely devoid of comfort, attractiveness and opportunity for recreation. Such villages have been deservedly called 'camps' and 'patches,' and whether they have existed at mines or factories, they have done incalculable damage to the spirit of American industrial labor.''[40] In 1916 the United States Bureau of Labor Statistics made a survey of communities maintained by bituminous-coal mining companies in Pennsylvania, West Virginia, Ohio, Indiana, Kentucky, Tennessee, Alabama, Colorado, and Wyoming, including almost exclusively the better types of communities. The findings were summarized as follows:[41]

1. The responsibility for the housing of a large proportion of the miners has been undertaken by the mine operators. The isolation of the average mining town, its dependence upon the one industry of mining, and frequently its impermanence and almost universal lack of local self-goverment, as well as the shifting character of the labor force, have compelled the mine owner to assume that responsibility.

2. The average company mining town has few of the amenities of ordinary community life. There is a dull uniformity in the appearance of the houses and an absence of trees and natural vegetation. Streets and alleys are open dirt roads almost without exception. Sidewalks are very rare.

---

[39] Victor S. Clark, *History of Manufactures in the United States*, 1917, p. 404, quoted by Leifur Magnusson, *Housing by Employers in the United States*, Bureau of Labor Statistics Bulletin No. 263, 1920, pp. 7-8. Morris Knowles, *Industrial Housing*, 1920, p. 6. Karl Schriftgiesser, ''Lowell,'' *American Mercury*, June, 1927, 11:42:234-240.
[40] Morris Knowles, *Industrial Housing*, 1920, p. 6.
[41] Leifur Magnusson, ''Company Housing in Bituminous Coal Fields,'' *Monthly Labor Review*, April, 1920, 10:4:215 ff.

3. The miner's house is without the ordinary inside conveniences found in the house of the city worker. Less than 2 per cent of the homes in the bituminous coal regions have inside toilets, and running water is rare. Stoves and grates are depended upon for heating.

4. The average house of the miner includes about four rooms, in which he must accommodate a family and frequently take in boarders when there is a housing shortage.

5. The rents of the miners' houses are comparatively low, most of them (65.4 per cent) renting in 1916 for less than $8 per month. The rent in some instances probably constitutes a subsidy to the wages of the miner who lives in a company house.

Decentralization of Industry and Housing.—A third example of company housing that has been prompted by necessity is afforded by the more recent movement of industries away from city centers out into suburbs or into new towns or smaller cities immediately adjoining—into what Taylor calls satellite cities. The reasons for this movement of industry away from the city, as was mentioned in an earlier chapter, are a desire for more land as well as for cheap land, lower taxes, lower rentals, and avoidance of congestion. To meet in a practical way the progress of the movement, the employer builds not only his factory plant, but also houses for his employees. The development of house and plant must be simultaneous so that operations may begin at once and continue steadily, for although rapid transit makes it possible for labor to live farther removed from its place of work than formerly, yet it is always necessary to have a certain nucleus of men near the plant or factory. When industry moves out from the city center it usually finds an actual shortage of houses in the new community. It may leave housing to haphazard real-estate enterprise, depend on traction to bring workers to the suburban shops, or, more generally, it may provide a made-to-order town, like Pullman, Illinois, and Gary, Indiana, or build rows of company houses. Decentralization of industry has led to industrial housing experiments on a more important scale than ever before. The fact that "practically all company housing developments recently undertaken are new-town developments or are located in the suburbs of cities" shows how extensively industrial decentralization underlies company housing.[42]

Industrial Housing and the Control of Labor.—Begun out of necessity, tempered somewhat by philanthropy, industrial housing has been extended through enlightened self-interest. To be sure, some

[42] Leifur Magnusson, *Housing By Employers in the United States*, 1920, pp. 17-18. Graham Taylor, *Satellite Cities*, 1915, ch. IV. Morris Knowles, *Industrial Housing*, 1920, pp. 6-7.

of the reasons assigned by manufacturers and mine operators housing their employees show clearly the exploitative character of the undertaking, especially where the purpose is to control the labor situation better, one employer emphasizing the desire "to have men concentrated so as to have proper supervision over them, to better control them in times of labor agitation and threatened strikes." Others express a vague and conventional humanitarianism. But in the majority of cases, the motive is enlightened self-interest. Employers have come to realize that a badly housed worker is an inefficient worker, and that they have a pecuniary interest in seeing that their employees have suitable homes. Although the housing of employees may require the expenditure of large sums of money which must be taken out of the business and which will bring less return, the diminished returns on this capital are made up by larger returns on the remainder of the capital due to better work done by more contented workmen. An official of the U. S. Steel Corporation says, "We firmly believe this, but it is not a thing which can be demonstrated by the books of account."[43] In one study where 180 different manufacturing and mining companies engaged in housing their employees reported as to the results obtained, 175, or 97.2 per cent, stated that the results on the whole were satisfactory both to the employee and to the company. Only 2.8 per cent declared the results to be unsatisfactory, or at least not positively satisfactory. As one or more favorable results were reported by each company, a total of 348 replies were received. Arranged in the order of the frequency with which certain results were mentioned, we have the following for all the 175 industries combined.[44]

1. Secured better class of workmen........................ 75
2. Find greater stability in the labor force................. 47
3. Secured necessary help................................. 43
4. Reduced number of floaters............................ 42
5. Secured better living conditions........................ 32
6. Secured greater loyalty and coöperation from labor...... 24
7. Have more contented labor force....................... 24
8. Have more efficient labor force........................ 19

[43] C. L. Close, "Housing of Employees at Industrial Plants," *National Housing Conference*, 1913, III, 65. *Cf.* Boyd Fisher, "Housing and Labor Turnover," *National Housing Conference*, 1918, VII, 171; Edith Wood, *Housing of the Unskilled Wage Earner*, 1919, p. 114; Lawrence Veiller, "Industrial Housing," *National Housing Conference*, 1916, V, 28; Morris Knowles, *Industrial Housing*, 1920, pp. 13-16; Leifur Magnusson, *Housing by Employers in the United States*, 1920, pp. 20-21.
[44] Leifur Magnusson, *Housing by Employers in the United States*, 1920, p. 247.

9. Better control of the labor situation...................... 9
10. Raised standard of living............................ 8
11. Married men attracted................................. 6
12. Greater regularity of employment...................... 5
13. Men supplied better houses for less money.............. 4
14. Profitable to company................................. 3
15. Very satisfactory 3
16. Facilitated part time................................. 2
17. Value in advertising.................................. 1
18. Control of drinking................................... 1

348

Under a system where only company houses are available the employer is able to select the class and type of workmen he desires. This facility, however, is limited by the existing state of the labor supply. Among the nine replies grouped under "Better control of the labor situation," it was noted that company housing tends to decrease labor troubles and that it has been possible to keep out labor agitators. More than half of the total replies may be grouped under the head of reduced labor turnover. Broadly speaking, company housing has been a factor in labor management and has had a certain influence upon the social and health conditions surrounding employees.

The Workman's Point of View.—Many workmen, on the other hand, dislike and resent company housing because it smacks of paternalism. In an investigation of the steel industry, many workers stated that in taking company jobs, living in company houses, buying at company stores, obtaining company loans, holding company stock, working toward a company pension, etc., they felt "all sewed up."[45] One mill operative referred to his employer as follows: "We work in *his* mill. We live in *his* houses. Our children go to *his* school. On Sunday we hear *his* preacher. . . . And when we die we are buried in *his* cemetery."[46] Some workmen object to living near the industrial plant, preferring to be away from the place where they have been working all day. One workman states: "It would interest you to see the workers in the industrial plants of Norwood as they undergo the discomforts of transportation in the city street cars from Cincinnati to Norwood. They hang on to those cars like angleworms and travel in and out in the cold of the winter and the stifling heat of the summer in

[45] *The Survey*, Aug. 2, 1920, 45:16:560.
[46] A. J. McKelway, *Child Wages in the Cotton Mill; Our Modern Feudalism*, 1913, quoted by Edith Wood, *Housing of the Unskilled Wage Earner*, 1919, p. 127.

order that they may live away from their work. They don't care to be around the plant. . . . Another thing that I object to in the housing around the industrial plant is the overshadowing feeling of ownership. The idea is that everything in the worker must belong to and center in the place where he works. Then if he happens to disagree with the company, why, his house is vacated for him and he finds himself without a home."[47]

More serious is the complaint that company housing handicaps the worker-tenant in his wage bargaining and restricts his right to strike. Consider, for example, the year of bitter warfare between miners and operators in Mingo County, West Virginia, which began when the miners and their families were evicted after a strike from houses owned by the operators. "It was claimed that the detectives acted without warrant in dispossessing the miners, and the mine companies claimed that when the miners struck the houses automatically reverted to the companies. The turning of these people into the streets led to the formation of the big tent colony near Williamson, the county seat of Mingo, which has since been the trouble centre of the West Virginia mine fields."[48]

The experience of other countries is similar. In England, for example, "work people have not as a rule been advocates of the movement for combining the functions of employer and landlord in the absence of a real necessity."[49] On the other hand, as opposed to the instances of exploitation, Magnusson[50] found in his study of 213 companies engaged in housing their workers that a very considerable proportion of them permit their employees to continue living rent free in company houses during sickness or shutdowns of the plant. "Practically all other employers defer the collection of rent in time of sickness, unemployment, or shutdowns. Many also take reduced rent at these times. It is quite common also to find disabled former employees or widows of employees occupying company houses free."

The location of company towns, as pointed out in the same study, has had unfavorable results, especially with reference to the recreational life of the workers. Proximity of the employee to his work has naturally been secured by company housing, but on the other hand, nearness to larger community life has not generally been attained. This is particularly true of mining towns, where the remoteness of

[47] E. L. Hitchens, "Housing of Employees," *National Housing Conference*, 1913, III, 166.
[48] New York *Times*, Aug. 26, 1921.
[49] Sydney J. Chapman, *Work and Wages*, 1914, III, 72.
[50] *Housing by Employers in the United States*, 1920, pp. 204, 242.

the mineral deposits takes the towns away from settled or community life. Manufacturing company towns are, as a rule, quite accessible to larger communities and group themselves on the outskirts of the metropolitan cities. ''The failure to provide recreational activities in the company towns or to locate the company towns in the neighborhood of larger cities, where recreation may be secured, has very frequently caused difficulty in retaining the labor supply. Workmen are likely to leave unless means of recreation are reasonably near at hand. In some instances in the bituminous-coal region of Pennsylvania workmen were found to be willing to commute from the larger cities to the mines, even as far as six or seven miles, rather than live in company houses.''

The Company Town.—The above objections to industrial housing apply with special force to those cases where the company owns the town and exercises public functions. Under these conditions company housing has wide social significance. In one study in which 224 communities reported, over one-half of them stated that street cleaning and lighting, fire protection, garbage collection, and sanitary regulations are functions of the employing company and not of the community. In 85 cases the company also provides the police protection of the community. The survey further found that, in general, employers controlling company towns merely assist in the provision of schools and churches, though the interest of some companies in the matter of providing educational facilities is controlling in the community. The real estate agent of one such company, which has built a trade school costing $500,000, a high school costing $100,000, a teachers' home, and a $50,000 building for a community art collection, all of which are rented to the state for the nominal sum of $1 apiece a year, states that there is considerable friction between the townspeople and the company by reason of the latter exercising too much control in local school matters. In the same study of company towns, playgrounds and hospitals where found are generally provided at the employer's expense. In over one-third of 205 communities reporting on this matter, no playgrounds are provided, and in about two-fifths of the 185 towns reporting, no hospitals are provided.

Control of community functions places undue power in the hands of companies; a heavy social responsibility rests upon them. ''Through their control of community streets, lights, public utilities, houses, recreational centers, and the industry which supports the economic life of their community, employers are in a position to control the character of the community. The rules promulgated by the employer are readily enforceable as they carry with them the threat of discharge from employment. . . . It is difficult to see how this responsibility can be avoided in a mining town. The isolation of mining towns, the impermanence of many of them, the shifting character of the labor force, the absence of local self-government, are all factors which throw the responsibility upon the employer. In a manufacturing community usually placed near populous centers where community life already exists, and where other agencies are already established to provide community needs, the responsibility of the employer is not so great. It is therefore not necessary for him so thoroughly to control or dominate the life of the community.''[51] Mr. Knowles,[52] an engineer who has made an extensive investigation of industrial housing, lays down a basic principle to be adhered to in the management of industrial towns, viz., ''make the town management as independent and separate from plant control as is possible.'' A step in this direction may be achieved by locating the town a reasonable distance away from the industry. Physical separation makes more readily possible the separate organization of the management, as well as of the financing and construction, of the town. Also, subsidiary land companies or housing organizations are a means of keeping town and plant management separate. Mr. Knowles urges further that the town be made self-supporting and that the plant keep out of the employees' personal and home affairs.

The Experience at Pullman.—The classic example which bears out Mr. Knowles's contention is the history of Pullman, Illinois. This experiment, which dates from 1881, was quite the most elaborate and expensive of the early ventures in establishing industrial towns, but in spite of many admirable features, it must be counted a failure. Its fault was excessive paternalism. The town was created for and by the Pullman Palace Car Company, which laid out the streets, sewers, water mains, all of the best quality, planted trees, and built houses, schools, libraries, churches, shops, etc. (but no hospital). No saloons were allowed. Three-story tenements were built with three- and four-room apartments, renting for $8 and $9 a month. There were single-family houses renting from $15 to $50. All rooms were light and every apartment contained a toilet. But beneath this attractive picture of the ''model town'' was the spirit and substance of paternalism. ''A cardinal point in the policy of the president of the Pullman Company

[51] Leifur Magnusson, *Housing by Employers in the United States*, 1920, pp. 39-40.
[52] *Industrial Housing*, 1920, pp. 375-376.

was the retention of the ownership of land and houses. Maintenance of utilities, care of houses and lawns, repair and cleaning of streets, management of hotel, theater and other community activities—all were controlled by the company. Thus was established that autocratic power, which scarcely was challenged until 1885, when Professor Richard T. Ely assailed it as feudalistic."[53]

"The Pullman employees objected to the restrictions, objected to the paternalism, objected to eating, sleeping, going to school and to church with the company as well as working for it and felt the inevitable check on the development of trade unionism and self-help."[54] Dr. Vincent[55] says: "When I visited Pullman, I found that the people of this model town didn't like to be model people and were looked upon with derision by those who lived outside of Pullman." Mr. Pullman felt that his employees were ungrateful for the many substantial benefits conferred. The experiment was the subject of the most fervent encomiums and the most bitter attacks.

Then began the steps toward dislodging the company's power and shifting it to the community. The annexation of Pullman to Chicago in 1889 was the beginning. "The vigor with which the company opposed this step indicated a realizing sense that it foreshadowed the end of company control of the town." The great strike was the next important factor in the disintegration of that control. "The trouble centered in a situation involving fixed rents and sliding wage scales, both controlled by the company." The third and final event was the Illinois Supreme Court decision in 1898 to the effect that the charter of the Pullman Company did not permit it to hold real estate beyond the necessities of its manufacturing business.

In many respects the development of Pullman shows the foresight of a pioneer mind. "Mr. Pullman early recognized the advantages of the removal of industry to the suburbs and saw the strategic possibilities of a Calumet harbor. He secured much land while yet it was cheap, and realized the economies of wholesale town and house building. And he provided recreation and tenements far in advance of the times, setting standards which Chicago failed to follow until years later, when hard struggle secured tenement laws and the movement for playgrounds and recreation centers became successful." But he failed to reckon with the human element. As Graham Taylor[56] suc-

[53] Graham Taylor, *Satellite Cities*, 1915, p. 32.
[54] Edith Wood, *Housing of the Unskilled Wage Earner*, 1919, p. 116.
[55] "Housing and Reconstruction," *National Housing Conference*, 1918, VII, 44.
[56] *Satellite Cities*, 1915, pp. 33 ff., 65-66, 67.

cinctly remarks, "The experience at Pullman has shown that while the men have not been able to dictate to the company as to work, the company has not been able to dictate to the men as to life."

Home-Ownership by Workmen.—Some of the difficulties connected with industrial housing that were cited above do not operate to the same extent where the workmen own or are in the process of buying their homes from the company. But selling of homes is not the customary method by which the employer houses his employees; it is as yet a comparatively untried experiment. Out of the 213 companies canvassed by Magnusson,[57] only 33 reported constructing and selling houses to their employees. It is least common in mining. Furthermore, there are many disadvantages to the ownership of homes by workmen. In the first place, home-ownership hinders mobility. In owning his house, a workman is tied to a particular locality, even to a particular dwelling. In order to better his position, any day he may be compelled to migrate to another part of the country; and even if he continues to work in the same town, his needs and tastes may change. Moreover, it takes too long for him to pay off the mortgage and secure title, and meanwhile he has to scrimp, which means a lowering of his standard of living or the taking of lodgers, with the consequent danger of overcrowding. An English observer of industrial housing conditions remarks: "The saving of the extra weekly payments needed to purchase the house may have created a habit of providence on the one hand, but in some places it certainly created over-crowding on the other hand and depressed standards of housing accommodations. Families were tempted to take lodgers when there was insufficient space for lodgers, in order to make up the payments for purchase of the house; and their action was imitated by neighbours without the same need."[58] Also, home owners of this class are not likely to keep up the place, they have not enough money to put into repairs and improvements. Their property rapidly deteriorates and health authorities have difficulty in getting them to comply with accepted standards of sanitation.[59] It is the experience of companies housing their employees that, whether houses are owned or rented, an urgent problem is that of maintenance and upkeep. Some have special sanitary departments in connection with the housing enterprise, others employ a staff of clean-up men, and still others issue circulars and notices to tenants and residents in the community to encourage proper upkeep

[57] *Housing by Employers in the United States,* 1920, p. 205.
[58] Sydney J. Chapman, *Work and Wages,* 1914, III, 66.
[59] Lawrence Veiller, "Industrial Housing," *National Housing Conference,* 1916, V, 44-46.

of the premises.[60] Nor has the plan of home-ownership by low-paid wage-earners worked out well in Great Britain and Germany.[61]

On the other hand, for the higher-paid workers who can manage it and who want to buy a home despite its check on their mobility, company housing aids them to secure a home at low cost and on easy terms. In addition, whether company houses are rented or sold, the plan has this advantage in these days of high prices, that building on a large scale reduces the cost per house. There are a number of cases of single firms or of housing corporations formed by industries or by chambers of commerce, building hundreds, even thousands, of houses at a time.[62] This is an important way of meeting the housing shortage and of reducing costs.

Industrial Housing in Europe Since the War.—In various European countries efforts have been made through industrial housing, among other means, to relieve the general housing shortage caused by the World War. Among the notable examples in Great Britain is the Industrial Housing Association, which was formed in 1922 by thirty big colliery companies following the suggestion by the Minister of Health that employers of labor on a large scale should recognize their obligation to provide decent houses for their workpeople. "These companies have formed what is, in effect, a coöperative society for housing, which has been registered under the title of The Industrial Housing Association, with an initial capital of £1,000,000 subscribed by the companies embraced in the scheme. No dividend will be paid upon the ordinary share capital and the directors will receive no fees from the Association. The entire scheme is for 10,000 houses to be built at the rate of 2,000 houses per annum; the balance of the capital required will be raised by mortgages on the houses erected and by a debenture issue upon the uncalled capital held by the colliery companies in the Association." The first building operations of the Association were at important collieries in the South Yorkshire coal-field and in Derbyshire and North and South Wales. "The underlying principle of the scheme is that an industry should undertake the housing of its own workpeople and not expect either the state or Local

[60] Leifur Magnusson, *Housing by Employers in the United States*, 1920, p. 228. C. L. Close, "Housing of Employees at Industrial Plants," *National Housing Conference*, 1913, III, 66.
[61] Sydney J. Chapman, *Work and Wages*, 1914, III, 66. Edith Wood, *Housing of the Unskilled Wage Earner*, 1919, p. 138.
[62] *Housing Betterment*, June, 1919, 8:2:25; Sept., 1919, 8:3:101; July, 1927, 16:2:119; March, 1928, 17:1:25. *American Year Book*, 1919, 248. W. H. Ham, "Housing Work in Bridgeport," *National Housing Conference*, 1920, VIII, 95-118. International Labour Office, *Housing Situation in the United States*, 1925, p. 29.

Authorities to provide houses for them. The scheme, however, has the special feature that it does not necessitate the withdrawal of large sums of money from the working capital of the industries concerned, but by coöperation of employers, providing moderate sums of money in the way of ordinary share capital, a security is available by which the greater proportion of the money required for building can be raised by loans and mortgages.''

In France, many thousand dwellings have been built since the War by the railway companies; the coal and metal mining, electrical, and engineering industries; and certain individual firms. A large proportion of these dwellings have been replacements of buildings destroyed during the War. Consider, for example, the mining companies. ''Up to 1913 French coal-mining companies had built 46,000 workers' dwellings providing accommodation for a population of nearly 200,000; 44,000 of the dwellings were in the mining district of the Nord and Pas-de-Calais and suffered considerably when those districts were invaded during the war. By the close of hostilities 18,000 houses had been entirely destroyed and 12,000 seriously damaged. The 14,000 houses owned by the mining companies of the Pas-de-Calais had not been reached by the invading armies, while 3,000 other houses were situated in places outside the war area. The mining companies thus had in the first place to rebuild the destroyed or damaged houses, and in the second to provide new houses for the additional workers required for restarting the mines.''

Many progressive employers in Switzerland, as elsewhere, have set a good example as regards the housing of their workers. In a number of instances on the continent the housing by employers is aided by government subsidy or other form of government aid.[63] This topic is discussed in a later section.

Summary.—By way of summary, a word may be said concerning the kind of accommodation furnished by companies housing their employees and the general characteristics of company towns. According to the findings of the most extensive survey that has been made in this country—one covering practically all sections and including 213 companies which operate 423 different establishments, employing 462,991 men, of whom 160,645, or 34.4 per cent, are accommodated in company houses—''the typical company house is a single or detached frame house consisting generally of four rooms, two of which are bedrooms, leaving a kitchen and one living room for general use. Stoves or fire-

[63] International Labour Office, *European Housing Problems Since the War*, 1924, pp. 106, 107, 134-135, 236, 348.

places form the heating equipment. Company houses are generally without modern sanitary plumbing. They are for the most part lighted by electricity. The company house tends to become standardized in each locality, as respects both plan and material of construction, and even with regard to the color of the exterior. Certain types, however, are characteristic of different sections of the country; and in the eastern States there is a further differentiation between the manufacturing and the mining town, which is not true in the northern and southern States. . . . On the whole, the companies in different sections of the country have adopted the type of house commonly erected by private home builders in the particular localities. Rents of company houses are moderate and well within the means of the low-paid wage earner.''

The chief characteristic of most company towns is their uniformity, due to a tendency to erect houses of similar plan and type and to arrange them along rectangular lines of survey. The possibilities of architecture and town planning have for the most part been neglected. The same skill and foresight displayed in adapting plant and machinery to manufacturing processes has not been applied to the development of the things through which houses may become homes, a construction camp a community, and livelihood life. ''Another feature of the company town, which it shares with most other communities, has been its disregard of the advantages of planting trees, grass, and shrubbery as beautifying elements. This is particularly true of the isolated mining town. On the other hand, company towns are quite generally characterized by relatively wide streets and ample lots. There is no tendency toward land overcrowding, save in two or three instances where companies have been compelled to buy land within city limits where speculative values have forced the price up. Generally speaking, company towns are unsewered and without a piped water system for a large majority of the dwellings. Dirt streets prevail, and many towns are without sidewalks or gutters. The smallness of these communities, however, and freedom from land overcrowding tend greatly to minimize the disadvantage from the lack of these utilities.''

Some notable examples of exceptions to the above statements are furnished by the industrial communities built along model lines by the Southern Pine Association. These are described with illustrations in a volume called *Homes for Workmen* published by the Association in 1919. Some of the housing developments of the U. S. Steel Corporation, in particular Morgan Park, Duluth, represent an appreciation of the advantages of architecture and city planning. The ideal of industry surrounded by a rich community life seems to have found fulfillment in the town of Kohler, Wisconsin.[64] Probably the model mining camp of the world is at Chuquicamata, Chile, where from 13,000 to 15,000 people are housed. The common laborers are provided with living quarters, medical service, and opportunities for pleasure and recreation. "They live in two- or three-room houses, systematically arranged on improved streets, well sewered and provided with water and electricity. Their living conditions are decidedly superior to those of the working class, generally, in Chile or other South American countries."[65]

From a governmental point of view, company towns, being private property, are "closed." Such general community functions as street cleaning and lighting, health and sanitary regulation, and administrative policing are vested in the controlling company. "There is a distinct absence of self-government in all company towns. It is rarely that company towns are found within the limits of self-governing communities; they are generally industrial satellites of larger cities or are isolated hamlets."

Company towns differ markedly in the matter of maintenance, even in the same section of the country and with the same class of employees. It is therefore reasonable to conclude that "these differences are due to the care and attention given the matter by the company and not, as has been asserted, to the tendency of the workman to keep the premises in an unsightly condition."[66]

Industrial housing has its field and it can contribute much to the solution of the housing problem. But there are many things which it must avoid. Mr. Boyd Fisher,[67] who has made a first-hand study of the subject, cautions the reader in these words: "It seems to me that the provision of houses to reduce labor turnover may be done in a fashion to create grievances which increase it; for instance, when the sale of houses to employees is made through deferred profit sharing, or any other plan which may cause the worker to lose credit for payments if he leaves the company; or if the company provides only un-

[64] U. S. Steel Corporation, *Safety, Sanitation and Welfare*, Bulletin No. 10, 1924, pp. 52-53; Bulletin No. 11, 1926, pp. 64-71. James C. Young, "A Model Town that Grew on a Prairie: Kohler's Industry is Concealed by Parks and the Homes of its Workers," *The New York Times Magazine*, Oct. 11, 1931, pp. 11, 22.

[65] R. H. Whitbeck, *Economic Geography of South America*, 1926, p. 181.

[66] Leifur Magnusson, *Housing by Employers in the United States*, 1920, pp. 12-13. *Cf.* Graham Taylor, *Satellite Cities*, 1915, pp. 7-8, 249.

[67] "Housing and Labor Turnover," *National Housing Conference*, 1918, VII, 173.

hygienic and uncomfortable houses in a community such as a mining town, where no other housing is available; or, if houses are rented, and the leases are made terminable automatically and immediately if an employee leaves or strikes; in any of these cases a housing plan interferes with the freedom and rights of the citizen, and will fall short of its purpose. Even in a plan otherwise ideal, if the company imposes too detailed restrictions on the use of the property, the employee is likely to resent his relations with a power which rules his conduct, not alone at work, but even in the privacy of his own home. The experience of Pullman is final on this point.''

4. GARDEN CITIES AND SUBURBS

In England there has developed a plan to improve housing conditions by getting the people out of the congested sections of old cities into rural districts. It is essentially a plan of decentralization. It has taken two forms: (*a*) the Garden Suburb or Village, which is purely residential; and (*b*) the Garden City, which is a self-sufficing community.

Garden Suburbs.—A Garden Suburb denotes an area in the outskirts of an existing important city, developed on ideal lines for residential purposes only, and designed for tenants from this city, irrespective of where they may be employed.[68] Since the residents of the Garden Suburb work in the big city, the development rests on cheap and adequate transportation facilities.

Hampstead Garden Suburb, located a few miles from London, is the best example. It owes its origin to the work of Mrs. S. A. Barnett, widow of the late Canon Barnett and his co-worker for many years in the East End of London. Reference will later be made to the part played by Canon Barnett in the social settlement movement. Hampstead was promoted by a limited-dividend company (the Hampstead Garden Suburb Trust, Ltd.) founded after an article by Mrs. Barnett, outlining an improved housing scheme for working people, had been published in the *Contemporary Review* of February, 1905. The objects as there set forth were:

1. To place within the reach of members of the industrial classes the opportunities of taking, within a 2d. fare of London, a cottage with a garden, where the family labour would produce vegetables, fruit and flowers, and add to health and pleasure.

2. To promote a better understanding between various classes, by arrang-

[68] George Hooker, ''Garden Cities,'' *National Housing Conference*, 1913, III, 17.

ing that people with all standards of income from 3s. 3d. a week to £300 a year should live on the same Estate.

3. To build not only a Church, a Free Church, and a Friends' Meeting House, but also an Institute where people of every section of Society and all sorts of opinions could meet, and by study, discussion, and recreation, become acquainted and form friendships.

4. To preserve all natural beauty, and so to lay out the ground that every tree might be kept, hedgerows duly considered, the foreground of the distant view preserved, and the buildings kept in harmony with the surroundings.

The estate was laid out by Mr. Raymond Unwin, the well-known English architect and town planner, and today it is a place of great beauty. The first sod was cut on May 2, 1907. The present position of this pioneer experiment of town extension (in spite of actual suspension of building operations for over six years) is as follows.

About 2,000 houses have been erected which accommodate some 10,000 people. Each house has a garden and a bathroom.

Three houses for worship, and three public institutions have been established and are maintained.

The Church, St.-Jude-on-the-Hill, and the Vicarage—£23,000.

The Free Church (where all sects worship together) and the Manse—£14,000.

The Friends' Meeting House—£5,000.

The Institute and temporary buildings, in which there is carried on a High School with Preparatory, Kindergarten and Montessori Departments; Schools of Art and Music, Classes for Senior and Junior Students in Languages, Domestic and Office Training, History and Literature; and self-governed Societies for study in various branches of learning or social service.

The Institute has about 1,200 members. Its work is recognised by the Board of Education, and is drawing public attention to the importance of pupils going out of, not into, towns to obtain teaching.

The Club House where the residents enjoy billiards, dancing, games and social pleasures—£5,000.

The Council Schools where 1,000 children are taught without fee by the Local Authority—£20,000.

The following Institutions for the old, weak, young or those needing assistance, have been built and are supported:

The Nursery Training School for the care of babies and the training of nurses—£6,000.

A Convalescent Cottage Home for nursing mothers—£5,000.

Three small separate Homes for orphans or neglected children—£1,000 each.

A Rest Home for girl servants—£1,000.

Twelve Tenements for widows of men who have fallen in the War—£2,500.

An 'Eventide' Home for the aged—£8,000.

A Quadrangle of 57 small tenements for old men and women—£6,000.

Two Communal Establishments have also been built. One for ladies who, earning their own livings, occupy their own apartments, as well as those used in commonalty. One for families, with separate flats, who organise co-operative service and take meals together.

Part of the Estate is built round an open space of 80 acres, and besides that there are woods, public gardens, playing grounds, spinneys, and sheltered seats which are enjoyed by all the tenants, whatever rents they pay.

Exceptional living conditions are provided here at a very nominal rent. The enterprise is not philanthropic but self-supporting.[69]

Several large employers of labor have built Garden Suburbs or Villages, primarily for their own employees. Where the residential community created by the proprietor of some large industry, near which it is located, is solely for the occupancy of the employees of that industry, it is sometimes distinguished by the term Garden Village instead of Garden Suburb. The first and best-known industrial garden community is Bournville, situated four miles from the heart of Birmingham, to which city it was recently annexed. It was begun in 1895 by Mr. George Cadbury, on a part of the site to which the Cadbury Brothers' Chocolate Works had been moved from a crowded district in Birmingham. About one-third of the houses are occupied by employees in these works, and the balance by people from the city at large. Although, therefore, the estate partakes somewhat of the character of a Garden Village, it is essentially a Garden Suburb, since it is open to persons generally. Also it is not an employer's enterprise in any narrow sense, like the cases of company housing cited earlier. The residential part of the estate now comprises nearly 1,000 acres and over 1,000 houses, occupied by about 5,500 people. The number of dwellings to the gross acre in different parts of the estate varies from seven to ten. Every dwelling has a garden. The entire residential estate, not including the works, was in 1900 turned over by Mr. Cadbury to a trust—the Bournville Village Trust. The specific aim set was that the houses should return 4 per cent on the capital invested. The Trust Deed enacts that, after making full provision for repairs and maintenance, the income shall be employed in laying out the

[69] Statement by the Hampstead Garden Suburb Trust, Ltd., Central Square, Hampstead Garden Suburb, London, N.W. 4. *Cf.* Edith Wood, *Housing of the Unskilled Wage Earner*, 1919, pp. 147-148; W. D. Cromarty, "English Garden Communities," *National Housing Conference*, 1920, VIII, 212-214; J. S. Nettlefold, *Practical Housing*, 1910, pp. 87-92.

Estate, building houses, and in purchasing other estates, either in the neighborhood of Birmingham or elsewhere, and in promoting housing reform. In pursuance of the last broad aim, the Trust has established a town-planning lectureship at the Birmingham University, and has aided toward the development of Letchworth and Hampstead Garden Suburb and other experiments in better housing.

The model village of Earswick, two and one-half miles from York and one mile from the Cocoa Works of Messrs. Rowntree and Co., Ltd., is another well-known example. The village had its genesis in the desire of Mr. Joseph Rowntree to make a practical contribution to the housing question. Like Mr. Cadbury, he was a Quaker and a cocoa manufacturer, and a benevolent type of employer. The essence of the experiment is the provision of a better house, and with it a garden in which the worker can enjoy a fuller and freer life. It was begun in 1904 with 120 acres and the provision that houses shall not occupy more than one-fourth of the sites on which they are built. An essential feature has been the development of a community of life and interest.

The classic English example of an employer's housing development, strictly for his own work people, is Port Sunlight, which was started in 1887. This Garden Village was built by Lord Leverhume, the soap manufacturer, adjacent to his factory in the outskirts of Liverpool. He had made architecture and building a lifelong hobby and firmly believed in the humanizing and refining influences of beautiful dwellings with healthy surroundings. There are about 140 acres in the village site and 90 reserved for the works. The village contains many hundred cottages of attractive appearance, occupied by the 3,000 or so employees of the company. The houses are rented at a price below what is necessary for an adequate return on the investment. The deficit is made up by the company, which regards this expenditure as one of its legitimate business expenses. Port Sunlight is the finest example of a Garden Village; there are probably a dozen or a score of less conspicuous examples in Great Britain. In Germany, Margarethenhöhe, on the outskirts of Essen, is a recent and beautiful example of the Garden Suburb. It is the fruit of an endowment fund set aside by one of the Krupps in honor of his daughter. It represents the best housing conditions that the Krupps, in their various endeavors, have provided for their employees.[70]

[70] Edith Wood, *Housing of the Unskilled Wage Earner*, 1919, pp. 117-119; *Housing Progress in Western Europe*, 1923, pp. 13-23. George Hooker, "Garden Cities," *National Housing Conference*, 1913, III, 17. W. Thompson, *Housing Up-to-Date*, 1907, pp. 221-230.

Garden Cities.—Unlike the Garden Suburb, which is attached as a residential section to an existing city, the Garden City is a self-contained community, in which provision is made for agriculture, industry and organized social life. It represents an attempt to solve the housing problem and relieve the congestion in crowded cities by an organized redistribution of the industrial population upon the land in new model towns, and by a concerted movement of manufacturers and others to some suitable site selected for the purpose. More inclusively, it is an effort to check the growth of big cities by prompting the creation of new towns, planned in advance to prevent congestion, voluntarily limited in size (usually to about 30,000), but containing all the essentials of complete community life—factories and business districts as well as dwellings, schools, and amusements.[71] An English definition is as follows: "A Garden City is a town planned for industry and healthy living; of a size that makes possible a full measure of social life, but not larger; surrounded by a permanent belt of rural land; the whole of the land being in public ownership or held in trust for the community."[72] Of the Garden City proper, fulfilling all the terms of the definition, there are at present only two examples in England, Letchworth and Welwyn.

The idea was conceived by Ebenezer Howard, who was born in England in 1850, the son of a baker and restaurant keeper. Upon reaching manhood he emigrated, largely for reasons of health, to Nebraska, where he took up farming. Later he moved to Chicago where he joined the staff of a firm of law stenographers. In 1876 he returned to England and became one of the official reporters for the House of Parliament. A few years later, greatly influenced by Edward Bellamy's book, *Looking Backward,* he was prompted to suggest a scheme of social reform, less ambitious and more practicable than that of reforming the universe. His plan was the building of a new town in which industrial, agricultural, and residential interests would be combined. The essence of his idea lies in the principle of beginning at the beginning. The whole city which is to be should be planned out from the outset with an eye to the convenience of the community as a whole. It is perhaps the most inclusive application of constructive city planning. Howard's idea for Garden Cities was developed and pre-

[71] Edith Wood, *Housing Progress in Western Europe*, 1923, p. 23. W. Thompson, *The Housing Handbook*, 1903, p. 187.

[72] C. B. Purdom, "Garden Cities," *The Survey*, May 1, 1925, 54:3:172. C. B. Purdom, *Town Theory and Practice*, 1921, p. 34. His definition, given above, has recently been adopted by the British Garden Cities and Town Planning Association. Edith Wood, *Housing Progress in Western Europe*, 1923, p. 24.

sented in a book called *Tomorrow*. This was in 1898. Later editions
were published under the title, *Garden Cities of Tomorrow*. Unlike
most Utopias, this one had foundations of solid reality. In 1899 the
Garden Cities Association was formed to promote the idea. In 1903
First Garden City, Ltd., was organized, and Letchworth was the
result.[73]

The Garden City of Letchworth, the pioneer attempt, is situated
34 miles from London. The general objects of the scheme, as explained
by Thomas Adams,[74] who was one of Howard's first collaborators,
were four in number.

1. The purchase of a large agricultural estate on which to establish an
industrial and residential town, principally by securing a concerted movement of manufacturers from crowded centers.
2. The restriction of the area set apart for urban development and the
permanent retention of the greater portion of the estate for agricultural
purposes.
3. The planning of the whole area in order to secure health, amenity,
convenience, and efficiency.
4. The limiting of the dividends to shareholders to 5 per cent per annum,
the balance of the profits to be used for the benefit of the town and its
inhabitants.

Despite the drawback of insufficient capital to start the enterprise
(the authorized capital was £300,000, of which £84,000 were subscribed at the start), much has been accomplished. Six square miles
of fine undulating farm lands, partially wooded, were purchased and
laid out, according to a town plan drawn up by Messrs. Parker and
Unwin, for a city that will have a maximum population of about
30,000 inhabitants. A population of about 14,000 is now living on an
area which consisted, in 1903, of bare cultivated fields. The city area
comprises about 1,200 acres; 2,600 acres of the original plot with an
additional 700 acres since acquired are reserved as a permanent agricultural belt around the city. Here farming is carried on and here
too are spaces reserved for golf, tennis, and other outdoor games.
About 150 factories and workshops are now established in the town.
There have been provided all the necessary appurtenances to community life: water works, gas works, electricity plant, sewage-disposal
system, railroad station, public buildings, hotels, parks, roads and

[73] George M. Harris, *The Garden City Movement*, 1906, p. 29. C. B. Purdom,
The Garden City, 1913, ch. II. Edith Wood, *Housing of the Unskilled Wage
Earner*, 1919, p. 147. *Housing*, June, 1928, 17:2:130-132.
[74] "House and Town Development in War Times," *National Housing Association*, Publication No. 49, June, 1918, pp. 7-8.

other utilities. Dividends of 5 per cent were first paid on the common stock in 1925; interest on bonds has been paid regularly from the start. Its financial position is now regarded as secure.[75]

Early in 1919, Ebenezer Howard, on his own responsibility and initiative, purchased an area of nearly four square miles as the site for the second experiment of this kind, Welwyn Garden City. In 1920, Welwyn Garden City, Ltd., was formed, with a capital of £250,000, and work upon the development was begun. It is planned for a population of 50,000 inhabitants. Unlike the case of Letchworth, the Welwyn experiment has been aided financially by the government, for the Housing Act of 1921 provided for loans for the development of Garden Cities. The government has lent between £250,000 and £300,000. The site of Welwyn Garden City, though only 21 miles from London, was in the midst of an almost inaccessible agricultural district. It had no water supply, drainage facilities, electricity or gas; it had few roads, and those in poor condition. At the end of 1930 Welwyn had a population of more than 7,500, with a modern railway station, many miles of newly built roads, industries, stores, a theatre, public schools, and playing fields.[76]

One unique feature in the development of Welwyn is what might be termed the industrial development of a community on the installment plan. "The great obstacle to the Garden City movement—as its founders recognized from the start and still recognize today—is the inertia and conservatism of industry, and the unwillingness of a well-established industry to pull up stakes and move from its existing location in a built-up community to a new community which has yet to prove itself. For this reason the industrial development of both Letchworth and Welwyn has naturally been slow, though Letchworth is now rapidly becoming an industrial community. A novel method of coping with this situation has been developed at Welwyn Garden City through the establishment of a series of what are termed 'sectional factories,' completed about a year ago and which have attracted much

[75] W. D. Cromarty, "English Garden Communities," *National Housing Conference*, 1920, VIII, 207-214. Edith Wood, *Housing Progress in Western Europe*, 1923, pp. 23-29. W. Thompson, *Housing Up-to-Date*, 1907, pp. 216-221. George Hooker, "Garden Cities," *National Housing Conference*, 1913, III, 16. Thomas Adams, "Housing and Social Reconstruction," *National Housing Conference*, 1918, VII, 29-30. George Vincent, "Housing and Reconstruction," *National Housing Conference*, 1918, VII, 44. George M. Harris, *The Garden City Movement*, 1906, pp. 57-68. A. R. Sennett, *Garden Cities in Theory and Practice*, 1905. C. B. Purdom, *The Garden City*, 1913 (well illustrated). *Housing*, Sept., 1928, 17:3:182.

[76] *Housing*, June, 1928, 17:2:134-139; Dec., 1930, 19:4:308. Edith Wood, *Housing Progress in Western Europe*, 1923, pp. 31-32.

attention. These permit the industrial development of a plant gradually and by installments. Several firms have already taken single sections of such factories with a view to future extension."[77] Although it is not likely that there will be a wholesale migration of industries to rural districts and small towns, there is nevertheless a definite tendency, as was pointed out earlier, for manufacturers to seek new sites for their works at a considerable distance from the crowded city, where they will find cheaper land, lower taxes, and other advantages. The Garden City plan is practicable in this respect. The decentralization of industry is a prerequisite to decentralization of residences, unless the worker is to spend much time and money in transportation. The worker in Letchworth lives within a few minutes' walk of his place of employment. "No costly transportation system takes him from a point 10 miles or so out in a suburb to a plant in the centre of the city requiring him to spend a couple of hours a day in going to and fro from his work."[78]

Perhaps the most novel and significant feature of the English Garden City idea is that of control of the land in perpetuity for the benefit of the people. The landlords of a Garden City are that body which has bought the land as a whole—a limited-liability company, in which the dividends to shareholders are restricted, usually to 5 per cent. If the company itself does not build, its chief income will be derived from rents for building leases and profits from enterprises carried on, such as furnishing water and electricity. The land is cheap to begin with; it is bought as a whole at agricultural value, and rises in value as population increases. In Letchworth, for example, the land was bought for $200 an acre; the value of it now has increased to $1,000 and $2,000 an acre. The company always maintains freehold in the land, which it will never part with unless it be to hand it over as a whole to the community itself. There is no individual private property in land; it is collectively owned. It may be leased for 99 years (in some instances for 999 years) with the right to renew at the end of that period subject to a revaluation. "It has been found that this system gives the practical feeling of ownership, while the important power to prevent misuse of the land by incongruous and undesirable development, is reserved to the trustees of the community." The profit realized by the company is

[77] *Housing*, June, 1928, 17:2:134.
[78] W. D. Cromarty, "English Garden Communities," *National Housing Conference*, 1920, VIII, 207-214.

retained for the benefit of the community after dividends of 5 per cent have been paid. It goes to the reduction of taxes or to the development of the estate and the provision of new public services. As the capital of the company is paid in, it will surrender its functions to the local government, in which case the community will be owned by the people. This is a device whereby the unearned increment goes to the benefit of the community which created it.[79]

In both Garden Cities and Suburbs, housing and other social conditions have been improved. Statistical studies show a startling difference in height and weight between Port Sunlight school children and those of the same age and economic stratum in Liverpool. The death-rate in these communities is lower than in the big cities. In 1921 in the Garden City of Letchworth the death-rate per 1,000 population was but 7.5, whereas in London it was 12.5. In 1922 the death-rate at Letchworth was 8.4 and in London 13.5. Similar discrepancies are to be observed in the infant mortality rates. In Letchworth in 1921 the infantile death-rate was 54.8 and in London 81. In the following year at Letchworth this death-rate was 66 and in London 75. Again, in Bournville the infant mortality rate was 54 in the year 1922 as contrasted with 77 in Birmingham. The general death-rate in Bournville for the same year was 8.3 as contrasted with 12.1 in Birmingham. To be sure, so many factors enter into both the death-rate and birth-rate that such evidence is not strictly scientific or conclusive, and the two types of communities are not entirely comparable, but the wide discrepancy between the rates may support what observation and examination of conditions attest, that living conditions are superior in the garden communities.[80]

The Garden City movement in England received great impetus from the unqualified endorsement given to it by Neville Chamberlain, when Minister of Health, and through the Housing Act of 1921 which permitted the government to aid such enterprises financially. Other Garden Cities are now being projected.[81] Ebenezer Howard was knighted in 1927, a year before he died. On this occasion George Bernard Shaw remarked: "Howard should have received a Knight-

[79] W. D. Cromarty, "English Garden Communities," *National Housing Conference*, 1920, VIII, 209, 210 (quoted). George M. Harris, *The Garden City Movement*, 1906, pp. 32-35. H. F. Burns, "Is America Ready for the Garden City?" *National Housing Conference*, 1920, VIII, 215-222.

[80] Lawrence Veiller, *Housing Reform*, 1910, p. 23. Edith Wood, *Housing Progress in Western Europe*, 1923, pp. 22-23. *Housing Betterment*, May, 1925, 14:2:-152. *Housing*, March, 1929, 18:1:41.

[81] *Housing Betterment*, May, 1925, 14:2:119. *Housing*, Mar., 1930, 19:1:31-33.

hood for his books, a Barony for Letchworth, and a Dukedom for Welwyn."[82]

The garden community idea has spread from England to the Continent, particularly to France and Germany, and to the United States, although for the most part it has been restricted to Garden Villages or Suburbs. A real Garden City, embodying all the essential features of the English plan, was established in France for the first time in 1926; it is located three miles northeast of Paris.[83] In the United States there are a number of Garden Suburbs, a recent example being Mariemont, built in 1927 on the outskirts of Cincinnati.[84] Although a Garden City experiment is desirable and probably practicable in America, it would be harder to create a Garden City here than in England. Our population lacks the homogeneity which simplifies the building up of a new community; the number and variety of races would create obstacles. In England the popularity of the coöperative store and the familiarity of the man in the street with coöperative methods have been of great advantage. Building on rented ground is foreign to our habits, and community ownership of land would probably be difficult to apply here.[85]

As an experiment in housing and town-planning, in the limitation of the number of dwellings to the acre, in health, in the practicability of a slumless city, Letchworth and Welwyn have proved their case, and their influence on housing standards has been great. As a sociological experiment in drawing the surplus population from big cities and in voluntarily limiting the size of the cities to be created, they still have their case to prove. Neither city has anywhere near reached its limit of growth. What will happen when one of them does? The development of regional planning may furnish an escape from the difficulty. Or, as Mrs. Edith Wood,[86] a leading housing authority, remarks, "if it should turn out that a self-limiting town proves unable to limit itself—well, in that case the formula will have to be recast.

[82] *Housing Betterment*, July, 1927, 16:2:120.
[83] *Housing Betterment*, March, 1926, 15:1:1-2; Dec., 1927, 16:4:299-300.
[84] Bleecker Marquette, "Mariemont, An American Garden Village," *National Municipal Review*, May, 1927, 16:5:296-301.
[85] Alexander M. Bing, "Can We Have Garden Cities in America?" *The Survey*, May 1, 1925, 54:3:190. Edith Wood, *Housing Progress in Western Europe*, 1923, p. 29. Edith Wood, *Housing of the Unskilled Wage Earner*, 1919, pp. 105-109. Lawrence Veiller, "Housing Progress of the Year," *National Housing Conference*, 1918, VII, 404. C. H. Williams, "How to Get Garden Suburbs in America," *National Housing Conference*, 1916, V, 107-110. *Housing Betterment*, Sept., 1919, 26 ff.
[86] *Housing Progress in Western Europe*, 1923, pp. 30-31.

Meanwhile the world is under an obligation to the British group who are trying it out."

5. CO-PARTNERSHIP TENANT SOCIETIES

Linked up with the Garden-City and town-planning movements in England is that of co-partnership in housing. This is founded on the thoroughly sound principle of mutual self-help. Coöperation has already achieved marvelous results in the production and distribution of all sorts of commodities for general consumption. Why not apply the same principle to house-building and home-ownership? There are many ways by which a man with small means is enabled to build a house for himself and gradually pay for it; an important method will be discussed in the next section. But there are also a number of disadvantages to individual ownership. Moreover, in house purchase, as in other business, collective operations are much more economical than individual action; it is just the difference between buying wholesale and retail. The advantages of joint action and collective ownership may be secured through coöperative housing societies.

The first step to be taken after the formation of such a society (in England they are registered and controlled under the Industrial and Provident Societies Acts as "public utility societies") is to secure an option to purchase or lease suitable land on the outskirts of an industrial center. The land is then planned as a whole in accordance with the hygienic, artistic, and economic principles of town planning. Thus the project may lead to a Garden Suburb, or land for building purposes may be leased in a Garden City. For example, one of these coöperative societies, the Hampstead Tenants, has constructed a number of houses in Hampstead Garden Suburb; and another, the Garden City Tenants, has done the same in Letchworth Garden City. The necessary capital is obtained chiefly through the sale of common stock (shares), the issuance of bonds (loan stock), and the flotation of mortgages. The latter two must be relied upon for the major portion of the capital at the start of the project. The loan capital has a prior claim to the assets of the society. The dividend on share capital is limited to 5 per cent. Also, a limit is placed on the number of shares which an individual may own. Payment may be made in any case on the installment plan. Surplus profits are applied in furthering the objects of the society and in the payment of a bonus to the tenants of the society, who are also shareholders. The division of profits among the tenant-members is in proportion to the rents paid by them. Each tenant-member's portion of the profits is credited to him in shares until his share capital equals the value of the house in which he lives, when it is paid in cash. The system solves the question of unearned increment without the slightest unfairness to any individual. The surplus profits due to unearned increment go to the tenant-members of the society in the shape of increased bonuses on their rentals. The tenants as a whole can gradually relieve themselves altogether of dependence on outside capital by accumulation of their own savings. It thus lies with the tenants to transfer the ownership from non-tenant shareholders, who take the main risk to begin with, to the tenant shareholders who may become, it is to be hoped, the ultimate owners. Each society is managed by a committee elected by the shareholders on the lines usually adopted by industrial and provident societies.[87]

Co-partnership housing has many advantages. It offers the tenant permanent occupancy on fair terms. The capital for building his house is provided at a cheaper rate than it could be obtained on any other system that is commercially sound. Should values go up, he gets the benefit, either by way of a dividend on his rent or by paying a rental that is below the market value. The unity of the neighborhood or town, whatever the development may be, is retained without paternalism or loss of sense of ownership. The tenant-member has the advantages of home-ownership without its disadvantages. Under this system the mobility of labor is not discouraged, for the system, in combining group-ownership with control of his own house by each occupier, affords some guarantee that the individual can retire from the district without incurring serious loss, such as would come from a sacrifice sale under individual ownership. When a member leaves the neighborhood, the society, not the tenant shareholder, possibly has a house on its hands. The tenant of the house has his shares in the society equal in value to the value of his house, which he can, if he likes, realize without any loss; or if he leaves his savings where they are, he will receive his interest as usual.

No tenant is in danger of having his property injured by the careless and untidy way in which his neighbor's house is kept. No member can say, "This house is mine." They can all say, "These houses are ours." One of the results of this is that public opinion on the estate is far too strong in favor of cleanliness and order for it to be possible that any tenant should neglect his house and garden, without being called to order by his partners. The co-partnership societies give

[87] J. S. Nettlefold, *Practical Housing*, 1910, pp. 129-132, 138, 152. W. Thompson, *Housing Up-to-Date*, 1907, pp. 210, 215.

the poorer classes an opportunity of gradually acquiring the value of the house they live in on easy terms, and at the same time guard them against all risks. Finally, it may be noted that under this plan there is complete merging of the interests of landlord and tenant.[88]

In England, Ealing Tenants, Ltd., built in 1901 the pioneer co-partnership village. Today there are over eighty coöperative tenancy societies of the limited-dividend, non-commercial type. Some of them are creating Garden Suburbs. One British company of co-partnership tenants in nine years increased its assets from $250,000 to $30,000,-000.[89] Many of the individual societies all over the country have joined Co-partnership Tenants Limited, which is a federation of branch societies, established in 1907, with headquarters in London. Coöperative housing societies are operating in Belgium, Holland, France, Italy, Spain, and Switzerland.[90] In the United States the only examples are the application of coöperative ownership to the purchase of moderate-priced apartments, such as the Jackson Heights plan in New York City, and the demonstration being made by Mr. John D. Rockefeller, Jr., in the case of the apartment house which he recently built in the Bronx.

In the first-mentioned American example, the advantages cited are as follows.[91]

1. A tenant-owner is protected against an increase of rent.

2. He obtains in semi-annual dividends all earnings above the actual fixed charges and operating costs of the building, which is estimated at 7 per cent on the amount he invests in the building.

3. He is protected against undesirable neighbors because he is a director of his own corporation and has a voice with the agent in their selection, and because the leases of the apartments are not assignable without the consent of the corporation and its agent. The tenant-owner may surrender the lease of his apartment at the end of any year on proper notice and still retain his investment in the building.

[88] J. S. Nettlefold, *Practical Housing*, 1910, pp. 127-129. Sydney J. Chapman, *Work and Wages*, 1914, III, 66-69. George Hooker, "Garden Cities," *National Housing Conference*, 1913, III, 26. A. C. Comey, "Co-partnership for Housing in America," *Annals*, Jan., 1914, 51:140:140-147. A. C. Comey, "Co-operative Housing," *National Housing Conference*, 1913, III, 29-36.

[89] Arthur Gleason, "The Lack of Houses: Remedies," *The Nation*, Aug. 24, 1920, 110:2860:548. Edith Wood, *Housing of the Unskilled Wage Earner*, 1919, pp. 147-148.

[90] Edith Wood, *Housing Progress in Western Europe*, 1923, pp. 84-88 *et passim*. International Labour Office, *European Housing Problems Since the War*, 1924, pp. 175-177, 210, 262, 394-396, 468-470.

[91] E. A. MacDougall, "Co-operative Housing," *National Housing Conference*, 1920, VIII, 46-55.

The Rockefeller experiment, which was begun in 1927, follows more closely the English co-partnership plan. The group of buildings, known as the Thomas Garden Apartments, covers one entire block; it contains apartments for 166 families and is said to have cost $1,-450,000. In this group of buildings, only stockholders may be tenants and only tenants may be stockholders. The amount of stock offered to each tenant is determined by the size of the apartment chosen. Payments are to be made over a term extending for twenty-five years or more. Owners of stock who desire to withdraw must offer their stock at par to the corporation, which will pay for it and sell it again to other prospective tenants. No tenant will be permitted to sub-let his apartment or assign his lease. In the event of a stockholder's death, his lease terminates and his stock is purchased by the corporation; but if his family desires to continue to live in the building, they have the first right to re-purchase the stock. In this connection, the corporation has announced that it has made an arrangement with a life insurance company to insure the lives of stock owners so that their families, in the event of the wage-earner's death, will be certain to be in a position to buy this interest for themselves. Mr. Rockefeller advanced the working capital for the corporation in return for preferred stock maturing in fifteen years; when this stock is retired, the building will be turned over to the tenants.[92]

6. HOUSING BY BUILDING AND LOAN ASSOCIATIONS

Among the more important influences on housing in America are the coöperative savings and lending societies known as building and loan associations. Their principal functions are twofold: First, they promote thrift by teaching economy in the saving of small sums of money in periodic installments. This is effected by the collection of dues or assessments, applying to the purchase of shares. Secondly, they encourage the ownership of homes by lending money for that purpose, making the interest and principal payable in small monthly installments spread over a long period of time. As Samuel Stern,[93] secretary of nine building and loan associations in Philadelphia, states, they differ from banks, trust companies and most other financial institutions in four principal ways.

First, they operate at a very much lower expense.

Second, their profits are divided mutually and equally among all their depositors who are also their shareholders.

[92] *Housing Betterment*, July, 1927, 16:2:128-131.
[93] "How Building and Loan Associations Can Aid Housing," *National Housing Conference*, 1923, IX, 118-120.

Third, only part of their receipts are applicable for withdrawals, thereby eliminating any possible so-called run on the bank.

And fourth—and this is the most important of all—all their funds available for investment purposes are used to make loans on mortgages.

The first building and loan association was organized in Philadelphia in 1831. At the present time more than 10,000 such associations are scattered throughout the United States, with assets of over eight billion dollars and with a membership of more than five million persons. They do a business of about a billion dollars annually. Their system of selling shares on which payments must be made weekly or monthly has proved an invaluable aid to hundreds of thousands of future home-buyers in accumulating savings and furnishing a sound and helpful scheme for paying off the principal of loans. Through careful administration and the practice of the amortization plan, in which they were the pioneers, loss is practically unknown. The cost of their operations is said to be about 0.75 per cent. The basic rate of interest, with few exceptions, is 6 per cent, and the completion of the payment period is sixteen and one-half years. The cost to the borrower is little more than the rental price of the mortgaged property for the same period; hence it is sometimes said by those who get homes with the help of a building and loan association that "the rent pays for the place."[94]

Dr. Wood[95] states in reference to this institution that "among skilled workers, clerks, book-keepers, teachers and other poorly paid professional groups, it has filled a large want in an acceptable way and certainly should disprove the often repeated statement that Americans are too individualistic to succeed in coöperative enterprises." She adds that although the system is useful for those of moderate means, it is out of the reach of the unskilled wage-earner, although it offers an instrumentality which, with government aid in the form of loans, might well be adapted to fit the needs of that group. The amount of lending capacity of these associations is limited to the weekly or monthly receipts from the savings of their members. Several bills have been introduced in Congress to permit them to borrow on their mortgages and thus make available larger sums for home building. If any plan of government aid in housing (the subject is discussed below) is developed in this country, it will undoubtedly

[94] F. T. Miller, *Housing Situation in England and the United States*, 1920, pp. 28-29. Charles Gide, *Principles of Political Economy*, 1903, pp. 397-398. Samuel Stern, "How Building and Loan Associations Can Aid Housing," *National Housing Conference*, 1923, IX, 119. *Housing*, March, 1931, 20:1:44-46.
[95] *Housing of the Unskilled Wage Earner*, 1919, pp. 233-234.

function in part through these associations. Their possibilities for usefulness should not be overlooked by the student of housing.[96]

7. TAXATION OF LAND VALUES AND ITS EFFECT ON HOUSING

A basic reason for the congestion of cities is the high cost of land. High land values, as was pointed out when discussing the causes of the housing problem, mean multiple dwellings and high rents. These result in overcrowding and inadequate housing. The larger the city, the more pronounced is this effect. Increase of population leads to greater demands on land and thus an increase of land values. This increment goes not to the people who produced it but to the land speculator and land owner. It is unearned, for it is not due, except in a slight degree, to the labor and care of the possessors. Many great unearned incomes have arisen out of land ownership.[97] A similar relationship exists between public improvements and land values. Suppose, for example, that a city builds a subway to distribute the population over a wider area. This provision of transit service raises the demand for land within easy reach of its stations, and thus leads to an increase in the value of the land. The increment, which is the result of the action of the community in building the subway and in making use of this new territory for residential purposes, goes to the land owners and speculators. It is charged as part of the cost of the house, either as rent or selling price.[98] There is no question that the community is chiefly responsible for increases in land values. Why, therefore, should not the community appropriate such values? This has been done in part by Germany and England through a tax upon the increase in the value of land.

Under the so-called "single tax," it is proposed to place the entire burden of taxation upon land alone, that is, on the site value of land, leaving buildings and personal property to go untaxed altogether. The tax is called single, because it is expected that so much revenue would be secured for the public as to enable all other levies to be dispensed with. Some single taxers, it may be noted parenthetically, have somewhat different views. Some would take only enough of the annual rent of the land to supply the needs of government, and others

[96] Charles Hennessy, "A Proposed Federal Building-Loan Bank System," *National Housing Conference*, 1920, VIII, 28-34. Edith Wood, *Housing of the Unskilled Wage Earner*, 1919, pp. 234, 268, 269.

[97] F. W. Taussig, *Principles of Economics*, 1921, II, 104-106.

[98] Lewis, Heydecker and O'Hara, *Land Values*, 1927, pp. 32-33. *Report of the Reconstruction Commission on Housing Conditions, New York*, 1920, pp. 39-40.

say that their doctrines do not necessarily exclude other taxes.[99] Substantially the same result would be attained if the community were to take possession of the land once for all and never part with the title, but lease the land to tenants for the amount of its rent. This principle of community ownership and control we have seen applied in the case of the English Garden Cities and the co-partnership tenant societies. The single-tax plan has many implications; it involves broad questions of basic economic policy; and difficulties would arise in determining a practical method of appropriation and assessment.[100] We are here concerned solely with its relation to the housing problem. It is important to consider, because the taxation of land values and the exemption of houses and improvements are being proposed in a number of states as a solution of the housing problem.

It is argued that if the community took the unearned increment in the form of a heavy tax on land values, or the full rental value of land exclusive of improvements and other products of labor, house rent would be cheaper, home-ownership would be promoted, and housing conditions would be improved. These beneficial results would occur in the following way. The effect of such a reform in taxation would be to stimulate building by forcing unoccupied land, favorably situated, into its most profitable use. Its advocates say that "the single tax would put an end to the holding of vacant land for speculative increases in value, as no one could afford to pay a heavy tax on land from which he was getting no revenue, especially as the tax would increase from year to year with the appreciation of the site value of the land, and wholly irrespective of the owner's expenditures for improvements."[101] The increase in the available supply and the reduction in the price of land which would result from forcing land into use would greatly reduce the cost of housing accommodation and increase its amount. The exemption of buildings and other improvements from taxation, which is involved in the program, would still further reduce the cost of housing. It is an accepted principle of economics that taxes on land, as for instance an urban site, rest definitely on the owner, whereas taxes on buildings tend to be shifted to the occupier. If the owner is also the occupier, the principle is the same; the burden must

[99] Herbert B. Dorau and Albert G. Hinman, *Urban Land Economics*, 1928, p. 373.

[100] Herbert B. Dorau and Albert G. Hinman, *Urban Land Economics*, 1928, pp. 348-378.

[101] Delos F. Wilcox, "Taxation of Real Estate Values and its Effect on Housing," *Annals of the American Academy of Political and Social Science*, Jan., 1914, 51:140:34. *Cf.* Joseph Fels, "Taxation, Housing and Town Planning," *The American City*, Nov., 1913, 9:5:425-427.

be borne by him.[102] To abolish altogether taxes on houses and improvements, as has been done in some Canadian cities, will therefore operate to lower rents for tenants and reduce expenses for homeowners. The shifting of taxation from improvements to land values encourages building operations and stimulates the use of land. There is no fear in the minds of the owners of being penalized for improvements. Where the value of the house far exceeds the value of the land, which is the usual case with one- and two-family dwellings, the reduction in the cost of housing is considerable. In districts such as unsanitary areas, in which the value of the land far exceeds the value of improvements on the land, the application of a heavy tax on land values would have a marked effect on housing conditions and would be the cheapest way in which the city could deal with the district. "If the tax were taken off the buildings within such a district, and the entire tax levied upon the land, the owners of this property would find it unprofitable to hold their land in its present wretched state. If the entire tax of the city were levied upon land values, the owners of all property that is improved would find their taxes reduced, but the holders of vacant land or of land uneconomically developed would be confronted with the necessity of building or of selling to some individual who would be willing to build."[103] If the complete single-tax program is not adopted, at least much may be said in favor of taxation which totally or partially exempts improvements. An example is furnished in the New York law which exempts new dwelling construction. This is discussed in the next section. It appears to be demonstrated that lower taxation on houses acts as an encouragement to building.[104]

There seems to be no question that taxation of land values could be used to stimulate, within certain limits, the building of houses, but as Professor Wilcox[105] points out, satisfactory results from the housing standpoint cannot be expected unless the single-tax scheme is supplemented by a comprehensive city plan and drastic public regulation of housing construction. "It is obvious that any force tending to close the open spaces and make a city compactly built must have

[102] F. W. Taussig, *Principles of Economics*, 1921, II, 539 ff.; this statement is qualified somewhat by Herbert B. Dorau and Albert G. Hinman, *Urban Land Economics*, 1928, p. 360.

[103] James Ford, "Some Fundamentals of Housing Reform," *The American City*, May, 1913, 8:5:475-476.

[104] Herbert B. Dorau and Albert Hinman, *Urban Land Economics*, 1928, pp. 372-373. Frederic C. Howe, *The Modern City*, 1915, pp. 282-287.

[105] "Taxation of Real Estate Values and its Effect on Housing," *Annals*, Jan., 1914, 51:140:38.

a fundamental effect on housing. Apparently, the adoption of the single-tax would throw upon the community as an organized unit of self-government the entire responsibility for the reservation of open spaces for all purposes. The natural tendency, so far as the private holder of land was concerned, would be to build as intensively as possible on the site controlled by him. Without a city plan and government regulation, this would mean high buildings, buildings covering the entire ground space, no parks or open squares and streets narrowed down toward the vanishing point. Obviously, these tendencies, if unchecked, would bring about the worst possible housing conditions." On the other hand, with more land made available for housing purposes and its price less, it may be argued that people will find it easier to have gardens and open spaces than under the present conditions of monopoly and high prices.[106] In any case, there should be coupled with the proposed adoption of the single tax as a social program a comprehensive scheme of city planning and community regulation.

8. GOVERNMENT AID IN HOUSING

The housing problem is two-fold in character: it has positive and negative, or constructive and restrictive sides. "In this two-fold aspect of the housing problem lies the reason for the two types of housing law which have been developed: (1) the constructive type, which aims to increase the supply of good houses, and (2) the restrictive, which aims to prevent the erection or the maintenance of bad houses. There ought to be no quarrel between them or their advocates. Both are essential to a well-rounded housing policy. The housing problem will never be solved without the aid of both."[107] The restrictive type of housing law is characteristic of the United States; it implies that houses will be built by private capital under regulations and restrictions laid down in housing laws. The constructive type of legislation is typical of European countries; it involves state intervention in a positive way to promote the erection of low-cost and sanitary dwellings for wage-earners. There are thus two schools of thought in regard to housing—the private-initiative group and the state-action group. In Europe, the former system was commonly followed until it was shown that private initiative and enterprise would not furnish a sufficient supply of wholesome homes for the people; the

[106] Joseph Fels, "Taxation, Housing and Town Planning," *The American City*, Nov., 1913, 9:5:427.
[107] Edith Wood, *Housing of the Unskilled Wage Earner*, 1919, pp. 18-19.

governments then undertook to stimulate or supplement the production of working-people's dwellings.

Most European countries, and Canada, Australia, and New Zealand as well, have, as the result of investigation and study, enacted legislation providing for government aid in one form or another for the better housing of the working people.[108] The method of granting this government aid differs greatly in detail in various countries, but the form in which aid is given is of three main classes:

1. Building directly for rental or sale.
   (a) For the government's own employees;
   (b) For working people generally.

2. Making loans of public funds (including also government guaranty of loans) to:
   (a) Local authorities;
   (b) Non-commercial building associations;
   (c) Employers;
   (d) Individuals.

3. Granting exemptions from or concessions in taxes or fees, or granting some other form of subsidy to building associations or others.

The agencies are either national, state or provincial, or municipal governments. The first type of aid is direct, the second two are indirect. It should be noted that classed under the loans of public funds are the loans which have been made of the funds of the state accident and sickness insurance associations in Austria and of the funds of the invalidity and old-age insurance institutes in France and Germany. These loans in Germany represent a most important financial aid to housing, having reached a total of over $100,000,000. By these various methods, European countries have expended millions of public funds to aid in the erection of low-cost and sanitary dwellings for wage-earners. "Most important among these methods of aid is that of loans to public-welfare building associations. These are associations in which the dividends which may be paid to the stockholders are limited

[108] *Government Aid to Home Owning and Housing of Working People in Foreign Countries*, U. S. Bureau of Labor Statistics Bulletin No. 158, 1915, pp. 10 ff. (11-12 quoted below). *Homesteads for Workingmen*, Massachusetts Bureau of Statistics, Labor Bulletin No. 88 1912. Massachusetts Homestead Commission, *2nd Annual Report*, 1914, Public Document No. 103, pp. 8, 130-144. Edith Wood, *Housing Progress in Western Europe*, 1923. Alfred Buckley, "Government Housing in Canada," *National Municipal Review*, Aug., 1920, 9:8:482-483. George B. Ford, "Housing in France," *National Housing Conference*, 1920, VIII, 141-152. Frederic C. Howe, *The Modern City*, 1915, ch. XX. *Housing Betterment*, June, 1919, 8:2:48-51. *Housing*, Oct., 1931, 20:3:187-228.

usually to 4 or at most 5 per cent on the paid-up capital. In many
cases it is also required that upon the dissolution of the association
any surplus which may exist shall not be divided among the stockholders but must go to some specified public purpose. In continental
European countries, where building associations operating under the
various housing laws have attained the greatest growth, as in Belgium, France, Germany, Italy, and Austria, their operations are
hedged about by many regulations and restrictions whose principal
objects are to safeguard the security of the capital and to see that
all the dwellings erected with the funds advanced are of a kind designed to carry out the purposes of the law and that they are so
managed that their benefits will be received by the class of persons
intended to be served."

The Housing Crisis Caused by the War.—The World War gave
a new aspect to the housing problem in European countries and led
to further government intervention. Even before the War there was
in some countries an actual numerical shortage of small dwellings.
This increased as the rise in prices due to general economic conditions
led to a rise in building costs. A good deal of housing accommodation
was absorbed by the transformation of the centers of large towns
into business quarters, and the erection of factories in the outlying
districts created a fresh demand. In general, therefore, the outbreak
of war came at a period when housing accommodation was becoming
increasingly inadequate, in spite of all efforts for improvement. It
precipitated the crisis, increased its intensity, and gave it the specific
form which makes it one of the most serious social and economic
problems of the present day.

The War profoundly affected both the demand for housing accommodation and the supply. The demand was increased by the movements of population. Refugees from the devastated areas flocked in
large numbers into the towns in the interior which had not been
affected by invasion. In addition to this, the rapid development of
war industries brought numbers of agricultural workers into the
towns and industrial districts. In this way there arose, even during
the second half of the war, a general housing shortage which could
be neither relieved nor removed, owing to the cessation of building.

The disastrous stagnation of the building industry was due to a variety
of causes, all intimately connected with the prosecution of the war. Large
numbers of building workers were called up for military service, and, as the
industry was not directly connected with the war, few were at first ex-

empted. Large quantities of building material were utilised for war purposes; some were regarded as indispensable for military purposes in certain countries, and were placed under government control. Some governments actually prohibited building in order to prevent the diversion of labour and materials from war purposes.

The building industry suffered even more severely from loss of capital than from loss of labour and materials. Capital was attracted to the war industries, which were working at full pressure and making large profits, especially when, as the war went on, the small returns which could be obtained from house property became insecure. Even in the early days of the war the special exemptions allowed in favour of tenants who were called up for military service considerably limited the obligation to pay rent. House building thus ceased to attract capital, and in face of the numerous difficulties which had to be met the supply of houses soon became inadequate.

But it was the movements of population which took place after the close of hostilities which rapidly increased the threatened housing shortage to the dimensions of a catastrophe. "The return of the soldiers, and then of the prisoners of war and interned civilians, led to a rapid increase in the number of persons who wished to have homes to return to or to set up a household. The changes brought about by the Peace Treaties and the formation of new countries led to further movements among some sections of the population, some of whom emigrated voluntarily, while others were expelled. Numbers of refugees came westward from the eastern European countries which were under Bolshevist control. An additional factor was the sudden increase in the number of marriages—a natural phenomenon of recovery which has been noted after every war. By 1920 the marriage rate had in many countries risen to nearly double the pre-war figure. On the other hand, the agricultural workers who had found urban employment in the war industries showed no immediate tendency to return, while families of refugees from the devastated areas only gradually returned to their homes as the work of reconstruction progressed." The size of the reconstruction problem was enormous. In the devastated areas about 300,000 houses had been entirely destroyed and more than 400,000 had been damaged.

In Belgium the number of dwellings required at the end of the war was estimated at from 90,000 to 240,000; in Great Britain the estimates ranged from half a million to a million; in Germany figures as high as one and one-half million have been quoted. In fact, the estimates were everywhere enormous. In view of the general economic situation it was not to be expected that such an immense shortage, which was, moreover, automatically increasing every day, could even approximately be made up in the near future. The necessary economic resources were lacking, and the resumption of building in particular was impeded by special difficulties. It is only necessary to mention the lack of building workers, the scarcity of materials, and the transport difficulties of the early post-war period, and in addition the general shortage of capital and the tendency to invest such capital as was available elsewhere than in building. Another great difficulty was the rise in prices and wages, which sent up building costs to an unprecedented extent, although it was assumed that after the post-war boom they would fall again.

If building was to be resumed at all, it was clear that the public authorities must intervene; and this they did in all countries.[109]

(a) Direct Government Aid

A permanent phase of the housing problem is the housing of the lowest-paid workers. Houses for them have never been built by private initiative, because it does not pay; they take the houses that have been abandoned by the better-paid workers. For example, a New York State Commission which investigated housing conditions reported: "It is economically unprofitable now, it has been economically impossible for many years past to provide a large part of the population of this State with decent homes according to American standards of living. Decent homes and wholesome environments in which to bring up children cost more than most workers can afford. . . . Houses for the lowest paid wage earners have *never* been built in the State of New York."[110] This has been the experience both abroad and in America. In Europe it has led to government aid in housing. When the government undertakes to build houses for the unskilled wage earners it, too, must do it at a loss.[111] But it may secure indirect gains in other respects.

[109] International Labour Office, *European Housing Problems since the War*, 1924, pp. 7-8 (quoted), 10-11 (quoted), 15, 151.
[110] *Report of the Reconstruction Commission on Housing Conditions, New York*, 1920, pp. 4, 45.
[111] The City of Vienna, under its Socialist government, has become the greatest and the best landlord of the municipality. Its apartment houses are extraordinarily attractive and model in every respect. The rents are so low that they do not include any return on the invested capital. The construction of residences is financed from current taxes, the amount of expenditure from 1925 through 1930 averaging $13,000,000 a year. Ernest L. Harris, "Workingmen's Housing in Vienna," *Monthly Labor Review*, May, 1931, 32:5:6-16. Dorothy Thompson, "Palaces for the Poor," New York *Herald Tribune*, May 17, 1931.

The Case of Great Britain.—Take the case of Great Britain which has set the highest housing standard for her working classes, and done the most to realize it, of any nation in the world. There are two main reasons why Great Britain has developed her housing program. The first is in the interest of public health. The nation has long been concerned over matters of national vitality, and the results of the medical examinations held under the Compulsory Service Acts showed a large percentage of the men of military age to be unfit for military service. This condition is attributed in part to inadequate housing conditions. The question of "slum clearance" and the rebuilding of the areas with modern sanitary structures has always been approached from the public-health standpoint. It is significant that the Housing Acts of Great Britain are administered by the Ministry of Health. Great Britain has demolished her slums with a ruthless hand. Millions have been spent in the endeavor for which there has not been nor will there be full return financially. The original cost of the land and destruction of the insanitary houses is either prohibitive or places too heavy an initial charge upon the undertaking, and it has been found impossible to build municipal tenements on the same area to house healthfully as many persons as were dishoused by the slum clearance scheme.[112]

But although slum clearance is costly, to leave the slums untouched is costlier. "How foolish we have been," comments Veiller,[113] "not to realize that we pay the cost anyhow, only in a different way. Instead of increasing the tax rate to pay the interest on bond issues to acquire slum property, we pay annual taxes to maintain hospitals, prisons, reformatories, police and all the intricate mechanism of modern municipal government, much of which is necessitated by the very slum that we hesitate to destroy. This is no fanciful view. Wherever slums have been cleared out the death rate, the sickness rate, the crime rate, the immorality rate, have immediately and permanently decreased. So, if we must pay the cost of getting rid of the slum in any event, how much better to grapple with the problem in a way that will produce not merely negative results, but positive ones." In some of the slum

---

[112] James Ford, "Some Fundamentals of Housing Reform," *The American City*, May, 1913, 8:5:475. Thomas Adams, "Housing and Social Reconstruction," *National Housing Conference*, 1918, VII, 18-20. U. S. Bureau of Labor Statistics, Bulletin No. 158, 1915, pp. 295-303. F. E. Fremantle, *The Housing of the Nation*, 1927, ch. IV. *Housing*, June, 1931, 20:2:90-96.

[113] "Slumless America," *National Municipal Review*, August, 1920, 9:8:496. *Cf.* C. E. Morrow and C. Herrick, "Blighted Districts," *City Planning*, Oct., 1925, 1:3:160-172.

areas of Liverpool which have been the subject of clearance schemes and where the displaced tenants have been rehoused upon the same areas, a death-rate ranging from 40 to 60 per thousand has, by the improved sanitary conditions brought about, been reduced by more than one-half. Similar results may be found in other cities.[114]

A second main reason why Great Britain has engaged so extensively in a housing program is political. The stability of a nation and its industrial efficiency rest in large part on the manner in which the people are housed. Since housing is so basic to general social conditions, questions of the supply, standard, and cost of dwellings are matters of national importance. The government has a direct interest in the adequate housing of the people. When the Housing Act of 1919 was being considered by the Lloyd George Coalition Government, the Prime Minister declared that nothing so contributed to social and industrial unrest as the housing problem. In 1924, John Wheatley, then Minister of Health, stated with reference to the housing situation in England that they were drifting, largely as the result of a shortage of suitable dwellings for wage-earners, into conditions under which it was impossible to produce or maintain an efficient industrial population; and without an efficient industrial population it would be impossible in the future for Great Britain to remain great in the competition which it would have to meet amongst the industrial nations of the world.[115]

The British Housing Act of 1919, which is the basis of the present system, required both town-planning and housing schemes to be prepared for their areas by the local authorities and submitted to the Ministry of Health for approval. The housing plans were to provide for the building, as soon as possible, of the number of houses needed in their districts to house the working classes. Financial assistance was to be given by the national treasury to meet any deficit resulting from a housing scheme beyond the product of a penny rate. A penny rate is a local tax of one penny on every pound, assessed on rental value. It is a very small contribution. Since then, different acts have fixed the amount of subsidy per annum per house to local authorities, to meet the loss which they might incur in building the houses, and also a flat subsidy to private builders as well as a subsidy on slum-clearance schemes. The law relating to housing was consolidated by

---

[114] *Government Aid to Home Owning and Housing of Working People in Foreign Countries*, U. S. Bureau of Labor Statistics Bulletin No. 158, 1915, pp. 12-13. *Housing*, June, 1931, 20:2:96.

[115] *Housing Betterment*, May, 1924, 13:2:132-133.

the Housing Act of 1925. The annual burden upon the taxpayers is about $100,000,000 a year.[116]

Despite red tape and other difficulties, the following has been accomplished. Over a million new houses (1,102,387 up to March 31, 1928) have been erected in England and Wales since the Armistice. Of these dwellings, 723,869 were built with state assistance, and 378,-518 were built without any assistance from the state. Of the total number of new houses, 690,586 were erected by private builders. The housing activities of the London County Council, the governmental body having control over the greater part of that huge metropolitan center known as London, have been especially noteworthy during this period. It is the leading exemplar of government housing in practice to be found anywhere in the world. It also illustrates how far a community may be led when once embarked upon the policy of government housing. Since 1918, this body has spent nearly ninety million dollars in building houses and has loaned another thirteen millions to enable people to buy or to build their own houses. "In this short period of less than 10 years the London County Council has provided 37,000 new dwellings—accommodations for a good-sized city. When all the existing schemes that are now arranged for are completed, without taking into account any additional projects which may be developed in the near future, they will have provided, on the basis of two persons per room, housing accommodations for 496,000 people, or in round figures half a million souls. Already the rent roll for the London County Council in its housing schemes exceeds £1,000,000 each year."[117]

"Slum Clearance" in the United States.—American cities have gone part of the way in slum-improvement schemes. The power of eminent domain has been invoked and the city has condemned the unhealthy area. But the destroyed section has been made into a park or open space and has not involved municipal housing. The federal Constitution and the constitutions of all the states require that the property in question must be taken for "a public use." That the clearing out of a vile slum is a public use there is no doubt, but whether the courts would hold the building of dwellings on such sites to be sold or rented out to citizens to be a public use is another ques-

[116] Edith Wood, *Housing Progress in Western Europe*, 1923, pp. 50-57. Lawrence Veiller, "Who Shall Provide Houses for the Workingman? The Government?" *National Housing Conference*, 1923, IX, 153-161. *Housing Betterment*, June, 1926, 15:2:73; May, 1927, 16:1:30 ff. F. E. Fremantle, *The Housing of the Nation*, 1927, chs. IV-VII.

[117] *Housing*, June, 1928, 17:2:107-108, 115 (quoted). *9th Annual Report of the Ministry of Health*, 1927-1928, p. 70.

tion.[118] To permit government housing would require an amendment to the constitution. The notorious Mulberry Bend in New York City was demolished a number of years ago; there was nothing else to do with it.[119] The tenements have been replaced by a park. Another American example of "slum clearance" is the destruction of the block known as the Morton Street District in Boston. "The block in question is bisected by the narrowest travelled thoroughfare in Boston, Morton Street, which ranged from 11 to 13 feet, including sidewalks. Two blind alleys into which face rows of tenements also penetrate the block, each with a three-foot passageway as its sole exit, and over one of these exits straddles a wooden building. Through this narrow pass scores of human beings would have to force their way in the event of fire if they were to get out at all. Covering one and one-half acres, the block would make six or eight suburban house lots for half a hundred people, but here it is cut into over 50 lots and has housed 1,100 people—and that, with three of the outside corners occupied by large factory buildings that monopolize the best exposures. There are said to have been no less than 700 children in this congested district." The City of Boston appropriated $200,000 to wipe out this plague spot. The experience of Boston furnishes an eloquent example of the extravagance of some civic "economies." Nearly fifty years ago attention was called to the growing menace of overcrowding in buildings unfit for residence. Twenty-five years ago, before the rebuilding of a large section of the block, the city was urged to take the interior for a local playground. In those days the block could have been redeemed at a cost far less than has been possible today.[120] American cities have much need of slum clearance, but the sentiment appears to be against any plan of municipal housing to replace the demolished dwellings. The case of New York, as cited in Chapter VI above, may prove to be an exception.

Should the United States Adopt Direct Government Aid?—The reasons advanced by those who are opposed to direct government aid in housing in the United States are mainly political. Against municipal or state housing is the fact that, as long as politics and administration are inseparable, as they appear to be in this country, there will be inefficiency, graft, higher costs, and other evils. Our scheme of

[118] Frank B. Williams, *The Law of City Planning and Zoning*, 1922, pp. 140 ff. Lawrence Veiller, "Slumless America," *National Municipal Review*, Aug., 1920, 9:8:497.

[119] Jacob Riis, *How the Other Half Lives*, 1890, ch. VI. Robert W. DeForest and Lawrence Veiller, *The Tenement House Problem*, 1903, II, 3, 5, 6.

[120] Ralph A. Cram, "Scrapping the Slum," *National Housing Conference*, 1918, VII, 249-250. *Housing Betterment*, May, 1917, 6:2:22-23.

government will not allow of an efficient housing program. We cannot guarantee the selection of expert men to operate a municipal housing department, nor their continued employment. "Municipal housing," states one authority,[121] "will not pay where long tenure of office cannot be guaranteed to efficient administrators, or where politics and slender appropriations can ruin the work of competent administrators." Dr. Wood[122] urges us not to be pessimistic, but there is not much in the political history of American cities to inspire confidence. We have not yet reached the idea that administration calls for specialists, not politicians. Certainly there is much evidence of the greater efficiency of private ownership and operation as compared with public.

In America it would prove to be very difficult for municipal authorities to insist upon the payment of arrears of rent in the face of the occupancy of municipal houses by the "deserving poor," and in the face of the pleas for leniency that would be made by politicians. In Sheffield, England, a large amount of arrears of rent has been accumulated, even after an appreciable amount has been written off as irrecoverable.[123] Then there is the doubt in many minds whether government houses will reach the people that they are intended to benefit. "The old contention that Government Housing is apt to result in the furnishing of houses at the expense of the taxpayer, to various groups in the community who are quite able to provide proper housing accommodations for themselves, and to pay for them, is finding illustration in complaints which have arisen at Glasgow in connection with some of the municipal houses built with government funds." Many of the people therein housed had incomes of £1,000 to £1,500. Among the tenants were 172 municipal employees, 11 town councillors, and 3 members of Parliament.[124]

On the other hand, it may turn out that we will be forced to government housing as the only alternative. "If our modern civilization," states Mrs. Wood,[125] "requires workers to congregate in cities and the great value of land there puts the control of their own housing out of the hands of these workers and good housing out of their reach, then it would seem logical that housing should be accepted as a community problem—as a public service, even as water, light, transit,

[121] James Ford, "Some Fundamentals of Housing Reform," *The American City*, May, 1913, 8:5:475. Lawrence Veiller, *Housing Reform*, 1910, ch. VIII. Lawson Purdy, "Exemption from Taxation and other Subsidies," *National Housing Conference*, 1920, VIII, 8-9.
[122] *Housing of the Unskilled Wage Earner*, 1919, pp. 253-256.
[123] *Housing Betterment*, Dec., 1927, 16:4:305-306.
[124] *Housing Betterment*, June, 1926, 15:2:96.
[125] *Housing of the Unskilled Wage Earner*, 1919, p. 239.

education or recreation—to be controlled and regulated and where necessary owned and managed by the community." To this point of view there is the opposing argument that "if it is once admitted that the providing of private shelter for individuals is a public function, and that the appropriation of money for such a purpose is a public use of money, there is no limit to which the State may not go, when once embarked upon this programme of State Socialism. It will indeed be easy to argue, and even more convincingly than in the case of housing, that the providing of food of the right quality and at low prices is a public function, and that the appropriation of money for that purpose is for a public use. From food and shelter the step to clothing will be but a slight one; and from clothing, to motors and other luxuries. One of our higher courts has already declared that the providing of theatre tickets is a public necessity, so it will not be strange to find that we shall even ultimately come to state control of our amusements." Again, "shall we go to the ultimate extreme in housing as they have in Soviet Russia and in Germany—the Nationalization of housing? the rationing of houses by which the public officials determine where individuals shall live, how many people shall be accommodated, what rents they shall pay, who shall live with whom?"[126]

Examples of Government Housing in the United States.—There have been a few experiments in government aid to housing in the United States, none of which has been successful.[127] The only one of a few municipal housing schemes that has had some success is that of Milwaukee under its Socialist mayor. A state act of 1919 empowered municipalities to subscribe to the stock of housing corporations under certain conditions. Thus far, no city other than Milwaukee has taken advantage of this enlarged power. A corporation was formed with authorized capital of $250,000 common and $250,000 preferred stock. The preferred stock, of which the city and county purchased $100,000 each, yields a 5 per cent cumulative dividend. The common stock is subscribed to by the house occupants. Legally, instead of buying their own homes, they purchase stock to the value of their homes. As the common stock is gradually purchased the preferred stock is retired, so that, it is figured, in about sixteen years the tenants will own all the property. "Inability to sell more preferred stock, yielding only 5 per cent, has caused the Garden Homes Company to suspend

[126] *Housing Betterment*, June, 1926, 15:2:74.
[127] Lawrence Veiller, "Government Housing," National Housing Conference, 1920, VIII, 120; *Housing Betterment*, June, 1926, 15:2:73.

further operations. In fact, the city and county bought twice as much stock as originally contemplated.''[128] Another experiment on a small scale has been tried at Cohoes, New York, involving an ingenious solution of the legal difficulties encountered. It was decided that the housing shortage was so serious that the municipality was justified in exercising the police power. The city set aside $150,000 to assist in building operations. ''The money is merely issued as a short-time loan with interest at 3 per cent. When the house is built and sold the obligation is cancelled, and the transaction as far as the municipality is concerned, is closed.''[129]

The first state housing enterprise in this country was that of Massachusetts. In 1911 the State Legislature created a Homestead Commission and instructed it to report to the Legislature of 1912 a bill embodying a plan ''whereby, with the assistance of the Commonwealth, homesteads or small houses and plots of ground may be acquired by mechanics, factory employees, laborers and others in the suburbs of cities and towns.'' The Commission in 1912 recommended that part of the unclaimed savings banks deposits held in the state treasury be lent to the Homestead Commission to construct houses in accordance with the provisions of the law creating the Commission. The Supreme Court, however, declared that the use of such funds or of any funds under public control, for the purpose of assisting people to acquire homesteads, was unconstitutional. This situation was altered by an amendment to the constitution which was voted by the people in 1914. It provides: ''The general court shall have power to authorize the Commonwealth to take land and to hold, improve, subdivide, build upon and sell the same for the purpose of relieving congestion of population and providing homes for citizens: *provided, however,* that this amendment shall not be deemed to authorize the sale of such land or buildings at less than the cost thereof.'' In 1917, building operations were commenced in Lowell. Twelve detached and semi-detached houses were built with state funds and sold on easy payments. This seems to be the extent of state housing in Massachusetts. A later report of the Homestead Commission states with reference to the Lowell project: ''It was never in the mind of the Commission more than a demonstration and a part of the educational work of the Commission.'' The labor group which had been most instrumental in securing the appointment of the Commission

[128] *Christian Science Monitor,* Oct. 1, 1924. International Labour Office, *The Housing Situation in the United States,* 1925, pp. 35-37.
[129] New York *Times,* Jan. 3, 1926.

and the adoption of the constitutional amendment lost interest in the project, some of them feeling that government housing is more properly a function of the municipality than the commonwealth. Among its other experiments it promoted and supervised the establishment of official town-planning boards by cities and towns having a population of more than 10,000 (Act of 1913). Massachusetts led the way in this respect. Since 1919 the work of the Commission has been taken over by the new Department of Public Welfare, and the Commission has been abolished.[130]

Oklahoma in 1915 passed a law which authorized the investment of certain state moneys in loans for building a home or paying off a mortgage on a home.[131] This is a form of indirect, not direct, government aid. What was to have been the most extensive state housing program was inaugurated in North Dakota in 1919 by the passage of two bills. The first authorized the state to establish and operate the North Dakota Home Builders' Association, to which was appropriated $100,000 for the purpose of enabling inhabitants of the state to acquire their own homes. The second bill provided for the issue of bonds to an amount not to exceed $10,000,000 to cover first mortgages on real estate which shall have been issued by the Bank of North Dakota. The Association was to be operated by the State Industrial Commission, which was authorized to acquire all requisite property rights and construct, repair and remodel buildings. No home was to be built or purchased and sold at a price to exceed $5,000, except in the case of a farm home, in which instance the selling price was not to exceed $10,000. Ten or more depositors in the Association could form themselves into a local body known as a Home Buyers' League. Whenever such a member deposited with the Association a sum equal to 20 per cent of the selling price of a home, the Association would buy or build such home and convey it to him upon a cash payment of 20 per cent, the balance to be secured by a purchase money mortgage upon the property and to be paid off monthly. A few houses were constructed under the terms of the act, but the whole scheme has apparently come to grief financially.[132]

[130] Massachusetts Homestead Commission, *2nd Annual Report*, 1914, Public Document No. 103, pp. 8-9; *5th Annual Report*, 1917, pp. 9-26; *6th Annual Report*, 1918, pp. 7-16; *7th Annual Report*, 1919, p. 10 (quoted). Edith Wood, *Housing of the Unskilled Wage Earner*, 1919, pp. 218-222.

[131] Arthur Gleason, "The Lack of Houses: Remedies," *The Nation*, April 24, 1920, 110:2860:547.

[132] C. R. Woodruff, "State Aid to Home Builders," *American Year Book*, 1919, 248. *Housing Betterment*, Sept., 1919, 8:3:83 ff.; June, 1926, 15:2:73.

The Federal Government's War Housing Program.—The United States Government took up the housing question during the World War for the purpose of furthering the production of war materials. A large movement of working population to the munitions centers had occurred, with resulting congestion and housing shortage, and hence high labor turnover, which meant a lessening of production.[133] In February, 1918, a bill was introduced in Congress with an appropriation of $50,000,000 to meet the housing needs of the War and Navy Departments. A bill had already been introduced authorizing the Emergency Fleet Corporation to construct houses for ship workers; and the Ordnance Department also was about to build houses. On May 16, 1918, a bill was passed authorizing the President to form a housing bureau, to which was later appropriated $100,000,000. On July 9 the United States Housing Corporation was incorporated under the laws of the State of New York. This was done so that the properties it would purchase and build would not be directly government owned but subject to local taxation laws. The ownership of all the stock of this corporation was in the Secretary of Labor, except that one share each was held by the president and treasurer of the corporation.

The United States Housing Corporation sought to meet the housing situation before it by five methods:

1. By making available housing facilities found by careful investigation to exist in or near the particular communities in question.

2. By connecting, through improved transportation, places where labor was needed with places capable of housing it.

3. By encouraging and aiding private capital to build.

4. By aiding in the distribution of labor and the placing of war contracts in such a manner that housing congestion might be avoided or reduced.

5. By construction and operation of houses, apartments, and dormitories.

The corporation lent or advanced $7,000,000 to local transportation companies, chartered a ferryboat system in one locality and put special trains in operation in another. It provided reduced fares for workmen by paying the difference between the regular fare and the reduced fare fixed by the corporation. It stimulated building by private capital by securing priorities for the delivery of the necessary material. "It was only as a last resort that the corporation proceeded to the acquisition of land and the construction of houses thereon."

[133] Philip Hiss, "Housing as a War Problem," *National Housing Conference,* 1917, VI, 18-25. C. H. Whitaker, "Housing as a War Problem," *National Housing Conference,* 1917, VI, 6-12.

Its plan was not to sell but simply to rent the houses it built for the duration of the war, so as to exclude profiteers who might inflate the rentals to match the paying power of the worker, as landlords did elsewhere.[134]

The large housing projects promoted by the government during the war were of two types: (a) temporary towns erected in remote wilderness locations for employees of explosive plants; and (b) permanent villages in places where there was a reasonable certainty of a market for the houses after the war. What was to have been the greatest housing undertaking in the world was begun on Neville Island near Pittsburgh. It was to have been the home of workers in the ordnance plant to be established there. The housing project meant that a complete city would have been built having a population of 50,000 inhabitants. It would have called for the construction of 15,000 separate dwellings.[135] The ending of the war curtailed the development. The largest permanent industrial town constructed by the government under the Emergency Fleet Corporation was Yorkship Village, Camden, New Jersey. The village was owned by a limited-dividend company with a capital stock of $250,000, the income being limited to $12,500. The government set aside for the construction of the village the sum of $10,000,000, and all the returns from this investment over and above that required for the amortization of the government loan and the possible $12,500 return on the capital stock was to go back to the inhabitants of Yorkship in the maintenance of the town and in increased physical, recreational, and educational facilities.[136]

At the end of the war the government had on its hands twelve wooden cities ranging from 1,500 to 30,000 in population, most of them being temporary towns erected in remote locations for the employees of explosive plants. These towns were promptly depopulated, the plants dismantled, and the houses and dormitories taken apart and sold. There were thirty completed, permanent villages constructed in places where there was some prospect of selling the houses after the war. Some were so small relative to the adjoining cities or so

[134] *Monthly Labor Review*, Feb., 1919, 8:2:247-249. Joseph D. Leland, 3d, "What the Federal Government has done to House the industrial Army," *National Housing Conference*, 1918, VII, 63. A brief record of progress in the government's war housing program will be found in the *Journal of the American Institute of Architects*, Sept., 1918, 6:9:445-448.

[135] C. R. Woodruff, "The Federal Government's Housing Policy," *American Year Book*, 1918, p. 260.

[136] E. D. Litchfield, "Recent Government Housing Developments," *National Housing Conference*, 1918, VII, 91-93.

scattered in small groups throughout the city that they were not separable from ordinary private property. These "building projects" were sold to individuals or to real estate companies. Other permanent properties were separate villages of such size and isolation as to constitute natural and complete social units. These "town projects" offered an unusual opportunity for trial in this country of the English plan of co-partnership or group ownership; but this did not occur.[137]

On November 1, 1918, the United States Housing Corporation had already under construction or ready to let, 18,747 permanent buildings, to house 23,319 families; 1,771 ready-cut buildings, to house as many families; and 300 buildings to house approximately 24,190 workers without their families. It had 82 large projects, the Emergency Fleet Corporation about 30, and the Ordnance Department had put up 16 towns.[138] The demobilization which followed so hard upon the Armistice hit first of all the Housing Corporation, which was abolished by act of Congress in 1919 and its properties ordered transferred to the Treasury Department for sale to private persons. The Federal Government spent $70,000,000 in building shipyard communities which were sold after the war to individuals living in them or to real estate operators, at 40 per cent of the original cost. When Yorkship Village was disposed of by the government, it was sold at a net loss of about 70 per cent.[139] Government housing was not a paying proposition, but much of this loss may be written off as a war cost. It was imperative that houses be constructed quickly, with cost a secondary consideration; then, too, the building was done in a period of inflated prices.

From a technical housing standpoint, what influence did this government experiment have? Three general principles guided the housing plans of the government: (1) That row or group houses are not normally to be more than two rooms deep. This avoids the dark, inner room. (2) That side yard space between adjacent buildings is to be at least 16 feet and preferably 20 feet. This sets a high standard for light and ventilation. (3) That tenement and apartment houses are considered generally undesirable and will be accepted only in cities where, because of high land values, it is clearly demonstrated that single and two-family houses cannot be economically provided or

[137] Richard S. Childs, "What Will Become of the Government Housing?" *National Municipal Review*, Jan., 1919, 8:1:48-49.

[138] Joseph D. Leland, 3d, "What the Federal Government has done to house the Industrial Army," *National Housing Conference*, 1918, VII, 68-69.

[139] *The Survey*, Sept. 15, 1920, 44:20:701. New York *Times*, Aug. 15, 1920. Daniel Crawford, "Who Shall Provide Houses for the Workingman?" *National Housing Conference*, 1923, IX, 136.

where there is insistent demand for this type of multiple housing.[140] According to Veiller,[141] "the standards adopted by the Government for the housing of workers will have a potent influence upon the housing of the workingman in this country for many years to come." This experiment in government aid in housing has led to no further activity on the part of the Federal Government. The only outcome of government housing during the war is the Division of Building and Housing created by Secretary Hoover on July 1, 1921, in the Department of Commerce. Its purpose is to "collect and disseminate such scientific, practical, and statistical information as may be procured, showing or tending to show approved methods in building, planning and construction, standardization, and adaptability of structural units, including building materials, and codes, economy in the manufacture and utilization of building materials and supplies, and such other matters as may tend to encourage, improve, and cheapen construction and housing." It coöperates with other agencies, public and private, but is not a competitor of private business enterprises.[142]

(b) Indirect Government Aid

Indirect government aid in housing consists in making loans of public funds and in granting exemptions from or concessions in taxes or some other form of subsidy. A policy of lending money at low interest rates for housing has been developed by almost every civilized county except the United States. It is the policy of lending the money or the credit of the state for the building of suitable homes for working-people. This does not mean that the state is to build such homes; it does not mean that the state is to own such homes and operate them; it does not mean that the state is to offer subsidies for the construction of homes. It means that the state shall lend money on its credit to limited-dividend corporations, to other organizations, and to individuals for the purpose of building houses. Such loans are to be made only on houses that will provide an acceptable standard of living conditions, the minimum of which is to be fixed by the proper authorities. To use state credit for this purpose in the United States will require a constitutional amendment.

The advantages to be gained from the use of state credit are many.

[140] John Nolen, "Housing Standards of the Federal Government," *National Housing Conference*, 1918, VII, 121. Harold G. Aron, "Some Problems of Management," *National Housing Conference*, 1918, VII, 234-241.

[141] "Housing Progress of the Year," *National Housing Conference*, 1918, VII, 396. Arthur Gleason, "The Lack of Houses: Remedies," *The Nation*, April 24, 1920, 110:2860:548.

[142] *The Survey*, July 15, 1922, 48:12:528.

"It will make loans available for a type of house for which no money can now be secured. It will make it available at the low rate of interest at which the private individual cannot borrow. The State can also afford to make these loans for a long period of years, with gradual amortization."[143] Banks, insurance companies, and other large lending institutions find that other forms of building offer much better returns than does housing. Federal and state income taxes reduce the income from mortgage loans to so low a figure that funds are withdrawn from this type of investment. Tax-exempt government bonds, federal, state and municipal, offer a better investment. In 1920 a bill was introduced in the New York Legislature to remedy this situation by exempting the interest on mortgages from the state income tax. It was similar in form and purpose to the McLaughlin bill introduced in Congress to exempt small holdings of real estate mortgages from the federal income tax. Both failed of passage.[144] The New York State Legislature, however, did pass a bill giving New York and other cities power to exempt until 1932 new buildings, whose construction is begun before April 1, 1925, from taxation for local purposes. New York City passed an ordinance in 1921 in accordance with the terms of the state enabling act, exempting new buildings erected exclusively for dwelling purposes, except hotels, from taxation up to a certain amount for local purposes other than assessments for local improvements. This ordinance unquestionably stimulated building, but it did so in the interest of the landlord rather than that of the tenant. It is claimed that its chief effect has been to put additional profits in the hands of builders. It did not bring relief to the class of citizens whom it was sought to relieve, the lowest paid workers.[145]

Some form of indirect government aid was secured for New York by the passage of the State Housing Law of 1926. It will be recalled that this Act provides for buildings to be erected by public or private limited-dividend corporations chartered by the State Housing Board. The tax-exemption provisions are thoroughgoing.

Any public limited dividend housing company formed hereunder shall be exempt from the payment of any and all franchise, organization, income, mortgage recording and other taxes to the state and all fees to the state or

---

[143] *Report of the Reconstruction Commission on Housing Conditions, New York,* 1920, pp. 45-46.
[144] *State of New York, Report of the Joint Legislative Committee on Housing,* Legislative Document (1922) No. 60, p. 1. *Housing Betterment,* May, 1920, 9:2:129; *The Survey,* Sept. 15, 1920, 44:20:699-700.
[145] *Housing Betterment,* May, 1924, 13:2:189-190; May, 1927, 16:1:28.

its officers. Bonds and mortgages and the income debenture certificates of all companies incorporated hereunder are declared to be instrumentalities of the state, issued for public purposes and shall, together with interest thereon, be exempt from taxation. The dividends on the stock of said companies shall be exempt from taxation by the state.

Furthermore, municipalities in which the housing projects authorized are located, are empowered to exempt from local taxation the buildings and improvements created under such projects. If this is done, they shall also be exempt from any and all state taxes, but "such exemption of said buildings and improvements from taxation by the municipality and state shall not extend to buildings erected after January first nineteen hundred and thirty-seven."[146]

Various suggestions have been made for tapping national credit power for housing purposes, and bills covering most of them have at different times been introduced in Congress. They are (1) a national housing fund, to be allotted to states with housing commissions, and by them granted to municipalities, and to limited-dividend non-commercial housing companies. (2) Postal savings deposit loans to individual workingmen. (3) An amendment to the Federal Reserve Act permitting national banks to make housing loans, thus rendering several billion dollars available. This is an extension of already existent permissions, for by the Act of 1916 national banks were permitted to make loans on real estate limited to one year in term and to cover improved and unencumbered property and to 50 per cent of its value. (4) An amendment to the Farm Loan Act, permitting housing loans. (5) State housing funds made available.[147] Passage of some of these bills would permit the building and loan associations to borrow on their mortgages and thus make available larger sums for home building, which experience has shown should be administered locally without governmental intervention or expense.

SUMMARY

The most obvious method of dealing with the housing problem is to hold the landlords responsible and to compel them to build and

[146] *Laws of New York*, Chapter 823, State Housing Law, 1926, § 39.
[147] Edith Wood, *Housing of the Unskilled Wage Earner*, 1919, pp. 262-276; "Using Postal Savings Funds," *National Housing Conference*, 1923, IX, 125-132. Arthur Gleason, "The Lack of Houses: Remedies," *The Nation*, April 24, 1920, 110:2860:547. F. T. Miller, *Housing Situation in England and the United States*, 1920, pp. 26-27. Edmund S. Wolfe, "Can National Bank Funds be Released for Housing?" *National Housing Conference*, 1920, VIII, 38. *Housing Betterment*, Sept., 1919, 8:3:41 ff.

maintain houses that meet the standards set for light, ventilation, sanitation, fire protection, and so forth. The means is restrictive legislation. This is the universal method and almost the only one utilized in the United States. Since no law is self-enforcing, it is necessary to provide for inspection and enforcement, which can best be secured by concentration of authority and responsibility in a housing department. So long as reliance is placed on private capital and commercial builders, this is the most important method. Semi-philanthropic activity along the line of building model tenements and lodging houses can help to set and raise the standards for restrictive legislation by experimenting and demonstrating.

Constructive housing legislation provides for government aid, either by building directly for rental or sale, or by lending of public funds or granting exemptions from or concessions in taxation. The indirect form operates mainly through non-commercial housing companies. This is the characteristic European method, of which Great Britain furnishes the best example. There are objections, chiefly political, to adopting direct government housing in the United States; the case is considerably different with indirect government aid.

Two root difficulties in the housing problem are high land values and the small income of the wage-earner. Government housing does not remove either but shifts the burden to the taxpayers. Decentralization will help with respect to high land values, and there appears to be a movement away from the large city because of the costs and disadvantages of living and doing business there. The Garden City idea is based on the plan of improving housing conditions by limiting the size of the city. The increase of land values is thereby checked. Congestion is also relieved by getting manufacturers and workers to move from the large city to the small town.

The idea of group-ownership as developed in the Garden City and also in the projects of co-partnership tenant societies reduces the cost of housing and turns the unearned increment to the advantage of the inhabitants. The single-tax proposal or some plan of shifting taxes from buildings and improvements to the land may promote house construction and lessen costs.

The development of transportation facilities is fundamental to housing reform; it is a chief way of relieving congestion by spreading the population over a wider area. Based on it is the plan of the Garden Suburb. It is also an essential feature of city planning. City planning attempts to remedy past mistakes and to avoid congested unsanitary conditions in the future. The remedial type of city planning leads to the destruction of unsanitary areas, what the British call slum clearance. The expansion of industry, involving its encroachment on tenement sections, also often eliminates much bad housing. The points at which constructive city planning and housing overlap and coalesce are chiefly in the fixing of depth of block and lot, width and treatment of street, height and thickness of permissible buildings to be used for housing, and the relations of all these to one another.[148] A well-planned city is a healthy and well-housed city.

Industrial housing is in some cases an absolute necessity; in others it can be a considerable aid chiefly through the advantage of large-scale construction, which is the most important way to combat high building costs and make the few dollars of the wage-earner go farther. If house building could ever be put on a factory basis, costs would be cut still more. By standardization, quantity production, and machine manufacture, housing might be made available to the wage-earner at a cost within his reach, just as modern methods of industry have already given to the poor man his ready-made clothes, his cheap shoes, his dollar watch, and his low-priced automobile.[149]

Since not all tenants are model, there is need of improving them in order to improve housing conditions. For those of low standard of living, the Octavia Hill plan and those like unto it are successful. There is here presented a problem of education in which the public schools can help.

The solution of the housing problem, or at least an improvement over present conditions, will come through using all the above methods and perhaps some other means not mentioned or even not yet thought of. There is obviously no panacea, no cure-all. There could not be, because the housing problem, like all social problems, is exceedingly complex. The housing problem is involved in the consideration of a great many other questions—questions of politics and administration,

[148] Frederick L. Olmsted, ''City Planning and Housing,'' *National Housing Conference*, 1911, I, 30-38. Andrew W. Crawford, ''The Interrelation of Housing and City Planning,'' *Annals*, Jan., 1914, 51:140:162-171.

[149] Grosvenor Atterbury, ''How to Get Low Cost Houses,'' *National Housing Conference*, 1916, V, 94-101. W. H. Ham, ''Lessons from Housing Work in Bridgeport,'' *National Housing Conference*, 1920, VIII, 95-118. D. K. Boyd, ''Standardization of Parts in House Construction,'' *National Housing Conference*, 1920, VIII, 74-86. Robert Tappan, ''Factory Production Applied to the Housing Problem,'' *National Housing Conference*, 1920, VIII, 56-64. John E. Conzelman. ''Ready-Made Houses,'' *National Housing Conference*, 1917, VI, 81-88. See also the papers on reducing the cost of housing, including the cost of labor, materials, and money, *National Housing Conference*, 1923, IX, 5-132.

of health, morality, and education, of poverty, standard of living, and birth-rate, of immigration, industrial relations, and wages, of city growth, land values, transportation, and so on. The one basic principle underlying the solution is adjustment to the factors and forces at work, the method of science.

Part III

HEALTH

CHAPTER IX

THE PUBLIC-HEALTH MOVEMENT

"THE public health," said Disraeli,[1] "is the foundation on which rest the happiness of the people and the welfare of the nation. The care of the public health is the first duty of the statesman."

The Social Importance of Health.—Historically, the interest of the state in the health of its members has been largely prompted by military consideration. "In a state of nature and surrounded by hostile tribes, the number of able-bodied warriors bore a direct and immediate relation to success in tribal conflict. Health had a distinct group survival value. So, too, in the warfare of more advanced groups, the nation able to make military use of the largest proportion of its members had, other things equal, the better chance in armed conflict."[2] This influence of war has not ceased. The nations engaged in the World War were shocked to find a high percentage of physical defects among the men examined for the army. In the United States approximately one-third of the recruits were rejected as physically unfit for full military duty. The results of the army medical examinations in England led Lloyd George to remark, "You cannot maintain an A-1 empire on a C-3 population." War, or the thought of war, has stimulated a good deal of the public-health measures of modern nations. In the field of child hygiene, for instance, Dr. S. Josephine Baker[3] states that war has been the greatest stimulus to organized efforts for child care.

Aside from military strength, the nation's health has utilitarian value. "In the economic competition between peoples physical health is an important item in deciding success. The numbers marked by defect or disease add but little to the labor force of the group, and detract from it to the extent that they must be protected and supported by the more efficient members. The economic significance of disease is not always realized. The losses are too common to attract attention, and too insidious to be at all generally understood."[4] Great Britain has checked up its industrial loss through sickness and disablement

---

[1] Quoted by S. Josephine Baker, *Child Hygiene*, 1925, p. 30.
[2] E. B. Reuter, *Population Problems*, 1923, p. 251.
[3] *Child Hygiene*, 1925, pp. 6 ff.
[4] E. B. Reuter, *Population Problems*, 1923, p. 251.

since the National Health Insurance Act went into effect. The figures show an annual average loss in England and Wales of at least 14,-000,000 weeks' work, or a period of upwards of 270,000 years. Put in another way, there is lost to the nation every year, among the insured population only, the equivalent of the work of 270,000 persons.[5] Studies made by Dr. Louis I. Dublin,[6] statistician of the Metropolitan Life Insurance Company, disclose that the average individual in the United States loses about seven days each year from sickness involving inability to work. There are additional days of discomfort which interfere more or less with a person's duties, but these are not included in the statistics. Converted into economic terms, this means that there is a loss of 2 per cent of total current production, amounting, in round numbers, to more than $1,250,000,000 annually. To this figure should be added the cost of such items as medical care, hospital service, drugs and appliances, and the like. The total cost of medical care, including all these items, would amount to more than a billion dollars a year. It may, therefore, be said with confidence that sickness costs directly in lost wages, in reduced production, as well as in the necessary care, a total of $2,250,000,000 a year.

This huge figure is occasioned by the need for an army of professional workers and lay assistants to care for the large number of sick. For 2 per cent of the population are at all times so ill as to require medical service of one kind or another. They employ approximately 150,000 physicians, whose average net income is a little more than $3,000 a year. About 50,000 dentists have a similar average net income. In addition, 140,000 nurses doing private bedside work average $1,500 a year; about 150,000 practical nurses and 100,000 more employees of various kinds such as orderlies, stenographers, and assistants in hospitals and in the offices of private physicians have an average annual income of about $1,000 a year. The total annual income of all concerned with the care of the sick is over a billion dollars. The cost of hospital service covering 860,000 beds adds 500 millions, and the cost of medicines and drugs is not less than 500 millions more. These figures are of necessity rough, but they total well over two billions of dollars a year.

Good health is no less important from the point of view of individual happiness and social welfare. Ill-health is responsible for a

[5] *Annual Report of the Chief Medical Officer of the Ministry of Health*, 1921, pp. 19-20.

[6] *Health and Wealth*, 1928, pp. 8, 9, 21. *Cf.* Harry H. Moore, *Public Health in the United States*, 1923, pp. 62-69; A. B. Mills, *The Extent of Illness*, 1929, pp. 3-15; Allon Peebles, *Medical Facilities in the United States*, 1929, pp. 3-14.

large proportion of the total amount of human misery. Sickness is an important cause of dependency. "Of all the cases that come before the relief societies of the City of New York, for example, some three-fourths are accountable for in terms of disease. It is an item of importance in vice and crime. It creates a lack of educational opportunity, or a stunted body and low vitality unable to profit by the school advantages. Disease and ill-health are major items in a vicious circle. Physical disability leads to poverty and so to the conditions favorable to the spread of disease. The children, because of poverty and its accompaniments are low in vitality, stunted in growth, and retarded in education, and become the socially indifferent, mentally retarded, and physically inefficient adults of another generation."[7]

Health is socially important for the further reason that the methods of eliminating disease and promoting health must be group-wise. They cannot be undertaken by the individual. The need of group action against disease converts the question of health into that of the public health. From the point of view of origin or causation, all disease may be classified as constitutional or environmental. In other words, the influences which affect health may be divided into those which are external to man's body and those which are internal. The internal influences or *intrinsic causes*, arising within the body proper, include communicable diseases, disease-germ carriers, immunity and susceptibility, education, and personal habits. The external influences, or *extrinsic causes*, are those of man's environment, and include such things as fresh air, pure water, sunshine, cleanliness of houses and yards, proper sewage disposal, control of infectious diseases, etc. There are thus two factors to be considered—the individual and his environment; the science of promoting public health, which may be divided into hygiene and sanitation, is concerned with each. Hygiene deals with the individual and his physical perfection, with measures which promote health and prevent disease. Sanitation deals with the causes and sources of those diseases which come from the outside, from the surroundings of the individual.[8] Sanitary science or hygiene has as its objects the prevention of disease, the prolongation of life, and the promotion of health and efficiency through organized community efforts. It is not a concrete intellectual discipline, but a field of social activity. It includes applications of chemistry and bacteriology, of engineering and statistics, of physiology, pathology, and

[7] E. B. Reuter, *Population Problems*, 1923, p. 252.
[8] H. W. Hill, *The New Public Health*, 1920, pp. 1-2. William T. Sedgwick, *Principles of Sanitary Science*, 1905, p. 10.

epidemiology, and of sociology and other social sciences. Upon these it builds a comprehensive program of community service.[9]

Sanitation—Our Sole Hope of Survival in Crowds.—The public-health movement is in the main a city movement. ''Throughout the ages it has been recognised that the aggregation of people in cities is accompanied by intensification of epidemic disease and by lowering of the standard of health; and social history consists largely in a statement of efforts to counteract these maleficent tendencies by regulation and improvement of housing, of sewerage, of water supplies, of ventilation, and of food.''[10] As contrasted with the country, man's environment in the city is inherently unhealthful. City-dwellers have less light and air, they do most of their work indoors, and some of them are engaged in occupations which, as in the dust industries, are injurious to health; they come into daily contact with large numbers of people, a factor which tends to spread disease. When the principal population of the country was rural, health was a private matter. Each family had its own well, its own milk and eggs and meat and vegetables, its own sewage-disposal system; people lived far apart and seldom came into contact. But it is different now, especially with the city-dwellers. The city brings him his water and takes away his sewage and garbage. People whom he never sees kill his meat, raise his vegetables, prepare his milk, bake his bread. Instead of fresh air and sunshine he gets the city's gas and smoke. He lives and works in places injurious to health. He comes into contact with people who carry the germs of infectious disease. Health is still a personal matter to a certain extent, but all the vigilance of the individual avails him nothing if the city happens to get its sewage mixed with its water supply, or its Board of Health mixed with politics. So many factors, most of them beyond the individual's control, enter the problem of keeping well that the effort to deal with them must be social, and the responsibility for disease, accident, and other factors which shorten life must also be social. The only protection the individual can get is that which the community gives him.

''Seventy-five years ago the large cities of Europe and America were unsafe for human habitation. In the middle of the nineteenth century birth-rates were almost twice as high as those prevailing in our cities today, yet the annual death-rates of London and New York not infrequently exceeded them. Only by immigration from the land

[9] C.-E. A. Winslow, *The Evolution and Significance of the Modern Public Health Campaign*, 1923, p. 1.
[10] Sir Arthur Newsholme, *Evolution of Preventive Medicine*, 1927, p. 88.

could the cities hold even. Then began the era of modern municipal sanitation which made their growth possible by the organization of services for disposal of human waste, the provision of safe food and water, some control of housing and work places, and specific measures for limiting the spread of communicable disease."[11] Within the experience of men and women still active and responsible for health services, deaths in cities in this country have been reduced by two-thirds. A death-rate of twelve per thousand is common in our cities instead of thirty-six. The death-rate is still higher and the expectation of life is less in the city than in the country, though the city has made tremendous gains on the country and in some respects enjoys distinct advantages. Municipal sanitation has, in fact, saved the life of the city, and though the toll is still heavy, the outlook is hopeful.

History of Public-Health Practice.—The earliest theory of disease known is that found among primitive peoples, who interpret fever, sickness, pain, madness, and hysteria as due to the temporary or prolonged occupancy of the affected body by an evil spirit or demon. It is called the Demonic Theory. The logical cure was to cast out the evil spirit, and it was universally applied. Hence the various exorcistic devices of the medicine man or priest, the sacrificial rites, the resort to incantations, charms and sorcery.

Among the ancient civilized peoples there were a number of public-health practices, some of which were purposeful, others without intention, but both nevertheless valuable in the preservation of mankind. The Egyptians filtered the muddy water of the Nile; this rendered it potable and in a measure prevented the spread of disease. "Their custom of mummifying the dead by keeping them in brine for seventy days, then drying and placing them in tombs in the hills above the over-flow of the Nile was not without sanitary significance. They had rules concerning meat inspection, bathing, clothing, diet, and care of infants."[12] Remains of the massive Babylonian drains show that the art of the proper disposal of sewage had been applied at this early date. The ruins of antiquity also give evidence that large reservoirs were common in ancient times. The Chinese for thousands of years have used alum as a coagulant in the clarification of muddy water. The inhabitants of India, over 4,000 years ago, knew that "it is good to keep water in copper vessels, to expose it to sunlight, and to

[11] Haven Emerson and Earle B. Phelps, "The City Gains on the Country," *The Survey*, August 1, 1929, 62:9:469. *Cf.* Haven Emerson, "The Robust City," *The Survey*, Nov. 1, 1925, 60:3:121.
[12] J. Howard Beard, "Progress of Public Health Work," *The Scientific Monthly*, Feb., 1922, 14:2:140.

filter it through charcoal.'' The ancient Hebrews were the real founders of public-health work, the first people to devote their attention to
disease prevention. They obtained excellent results in wholesome living
by making hygiene a part of their religion. The high priests were
sanitary police. Their mandates, minutely detailed in the book of
Leviticus, covered diet, the touching of unclean objects, prevention of
contagious disease, isolation, disinfection, sanitary inspection, removal
of nuisances, certain industrial practices, personal hygiene, and medical jurisprudence.

The Greeks contributed little to sanitation, but their attention to
individual hygiene places them in the front rank of both ancient and
modern peoples in this respect. ''The teachings of the Greek philoso-
phers and physicians contained principles which promoted the well-
being of the people as a whole. The laws of Solon and Lycurgus were
especially helpful in improving the health of the masses. The Spartan
requirements for warriors, the Olympic games and the emphasis
placed upon the winning of distinction in them, together with the
prominence given to physical perfection in sculpture, art and literature inspired the youth to maintain a high degree of health.''[13] The
Greek conception of the causes of disease was such that it precluded
measures directed toward public disease prevention. ''According to
their view disease arose when any derangement occurred in the proportions or combinations of the four elements, fire, water, air, earth, and
the four qualities, moist, dry, hot, cold, and the four humors, blood,
phlegm, yellow bile, black bile. This conception logically assumes that
disease comes from within and hence is not due to something which
enters from the outside world. Prevention, therefore, was a matter
of individual and not public concern.''[14] Much of the language of this
famous theory of the four humors still lingers, as when we speak
of a ''bilious'' condition, a ''sanguine,'' ''phlegmatic,'' or ''melan-
cholic'' (black bile) temperament. The theory had the high merit,
under Hippocrates, of fixing attention upon natural rather than
supernatural causes, upon the patient rather than the demons. Hippocrates, the father of medicine, about 400 B.C., held that disease was
caused by morbid secretions of the atmosphere, and denied that it
arose through demons, spirits or other supernatural agencies. He was
believed to have controlled the plague of Athens by lighting fires as
an atmospheric corrective. Thucydides is the first writer to enunciate
the doctrine of contagion, and from his time on the conception was

[13] *Ibid.*, pp. 140-141.
[14] Herbert H. Waite, *Disease Prevention*, 1926, pp. 2-3.

never wholly lost. It was consistently subordinated, however, to the miasmatic theory.[15] Galen recognized the contagiousness of several diseases, such as itch, ophthalmia, rabies, plague, and consumption.[16]

As personal hygiene flowered in Greece, so public sanitation reached a comparatively brilliant development in ancient Rome. Although in ancient and even in medieval cities the conditions as regards filth were almost indescribable, the Romans formed a partial exception. To their chief cities they brought supplies of water through aqueducts which can still be seen. They constructed sewers; in fact, their cloacae were the forerunners of our modern sewerage systems. They also had a system of periodical removal of refuse. They were among the first of the ancients to provide methods for good ventilation of houses. Cremation and public baths were among their other important sanitary practices, but their greatest achievements were in the field of sanitary engineering.[17]

In the Middle Ages there was one phase of public-health work which grim necessity forced upon the attention of the rulers of that period—the problem of controlling epidemic disease. "The Crusades, mis-rule, and innumerable wars prepared the soil and sowed the seed of the great epidemics in the Middle Ages which threatened man with extinction and gave the fatal thrust to tottering civilizations. Crowded conditions, the bad sanitation of the walled medieval towns, and gross immorality were the great predisposing factors. Gorton tells us that as late as the 16th century the English housewives swept the refuse from their dwellings into the streets. People seldom bathed or washed their clothes. Even eminent ecclesiastics swarmed with vermin. The garbage was emptied into unpaved streets and ground to mush when it rained. At nightfall shutters were opened and sewage poured into the streets." According to the early teachings of this period a wound was considered unhealthy if pus did not appear in it, a doctrine which did not disappear until very recently. Superstitions regarding infectious diseases were rife. The intellectuals of the time were lost in a maze of theological controversy. "Epidemics were regarded as a 'visitation from God' inflicted alike upon the innocent and the guilty, to chasten a sinful world. As a result, no great effort was made to prevent them. Humanity escaped from the severe ravages of ergotism,

[15] C.-E. A. Winslow, *The Evolution and Significance of the Modern Public Health Campaign*, 1923, p. 29. William T. Sedgwick, *Principles of Sanitary Science*, 1905, p. 26.

[16] Herbert H. Waite, *Disease Prevention*, 1926, p. 3.

[17] J. Howard Beard, *op. cit.*, 141. Sir Arthur Newsholme, *Evolution of Preventive Medicine*, 1927, p. 89.

scurvy, and influenza to be swept off by black death. Bubonic plague appeared in 1346 and killed sixty million people, over one-fourth of the earth's inhabitants. Plague visited London many times and would have depopulated it had not the people fled. Burning of the city killed the rats and reduced the plague.''[18] Boccaccio's *Decameron* gives a most graphic description of this epidemic. In the midst of the ravages of the plague, the first guardians of public health were appointed, and quarantine was attempted. It was tried in Venice (the term quarantine is derived from *quaranta giorni*, which means forty days, the length of time established for this particular epidemic) and later extended to other Mediterranean ports and to the North and Baltic seaboards. Health ordinances were promulgated and pest houses erected. During this period leprosy was at the height of its virulence, and leprosaria were founded for the isolation of its victims. Each leper was compelled to carry a rattle, and to give notice of his presence by sounding an alarm.

The Discovery of Disease Germs.—The crude quarantine of the Middle Ages was later replaced by the modern procedure, which is based on scientific knowledge. Superstition gradually gave way to science, and knowledge of the causes of disease and epidemics took the place of theory. An important first step was the invention of the microscope or, rather, great improvements on this instrument, which furnished the means for more intensive investigations concerning the causes of disease. For this development credit is due to Anton van Leeuwenhoek (1632-1723), a linen draper in the town of Delft, Holland. He became interested in lens grinding as a hobby, and developed great proficiency in this art, finally turning his attention to the microscope. He succeeded in making a lens which was so powerful that he was able to see objects so minute they had never been seen before. Meticulously he examined rain water, scrapings from his teeth, the intestines of frogs and horses—anything he could get hold of—and accurately described what he saw—swarms of minute moving creatures. He had discovered microbes. He has been rightly called the Father of Bacteriology. His discovery was that of an observer of facts in no way influenced by subjective assumptions. He was the embodiment of the scientific spirit.[19]

[18] J. Howard Beard, ''Progress of Public Health Work,'' *The Scientific Monthly*, Feb., 1922, 14:2:141. *Cf.* Herbert H. Waite, *Disease Prevention*, 1926, pp. 3, 4; Sir Arthur Newsholme, *Evolution of Preventive Medicine*, 1927, pp. 6-10; Howard W. Haggard, *Devils, Drugs, and Doctors*, 1929, ch. VIII.

[19] Paul de Kruif, *Microbe Hunters*, 1926, ch. I. Herbert H. Waite, *Disease Prevention*, 1926, p. 4.

What is the nature of these minute forms of life which Leeuwenhoek discovered? Many hundred different types exist, but only a small proportion of them produce disease. They are all simple single-celled organisms, either microscopic plants (bacteria) or animals (protozoa). They may be collectively called germs or microbes. "Each of the bacterial cells has a wall on the outside and a mass of living stuff or protoplasm within. They are shaped like sticks (the word *bacterium* in Latin means a stick or rod), or balls or spiral threads, and are so small that 400,000,000 could be packed into a grain of granulated sugar. Some of them have wavy processes or flagella which they use like fins to swim about in liquids. They normally reproduce by the simple process of growing larger and then splitting in half, so that two bacteria are present where there was only one before; and under the most favorable conditions this reproduction may take place as often as once in twenty minutes. The application of simple arithmetic will show that a single germ may at this rate produce a billion descendants in ten hours."[20] In the economy of life these organisms are of the highest importance. Many species are active agents in converting dead organic matter into soluble food material for plants; some oxidize nitrites into nitrates; others possess the power of fixing atmospheric nitrogen; many are concerned in the various processes of fermentation. But there is also a certain group which is pathogenic, giving rise to various diseases in man and animals as well as plants. They are able to grow in the tissues of the human body, a power which most of the group as a whole do not possess. A parasitic microbe capable of growing in the human body can thrive only in the human body or, in certain instances, in the body of some other animal. It may and often does survive for a time in water or soil or filth, but only for a time.[21]

The discovery of microbes by Leeuwenhoek immediately led to a controversy concerning the source whence these microörganisms emanated. Speculation ran riot, many affirming that they arose spontaneously from the matter in which they were found. Opponents of this theory maintained that life could not arise from inanimate substances but must arise from preëxisting life. The controversy over spontaneous generation did not reach its culmination until the middle of the eighteenth century, and was not completely subverted until the latter half of the nineteenth. The theory was not entirely over-

[20] C.-E. A. Winslow, *Man and the Microbe*, 1924, p. 8.
[21] *Ibid.*, pp. 9, 11. Jean Broadhurst, *Home and Community Hygiene*, 1923, pp. 1-11.

thrown until Pasteur, through his epoch-making experiments on fermentation, showed conclusively that spontaneous generation was a myth. In a brilliant series of investigations which began in 1857 and were pursued intermittently for nearly twenty years, Pasteur demonstrated that the process of fermentation was due to microbes, that each particular fermentation was caused by a particular kind of microbe, and that these microbes themselves were produced only by biogenesis and were not spontaneously generated. By 1867 he had definitely reached the parasitic hypothesis, and by 1870 he had shown how the serious economic problem of silkworm disease could be practically controlled, essentially by the application of isolation and quarantine. From fermentation to silkworm disease was a long but a natural step. From silkworm disease to the contagious maladies of the higher animals was a short and inevitable one. The general theories of Pasteur had already been applied by Lister to antiseptic surgery and by Davaine to the etiology of anthrax. In 1877 Pasteur himself, and Robert Koch, simultaneously and independently, demonstrated beyond doubt that the germ of anthrax is actually the cause of this disease. They did this by cultivating the germ in pure cultures and then artificially infecting animals. Finally by his studies on the chicken cholera (1880), on anthrax (1881), and on rabies (1885), Pasteur succeeded in producing artificial immunity against microbic diseases by the attenuation of the specific viruses concerned. ''In a quarter of a century, and by the labors of one man, the mystery which for time immemorial had shrouded the plagues and pestilences was rent away, and there was established on the one hand the science of bacteriology which was to make it possible to check the spread of microbic invaders and on the other the science of immunology which opened the way for building up specific resistance against their ravages.''[22]

The year 1877 may be taken as the beginning of modern preventive medicine, for it was then demonstrated for the first time and beyond the slightest doubt that anthrax, a disease of animals and occasionally of man, was caused by living germs. Pasteur and Koch had given to the world the new science of bacteriology. The discovery of germ

        [22] C.-E. A. Winslow, *Evolution and Significance of the Modern Public Health Campaign,* 1923, pp. 32-33 (quoted). Herbert H. Waite, *Disease Prevention,* 1926, p. 5. Charles V. Chapin, ''The Science of Epidemic Diseases,'' *The Scientific Monthly,* June, 1928, 26:6:483. Paul de Kruif, *Microbe Hunters,* 1926, chs. III, V. René Vallery-Radot, *The Life of Pasteur,* 1902, translated from the French by Mrs. R. L. Devonshire.

after germ came in rapid succession until now it has been clearly proved that about a hundred infectious diseases are caused in this way. Although to Louis Pasteur belongs the high honor of having been the founder of bacteriology, it was Robert Koch who definitely established it as a science. Koch introduced those technical methods, such as the use of the solid, transparent medium, which led, during the eighties, in his hands and those of his followers, to a marvelous series of discoveries of the parasitic microörganisms causing disease. Previous to 1880 in only three diseases—anthrax, gonorrhea, and leprosy—had a bacterial cause been demonstrated. During the decade 1880 to 1890 there was discovered the causal relationship of bacteria to typhoid fever, cholera, lobar pneumonia, pus infections, tuberculosis, glanders, diphtheria, tetanus, Malta fever, cerebro-spinal meningitis, and other infectious diseases. "The following decade, scarcely less remarkable, was marked by the introduction of vaccine and serum therapy and prophylaxis, the discrimination between human and bovine tubercle bacilli by Theobald Smith, who had already by his studies of Texas cattle fever opened to exploration the highly important domain of insect-borne diseases, to which malaria, yellow fever, trypanosomiasis, and typhus belong. The close of the century was worthily crowned by the conquest of yellow fever by the discoveries of Walter Reed and his colleagues of the Army Yellow Fever Commission. The rôle of human carriers in the transmission of infection was made known, although full appreciation of the perplexing epidemiological problems thereby created did not come until the present century, which has continued to enrich our store of knowledge in the fields of hygiene and preventive medicine, as well as in other departments of medical science."[23]

Phases of the Public-Health Movement.—The modern public-health movement was born not quite one hundred years ago in Europe. It has improved its practice as advancing science has widened our knowledge concerning the causation of disease. The movement has gone through three distinct phases. The first covers the period of empirical environmental sanitation, and extends roughly from 1840 to 1890. It was inaugurated in England by the work of Sir Edwin Chadwick and Sir John Simon, who initiated the great sanitary awakening campaign which resulted in the construction of water and

[23] W. H. Welch, *Public Health in Theory and Practice*, 1925, pp. 32-33 (quoted). Herbert H. Waite, *Disease Prevention*, 1926, pp. 25-26. Charles V. Chapin, "The Science of Epidemic Diseases," *The Scientific Monthly*, June, 1928, 26:6:483-484. Paul de Kruif, *Microbe Hunters*, 1926, ch. VIII.

sewerage systems for the City of London and the passage of public-health laws.[24]

The impulse of the "great sanitary awakening" came to the United States from London. "Although measures for the prevention of nuisances and for the imposition of quarantine were adopted in colonial days, as far back as 1647, it was not until 1849 that the State authorities began to consider seriously their duties in connection with public health. In May of this year the Governor of Massachusettts appointed a commission under Lemuel Shattuck to ascertain the health needs of the commonwealth and to make recommendations. The Shattuck commission advised the establishment of a central Board of Health charged with the general execution of the health laws of the State, the creation of local Boards of Health, the taking of a census of the people, and a systematic registration of marriages, births, and deaths. It recommended an investigation into the cause of disease, abatement of the smoke nuisance, adoption of means for public health education, and other far-reaching measures. The report of the committee to the legislature was pigeonholed for twenty years, but in 1869 the State Board of Health of Massachusetts began work under a broad charter, which has been the model for other states. In 1877 Illinois became the second state to establish a Board of Health."[25]

Permanent governmental health organizations in this country came into existence to combat repeated outbreaks of cholera, typhus and yellow fevers. They were created at a time when disease was supposed to have its origin in filth, when sewer gas and foul odors were thought to be the cause of epidemics, and night air to carry illness and death. Under the influence of the filth theory of disease, the efforts of public health officials were concentrated on the abatement of nuisances by scavenging, by constructing sewers, and by building water-closets. They enforced measures to prevent overcrowding, to insure better housing, to promote ventilation, and to provide for a supply of safe milk and of unpolluted water. That is, the public-health movement first concerned itself with the control of the environment. Such was the nature of public-health work until the decade of the eighties, when the rapid, brilliant discoveries of bacteriology, showing the relation of microörganisms to disease, gave to the world a different conception of the cause of contagion.

The "sewer-gas-foul-odor-night-air era" of public-health work, as

[24] C.-E. A. Winslow, *Evolution and Significance of the Modern Public Health Campaign*, 1923, pp. 24-25.
[25] J. Howard Beard, "Progress of Public Health Work," *The Scientific Monthly*, Feb., 1922, 14:2:142.

Dr. Beard[26] styles it, was one of considerable progress. "In their vigorous attempts to eliminate 'emanations which polluted the air,' sanitarians made great contributions to comfort, common decency, and public health. We know now the safe disposal of sewage and the provision of pure water supplies were great factors in the eradication of cholera, and in the reduction of typhoid fever and the 'diarrheas.' Less crowded living conditions and cleaner houses did much to decrease vermin and louse-borne typhus fever. General cleanliness may have slightly diminished the incidence of disease spread by the secretions from the nose and throat. It had little effect upon the occurrence of yellow fever. While the pioneers in public health did much for comfort, convenience, and civic betterment, their erroneous conception as to the cause of disease has remained an unhappy legacy to succeeding generations. There are many today who fail to distinguish between filth, contaminated with disease germs, and unsightly rubbish, in itself incapable of causing illness. Believers in sewer gas are not entirely extinct even among the medical profession. Emphasis upon air as a carrier of disease kept down bed-room windows and delayed the building of sleeping-porches for several generations. Fear of air-borne disease still causes a great waste of formaldehyde gas in fumigation which is often more effective in the production of psychic calm than in the destruction of pathogenic bacteria."

The second phase of the modern public-health movement includes measures for the control of infections transmitted from one person to another. Here the bacteriologist rather than the engineer has assumed the leadership. The discoveries of Pasteur and Koch led to isolation and disinfection as measures for preventing the spread of disease; the work of Jenner and of Pfeiffer and Kolle brought in the use of vaccines; and the researches of Behring and Kitasato, the utilization of serums for the treatment of disease.[27] "Following the demonstration that communicable disease was due to specific micro-organisms, over-emphasis on the environment as the origin of disease gave way to control of man in preventing it. Rules and laws for the isolation of patients and carriers were enacted. Enforcement of these regulations gave rise to compulsory notification of communicable disease and the establishment of laboratories to ascertain the presence or absence

[26] "Progress of Public Health Work," *The Scientific Monthly*, Feb., 1922, 14:2:142-143. Charles V. Chapin, *Sources and Modes of Infection*, 1910, pp. 27-28, "The Science of Epidemic Disease," *The Scientific Monthly*, June, 1928, 26:6:482, 485, 492. Harry H. Moore, *Public Health in the United States*, 1923, pp. 5-6.
[27] Harry H. Moore, *Public Health in the United States*, 1923, pp. 6-7.

of the specific bacteria. The length of incubation, the period of communicability, and the manner in which the disease is transmitted became the factors determining the length and nature of quarantine. . . . Experience with isolation in the prevention of disease has shown that to be effective it must be early.''[28] Thus within the last half century bacteriology, by revealing the microörganisms concerned in those diseases which are of the greatest racial and social importance to mankind, and by providing methods for the study of their characters and behavior, transformed hygiene and sanitation from a blundering, empirical set of doctrines and practice to a science and laid secure foundations for their further development along scientific lines.[29]

The problems of infant mortality, tuberculosis, and various other diseases have led to the development of a third phase of the public-health movement—the education of the individual in the practices of personal hygiene—which is the dominant motive in the present-day campaign. ''The discovery of popular education as an instrument in preventive medicine, made by the pioneers in the tuberculosis movement,'' says Winslow,[30] ''has proved almost as far-reaching in its results as the discovery of the germ theory of disease thirty years before. . . . Tuberculosis and infant mortality are pre-eminent among all the causes of preventable disease and death as the two greatest scourges, from the abatement of which the largest results for humanity are to be attained. In each case the fight must be won, not by the construction of public works, but by the conduct of the individual life. The same thing is true with regard to the spread of the acute contagia, the burden of venereal disease, the obscure ill effects of defective eyes and ears and teeth, and a dozen other problems which in greater or lesser degree concern the public health. In every one of these cases the results we are striving for can only be reached by spreading a clear knowledge of the ways in which disease spreads, and the ways in which it is prevented, among the mothers who bring up the babies and the men who pay rent in the tenements and work in the stores and factories. With the growth of this conception of education as the dominant motive in the public-health campaign, there came the need for new machinery through which such education could be accomplished. An elaborate technique of

[28] J. Howard Beard, ''Progress of Public Health Work,'' *The Scientific Monthly*, Feb., 1922, 14:2:144.
[29] W. H. Welch, *Public Health in Theory and Practice*, 1925, pp. 33-34.
[30] *Evolution and Significance of the Modern Public Health Campaign*, 1923, pp. 53, 55.

health bulletins, health news services, health lecture bureaus and institutes, health cinemas, health exhibits, and health radiograms has been created to meet this need. These instruments are all of assistance in their twofold object, of securing popular support for the community health program, and of bringing into contact with health clinics of various types the individuals who are in need of their services." This most recent phase of the public-health movement has assumed a more positive aspect than have the others. As Sir George Newman,[31] Chief Medical Officer of the British Ministry of Health, has said, "In recent years we have learned that the public health is not only a matter of the postponement of mortality and the prevention of sickness, but of the positive side of health—the increase of vitality, capacity and efficiency of the human body. Our aim is not only to oppose disease but to advance and develop physical fitness and well-being."

The Sources and Modes of Infection.—The teachings of the new science of public health may be expressed in the following trichotomy:[32]

The sources of infection are in man.

The routes of infection are the routes of man's discharges.

The discharges are harmless until they enter man again.

Infectious diseases are infectious because they are due to the growth, in the body, of minute animal or vegetable forms (germs), the transmissibility of these germs from body to body being the sole explanation why these diseases are "catching."

Regardless of where the germs *develop* in the body, they leave it chiefly in the discharges of the nose and throat, bladder or bowel.

Outside the body, disease germs do not multiply in nature, except rarely and temporarily in milk, water, or similar fluids. To live they need moisture, darkness, the right food, temperature, and atmosphere. These differ for different kinds of germs. Most disease germs find the living body the most favorable environment; when they leave it, sunlight and desiccation soon kill or weaken them.

The main routes by which the discharges of the sick person pass to others are five in number.

1. Contact—the more or less direct transfer of discharges by mouth spray, by the hands, and by objects which have been recently handled. For nose and mouth discharges the routes are mouth spray, and

[31] In Introduction to *The Health of the Industrial Worker*, by Collis and Greenwood, 1921.

[32] The following is adapted from H. W. Hill, *The New Public Health*, 1920, ch. III. *Cf.* C.-E. A. Winslow, *Man and the Microbe*, 1924, pp. 15-16.

sputum conveyed through direct contact (as in kissing), and by the hands; for bowel and bladder discharges, the hands chiefly; and for all discharges, the things infected by them directly or through the hands, especially those things which then go to the mouth or touch things which go to the mouth, as food, water, eating utensils, towels, pipes, etc., etc.

2. Water supplies, which are peculiar because they are frequently polluted by serving as a means of sewage disposal.

3. Milk, which is regularly consumed in the raw state and which is subject to many sources of contamination.

4. Food, which may be exposed to pollution and then consumed within a short space of time without cooking.

5. Certain insects, like the fly and mosquito, which may carry the microbes, on or in their bodies, from one person to another. Flies furnish an effective route, especially from feces to food.

The first may be termed the private route of infection, the last four the public routes. Control of the public routes, which involves the problem of municipal sanitation, will be referred to in the following chapters. Here consideration will be given to contact infection. In general it may be said that the chief official public-health activities are the search for and supervision of infected persons, and the control of the infected discharges. "Prompt intelligent disinfection of all the excreta *immediately after their discharge from, the body* (concurrent disinfection), is the best weapon in the supervision of infected persons. Isolation of the infected person is the next best, and is more universally practicable, because immediate intelligent disinfection of discharges can rarely be secured outside of the very best hospitals for contagious disease. The search for and supervision of mild, early, convalescing, unrecognized, and concealed cases and carriers, as well as of frank cases, is necessarily an essential item in the scheme."[33]

Contact Infection.—As a result of the collaboration of epidemiologists and public-health laboratory men, it has been determined that the common contagious diseases are spread chiefly by means of the quite direct transfer of infective material from person to person. In such contact infection the problem of control is very much greater than it is in the case of the public routes of infection. The paths by which contact infection may spread are almost infinite in number. The most direct type of transfer is that which occurs when an infected

[33] H. W. Hill, *The New Public Health*, 1920, pp. 24-25.

person coughs or sneezes in the face of a susceptible victim, as may especially happen whenever people are crowded together in a street car or in some congested place of public assembly. More roundabout types of transfer occur in the case of fomites, or infected objects, which retain the infection for some time; this mode of transference should properly be considered a form of contact infection.[34] "The contact-borne diseases *par excellence* are, however, those in which the specific germs are present in the discharges from the nose and throat; and a moment's consideration will indicate that in this class are included the great majority of the communicable diseases with which we have to deal. Discharges from the upper respiratory tract are the primary sources of infection, not only in such diseases as the common cold, diphtheria, influenza, mumps, pneumonia, septic sore throat, tuberculosis, and whooping cough whose symptoms are obvious in throat, nose, and lungs, but also in the eruptive diseases, chickenpox, German measles, measles, scarlet fever, and smallpox, and in infant paralysis and epidemic cerebrospinal meningitis where the seat of the actual disease is in the central nervous system. The control of the diseases spread by contact dissemination of the discharges from the upper respiratory tract is, therefore, the major problem of modern epidemiology (the science of studying epidemics). Its solution can not be attained by any simple procedure such as the pasteurization of milk or the drainage of mosquito-breeding marshlands; but only by the far more difficult task of detecting and isolating human cases and carriers of disease."[35]

The first essential is, of course, that the health department should be notified of the existence of cases of communicable disease, which may prove a source of infection for others, at the earliest possible moment. As soon as a case of communicable disease is discovered it is the duty of the health department to establish isolation—that is, to see that the case is so cared for as to give every possible security against the transmission of the infective material. Quite as important as the care of the first case of disease is the supervision of other members of the family, schoolmates, or associates, who have been in contact with the patient and may already have become infected by him before his condition was recognized. This is known as concurrent epidemiology. The duty of the health officer is to exclude these persons from school and places of assembly and to keep them under observation

[34] Charles V. Chapin, *The Sources and Modes of Infection*, 1910, ch. V; "The Science of Epidemic Diseases," *The Scientific Monthly*, June, 1928, 26:6:485.
[35] C.-E. A. Winslow, *Man and the Microbe*, 1924, p. 45.

until it is certain that they are not coming down with the disease.[36] Winslow[37] states that the actual carrying out of the following two simple rules would probably do more than anything else for the prevention of communicable disease.

1. Nothing should ever go into the mouth, except things to eat and drink and the toothbrush. Nothing should ever go to the nose except a clean handkerchief.

2. The hands should be thoroughly washed before meals and before eating any food handled with the fingers.

It is a surprise, and rather shocking, to learn that the human hands are so often the carriers of excrement, yet this fact has been abundantly proved by both bacteriologists and epidemiologists. The following graphic statement by Dr. Chapin[38] will quickly dispel any doubt that the fingers play the chief part in the spread of our most common diseases, in which the secretions of the mouth are the main source of infection.

Probably the chief vehicle for the conveyance of nasal and oral secretion from one to another is the fingers. If one takes the trouble to watch for a short time his neighbors, or even himself, unless he has been particularly trained in such matters, he will be surprised to note the number of times that the fingers go to the mouth and the nose. Not only is the saliva made use of for a great variety of purposes, and numberless articles are for one reason or another placed in the mouth, but for no reason whatever, and all unconsciously, the fingers are with great frequency raised to the lips or the nose. Who can doubt that if the salivary glands secreted indigo the fingers would continually be stained a deep blue, and who can doubt that if the nasal and oral secretions contain the germs of disease these germs will be almost as constantly found upon the fingers?

All successful commerce is reciprocal, and in this universal trade in human saliva the fingers not only bring foreign secretions to the mouth of their owner, but there exchanging them for his own, distribute the latter to everything that the hand touches. This happens not once but scores and hundreds of times during the day's round of the individual. The cook spreads his saliva on the muffins and rolls, the waitress infects the glasses and spoons, the moistened fingers of the peddler arrange his fruit, the thumb of the milkman is in his measure, the reader moistens the pages of his book,

---

[36] C.-E. A. Winslow, *Man and the Microbe*, 1924, p. 46. H. W. Hill, *The New Public Health*, 1920, ch. VIII.

[37] C.-E. A. Winslow, *Man and the Microbe*, 1924, pp. 50-51. See also Allan J. McLaughlin, *The Communicable Diseases, How they spread and how they may be controlled*, 1923.

[38] *The Sources and Modes of Infection*, 1910, pp. 146-147. See also his ''The Science of Epidemic Diseases,'' *The Scientific Monthly*, June, 1928, 26:6:486.

the conductor his transfer tickets, the 'lady' the fingers of her glove. Every one is busily engaged in this distribution of saliva, so that the end of each day finds this secretion freely distributed on the doors, window sills, furniture and playthings in the home, the straps of trolley cars, the rails and counter and desks of shops and public buildings, and indeed upon everything that the hands of man touch. What avails it if the pathogens do die quickly? A fresh supply is furnished each day.

Importance of "Carriers" and "Missed" Cases.—"The laboratory has taught the epidemiologist not only where not to search for the source of disease, but where he should search. The laboratory has shown that when disease germs gain access to a person, they do not always make him sick. He may feel perfectly well, and go about, a healthy 'carrier' of disease germs. Again the germs may make their host only slightly ill, causing such atypical symptoms that, even if seen by a physician, the disease would not be recognized, would be 'missed' by the doctor. The laboratory has given the physician and the epidemiologist many methods of the greatest value as aids to diagnosis and which help greatly in the search for and study of carriers and missed cases."[39] There is ample epidemiological evidence that healthy carriers as well as mild unrecognized cases are the source of well-marked outbreaks. The story of "Typhoid Mary," the first of its kind to be reported, is a classic illustration of the importance of carriers in the transmission of disease. Between 1902 and 1907, while employed as cook in six different families, Mary Mallon was the cause of typhoid cases in each family, infecting 26 persons in all. In 1907 she was taken to a hospital and found to be a chronic typhoid carrier. She was released and was lost to sight for some time. In October, 1914, she was engaged as cook in the Sloane Hospital for Women in New York, and a few months later an outbreak of typhoid occurred, principally among the doctors, nurses, and help of the institution, involving 25 cases. A subsequent study of her career showed that she had infected still other individuals and that she may have given rise to the water-borne outbreak of 1,300 cases at Ithaca, New York, in 1903.

Another carrier whose story is even more surprising was a farmer who had typhoid fever in Wisconsin in 1864. He recovered and moved to Camden, New Jersey, where he set up in the milk business. In 1878 his daughter had typhoid, in 1886 his son-in-law, in 1893 another daughter, in 1897 another, in 1903 and 1909 two hired men. Meanwhile Camden became notorious for its generally high typhoid

[39] Charles V. Chapin, "The Science of Epidemic Diseases," *The Scientific Monthly*, June, 1928, 26:6:485.

rate, three-quarters of the cases being among the users of this farmer's milk. Finally, in 1900, some of this milk was sent to New York and caused an epidemic of 380 cases, when the New York authorities investigated, found the man to be a typhoid carrier and thus solved the problem.[40]

It is obvious that any scheme of prevention which fails to take into account carriers and missed cases is doomed to partial and perhaps complete failure.

Immunity.—From ancient times it has been known that in most contagious diseases one attack protects against another. This is the specific immunity which almost universally follows an attack of some communicable disease. When a person recovers from almost any such infection he will have acquired an immunity which protects him against another attack, sometimes only for a few weeks but frequently for life. "Even influenza seems to produce some immunity in many of its victims, though it is usually far from complete or lasting. It is only in quite recent years that we have learned that it is by no means always necessary for a person to have a typical attack of a contagious disease to acquire immunity. Many times, persons have such a mild attack of diphtheria or scarlet fever that it is unnoticed, but the immunity may be as complete as that following a severe case. Again, it is now well known that, in most contagious diseases, a still larger portion of the population acquires the germs without being sick at all. They are merely carriers, but are, nevertheless, immunized by their germs. It is believed that the amount of such natural immunity in a community is one of the important factors in determining the course of outbreaks. In large towns and cities, where one's contacts with others are so frequent, the number of such immunes is usually very much larger than in rural districts."[41]

From these facts it is obvious that if we had some way of producing such specific immunity at will and without waiting for a natural attack to occur, in mild or in severe form, we should possess a most potent weapon in the war against disease. In a number of the communicable diseases exactly this result has been accomplished by the procedures of vaccine and serum treatment. Ever since the discovery by Jenner of vaccination against smallpox, medical men have sought immunization against other diseases, but it remained for Pas-

[40] C.-E. A. Winslow, *Man and the Microbe*, 1924, pp. 13-14. M. J. Rosenau, *Preventive Medicine and Hygiene*, 1927, pp. 106-107. Charles V. Chapin, *The Sources and Modes of Infection*, 1910, ch. II.

[41] Charles V. Chapin, "The Science of Epidemic Diseases," *The Scientific Monthly*, June, 1928, 26:6:486-487.

teur to show the way. Successful methods are now employed against several diseases, as diphtheria, typhoid fever, scarlet fever, dysentery, cholera, plague, measles, and rabies, and the number is increasing year by year.[42]

Results.—The science of epidemiology has profoundly modified our methods of dealing with contagious diseases. Terminal fumigation has been abandoned, and emphasis has been placed on the search for carriers, the quarantine of contacts, and the prompt isolation of early cases of disease, which are the distinguishing characteristics of present-day practice. Where the causative organisms can be detected or where the period of communicability and avenues of infection have been determined, the modern methods of concurrent epidemiology are beginning to yield results of substantial importance. "The old methods of arbitrary detention and destructive disinfection of incoming vessels has given way to effective inspection and removal of contacts. Fumigation is reserved only for plague ships, and is not destructive. On shore the fumigation of dwellings and schools also has been abandoned. The useless search for disease in drains and cesspools has ceased, and the search for human carriers in homes, schools, institutions and dairies finds the true sources of infection and permits control. A wet sheet is no longer hung before the door of the sick room, but the attendants are taught to wash their hands even as the surgeon does. Persons do not cross the street when they see a scarlet fever warning sign, nor is it necessary to place an isolation hospital in a lonely spot. All our methods of isolation are becoming more rational and effective and less of a burden on the afflicted."[43]

More important has been the gain in reduction of sickness and prolongation of life. A number of infectious diseases have been conquered; others are rapidly vanishing. Widespread epidemics have become a thing of the past, at least in advanced countries. A successful war is being waged against the invisible foes of mankind. But that is a story which belongs to another chapter.

[42] *Ibid.*, p. 487. C.-E.A. Winslow, *Man and the Microbe*, 1924, p. 53; see ch. XIV, below.
[43] Charles V. Chapin, "The Science of Epidemic Diseases," *The Scientific Monthly*, June, 1928, 26:6:493. *Cf.* C.-E.A. Winslow, *Evolution and Significance of the Modern Public Health Campaign*, 1923, p. 45.

CHAPTER X

THE PUBLIC WATER-SUPPLY

THE chief sanitary measures requiring community action are those which come under the head of Public Works, including the provision of an adequate and safe water-supply, the disposal of sewage, and the removal of general refuse. The most important and earliest of these provisions is that of the public water-supply. It is the first basic essential of municipal sanitation. The water-supply, says Geddes[1] in reference to the public systems of English cities, is "precisely the most important, the ultimate and determinant condition of population, and the inexorable limit of their growth. Coal will still last a long time, and cotton might expand accordingly; but water is the prime necessity after air itself, and, unlike it, is limited in quantity. Food can be brought for almost any conceivable population as long as ships can sail the seas, and we have the wherewithal to buy; famine one can survive for months; total starvation even for weeks; but without water we last barely three days. Parish Pump indeed! the prime necessity of regional statesmanship, since even of bare survival. For life and health, for cleanliness and beauty, for manufactures too, what more need be said?"

The Relation of Water to Life.—The importance of water, as of other absolute essentials, is so obvious that it is little appreciated. We accept such things without questioning, until some emergency forces them upon our attention. We may know, but ordinarily we do not stop to consider that "nothing can live without water. Where there is no water there can be no life of any kind, vegetable or animal. There is no water on the moon, therefore no living thing can exist there. If there were no water on the earth, there would be no trees, plants, or vegetables of any sort; no food to eat; nothing to drink; and therefore no human beings or lower animals. Everything would be a vast desert of rocks or sand."

As water is necessary for life, so it is necessary for health. "When a person eats and drinks, the food is digested and changed in the body; the useful part goes to nourish the body and the useless part is carried off. The useless and unhealthy particles are carried away

[1] *Cities in Evolution*, 1915, pp. 42-43.

234

by the aid of water just as the good particles are distributed in the body by the aid of water." Water is essential to health in another way. Just as it serves to carry useless and unhealthy matter out of the body, so it serves to carry the dirt and filth out of the house and city through the sewers. There could be no sewer system without an adequate water-supply. Without sewers and a water-supply there could be no sanitary arrangements in our houses; the streets could not be washed; filth would accumulate; and disease and death would be the result. Great epidemics, killing thousands of people, have been caused by the lack of proper water-supply and sewerage.

Water is nature's great provision for extinguishing fires. The great damage in San Francisco in 1906 at the time of the earthquake was not due primarily to the earthquake, but to the breaking of the water pipes which prevented extinguishing the fire which started. Water is necessary in industry, being utilized for power and in many manufacturing processes. "So universal is the use of water in industry that it may be said in literal truth that not a thing is manufactured —for food, clothing, housing, transportation, or any other purpose— of which water does not form a part or in the making of which water does not help. If we had only enough water for food and drink and none for mechanical and manufacturing purposes, nearly all forms of modern industry and almost all the manifold activities of our lives would come to a standstill." In short, water is necessary for life, for food and drink, for health, for sanitation, for protection from fire, and for industry.[2]

The Development of Public Water-Supplies.—The human race recognized, even in its earliest days, the relation of water to life. Early nomadic tribes had their movements guided by the location of oases and streams, and it is well known that the first civilizations developed along the shores of such rivers as the Nile and the Euphrates. Wells were common in ancient Egypt, and some of them appear to have been of great antiquity. The most famous of these, Joseph's well at Cairo, was excavated in solid rock to a depth of nearly three hundred feet. Likewise the practice of impounding water in reservoirs and holding it for times of need is known to have existed long before the beginning of the Christian era. The ancient Egyptians, as is evidenced by traces of great canals and storage lakes, impounded the waters of the Nile at flood periods not only for irrigation during drought but also for regular domestic use. There were great rain-

[2] Edward H. Hall, *The Catskill Aqueduct*, 1918, pp. 657-661.

water cisterns in Carthage as early as 150 B.C., and at Athens there were infiltration galleries for collecting ground-water supplies.

Water-supply may therefore be regarded as one of the oldest among community requirements. It was one of the essentials to the inception of the human community. The institution of the city, indeed, was founded upon the institution of the well or the spring. "To this day the traveler in the Far East, in the center of China, who comes at dusk to a walled town, knows that the town is there because of a well—a water storage; to this day the traveler who sights a gray stony medieval-founded city in Italy or Spain knows that it has stood there these hundreds of years for one reason only—a spring has not failed."[3] But as towns and cities grew, the supply of spring or well at the site became inadequate, and the need of aqueducts arose. The greatest of the aqueduct systems of the ancient world was the Roman. In early times, the Romans obtained their water from the polluted Tiber, but they soon recognized the danger of using such water and expended large sums of money in constructing aqueducts. The Roman aqueducts, built from 312 B.C. to A.D. 52, nine in number, varied in length from 10 to 62 miles. When all were in operation, they had an aggregate capacity of about 84,000,000 gallons a day. Pliny[4] said concerning the aqueducts supplying Rome with water: "If we only take into consideration the abundant supply of water to the public, for baths, ponds, canals, household purposes, gardens, places in the suburbs, and country-houses; and reflect upon the distances that are traversed, the arches that have been constructed, the mountains that have been pierced, the valleys that have been levelled, we must of necessity admit that there is nothing to be found more worthy of our admiration throughout the whole universe."

The water facilities of medieval cities, like their other municipal services, were very primitive. No city of medieval Europe approached either Athens or Rome in the quality or the amount of water used. In fact, "from the fall of Rome to the Industrial Revolution no progress was made in the art of giving urban communities an adequate supply of water for human use. London was worse off in 1750 than Rome had been at the beginning of the Christian era. But the great changes which marked the incoming of the nineteenth century soon worked a revolution in this field." Rapid urban growth, new inventions (such as the steam engine, which permitted water to be pumped

[3] R. W. Child and H. Nawn, "Civilization and the Water Tap," *Saturday Evening Post*, Nov. 13, 1926.

[4] *Natural History*, Bk. XXXVI, ch. 24 (translation by Bostock and Riley).

in large quantities at relatively small cost, and cast-iron pipes, available after 1800, which replaced wood or lead ones), and a wider diffusion of sanitary knowledge among the people created everywhere a demand for an enlarged and improved water-supply. "Where the regular municipal authorities could not respond to this demand private companies were organized to build reservoirs and bring water into the cities for sale to the householders. The first modern water systems in many European cities, and in some American cities as well, were planned and built by private companies. It did not take the municipalities long to realize, however, that public water supplies ought to be publicly-owned, and consequently very few water franchises were granted to private companies after the middle of the nineteenth century. Since that time the expansion in this field of municipal service has been extraordinarily rapid. In 1850 there were only eighty public water systems in the United States, in 1880 only six hundred, and today there are nearly six thousand. In Western Europe the progress has been almost as remarkable."[5]

Munro[6] thinks that public ownership of the water-supply system is demanded by various considerations which do not apply to other public utilities such as lighting plants, street railways, and telephones. "The water supply, in point of adequacy and purity, has a relation to the public health which the others have not. The city cannot leave the control of its illness-and-death rates in the hands of any profit-seeking concern and should not be asked to do so. Again, the city itself is the largest individual customer of the water plant. The park department, the street-sprinkling service, the sewer-cleaning division, the fire department and many other branches of municipal administration are all large users of water; they sometimes take as much as one-fifth of the entire daily supply. Finally, there is a public interest that may be adversely affected by a private company's rate-making policy. One method of charging for water may encourage the coming of new industries; another may drive them away. One schedule may discourage the owners of crowded tenements from putting in proper sanitary arrangements; another may make it more easy for them to do so. Water should be supplied to the people at cost, or nearly at cost, and a private company cannot be expected to operate the plant on this basis. For these various reasons water supply is a public utility that stands in a class by itself. The issue of public or private

[5] William B. Munro, *Municipal Government and Administration*, 1923, II, 139, 141.
[6] *Ibid.*, II, 161.

ownership cannot here be settled on economic grounds alone. Social considerations bulk large. One may therefore be a strong advocate of public ownership in this field, and yet be strongly opposed to the municipalization of gas plants or street railways.''

The Source of Water-Supply.—All water is either *ground water*, that which has passed through the soil and is made available for use in wells or springs, or *surface water*, that found in lakes, ponds, rivers, streams. In the case of ground water, a high degree of organic purity is established by natural processes; such water is sanitary provided no pollution has entered it. Surface water, on the other hand, is usually less pure, for it is affected by surface drainage. In rural communities the source of supply is usually ground water, and each household provides for its own needs. As population increases and rural conditions give way to urban, ground water becomes limited in quantity and polluted by surface washings, and the community must turn to larger sources of supply and introduce methods of purification.[7] The history of every city has shown first the use of wells, then their pollution and inadequacy as population increases, and finally the development of a public system of surface-water supply.

One of the first instances of a clearcut demonstration of the causation of sickness by infected ground water was that of the famous Broad Street Well, in St. James's Parish, London, in 1854, which was responsible for a serious outbreak of cholera. This occurred at a time when it was almost universally believed that cholera is spread by a miasma from polluted soil. The demonstration by John Snow of the real source of the epidemic has been called by Sedgwick[8] "a monument of sanitary research, of medical and engineering interest and of penetrating inductive reasoning." During the outbreak there was an enormous concentration of cases in a very limited area just east of Regent Street, there having been reported, during a period of about six weeks, over 600 fatal cases. A careful study of the site, soil, subsoil, streets, density and character of population, dwellings, yards, closets, cesspools, vaults, drains, conditions of cleanliness and atmospheric conditions, revealed nothing of significance. But a study of the water-supply disclosed most interesting facts. Nearly all the cases were nearer a certain public pump in Broad Street than any other well, and most of them gave a definite history of getting water from this pump. Investigation further showed that a privy vault and

[7] William T. Sedgwick, *Principles of Sanitary Science*, 1905, pp. 226 ff.

[8] *Ibid.*, 170-181. *Cf.* Charles V. Chapin, *The Sources and Modes of Infection*, 1910, pp. 266-267.

cesspool in an adjoining house discharged through a leaky drain which ran within two feet of the well. There were four fatal cases of cholera in this house at the time of the outbreak and obscure earlier cases which were probably cholera. Snow rightly concluded that the well was the source of cholera, and had the pump handle removed. The outbreak, which was declining, soon ceased.

Chicago provides a typical example of the water-supply problem which faces every growing community. When the old household wells became polluted owing to growth of the population and increase of the city's wastes, certain enterprising citizens began hauling water from Lake Michigan and selling it to the inhabitants. In 1834 the village council undertook to meet the demand for better water-supply by appropriating $95.50 for digging a public well. It supplied only a small section on the north side. On the south side a water company was formed which laid pipes out 500 feet into the lake and constructed a tank of a capacity of 500 or 600 barrels. Water was pumped into the tank and then distributed. This proved very inadequate, and water-cart distributors were still able to do a good business. In 1854 the city opened its own waterworks. Water was taken from the lake and pumped into two reservoirs, one on each side of the city. Ten years later extension was necessary. A tunnel was built under the lake for two miles. After the fire of 1871 the city built a four-mile tunnel. These extensions of the tunnel for the intake of water were necessitated by the fact that the water was being increasingly polluted by the disposal of sewage into the lake. The situation was later improved by the construction of the Chicago Drainage Canal to carry sewage away from Lake Michigan into the Mississippi River. Despite all the city's efforts, the water-supply is not yet entirely satisfactory.[9]

Purposes of a Water-Supply.—The water-supply of a community serves three main purposes. As we have seen, water is needed for various industrial uses. In this case it must be free from substances which incrust boilers or hinder manufacturing processes, such as in paper making. Then there are the public uses of a water-supply—for fighting fires, flushing streets and sewers—in which quantity is of more importance than quality. Finally, there is the domestic use, for which purity and clearness are essential. Such water must be chemically and bacteriologically pure for drinking and culinary purposes. The chief danger in domestic use of water is that it may contain

[9] Charles Zueblin, *American Municipal Progress*, 1915, p. 103. A. E. Gorman, "Chlorination Control in Chicago," *American City*, November, 1927, 37:5:613-621.

disease germs. In the past, water has been responsible for the most widespread epidemics of intestinal diseases, particularly typhoid fever and Asiatic cholera. There is universal evidence that where a water-supply is improved, these and other diseases decrease.

Probably not more than 1 per cent of the water is used for drinking and cooking purposes, nor more than 10 per cent for all domestic uses. "So far as ninety per cent of a city's water consumption is concerned, there is no need for bacteriological purity. Germ-free water is not essential for putting out fires, watering streets, cleaning sewers, dyeing silk, filling steam boilers, sprinkling lawns, and flushing toilets."[10] This situation has led to a double water-supply in some cities, notably Paris—a good potable water for drinking and general household purposes, and a less costly water for civic and other uses. The duplicate system, however, has certain drawbacks, the principal one of which is the danger of mistake or misuse. Therefore cities go to the great expense of protecting their watersheds, storing water in reservoirs to improve its quality, filtering it, and guarding it at every point against pollution.

Water Purification.—Since, as we have seen, water may act as a public route of infection, measures must be taken to render it harmless from the public-health standpoint. It is important to get rid of disease germs, particularly the typhoid bacillus, suspended matter, color, and disagreeable tastes and odors. The various processes of water purification may be classified as natural and artificial or mechanical.

Natural purification takes place through the action of several agents. The bacteria in the polluting substances may die for lack of food if sufficient dilution with pure water takes place. The penetrating sunlight also aids in the destruction of bacteria, though in open reservoirs sunlight may favor the growth of various green water plants (mainly algae) and lead to the accumulation of undesirable gases or odors. Aëration—the thorough mixing of air with the water—is a common method of removing these objectionable qualities. Purification is also effected by sedimentation, the suspended matter settling at the bottom. This is promoted by storing the water, since quiet, not running water, purifies itself. River waters stored in large reservoirs commonly lose in a few weeks 90 to 95 per cent of their bacterial contents. The above-mentioned natural agents of purification are taken advantage of in every water system.

Artificial means of water purification consist, first of all, in sand

[10] William B. Munro, *Municipal Government and Administration*, 1923, II, 144.

filtration. Two types are common, slow sand filtration and rapid or mechanical filtration. The method of slow sand filtration is modeled after the natural filtration which takes place through the soil. A bed is constructed of different grades of material, ranging from very fine sand on top to gravel at the bottom. The sand grains on top soon become covered with a film of matter like gelatine—in reality, a layer of scum. This holds a form of bacteria hostile to the disease-producing germs in the water, so that in general only a fraction of 1 per cent of the latter survive to pass through the filter. These more vigorous bacteria, utilizing the oxygen in the filtering water, reduce not only the total organic matter in it, but aid in the final destruction of the water bacteria caught and held in the sand bed spaces. The action of the filter is not so much mechanical as bacterial. In time the film of scum on top of the sand bed becomes impervious and must be removed; this is done by scraping it off. The filter is useless until a new film forms.

In mechanical filtration (often called the American Method to distinguish it from the slow process known as the English Method) coarser sand is used and there is a higher rate of action. A coagulant such as aluminium sulphate, alum, and iron sulphate, is added to the water to increase precipitation. This forms a jelly-like mass or coagulum, which mechanically carries down all matter in suspension, including bacteria. The coagulum, after it has settled, forms a layer on the sand which acts in a manner similar to the biological layer of the slow sand filter. The mechanical filters become clogged more frequently than do the slow sand filters; they require cleansing several times daily. This is readily accomplished by reversing the flow of water through the filter. Mechanical filters act much more rapidly, water passing through them generally at a rate of 150 million gallons per acre per day. By the slow process at best not more than 3 million gallons per acre pass through per day. In turbid waters containing fine clay, slow sand filtration is not effective, since the clay passes through the sand, carrying with it sewage bacteria. It is in waters of this kind that the rapid mechanical filter is most useful. Mechanical filters are usually less expensive to install than slow sand filters, but more expensive to operate. The selection of one or the other method depends upon local conditions; it cannot be determined by any general rule. The nature of the raw water, whether clear or turbid, discolored or not, badly polluted or not, is the most important factor but not the only one. Consideration must be given also to what sites

are available and what they cost, likewise to what the city can afford
to spend.

The following table summarizes some of the relative values of the
two methods.

SLOW SAND FILTRATION	RAPID SAND FILTERS
Action mainly bacterial; mechanical filtration also.	Mechanical filtration.
Bacterial removal uniform; 99%.	Bacterial removal less uniform; 95 to 99%.
Rate: 1,500,000 to 5,000,000 gallons per acre daily.	Rate: 100 to 200 times slow sand filter.
Cleaned by scraping off surface layer.	Cleaned by reversing flow (with agitation).
Serviceable for less turbid waters.	Helpful in turbid waters (clay, silt; also coloring).

Another method of purification is by chemical disinfection, chiefly
with chlorine, an effective germicide. It is sometimes employed without
previous treatment of the water by filtration. Where the water is
filtered, chlorination of the effluent always terminates the purification
process. The amount used varies with conditions; commonly it is
from one-half to three pounds of liquid chlorine per one million gallons of water.

Daily bacteriological analyses are made as an added safeguard.
The results of the tests are commonly expressed by saying that colon
bacilli (B. coli) are present or are not present in so many cubic centi-
meters of water. The finding of B. coli in water is accepted as a definite, although not as an absolutely conclusive, indication of pollution
by sewage. The attempt to detect the actual presence of typhoid bacilli
(B. typhosi) is not usually made because the task of isolating and
identifying these particular members of the colon group is somewhat
difficult. The introduction of filtration and disinfection processes has
everywhere greatly reduced the prevalence of typhoid fever and other
water-borne infections.[11]

Per Capita Water Consumption.—The water consumption of different cities shows considerable variation. European cities do not use,
on the average, more than 50 gallons per capita each day; some of

[11] William T. Sedgwick, Principles of Sanitary Science, 1905, pp. 223 ff. Jean
Broadhurst, Home and Community Hygiene, 1923, pp. 92-114. Herbert H. Waite,
Disease Prevention, 1926, pp. 61-62. William B. Munro, Municipal Government
and Administration, 1923, II, 149, 153-154. Charles V. Chapin, Municipal Sanitation in the United States, 1901, ch. VI. C.-E. A. Winslow, Man and the Microbe,
1924, pp. 25-26. M. J. Rosenau, Preventive Medicine and Hygiene, 1927, pp.
985-1030.

them use much less. The figures are lowest in cities like Constantinople and Warsaw; highest in the municipalities of Great Britain, France, and Germany. In the cities of the United States the daily per capita consumption rarely runs below 100 gallons and it is frequently much higher, in some of the larger cities amounting to as much as 250 gallons. Water consumption depends on a number of factors—the relative amount of waste, the number and nature of the industries in the city, the percentage of the service that is metered, and the general sanitary traditions of the people.[12]

Location of Cities and the Water-Supply.—The problem of a given city in securing a satisfactory water-supply varies with a number of conditions, including the location of the city, its topography, the nearness or remoteness of available sources, and the degree of contamination. Cities that are seaports are in the condition of the Ancient Mariner with "Water, water everywhere, nor any drop to drink." They must turn to inland supplies of fresh water. Cities located on lakes and rivers have an adequate supply at hand, but such water is usually polluted through serving as a receptacle for sewage. In cases where there is no body of water that can be used, the city must develop and tap a watershed. The character of surface water depends largely on the conditions of the watershed—the degree to which it is inhabited, the nature of the soil, and the amount and kind of polluting substances that enter the water collected there. Surface water is polluted organically by sewage and by drainage from roads, stables, and woolen mills; and inorganically by the wastes from factories and other mills. The ideal would be for each city to have an uninhabited area from which to draw a water-supply kept free from organic matter. Since this is usually impossible, the next best thing is to safeguard the watershed as much as possible by patrolling it and by controlling all the sanitary arrangements.

The Water-Supply System of New York City.—The history of the public water-supply system of America's largest city is an absorbing account of municipal achievement. The present developed system is a striking example of the extreme efforts which large cities must make to satisfy common needs. It is also a monument to the skill of sanitary engineering, upon the accomplishments of which depend the life and growth of the city. It is, indeed, one of the marvels of the modern world.

[12] Jean Broadhurst, *Home and Community Hygiene*, 1923, pp. 110-112. William B. Munro, *Municipal Government and Administration*, 1923, II, 142.

The Era of Wells and Pumps.—Throughout the history of the water-supply of New York City, from the earliest days to the present, two considerations have been uppermost: the public-health aspect, and the constant pressure for new supplies due to the rapid growth of the city. The natural water-supply of New Amsterdam and of New York City in its early years was derived from the ponds, brooks, and springs which abounded on the island of Manhattan before they were obliterated by the construction of streets and buildings. The earliest artificial supply was derived from wells. In 1677, under English rule, the Common Council began the systematic construction of wells in the public streets. Pumps came into fashion in the first half of the eighteenth century and rapidly displaced the old well-sweeps. "Other than wells, with hand pumps, the first municipal waterworks within the limits of New York City were those for the lower part of Manhattan Island, which, commencing in 1776, with a population of 25,000, was supplied with well water pumped by a steam engine into a reservoir near Pearl street and Broadway and distributed through pipes made by boring logs." These works were soon abandoned on account of the Revolution. A similar service was furnished after 1800 by a private corporation, the Manhattan Company, and in 1830 by the town. By this time the population had mounted to 200,000. The Manhattan Company, which operated the first successful pipe-line system of waterworks, continued in business until about the time the Croton system—the city's first extensive undertaking—came into use in 1842. It had about 25 miles of mains and supplied approximately 2,000 houses, the maximum amount of water furnished being roughly 700,000 gallons a day. In 1829 the city built a reservoir for the distribution of water for fire-extinguishing purposes. The water came from a well and was not good enough for domestic use. In fact, not one of the early supplies was ever satisfactory in either quantity or quality. The movement for a municipal water-supply received powerful stimulus from a series of fires and epidemics. Finally a commission was appointed to draw up plans. It recommended the utilization of the Croton River, about 38 miles north of the city, and in 1834 this proposal was ratified by popular vote.

The Croton System.—Construction of the Old Croton aqueduct was begun in 1837 and was sufficiently advanced to supply the city in 1842. A diverting dam was built across the Croton River 6 miles from its mouth. It impounded the water of the river in a reservoir 5 miles long and about 400 acres in area. From it an aqueduct 34 miles long, of 80 million gallons daily capacity, was built along the slopes of the hills on the eastern side of the Hudson River to Yonkers, thence turning inland and passing southward through the Bronx to the Harlem River, and crossing upon the High Bridge. Another reservoir, for distributing purposes, was built within the area that is now Central Park, between 79th and 86th Streets.

It was thought at the time that this system would supply the needs of the city for a great many years to come, but within a generation the original Croton system was outgrown. Severe droughts in 1880 and 1881 proved the inadequacy of the supply and the need of additional waterworks. On account of the phenomenal growth of the city, it became necessary not only to build additional reservoirs from time to time, but also to construct another aqueduct from the Croton valley. In 1885 construction was begun on this conduit, and in 1891 it was put into regular service. The New Croton aqueduct is almost entirely of tunnel construction, in virtually a straight line from the Old Croton dam to Jerome Park reservoir. Its length is 31 miles to its terminus at the 135th Street gate-house, whence lines of 48-inch cast-iron pipe are laid to a new distributing reservoir in Central Park between 86th and 96th Streets, and to other points. The rated capacity of the New Croton aqueduct is 300 million gallons daily.

The Croton system as completed embraces the two aqueducts, ten reservoirs and six controlled natural lakes, providing a total storage of 104 billion gallons. As thus developed, the Croton River will yield, even in periods of drought, a daily supply of 336 million gallons.

Other Borough Water-Supplies.—Meantime different arrangements were made by the other boroughs of New York City prior to 1917, when they were brought in under the new Catskill system. Brooklyn was able longer than Manhattan to use natural sources, relying exclusively upon springs, streams, ponds, and wells up to the year 1859 (when the public supply began) and largely so up to the present time. These sources yield about 150 million gallons a day and involve much pumping, at great expense. Queens has had municipal pumping stations and private water companies, whose entire sources were ground water collected by means of driven wells. The Bronx in 1880 developed the Bronx and Byram watersheds; in 1884 connection was made with the Kensico reservoir and in 1902 with the Old Croton aqueduct. Richmond, prior to 1917, was dependent upon wells. It was served by private water companies until 1909, when the principal water systems were acquired by the city.

The Catskill System.—The New Croton system in time proved inadequate, owing to the growth of the city, and it became necessary to tap a new watershed. In 1907 the city undertook to draw off water from the Catskill Mountains, about 120 miles from the city, west of the Hudson River. The Catskill Water-Supply system was opened in 1917, though it was not brought to completion until 1929, by which time it had been extended an additional 30 miles northward. It has cost roughly $200,000,000. Several different watersheds, with a total drainage area of over 500 square miles, were tapped, reservoirs were constructed, and an aqueduct nearly 120 miles long was built to carry the water to the city. The largest reservoir in the Catskill system is the Ashokan, about 14 miles west from Kingston, New York. "From the Ashokan reservoir it is almost a three-days' journey for the water at the average velocity to flow through the aqueduct to the Silver Lake terminal reservoir on Staten Island, in the course of which it flows along many a steep hillside, crosses several broad plains, pierces mountains, descends beneath rivers and wide, deep valleys, traverses the Boroughs of The Bronx, Manhattan and Brooklyn, and crosses the Narrows of New York harbor." A few of the outstanding features of the system are as follows:

The Ashokan reservoir, about 12 miles long and from 1 to 3 miles wide, has an available capacity of 128 billion gallons, a quantity sufficiently great to cover all of Manhattan Island to a depth of 30 feet. It is the largest in the world. Within the area selected for the reservoir were nine villages with private houses, boarding houses, stores, churches, school houses, and all the activities of country life. There were also 32 cemeteries, containing over 2,800 graves, some dating back more than two hundred years. It was necessary to acquire all this land, remove the villages and cemeteries, re-locate 11 miles of the Ulster & Delaware railroad track, discontinue 64 miles of old highways, build 40 miles of new highways, and construct 10 highway bridges, to make way for the reservoir.

The most northerly of New York City's waterworks is the Schoharie reservoir, developed by construction of the Gilboa dam on the Schoharie creek. It has an available capacity of 20 billion gallons. This project was completed in 1927. From the Schoharie reservoir the water is diverted through the Shandaken tunnel to the Esopus creek, whence it flows into the Ashokan reservoir for storage and subsequent delivery through the Catskill aqueduct to New York City. The tunnel, which extends 18.1 miles under the Shandaken Mountain range, is the longest in the world.

From the Ashokan reservoir the water is brought by aqueduct about 45 miles to the Hudson River, at Storm King Mountain, where

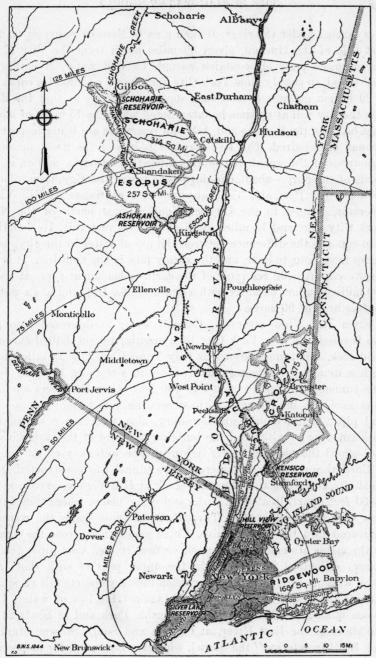

(Courtesy of the Board of Water Supply of the City of New York)
NEW YORK WATER-SUPPLY SYSTEM

it is carried under the river. It then goes to Kensico reservoir on the east side of the Hudson, about 30 miles north from the City Hall. The Kensico reservoir contains enough Catskill water, if carefully husbanded, to supply New York City for several months. Its capacity is 29 billion gallons. It acts as a storage reservoir, so that the flow into the city will at no time be interrupted while the 75 miles of aqueduct between the Kensico and Ashokan reservoirs are being inspected, cleaned or repaired. The Kensico dam is one of the great masonry structures of the world. It contains altogether nearly a million cubic yards of masonry—about one-third that which the Egyptians placed in the Great Pyramid. The aqueduct then continues to Hill View reservoir, located in the City of Yonkers, just north of the New York City line, and 15 miles south of Kensico reservoir. Its function is to equalize the difference between the use of water in the city, as it varies from hour to hour, and the steady flow in the aqueduct. It is an uncovered, artificial reservoir of the earth-embankment type. It holds 900 million gallons of water with a depth of 36.5 feet, and has a water-surface area of 90 acres.

From Hill View reservoir, Catskill water is delivered into the five boroughs of New York City by a circular tunnel drilled through solid rock. The tunnel, known as City Tunnel No. 1, is 18 miles long, with a diameter that gradually reduces in size from 15 to 11 feet. The tunnel is at depths of 200 to 750 feet below the street surface, thus avoiding interference with streets, buildings, subways, sewers and pipes. These depths are necessary, also, to secure a substantial rock covering to withstand the bursting pressure of the water inside and afford the requisite water-tightness. The waterway of the tunnel is lined throughout with concrete. The tunnel was constructed from 25 shafts, including the Downtake shaft at Hill View reservoir, about 4,000 feet apart, located in parks and other places where they interfere very little with traffic. Through 22 of these shafts the water is delivered into the street mains. These connections from the tunnel to the mains are made by means of vertical riveted steel pipes (called risers) embedded in concrete in the upper part of each shaft and lined with concrete to prevent corrosion inside. Concrete fills all spaces outside the risers, sealing the shafts against the loss of water. Provision is made at Shaft 11 in Morningside Park and at Shaft 21 on the shore of the East River, at Clinton and South Streets, Manhattan, for "unwatering" the tunnel, whenever necessary, for inspection, cleaning or repairs. Shaft 21, at a depth of 752 feet, is deeper than the Woolworth building is high.

The aqueduct passes from Manhattan Island at Clinton and South Streets to Long Island at Sands and Bridge Streets, under the rotten rock of the East River, at a depth of 704 feet below sea-level and 752 feet below the surface of the ground on the Manhattan side. On the Brooklyn side, the aqueduct comes up to above sea-level, and continues at varying heights to Fort Greene Park. From this and another terminal shaft, the water is conducted through steel and cast-iron pipe-lines to the Boroughs of Queens and Richmond. The crossing of the Narrows, from Brooklyn to Richmond (Staten Island) was accomplished by the construction of a flexible pipe-line. From the Staten Island end of the Narrows siphon, a 48-inch cast-iron pipe was laid to the Silver Lake reservoir, the terminal reservoir for the Catskill water system, which has a capacity of 435 million gallons.

The Catskill Water-Supply system is a gravity system throughout. Water in the Ashokan reservoir is nearly 600 feet above tide level. Water can be delivered in lower Manhattan at an elevation of 260 feet and in Brooklyn at about 240 feet above tide level. The Catskill system now supplies the city with 600 million gallons of water a day. It is the greatest water-supply system in the world.

The Catskill Aqueduct.—Though the reader ordinarily finds little excitement in technical details, nevertheless he cannot but be impressed by the engineering skill displayed in constructing the Catskill aqueduct and by a comparison of this greatest of modern aqueduct systems with the Roman, the greatest of the ancient.

The aqueduct which conveys the water from the Ashokan reservoir to the City of New York is of five different types of construction, namely, cut-and-cover, grade tunnel, pressure tunnel, steel pipe siphon and flexible-jointed pipe siphon—the latter being used only at one place, namely, across the Narrows of New York harbor.

1. The term "cut-and-cover" is used to describe that type of aqueduct which is built by cutting a trench in the surface of the ground, laying the conduit in the trench, and covering it with earth. In section it is horse-shoe shaped, with a slightly curved bottom called the "invert" and a high arched top. The interior diameter is 17 feet 6 inches wide and 17 feet high. The conduit is made of concrete, varying in thickness from 1 foot at the top and bottom to 5 feet at the bottom of the arch. This is the least difficult and least expensive type, and has been used wherever the elevation and nature of the land permitted, where the grades are comparatively moderate, and therefore where the bursting pressure of the water is not great. The gradient of the cut-and-cover tunnel is about 1 foot to the mile. An aggregate of 55 miles of the aqueduct is of this type. Most of the old aqueducts which supplied the City of Rome were built by the cut-and-

cover method, although the Roman conduits were made generally of stone or brick, lined with concrete.

2. Grade tunnels were driven through hills and mountains where it would have been impracticable or uneconomical to circumvent them by the cut-and-cover method. They followed the general grade of the aqueduct, but had a gradient of about 2 feet to the mile. They are also horse-shoe shaped, and the same height as the cut-and-cover type, namely, 17 feet, but are narrower, being only 13 feet 4 inches wide. There are 24 of these grade tunnels, aggregating 14 miles.

3. Pressure tunnels were built where it was necessary to pass under broad valleys and deep rivers, and in the City of New York, and where suitable rock could be found through which to build them. It may be stated in passing that all rock is not suitable rock for an aqueduct tunnel, for it is impracticable to construct through disintegrated and badly fissured rock a tunnel which has to stand great bursting pressure due to the depth of the tunnel below the initial level of the water. The pressure tunnels are circular in form, built of concrete and are generally 14½ feet in diameter in those portions north of New York City. The city tunnel begins with a diameter of 15 feet which is gradually reduced as it goes southward to 11 feet. There are 7 pressure tunnels aggregating 17 miles in length north of the city, and the city tunnel is 18 miles long, being the longest tunnel in the world for carrying water under pressure. The normal gradient of the pressure tunnels is about 3 feet to the mile.

Great skill was shown by the aqueduct builders in constructing the grade and pressure tunnels. The precision of the engineers in the single matter of surveying may be illustrated by a comparison with the old Romans. When, in the first century, the Aqua Claudia was being built, the Romans decided to drive a tunnel 3 miles long through Mount Affliano. Their chief engineer set the line for the tunnel and put two parties of men at work, one at each end, to tunnel toward each other, in the expectation of meeting in the middle of the mountain. While they were thus at work, the chief engineer was captured by bandits and held a prisoner for a long time. When he was released and went to see how the tunnel was progressing, he found that the two working parties had passed each other and did not know it. He said that if he had not discovered their error in time they would have had two tunnels instead of one. In contrast with this experience may be mentioned two typical examples of Catskill aqueduct engineering. In tunneling under the Hudson river at Storm King, two parties of workmen on opposite sides of the river, over 3/5 of a mile apart, bored vertically down to a depth of 1,114 feet below sea-level, then started toward each other, and met under midstream with the variation of not more than ½ inch. In building the Bonticou grade tunnel through the mountain between the Rondout and Walkill creeks on the west side of the Hudson, two parties started from opposite directions and met under Bonticou Mountain with equal precision, each having worked a distance of about 3,500 feet, or a total distance of over a mile and a quarter.

4. The fourth principal type of construction is the steel-pipe siphon. This form of construction is used to pass under valleys where the rock is not sound and where for other reasons pressure tunnels would be impracticable. Each siphon consists of 3 cylindrical steel pipes from 9 feet to 11 feet in diameter made of plates varying from 7/16 to ¾ of an inch thick riveted together. They are lined with 2 inches of cement mortar and are enveloped with concrete. There are 14 steel-pipe siphons, aggregating 6 miles in length. They are not true siphons but are so called because of their resemblance in shape to an inverted siphon. The Romans knew the principle of the inverted siphon, but, not having cast iron and steel, were unable to employ it on their main aqueducts. The best they could do was to use small lead pipes as inverted siphons in their distribution system.

5. The fifth type of Catskill aqueduct construction is the flexible pipeline, which was used in a very ingenious way to cross the Narrows of New York harbor, from Brooklyn to Staten Island. Instead of tunneling under the Narrows, where the rock is at an unknown depth, a 36-inch flexible jointed cast-iron pipe was laid in a trench dredged in the bottom of the harbor. This pipe was made in 12-foot lengths, the joints being designed on the ball-and-socket principle, allowing for a maximum deflection of 10°50′ more or less. The joints were filled with lead, about 300 pounds of lead being used in each. Starting from the gate chamber on the Brooklyn side, the pipe was laid from a derrick scow which moved toward Staten Island as joint after joint was added to the inboard end of the scow. The portion of the pipe between the scow and the bottom of the harbor was sustained in a curve by temporary rigging which was carried along by the scow as the work progressed. When Staten Island was reached, connection was made with the gate-house on that shore. The total length of this siphon is 9,830 feet, or nearly two miles. Meters at each end indicate the leakage, if any.

About 8 miles of by-pass and miscellaneous construction brings the total length of the aqueduct at present up to about 120 miles. The Roman aqueducts varied in length from 10 to 62 miles. Thus the longest of them was only about half the length of the Catskill aqueduct. Other details show that even the best of them was not comparable with the Catskill aqueduct as an engineering achievement. The cross-section of the Catskill aqueduct is six or seven times the size of the largest Roman aqueduct. When all nine Roman aqueducts were in operation, they had an aggregate capacity of about 84,-000,000 gallons a day. The single Catskill aqueduct has a capacity of 600,-000,000 gallons a day.[13]

[13] The above account has been adapted largely from Edward H. Hall, *The Catskill Aqueduct*, 1918, ch. III; also Board of Water Supply of the City of New York, *Catskill Water*, 1917, pp. 7-13, 25-45; *Catskill Water Supply*, 1928, pp. 12-26. See *Annual Report of the New York Board of Water Supply*, 1924, XVIII, 100-119, for a description of the Shandaken tunnel, and XXII, 49-60, 83-126 (1927) on the Schoharie development.

Protecting the Quality of the Catskill Water.—Several different processes are used to make sure that the supply of water is clear and pure. They constitute a combination of natural and artificial means.

1. Aëration.—In connection with the Headworks of the Catskill aqueduct, at the Ashokan reservoir, and also at Kensico reservoir, aërators capable of treating all the water which flows in the aqueduct have been built. These two aërators, which are substantially alike, are great fountain basins, approximately 500 feet long by 250 feet wide, each containing about 1,600 nozzles, through which jets of water are thrown vertically into the air. The nozzles are so designed that the water is divided into fine spray, permitting thorough admixture of oxygen from the atmosphere and thus the removal of undesirable gases and other matters causing tastes and odors.

2. Coagulation.—At a number of places in the Catskill watersheds there are banks of very fine clay-like earth on the hill slopes or along the streams and margins of the reservoirs. Under certain conditions of storm or very rapid run-off of water from the steep surfaces of the hills and mountains, some of this fine earth is carried into the streams and by them into the reservoirs, making the water turbid. Most of this turbidity settles in the reservoirs during the period of storage of the water. At times, however, some of the finest turbidity may be carried into the aqueduct, rendering the water unattractive in appearance. To correct this fault whenever it may occur, a coagulating plant has been installed on the aqueduct about two miles north of Kensico reservoir. This plant is so arranged that it can mix into the water flowing in the aqueduct small quantities of a harmless coagulant (alum) which will cause the very fine clay particles to settle out of the water while passing through Kensico reservoir.

3. Sterilization.—In order to eliminate any pathogenic or harmful bacteria that may be present, the water is sterilized by the introduction of chlorine. Chlorinating plants have been installed at the Ashokan, Kensico, and Hill View reservoirs, and all the water at those points is sterilized and rendered entirely pure. The control of the gas through the chlorinating apparatus is so complete that only sufficient gas is introduced to effect the desired sterilization, all the gas being taken up by reaction on the organic life or other foreign material in the water.

4. Storage.—In addition to the above methods of treatment, Catskill water constantly receives benefit from its long storage in the great reservoirs of the system. In them sedimentation, bleaching by the sun, oxidation by the winds, and sterilization by natural processes, all go on more or less continually. Treatment by filtration is not required. From each reservoir the water can be drawn at the depth at which the water is in the best condition at the time.

5. Sanitary Improvement of the Watershed.—The Esopus watershed is sparsely settled, but the few villages and hamlets and many of the scattered houses, owing to the steep mountainous slopes, are situated at the bottom of the narrow valleys close to the creek and its tributaries. The all-the-year-round population of the whole watershed is only about 5,300. The summer population is increased to about 11,000 by the great influx of visitors between the middle of June and the middle of September. In order to prevent pollution of the streams by sewage, the sanitary facilities on hundreds of premises have been improved. Efforts have also been made to raise the sanitary standards of the communities and secure their coöperation along these lines for local benefit as well as for the improvement of New York City's water-supply.[14]

New York City Reaches Out for More Water.—So fast has New York City grown that, despite the huge Catskill development, the water-supply will in a few years be insufficient. "To state the growth in population in bare figures suggests but little. Instead it may be written that each year New York adds people enough to make an Atlanta, a Hartford, a Memphis or a New Haven; or every three years a Buffalo, a Cincinnati or a San Francisco; or in four years, a Baltimore or a Pittsburgh, or enough to populate the State of Rhode Island."[15] The present water-supply system can be forced to yield about a billion gallons a day. The annual consumption of water in the city now amounts to over 850 million gallons daily. The rate of increase in consumption each year, owing to population growth, is at least 30 million gallons daily. According to official forecasts, it will be necessary to provide an additional supply of water by 1935.

Already the city has been forced to build a second delivery tunnel, construction of which is now well under way, at an estimated cost of $64,000,000. It is being built primarily to serve adequately the needs of the fast-growing Boroughs of Brooklyn, Queens, and Richmond by delivering to them larger quantities of Catskill water and of such other sources as may be developed in the future. This new tunnel, known as City Tunnel No. 2, will extend from the Hill View reservoir in the city of Yonkers, through the Borough of The Bronx, under the

[14] Board of Water Supply of the City of New York, *Catskill Water,* 1917, pp. 45-47.
[15] *Ibid.,* p. 23.

East River at Rikers Island to the Borough of Queens, and thence to a point near the intersection of Hamilton Avenue and Hicks Street in the Borough of Brooklyn. The tunnel will be 20 miles long, with a finished interior diameter of 17 feet for a distance of about 18 miles and then decreasing to 15 feet for the rest of the distance. It will everywhere be at a depth of not less than 475 feet below sea-level. Seventeen shafts will be sunk for construction purposes and for permanent waterways. The capacity of this tunnel will be sufficient to meet the probable needs and requirements of the city until 1950, when the consumption of water will be in excess of 1½ billion gallons daily, a quantity nearly twice as great as at present.[16]

To provide for the future water needs of the city, one or both of two lines of action may be taken: either conservation of the present supply or development of new sources. Under the first, consideration is being given to metering and to an increase in rates. With the exception of business premises, the city is unmetered. Water for domestic use is sold on a flat or frontage rate basis. The installation of meters throughout the city, according to engineers, would save the taxpayers of the city millions of dollars by making it unnecessary to go ahead with other plans for an increased supply of water for some time, since the enormous wastage of water occurring at the present time would be almost eliminated. Allied to this is the proposal to raise the rates. There has been no change in the charge for water in the city since 1857. The consumer pays the remarkably low price of about "one cent for forty pails." Both these projects, however, are faced with more difficulties than that of tapping new sources. "On many occasions they have been brought up and defeated. There have been numerous campaigns for the purpose of showing that they are the best and most reasonable methods of water conservation—benefiting the public at all points—but without avail. Politics is brought to bear here with particular emphasis; the belief that metering or higher charges would greatly increase the actual cost of water used, is, according to those familiar with the situation, almost impossible to dispel."[17]

The other line of action includes the development of new supplies. The total cost of construction of the Municipal Water Works up to January 1, 1929, was already more than $450,000,000. Several more

[16] *Annual Report of the Board of Water Supply of the City of New York*, 1927, XXII, 5-6, 173-175.

[17] C. G. Poore, "New York Reaches Far Out for More Water," New York *Times*, April 10, 1927. Department of Water Supply, Gas and Electricity, City of New York, *Annual Report for 1925-26-27*, pp. 73-76.

hundred millions are involved in the new proposals. One plan is to develop the Long Island sources through the medium of artesian wells. About 150 million gallons daily could be made available through this means for certain sections of the city.

Another and more extensive plan, put forward by the New York City Board of Water Supply in 1926, is to utilize the streams tributary to the Hudson River on the east side beyond the Croton watershed. This would mean extending the present system of reservoirs and aqueducts east of the Hudson for a distance of 150 miles, through Dutchess, Columbia, and Rensselaer Counties, veering toward the Connecticut and Massachusettts borders. An outlay of about $350,000,000 would be involved, and the development would take about 15 years. It would add from 400 to 500 million gallons daily. In 1927 the New York State Legislature rebuffed the City of New York in this plan because the supply was being reserved for other upstate cities.[18]

A third plan is to develop the Delaware River sources. This watershed lies within the boundaries of the three states of New York, New Jersey, and Pennsylvania, and its development would entail joint action by the legislatures of the three states. A tri-state compact to develop these sources was approved in 1927 by the commissioners of the three states and adopted by the legislature of New York State; it failed of ratification by the legislatures of New Jersey and Pennsylvania. The New York City Board of Water Supply then proposed to take part of the flood waters of those tributaries of the Delaware River lying wholly in the State of New York. This plan, which was to add 600 million gallons a day, was approved and the necessary legislation secured in 1928. Whereupon New Jersey, with Pennsylvania intervening to the same end, brought suit to prevent New York from diverting any water whatever from the Delaware. In 1931 the United States Supreme Court denied New Jersey's plea and permitted New York City to divert from the Delaware 440 million gallons daily. It will take from 8 to 10 years to develop this new source, and it will cost about $272,000,000. Meantime New York City is facing a probable deficiency in its water-supply, due to recent droughts, the increased consumption arising from the growth of population, and the delay in developing new sources.[19]

[18] New York *Times*, Nov. 3, 1927. *Annual Report of the Board of Water Supply of New York City*, 1926, XXI, 103-104. *Regional Survey of New York and Its Environs*, 1929, VIII, 44.

[19] *Annual Report of the Board of Water Supply of New York City*, 1927, XXII, 4-5; 1928, XXIII, 3-5. *Regional Survey of New York and Its Environs*, 1929, VIII, 44-45. New York *Times*, May 5, 1931. Arthur Warner, ''New York's Water Problems to Continue for Eight Years,'' New York *Times*, April 19, 1931.

Here, then, is the most extensive and costly water-supply system in America, if not in the world. And yet, owing to its continued growth, New York City is still faced with an urgent problem of developing additional sources. Boston, Los Angeles, San Francisco, and other large cities have experienced the same difficulty of providing for the needs of a rapidly growing community, and they too have vast projects for future development, undertakings which likewise involve brilliant engineering operations.[20] How far can this procedure go? No city can live without water; will the future size of cities be limited by the difficulty and cost of satisfying this elemental need?

[20] Robert M. Brown, ''The Water Supply of Cities in the United States,'' *The Scientific Monthly*, August, 1931, 33:2:137-141.

CHAPTER XI

MUNICIPAL HOUSECLEANING

IF THE most imperative need of a modern city is its water-supply, the daily requirement next in point of urgency is the removal of waste. The modern city throws off an enormous amount of waste material from day to day. To dispose of all objectionable wastes in the most unobjectionable way is the object of municipal sanitation. This branch of sanitary engineering has some relation to the public health, but more largely is it a contribution to public decency and convenience.

Municipal waste may be classified into organic and inorganic materials, the first including sewage, garbage, and offal or the refuse from abattoirs; the second, ashes, rubbish, and part of street-sweepings. Another and more practicable grouping is (a) the liquid portion of the community wastes, e.g., sewage; and (b) general refuse or solid wastes (ashes, garbage, rubbish, street-sweepings). The disposal of sewage presents the only real problem from the public-health standpoint.[1]

SEWAGE DISPOSAL

The word *sewerage* means a system of sewers or the systematic removal and disposal of that waste matter which is carried in sewers. The term *sewage* refers to the contents of a sewer or drain, the matter discharged from sewers. Sewage consists of the waste water of the public water-supply with the addition of such household filth and refuse matter as is water-borne. A considerable portion of the sewage is also composed of industrial waste—the liquid output from laundries, dyeworks, and industries of all sorts. Some industries do not empty their trade wastes into the public sewers but dispose of them directly into the river, lake, or ocean. Moreover, after a rainfall an enormous volume of waste water must be handled either in combination with the ordinary sewage or separately in special drains. Since this heavy precipitation sometimes comes upon a city within the space of a few

[1] William B. Munro, *Municipal Government and Administration*, 1923, II, 163. William F. Morse, *The Collection and Disposal of Municipal Waste*, 1908, p. 13. H. Parsons, *Disposal of Municipal Refuse*, 1906, p. 14.

hours, the sewerage system must have the capacity to carry several times its normal load, for the wet-weather flow in the sewers may more than quadruple that of a dry-weather period.[2]

Sewage must be adequately disposed of chiefly because of its close connection with the spread of disease, mainly through contaminating the public water-supply. Evidence from all over the world indicates that where sewage is properly treated, the death-rate from typhoid fever, Asiatic cholera and other intestinal diseases has been greatly lowered.

The volume of sewage in the modern city is very large and is constantly increasing. It varies with the seasons of the year. In the larger American cities it may range from 50 to several hundred gallons per capita daily; the average is slightly above 150 gallons per head of population. If the daily sewage discharge from New York City were collected in the bed of a river 100 feet wide and 10 feet deep, it would in one day completely fill the river for a distance of 13 miles; the solid matter alone, though less than one one-thousandth of the total, would be equal to 600 tons a day.[3]

Methods of Sewage Disposal.—After a sewerage system has been designed, the question arises as to what disposition is to be made of the outflow or effluent. The problem varies according to local conditions, such as the volume of sewage, the location of the city, and the availability of different means of disposal. The simplest and most primitive method is to turn it into the nearest body of water. "This may be permissible if the body of water is large enough to so dilute it that a nuisance is not created, and if it does not prevent the continuation with safety of the uses of the water which prevailed before sewage was emptied into it. If it is reasonably certain that it renders the water inimical to health, or that it destroys animal life, its use as a receptacle for raw sewage should be prohibited."[4]

When raw sewage is discharged into the ocean, as is the general practice among the cities on the Atlantic and Pacific coasts, the health menace is not great, especially if the sewage is discharged on an outgoing tide and at a considerable distance from the shore. Otherwise, the tide may bring it back and thereby spoil the bathing beaches. The contamination of sea food may also result. In the case of cities located on lakes and rivers, this method of disposal has been a great cause of trouble owing to the fact that these same bodies of water are the

[2] William B. Munro, *Municipal Government and Administration*, 1923, II, 170-171.
[3] C.-E. A. Winslow, *Man and the Microbe*, 1924, pp. 19-20.
[4] Herbert H. Waite, *Disease Prevention*, 1926, p. 68.

sources of the public water-supply. The proximity of the outlet of sewers to the intake of water has been the cause of many serious epidemics. Inter-city and even inter-state controversies have resulted from sewage disposal of this type.

The amount of danger arising from the discharge of sewage into lakes and rivers depends upon the volume of sewage and the size of the water-course. Where a small volume of sewage is discharged into a large body of water, the intestinal bacteria may die out and the organic matter be disposed of by natural processes without danger of offense. "Large bodies of fresh water can digest an enormous daily diet of sewage, and by the process of dilution render it reasonably harmless. This process requires, however, that there shall be a sufficient volume of diluting water, containing enough oxygen to ensure the nitrification of the sewage. Under favorable conditions water will always rid itself of pollution by converting the putrescible matter into nitrates or other mineral substances. The bacilli, in this process, are destroyed. . . . Duluth, Detroit, Cleveland, Toledo, Buffalo, Rochester and other cities have been emptying their sewage into the Great Lakes without any preliminary treatment other than screening to intercept the larger masses of floating matter, yet at Montreal the St. Lawrence River is as free from pollution as is any ordinary surface stream which flows through well-settled areas. The dilution in these instances is very great.''[5]

As the amount of sewage becomes greater in relation to the volume of diluting water it becomes necessary to reduce the burden of polluting material. Several different methods are used. As a rule, preliminary removal of the larger bodies in suspension is necessary if the best results are to be secured. This is accomplished chiefly by screening and by sedimentation.

Screening.—This is the simplest of all sewage-treatment methods. The sewage is merely passed through coarse or fine screens to remove the larger particles floating in it. Only a small proportion, rarely over 15 per cent, of the bodies in suspension is removed by screens. The screened material is taken away daily and after being pressed to remove water and diminish bulk, the resulting mass, called sludge, is then burned, used for filling purposes, or buried.

Sedimentation.—Of more importance than screening is the process of sedimentation. There are five common methods of accomplishing this object.

1. Grit Chambers—These are small settling basins in which the sewage is

[5] William B. Munro, *Municipal Government and Administration*, 1923, II, 176-177. C.-E. A. Winslow, *Man and the Microbe*, 1924, pp. 20-21.

allowed to remain for a short time, often for only a few minutes. The velocity of flow is from 10 to 20 inches per minute. The sediment which collects is composed chiefly of sand, gravel, and other heavy materials. Some organic matter is also incorporated, the amount usually being sufficient to render the sludge offensive. Grit chambers remove only the heavier bodies which constitute a small part of the solids, from 15 to 25 per cent being removed in 1 hour.

2. *Plain Sedimentation Tanks.*—In 6 hours plain sedimentation removes from 25 to 60 per cent of the suspended matter, depending on the strength of the sewage. In these tanks the flow is slow, usually not over $\frac{1}{2}$ inch per minute. Sewage is retained from 1 to 12 hours. The sludge must be removed at frequent intervals to prevent it from becoming offensive.

3. *Septic Tanks.*—In this process the basin is made sufficiently large to retain sewage from 8 to 24 hours or longer. The flow is usually from $\frac{1}{10}$ to $\frac{3}{10}$ or more inches per minute. Oxygen is excluded, the decomposition being brought about almost exclusively by anaërobic bacteria, those which can live without free oxygen. By bacterial activity some of the solid organic matter is liquefied or converted into gas. A scum forms on the top, and there is a continual movement of the sludge from the bottom to the top and in the reverse direction. From 10 to 40 per cent of the solid organic matter is decomposed. Septic tanks may take care of the small amounts of sewage for a single household or for a small number of residences. It is not safe to empty the untreated effluent in streams, since disease-producing bacteria may be present to almost as great an extent as in raw sewage. In septic tanks from 30 to 75 per cent of the suspended matter is removed in 24 hours, depending on the strength of the sewage. The sludge which is formed must be disposed of at regular intervals.

4. *Digestion Tanks.*—The best-known and probably the most efficient form of digestion tank in use today is the Imhoff or Emscher tank, or one constructed on the same principles. The Imhoff tank consists of two intercommunicating tanks, an upper flow chamber in which sedimentation occurs, and a lower chamber in which the sediment and larger solid portions settle in the form of sludge. In the lower chamber the organic matter is decomposed by bacterial action. The advantage which this method has over others is that it confines the septic action to the lower compartment, does not allow the decomposition products to mix with the sewage in the upper compartment, and more completely decomposes the organic matter, thus improving the character of the sludge. From 40 to 85 per cent of the suspended matter is removed, the amount depending on the strength of the sewage and the length of time it is kept in the tank.

5. *Use of Chemicals.*—To hasten sedimentation and to remove more of the substances in suspension, chemicals such as lime, copperas, and alum are often used. When lime is used alone, from 500 to 1,000 pounds are required per million gallons of sewage; when used with copperas, from 100 to 1,000

pounds of the latter are added. From 500 to 1,500 pounds of alum are required per million gallons of sewage.

In all processes of sedimentation a large amount of sludge is formed, creating a troublesome problem. The water in it may be removed by evaporation or by pressing. Both methods are costly, and each may create a nuisance. After the drying or pressing, the solid remains must be disposed of. This is usually done by burying or burning the sludge or using it as a fill for low places. The Miles process, in which sulphurous acid is used primarily to remove grease and to extract fertilizing substances from the sludge, gives promise of being so developed that sewage treatment may become economical, and, in individual instances, where conditions are favorable, may actually become a source of profit.[6]

Purification Processes.—In many instances the effluent from the sewage, which has been subjected to the processes described above, cannot be directly discharged into a stream or otherwise disposed of without further treatment. Where the amount of sewage is small and the conditions are favorable sub-surface irrigation may suffice. By this method pipes receive the effluent from cesspool or septic tank and distribute it to the upper layer of soil. Larger amounts require further treatment to prevent nuisance and danger from disease. Various methods are used, the aim being to employ the one best suited to local conditions. Five recognized methods of treatment are in use, namely broad irrigation, intermittent sand filtration, contact beds, trickling filters, and activated sludge tanks.

In all these methods a higher degree of purification is obtained mainly through bacterial action. The organic material in the sewage may be oxidized and turned into a harmless and inoffensive mineral form (nitrates) by the action of nitrifying bacteria. "This sort of purification takes place in nature whenever manure is ploughed into the soil or when the untidy housewife throws kitchen slops out from the back door. On a large scale we can make it more effective by disposing of sewage on special beds of sand or broken stone or in aëration tanks. All these devices involve the cultivation in the sand beds, or on the stone filters, or in the aëration tanks, of special types of bacteria which, in the presence of sufficient oxygen, oxidize the organic matter of the sewage into nitrates." The broad irrigation method involves the discharge of raw sewage upon land requiring irrigation. Bacteria in the soil act as purifying agents. "In the case of

[6] Adapted from Herbert H. Waite, *Disease Prevention*, 1926, pp. 68-70. *Cf.* William B. Munro, *Municipal Government and Administration*, 1923, II, 177-178.

the sand filter the sewage is applied in intermittent doses, the air being drawn in after each application. In the stone filters, called trickling beds, the sewage is discharged from spray nozzles up into the air, and then allowed to trickle downward over the stones which are covered with bacterial films. In the aëration tanks air is blown directly in through porous plates at the bottom and sewage, oxygen, and nitrifying bacteria are thus intimately mixed."[7] For the benefit of those readers who desire more specific details as to the operation of these various methods, the following account is presented.

1. Broad Irrigation.—This method is similar to an irrigation system, the sewage being distributed through ditches or similar devices to improve farm land. It is practically confined to Europe. Berlin and Paris, for example, have extensive farms on which their sewage is deposited; it is said that half of the fresh vegetables used in Berlin are raised on these sewage farms. Sufficient revenue is derived from the crops to aid in paying the cost of operation. There is relatively little value derived from the sewage as a fertilizer, the principal advantage coming from the water which serves as an irrigant. The purification achieved by this method, crude though it be, is usually satisfactory. Sometimes an offensive odor is produced, which, though harmless, creates a nuisance.

2. Intermittent Sand Filtration.—In intermittent sand filtration the sewage is allowed to flow at intervals over especially prepared beds of sand. The amount applied is so regulated in quantity that it disappears quickly in the sand. Air is taken in and this aids in the decomposition which is brought about by bacteria. The organic matter becomes completely nitrified if the filter is properly constructed and operated. Beneath the filter are under-drains which carry away the effluent, the latter being clear and almost free from sewage bacteria. Where local conditions are favorable, this method is the most efficient of all those in use. It can be used only in regions where there are convenient areas of sandy soil and where the climate is temperate.

3. Contact Beds.—Contact beds consist of water-tight compartments usually filled with broken stone from $\frac{1}{8}$ to 2 inches in diameter, though sometimes slag, coke, broken bricks and coarse gravel are employed. These beds are from 2 to 8 feet in depth and are generally built in series, the effluent from the first flowing into the second, that from the second into the third, and so on if there are more in the series. The usual procedure at the present time is to allow the effluent, which has passed through a septic tank, to fill the contact bed slowly. It is then held in the bed for about 2 hours to permit the suspended matters to settle in the interstices. During this period oxidizing bacteria act upon the organic matter which settles to form a film on the surfaces of the stones or other substances in the bed. An hour is the usual time allowed for emptying the bed. It now stands idle for about 4 hours,

[7] C.-E. A. Winslow, *Man and the Microbe*, 1924, pp. 20-21.

when it is again filled. While standing empty, still further oxidation of the organic matter incorporated in the film occurs. When sewage is passed from properly constructed and operated septic tanks through a series of contact beds, as much as 70 per cent of the organic matter, 85 per cent of the bacteria, and 90 per cent of the sediment may be removed. After several years' operation, contact beds must be cleaned. At best, contact beds are not very satisfactory on account of the cost of operation and the character of the effluent, hence they are seldom used.

4. *Trickling or Sprinkling Filter.*—The trickling filter, also known as sprinkling filter and percolating filter, is a modern improvement on the contact-bed method. It has a contact bed similar to that just described. The sewage is delivered to the beds through fixed or traveling, rectangular or rotary sprinklers. The object of using the trickling filter is to furnish a large surface for the incorporation of oxygen. The oxygen obtained in this way is used by aërobic bacteria which so decompose the organic matter that the effluent is not putrescible. If the filter receives the effluent from a sedimentation or septic tank, as much as 90 per cent of the sediment and 95 per cent of the bacteria may be removed. The effluent is usually not clear and should, therefore, be passed through settling basins before it is discharged. This method is especially useful in places which lack sandy areas and hence cannot utilize intermittent filtration except at great expense. Each acre of a properly constructed and operated trickling filter will take care of from 1 to 2 million gallons of sewage per day, or twice as much as the plain contact bed.

5. *Activated Sludge Process.*—This method is based on the fact that sludge furnishes a favorable environment for the growth of aërobic bacteria. Sufficient oxygen for this purpose is introduced artificially. In operation, compressed air is forced through the sewage confined in a tank. After a few weeks the particles in suspension form a colloidal mass. The bubbles of air keep these little masses in a continuous state of agitation. After the preliminary activating process has reached the proper stage, sewage is admitted. Sometimes the continuous flow, at other times the fill and draw method, is used. Some nitrification occurs, but it is not complete. The sludge which is formed has more manurial value than that obtained through other methods. As yet this method may be said to be somewhat in the experimental stage. As it proves successful it will replace other methods now in use because of the simplicity of plant construction and operation. Other factors, however, which will have to be considered, are the cost of aëration and the removal of sludge.

Whatever method is used for purification, the final step in the process should be disinfection of the effluent. Calcium hypochlorite (chloride of lime) and liquid chlorine are both effective and economical.[8]

[8] Adapted in the main from Herbert H. Waite, *Disease Prevention,* 1926, pp. 70-72. See also William T. Sedgwick, *Principles of Sanitary Science,* 1905, pp. 135 ff. Charles V. Chapin, *Municipal Sanitation in the United States,* 1901, ch. VI.

The Problem of Sewage Disposal Still Urgent.—Although the handling of relatively small amounts of sewage is now effectively done, we are still in the experimental stage so far as the disposal of huge volumes of sewage is concerned. Very exceptional is the large city which has a satisfactory and adequate system.

New York City, for example, is faced with an acute situation. Its present method is to dump the sewage, which amounts to about 880 million gallons a day, into the rivers and harbor. There is no previous treatment of the sewage except that a small proportion is screened. The effect has been such that Manhattan may be defined as an island surrounded by sewage. Serious nuisances and danger to health have resulted from this crude method of disposal. The capacity of these waters to assimilate the filth has long been overburdened. Tests for oxygen content have shown that the waters have progressively become septic. If this method of disposal is continued, the oxygen will soon be entirely gone, causing the water to become black and odoriferous. Many beaches have become so unsafe that they have been condemned by the public-health authorities, which have forbidden the operation of any public bathing establishment thereon. Fish life has been practically driven out of the waters in the main parts of the harbor. The taking of oysters from its waters for consumption in New York City has been prohibited by the City Health Department. Offensive odors and sights accompany the discharge of large amounts of sewage at points where they cannot be readily absorbed. Land values along certain waterways have depreciated.

In 1914 the public was notified by the Metropolitan Sewerage Commission that the time had come to build works for the proper disposition of the dangerous and offensive wastes, and it was supplied with a comprehensive plan and policy by which protection could be afforded. These recommendations were not adopted. Instead, New York City has meanwhile been greatly adding to the pollution through increase in population. There are several reasons why this comprehensive program has not yet been put into operation. First is the enormous sums which will be required to carry out the modernization of the disposal system. In New York City the cost of the land is certain to be a heavy item. Furthermore, the public has little appreciated the urgency of the situation. Fear of a malodorous neighborhood has brought about much popular objection to the location of sewage works near property which is occupied or likely to be occupied.

Extensive as are the works planned, they by no means represent the complete solution that will ultimately be required. The sanitary disposal of the sewage of the metropolitan district calls for a well-coördinated plan of main drainage and treatment works for the entire territory. The population to be cared for, approximately 10,000,000 today, is expected to be about 13,000,000 by 1940 and 21,000,000 by 1965. The quantity of sewage to be disposed of will be more than doubled in the next forty years. The capacity of the harbor, already overtaxed, cannot be increased. New York City is thus faced with the grave necessity of modernizing her methods of sewage disposal at the earliest possible moment. The plan which, according to the Sanitary Commission of New York, would give the most complete treatment that now appears practicable, would necessitate a cost of $378,000,000 by the year 1960.[9]

The Chicago Drainage Canal.—The city of Chicago is an outstanding example of the extensive efforts made to solve the problem of sewage disposal and thus lessen the incidence of water-borne disease. The first sewers of Chicago were built in 1856. They took care of the population of 80,000 by depositing most of the sewage into the Chicago River, which flowed into Lake Michigan and succeeded most effectively in polluting the waters and causing typhoid epidemics. As the population grew, the condition got worse. By the time the population had reached the 800,000 mark, in 1886, it was decided that something had to be done to meet the present and future needs of the city. An engineering commission was appointed to make a survey and recommend methods of improvement.

An important factor in the solution of the problem is the location of Chicago near the apex of two watersheds, the St. Lawrence and the Mississippi. Her waters naturally drain down to the lake, from which extend the various cribs which lead the drinking water back into the city. Chicago's answer to her sewage problem, and simultaneously to her health problem, lay in putting herself on the Mississippi instead of the St. Lawrence watershed. If the city should continue to take its water supply from the lake, but dispose of its sewage down the Mississippi, the problem, said the engineers, would be solved. To divert the sewage this way would necessitate reversing the flow of the Chicago River, from north to south.

The recommendations of the engineers were adopted, and the State of Illinois authorized the organization of the Sanitary District of Chicago, including besides Chicago about fifty other towns and villages

[9] *Regional Survey of New York and Its Environs*, 1929, VIII, 54-74. George A. Soper, ''Fouled Harbor Makes Sewage Problem Acute,'' New York *Times*, May 26, 1929; ''New York City at Last Moves to End Pollution of Its Harbor,'' *ibid.*, July 12, 1931.

and embracing an area of 430 square miles with a population of over 3 million. A drainage canal 28 miles long was built to connect the Chicago River with the Des Plaines River, which flows to the Illinois and thence to the Mississippi. The canal was opened in 1900, after eight years had been spent in construction. The cost of the entire undertaking, including the deepening of the rivers and the construction of locks, dams, and power plants to supply electric current, has amounted to about $70,000,000. The drainage canal has a capacity of 10,000 cubic feet of water per second, sufficient to dilute the sewage of 2,500,000 people at the rate of 4 cubic feet of water per second per 1,000 people, and also sufficient to keep storm flows from flushing the reversed Chicago River back into Lake Michigan. The diversion of water from Lake Michigan for this purpose is authorized and regulated by the Secretary of War under grant of power by Congress. The existing permit of March 3, 1925, authorizes the sanitary district to divert, on the average, not more than 8,500 cubic feet per second, and at no time to exceed 11,000 cubic feet per second.

By the time the sewage reaches a city where the river water is needed for drinking purposes, it has been purified by natural processes. The capacity of large bodies of fresh water to absorb sewage is great. "It has been estimated that the Mississippi River receives nearly two billion gallons of sewage a day, including the entire output of Chicago and St. Louis. Yet at New Orleans the Father of Waters is no more contaminated than many smaller streams which receive the sewage of a single community. It has been demonstrated by elaborate tests, indeed, that the organic matter in the sewage of Chicago is entirely nitrified in the Des Plaines and Illinois rivers before it even reaches the Mississippi."[10]

Artificial treatment sewage plants to supplement the work of the canal were started in 1914. In 1921 the State Legislature passed an act making obligatory, beginning with 1925, the construction of additional sewage plants each year until a sufficient number are built to care for the sewage of approximately 1½ million people. The rest will be handled by dilution in the canal One hundred and twenty-five million dollars were voted for this purpose. In 1928 the city opened a huge sewage-treatment plant, covering 70 acres, with a capacity of 400 million gallons of sewage daily. It utilizes the activated sludge process, and was built at a cost of $32,000,000.

Complaint has been brought against Chicago by neighboring states

[10] William B. Munro, *Municipal Government and Administration*, 1923, II, 177.

and by Canada for diverting the waters of Lake Michigan. In recent years the Great Lakes have been lowered an average of 25 inches below their normal levels. This has seriously hampered the barge business and the operation of docks and wharfs built for a higher level. It has also decreased the Niagara Falls water power used to generate electricity. Chicago's drainage system has been held responsible for this. The fear has even been expressed that the Great Lakes will be drained, but the sanitary commission has replied that the inflow into the lakes is normally about eighteen times as much as the flow of 8,500 cubic feet per second which goes out to the sewage canal. It has also maintained that the lowering of the lake levels has been caused primarily by shortage of precipitation and a rate of evaporation above the average. This explanation has been substantiated by a study made by American and Canadian engineers. In a report filed with the Supreme Court of the United States in November, 1927, Mr. Charles Evans Hughes, acting as special master, stated: "I find that the full effect of a diversion of 8,500 cubic feet a second of water from Lake Michigan at Chicago through the drainage canal of the sanitary district would be to lower the levels of Lakes Michigan and Huron approximately 6 inches at mean lake levels; the levels of Lakes Erie and Ontario, approximately 5 inches at mean lake levels; and the levels of the connecting rivers, bays and harbors, so far as they have the same mean levels as the above mentioned lakes, to the same extent, respectively."[11]

An additional drain is made on the lake for the water-supply of the city of Chicago. Chicago uses about 800 million gallons daily, most of which is eventually disposed of through the drainage canal. The per capita consumption of water in Chicago is unusually high, amounting to 278 gallons a day. With other Great Lake cities to the east of her complaining that Chicago is using more than her share of the water, it seems an unsuitable time for her to announce in proud accents that "Chicagoans bathe more often and more diligently, whether from the feeling of necessity or choice, than the inhabitants of any other of the world's great cities." The high consumption may be accounted for in part by the statement that whereas in the rest of the country about a third of the urban dwellings are without bath equipment, in Chicago 90 per cent of the families have tubs, or showers, or both. Lack of metering may also play a part. By metering the water service, which, it is estimated, will cut down the daily consumption

[11] New York *Times,* Nov. 24, 1927.

from 278 gallons per capita to about 125, there will be less pressure on the sewage system.[12]

Chicago pleads partially guilty to the charge of lowering the levels of the Great Lakes, but upholds her position on the ground that the decrease in disease which finds its origin in polluted water is sufficient justification for her act. "In the years 1890, 1891 and 1892 the number of deaths from typhoid fever in Chicago was 1,008, 997 and 1,489 respectively. In 1920 the total number of deaths from typhoid fever in Chicago was 31, a marked contrast with 1,489 in 1892, when the population of Chicago was very much less than it is now."[13]

DISPOSAL OF GENERAL REFUSE

Under the term refuse are included all solid wastes such as ashes, garbage, rubbish, and street-sweepings. All these substances belong to a city's waste, and their disposal is a municipal problem requiring a social adjustment to urban conditions. The problem has been present ever since the beginning of settled community life, but it has been handled in an efficient and scientific way only in quite recent times. In early communities, refuse was commonly thrown in the fields, on low areas, or on the roads. Some of the streets in the oldest European cities have been gradually raised several feet by the rubbish dumped on them during centuries. The rapid growth of modern cities, particularly since the development of sanitary science, brought the refuse-removal problem into prominence. England led the way by starting works for the removal and disposal of municipal waste. Germany followed, and advanced the subject in essential directions. France also followed, and was interested chiefly in utilizing the valuable parts of the refuse. America then took up the question and, after trying most of the European methods, developed others.[14]

The disposal of municipal refuse must be made under two conditions: in a sanitary manner, and at a reasonable cost. It is interesting to note that certain economies are obtainable from each of the items of general refuse. Strictly speaking, the disposal of solid refuse is not a sanitary problem since only in very rare instances is it capable of directly transmitting disease. Rubbish and garbage may serve as breeding places for flies and mosquitoes, which are sometimes carriers of

[12] New York *Times*, Oct. 21, 1926; Feb. 3, 1927. *Scientific American*, Oct., 1926.

[13] Herbert H. Waite, *Disease Prevention*, 1926, p. 563. New York *Times*, Sept. 30, 1928.

[14] R. Hering and S. A. Greeley, *Collection and Disposal of Municipal Refuse*, 1921, pp. 1, 11.

disease. The odor from decomposing garbage, dead animals, or manure is offensive and creates a nuisance, but the odor has very little significance as far as disease is concerned. Disposal is rather an economic problem; it is done for convenience, for cleanliness, and for the sake of appearance.[15]

Refuse materials, especially those coming from residences, are produced in varying quantities. They are disposed of under varying conditions. These variations are determined by four main factors.

1. *The Geographical Location of the City.*—There is more garbage per capita in the South because larger quantities of fruit and vegetables are consumed; there are less ashes, for the coal consumption is smaller than in the North. Conditions of disposal are affected by the presence or absence of ravines, swamps, or large bodies of water where the refuse may be dumped, and by the length of haul required.

2. *Season of the Year.*—The maximum garbage is produced during the summer when vegetables and fruits constitute the principal diet; the minimum during the winter months. Garbage must be collected and disposed of more frequently in a hot climate than in a cold one and in summer as contrasted with winter.

3. *Character of the Population.*—The production of garbage is larger in a residential than in a manufacturing city, and in the wealthier than in the poor districts of the average city. There are more ashes in industrial cities.

4. *Administrative Efficiency.*—Of the two methods of operation— by the municipality and by contract—the first is generally to be preferred. In the majority of large cities throughout the United States, and in Europe almost exclusively, the collection is done by the municipality. In the United States, short tenure of office and election by popular vote often interfere with an economical and farsighted plan for disposing of a city's general refuse; this is a technical task and should be intrusted to experts.

Refuse collection and disposal have been developed with special success in England and Germany. It is the common practice in Europe to place house refuse of all kinds in the same can and to collect it in the same wagon, so that it is dealt with as mixed refuse. It is not as objectionable a material as garbage generally is in America. Europeans are less wasteful than Americans and produce materially smaller quantities of refuse per capita. Since the common practice in Europe is to burn all refuse in incinerators, the one-can or receptacle method is adaptable. The most common practice in American cities

[15] Herbert H. Waite, *Disease Prevention*, 1926, pp. 76-77.

is the two-can system, whereby the garbage is kept in one receptacle and the ashes and rubbish in another. This method of collection is prompted by the fact that the two classes of refuse are treated differently.[16]

The following table summarizes the main methods of disposal applied to each of the items of general refuse.

METHODS OF DISPOSAL	APPLICABLE TO
1. Dumping on land.................	All subdivisions (*i.e.*, ashes, garbage, rubbish, street-sweepings).
2. Dumping into large bodies of water..	All subdivisions.
3. Ploughing into the soil............	Garbage and some street-sweepings.
4. Feeding to swine.................	Garbage.
5. Reduction.....................	Garbage.
6. Incineration....................	All subdivisions.

Garbage.—The most difficult of all refuse matter to handle is garbage, for the reason that it is organic and will quickly ferment or putrefy. It has to be collected more frequently and disposed of more quickly. In large cities, hundreds of tons are collected daily. Among the cruder methods of disposal is dumping it on land, sometimes ploughing it in for its fertilizing value. Dumping garbage, especially in large quantities, without mixing with other materials, creates offensive conditions. Putrefaction and fly breeding may soon produce quite serious nuisances. When the garbage is mixed with a sufficient quantity of ashes, rubbish, or street-sweepings, the dumping is less objectionable, depending on the quantity and character of such added materials and on the climate. Garbage may also be dumped in large bodies of water, in which case it should be carried out sufficiently far so that it will not float inshore to the detriment of beaches.

Another method of disposal is to feed garbage to swine. The food value of fresh garbage is sufficiently great to have made this an old and very common method of final disposal. Hotels and eating houses generally have private collections for this purpose, and realize a profit therefrom. In nearly all cities some of the garbage is disposed of in this way. It constitutes the chief method in many cities, among them being New Haven, Worcester, Baltimore, Buffalo, Los Angeles, and San Francisco. In late years the use of this method has been greatly extended, and it promises further satisfactory development along both sanitary and economic lines. The chief requirements in feeding garbage to hogs are to keep it as fresh as possible, so as to

[16] R. Hering and S. A. Greeley, *Collection and Disposal of Municipal Refuse,* 1921, pp. 27, 69, 104. H. Parsons, *Disposal of Municipal Refuse,* 1906, p. 4.

preserve the highest food value, and to safeguard and maintain the health of the hogs. Both these requirements call for special sanitary care in the house treatment, collection service, transportation system, and the farm. There are about 300 community piggeries in the United States, which together are credited with an annual production of 52 million pounds of pork. Some of these pay the whole cost of garbage removal, others more. They are not always popular locally, and should be subject to the supervision of the health board.[17]

Garbage, along with other refuse, may be burned. The most scientific method of dealing with it, especially in America, is to reduce it, which saves some of the material destroyed in the incinerating plants. The reduction of garbage into grease and fertilizer originated in Vienna, where the Merz process was first introduced experimentally, but it was not developed successfully on a working scale for large cities until its introduction into America at Buffalo in 1886. Conditions in America were favorable to the development of garbage reduction, chiefly on account of the high percentage of grease obtainable. As inoffensive burning of garbage, unmixed with other kinds of refuse, was found to be expensive, the possibility of obtaining a revenue by using the reduction process for its disposal became attractive, and the Austrian invention was received favorably by Americans.

By the reduction process, the garbage is passed through a series of digesters where it is kept from 6 to 12 hours or longer under a steam pressure of about 60 pounds. It is next pressed to remove the water and grease, which are then conducted into settling tanks where the grease is skimmed off the top. The water is allowed to flow into the sewer or it is evaporated. Sometimes naphtha is used as a solvent, which is afterwards recovered from the grease. The solid residue, called tankage, is a dry vegetable, animal, and mineral material, which is fairly stable and mostly fibrous. Sometimes the grease is partially purified at the plant, but it is usually sold without much refining. The grease is used in the manufacture of soap, candles, glycerine, and other materials, and has been selling at from 3 to 10 cents per pound. The tankage is used as a filler or base for certain fertilizers, and has been selling at from $5.00 to $10.00 per ton, generally according to its ammonia content. Usually there is produced from 40 to 60 pounds of grease and 400 pounds of tankage per ton of garbage. In some of the large cities of the United States, notably Cleveland and

[17] R. Hering and S. A. Greeley, *Collection and Disposal of Municipal Refuse,* 1921, pp. 258-289. Jean Broadhurst, *Home and Community Hygiene,* 1923, p. 170.

Indianapolis, the reduction method has been economical and satisfactory.[18]

Rubbish.—Rubbish comprises miscellaneous materials from houses, stores, and other places. The usual methods of disposal are incineration and dumping on land or in large bodies of water. More than other kinds of refuse, rubbish contains articles—like paper, rags, rubber, bottles, tin cans, bits of metal, and old shoes—which may be picked out, sorted, and sold. At disposal works, laborers occasionally find silver spoons, coins, jewels, and other valuables in the collected material. "Picking over this rubbish, and marketing the salable portions, is an old custom, and is practiced with many variations. In Paris, members of the historic company of 'Rag-pickers' (*Chiffoniers*) examine the house cans before collection, and take out that which they can use or sell. They remove from the refuse all materials that have any value before it is collected for final disposal. Therefore, there is very little material left to be picked out at the delivery point. It is estimated that the annual receipts of this ambulating Parisian rubbish picking establishment have amounted to many thousands of dollars. Some picking over or scavenging is done at most of the refuse dumps in American cities by unlicensed scavengers, and frequently without municipal supervision. It is generally an unsightly activity, because the pickers are often slovenly and unclean, and allow small children to assist them. Under proper control, however, this work at dumps may be fairly satisfactory and bring a substantial revenue to the municipality. The total weight of rubbish systematically picked out and sold has occasionally ranged from 30 to 50 per cent of the total rubbish collected. . . . When carefully developed, the sorting is carried on in buildings fitted with conveyors on which the rubbish is spread out before the pickers. There are also bins for temporary storage, and presses and other machinery for preparing the sorted materials for shipment. An incinerator usually adjoins the building, and in it the residue is burned. . . . In addition to the sorting plants, New York City has for many years sold the privilege of picking over the garbage and rubbish, at the dumps and scow transfer stations along the water front, for which contractors have paid approximately $1920 per week. The estimated quantity was 1800 tons per week, from

[18] R. Hering and S. A. Greeley, *Collection and Disposal of Municipal Refuse*, 1921, pp. 444-445. Herbert H. Waite, *Disease Prevention*, 1926, pp. 78-79. William F. Morse, *The Collection and Disposal of Municipal Waste*, 1908, pp. 90, 290-419. H. Parsons, *Disposal of Municipal Refuse*, 1906, pp. 95, 113. Charles V. Chapin, *Municipal Sanitation in the United States*, 1901, pp. 703 ff. E. M. Reid, "Indianapolis Reaps Profit in Garbage," *The American City*, Dec., 1927, 37:6:753-757.

which about 35 per cent was picked out and sold. The value of rubbish to the city was thus about $1.06 per ton."[19]

Ashes.—The problem of ash disposal is a relatively easy one to solve. Ashes are used for filling in marshes or they may be dumped in water though not near a harbor. New York City ashes are dumped in the water at Rikers Island, where new and valuable land is being made. Ashes may be used for road building or they may even be burned. It is said that 4 per cent of steam ashes and 15 per cent of household ashes consist of unburned coal. In cases where all combustible waste materials are burned in specially designed furnaces, the mixed refuse often contains sufficient quantities of unburnt coal and of rubbish or litter to burn readily without additional fuel. The utilization of the steam and clinker produced by the incinerators may yield a substantial revenue and thus reduce the net cost of incineration. In England and Germany particularly, crushed clinker is made, to be used in place of broken stone or gravel, for ballast or aggregate in concrete, for paving and building blocks, flagstones, and bricks.[20] The commercial value of ashes is never sufficient to offset the cost of collection and disposal.

Street-Sweepings.—The waste materials collecting on the streets— manure, dirt, leaves, paper, building wastes, etc.—are disposed of by burning or by dumping on land or in water. The manure has some value as fertilizer if separated from the rest.

To keep the streets of a city clean is a necessary task but one which has not been very satisfactorily done. "Sanitary engineers look upon street cleaning as the least developed branch of their profession. It calls for a minimum of plant and apparatus and the direction of a large force of unskilled or relatively unskilled labor. It is an art rather than a science, and never properly developed. There is no adequate body of principles to guide it, such as are employed in most engineering and industrial undertakings. The conditions to be encountered vary greatly in different cities, in different parts of the same city; with changing seasons and conditions of weather, of traffic and other uses of the streets; and with the occupancy of the houses, whether for residence, office, manufacturing, shopping or amusement purposes."[21] In this country the first person of exceptional ability to undertake the scientific management of such a task was Col. George E. Waring,

[19] R. Hering and S. A. Greeley, *Collection and Disposal of Municipal Refuse*, 1921, pp. 9, 290, 291, 303.

[20] *Ibid.*, pp. 311–443.

[21] George A. Soper, "New York City Faces Reforms in Refuse Disposal," New York *Times*, March 17, 1929.

under a reform administration in New York City in the late nineties. He was a leading sanitary engineer and had had experience in directing a large force of men. He organized the street-cleaning army of the city, put men instead of voters behind the brooms, and introduced the custom of street-cleaners wearing uniforms—whence the term "white-wings." The task, which was no small one, was handled in a very business-like and efficient way.[22] There are about 1,000 miles of streets in New York City to be regularly cleaned. Taking the average width as 60 feet, this means an area of 55 million square yards that must be constantly cared for.

Related to street-cleaning is the problem of snow removal. "In northern cities, especially during winters when the precipitation is heavy, the removal of snow from the streets is a tedious and costly enterprise. Most of the city's attention is devoted to the business thoroughfares and the vicinity of fire hydrants. Apart from waiting for a change in temperature there is only one practical way of getting snow removed from the streets, which is by carting it away. A certain amount of it can be scraped or dumped into the sewer manholes; but if the quantity is too large for disposal in this way the only alternative is to haul it into the nearest waterway or to vacant land which has proper drainage facilities."[23] The cost of removing snow in this way will usually run from 20 to 40 cents per cubic yard. A heavy snow fall costs the City of New York a million dollars.

Refuse Disposal in New York City.—Although New York City has a marvelous water-supply system, it is still using primitive methods for the disposal of sewage and refuse. The problem is especially acute on account of the huge amounts of refuse produced. The total ashes, garbage, and rubbish collected in the five boroughs of New York City in 1925 was over 15 million cubic yards. Its composition was approximately as follows:

	Cubic yards	Per cent by volume	Per cent by weight*
Ashes	6,786,000	44	70
Garbage	2,074,000	14	21
Rubbish	6,443,000	42	9

* Assuming ashes and garbage to weigh 1,100 pounds per cubic yard and rubbish to weigh 150 pounds per cubic yard.

[22] George E. Waring, *Street-Cleaning*, 1899.
[23] William B. Munro, *Municipal Government and Administration*, 1923, II, 164.

The solid wastes produced yearly in the metropolitan district of New York have been estimated, in weight, as follows: ashes, 4,680,000 tons; garbage, 905,000 tons; and rubbish, 465,000 tons.

As to the disposition of this huge amount, about one-fourth is incinerated; the rest is dumped at sea, at Rikers Island or on various borough land dumps, where the resulting odors and dust constitute a serious nuisance since the dumps are in the midst of rapidly growing communities. The disposal of garbage by dumping at sea has, during the past few years, been strongly objected to by the communities on the New Jersey coast and on the south shore of Long Island. Garbage and other refuse appear in considerable quantities on the beaches in these sections after prevailing easterly winds. The supervisor of the harbor, a federal official, has notified the City of New York that the dumping of solid refuse at sea must be stopped.

Progress toward the substitution of improved methods has been slow and has been impeded by the lack of public interest. A study of the problem by the Regional Plan of New York and Its Environs concludes that the practice of dumping garbage and rubbish at sea is both wasteful and unsanitary. It urges that garbage treatment plants, either by incineration or reduction, be built in different parts of the city to take care of the refuse collected. The city has a few incinerators and has appropriated money for more. Its program in 1931 called for the erection of fifteen new incinerators, at a cost of $17,375,000. It has experienced difficulty, however, in obtaining approval of sites. "Local residents and business men have considered such plants as nuisances and have opposed their construction. This is a natural but selfish point of view which public sentiment should not support. A well-built and well-operated plant need be neither unsightly nor obnoxious, and each community should recognize its responsibility for taking care of its own wastes on sites best suited to that use."[24]

There are indications that the problem of refuse disposal in New York City will soon receive long-deserved and serious consideration. A bill has been introduced in the New York Legislature providing for a Sanitary Department and Commission for New York City, to have control of the questions of sewage and refuse disposal and street cleaning. If the proposed program is pushed with all possible speed, the city may soon be equipped with an adequate refuse disposal sys-

[24] *Regional Survey of New York and Its Environs*, 1929, VIII, 92-105 (103-104 quoted). James C. Young, "New York City Faces a Crisis over Disposal of Waste," New York *Times*, March 13, 1927; May 20, 1931.

tem for all classes of waste, obviating the necessity of sending refuse to be dumped at sea, and removing all cause for complaint of littered beaches so far as the City of New York is concerned.[25]

PURIFICATION OF CITY AIR

A problem closely related to those discussed above is that arising from the pollution of city air. In addition to those physical properties of air which affect comfort and health (temperature, humidity, and air movement), the atmosphere determines the character and extent of the sun's rays which reach the earth's surface. Its pollution, then, becomes a matter for consideration. "About 20 per cent of the light of the visible spectrum, 'light' in the common use of the word, is absorbed by a clear atmosphere at sea level. Only a small part of the total ultra-violet radiation of the sun ever reaches the earth's surface, while a large proportion of the infra-red spectrum and the heat rays do come through. This selective screening effect is modified by the thickness of the air layer (altitude of the place), and by the clouds, fog, smoke and dust." The ultra-violet rays, which, as we shall see, are so significant from the health standpoint, constitute less than 2 per cent of the sun's total radiation. "These rays are very sensitive to the media through which they pass and are readily absorbed. The atmosphere surrounding the earth is a great barrier. Obviously, more of them reach the earth in summer when the sun is near the zenith than during the winter. Likewise there are more of them on the top of a high mountain than at sea level. There are more of them on bright than on cloudy days; more reach the country than the smoke covered cities, for they are absorbed by dust, moisture and gases."[26] Practically all the smoke in an ordinary city is produced during the day. It is during these smokiest hours that the sun attempts to send through its vitalizing rays. Why this reduced permeability is, from the health standpoint, the most serious consequence of polluting city air, will be seen below.

Great progress has been made in purifying our food and water supplies, but little has been done to purify our air. The solution of the menace of impure air is the purification of all the air we breathe. This can be done by preventing contaminating substances from entering the air.

The Smoke Nuisance.—The chief contamination of the air of cities comes from smoke. In large manufacturing centers using bitumi-

[25] George A. Soper, ''New York City Faces Reforms in Refuse Disposal,'' New York *Times*, March 17, 1929.

[26] W. W. Peter, ''Sunlight and Health,'' *The Survey*, March 15, 1928, 59:12:773.

nous coal, the great quantities of smoke issuing from the factories and buildings give the effect of a cloud hanging over the city. The problem is not a new one. "Soft coal was introduced into London about the end of the thirteenth century and almost at once an agitation against the 'smoke nuisance' began, leading even in the reign of Edward I to a prohibition of the use of soft coal during the sessions of Parliament. English authorities have devoted much attention to this problem during the past few years and have demonstrated the astounding fact that between 80 and 400 tons of solid matter per annum are deposited from the air of English cities on every square mile of territory. In Manchester, Glasgow, and Leeds it has been shown that the average amount of winter sunlight is diminished about 40 per cent as compared with adjacent rural districts, while Besson reports that the smoke of Paris causes a reduction in sunlight of 15 to 25 per cent as far as 10 kilometers from the city."[27] According to an official statement the obstruction to sunlight results in the loss of 20 per cent of sunshine in the towns of England, and probably at least 65 per cent of the possible ultra-violet rays are lost.[28]

Conditions are as bad in American cities. In Pittsburgh as much as 1,000 tons of soot per square mile were deposited throughout the city in 1912 and 1,400 tons in 1924. The worst offenders were the 100,000 homes. In its smokiest area, Pittsburgh carries 1,950 tons to the square mile. The chemical action of daylight in Pittsburgh is about 60 per cent of that in Sewickley, a small residential town nearby. St. Louis averages 775 tons of soot to the square mile. On an average-bright day the clouds of smoke particles that hang over New York like floating curtains deprive the city of 37 per cent of its sunshine in the early morning and 14 per cent at high noon. Averages for the whole year show that smoke steals about one-fifth of New York City's natural light. In Cleveland, four observation posts were set up on the roofs of hospitals or adjacent buildings; the total yearly deposit of solids of fuel origin, calculated per square mile, varied from 353 tons in the best case to 1,432 in the worst. Cleveland obtains annually only 53 per cent of the sunshine that, according to the United States Weather Bureau, she ought to get. From December to March, the city has the benefit of only 34 per cent of her possible hours of sunshine.[29]

[27] C.-E. A. Winslow, *Fresh Air and Ventilation*, 1926, pp. 15-16.
[28] Sir Arthur Newsholme, *The Story of Modern Preventive Medicine*, 1929, p. 212.
[29] W. W. Peter, "Sunlight and Health," *The Survey*, March 15, 1928, 59:12:- 773-774. New York *Times*, Oct. 30, 1927; *The Survey*, Feb. 15, 1922, 47:10:782; Jan. 15, 1931, 65:8:443.

Ultra-Violet Rays.—Atmospheric pollution resulting from smoke and dust affects the public health chiefly by reducing the permeability of the air for the short rays of light. Fog, which is increased by the presence of these polluting substances, has the same effect. It is the ultra-violet rays which make sunlight one of the best germicides, although the heat rays are also of importance in the drying which helps kill exposed bacteria. In direct sunlight the tubercle bacillus, if not buried in a mass of other substance, dies in a few hours. In particular, the short rays of light, which are reduced by atmospheric pollution, have a vital relation to rickets.

Rickets.—''While rickets may occur in any latitude if there is interference with the metabolic processes which determine normal development, it is found most abundantly, indeed almost universally, among babies in their first year of life in all the large northern cities of Europe and America, where, in addition to the limitations of the sun's rays by low inclination and cloud, children are housed and fed unsuitably.''[30] Rosenau[31] says of this disease: ''Rickets is a nutritional disorder due to lack of sunshine and faulty diet. It is a disease of civilization brought on by artificial living. The disease is characterized by an alteration in the structure and growth of bones, which become enlarged at the extremities and so soft that they bend under the weight of the body. It occurs during the first two years of life, when growth is most rapid. . . . Rickets is responsible for bowed legs, knock knees, flat feet and saber legs; and is associated with the rickety rosary, pigeon breast, square head and pot belly, a strange medley that find their most exaggerated expression in misshapen dwarfs. . . . Rickets is one of the penalties of living in houses on a denatured diet. Primitive man lives in the sunshine and on natural food. Tropical races are spared; the Eskimos, deprived of the sun's rays for long periods, are protected by a diet rich in fish oils and liver. . . . Rickets is the most common chronic nutritional disorder occurring among infants of the temperate zones; it is mild or absent in the tropics. It is more particularly a disorder of cities and of the large industrial centers, although it is by no means absent among the rural population. Its frequency is roughly proportional to the density of population. . . . Rickets is much more prevalent than is indicated by the meager figures found in vital statistics. For various reasons it is more often overlooked than recognized. It does not appear

[30] Haven Emerson and Earle B. Phelps, ''The City Gains on the Country,'' *The Survey*, Aug. 1, 1929, 62:9:472.
[31] *Preventive Medicine and Hygiene*, 1927, 629-630, 632, 633.

in the mortality tables because it is seldom a direct cause of death. . . . The greatest recent advance in our knowledge of rickets has been an understanding of the precise nature of the hygienic factor. This has been shown to be sunlight rather than fresh air, exercise, cleanliness, etc. Infants do not develop rickets in the summer on account of the protective effect of the sun's rays. This is due to the ultra-violet radiations and not to the visible rays.'' One of the main dangers of the disorder is that rachitic children are predisposed to infections of the respiratory tract. More serious than the deformities of limbs is the deformity and constriction of the pelvis which occurs in female rickety children. ''In women this becomes the most common cause of difficult, protracted, and complicated parturition: thus infantile rickets is an important cause—twenty or more years later— of mortality of mothers in childbirth, which is entirely avoidable.''[32]

Recently it has been shown that rickets can not only be cured but prevented by treatment with sunlight or with light from artificial sun lamps. This has led to a program, which the Children's Bureau among others has been popularizing, of sun baths for infants. It has also been discovered that cod-liver oil has the same curative and preventive effect. When we give cod-liver oil to cure rickets, we are really administering ''bottled sunlight.'' Cod-liver oil has been called civilization's excellent, economical and practical substitute—at least during the colder and darker half of the year—for exposure to sunlight.

''For the practical hygienist the chief immediate point is that we have now at last a rational justification of our instinctive belief in the value of sunlight, a new ground for controlling the smoke nuisance, demanding sound building laws and advocating the outdoor life. The superiority of scientific knowledge over empiricism is well illustrated, however, by the fact that sunlight admitted through glass is robbed of its most valuable radiations and as Bovie has shown in his studies of diseases of fowls this problem may perhaps have to be solved by the use of windows made of fused quartz.''[33] ''The flood of sunlight outside our windows is a flood of health, yet only visible light and some invisible heat come through. So far as ultra-violet radiation is concerned, our houses and office buildings are all dungeons. City dwellers grow and work under glass, but glass of the wrong kind. Ordinary glass literally skims sunlight of its life-sustaining, healing, disease-resisting, invisible ultra-violet rays. It is dena-

[32] Sir Arthur Newsholme, *The Story of Modern Preventive Medicine*, 1929, pp. 257, 266.
[33] C.-E. A. Winslow, *Fresh Air and Ventilation*, 1926, p. 18. *Cf.* Martha M. Eliot, *Sunlight for Babies*, 1925.

tured light—near light. Sunbeams travel 93,000,000 miles to reach us and then we rob them of their most valuable property."[34] Even with the widespread use of cod-liver oil and artificial sunlight to correct and prevent rickets there was in 1920 a ratio of 1.75 cases per child population in cities to every one among country children in the United States.

Respiratory Diseases.—Along with rickets, tuberculosis is part of the price "the modern paleface has to pay for living in herds, shut within walls or underground, with artificial lights and on denatured foods."[35] Dr. Rosenau[36] says of tuberculosis: "It is a disease of cattle in barns, not on the range; chickens in coops, not birds in nature; monkeys in zoos, not in the jungle; man in houses, not primitive races." Excess of coal smoke is a cause of the high death-rate from acute diseases of the respiratory organs. "In manufacturing countries the highest mortality from acute lung disease is found in those districts where coal smoke is most abundant. Smoke not only tends to produce pulmonary disease but it hastens the course of tuberculosis." Sir Arthur Newsholme,[37] formerly principal medical officer of the Local Government Board of England and Wales, states: "The effect of a few days of smoky fog in increasing the death rate in the following week, especially from bronchitis and other respiratory affections, is well known. . . . It is the combination for several days of fog, frost, deprival of sunlight and still air which is especially lethal. As a practical problem in preventive medicine, we know that removal of coal dust from the air would diminish the density and duration of the fog, reduce its irritant effect, and possibly admit a certain proportion of the sun's rays."

Air Pollution by Carbon Monoxide.—A special problem of air pollution is that occasioned by the exhaust gas of motor vehicles. In industry carbon monoxide poisoning is fairly common, but Henderson and Haggard[38] believe that, even outdoors, dangerous concentrations of carbon monoxide may be reached under conditions of crowded street traffic. Tests made in Manhattan have shown that 1 part of carbon monoxide in 10,000 of air is a quite frequent condition in streets where traffic is heavy and that 2 parts of carbon monoxide are not unusual. Even more than this occurs in limited areas and for

[34] Waldemar Kaempffert, quoted in *Housing Betterment*, July, 1927, 16:2:110.
[35] W. W. Peter, "Sunlight and Health," *The Survey*, March 15, 1928, 59:12:772.
[36] *Preventive Medicine and Hygiene*, 1927, p. 157.
[37] *The Story of Modern Preventive Medicine*, 1929, p. 213.
[38] "Health Hazard from Automobile Exhaust Gas in City Streets, Garages and Repair Shops," *Jour. American Medical Assn.*, Aug. 4, 1923, 81:385-391.

short periods. Conditions are worse in the streets than in the Holland vehicular tunnel on its busiest day. Four parts in 10,000 is a danger point when individuals are exposed to this concentration of gas for any length of time. The remedy suggested by these investigators is the requirement of vertical exhaust on all cars with fixed tops, unless such drastic steps are to be taken as enforcing the substitution of electric- for gasoline-propelled vehicles for exclusive city use.

Effect of Smoke on Vegetation.—In addition to its injurious effect on health, there are other reasons for condemning the smoke nuisance. It has a similar effect on vegetation. "Soot may exert a detrimental effect on the growth of plants in three ways, namely, by blocking up the stomata and thus impeding the process of transpiration; by coating the leaf and so reducing the intensity of sunlight, and at the same time affecting the assimilation of carbon dioxide, and lastly by the corrosive effect of the acid it contains."[39] The well-known architect Frederick Law Olmstead, Jr., has said: "You can draw plans for the most beautiful park in the world, but you cannot have grass and trees while you have smoke." New York City is spending over $870,000 to rehabilitate Central Park, which is said to have been smothering under a blanket of black smoke that has been killing off the trees and shrubbery.[40] The Missouri Botanical Garden at St. Louis and the Brooklyn Botanic Garden have reported that smoke has shortened and, in some instances, destroyed plant life.

Economic Cost of the Smoke Nuisance.—The smoke nuisance is also to be condemned on aesthetic grounds. Smoke nullifies efforts to construct attractive buildings by blackening the walls and decorations. Smoky cities have spent many thousands of dollars in cleaning the grime from buildings and monuments. It is stated that priceless pictures in the British Museum and National Gallery are suffering slow destruction. "We are the dirtiest museum in the world," says the director of Chicago's famous Art Institute. Recently thirteen tons of soot and cinders were taken from its roofs.

The smoke nuisance also causes considerable money loss: to the individual for laundry and cleaning bills; to the household for extra painting, sheet metal work, cleaning and renewing wall paper and curtains, and for artificial lighting; to wholesale and retail stores for damage to merchandise, especially white goods exposed for sale, for cleaning and artificial lighting; to public and quasi-public buildings for cleaning and extra lighting; and to the smoke makers themselves,

[39] J. B. Cohen and A. G. Ruston, *Smoke*, 1912, p. 20.
[40] New York *Times*, April 1, 1928.

since smoke arises from the imperfect combustion of fuel.[41] It has been estimated that in a single year smoke costs the people of the United States more than $500,000,000, in the destruction of merchandise, the defacement of buildings, tarnishing of metals, injury to human and plant life, the greatly increased labor and cost of housekeeping, and the losses to manufacturers and householders due to imperfect combustion of coal.[42] The waste due to half-burned coal is placed at 60 million tons—or more than enough to supply all the fuel needs of a great city like Chicago for an entire year. Smoke abatement is a first cousin to fuel conservation from an economic standpoint.

Smoke Abatement.—Some cities have attempted to solve the problem by ordinances prohibiting factories from belching forth clouds of smoke; some force the railroads entering the city to electrify their roads; some have smoke abatement or inspection departments; some states have anti-smoke laws. Generally such legislation is not well enforced or administered. A few cities have had some success through a reasonable anti-smoke ordinance, properly enforced. Smoke exceeding a certain density (usually stated in terms of the Ringlemann chart devised by the United States Bureau of Mines), emitted for more than a limited period, should be prohibited. The time limit for permissible dense smoke (60 per cent black) varies. Before a boiler, furnace or fuel-burning apparatus may be installed, a permit must be secured. A survey made by the Mellon Institute of Industrial Research in 1923-24 indicated that in Pittsburgh, smoke prohibited by law had decreased approximately 80 per cent since 1912-13, when the first survey was made.[43]

The technical phase of the program of smoke abatement centers about the fact that smoke depends upon the character of the fuel, the nature of the combustion equipment, and the management of that equipment. The best way to abate the nuisance is to get at the heart of the matter, which is imperfect or incomplete combustion. Combustion is rapid chemical combination with the evolution of light and heat. "The two substances most commonly used for developing heat are carbon, found in wood or coal, and oxygen, found in the air. When combustion takes place a certain fixed amount of one of these substances always unites with a certain fixed amount of the other. A

[41] J. J. O'Connor, *The Economic Cost of the Smoke Nuisance to Pittsburgh,* 1913.

[42] H. M. Wilson, "Smoke Worse than Fire," *The American City,* May, 1911, IV, 210-212.

[43] H. B. Meller, "How Cities Can Control the Smoke Nuisance," *National Municipal Review,* May, 1926, 15:5:270 ff.

certain temperature, called the ignition temperature, must be reached and maintained before combustion will take place.'' If combustion is hindered (as by cutting off the air supply, increasing the fuel supply beyond that for which the air supplied is sufficient, or if the temperature of the gases is suddenly lowered below the ignition point), smoke results, and particles of unburned carbon are deposited as soot or are carried up the chimney and become visible as dense black smoke. The remedy is obvious: keep the gases heated above the ignition point and continue to supply the proper amount of air until combustion is complete. Thus smoke prevention simply means perfect combustion. The necessary factors for the smokeless burning of coal are proper equipment, efficient labor, and intelligent supervision.[44] These are often hard to secure.

In the interest of conserving the fuel resources of the country, the Federal Government has made many successful experiments in burning coal without smoke. Several hundred factories are running without producing any smoke, which means a considerable saving to them because of complete combustion. The railroads have, in the interest of economy, greatly reduced the amount of smoke produced by locomotives. It is the opinion of experts in the Bureau of Mines who have made extensive investigations that ''although hand-fired furnaces can be operated without objectionable smoke, the fireman is so variable a factor that the ultimate solution of the problem depends on the mechanical stoker—in other words, the personal element must be eliminated.''[45] A smokeless city is entirely possible, and it will come when the public has thoroughly awakened to the enormous waste of natural and human resources through the smoke nuisance.

[44] H. M. Wilson, ''The Cure for the Smoke Evil,'' *The American City*, June, 1911, IV, 264-265.

[45] D. T. Randall and H. W. Weeks, *The Smokeless Combustion of Coal in Boiler Furnaces*, Bulletin 40, 1912, Department of the Interior, Bureau of Mines. H. M. Wilson, ''The Cure for the Smoke Evil,'' *The American City*, June, 1911, IV, 263-267.

CHAPTER XII

PROTECTING THE CONSUMER OF FOOD AND DRUGS

UNDER modern urban conditions the consumer is far removed from the source of food supply. He is unacquainted with the conditions under which his food is produced and handled, and even if he were familiar with them he would be powerless to exercise any control. He is himself unable to ascertain the true worth of the many articles of consumption. Thus the city-dweller may be the victim of fraud or, more seriously, he may become sick through consuming contaminated goods. Adjustment to modern conditions of production and distribution calls for some kind of social control for the protection of the consumer. This is furnished by society, acting in its organized capacity, chiefly through its public-health departments.

THE MILK QUESTION

The Importance of Milk.—Of all foods the most important from the public-health standpoint is milk. No other article of food contains to so complete an extent all the elements of a well-balanced diet. Valuable to adults, it is the indispensable food for children. On the other hand, milk is responsible for more disease than all other foods. There are several reasons why milk occupies this position. It is the only important food derived from animals which is regularly consumed in the raw state. Cooking destroys germs; uncooked articles may convey infection. No other single food is subject to so many sources of contamination as is milk, or is so difficult to produce and distribute to the consumer with safety. "It requires scrupulous care from pasture to pail, and from pail to palate. It is the most difficult of all our foods to gather, handle, transport, and deliver in a fresh, clean, safe, and satisfactory manner. Furthermore, milk decomposes more quickly than any other food. It spoils even more quickly than fresh fruit and berries."[1] Milk is one of the best media for the growth of bacteria. The great difference between milk and water from a sanitary standpoint is that bacteria tend to die in water whereas they grow well in milk—even more quickly in milk than in the body.

[1] M. J. Rosenau, *The Milk Question*, 1912, p. 2.

Dilution, sunshine, aëration, sedimentation, and other factors which are unfavorable to germ life in water, have no chance in milk. Clean water does not furnish sufficient food even for the humble germs. Milk, on the other hand, is a rich culture medium.

Milk As a Route of Infection.—There are two principal ways in which milk may become contaminated and thus convey infection to the consumer. (1) The animal from which the milk is obtained may be diseased and the germs causing the disease may get in the milk. (2) The milk may be infected by germs from diseased milkers or other persons who handle it. The diseases known to be conveyed by milk are tuberculosis, typhoid fever, scarlet fever, diphtheria, septic sore throat, foot-and-mouth disease, Malta fever, milk sickness, and occasionally others. This list does not include the dysenteries and gastro-intestinal diseases of babies that are also associated with impure milk. Some of the diseases mentioned come from the lower animals; some from man. Thus "bovine tuberculosis, foot-and-mouth disease, and milk sickness come from the cow; Malta fever is primarily a disease of goats. The more serious infections in milk, however, come from human origin. Man contracts most of the diseases to which he is heir from his fellow man. Cows do not have typhoid fever, scarlet fever, or diphtheria, so that when milk contains the viruses of these diseases the infection usually gets into the milk either directly or indirectly from human sources."[2] Infected milk has caused numerous and, at times, extensive epidemics. These are the reasons why there is a milk question. In fact, the milk question as we understand it today began only when it was shown that impure milk is apt to convey disease.[3]

Governmental Regulation.—For the protection of the public health, then, it is desirable and necessary that the state and its local subdivisions should regulate the production, handling, and distribution of milk. It is also important to do this so as to protect the purchasers of milk against fraud. "The definition of milk formulated by the United States Public Health Service requires that it shall contain not less than ½ per cent of solids not fat and not less than 3¼ per cent of milk fat. The amount of fat contained in milk is ascertained by the so-called Babcock test. The principal regulations to protect the public against fraud are designed to eliminate the watering of milk

[2] M. J. Rosenau, *The Milk Question*, 1912, p. 89. *Cf.* Herbert H. Waite, *Disease Prevention*, 1926, p. 63.

[3] M. J. Rosenau, *The Milk Question*, 1912, pp. 11, 89-91. Jean Broadhurst, *Home and Community Hygiene*, 1923, pp. 62-91.

to increase the quantity, or introduction of preservatives or coloring matter. Watering naturally decreases the percentage of solids and fats in the milk. Standards may also be fixed for cream, requiring that it shall contain not less than a certain percentage of milk fat. The percentage usually adopted is 18 per cent, although several dairy States use 20 per cent instead. Some ordinances require that the capacity of milk containers be plainly shown upon them. Such regulations have been uniformly upheld as a proper exercise of the police power.''[4]

Three general types of control are used in the enforcement of statutes and ordinances regulating the production and handling of milk. The first method of control is to require that no milk be sold by any person who does not possess a license from the state or municipality to sell or distribute milk. As a condition prerequisite to the granting of the license, the plant and equipment of the applicant are usually inspected to ascertain whether or not they comply with the provisions of the law. For certain specific violations, the license may be revoked or suspended, and the producer or distributor thus denied the privilege of selling or distributing milk in that territory. The second method, which is used in some states, is to provide for the grading of milk into several different types, with varying degrees of desirability as food products. If a producer fails to maintain the standard of production required by the ordinance, his milk may be placed in a lower grade, thus affecting its sale value. There are very few ordinances which do not define at least two classes of milk—raw milk and pasteurized milk. Many of them add certified milk to the types included in the definitions. A third method of control is penal. Practically every ordinance utilizes this method, and most of them employ it in conjunction with one or the other of the methods just mentioned. For example, ordinances providing for the granting and revoking of licenses regularly impose a penalty for selling milk of a lower grade (or in some cases of a different grade) than that indicated by the cap or label. The most widely used type of ordinance is that which combines the grading and penal methods.

In the case of large cities drawing their milk supply from other states, the licensing method is of peculiar value in that it permits the exercise of inter-state control. Neither the local nor the state authorities have direct power to inspect dairies in another state, but through a system of licensing they can accomplish the same end. A milk

⁴ Harvey Walker, *Regulating the Production, Handling, and Distribution of Milk*, Public Health Reports, Aug. 10, 1928, 43:32:2095-2097.

dealer in Vermont, for example, need not submit to inspection by an agent from the State of Massachusettts or from the city of Boston, but either the city of Boston or the State of Massachusetts can say to the Vermont farmer: "You cannot sell your milk in our city or state unless you permit our inspection and comply with our sanitary requirements." The refusal to permit the inspection may be taken as *prima facie* evidence that the dairy is in an unsanitary condition or that the methods are unsatisfactory, and the milk may therefore be excluded. As a great proportion of the milk of all large cities comes from other states, the control of this inter-state traffic through the indirect method of the license becomes an essential part of the system of milk inspection.[5] In New York City, for example, the daily supply of milk, which averages about $2\frac{1}{2}$ million quarts, comes from some 50,000 farms scattered through 8 different states.

Inspection.—The milk regulations are usually enforced by the local board of health. Inspectors visit the farms where the milk is produced and the plants in the city which distribute it. They inspect the machinery and utensils and also the workmen. They take samples of milk which they subject to chemical and bacteriological examinations to ascertain whether the milk attains the standards set by the law. Of all the routine laboratory tests, the simple enumeration of the number of bacteria in milk tells most concerning its general sanitary quality. A large number of bacteria in milk, regardless of their kind, means that it is old, that it has not been kept cold, or that it is dirty. With bacterial counts as a guide, it is comparatively easy to determine the cause of trouble or to locate just where the trouble takes place. With a proper diagnosis it becomes easy to institute treatment and to prevent the recurrence of the difficulty.[6]

Pasteurization.—The greatest device for protecting the milk supply is pasteurization, by which is meant simply the heating of milk to a temperature below that of boiling for a short period of time, followed by rapid cooling. It renders harmless all disease bacteria which may be in the milk, without producing undesirable or harmful changes in the milk itself. The process is called after Louis Pasteur, who first used it for the preservation of organic fluids. It was applied to milk by the distinguished chemist, Soxhlet, who in 1886 advised the heating of milk for infant feeding and described an apparatus for carrying out the process in the home.

[5] M. J. Rosenau, *The Milk Question*, 1912, pp. 182-183.
[6] F. Overton and W. J. Denno, *The Health Officer*, 1920, pp. 347-350, 358-370. M. J. Rosenau, *The Milk Question*, 1912, pp. 61-88.

Milk may be pasteurized commercially in three ways.

1. *The Flash Method.*—This consists in raising the milk to a high temperature (170° or 180°F.), keeping it at this temperature for a minute or so, then rapidly cooling it. This method is not satisfactory, and sanitarians do not endorse it. It cannot be depended upon to kill the tubercle bacillus. It is difficult to make sure that every particle of the milk is heated to the desired temperature; in fact, it is quite certain that some of the milk escapes. The results, therefore, are irregular and unreliable.

2. *The Holding Method.*—This is the method most in vogue, and, when properly carried out, is entirely satisfactory. The milk is heated to a temperature of 140° to 145°F. and held at that point for 20, 30, or 45 minutes. It is then immediately cooled and filled into sterilized bottles by machinery. With a good holding device, there is not a loophole by which any harmful bacteria may escape destruction. Every possible precaution, however, must be exercised to prevent contamination after the milk has been heated.

3. *Pasteurization in the Bottle or Final Container.*—This is the best way to pasteurize milk. It has the advantage of eliminating the possibility of reinfection. Clean bottles are filled with milk, capped, then placed in a tank where the holding method is employed to pasteurize the milk. When this process is used, the consumer receives a bottle of milk which he can depend upon as being entirely free of infection.

Pasteurization does not in any way injure the nutritive value of milk. It does not affect the fat-soluble vitamin, though it lessens the amount of antiscorbutic vitamin. The loss, however, is no greater than results from keeping milk for too long a time. Any deficiency in vitamins resulting from pasteurization is readily offset in the case of older children through the consumption of additional foods, and in case of bottle-fed infants through supplementing their diet with orange juice and tomato pulp.

Pasteurization should be used only to destroy the harmful bacteria in milk and for no other purpose. It must not be used as a redemption process. It cannot atone for filth. It should never be used to bolster up bad milk. It should never be used as a preservative; heated milk keeps somewhat longer than raw milk. It is the cheapest form of life insurance the consumer can take out. The sanitarian asks of the consumer but a trivial amount for this safety check which he puts on the most indispensable of foods. The price of one glass of milk a year is all it costs the city-dweller to have his officer of health guard him against milk-borne infections. This small per capita rate suffices to provide a public service which has thousands of lives to its credit each year.[7]

Summary.—The solution of the milk problem thus lies in inspection and in pasteurization. Inspection goes to the root of the problem. Through an efficient system of inspection, the milk supply should be cleaner, better, fresher, and safer. Inspection, however, has limitations. These limitations may be guarded against by pasteurization. A milk supply, therefore, that is both supervised and pasteurized is the only satisfactory solution of the problem. Rosenau[8] summarizes this by saying: "To keep milk clean, we need inspection. To render milk safe, we need pasteurization." In the solution of the milk problem we see again the contribution of science to social problems. We are indebted to bacteriology, chemistry, immunology, and the advances in the sanitary sciences generally, not only for indicating but for solving the milk question. The scientist in the laboratory has pointed out the dangers, has led the way, and has given the power of prevention and cure.

FOOD SANITATION

If the first requisite in a food supply for a community is that it shall be sufficient in amount, of good quality, and well balanced, the second is that it should not convey pathogenic organisms nor be preserved, stored, or prepared in any way injurious to man. The conditions of food which may be detrimental to health are its impurity or adulteration, its decomposition, and the presence of poisons or disease germs. To protect the consumer against these conditions is a further duty devolving upon the health officer.

Adulteration.—The adulteration or sophistication of many articles of food has been commonly practiced. "It goes back to ancient times. Pliny alludes to the frauds practised by bakers; and both in ancient Athens and Rome wine was much tampered with. Bread was the subject of legal regulation in England as early as the reign of King John, the chief object being to limit the profit of the baker. In 1582 provisions were inserted against the adulteration of meal, as well as against the sale of 'mesell pork,' etc., punishment being inflicted of a fine, or the pillory, or for a third or fourth offense that the offender shall 'forswere the towne.' In France in 1382 there were ordinances

[7] Haven Emerson, "The Robust City," *The Survey*, Nov. 1, 1925, 60:3:123. Herbert H. Waite, *Disease Prevention*, 1926, p. 64. M. J. Rosenau, *The Milk Question*, 1912, pp. 185 ff. F. Overton and W. J. Denno, *The Health Officer*, 1920, ch. XXXII.

[8] M. J. Rosenau, *The Milk Question*, 1912, pp. 288, 297.

against the use of damaged flour, the substitution of other materials for corn, or light weight. In Germany there were similar regulations. . . . In the early part of the 19th century there was much activity against adulteration of foods; and in most civilized countries there are now public analysts and food inspectors to secure the examination of suspected foods, and the prosecution of offenders.''[9]

In this country the conditions which are considered to be adulterations are set forth in the Federal Pure Food and Drugs Act of 1906 and include the following.

1. Foods containing substances which are added in order to reduce their quality or strength (*e.g.*, watered milk).

2. Foods in which cheap substances are substituted for more expensive articles (*e.g.*, cottonseed oil for olive oil).

3. The meat of diseased animals, or foods containing filthy, decomposed, or putrid substances or products (*e.g.*, oysters contaminated with sewage, and eggs on the verge of decay).

4. Foods from which any valuable constituents have been removed (*e.g.*, skimmed milk). But the sale of such foods is permitted provided their actual nature or composition is stated on the labels or is told to the buyers.

5. Foods colored or otherwise treated in order to disguise damage or inferiority (*e.g.*, old meat colored red to resemble fresh meat).

Fraud is the principal ground on which adulterations are condemned. The food has a composition different from that which it is purported to have, and the consumer is cheated. A health department has no jurisdiction over adulterations on the ground of fraud alone, without authorization by law; but it may properly take action when the adulterations have an effect on the public health.[10]

The Pure Food and Drugs Act, applying to the District of Columbia and to inter-state commerce, is designed to prevent the manufacture, sale, or transportation of adulterated or misbranded or poisonous or deleterious foods, drugs, and medicines. The examination of specimens of foods and drugs is made by the Bureau of Chemistry of the Department of Agriculture. Though the act has been beneficial in many respects, its value is economic rather than hygienic. It is an honest-label law more than a pure-food act.

Bacterial Food Poisonings.—The severe forms of food poisonings are usually caused by specific bacteria, which are characterized by the production of toxins and by the ability to grow in meat and other foods. Two main classes may be distinguished: food infections and

[9] Sir Arthur Newsholme, *The Evolution of Preventive Medicine*, 1927, p. 201.
[10] F. Overton and W. J. Denno, *The Health Officer*, 1920, pp. 371-372.

food intoxications. In the first instance, the causal agent is the *Bacillus enteritidis*. The usual article of infected food is meat, though other articles, especially milk and its products, may occasionally be implicated. The infection may come from consuming the meat of an animal infected before it was slaughtered, or it may arise from meat which has become infected subsequent to slaughter. Prevention is based upon proper methods of slaughter-house sanitation, cleanliness and care in the preparation of foods, and protection from contamination in the interval between cooking and consumption.

Another form of food poisoning is known as botulism, a specific intoxication due to a toxin formed by the *Bacillus botulinus*. It is quite generally believed that this bacillus cannot grow in the living animal body. If this is true, botulism is never an infection, since no multiplication of the organism takes place after it has entered the living body. Its effects are therefore believed to be wholly due to poisons already elaborated through the growth of the bacillus in the food before it is consumed. This type of poisoning is less common in the United States than in Europe, where it is due generally to the consumption of contaminated meat. In the United States it has been caused more frequently by the consumption of ripe olives and canned goods. The prevention of poisoning from eating canned goods is a simple matter, the only requirement for removing danger being that of boiling the contents of the can for 10 minutes before eating.[11]

Meat Inspection.—The inspection of meat at slaughter-houses by trained inspectors is a necessary measure for the protection of the public health. The regulations aim to insure safe meat to the consumer. The departments of health of the larger cities require that animals to be used as food shall be slaughtered at licensed abattoirs in the presence of qualified inspectors. In the case of meat prepared in other states, regulation is effected by the Federal Meat Inspection Law of 1906. This act was passed following an investigation of the Chicago slaughter-houses, insisted upon by popular demand after the exposure by Upton Sinclair in *The Jungle*. The law provides that no meat shall enter into inter-state commerce except when inspected and certified to be clean, free from dangerous diseases, untainted, and wholesome, and so stamped or labeled by government seal ("U. S. Inspected and Passed"). It is enforced by the Department of Agriculture through its Bureau of Animal Industry. An inspection is made of the living animals and also of their carcasses and internal organs. Living animals are condemned when they are evidently diseased or

[11] Herbert H. Waite, *Disease Prevention*, 1926, pp. 66, 543-556.

show signs of sickness. When a slaughtered animal shows signs of disease, its body and internal organs are laid aside and examined in detail later. If the disease is localized, the affected parts are removed, and the remainder of the carcass is usually allowed to be sold. There seems to be no sanitary reason for condemning any healthy edible part of an animal, since a thorough cooking will prevent the transmission of disease by the meat.

The principal animal diseases which have a relation to human food are trichinosis, tapeworm, and tuberculosis. Human infection by the bovine tubercle bacillus very rarely occurs from any other source than the ingestion of milk or milk products. Tapeworm disease is transmitted to man by the ingestion of meat from infected cattle and hogs. Trichinosis arises from the consumption of the raw or insufficiently cooked meat of infested hogs.

To guarantee the cleanliness of meat, precaution must be exercised in the butchering, handling, storage, transportation, purveying, and preparation of meat as food. The most certain means of prevention, however, is thorough cooking.[12]

Food Infection.—Foods are sometimes infected with the bacteria of human diseases, the principal sources of infection being sewage, contaminated water, and human carriers. The foods which are most likely to become infected are shell-fish and green vegetables. The danger is greatest where the foods are eaten raw. Outbreaks of typhoid fever have been caused by eating raw oysters and other shell-fish taken near the mouths of sewers or in water that is heavily contaminated with sewage. Vegetables which are eaten raw may become infected with typhoid bacilli when they are fertilized with sewage or human excretions, or are washed in contaminated water, or handled by a carrier. Persons who are afflicted with communicable diseases, or are carriers of disease germs, may introduce these germs into foods which they handle.

The prevention of food infection and of food-borne disease consists in the education of the public and the inspection of places where food is prepared and sold. The first includes instruction regarding the preparation of foods so as to destroy whatever infection may be in them, and the arousal of public demand for cleanliness and sanitary methods of food handling by the producer and distributor. The inspections generally include restaurants, lunch counters, hotels, bak-

[12] Jean Broadhurst, *Home and Community Hygiene*, 1923, pp. 43-48. F. Overton and W. J. Denno, *The Health Officer*, 1920, p. 377. Herbert H. Waite, *Disease Prevention*, 1926, ch. VII.

eries, candy stores, soda fountains, meat markets, macaroni factories, and grocery stores. In many cities the supervision of the sanitary conditions of the food stores is supplemented by routine medical examination of the food handlers themselves, to protect the public against possible infection from persons affected with communicable diseases. Diseased individuals constitute a more serious danger to food than uncleanly surroundings.[13]

PROTECTION FROM NOSTRUMS AND QUACKERY

The United States is suffering, among other things, from so-called patent medicines. Hundreds of millions of dollars are invested in the nostrum industry, and many millions are spent annually for these preparations. The sale is considerable in country districts, since farmers have of necessity acquired the habit of doing much of their own medication. It is also very prevalent in cities, especially among the foreign-born and the less sophisticated. A large proportion of these prepared "medicines" are either worthless or grossly overvalued. America probably leads all other countries in the production and consumption of fraudulent or misleadingly branded drugs and medicines. The industry is well termed the Great American Fraud.

Proprietary Medicines.—We commonly think of nostrums as "patent medicines," but actually most of them are proprietary articles. There are several reasons why very few of the nostrums on the market are patented. A patent represents a limited monopoly; in seventeen years it becomes public property. This does not attract those who intend to exploit the public. There is the added inconvenience, from the manufacturer's standpoint, of having to give in detail all the facts regarding the ingredients, quantities, and method of compounding the product. The publication of the formula would dissipate the mystery which is the sheet anchor of nostrum exploitation. Further, patents are supposed to be issued only on products that can be shown to be both new and useful. Few of the medicinal preparations would qualify under these requirements. A much simpler and more effective way of obtaining a monopoly is utilized. A fancy name is given to the drug, or mixture of drugs, and that name is registered as a trade-mark. The name then becomes the inventor's property for all time. In granting a trade-mark, the government asks no embarrassing questions about the composition of the thing to which the name is applied. The owner may change the formula or process as often as he likes, but his proprietorship in the name remains intact. Some of these

[13] F. Overton and W. J. Denno, *The Health Officer*, 1920, ch. XXXIII.

names, such as "Peruna" or "Tanlac," have been worth in their time millions of dollars.[14]

Even legitimate drugs, when sold under trade names, cost more than when purchased under their official names. Take, for example, the case of aspirin (acetylsalicylic acid). "One brand of acetylsalicylic acid is as good as another, for aspirin is aspirin, just as quinine is quinine. Yet we find that the aspirin put under the name of Bayer has a wholesale price of 85 cents an ounce, whereas aspirin purchased under its official name, acetylsalicylic acid, can be had for 17 cents an ounce. . . . Veronal is the trade-marked name for a hypnotic known officially as barbital. The price charged for the drug under its proprietary name is $3 an ounce, as against 70 cents an ounce for exactly the same substance sold under its official name, barbital."[15]

Examples of Medical Frauds.—In the hope that the data it contains will be helpful in discouraging the use of nostrums and worthless preparations, the Indiana State Board of Health, among others, publishes a pamphlet on medical frauds, from which the following illustrations are cited.[16]

Am-O-Tone.—That anyone would be so foolish as to pay seventy-five cents for five cents' worth of borax is rather hard to believe, yet this is precisely what many do when they buy Am-O-Tone to use as a "dry shampoo."

Anti-Freckle Lotion.—E. B. Gustin manufactures this preparation in Logansport, Indiana, and guarantees it to remove freckles. Inasmuch as it is a simple solution of corrosive sublimate, we will not deny his claim, but rather supplement it by adding that the skin and some flesh will follow the freckles into oblivion.

Beecham's Pills.—According to the British Medical Association, these pills consist of aloes, powdered ginger and soap. One-half cent would be a high price to pay for the ingredients of a twenty-five cent box.

Bromo Seltzer.—An effervescent mixture containing a strong heart depressant and therefore dangerous.

Canthrox.—If we condense the elaborate statement of the manufacturer that Canthrox "gives to the hair that exquisite fluff and wavy softness that will insure a lovely growth," we find that he means that it cleanses. Obviously we do not deny this claim, but prefer to buy soap as soap at soap prices and not Canthrox at twenty-five times its actual value.

Castoria.—The Journal of the American Medical Association, in summarizing the patent of this preparation, which has now expired and is public

---

[14] Arthur J. Cramp, "Debunking Drugs," *The American Mercury*, March, 1928, 13:51:347. Stuart Chase and F. J. Schlink, *Your Money's Worth*, 1927, p. 122.

[15] Arthur J. Cramp, *op. cit.*, p. 350.

[16] H. E. Barnard, *Medical Frauds*, pp. 1-34.

property, states that "it appears to be a syrup containing an aqueous extract of senna with aromatics." The continued use of senna by an adult is dangerous, but for infants, as Castoria is advertised, it is doubly so.

Clearola.—G. W. Carpenter, of Jaffrey, N. H., has discovered how to sell one cent's worth of sulphur for fifty. His method consists of putting it in a pasteboard box, calling it Clearola and advertising that it "whitens the skin."

Cuticura Ointment.—The British Medical Association reports on this product as follows: "It consists of a mixture of hard and soft paraffin, slightly perfumed with rose and colored green." In our analysis, also, no other ingredients could be detected, and we must conclude that the purchaser of this salve pays an outrageous price for vaseline.

Eckman's Alterative.—*Collier's Weekly* recently tabulated the patent medicines that had been taken by the patients of a hospital for the tuberculous prior to their admission and found that more had consumed Eckman's Alterative than any other fake. When we learn that this fraudulent mixture of cloves, alcohol and calcium chloride sells for two dollars a bottle and that each patient probably takes ten or twelve bottles, we must realize that the public is paying quite a bonus for its patients in the tuberculosis hospitals.

Fat-Off.—This silly product of M. S. Borden, Brooklyn, N. Y., is soft soap. When sold as Fat-Off, five cents' worth rises in price to a dollar and a half.

It may be stated parenthetically that Dr. Arthur J. Cramp, director of the Bureau of Investigation of the American Medical Association, summarizes the fat reduction field as follows: "It can be laid down as a broad principle that all 'obesity cures' come under one of two classes: those that contain thyroid extract and will actually reduce weight but are exceedingly dangerous, and those that do not contain thyroid and will not under any circumstances reduce weight."

Father John's Medicine.—We find this preparation to consist approximately of one third cod-liver oil, one third water and one third balsam tolu and emulsifying agents. The United States District Court has declared this stuff misbranded because it is not "without an equal as a body builder, health food and for consumption, coughs, colds, croup, la grippe, pneumonia, whooping cough, bronchitis, asthma, night sweats, catarrh, rickets, thin blood, hoarseness and weak voice."

Hall's Catarrh Cure.—Potassium iodide, apparently, is the very life of a host of patent medicines that are advertised to cure almost anything from barber's itch to rheumatism. We have found it in so-called "cures" for consumption, eczema, syphilis, asthma, pneumonia, dropsy and now catarrh, for it is the principal ingredient of Hall's Catarrh Cure. Potassium iodide no doubt has value in some diseases when properly administered, but most of the wonderful virtues ascribed to it by the patent medicine manufacturers, when sold under a coined name, are impossible.

Kargon Compound.—The purchaser of a bottle of this hodgepodge finds the following statement in the accompanying circular: "As an act of humanity, recommend this to your suffering relatives." It seems to us that the "act of humanity" would affect the manufacturer more than the "suffering relatives" as additional unearned profits would then be added to his exchequer. The "compound" sells for fifty cents and contains four cents' worth of potassium acetate, alcohol and vegetable extracts.

Mother's Friend.—The Federal Government declared this stuff misbranded because it consisted of oil and soap and therefore would not "shorten the duration of labor" or "assist in the safe and quick delivery." Oil may smooth troubled waters and "soft soap" may be used to advantage under some conditions, but we fail to see how either can materially aid child birth.

Peruna.—Several years ago, according to the *Journal of the American Medical Association*, the federal authorities ruled that Peruna did not contain sufficient medicine to prevent it being used as a beverage. The manufacturer thereupon added a laxative and the sales diminished. This seems to prove that Peruna possesses no medicinal qualities, other than laxative, and is an alcoholic stimulant.

Tanlac.—Tanlac contains extracts of barberry, pareira brava, buckthorn, licorice and gentian together with 18 per cent of alcohol. The principal effect of this concoction, therefore, is simply that of a physic and stimulant. The continued use of it is harmful and the price charged exhorbitant, being ten times the cost of the ingredients.

Sanatogen.—This so-called "Re-Creator of Lost Health" consists of 95 per cent casein and 5 per cent sodium glycerophosphate. Casein is probably better known as cottage cheese, and the other ingredient, although of imposing name, can be purchased for twenty-five cents an ounce. Cottage cheese, no doubt, is a good food, but why buy Sanatogen at the rate of $4.50 a pound when a mixture of cottage cheese and sodium glycerophosphate in the same proportion can be had for thirty cents?

The last-mentioned preparation illustrates the dictum that the value of an advertised medium depends upon what is put *on* the bottle rather than what is put *in* it. Through the eloquence of advertising, a few cents' worth of casein is reared to lofty pinnacles—a "gift from the Goddess of Health." The advertisement follows:

Sanatogen is a scientific compound, every particle of which represents the finest concentrated tissue-constructing nutriment, endowed with unique revitalizing and rejuvenating powers. Sanatogen contains over 700 per cent more tissue-building, life-sustaining nourishment than wheat flour.

To this claim, Chase and Schlink,[17] in their fascinating book, *Your Money's Worth*, reply: "Laboratory analysis showed that one dollar's worth of wheat flour contains as much energy as $197 worth of

[17] 1927, pp. 128-129.

Sanatogen. The stuff is the equivalent of modified cottage cheese. For one dollar the consumer receives 332 calories of energy in Sanatogen; for the same dollar spent for cheese he receives 11,850 calories; and for wheat flour 65,400 calories."

The mystery of their composition and the false and misleading claims that are made for them account in large part for the sale of these nostrums. Through the power of advertising, Listerine has some reputation as an antiseptic, yet according to the *Journal of the American Medical Association* (July 4, 1925), "four hundred and ninety-five dollars' worth of Listerine has the antiseptic action of a cent's worth of corrosive sublimate; or fifteen dollars' worth of Listerine equals a cent's worth of carbolic acid." High-sounding names and scientific appearance help in inducing the public to buy commonplace and cheap articles at fancy prices. The manufacturers of a widely advertised poultice vouchsafed the information that the base of their preparation was "composed of the finest anhydrous and levigated argillaceous mineral." "Few vocabularies," comments Dr. Cramp,[18] "run this far, and no doubt inertia was counted on to keep the rank and file from consulting the dictionary and there finding that this awe-inspiring word-picture described only dried and powdered clay!"

Testimonials.—How are testimonials secured, and how valuable are they? Many come in voluntarily, sometimes being prompted by vanity. As the Toronto *Star* states, "If your brains won't get you into the papers, sign a patent medicine testimonial. Maybe your kidneys will." Sometimes the present of 12 cabinet photographs will fetch a testimonial; sometimes it takes cold cash. A service called Famous Names, Inc., headquarters Chicago, furnishes testimonials or special posings of celebrities at fees ranging from $150 to $2,500 depending upon the standing of the star and the length of time the exclusive use is desired. This fee includes the special posing and signed endorsement. Chase and Schlink[19] cite an example of celebrity endorsement in the case of Nuxated Iron, "which has thriven, and thrives, on the psychological effect of the word 'iron.' One's associative mental processes jump to iron muscles, iron endurance, iron manhood. When Jess Willard whipped Jack Johnson, it was Nuxated Iron which did it, according to the advertisement; when Dempsey knocked out Willard four years later, it was Nuxated Iron which ac-

[18] "Debunking Drugs," *The American Mercury, March,* 1928, 13:51:345.
[19] *Your Money's Worth,* 1927, pp. 135-136.

complished the feat, according to another great advertisement series. What happened to Willard's iron in the interim is not disclosed."

Said Willard in 1915:

"Without Nuxated Iron I am sure that I would never have been able to whip Jack Johnson so completely and easily as I did."

Said Dempsey in 1919:

"Nuxated Iron put added power behind my punch and helped to accomplish what I did at Toledo."

The series stopped with Tunney. What is the actual value of the preparation? "A dollar bottle of Nuxated Iron was found by the chemists of the American Medical Association to contain less than $2\frac{1}{2}$ grains of iron. If an individual really needs iron—and the need is rare—he can get nearly 100 grains in a dollar's worth of Blaud's Pills—which is a non-secret official remedy. In a Nuxated Iron tablet was found only one-twenty-fifth of a grain of iron, while the amount of Nux Vomica—the other drug ingredient—was practically negligible. 'The claim that Nuxated Iron possesses great advantages over other forms of iron is the sheerest advertising buncombe. The indiscriminate use of iron is illogical and unwise. Few drugs have been more abused and taken with less discrimination than has iron.'"

An obesity cure, a mail-order swindle, published the alleged endorsement of Texas Guinan, an actress. "It was brought out in court that Miss Guinan never saw the letters to which her name was signed, but she was paid $500 down and $50 a week for the use of her name. The 'cure' contained 30 cents' worth of alum, alcohol, and water and sold for $20."[20] "Within the past year, eighteen thousand physicians are alleged to have testified that the 'toasting process' to which a certain brand of cigarettes are allegedly submitted, is likely to free these cigarettes from throat-irritating properties. Of course not one physician in a thousand is competent to express such an opinion, but a questionnaire, accompanied by the persuasive power of a free gift of a carton of a hundred cigarettes, seems to have brought a lush response from an easy-going and tolerant profession—a record that does not redound to its credit."[21]

All the evidence indicates that testimonials, even the voluntary and sincere ones, mean little. Those that are honestly given come from one of two classes of individuals: first, people who are really

[20] Harry H. Moore, *Public Health in the United States*, 1920, p. 177.
[21] Arthur J. Cramp, "Testimonials—Mainly Medical," *The American Mercury*, Aug., 1929, 17:68:450.

dangerously ill, and who, in the optimism that every new "treatment" inspires, write praising the "cure"; secondly, those who, having nothing seriously the matter with them, naturally recover from the passing indisposition and credit their recovery to whatever they may have taken. Thus the bulk of testimony in the medical field that is commercially valuable is scientifically worthless. "It is valuable commercially because the public thinks it represents experience; it is worthless scientifically because, at its best, it details but a sequence of events and not a casual relationship.In other words, it comes from those whose testimony is incompetent."[22]

Some testimonials are self-canceling. In the files of the Bureau of Investigation of the American Medical Association are large numbers of testimonials for remedies for cancer, tuberculosis, diabetes, Bright's disease and other conditions, and filed with them are the death certificates of the individuals who gave the testimonials. A few examples are as follows:

Miss Ida S. of Wisconsin fell into the hands of a Michigan consumption-cure quack who published the girl's testimonial and added the claim: "She is now cured." Investigation brought a death certificate showing that the young woman had died of consumption more than a year prior to the time her testimonial was being circulated.

A California concern that sells "cures" for diabetes and Bright's disease has published many glowing testimonials. Take the case of Edward Z. of Iowa. Mr. Z. took thirty bottles of the diabetic remedy and was willing to have the company refer anyone to him, but the death certificate records that Mr. Z. died of diabetes. The case of Mort G. of California was described by the diabetes-cure concern as "a pleasing incident." Mr. G. took about forty bottles of the remedy; he died some months later. Cause of death: "uremic poisoning from diabetes." Daniel McH. of Virginia took the company's remedy for kidney disease and his testimonial was published, and the case recorded by the company as a "nice recovery." Mr. McH.'s death certificate records "interstitial nephritis" as the cause of death.

"Sometimes the god of chance gives the public a break in the testimonial game. Take, for example, the testimonial of W.A.M. of Nashua, Iowa, that appeared in the Nashua *Reporter*, gratefully endorsing Doan's Kidney Pills. The pulling power of this advertisement was seriously impaired by the fact that the death notice of Mr. M. appeared in the same issue of the paper. Nostrum vendors who use the local testimonial method of advertising need to keep check on their

---

[22] *Ibid.*, p. 444. American Medical Association, *Nostrums and Quackery*, 1911, p. 126.

endorsers.''[23] Doan's Kidney Pills have in more than one instance been endorsed by persons dead and buried. "After several such coincidences, the manufacturers instructed newspapers carrying their advertisements to return 'copy' containing testimonials of local persons who had died.''[24]

There are some testimonials that are never given out. The following samples referring to a consumption "cure" were collected by the Board of Health of Columbus, Ohio.[25]

I took Nature's Creation last summer because it was claimed a cure for tuberculosis. Took two bottles without benefit. Wish I could get my $9 back. They gave me two bottles for $9, but I do not consider that the two bottles were worth 9 cents.

I took Nature's Creation on the advice of a friend. Took three bottles. I was far worse off when I quit than when I started taking it. I decreased in weight and felt worse generally. I was able to be up and about when I commenced taking it, but was unable to leave my bed after taking two bottles. Wish that I could recover $15 they took from me without benefit.

My son, Gussie Jones, was suffering with tuberculosis for about a year. Nature's Creation was recommended to him as a cure, and finally he began taking it. He took two bottles of the medicine, but before he had finished the first he suffered terribly with his stomach as a result of it. I firmly believe that it did him more harm than good, and hastened his death, and I am free to make this statement of the facts of the case.

Medical Quacks.—Closely related to the problem of nostrums is that of the quack doctors who advertise, frequently in the foreign-language newspapers, as "medical specialists." Some of them also do business through purchasing "sucker lists" of prospective patients. "For years 'letter brokers' have done an extensive business in the purchase and re-sale of letters written in confidence to various mail-order quacks. Over 140,000 such letters were written to 'Mrs. Harriet M. Richard,' a name under which certain quacks advertised. They were rented at the rate of $5.00 a thousand, in bundles of 500, to other quacks in the same line of business who used them to circularize the sick. This method of obtaining a 'sucker list' has been widely used.''[26]

To test the analytical and diagnostic powers of the Van Bysterveld

[23] Arthur J. Cramp, "Testimonials—Mainly Medical," *The American Mercury,* Aug., 1929, 17:68:449.
[24] Harry H. Moore, *Public Health in the United States,* 1923, p. 167.
[25] American Medical Association, *Nostrums and Quackery,* 1911, p. 142.
[26] Harry H. Moore, *Public Health in the United States,* 1923, p. 177.

Medicine Co., "Inspectors and Examiners of Urine," Grand Rapids, Michigan, the chemists of the American Medical Association[27] submitted a mixture of hydrant water and glucose. The following reply was received from the company.

Dear Madam: Careful examination of the urine shows there is poor circulation of the blood which will cause a general weakness, the liver is not working properly which will cause gas in the stomach and bowels and you will have a weak, tired nervous feeling, also headache and backache spells. We can see no reason why a few weeks' treatment should not show you very beneficial results and trust that you may see your way clear to favor our method with at least a trial, which we feel confident will convince you of its merits.

The following letter was sent to Dr. Bertha C. Day, "specialist" in diseases of women:

Dear Doctor:—Will you please write and tell me about your cure for female trouble?

This is all that was written, yet the information was sufficient for the diagnostic powers of Dr. Day, who wrote back:

A careful diagnosis of your case shows you have Female Weakness.

Still another letter was written as follows:

Dear Doctor:—Will you please write and tell me if you can do anything for rheumatism?

By return mail came the stock diagnosis letter with the statement:

A careful diagnosis of your case shows you have rheumatism and associated conditions.

Organizations Engaged in Debunking Drugs.—"Among the first persons to appreciate the extensive harm done by nostrums and quackery were the editors of *The Ladies' Home Journal* and *Collier's Weekly*. These magazines enlisted the assistance of Mark Sullivan and Samuel Hopkins Adams, and conducted vigorous and effective campaigns in an attempt to enlighten the people of the country regarding the true nature of the business. Later, when the fraudulent nature of some eight or ten firms was exposed in Portland, Oregon, various papers quickly responded and voluntarily gave up many thousand dollars' worth of advertising. As a result, these firms soon closed their doors. The Chicago *Tribune* did aggressive work in running out of

[27] *Nostrums and Quackery,* 1911, p. 210.

that city several firms of 'specialists' in the private diseases of men. The New York *Tribune* also has done effective work in this field.'"[28]

In 1905 the American Medical Association definitely took action by authorizing the creation of a board known as the Council on Pharmacy and Chemistry. Its essential function is to gather and disseminate such information as will give the medical profession the facts regarding proprietary medicines sold for prescription purposes. Through the efforts of Dr. Arthur J. Cramp, on the editorial staff of the Association's *Journal*, a Bureau of Investigation has been developed in the American Medical Association. It is a clearing-house for information on the nostrum evil, quackery, and allied subjects, and has been of invaluable service in the war against medical frauds.

Officially the war is also being waged by public-health departments; by the Post Office Department, which withholds the use of the mails from persons and firms guilty of fraud; and by the Federal Government under the Pure Food and Drugs Act. All have been effective in the fight against quackery, and the government has successfully prosecuted many cases. The chief weakness in the Pure Food and Drugs Act is that although the act prohibits the use on bottles of labels which make false claims, it does not prevent the most extravagant advertising in newspapers; it is even permissible under the law to inclose with the bottle a circular claiming far more for the nostrum than does the label. Control in this respect may come through soliciting the coöperation of newspapers to prohibit false or extravagant advertising and that of the retail druggists association to stop the sale of fraudulent or misleadingly branded medicines and drugs. The only real solution, however, lies in educating the public regarding the perpetrations of which it is the victim.

[28] Harry H. Moore, *Public Health in the United States*, 1923, p. 181.

Chapter XIII

OTHER PUBLIC-HEALTH PROBLEMS

1. VITAL STATISTICS

VITAL statistics are statistics respecting the duration of life and the circumstances affecting its duration. They represent the application of the statistical method to the fundamental events of human lives, such as birth, marriage, sickness, and death. They are important to the worker in any field of public health, since they furnish him with the means of measuring the need for any particular kind of work as well as the success or failure of his efforts. "There are very few, if any, better methods of learning about the sanitary conditions of a given population than by turning to the best available vital statistics. The sanitary or biological condition or state of affairs of a given community is expressed statistically by the ratios of deaths and of diseases to the population. There are, therefore, two fundamental statistical elements to consider: First, the statistics of *population*; and second, the statistics of *morbidity* (sickness) and *mortality* (deaths)."[1]

The Census.—Population is the basis of all vital statistics. Statistics of population are obtained by the process of enumeration. Besides the total number of people in the community, a census usually includes information about other characteristics of the population, important among which are its distribution and its composition by age, sex, color, race, nativity, and parentage. These data are essential to the interpretation of other statistics and to the analysis of special problems.

Like all statistics, vital statistics must be correctly used and interpreted. Many elements enter into their interpretation, and erroneous conclusions will be drawn unless all the elements are considered. The death-rate among college students, for example, is extremely low in comparison with the death-rate among the whole population. The comparison, however, to be of value, must be made not with the death-rate among people of various ages but with that among young men of the same age as the college students. A community that boasts of

---

[1] I. S. Falk, *Essays on Vital Statistics*, 1922, p. 3.

the universally great age at which its inhabitants die may be one from which the young and active people have moved away, leaving only the older folk.

The Birth-Rate.—Fundamentally related to statistics of population are those of births and birth-rates. The number of births in a community is ascertained by means of the compulsory registration of every child that is born. The law usually imposes this duty on physicians and midwives. Relating births to the total population gives what is termed the crude birth-rate, usually expressed as the number of births per 1000 population. Since the birth-rate is dependent upon the fecundity of the female population of child-bearing age (ordinarily taken for statistical purposes as 15 to 45 years), the crude birth-rate may be refined to the number of births per 1000 married women between the ages of 15 and 45 years. Birth-rates are used as the basis for calculating infant-mortality rates and for testing the results of child-hygiene work.

The Morbidity Rate.—The morbidity rate, sometimes called the sickness or the case rate, is the number of cases of a specific disease or group of diseases occurring during the year, taken generally per 100,000 persons in the average population for the year. It is expressed, for example, as 125 (cases) per 100,000 (persons). "With the problem of morbidity, as will be seen to be the case with that of mortality, before accurate preventive or curative steps can be taken it is essential to have at hand the facts with which to evaluate the seriousness of the problem, to know its extent, its chief characteristics. To prevent sickness we must have at hand accurate data on the extent of sickness in an ordinary population; in special types of population; the severity of sickness; the available organizations to care for the sick; the causes; the forms of sickness; its incidence by sex, age, color, nationality and race. We must know the influence of specific industrial and social conditions upon sickness. To carry on sickness prevention programs we must know the cost of sickness and must learn the cost of prevention. These are the starting points in the campaign against sickness."[2] The statistics which have the most value to a health officer are those relating to the number of cases of communicable diseases in his jurisdiction. Most states require physicians to report cases of contagious diseases to the department of health, but the list of diseases and the manner of reporting vary widely.

The Death-Rate.—In the United States the ultimate source of mortality statistics is the death certificate, required in most states

[2] I. S. Falk, *Essays on Vital Statistics*, 1922, p. 23.

before burial. The crude death-rate is the number of deaths occurring annually in each 1000 of population. The death-rate of a community is influenced by a number of factors, among which sanitation and the prevalence of diseases are the most important. The crude death-rate is often taken as the standard by which the healthfulness of a place may be judged, but it is not a true index unless all other factors which influence the death-rate are excluded. For example, a factor which may have great influence on the death-rate of a community is the presence of a large almshouse, hospital, or other institution. A state hospital for the insane may have 2,000 inmates with 100 deaths annually. The corrected death-rate would be calculated upon the deaths remaining after those of non-resident inmates have been deducted; and the population would be that of the town after the number of non-resident inmates had been deducted. Also, correction must be made for age. "An allowance for the age distribution of population, and for deaths among various age groups, must be made in interpreting the death-rate of a community, or in comparing the rate of one municipality with that of another. If a municipality contains an excess of young persons, it will have a low death-rate. An excess of the number of babies, or of old people, will increase the death-rate. The differences among cities, states, and countries are so great in this respect that the effect of the age grouping of the population must be considered in comparing their death-rates."[3]

Thus the problem of mortality demands the use of more refined indexes than the crude death-rate. It is necessary to ascertain the specific death-rates of special groups in order to learn something about the part which factors such as sex, age, specific causes of death, season of the year, or occupation play in the causation of mortality.

The registration of deaths is indispensable to the development of public-health and social-welfare programs and the measurement of their results. Of particular value are the statistics regarding infant mortality (the death-rate among children under one year of age), which is the most sensitive index of social welfare and of sanitary administration, especially under urban conditions. "It is to the health propagandist what the clinical thermometer is to the physician. Childhood is ushered in with the highest and out with the lowest rates of mortality of all the span of life. Coupled with its enormous severity, infant mortality bears the additional characteristic that—like the thread of mercury in the thermometer—it goes up and down with

[3] F. Overton and W. J. Denno, *The Health Officer*, 1920, pp. 105, 106.

deleterious or salutary changes in the social, sanitary and economic conditions of the people.''[4]

Other Values of Vital Statistics.—In addition to these strong arguments from the public-health standpoint for the registration of vital statistics, there are other good reasons why such data should be kept. Consider, for example, the registration of births and deaths. Birth certificates are valuable to establish identity, to prove nationality and receive a passport for foreign travel, to prove legitimacy, to show when the child has the right to enter school or to seek employment under the child-labor laws, to establish the right of inheritance to property, to prove age of consent in court, to establish the right to the protection of the juvenile court, to prove the age at which the marriage contract may be entered into, to establish liability to military duty as well as exemption therefrom, to qualify to hold title to real estate, to establish the right to vote and to hold public office. The registration of deaths is of great legal and commercial importance for several reasons, chief of which are the protection of the persons and property of individuals, particularly with respect to pensions, life insurance, titles and rights to inheritances; and the prevention of crime by the legal requirements of the certification of a death certificate prior to the burial of a body.[5]

How Completely Are Vital Statistics Kept?—In view of these facts, it might be imagined that vital statistics would everywhere be fully and accurately kept, yet only a fraction of the world's population compiles such records. Some countries are not sufficiently advanced to realize their importance; some consider them unnecessary. For example, the head of an Oriental town, a Mohammedan, upon being asked by the British Government certain questions relating to his city, sent in the following reply:

Question: What is the death-rate per thousand in your city?
Answer: In my city it is the will of Allah that all must die; some die old, some young.
Question: What is the annual number of births?
Answer: We don't know, only God can say.
Question: Are the supplies of drinking water sufficient and of good quality?
Answer: From the remotest period no one has ever died of thirst.
Question: What is the general hygienic condition of your city?
Answer: Since Allah sent us Mohammed, his prophet, to purge the world

---

[4] I. S. Falk, *Essays on Vital Statistics*, 1922, pp. 17, 38, 39.
[5] *Ibid.*, p. 35. F. Overton and W. J. Denno, *The Health Officer*, 1920, p. 102.

with fire and sword, there has been great improvement. And now, my lamb of the West, cease your questioning, which can do no good either to you or anyone else. Man should not bother himself about matters which concern God alone.

Even in the United States registration is still incomplete in many parts of the country. We do not know and we never have known exactly how many children are born annually in the United States. We do not know the death-rate of the country at large. The collection of both birth and death statistics was authorized by the permanent census act, approved March 6, 1902, but until recently very few states have maintained reliable registration systems. It was not until 1915 that the first annual birth report could be compiled, and then it included data for only ten states and the District of Columbia. The standard set by the Bureau of the Census is the registration of 90 per cent of the births. States attaining this standard constitute the Birth Registration Area. This area has steadily grown until by 1929 it included forty-five states, containing approximately 95 per cent of the total population. Three states—New Mexico, Texas, and South Dakota—remain as fields of missionary endeavor.

Accurate statistics of mortality are not yet available for the whole country, though annual reports covering certain sections have been published since 1900. The United States Census Bureau confines its mortality data to those states which have been admitted to the Death Registration Area. States are "admitted" when they have made adequate legal provisions for the compulsory registration of accurate and complete death certificates and when they can demonstrate to the satisfaction of the Census Bureau officials that 90 per cent or more of all deaths which occur are being registered. The registration area now includes forty-five states (identical with the birth registration area), the District of Columbia, and ten cities in non-registration states. The completeness and the accuracy of these statistics are dependent upon the proportion of all deaths which are reported and the correctness with which the death certificates are filled out. Many errors creep into mortality statistics, one of the most outstanding being their incompleteness. In part this is due to failure of registration and in part to the complicating problems which arise when individuals die while they are away from their home community, in the hospitals, for example, of another city. "No adequate system for properly charging back institutional deaths to the proper places of residence has been devised as yet, and to avoid the chance of duplicating death registries the United States Census Bureau still adheres to the plan of charging deaths against the state, city or county in which they occur. Thus, communities with large institutions in which people die have unusually high mortality rates. Another common source of error in mortality statistics is the inaccurate statement of information on the death certificate. Age of the deceased, place of residence and occupation are very commonly given inaccurately. One of the most important items of information on a death certificate is the statement of cause of death. Also, it is the one in which there is the greatest opportunity for error. . . . Either because of the difficulty of diagnosis or sometimes because of the conscious desire to mis-state the cause of death to avoid odium or to shield the family of the deceased, or often because two or more pathological conditions have operated simultaneously to cause death, the statement of cause of death is liable to frequent error."[6] If autopsies were regularly performed, as is the case in certain European countries, the causes of death would be reported more accurately.

Hospital statistics in this country are even more incompletely developed. In no American city of any size is it possible to give the total number of cases admitted to hospitals, both public and private, the diseases for which entrance was sought, the age and sex distribution of the patients, the duration and results of the treatment. It is a blemish on the excellent work done by hospitals that this phase of their activities has almost without exception been left undeveloped.

Vital statistics are perhaps better kept and put to better use in England than anywhere else. This is owing to the employment of university men with specialized training and the high traditions of public service. In the United States, by contrast, the registration of vital statistics is commonly intrusted to persons with no special training in this field; it is often a political office, and voters unable to judge the qualifications of the candidates are asked to select the incumbent.

The importance of the whole subject has been excellently expressed by Dr. Chapin,[7] whose words may be quoted in summary. "The registration of vital statistics is the firm basis on which the whole structure of sanitary science and practice must rest. In order to learn the laws of disease, to devise remedies, and test them, we must have an approximately accurate knowledge of the movement of population and of the causes of death. Not only is a knowledge of these required, but also an

[6] I. S. Falk, *Essays on Vital Statistics,* 1922, p. 37. *Cf.* F. Overton and W. J. Denno, *The Health Officer,* 1920, pp. 104-105.
[7] *Municipal Sanitation in the United States,* 1901, p. 52.

accurate census showing the distribution of the population as to age, sex, civil condition, race, etc. Correct knowledge of population and its movements is valuable, not alone to sanitary science, but to the economist, the educator, the penologist, and indeed to the student of every branch of social science. A subject which is of such vast scientific importance should receive most careful governmental attention, and every aid should be given in assisting its investigation.''

2. INDUSTRIAL HYGIENE

It is a well-established fact that persons habitually engaged in hard work, especially in factories and indoors, present a greater amount of sickness and a higher mortality than persons more favorably situated, and that the character of the occupation influences to a great extent not only the average expectation of life, but also the prevalence of certain diseases. This unfavorable situation has been enhanced by the development of new industrial processes. From the mechanical and scientific point of view modern industry represents a marvelous development; a concomitant of this development, and one which is not always fully appreciated, is the human cost of industry. ''The wide use of chemistry in industry, the substitution of steam for water-power, the evolution of refrigeration, the increasing application of very high temperatures in working metals, the necessity of working in rarefied and compressed air, the almost universal use of electrical energy in the mechanical arts, the development of rapid transportation, the extensive employment of artificial light, the strenuousness of a machine-set pace, and the overcrowding in manufacturing centers and in factories have produced new types of illness, have intensified the ravages of communicable disease, and have created industrial hygiene as an important branch of public health work.''[8]

The Expectation of Life of Industrial Workers.—The industrial workers of the country, taken by and large, may be distinguished by a marked diminution in their longevity from those who are engaged in other forms of employment, such as agriculture and the commercial and professional pursuits. It thus becomes evident that the business or ''white collar'' class not only enjoys a higher social status but is also rewarded with a longer duration of life.[9] ''At the

[8] J. Howard Beard, ''Progress of Public Health Work,'' *The Scientific Monthly*, Feb., 1922, 14:2:148.

[9] See Robert and Helen Lynd, *Middletown*, 1929, esp. ch. VII, for a discussion of the disparity between the accompaniments of getting a living for the working class and for the business group.

present time the expectation of life of men at age twenty engaged
in industrial pursuits is forty-two years. This means that they may
expect on the average to attain the age of sixty-two. On the other
hand, those who are not engaged in industry may expect an additional
forty-nine years at age twenty. There would, therefore, seem to be
a difference of about seven years in the average expectation of the
two groups. This difference should not be charged altogether to the
effects of industry, because such items as economic status, nationality,
and the general level of intelligence all influence greatly the expectation of life. But if a single item were to be selected as the most important determining factor in the lives of men, occupation would
probably come nearer to expressing the truth than any other. The
handicap of seven years in the expectation of life is in the nature of a
tax which millions of men who are engaged in industry pay under
present conditions. It is measurable and a very real burden which
might readily be expected from the very nature of industrial employment and the mode of life of workers. This is, however, not the
only tax which they pay. Possibly more important, but unfortunately
less easily measured, is the tax of illness and of disability which
is laid upon men in industrial pursuits."[10] Studies made by the
Metropolitan Life Insurance Company of the amount of sickness
prevailing among policyholders have disclosed an average loss of
working time of eight days per annum for gainfully employed men.
The actual loss is probably a great deal heavier, since much illness
goes unrecorded.

What items account for the reduction of seven years in the expectation of life among those engaged in industry? The extra hazard from
accident is important, and probably decreases the life span of all
workers by about one year on the average. Among industrial workers
the death-rate from accidental causes is about two and one-half times
that for the non-industrial group. Tuberculosis is probably responsible for a loss of between eighteen months and two years in the
longevity of workers. Dr. Dublin[11] holds that industrial employment
is the most important single factor in the tuberculosis death-rate.
Age period for age period, the death-rates from tuberculosis still
remain from two to three times as high among industrial as among
the professional, mercantile, and agricultural groups. Pneumonia is
twice as high among industrial as among non-industrial workers and
may, therefore, be considered an added occupational hazard, result-

[10] Louis I. Dublin, *Health and Wealth*, 1928, pp. 273-274.
[11] *Ibid.*, 1928, pp. 276-278.

ing in a loss of life expectation as great as that from industrial accidents. The degenerative diseases, such as cerebral hemorrhage, Bright's disease, and organic heart disease, show strikingly the effects of industrial exposure. The death-rates are two and three times as high as in the non-industrial groups during the active working years of life. Other important factors are the particular hazards inherent in certain industrial processes, giving rise to definite occupational diseases. The number of immediate deaths owing to these diseases is probably not large, but the indirect effects can be noted in the curtailed efficiency of workers in these trades, in long periods of illness and disability, and especially in cases of heart disease and kidney disease which strike men down prematurely—often without disclosing the original occupational cause of the fatal illness.

Occupational Diseases.—What are the conditions of employment and the particular occupational hazards which so detrimentally affect industrial workers? They may be classified according to cause and nature of injury as follows.

1. Industrial Poisons.—The commonest occupational intoxication is lead poisoning, the danger of which lurks in over a hundred different industries. "Metallic lead, itself, is not poisonous because it is not soluble in the body fluids but the carbonate (white lead), the acetate (sugar of lead) and the oxides (red lead, litharge, etc.) are all exceedingly toxic. The hazard involved in the use of these substances is greatly increased by the fact that lead is a 'cumulative' poison; instead of producing an acute effect and then being excreted it is, to a large extent, stored up in the body, being liberated when the reaction of the blood is slightly changed to produce serious and far-reaching effects. Poisonous lead salts, for the most part, enter the body by way of the digestive tract or as a result of dust breathed into the lungs although it also is possible for poisoning to take place by absorption through the skin. The normal way by which lead gets to the digestive tract is, however, by swallowing of inhaled atmospheric dust."[12] Among the symptoms are a peculiar bluish line (the "lead line") on the margin of the gums close to the teeth, sharp attacks of pain in the abdomen ("painter's colic") and paralysis of the wrists ("wrist-drop") or other joints. Meanwhile, far-reaching toxic effects are exerted upon the blood vessels and kidneys, and there can be no doubt that many deaths which are attributed, perhaps years afterwards, to degeneration of the circulatory system are really the ultimate effects of lead poisoning.

[12] C.-E. A. Winslow, *Fresh Air and Ventilation*, 1926, pp. 144-145.

A very serious form of industrial poisoning, but one which has now been happily eliminated, is white phosphorus poisoning in the match industry. It produces one of the most loathsome of occupational diseases—phosphorus necrosis or "phossy jaw." The use of poisonous phosphorus in the match industry has been definitely prohibited throughout practically the whole civilized world. In 1912 the United States through act of Congress placed a prohibitive tax on matches made of white phosphorus. Their importation and exportation were also absolutely forbidden after 1913 and 1914 respectively.[13]

There are numerous other industrial poisons. "Mercury salts which cause the 'hatter's shakes,' arsenic and other heavy metals, the fumes of brass and zinc, the oxides of nitrogen which produce acute and often fatal injuries to the lungs of munition and chemical workers, the irritant halogens, and a whole host of organic poisons such as wood alcohol, carbon bisulphide, anilin and benzene and their derivatives, the nitro-benzols and trinitrotuluene, are all common and serious industrial poisons."[14] Dr. Alice Hamilton[15] mentions as factors which influence the incidence of industrial poisonings: hot and humid air, which facilitates the absorption of those poisons that pass through the skin; long hours of work, which increase the actual dose of poison and lessen the chance of completely eliminating one dose before another is taken; food, since poisons like medicines are absorbed more quickly by the fasting stomach than when administered after a meal; certain constitutional defects like anemia and nephritis, which render a person unfit for employment in poisonous trades; and the factors of race, sex, age, and individual susceptibility.

2. Diseases Due to Dusts and Fumes.—"The greatest enemy of a worker in any trade is dust. If we could get rid of dust and have our people working in a clear and, comparatively speaking, dustless atmosphere we would hear less of occupational diseases. The dust given off in any particular trade may be of an organic nature like the fine fluff from cotton, or be inorganic like the particles of stone evolved in steel grinding, or particles of lead arising in the manufacture and handling of white lead. Some kinds of dusts are soluble in the juices of the animal body, others are insoluble. The dust given off during work may be inhaled during respiration or it may become caught in the saliva of the mouth and be swallowed. Some dusts

[13] John B. Andrews, "Phosphorus Poisoning in the Match Industry," Bulletin 86, U. S. Bureau of Labor. "The Prevention of Phosphorus Poisoning," Sec. X, ch. I, of G. M. Kober and W. C. Hanson, *Diseases and Occupation*, 1916.
[14] C.-E. A. Winslow, *Fresh Air and Ventilation*, 1926, p. 147.
[15] *Industrial Poisons in the United States*, 1925, pp. 3 ff.

irritate the mucous membranes and induce coughing and running at the eyes, others owing to their chemical constitution, e.g., chrome salts and arsenical compounds, act as destructive agents and cause ulceration or they cause general poisoning. The dust given off in mines during rock drilling is, when inhaled, a source of pulmonary diseases."[16]

In a wide variety of industrial processes atmospheric fumes and dusts are the agents by which various poisonous materials are most commonly distributed. The control of these hazards by special ventilation is a problem of pressing moment. Professor Winslow[17] describes as follows the preventive measures for the mitigation of dangers from industrial dusts and fumes.

The first problem to be considered in connection with such hazards as those which have been discussed . . . is the possibility of eliminating the original source of the danger. In the case of lead poisoning among painters, for example, the only really satisfactory procedure is the substitution of zinc paints for the poisonous lead compounds, such as has been brought about to a limited degree through legal regulations in force in France. . . .

In the manufacture of white lead, many processes are now carried out under water or oil so that practically no dust need be present in the air of the workroom; and many benzol processes are rendered safe by carrying them out in a system of closed containers. . . . In the South African mines the use of water sprays has cut the dust content of the air to less than a tenth of its former figure. . . .

The method which is most generally available for protection against the industrial hazard of fumes and dusts is the installation of local exhaust ventilation, sufficiently powerful to remove the toxic or otherwise harmful substances from the point where they are produced. . . . It is, above all, in connection with grinding and polishing wheels and similar dust-producing devices that the principle of local exhaust ventilation finds its most general application. . . .

In certain industrial processes as in packing operations, in marble and granite working, and in the sand blasting of large castings, it is impossible by any of the means previously described to keep the air of the workplace free from dangerous concentrations of mineral and metallic (or poisonous) dusts. In such cases as this, the only alternative is the wearing of respirators which filter out the dust particles from the air before it is drawn into the respiratory tract, or of helmets which exclude the dusty atmosphere more or less completely from the mouth and nose and supply pure air for breathing from some other source. All such devices are uncomfortable and irksome to the wearer and the necessity for using them should be avoided wherever

[16] Sir Thomas Oliver, *Occupations*, 1916, pp. 71-72.
[17] *Fresh Air and Ventilation*, 1926, pp. 159-164.

possible by the installation of the other devices which have been considered above. In certain employments, however, the respirator or helmet offers the only possible means of protection. . . . For protection against chemical fumes devices are provided like the gas masks used in the war, with a layer of some absorptive chemical in the chamber through which the incoming air enters, selected to take care of the particular toxic gas likely to be present.

3. *Industrial Infectious Diseases.*—A typical example is anthrax. The intestinal form of anthrax is rare in man; it is caused by the ingestion of infected meat, or it may arise from eating with hands not properly cleansed after handling infectious material. Pulmonary anthrax is more common; it arises from the inspiration of dust from infected wool, rags, hair, etc., which contains anthrax spores—hence the names "wool-sorter's and rag-picker's disease." The mortality from pulmonary anthrax is about 50 per cent. "The more usual form in man is the carbuncular, the so-called malignant pustule, and is the result of skin infection, bacilli or spores gaining access through cuts or abrasions of any kind, and probably in some instances directly introduced by insect bites. The pure septicemic form is rare. It is, therefore, evident that certain occupations favor infection and the disease is usually met with among workers on hides, hair, bristles, wool, etc., and in laboratory workers, veterinarians, meat inspectors, herders, farmers, cattle men, and butchers."[18]

4. *Compressed-Air Illness.*—Frequently the industrial worker is affected by injurious environments, with unfavorable conditions of ventilation, temperature and humidity, light, and certain abnormal atmospheric conditions. A special occupational disease arising from abnormal atmospheric conditions is compressed-air illness, or caisson disease, sometimes known more popularly as "divers' palsy," "bends," or "screws." It occurs among divers, caisson workers, sub-aqueous tunnel workers, and others, following exposure to compressed air, the symptoms arising only after the too rapid removal of pressure, which liberates bubbles of gas in the supersaturated body fluids and tissues. It is essentially a disease of modern civilization. The pathology of this disease appears to be a relatively simple one. Under high atmospheric pressure, as in a diving-bell or caisson, nitrogen is dissolved in the blood and in the tissues. If the pressure is suddenly released, the gas cannot remain in solution but forms bubbles within the blood vessels or tissues, with inevitable mechanical injury.

[18] G. M. Kober and W. C. Hanson, *Diseases of Occupation*, 1916, p. 168. Herbert H. Waite, *Disease Prevention*, 1926, pp. 257-264.

This condition can, of course, be controlled by regulated and gradual decompression.[19]

5. *Abnormal Positions of the Body.*—The effects of a constrained working position, combined with a sedentary life, are especially harmful in youthful workers whose osseous system is not fully developed, and there is little doubt that most of the bone and joint deformities are developed in the earlier years of work and aggravated by habit. "Among the more important should be mentioned the hollow chest and round stooped shoulders, caused by a stooped and cramped position, as seen especially in tailors, engravers, lithographers, watchmakers, metal grinders, shoemakers, and all others obliged to assume a more or less bent-over posture. . . . All thoracic postural deformities naturally interfere with free expansion of the lungs, and hence with the respiratory functions. A stooped or bending posture also interferes with the proper distribution of the blood supply, and invites congestions of the abdominal and pelvic organs. As a matter of fact, a large number of this class of artisans show a peculiar predisposition to consumption, many suffer from anaemia, constipation, dyspepsia, and hemorrhoids, and the majority have a low average duration of life. . . . Abnormal position combined with pressure is responsible for muscular cramps, sciatica, and neuralgic affections."[20]

6. *Overexercise of Certain Parts of the Body.*—Constant local pressure, friction, and overuse of the arms and hands are productive of much harm. Occupations involving constant jarring of the entire body are conducive to the development of neurasthenia, insomnia, and gastro-intestinal neurosis. "As an example of overstrain of certain groups of muscles should be mentioned the distended, yet flabby condition of the cheek, as observed in glass-blowers and performers on wind instruments. In these cases there is at first a hypertrophy of the muscular fibers, followed later by a partial atrophy which not infrequently results in actual rupture."[21] The prevalence of hernia is noticeable among persons engaged in hard work, especially those who lift or carry heavy weights on ladders.

7. *Overwork or Fatigue.*—One of the most important predisposing causes of disease is overwork or fatigue, because the accumulation of waste products in the blood, from muscular wear and tear, together with the expended nervous energy, combine to render the sys-

[19] C.-E. A. Winslow, *Fresh Air and Ventilation*, 1926, p. 8. G. M. Kober and W. C. Hanson, *Diseases of Occupation*, 1916, pp. 187-210, 436 ff.
[20] G. M. Kober and W. C. Hanson, *Diseases of Occupation*, 1916, pp. 443-444.
[21] G. M. Kober and W. C. Hanson, *Diseases of Occupation*, 1916, p. 446.

tem more susceptible to disease. Fatigue has been defined as the sum
of the results of activity which show themselves in a diminished capacity for work. Activity must then precede fatigue, and a diminished
capacity for work is its measure. Moderate activity is followed by
healthy fatigue, that is, by fatigue which entirely disappears during
rest; but activity systematically pursued despite feelings of tiredness
carries fatigue past the limits of perfect recovery into the regions of
disordered metabolism.

The influences contributing to industrial fatigue can be placed in
two groups. The first comprises influences not generally considered to
be under the control of employers. They concern time spent outside
hours of work, and include housing conditions, facilities for transit
to and from work, and means for healthy recreation. The second includes the number of hours of labor and their distribution, the conditions of employment and methods of work. The latter group, which is
more intimately under control, has been the subject of much inquiry
and research. Modification of any of these influences may have a
great effect upon the occurrence of fatigue. Of all the fatigue factors,
none is more potent than the pernicious practice of "speeding up."[22]

Compensation for Industrial Diseases.—In most industrial countries occupational diseases are either compensable under the accident
insurance laws (compensation acts) or are taken care of through
sickness and invalidity insurance systems. In the United States, however, with a few noteworthy exceptions, occupational diseases are not
only excluded from the operation of the various compensation acts,
but because of the absence of health and invalidity insurance laws,
receive no official consideration whatever. Only about a dozen of the
workmen's compensation laws provide for the payment of compensation for disabilities due to industrial diseases, as "personal injuries."
Approximately half of these cover only specified diseases, such as lead
poisoning, anthrax and caisson disease; others compensate all disabilities clearly caused by the employment. Group insurance schemes
in some industries cover sickness among employees, but a state health
insurance act is the only means of assuring universal protection.
Health insurance, to be effective, must be made compulsory upon
the individual worker.[23]

[22] *Ibid.,* pp. 249-269, 447. E. L. Collis and Maj. Greenwood, *The Health of
the Industrial Worker,* 1921, pp. 79, 80, 109.
[23] John R. Commons and John B. Andrews, *Principles of Labor Legislation,*
1927, p. 441. Carl Hookstadt, "Workmen's Compensation and Social Insurance,"
Monthly Labor Review, April, 1919, 8:4:200. Harry H. Moore, *Public Health in
the United States,* 1923, p. 352.

Prevention of Occupational Diseases.—"Clean workmen, clean industrial establishments, and frequent periodical examination of employees are the most important factors in the prevention of occupational diseases."[24] Among the agencies are the state and the employers. Some improvement has been effected through labor legislation which excludes from employment those most susceptible to danger, whether children, women, or certain classes of men, and outlaws the substances or instruments which render employment dangerous. Protection of the health and safety of industrial workers is also provided by regulations which limit the number of working hours and require the installation of machine guards, fire-escapes, dust and fume removal systems, separate wash-rooms and eating rooms, and other sanitary and protective devices.[25] Further safeguarding has been voluntarily provided in some instances through medical service in industry, a form of industrial welfare work.

Medical Service in Industry.—Important among the health services in industry is the physical examination of applicants for the purpose of excluding those with contagious diseases or pronounced physical unfitness for the work and of aiding in the proper placement of those accepted. According to the records of a number of industries, from a little over 1 to slightly under 10 per cent of applicants are rejected on physical examination. The average of rejections is about 5 per cent.

Some industries provide for the periodical examination of employees to discover and remedy ailments and defects so that the worker may become more efficient. A number of concerns are equipped with medical departments, clinics, and dispensaries for the service of employees.

The physical examination has a number of mutual advantages. "It is primarily intended as a means of increasing efficiency and production and it has been found to accomplish these ends. It keeps undesirables and poor risks out of the plant, prevents or lessens epidemics, enables the early discovery of disease and thereby increases the chance of recovery. By its means absentism is considerably reduced. . . . The discovery of the exact physical condition of the worker at the time of entrance and subsequently prevents accidents and enables the employer to resist unjust claims for injuries. The worker benefits primarily by having his general health supervised without cost. He is

[24] Herbert H. Waite, *Disease Prevention*, 1926, p. 605.
[25] John R. Commons and John B. Andrews, *Principles of Labor Legislation*, 1927, pp. 366-418.

made aware of the dangers of disease, his periods of sickness are reduced, and he is enabled to become a steady wage-earner. He saves
money on doctors' bills and, at the same time, increases the amount
in his pay envelope. By the exclusion of applicants with contagious
diseases the regular force is protected and its exposure is reduced.
An intelligent knowledge of a man's physical condition enables the
doctor to place him where he can produce most, with the least physical
strain, and with resulting content.''[26]

On the other hand, the physical examination may be objected to by
the wage-earner, especially if it results in scrapping him. ''The applicant objects to physical examination because it may exclude him from
work on account of physical defects which, if discovered, bring no
treatment or even advice. He feels that, even if hired, he does not
want to be lectured as to how he should live. Should he leave, having
disabilities, his chances of reemployment are small. It is further
claimed that physical examination is used as a means of discriminating
against trade unionists by discovering fancied ills. . . . Whether this
is a valid claim or not the situation undoubtedly exists and objection
to physical examination was one of the ostensible grievances set forth
in the great steel strike a few years ago.''[27]

Other phases of health maintenance in industry include the provision of dispensaries and medical treatment, emergency and company hospitals, first-aid treatment and accident-prevention work,
plant hygiene and sanitation. A recent development has been the employment of industrial nurses. ''It has been shown that industrial
nurses have actually increased the working time of the individual em-
ployé by means of instruction which prevents illness, by advice which
leads to the correction of physical defects, by the care of minor ailments which will permit those suffering from them to remain at their
work, by the prevention of the spread of contagion, by looking up ab-
sentees, and sometimes, by the home care of members of the family
whose illness has kept them at home, by insistence on the observance
of the simple rules of hygiene and of suitable precautions in the
dangerous trades, and by shortening the periods of actual illness by
first aid assistance or by skilled nursing care.''[28]

About nine hundred plants have medical departments with full or
part-time nurses and doctors.[29] Medical welfare work pays in in-

[26] J. D. Hackett, *Health Maintenance in Industry*, 1925, pp. 211-212, 228.
[27] *Ibid.*, p. 213.
[28] Mary S. Gardner, *Public Health Nursing*, 1923, p. 317.
[29] Ordway Tead, ''The Progress of Personnel Management,'' *The Survey*, Dec.
15, 1924, 53:6:351.

creased efficiency and reduced labor turnover. It is sound business practice.

3. HOSPITALS AND CLINICS

One of the most striking of recent developments in the care of the sick has been the growth of hospitals and clinics. Not only has there been an upward trend in number, but also a change in methods and purpose—all in adjustment to modern social conditions and the advance of medical science. They have become essential features in the general program for the treatment and prevention of disease. They are medical social agencies; and it is this aspect in which we are especially interested.

History of Hospitals.—The idea of a hospital as a place to which the sick may come for treatment is not new. It dates back to distant ages. The Egyptians, Greeks, and other early advanced peoples had institutions which we may regard as the prototype of hospitals. A number of hospitals were founded during the early centuries of the Christian era, largely the outcome of the spirit of charity. They were for the destitute and homeless, and for the traveler who might not be destitute but who had no home to which he might go if taken ill. They were originally developed in connection with monasteries, and later through the work of the Order of the Knights Hospitallers. "Hence also arose the name of *hospital*, though the original significance of the title as a place for receiving travelers has long since passed away. The Hôtel Dieu in Paris, founded A.D. 600, was the first known to have been established apart from monasteries. A second origin of hospitals was military, as they were required both for wounded or acutely sick soldiers and for the old or chronically ill. The Hôtel des Invalides at Paris is of the latter type. For many centuries the primary incentive to the founding of hospitals was the spirit of charity, supplemented at times by the military demands and by fear of pestilence. St. Bartholomew's in London, established over a thousand years ago, held as its chief purpose the service of 'poor diseased persons until they got well.' "[30] In the United States the earliest hospitals, established in the eighteenth century, were likewise for those unable to pay. For example, Bellevue Hospital, New York, arose out of a combination of poorhouse and "pest-house." This was generally the situation up to the third quarter of the nineteenth century; hospitals were simply institutions for the relief of the sick poor. At the end of the first quarter of the twentieth century hospitals had

[30] Michael M. Davis, *Clinics, Hospitals and Health Centers*, 1927, pp. 10-11.

come to be institutions for the practice of medicine and were approaching self-support. A modern hospital may be defined as an institution in which there is joint use of medical equipment and coöperative organization of medical skill for the diagnosis, treatment, and prevention of disease.

What are the reasons for this change of emphasis? What factors account for the growth of institutional practice? First is the advance of medical science, which has necessitated an increasing capital investment for efficient practice and has called for a greatly increased technical personnel. The average single physician could not keep busy a fully equipped set of laboratories, nor could he utilize the full time of such aides. Furthermore, this elaboration of equipment and of personnel requires organization. In addition, medical education is now carried on under conditions of institutional practice; also social and economic conditions cause many persons to seek institutional care in illness.[31] Urban housing conditions are not readily adaptable to the care of the sick; in hospitals better medical or surgical care can be secured than at home.

The hospital thus represents an adjustment to modern conditions. And as the above-mentioned factors have become of increasing importance, the number of hospitals has multiplied. In 1873 there were only 149 hospitals and allied institutions in the United States; fifty years later there were 6,762. The number of beds in the former year was 35,453, and half a century later there were 770,375 beds. In 1928 there were 6,852 hospitals, with 892,934 beds, caring for a daily average of 700,000 patients. The investment is over 3 billion, the annual maintenance cost about 250 million dollars. During the past twenty years the rate of growth of hospitals has been more rapid than that of physicians or that of the general population.[32]

Sickness surveys made by the Metropolitan Life Insurance Company show that about 2 per cent of the population at any time are incapacitated by illness. This excludes minor illness and diseases not causing incapacity. These people have various resources in case of sickness: a home remedy, the advice of a friend or grandmother or a neighbor of reputed wisdom, the private physician, the drug store, the nurse, the midwife, the quack doctor or medical institute, or the hospital. Studies indicate that about 12 per cent of the cases of in-

---

[31] Michael M. Davis, *Clinics, Hospitals and Health Centers*, 1927, pp. 6-9.
[32] Harry H. Moore, "Public Health and Medicine," *American Journal of Sociology*, May, 1929, 34:6:1069. Allon Peebles, *Medical Facilities in the United States*, 1929, pp. 8-9. C. Rufus Rorem, *Capital Investment in Hospitals*, The Committee on the Costs of Medical Care Publication No. 7, 1930.

capacitating illness are regularly hospitalized. In large cities the percentage is probably higher.[33] From these figures, and the average length of hospital stay, it is possible to estimate with some accuracy the hospital requirements—the number of beds per thousand population—of a given community.

Classification of Hospitals.—Hospitals are either general or special. The first class, which is more common, takes care of various types of illness; the second is restricted to the care of special diseases or related groups, such as surgical, tuberculosis, maternity, ear, nose and throat. Modern hospitals may also be classed as proprietary or public service. Both are incorporated: the first for profit, the second not for profit. Proprietary hospitals, which are frequently special hospitals, are interested chiefly in pay patients. Public-service hospitals exist to provide general hospital facilities for the public; they receive patients as a public service, whether pay, part-pay, or free patients. Public-service hospitals may be further divided into two types: the privately founded and supported, and the publicly supported. The first is the more general type in a community and is often a religious or charitable institution. It represents a desirable form of charity or social work. Public hospitals may be for the care of special types of patients, as the tuberculous or the insane; or they may be general, such as the municipal hospital. A city hospital, supported by taxation, is a general hospital differing from other hospitals in a number of respects. It has a higher percentage of free patients and of chronic and incurable cases, often it is the only hospital taking contagious cases, alcoholics, drug addicts, and mental patients, and it generally provides for police cases.

Functions of the Modern General Hospital.—The modern general hospital has three chief activities: (1) The in-patient department, or hospital proper, for the care of persons with incapacitating illness. These are the bed patients, who are provided for in private or semi-private rooms or wards. (2) The out-patient department, or dispensary or clinic, for ambulatory cases; that is, those having various kinds of ailments but able to be about. They are the vertical patients as contrasted with the bed or horizontal patients. (3) The social service department, which considers the medical case as a human social unit, which is a person and not a disease.

Public Attitude toward Hospitals.—The history of the in-patient department, as we have seen, has been marked by a change of emphasis from charity to medical service, by a broadening of its range to

[33] Louis I. Dublin, *Health and Wealth*, 1928, pp. 8, 27.

include other social classes than the destitute, and by the institution of payment by patients. The development of hospitals is by no means complete. They are occupying a larger and larger place in the community structure as more and more people come to them for relief in illness. In turn, the hospital as it grows larger in size and multiplies in number reaches out for a wider basis of support. The public attitude toward hospitals thus becomes a factor to be considered. What is the attitude of the average man? In particular, what complaints has he about the way the institution is conducted? What is the perspective of the hospital and its varied activities as viewed by the proverbial man in the street?

The latter wonders why, since the rates for room and board in hospitals are so much higher than in hotels, the hospitals cannot make ends meet, particularly with free work decreasing and the percentage of pay work increasing. He believes he sees a real need for cost accounting, for more strict enforcement of business methods in the management of hospitals. Especially is the middle class affected by the high rates. This group eschews the associations of a public ward and of free medical service, yet finds the prevailing rates for hospital accommodations and nursing service, as well as for medical and surgical fees, a great problem when serious and protracted illness develops. It regards the question of the provision of moderate-priced hospital facilities as a matter of paramount importance.

Another thing for which hospitals are often criticized is their food. Despite the greater problem of the hospital in this respect as contrasted with the hotel, many hospitals are nevertheless defectively organized for the proper distribution of food among the patients and the cuisine is not always of the best, nor is the importance of scientific dietetics in relation to the treatment of disease always realized.

Furthermore, "sick people and their relatives and friends will never get used to the indifference of nurses and other officials in hospitals. No other single factor makes so many friends for a hospital as courtesy and considerateness and many enemies are made through a lack of these qualities. Yet hospitals where these qualities of courtesy and considerateness are prevalent are few, indeed."

The average man is surprised to learn that hospital privileges are as a rule limited to selected groups of men. "There is need of repeated explanations concerning the impossibility of proper staff organization and control over the medical and surgical work, when hospitals are run as medical hotels open to any one who applies. There is, however, need of some reform in the present practice. More men should have hospital affiliation than the present rigid system permits.''

Among the recognized functions of the hospital is the advancement of medical and hospital science. ''We have been particularly negligent in this respect. We have not educated the public to the importance of that phase of the work, and we have not instilled in many hospital staffs the necessary scientific spirit.'' Hospitals more than any other social medical agency accumulate the evidence against the dangers to life in the community—dangers from contagion, from ways of living, and from industry—and they must feel the responsibility of studying this evidence and becoming leaders in the progress of preventive medicine. Yet ''the medical and social service records of many hospitals are utterly inadequate.'' Hospitals could make contributions through a proper and uniform presentation of statistical facts. Take the case of New York City where about half a million persons go through the hospitals annually. What tremendous value the compilation of the medical statistics relating to this mass of humanity would have, if it were properly done. Could not hospitals engage in more self-analysis and in scientific comparisons between institutions, and would not these be valuable and enlightening?

Hospital executives are aware of these conditions, and in the new rôle of the hospital as part of the community team for better health and better civic conditions are giving their attention to them.[34] Adjustment is also being effected through certain recent developments in the field of hospital clinics and medical social service and in the efforts to lessen the burden of the cost of medical care.

Clinics and Dispensaries.—Following the great fire which devastated London in 1665, the College of Physicians voted that its members give their services to the poor without charge. ''When, however, the charitable-minded sought to call the good physicians to the service of the poor, no means was found of providing the medicines which the doctors wished to prescribe. The pharmacists of London were at that time organized as a guild, the so-called Apothecaries' Hall; and Apothecaries' Hall would not lower its prices, even when the College of Physicians requested it on behalf of the poor. The physicians did not sit idle under this monopoly in the prescription market. Fifty-three leading spirits signed an agreement on December 22, 1696, to pay ten pounds apiece to Dr. Thomas Burwell, one of

[34] F. H. Lewinski-Corwin, ''What's the Matter with our Hospitals?'' *The Modern Hospital*, Nov., 1925, 25:5:1-4. Niles Carpenter, *Hospital Service for Patients of Moderate Means*, The Committee on the Costs of Medical Care Publication No. 4, 1929.

their number, which sum Dr. Burwell was to use for medicines for the poor. Thereupon the first Dispensary in the English-speaking world was opened in the building of the College of Physicians.''[35]

In the United States, the first dispensary was started in Philadelphia in 1786; the second in New York in 1790; the third in Boston in 1796. The primary motive leading to the establishment of all early dispensaries was the benevolent desire to help the sick poor. The term ''dispensary'' originally meant a place where medicine was given out to the poor on the prescription of a physician, and later where medical treatment was provided. Medical diagnosis, advice and treatment are now given in a great variety of fields covering practically every branch of medical service; the dispensing of medicine is but a minor function. The organization is better termed a clinic, which may be defined as an institution which organizes the professional skill of physicians and special equipment for the diagnosis, treatment, and prevention of disease, or for the promotion of health, among ambulatory patients. More briefly stated, a clinic is an institution receiving ambulatory patients for diagnostic, therapeutic, or preventive service. When attached to a hospital it is known as the out-patient department. The term dispensary may thus be restricted to that portion of a clinic concerned with the dispensing of medicine, that is, the pharmacy. From the standpoint of medical education the word clinic has been used to mean an examination or demonstration of a patient before students, and may apply either to bed or to ambulatory cases.[36]

Classification of Clinics.—The various types of clinics to be found today may be classified, according to organization, as out-patient departments of hospitals; unattached clinics; teaching clinics, attached or unattached; health stations and health centers. A health center is an organization which provides, promotes, and coördinates medical service and related social service for a specified district. Clinics are grouped, according to the range of diseases treated, into general and special; according to their community purpose, into public and proprietary; and according to function, into curative or preventive.[37]

Motives Affecting the Development of Clinics.—The original motive leading to the establishment of clinics was the charitable desire to help the sick poor. During the first part of the nineteenth century a new element entered to reinforce this charitable desire, namely, the interest of physicians in acquiring medical experience and in

[35] Michael M. Davis and Andrew R. Warner, *Dispensaries*, 1918, pp. 1-2.
[36] Michael M. Davis, *Clinics, Hospitals, and Health Centers*, 1927, pp. 42 ff.
[37] *Ibid.*, pp. 45, 357.

teaching medical students at a clinic. "In the early part of the nineteenth century the teaching of medical students was carried on by physicians who took apprentices, as it were, so that the student learned the practice of medicine by taking part in it, under the tutelage and practical guidance of an established physician. In connection with the Boston Dispensary students were allowed to attend patients almost from the beginning, as regulations governing the activities of students appear in the records as early as 1827. With the advance of medical science and the development of medical schools, teaching was reorganized. The emphasis upon clinical teaching in the latter part of the nineteenth century, instead of mere didactic instruction, has been one of the most powerful factors in increasing the number of dispensaries and improving their work. The desire to provide material for medical students is supplemented in the physician's mind by the endeavor to increase his own skill and knowledge. The teaching motive (or medical-experience motive) is the second important force which has shaped the development of dispensaries."[38] The modern demand that medical students be taught diagnosis and treatment of disease by personal contact with patients has required the extensive development of hospitals and clinics in connection with medical schools.

The two motives thus far analyzed, to do charity and to advance medical knowledge and education, were responsible for the establishment and development of the majority of the general clinics until recent years. In 1800 there were only 3 dispensaries in the United States. In 1900 there were about 150. Shortly thereafter a new force entered the field, developing many hundreds of new clinics and transforming many of the old.

The new motive affecting the development of clinics arose from the inauguration of national movements for disease prevention. The conscious establishment of clinics for public-health reasons may be regarded as having originated in this country through the anti-tuberculosis movement. This movement assumed organized shape in 1905, when the National Association for the Study and Prevention of Tuberculosis was formed. In the ten years immediately following, over 500 tuberculosis clinics were established. The motive underlying this development was not that of providing care for the poor, nor medical advantages for physicians and students, but it was a direct endeavor to combat disease and promote public health. Other national move-

---

[38] Michael M. Davis and Andrew R. Warner, *Dispensaries*, 1918, pp. 7-8. *Cf.* Michael M. Davis, *Clinics, Hospitals and Health Centers*, 1927, p. 32.

ments, combating infant mortality, maternal mortality, mental disease, venereal disease, etc., have followed a similar course. In each, two essential programs are manifest: first, the education of the public; and second, the increase of facilities for the detection, care, and control of these diseases or conditions.

The growth of clinics following the entrance of the public-health motive has been spectacular. It represents the most striking development of group medicine today. In 1900, as has been said, there were only about 150 clinics in the United States. Today there are about 6,000. They have increased more rapidly than hospitals. The number of hospitals has increased about 45 times in 50 years; the number of clinics about 40 times in 25 years. In certain fields, such as tuberculosis sanatoria and many branches of clinic service, the entire development has taken place within 20 years. At the present time about 10 million people throughout the country receive clinic care. There are about 100,000 visits per day to the clinics of the United States. About 5 per cent of all ambulatory cases are cared for in clinics. Combining this institutional care with the hospitalization of about 12 per cent of cases with incapacitating illness, we find that about 17 per cent of medical practice is now conducted in institutions. This growth of clinics has taken place especially in the large medical centers where hospital facilities are ample. The smaller towns and the rural areas have as yet scarcely any such service. It has been estimated that as high as 15 per cent of all ambulatory cases in many large communities are treated at clinics. In New York City 1¼ million persons annually receive service from clinics. This number is equivalent to 1 in every 5 of the population, whereas in 1862, the earliest year for which figures are available, clinics served only about 1 in every 25 inhabitants.[39]

A revolutionary change has thus occurred in the clinical field. The clinics which now render curative and preventive service have evolved, almost within a generation, from practically a medical "soup-kitchen" in which patients stood before the doctor for perhaps three minutes, seldom more, in order to obtain a prescription for medicine. This change is the result of a widespread public demand, which has arisen from four main sources, namely, "the *higher cost* of medical service, which has made it more difficult for persons of moderate means to obtain; the *greater efficiency* of medical service, which has made it

    [39] Michael M. Davis, *Clinics, Hospitals and Health Centers*, 1927, pp. 5, 34 ff. Michael M. Davis and Andrew R. Warner, *Dispensaries*, 1918, ch. II. Allon Peebles, *Medical Facilities in the United States*, 1929, pp. 11-12. Louis I. Dublin, *Health and Wealth*, 1928, pp. 30-31.

more worth obtaining; the *enhanced interest* on the part of individuals and communities in securing good medical care; and the *organized health work*, which has established clinics and other facilities for the care of the sick and the prevention of disease, and has actively promoted their use. This changing and broadening social scope is the outcome of the new conception of the clinic as a place for rendering medical service—a conception consistent with, but much more comprehensive than the old idea of mere charity. Specialization in medicine has accompanied and stimulated this development. In 1862 the services in clinics were usually of the sort which a general practitioner would have rendered in his private office. At the present time . . . two-thirds to four-fifths of the services in New York clinics are of the kind that in private practice would be obtained from a consultant or specialist. The kinds of service have become more numerous and more varied, and—which is much to the point—generally much more expensive. They are nevertheless more in demand, due to an enhanced appreciation of their value.''[40]

Innovations in the management of clinics have further adapted them to the needs of patients. Some clinics are now held in the evening, to the saving of time and money of those employed. The appointment system has been successfully introduced in a number of cases, and pay clinics have arisen to meet the need of people of moderate income.[41]

The Rise of Pay Clinics.—Whereas the early clinics were established for the destitute poor and did little more than dispense set prescriptions instead of giving medical service in the modern sense of the term, today clinics are giving fair medical service and are becoming self-supporting at the same time. A number of clinics where the patients are expected to pay the full cost of the service, including the salaries of the attending physicians, have already been organized to provide better and more economical medical care for middle-class families. They are intended for patients more prosperous than those entitled to out-patient hospital care, but with incomes insufficient for consultation with private specialists.

The first pay clinic was started at the Boston Dispensary in 1913. It was for eye diseases. In subsequent years this institution opened pay clinics for genito-urinary, syphilis, ear, nose and throat, and general medical and surgical diseases. Pay clinics for venereal dis-

[40] Committee on Dispensary Development, *Medical Care for a Million People*, 1927, pp. 23-24.
[41] Michael M. Davis, *Clinics, Hospitals and Health Centers*, 1927, pp. 156-162.

eases were opened in Brooklyn in 1915, in Chicago in 1916, and in Cleveland in 1917. Since then the number of pay clinics has increased.

The Cornell Medical College pay clinic in New York City has attracted wide attention, both as a demonstrably successful experiment in self-supporting medical service to ambulatory patients of moderate means, and as an example of efficient medical service, demonstrating effective methods of out-patient administration and clinic management. Conjointly with its service to patients, it is used by the Medical College for the teaching of students and for research. The clinic was opened on November 1, 1921, and on that day over 1,000 persons applied for treatment. During its first 6 years, about 115,000 patients were registered. Together with the old patients on the books, about 21,000 people are treated each year and about 475 patients now come to the clinic each day. For the most part, patients belong to families having an income of about $2,400 a year. The clinic is now said to be self-sustaining. Patients are charged a flat fee of $1.50 per visit, but pay supplementary fees (at cost) for x-ray plates, for laboratory tests, appliances, eye-glasses, medicines, and other special items. Services are offered in 22 departments or subdepartments of medicine and surgery, and in dentistry. Patients are receiving excellent medical service for about a third of what they would have to pay to the same physicians at their private offices.[42]

Medical Social Service.—Fully as important as the medical facts in a case of sickness are the individual and social factors involved. Indeed, in many instances the latter must be known in order to diagnose the case correctly and secure effective treatment.

A patient for whom a back brace was ordered by an orthopedic surgeon was found subsequently by a social worker to be starving herself to pay for the brace. Later a general physical examination showed that she was suffering from pernicious anemia. One thing is certain: a patient with pernicious anemia will not long wear a back brace.

Another patient, markedly debilitated, came to a hospital for a tonic, but received little benefit from the physician's prescription because she was struggling to care for herself and her young son on the $4.50 a week provided by a so-called "relief society."

The social worker, whose function is the diagnosis and treatment of those who need social readjustment, has a contribution to make to medical work. The medical social service movement emphasizes the

[42] Committee on Dispensary Development, *Medical Care for a Million People*, 1927, pp. 24-27. Louis I. Dublin, *Health and Wealth*, 1928, pp. 32-33. Michael M. Davis and Andrew R. Warner, *Dispensaries*, 1918, pp. 329-344.

interdependence of medical and social work, not only in treatment but also in seeking the causes of disease. "It strives to find the common ground of medicine and sociology and to relate effectively the functions of doctor and social worker. . . . The hospital social service movement aims to throw a new light on medical practice in institutions. It seeks to understand and to treat the social complications of disease by establishing a close relationship between the medical care of patients in hospitals or dispensaries and the services of those skilled in the profession of social work; to bring to the institutionalized care of the sick such personal knowledge of their social condition as will hasten and safeguard their recovery."[43] "Conditions of the patient's environment as well as his state of mind—his ignorance, his prejudices—need to be altered or controlled in order to render efficient treatment possible. To ascertain facts concerning the patient's personality and environment and to apply this knowledge so as to help in achieving medical results, is the scope and function of medical social service."[44]

Medical social work represents an application of the principle of individualization in medical-social treatment. Too commonly in hospital and clinic the individual has been overlooked in the interest of the "case." Indeed, "the content and atmosphere of the present-day medical curriculum and hospital interneship render the average graduate little able to appreciate the significance of the aphorism said to have been a favorite of Sir William Osler: *It is much more important to know what sort of a patient has a disease than what sort of a disease a patient has.*"[45] Medical social work tries to give consideration to the human factor. "A patient presenting himself at clinic or hospital is a human being moulded and shaped by the play of many forces, hereditary, educational, industrial, sexual, economic, environmental. These may have contributed in the past to his present condition and should be known and appraised in order to understand each individual patient and to plan his treatment intelligently."[46]

Like other forms of social and philanthropic work, medical social service has sprung into existence to fill a modern need. "The old time family physician, driving about from house to house, needed no social worker to assist him. His patients and his patients' families were so well-known to him that there was no danger of his ordering the im-

[43] Ida M. Cannon, *Social Work in Hospitals*, 1923, pp. 1-3.
[44] Michael M. Davis and Andrew R. Warner, *Dispensaries*, 1918, p. 100.
[45] Michael M. Davis, *Clinics, Hospitals and Health Centers*, 1927, p. 169.
[46] Edith M. Baker, "Social Case Work in Hospital and Clinic," *Journal of Social Hygiene*, Nov., 1927, 13:8:478.

possible, because his advice was founded on an intimate knowledge of family conditions financial and otherwise. All this has been greatly changed by the growth and increasing popularity of the great hospital, with its attendant out-patient department, where the individuality of the patient is necessarily somewhat lost and where his disease becomes the most important thing about him. . . . The frequent return to the wards of patients suffering with the very difficulties of which they had once been cured, forced upon the doctors a recognition of the fact that more than hospital care was needed to establish permanent health. In the out-patient department failures were even more apparent, for there, home conditions exert a still more powerful influence. In considering economy of effort it is quite evident that a doctor who, after a painstaking diagnosis gives advice which is not followed, has made poor use of his time as far as that particular patient is concerned."[47]

To the development of this new hospital and clinic social service, a service quite different from any that preceded it, contributions were made both here and abroad. The most significant contribution in this country was that of Dr. Charles P. Emerson, of Johns Hopkins University, who recognized that truly effective medical training must include an understanding by the physician of the background and the standards of living of his patients, and who therefore inaugurated, in 1902, social training for medical students. The organization of a social-service department in a dispensary and the beginning of organized and trained social work in medical institutions in the United States did not come until 1905. "It is well known that to Dr. Richard C. Cabot of Boston is due the credit of introducing the social worker as a definite factor in hospital and dispensary treatment. Not alone for the sake of the patient's spiritual welfare, not for the training of medical students, not for the instruction of nurses, nor simply for the extension of medical care into the homes was this form of work created. Rather was it conceived by a physician who, in seeking the improvement of dispensary practice, found in the social worker a potent means for more accurate diagnosis and more effective treatment."[48]

Summary and Illustrations.—The objects of medical social service may be summarized as follows: to discover and report to the physicians facts regarding the patient's personality and environment, which relate to his physical condition; to overcome such obstacles to successful

[47] Mary S. Gardner, *Public Health Nursing*, 1923, pp. 322-323.
[48] Ida M. Cannon, *Social Work in Hospitals*, 1923, pp. 6, 12-14.

treatment as may exist or arise in the patient's home or his work; to educate the patient in regard to his physical condition in order that he will coöperate to the best advantage with the doctor's program for the cure of the illness or the promotion of health; to bring to the patient that touch of personal interest in his affairs which will lessen his fear of the big institution; to simplify the work of other social agencies and to interpret the hospital to them; and to collect and tabulate data which will aid in the study of the social causes of disease.[49]

Every conceivable human problem is faced in the course of a year in the social-service department of a large clinic or hospital. The following are a few illustrations cited by Davis and Warner.[50]

A woman needs an operation—but at home are four young children, and the father earns but $12 a week. The mother can neither leave her little ones, nor afford a servant. The doctor may make his diagnosis and advise the operation, but unless the social worker finds out the woman's home situation and secures a friend or relative to act as caretaker, or a charitable agency which will hire one if necessary, the woman will not go to the hospital for what she needs.

A man comes with syphilis. His wife and children ought to be examined, and perhaps when they meet the doctor the family situation which faces the physician and the social worker will require the wisdom of Solomon to solve.

A mother brings a sick baby wrapped in many clothes and fed on condensed milk. Ignorance and not lack of income must be patiently wrestled with.

Sometimes the doctor's advice may be modified by social facts disclosed by the worker's investigation.

A woman of forty was referred who was found to have incipient tuberculosis, and sanatorium treatment was advised. The social worker talked with the patient, visited the home, conferred with the husband, and then brought to the doctor for consideration the following facts: The home was a single house with four rooms in the outskirts of the city. There were no children. The patient was intelligent and very eager to do her part in the treatment, provided she would not have to break up her home. The husband, while fond of his wife, had caused her considerable anxiety by occasional drinking. A previous history of hospital care for the wife had resulted disastrously, for he had become involved with undesirable companions. The man had been critical of his wife's inertia, which the social worker could now explain to him as due to her physical condition. When he understood, he was willing

[49] Michael M. Davis, ''Searchlight on Hospital Social Service,'' *The Survey*, Nov. 20, 1920, 45:8:284. Mary S. Gardner, *Public Health Nursing*, 1923, p. 341.
[50] *Dispensaries*, 1918, pp. 102-103.

and glad to pay to have the laundry and cleaning done by a neighbor, if the patient would try home treatment. As a result of this consultation, the patient was recommended by the doctor for admission to a tuberculosis class. She followed directions faithfully, reported each week at the class meeting, and after two years was discharged cured. Now, after ten years, she is still well, doing her work, and the home has throughout this time been kept intact.[51]

Since 1905, the year of the initiation of the movement, nearly 400 social-service departments have been introduced into hospitals and clinics in this country. This is not a large percentage of the total number of public-service general hospitals. Medical social service has done splendid work in humanizing the hospital as well as making diagnosis and treatment more effective. The whole hospital should be organized on that basis, and students, nurses, and doctors should have knowledge of the personality and environmental factors which are so important in the treatment and prevention of disease.

The Cost of Medical Care.—''The delivery of adequate, scientific medical service to all the people, rich and poor, at a cost which can be reasonably met by them in their respective stations in life'' is, according to the Secretary of the American Medical Association, the one great outstanding question before the medical profession today. An eminently qualified Committee on the Cost of Medical Care has been created to study this problem. It adopted in 1928 a five-year program consisting of the three following groups of study:[52]

I. Preliminary surveys of data showing the extent of disease and disability requiring medical services and of generally existing facilities for dealing with these conditions.

II. Studies on the cost to the family of medical services and the return accruing to the physician and other agents furnishing such services.

III. Analyses of specially organized facilities for medical care now serving particular groups of the population.

Among the specially organized facilities for medical care now serving particular groups of the population are pay clinics and private group clinics, organized medical service in industry and in universities, visiting nurse associations, school health service, and health insurance. We have already discussed pay clinics and organized medical service in industry. Visiting nurse societies and school health service

[51] Ida M. Cannon, *Social Work in Hospitals*, 1923, pp. 34-35.
[52] *The Five-Year Program of the Committee on the Costs of Medical Care*, Publication No. 1, 1928. *The First Two Years' Work of the Committee on the Costs of Medical Care*, 1929.

will be discussed below. Here consideration will be given to the other facilities, which are closely related to clinics.

In the United States, chiefly in the Middle West, there are over 200 "group clinics," wherein a group of associated physicians carry on private practice with joint use of plant, equipment, and assistant personnel; in other words, a clinic organized on a business basis. Some of them, such as the Mayo Clinic and the Cleveland Clinic, are nationally known. "The essential distinction between the group clinic and the ordinary clinic (or hospital) is that the group clinic is a business enterprise of the participating physicians; the capital for building and equipment is provided by them or loaned by others with the expectation of financial return, whereas in the ordinary hospital or clinic the capital is given for the purpose of public service, even though the institution may (because of a large proportion of paying patients) be self-supporting as far as annual maintenance is concerned. . . . The studies of group clinics have thus far given no indication that such economies as result from the joint use of plant, equipment, and personnel have been passed on to patients in the form of lower costs. There appears to have been a gain to the public from the point of view of efficiency, but not from the standpoint of economy, and there are as yet no indications that the fundamental problem of cost, vital as it is to the interests of the middle-economic groups, can be solved in this way."[53]

An interesting example of a method of supplying effective and economical medical service is the development of student health work in American secondary schools, colleges, and universities. "Many educational institutions are located in small towns where private medical facilities are inadequate to care for the large number of students. The school authorities have, therefore, found it necessary to provide facilities of their own, using largely the excellent personnel and medical equipment of their own medical faculties. Such service is now very widely available; perhaps the most interesting examples being found in the Universities of California, Michigan, and Minnesota, each of which cares for about ten thousand students. In these institutions, the service is all-inclusive." Figures from clinics at 10 of the largest universities in the country show the interesting fact that an average of 677 per 1000 students make use of the service during the course of a year, each student making 6 visits. "What interests us particularly in these demonstrations is the very low cost

[53] Committee on Dispensary Development, *Medical Care for a Million People*, 1927, pp. 27-29.

of the service. Dr. Sundwall, describing his work at Ann Arbor, says that each student is taxed $6 a year for health service and that this amount is adequate to cover medical and nursing expenses, together with the cost of equipment. This small sum is also the amount of the annual fee per student at the University of Minnesota where an excellent service is rendered. The fee will be increased to $9 with the new semester. At the University of California, the actual cost of the service is more nearly $12.30 a year. These college health organizations prove that a reasonably complete medical service can be rendered at an extraordinarily low cost. . . . In a few institutions the faculty members are receiving similar care, and in a few others a movement is on foot to make the service available to families of the faculty."[54]

According to Dr. Michael M. Davis,[55] two truths lie at the root of the financial problem of sickness and at the basis of its solution. The first is that our spending habits for sickness are less than our spending ability. The total amount spent for the care of sickness and the promotion of health in the United States is about 3 billion dollars a year, or approximately 3 1/3 per cent of our gross national income. Only about 100 millions, or 1/30 of the 3 billions, goes for preventive work. Our spending habits and standards in relation to sickness have been carried over from a time when there was generally less margin of income over necessities than there is today, and when the power of medicine to cure or to prevent disease was far less than it is now.

The second truth underlying the financial problem of sickness is that it is the unevenness of the burden, not its total amount, which creates most of the present financial problems. This being the case, the solution must lie in the application of the principles of insurance, which is the only sound way of dealing with an uneven and uncertain financial burden. Even if it does not reduce the cost of medical treatment, health insurance will assure funds with which to meet medical bills conveniently when serious and expensive sickness occurs. "It is not concerned with medical organization—whether doctors work privately or in groups. It does, however, supplement group organization of physicians with group organization of patients.

---

[54] Louis I. Dublin, *Health and Wealth*, 1928, pp. 36-37.
[55] "How Pay Sickness Bills?" *The Survey*, Sept. 1, 1928, 60:11:541-543. An excellent discussion of the cost of health, considered from various points of view, is presented in *The Survey*, Jan. 1, 1930, which devotes the entire number to this subject. E. E. Muntz, "Health vs. the High Cost of Medical Care," *Hospital Social Service*, XXIII, 1931, 494-503, summarizes the data on the cost of the various items of medical care and suggests economies which may well be instituted.

By this means, people in vast numbers join together and by the payment of fixed premiums while they are well provide a fund adequate to pay sickness costs. This is essentially health insurance—the best method yet proposed for meeting the cost of disabling sickness. There are fortunately enough private insurance companies in the United States to conduct this type of business both efficiently and economically. In fact, many persons in comfortable circumstances are now carrying sickness and accident insurance in existing insurance organizations. A half million Amerian wage-earners are now covered by group health insurance contracts in strong life insurance companies, and possibly several million more are affiliated with lodges and mutual benefit associations which to a greater or less degree provide medical service. The solution of the economic problem we have been discussing will come only when sickness insurance becomes as popular among working-men and their families as industrial life insurance is now. Such a system will leave people entirely free to choose their own physicians just as they do now. Doctors will likewise benefit; for under this plan they will be assured of compensation for services rendered. The cost of such insurance, if limited to cases of serious illness involving disability, will not be excessive. Nondisabling ailments, although of frequent occurrence, do not lend themselves to insurance coverage. The mechanics of handling enormous numbers of claims for petty amounts would add heavily to the cost of the insurance and could, therefore, be of little advantage to the patients. It may be good practice in the early stages of this development to scale premiums down to cover only from two-thirds to three-quarters of the actual present cost of medical service in serious cases. The cost of such health insurance would be still further reduced and brought within the means of virtually all families if it could be written on large numbers of persons at one time (group or wholesale insurance)."[56]

On the other hand, a system of social insurance of the compulsory type will much more readily and easily reach the mass of the people. The lesson of history is strongly in favor of the compulsory principle in connection with sickness insurance. The considerations which have led to this conclusion are as follows: first, the demonstrated inability to bring the neediest strata of the working class into the system by any measure short of compulsion; second, a study of the social causes of disease establishes at least a partial responsibility for illness on the part of industry and society, and justice would require that industry

[56] Louis I. Dublin, *Health and Wealth*, 1928, pp. 42-43.

and society should share in the cost of sickness insurance. Further-more, the compulsory plan will more readily promote standardiza-tion of the insurance system. Health insurance has proved successful in those European countries which have adopted it, and might well be instituted in the United States.[57]

4. THE EVOLUTION OF PUBLIC-HEALTH NURSING

Public-health nursing is an outgrowth and development of visiting nursing. The latter has existed since early times, but it was not until recently that the public-health aspect came into the work. "When we read of the care given the sick in the centuries before Christ in such enlightened countries as India, Egypt, Greece and Rome, we cannot believe that this care was strictly confined to the hospitals. Visiting the sick is not only spoken of in the New Testament as one of the forms of charity, but long before the Christian era the Rabbis de-clared it to be incumbent on every Jew 'to visit the sick, in order to show them sympathy, to cheer and aid and relieve them in their suffering,' and since the founding of the primitive Church, such work has been a recognised part of its activity."[58] The real beginning of visiting nursing occurred in the first century of the Christian era, when the first organized visiting of the sick in their homes began un-der the auspices of the primitive church, which established the order of deaconesses and placed upon them the Christian duty of visiting and caring for those of their brethren who were sick or in need. In the centuries immediately following, institutional care largely sup-planted the care of the sick in their homes, and monks and nuns took the place of the old-time deaconess. Many nursing orders were founded, usually within the church or under its control. From the Crusades sprang the military nursing orders, prominent among them that of St. John of Jerusalem. Throughout the Middle Ages, visiting the sick was not a science, it was a work of mercy. It was an example of what Bertrand Russell[59] calls love without knowledge.

One of the most prominent figures in the history of public-health nursing is St. Vincent de Paul, who, in the middle of the seventeenth century, with the help of Mlle. Le Gras founded the world-famous order of the Sisters of Charity. He was determined that the Sisters should not become religious in the monastic sense; he recognized the necessity of instruction; and he realized the importance of what we

[57] W. H. Hamilton, *Current Economic Problems*, 1921, pp. 581 ff. John R. Com-mons and John B. Andrews, *Principles of Labor Legislation*, 1927, pp. 465-468.
[58] Mary S. Gardner, *Public Health Nursing*, 1923, p. 4.
[59] *What I Believe*, 1925, pp. 28-29.

now call social work. His work was all the more brilliant because in the latter part of the seventeenth century nursing entered upon the dark period of its history, which lasted to the middle of the nineteenth century. "As we read of the early history of nursing, of the work of St. Elizabeth of Hungary, of St. Catherine of Siena, of the secular orders of the Beguines and the Santo Spirito, and of the later religious orders, both Roman Catholic and Protestant, it seems almost incredible that nursing should have sunk to the level at which we find it in the middle of the nineteenth century, when modern secular nursing was brought to life by Florence Nightingale, who in turn received her impetus from the Fliedner's Training School for Deaconesses at Kaiserswert."[60] All the world knows of the dramatic character of the work of Florence Nightingale (1820-1910) in the Crimea, and of how she later led both in making nursing a profession allied with science, and in calling to its ranks women of education and refinement.

With her help the first District Nursing Association in the modern sense of the word was founded in Liverpool in 1859 by a Quaker, William Rathbone, who is known as the father of the present movement. Recognizing the need for trained nursing service among the poor, he erected a home for nurses on the grounds of the Liverpool Royal Infirmary and arranged for systematic training to be given to nurses in order that they might supply the Infirmary and also give care to both poor and rich in their own homes. Four years later the city was divided into eighteen districts, each supplied with a trained nurse. Other large cities of England soon followed the example of Liverpool, and visiting-nurse associations were organized in other countries. In 1887 the work of district nursing in England was thoroughly established and given substantial recognition by Queen Victoria, who devoted part of her Jubilee Offering from the women of England to founding an institute for nursing the sick poor in their own homes. The work of the Queen Victoria's Jubilee Institute for Nurses is founded upon two fundamental principles: special training of the nurses, and expert supervision of their work. The Institute has also undertaken to systematize and extend visiting nursing throughout the United Kingdom.[61]

In America, the sick have been cared for by nuns and sisters, both in and out of hospitals, since Colonial days. The early hospitals had

[60] Mary S. Gardner, *Public Health Nursing*, 1923, p. 7.
[61] Mary S. Gardner, *Public Health Nursing*, 1923, pp. 6-17. Annie M. Brainard, *Evolution of Public Health Nursing*, 1922, chs. VIII, IX, XII.

nurse attendants, who were, however, untrained. "It was the Civil War which was destined to give the greatest impetus to nursing in the United States. Its effect was almost as far-reaching as had been that of the Crimean War on English nursing. True, no great personality like that of Florence Nightingale emerged, but many women of real ability came to the fore, showing genuine executive power and doing admirable work, both as members of the Sanitary Commission and as nurses in the field. Their energies once aroused could not in the nature of things die away into inactivity, and after the war women everywhere began to interest themselves in the better care of the sick in times of peace. The result was the opening of training schools for nurses in various parts of the country."[62] The first American organization systematically to send trained nurses into the homes of the sick poor was the New York City Mission in 1877. The work of the missionary nurses, however, was more religious than scientific, curative than preventive. By 1890, twenty-one organizations were engaged in the work of visiting nursing. The growth of health nursing was slow and somewhat apathetic until 1905, when the development became more rapid by sharing in the national public-health movements in the fields of tuberculosis, infant and child welfare, mental hygiene, etc. New associations sprang up, many more nurses were employed, national nurses' organizations were formed, and the strength of the whole movement increased in other ways than merely numerical. These district or visiting-nurse associations were privately founded and supported for the purpose of providing skilled nursing care of the sick in their homes and teaching cleanliness, proper care of the sick, and means of preventing the spread of disease. Because of their emphasis on health instruction and the prevention of disease, a more truly descriptive name would be public-health nursing associations.

As the complexities of public-health nursing grew, the truth that had been recognized from the first by the Queen's Institute in England forced itself upon those interested in the subject in America, namely, that a hospital training was not by itself sufficient, but that a public-health nurse needed special training to fit her for the work. That all public-health nurses should be graduates of hospital training schools has been accepted as a foregone conclusion, but something in addition to this training is required. Hospital training, the essential foundation for any nurse, teaches the care of the sick patient, but up to the present time it has left almost wholly untouched those social aspects of sickness and health which loom so large on the horizon of

[62] Mary S. Gardner, *Public Health Nursing*, 1923, p. 20.

public-health nursing. It is an undisputed fact that the nurse with only hospital training cannot be intrusted with the real responsibility of public-health work. Post-graduate courses in public-health nursing have been offered by visiting-nurse associations, in conjunction with colleges or social agencies, or by colleges and universities themselves. Undoubtedly the tendency at the present time is toward an assumption of the responsibility by purely educational institutions.

From the point of view of payment, the patients served by the public-health nurse may be divided into four groups: those who can make no payment; those who can make partial payment; those who can pay cost price, but cannot afford a private nurse; and those who can afford anything, but call upon the public-health nurse for convenience. The fundamental principle having to do with payment is twofold: first, nursing care shall be given free to those unable to pay for it; second, those who can afford to do so shall pay according to their means. The first part of this principle is as old as the first visiting-nurse association. The second is a much later development. In this respect, public-health nursing has paralleled the development of hospitals and clinics. In 1909 a modest experiment was first made in Brattleboro, Vermont, which has had its effect on the development of nursing services organized to meet the needs of that great body of people of moderate means who require continuous nursing care and household assistance on a paying basis. The extension of service to those who can pay has been one of the most important recent developments.

Concomitantly with the development of the public-health movement has occurred the development of specialization in public-health nursing. The tuberculosis nurse, the school and infant welfare nurse, the medical social worker, and the industrial nurse arose as these phases of the public-health campaign developed. Both specialization and what, for want of a better word, may be termed generalization, have their weak as well as their strong points, about which there has been much discussion.[63]

A new aspect of public-health nursing was presented in 1909 when, at the suggestion of Miss Lillian D. Wald, of the Henry Street Settlement, the Metropolitan Life Insurance Company undertook, at first experimentally, to offer home nursing to its industrial policyholders. This work has been extended throughout the United States and Canada and has proved a good economic investment. Arrangements have

[63] Mary S. Gardner, *Public Health Nursing*, 1923, pp. 50-52, 57 ff., 66 ff. Annie M. Brainard, *Evolution of Public Health Nursing*, 1922, ch. XVIII.

been made, where possible, with existing visiting-nurse associations to furnish this service, payment being based on the exact cost to the association of the visits made.[64]

One of the most conspicuous changes in the status of public-health nursing today is the increasing number of public-health nurses found working under state and city health departments. The nurse has become a "public servant." In the past, public-health nursing has almost everywhere been started as a private enterprise. Even the branches of the work now usually undertaken by municipalities, such as school nursing or the care of the tuberculous, were first demonstrated as successful experiments by visiting-nurse associations. There is undoubtedly at the present time a very general tendency in many directions toward an increased assumption of responsibility by both states and municipalities. There are certain inherent advantages and disadvantages to both public and private administration of public-health nursing work. As to the future, private organizations will continue to inaugurate new work and maintain old work, and municipalities will continue their responsibility for certain of the special branches, entering perhaps new and as yet unexplored paths, while the state will concern itself more and more with public-health nursing in rural districts through county organizations. The latter extension of the work is of great moment, since rural nursing in the United States has for years been the weakest point in the system. Further assistance has come from the American Red Cross which a few years ago inaugurated a plan of rural nursing similar to that of the Victorian Order in Canada. The nurse in rural districts and small towns, in the absence of organized social work, must often perform social activities of varied nature.[65]

The need of the public-health nurse has been generally accepted by the community. "We find other agencies counting, not only on her help in individual cases, but upon the knowledge of social conditions which she has gained from her unique position. We see that she has actually had her effect on state and city legislation, and in other instances has influenced public opinion to effect non-legislative reform. We find her valued as a preventive agent and health instructor by municipalities and state bodies, and the usefulness of her statistics acknowledged by research workers. We find her acting as probation officer, tenement house and sanitary inspector, county bailiff, do-

[64] Lillian D. Wald, *The House on Henry Street*, 1915, pp. 62-63.
[65] Mary S. Gardner, *Public Health Nursing*, 1923, pp. 24, 63. Annie M. Brainard, *Evolution of Public Health Nursing*, 1922, ch. XXV.

mestic educator and hospital social service worker. She is to be found in the juvenile courts and public play grounds, in the department stores and big hotels, in the schools and factories, in the houses of small wage earners and in the swarming tenements of the very poor. We find her in the big cities, the small towns, the rural districts and the lonely mountain regions. We find her dealing with tuberculosis, babies, mental cases, industrial workers and expectant mothers, midwifery and housing conditions. She instructs by means of public lectures and classes.''[66]

Thus has the public-health nurse evolved through the centuries. ''We have seen her as the deaconess of the early church; as the Lady Bountiful of the middle ages; as the district nurse of modern times; and, finally, as the highly trained public-health nurse of today. No longer is she content to give only passing relief; she aims to give permanent cure; no longer does she confine her attention to the individual and the poor; she takes the whole community under her care.''[67]

5. HEALTH SUPERVISION OF SCHOOL CHILDREN

The Argument for Medical Inspection of Schools.—''Medical inspection is an extension of the activities of the school in which the educator and the physician join hands to insure for each child such conditions of health and vitality as will best enable him to take full advantage of the free education offered by the state. Its object is to better health conditions among school children, safeguard them from disease, and render them healthier, happier, and more vigorous. It is founded upon a recognition of the intimate relationship between the physical and mental conditions of the children, and the consequent dependence of education on health conditions.''[68]

It was started as a means of preventing the spread of infectious diseases, being adopted by many cities only after epidemics had occurred. In many instances the recognition of the imperative necessity for safeguarding the physical welfare of school children grew out of the discovery that compulsory education under modern city conditions meant compulsory disease. The state, to provide for its own welfare, has decreed that all children must attend school, and has put in motion the all-powerful but indiscriminating agency of compulsory education, which gathers in not only the rich and the poor, the bright

[66] Mary S. Gardner, *Public Health Nursing*, 1923, p. 29.
[67] Annie M. Brainard, *Evolution of Public Health Nursing*, 1922, p. 419.
[68] L. H. Gulick and L. P. Ayres, *Medical Inspection of Schools*, 1913, p. 1.

and the dull, but the healthy and the sick. "The object was to insure that these children should have sound minds. One of the unforeseen results was to insure that they should have unsound bodies. Medical inspection is the device created to remedy this condition. Its object is prevention and cure."[69] Where the work has been done successfully and adequately the number of cases of contagious disease among the children has been greatly reduced, epidemics have been checked or avoided, and the necessity for closing schools because of epidemics has been largely done away with.

But medical inspection does not confine itself to dealing with contagious disease. Its aid has been invoked to help the child who is backward in his studies. "School men discovered that the drag-net of compulsory education was bringing into school hundreds of children who were unable to keep step with their companions, and because this interfered with the orderly administration of our school systems, they began to ask why the children were backward. The school physicians helped to find the answer when they showed that hundreds of these children were backward simply because of removable physical defects."[70]

Accurate estimates, based on the examination of several million children, are available as to the prevalence of physical defects among children of school age. Dr. Thomas D. Wood[71] summarizes them as follows: "In present school groups not more than five or ten percent of all children, whether in country or city, are entirely free from physical defects, actually or potentially detrimental to health. One or two percent are mentally defective; a similar number have heart defects; between five and ten percent have had or now have some form of tuberculosis; twenty to thirty percent or more are malnourished; ten to thirteen percent have defects of vision; more than thirty percent have some defect of nose and throat, such as diseased tonsils, adenoids, etc.; thirty to forty percent have defects in posture, such as round shoulders, weak foot arches, etc.; from fifty to ninety-eight percent have neglected defective teeth." Thus the great majority of school children suffer from physical defects sufficiently serious to require the attention of the physician, oculist, or dentist.

[69] Ibid., p. 2.
[70] Ibid., p. 3.
[71] T. D. Wood and H. G. Rowell, Health Supervision and Medical Inspection of Schools, 1928, pp. 260-261 (quoted). T. D. Wood, Health Education, 1929, pp. 16-17. S. Josephine Baker, Child Hygiene, 1925, pp. 354-356. F. Overton and W. J. Denno, The Health Officer, 1920, p. 499.

The discovery of the relation of physical defects to educational retardation led to an extension of the scope of medical inspection to include the physical examination of school children with the aim of discovering whether or not they were suffering from such defects as would handicap their educational progress and prevent them from receiving the full benefit of the free education furnished by the state. "The theory on which physical examinations are based rests on a different foundation from that underlying medical inspection for the detection of contagious diseases. The latter is primarily a protective measure and looks mainly to the immediate safeguarding of the health of the community. The former aims at securing physical soundness and vitality and looks far into the future."[72] Many problems of the school, such as retardation, irregular attendance, loss of interest, and truancy, have been traced to ill health among the children. The school perceived that John cannot grasp arithmetic because he does not see the blackboard and Mary has difficulty with grammar because she has adenoids; Joseph has been considered stupid because of deafness, has neglected his studies, hates his school, and leaves before he has completed the course. Education must comprehend the whole man, and the whole man is built fundamentally on what he is physically.

The advancing public-health movement still further broadened the scope of medical school inspection with its emphasis on the positive side of health—the increase of the vitality, capacity, and efficiency of the human body and the education of the individual in the practice of personal hygiene. Because of this enlarged concept a better term than medical inspection of schools would be health supervision of school children. The one essential object of the program is to assure sound health to all children of school age. To accomplish this, certain fundamental provisions are considered necessary. The broad program of health administration of schools includes not only inspection for contagious disease and detection of physical defects, but supervision over the physical development of the child, education of the children in habits pertaining to their own health, and sanitation with regard to school buildings and surroundings.[73]

The Opposition to Medical Inspection.—"Medical inspection is essential in country districts as well as in large cities, and in rich communities as well as in poor ones. The locality has yet to be discovered in which the medical inspection of school children is unneces-

[72] L. H. Gulick and L. P. Ayres, *Medical Inspection of Schools*, 1913, p. 35.
[73] S. Josephine Baker, *Child Hygiene*, 1925, pp. 282-283.

sary or undesirable."[74] Nevertheless, certain objections have been raised to it, though they will be found on analysis to be untenable.

It has been objected that the school has no right to permit or require medical inspection of the children, but the authority which has the right to compel attendance at school certainly has the added duty of insisting that no harm shall come to those who go there. "The exercise of the power to enforce school attendance is dangerous if it is not accompanied by an appreciation of the duty of seeing that the assembling of pupils brings to the individual no physical detriment."[75] The child himself is too young to realize the permanent consequences of ill health and remediable defects and to take care of the matter himself. Parents have the right and the duty to care for their children, but through ignorance or neglect they may fail to exercise it. The rights of the state are paramount. The state, on the principle of *parens patriae*, is the ultimate parent, and all children are its wards. This is the basis and justification of all social legislation affecting children.

Nor are the schools, in assuming the medical oversight of the pupils, trespassing upon the domain of private rights and initiative. "Under medical inspection, what is done for the parent is to tell him of the needs of his child, of which he might otherwise have been in ignorance. It leaves to the parent the duty of meeting those needs. It leaves him with a larger responsibility than before. . . . School physicians are forbidden to make any suggestions as to treatment and management of sick pupils. This rule is nearly universal and is made imperative."[76] It is difficult to find a logical basis for the argument that the school has not the right to inform the parents of defects present in the child, and to advise as to remedial measures which should be taken to remove them.

More broadly, "the justification of the state in assuming the function of education and in making that education compulsory is to insure its own preservation and efficiency. . . . But the well-being of a state is as much dependent upon the strength, health, and productive capacity of its members as it is upon their knowledge and intelligence. In order that it may insure the efficiency of its citizens, the state through its compulsory educational enactments requires its youth to pursue certain studies which experience has proved necessary to secure that efficiency. Individual efficiency, however, rests not alone

[74] L. H. Gulick and L. P. Ayres, *Medical Inspection of Schools*, 1913, p. ix.
[75] *Ibid.*, p. 5.
[76] *Ibid.*, pp. 5, 31.

on education and intelligence, but is equally dependent on physical health and vigor. Hence, if the state may make mandatory training in intelligence, it may also command training to secure physical soundness and capacity."[77] The interest of the state in national vitality may also be military. The examination of recruits for the American army showed that one-fourth of all men of draft age had serious physical defects which disqualified them for service. Over half of these defects could have been remedied completely, and half of the remainder lessened, if the men had been examined and treated during their school days.[78]

On the basis of personal rights and liberties and on that of a different theory of the cause and treatment of disease, certain organizations have opposed the health supervision of school children. In Massachusetts the Medical Liberty League has appeared (to quote the *Christian Science Monitor* of Nov. 1, 1922) to champion "the right of the school child to enjoy the advantages of free education without being subjected to offensive and humiliating physical examinations. The league has worked steadfastly to change the compulsory vaccination laws, not wholly because of the evils of vaccination, but because compulsory medicine is indefensible on the basis of fundamental human rights." Under the caption, EMANCIPATION FOR THE CHILDREN, the same paper (Nov. 2, 1922) stated that the Medical Liberty League was conducting a campaign against the employment in schools of the Schick test for diphtheria and the use of various serums and antigens. "There is growing popular resentment against that tendency, fostered by experimenters, to engender among children who attend the public schools, hatreds and divisions between those who have been 'immunized' and those who put their own welfare, good health, cleanliness, and independence above slavery to fear and superstition." This journal also relates that the Public School Protective League of Washington, "composed of Christian Scientists and numerous other persons whose convictions forbid medical experimentation on school children," has favored the passage of a bill to provide that parents or guardians may forbid physical examinations of their children by school authorities, except when the children show symptoms of contagious or infectious diseases. The League "has emphasized the fact that, under the Constitution, a child has a right to freedom from medical exploitation and has pointed out that those who oppose the bill are seeking to preserve jobs for young doctors seeking a quick

[77] *Ibid.*, p. 5.
[78] F. Overton and W. J. Denno, *The Health Officer*, 1920, p. 498.

practice and for old doctors who otherwise would lack patients and to promote in the minds of parents a belief in sickness which will enthrone medical men."[79]

Opposition has also occurred in California. "Christian Science anti-science in California has centered its principal activities in the Public School Protective League, an organization with a very able attorney whose purpose is to interpose legal obstruction to what they regard as baleful health measures, and at times even to physiological and hygenic instruction in the public schools. They regard bacteriology as a sectarian doctrine, and have a decision of some court, on which they rely, that the physical examination of the throat of a child, during a diphtheria epidemic, unless by express consent of parents, is assault and battery. They have also joined with other anti-scientists in their various anti-scientific crusades, and have gone into active politics, especially in southern California, against health measures, except those which confine themselves strictly to the promotion of cleanliness. That, it seems, is a spiritual virtue, and therefore permissible."[80]

Another type of opposition is born of more blissful ignorance. It is the sort of attitude which the medical experts of the Rockefeller Foundation encountered when attempting to eradicate the hookworm disease in the southern mountains. A mountaineer addressed the physicians: "Who fetched youn's? What air you furriners pesterin' us fer? I reckon this here is *our* hookworm!" Among the answers of some London parents to the notification by school doctors that their children's teeth or eyes were in need of attention, were the following. One says: "I desire my daughter's teeth to remain as they are. The same Power that placed them there, will make due change when necessary." A mother writes: "Father has had toothache all his life, so the child will have to put up with it." Says another parent: "Squint is God-given. It is wrong to tamper with it." These recall the reply of a Kentucky mountain mother when warned that her boy's adenoids ought to be removed: "I reckon on burying him with all his natural parts."[81]

History of School Medical Inspection.—The earliest history of any governmental attempt to control or supervise the health of children in school occurred in France in 1833, but it was not until 1897 that France had any system of school medical inspection that might

---

[79] *Christian Science Monitor*, Oct. 26, 1922.

[80] Chester H. Rowell, "The Cancer of Ignorance," *The Survey*, Nov. 1, 1925, 60:3:161.

[81] E. A. Ross, *Standing Room Only?* 1927, p. 192.

be called satisfactory. Germany's system of control of the health of school children was instituted in Dresden in 1867. It consisted only of test of vision. The modern type of inspection was begun in Frankfort-on-the-Main in 1889. Since then medical inspection of schools has assumed the proportions of a world-wide movement. It is found in all the continents, and the extent of its development in different countries is in some measure proportionate to their degree of educational enlightenment. Medical inspection is a movement national in scope in England, France, Germany, Norway, Sweden, Austria, Switzerland, Belgium, Japan, Australia, and Tasmania. It is found in the more important cities in Denmark, Russia, Bulgaria, Egypt, Canada, Mexico, the Argentine Republic, and Chile. In the United States, thirty-nine states and the District of Columbia have medical inspection laws. Some merely permit examinations, others make them mandatory. In the nine other states where there are no specific laws relating to school medical inspection, most of the cities in these states have organized such systems, acting under their general health powers.[82]

Medical Inspection in the United States.—The first city in the United States to establish a regular system of medical inspection was Boston, which started in 1894 with a staff of fifty school physicians. The movement came as a result of a series of epidemics among the school children. Chicago followed in 1895, New York City in 1897, and Philadelphia in 1898. In all these instances medical inspection in its inception had as its sole object the reducing of the number of cases of contagious disease among the pupils. In 1905, New York City entered the second phase of medical inspection with the inauguration of the system of examining each school child to determine the presence of non-contagious physical defects. The first state law relating to medical inspection was passed in Connecticut in 1899; it required the teachers to make a test of the eyesight of each pupil every three years. The first mandatory legislation providing for state-wide medical inspection in all public schools was passed by Massachusetts in 1906.

According to the latest available information, nineteen states and the District of Columbia have school medical-inspection laws which are mandatory for all school districts; four states have laws which are mandatory for certain districts but make no provision for inspection in other districts; five states have laws mandatory for certain school

[82] L. H. Gulick and L. P. Ayres, *Medical Inspection of Schools*, 1913, p. vii. S. Josephine Baker, *Child Hygiene*, 1925, pp. 275-277.

districts and permissive for all others; five states have permissive laws for all districts; one state has a permissive law for first-class school districts, with no provision for other places; the remaining states either have no medical-inspection laws or have laws which do not specify whether the inspection is mandatory or permissive. The extent and character of the medical examinations that are to be made of the school children are specified by law in twenty-four states and the District of Columbia, and vary from the laws which require only dental examinations or those that contain the broad provision for a "proper medical and dental examination" to those laws which specify in detail the character of the defects for which an examination is to be made.[83] This great confusion results from our federated form of government and stands in marked contrast to the method of other nations where a national law establishes medical inspection at once throughout the land.

The Organization of Medical Inspection in the Schools.—In this country it has long been a mooted question as to whether the board of health or the board of education should have control of medical inspection of schools. Some states have decided one way, some another, and some have compromised by placing the responsibility on both. In cities where medical inspection is of longest standing the work is commonly done by the health department. Since medical inspection in its inception was confined to examination for contagious disease, this work naturally came under the board of health. This department, having obtained a foothold, has been reluctant to relinquish it.

Public-health authorities contend that medical work in the schools is just a part of the general public-health work which concerns people of all ages. They see no good reason why children of a certain age group and for a certain part of the year should be taken from the hands of the health department and placed under the jurisdiction of the board of education. They also point out that some children attend parochial schools over which the board of education has no jurisdiction.

The educational authorities, on the other hand, contend that the health and physical condition of school children are closely related to school work. Contagious diseases, they admit, properly come under the work of the board of health, but such cases compose only 4 or 5 per cent of the total number needing attention, whereas probably

[83] S. Josephine Baker, *Child Hygiene*, 1925, pp. 278-279. T. D. Wood and H. G. Rowell, *Health Supervision and Medical Inspection of Schools*, 1928, pp. 17-25.

three-fourths of the children suffer from non-contagious physical defects. The great proportion of the inspector's work is more closely allied to the functions of the teacher than to those of the public-health officer. Defective vision, deafness, adenoids, defective teeth, etc., directly affect capacity for education and determine the methods of instruction that should be applied. The promotion of health, therefore, means the promotion of education, and medical inspection becomes an extension of the work of the school hygiene and physical exercise departments. There will be less friction and better administration if the nurses and physicians are employed by the department of education.

As matters actually stand, in most cities and towns the work is carried on by the board of education. In the smaller cities, towns, and country districts the school boards are better organized and in many cases more efficient than the local boards of health and this fact accounts for the pronounced tendency toward board-of-education control. In fifteen states the responsibility is lodged in both the department of education and the department of health. Usually there is a division of labor: medical inspection for the detection of contagious diseases being a function of the board of health, and physical examinations for the detection of non-contagious defects being conducted by the educational authorities or at least with their full cooperation. The reason why there are valid arguments on both sides is that the question is really on the border line between public-health work and educational work.[84]

The School Nurse.—In either case the actual work is done by physicians and nurses, either together or separately, sometimes assisted by the teachers. In many respects the most effective part of medical or health work in schools is that done by the school nurse.

School nursing had its inception in London in 1894 when the managers of a school in a very poor section asked a district nurse to visit the school to promote the physical welfare of the children. This beginning was followed in 1898 by the formation of a volunteer School Nurses' Society with the object of supplying visiting nurses to elementary schools in four districts. These early experiments demonstrated so conclusively the value of the nurse's service that in 1904 the system was taken over by the city and supported by municipal funds. From the work in London came the suggestion for a nursing staff in the schools of New York City. Lillian D. Wald, head worker

[84] L. H. Gulick and L. P. Ayres, *Medical Inspection of Schools*, 1913, p. 151. Lina R. Struthers, *The School Nurse*, 1917, ch. V. S. Josephine Baker, *Child Hygiene*, 1925, pp. 280-282. T. D. Wood and H. G. Rowell, *Health Supervision and Medical Inspection of Schools*, 1928, pp. 40-42.

of the Henry Street Nurses' Settlement, called attention to the work of the school nurses in England and offered to lend the services of one of her staff for an experimental demonstration of one month. This first American school nurse was Lina L. Rogers, now Mrs. Struthers.[85] The board of health, the educational authorities, and the public were at once converted to the idea, and in 1902 school nursing was placed under municipal direction and control. New York City was thus the first municipality to undertake school nursing.

The duties of the school nurse include assisting the school physician in his examinations, treating minor ailments in the school and clinic and furnishing aid in emergencies, following up cases to insure remedial action, giving practical demonstrations of required treatments in the home, and educating the teachers, pupils, and parents in practical applied hygiene. The following record, taken from the Cleveland school survey, represents a typical day's work for a typical school nurse.[86]

8:30 A.M.

Home call to get permission to take child to school headquarters for mental examination.

Called at Case-Woodland School to examine child with sore throat.

Took a child home to have mother clean her up.

Called at Harmon School.

Treated ten cases of impetigo, three of toothache, two of ringworm.

Took two children home to be cleaned up.

Inspected 50 children.

Gave health talk.

Tried to locate a boy who is to attend partial blind class at Harmon School.

Found boy was transferred from Harmon School to Marion School last year.

Called at Marion School but found no trace of boy.

Called at address to which child was supposed to have moved; no such number.

Called at Kennard School to see if Miss O'Neill remembered him at Marion School; found no trace of him.

Called at two homes in regard to enlarged tonsils and defective vision.

1:15 P.M.

Mayflower School: boy with sprained ankle, soaked in hot water, strapped with adhesive.

[85] Lina R. Struthers, *The School Nurse*, 1917, pp. 13-30. L. H. Gulick and L. P. Ayres, *Medical Inspection of Schools*, 1913, ch. V.
[86] L. P. Ayres and M. Ayres, *Health Work in the Public Schools*, 1915, pp. 23-24.

Treated four cases of impetigo, one cut finger, opened two boils.
Conference with mother at school.
Instructed her in care of child's discharging ear.
Inspected 62 children.
Called at two homes to secure treatment for defective teeth.
Advised mother to send children to Marion Dental Clinic.

Valuable as is the contribution of the nurse to the health work actually carried out in the schools, probably her most important function is that of making visits to the homes of children who have been found to have physical defects or who are in need of any kind of health care. The care given in school is the ameliorative, that in the homes the preventive, part of the service. The work of the nurse prevents loss of time on the part of the pupils and vastly reduces the number of exclusions for contagious diseases. This was clearly demonstrated by the experience in New York at the very start of the work. During the single month of September, 1902, 10,567 children were excluded from the city schools, whereas in September, 1903, with the nurses in attendance, there were but 1,101 exclusions. Secondly, with regard to giving effectiveness to school inspection through follow-up work, "in New York City, before nurses were employed in school health work, it was the common practice to send a postal-card notification to parents, informing them that their child had been found to have a certain type of physical defect. A careful investigation of the results of this method showed that approximately 6 per cent of the children received treatment after this notification. With the employment of school nurses who make visits to the homes to tell parents personally of physical defects in their children and to explain to them the need for adequate treatment, the percentage of such children receiving proper treatment almost immediately rose to 86 per cent."[87]

Thus the school nurse is the most important adjunct of medical inspection, the most effective possible link between the school and the home. She supplies the motive force which makes medical inspection effective. "The school physician's discovery of defects and diseases is of little use if the result is only the entering of the fact on the record card or the exclusion of the child from school. The notice sent to parents telling of the child's condition and advising that the family physician be consulted, represents wasted effort if the parents fail to realize the import of the notification or if there be no family physician to consult. If the physical examination has for its only result the

[87] S. Josephine Baker, *Child Hygiene*, 1925, pp. 286-287. Mary S. Gardner, *Public Health Nursing*, 1923, pp. 267-268.

entering of words upon record cards, then pediculosis and tuberculosis are of precisely equal importance. The nurse avoids such ineffective lost motions by converting them into efficient functioning."[88] The value of the school nurse is one feature of medical inspection of schools about which there is no division of opinion.

The Problem of Malnutrition.—Investigations of physical deterioration in England, published in 1904, disclosed much evidence concerning the physical needs of necessitous and underfed school children. To meet this need, there was passed in 1906 the Education (Provision of Meals) Act which gave power to local educational authorities to take steps for providing school children with meals. This act was supplanted in 1921 by a more comprehensive law. The object of school feeding as incorporated in the Education Act of 1921 is to help those children who are "unable by reason of lack of food to take full advantage of the education provided for them." This implies some kind of medical or physical test. About 4.5 per cent of the children in average attendance in the areas in which school feeding is provided receive this assistance. There is more school feeding in London than elsewhere.[89]

The English investigations led to an agitation in New York City, prompted by the publication of Robert Hunter's *Poverty* and John Spargo's *Bitter Cry of the Children*, concerning the supposedly large number of school children who were underfed. There was a wild effort to do something about it, chiefly by providing free meals, until careful investigation disclosed that the estimates of underfed children were greatly exaggerated. The agitation, however, made Americans interested for the first time in the physical examination of school children, and in 1905 New York City led the way, as we have already noted, by providing for the examination of school children for noncontagious defects.[90] Scientific men then began to find out the facts about malnutrition, to give undernourishment a technical meaning, to discover its causes and its actual relation to economic conditions.

Malnutrition is a clinical entity with a characteristic history, definite symptoms, and pathological physical signs. Among the specific causes are improper diet ("a diet insufficient or unsuitable is generally conceded to be the most common cause of malnutrition"), wrong food habits, insufficient sleep, chronic fatigue, lack of exercise, and diseases and defects such as enlarged or diseased tonsils or adenoids, de-

[88] L. P. Ayres and M. Ayres, *Health Work in the Public Schools*, 1915, p. 22.
[89] *Annual Report of the Chief Medical Officer of the Board of Education for the Year 1927*, pp. 101, 102.
[90] William H. Allen, *Civics and Health*, 1909, p. 86, ch. XVII.

cayed teeth, and tuberculosis. The only sure way to decide whether a child is malnourished is to have him examined by a physician who takes into consideration all the signs that may point to malnutrition. A thorough examination by a physician is not yet available to all children. The custom has arisen, therefore, during the past few years, of using increase in height and weight as a rough index of nutrition. Emerson holds that any child habitually 7 per cent or more underweight for his height is malnourished. Holt, Wood, and a large majority of other workers in this field consider 10 per cent a safer limit to use in routine examinations. Most authorities agree that the age of the child should be considered in deciding what his normal weight should be for his height. The Baldwin-Wood-Woodbury table, which is generally regarded as the best available measuring stick for this purpose, gives the average height and the average weight for children at different ages.

What is the extent of malnutrition? A study of over 170,000 school children in New York City showed the following results:

> 17.3 per cent excellent.
> 61.1 " " good.
> 18.5 " " requiring supervision.
> 3.1 " " requiring medical treatment.

From extensive observations of thousands of children in widely separated localities, it is safe to conclude that from one-fourth to one-third of the children in the United States are definitely malnourished, and that the number of children of really superior nutrition is small.[91]

At the beginning of the nutrition movement practically all the blame for the prevalence of malnutrition was laid on poverty. Experience soon showed the importance of ignorance and lack of parental control, and a tendency arose to minimize the importance of poverty as a factor in malnutrition. In fact, wherever comparison has been made, it has been found that the proportion of malnourished children among the so-called better classes is as great as or even greater than among the poorer and immigrant groups. Studies made in many places, notably Chicago, Grand Rapids, and New York, have given definite information to the effect that undernourishment among children of school age is distinctly more prevalent among the children of the wealthy or well-to-do than among children in the more crowded tenement districts belonging to families whose standards of living are be-

---

[91] William Emerson, *Nutrition and Growth in Children*, 1922, p. 6. Lydia J. Roberts, *What is Malnutrition?* Children's Bureau Pub. No. 59, 1927, pp. 3, 5-9.

low the so-called poverty line. Improper diet, as well as insufficient diet, is an important cause of malnutrition. If a child "indulges in sweets and highly seasoned foods, or eats irregularly between meals, or keeps late hours, or sleeps in a poorly ventilated room, or gets too little exercise, he will have a finicky appetite, and this will result in his taking too little food. Whenever the food eaten habitually by a child falls below his actual need, no matter for what reason, malnutrition follows."[92] These factors have no direct connection with income. Children of the wealthy have money to buy candy and ice cream sodas and food which is pleasing to the palate but not body building; they are often permitted to indulge their appetites freely in cake, candy, and sundaes to the exclusion of the plain and nourishing foods necessary to their physical development and long life. Some of these facts are well illustrated in the following skit which appeared in the *Journal of the American Medical Association.*

THE TALE OF AN OVERWORKED TUMMY

The Sad Story of What Happened Between 10 A.M. and 9.45 P.M.,
As Told by "Little Mary"

10 A.M.—Oh, dear! Another warm day. Wonder if I'll be abused as I was yesterday. If I am, I'm going to strike. Just disposed of a half-chewed breakfast. We ran for the train, which meant that I was so jiggled about and so tired that it took me twice as long to do my work. Hope she gives me an hour or two of complete rest before anything more comes my way.

10.30 A.M.—Two glasses of ice water have just arrived. It will take all the energy I can pump up in the next hour just to warm me up to normal again.

10.50 A.M.—Half-chewed breakfast did not satisfy her and she has bought some peanuts and started again.

12 M.—Peanuts have been drifting along steadily ever since. Think she has finished them, though.

12.30 P.M.—Decided she wasn't very hungry, and instead of a good solid dinner sent me down a cold eggnog heavy with chocolate. Could have managed it all right if it hadn't been so unnaturally cold, but that made it terribly difficult to deal with.

1.10 P.M.—More ice water.

1.40 P.M.—Was mistaken about the peanuts; she has found another handful in the bottom of her vanity bag, and now I am getting them again.

2.05 P.M.—More ice water.

3.10 P.M.—She has been lifting some heavy books, and as usual used my muscles instead of her arm muscles. You see, she's never had any proper

[92] Lydia J. Roberts, *What is Malnutrition?* Children's Bureau Pub. No. 59, 1927, p. 6.

physical education—soft, flabby, slouchy sort. Tired me almost as much as a six-course dinner.

3.20 P.M.—Furtive fellow has brought us a box of caramels, and she has started right in on them.

4.30 P.M.—Have received something like half a pound of caramels. Just heard her say: "Oh, dear, I don't feel a bit well. The milk in that eggnog must have been sour."

6.30 P.M.—We played a set of tennis before dinner, and here I am all tired out and a lot of work to do.

6.50 P.M.—We were invited by a sissy sport with a belt on his coat to have a soda before going home. Had a lemon phosphate and then had to run for the car.

7 P.M.—Fried taters, cucumbers, veal cutlets, catsup, cookies and canned blueberries. What do you know about that?

7.45 P.M.—We are strolling down to the corner with a knock-kneed guy in a sport shirt and white pants for a pineapple walnut college ice.

8.20 P.M.—Got home and found somebody had made some iced tea. She drank two glasses. I tried hard to keep the tea and the college ice separated, but they mixed it in spite of me. I go on strike.

8.30 P.M.—Have sent back the college ice and the iced tea.

8.40 P.M.—Returned the blueberries.

8.45 P.M.—And the peanuts.

9 P.M.—The devil to pay—can't get the doctor.

9.17 P.M.—Doctor found at the movies. Mother thinks it is a weak stomach she inherited from her father. Knock-knee suggests it is the beastly weather— the big boob!

9.45 P.M.—Doctor says it is from a bilious temperament. *Good night!*

Several agencies have been established to cope with the problem of malnutrition. These are: (1) School lunches, that is, extra meals provided by school authorities, and properly selected for their nutritional value. (2) Nutrition clinics and classes for underweight children, conducted by the regular clinical methods, with visits to the home. (3) Health education for all children, in an endeavor to institute preventive health habits. (4) Nutrition work for preschool children, conducted through child-health centers, nursery schools, home demonstration work, and parent education.[93]

Open-Air Schools and Classes.—Open-air schools represent a special phase of school hygiene, giving special care to anemic and tubercular children in order to develop and strengthen them for their school work. The first open-air school was started in Charlottenburg,

[93] Lydia J. Roberts, *What is Malnutrition?* Children's Bureau Pub. No. 59, 1927, pp. 11-16. Arnold L. Gesell, *The Preschool Child*, 1923, chs. I, III, XI, XII. William Emerson, *Nutrition and Growth in Children*, 1922, Part III.

a suburb of Berlin, in 1904. In England the first was established in London in 1907. The first in the United States were in Providence, Boston, New York, and Chicago. The movement was initiated largely by private societies, like the tuberculosis committee; it later secured the assistance of the educational authorities. In many cases even now some private philanthropy is assisting in financing the enterprise. Private associations pay for the cots, quilts, special clothing, extra food, nurses, and cooks; the school board provides the building and equipment and pays for the teacher. A regular health program is instituted along with the school work. The hours of study are limited and interrupted by frequent rest or lunch periods.

Though the open-air school or room was started for the tubercular and pretubercular, it has been extended until there has arisen a demand for open windows and low-temperature school rooms for all children. The effect of this open-air life upon the health of the children has been marked. Wherever such classes are maintained, the statistical and clinical data obtained show a continued and marked improvement in the health of the children. "They gain in weight; their nervous stability is restored and the progress of nervous disease arrested; their capacity for school work is increased; absences caused by illness are markedly decreased; there is a lessened possibility of spread of infectious diseases and the actual cases are fewer in number; tuberculosis is prevented or arrested in its development; correct habits for health and feeding are established; and the home environment of the children is greatly improved by force of example."[94]

Dental Inspection.—The commonest of all physical defects among school children is defective teeth. They cause more trouble than any other defect. Bad teeth are closely related to malnutrition, ill-health, and retardation. No other single ailment of school children is directly or indirectly responsible for so great an amount of misery, disease, and mental and physical handicap.

To meet this great need dental inspection has been introduced. It is rapidly becoming one of the most important branches of medical inspection. First in Germany, next in England, and more recently in the United States, dental inspection has been inaugurated and school dental clinics established. The work is now being carried on in over 200 American cities. In nearly all cases dental inspection in

[94] S. Josephine Baker, *Child Hygiene*, 1925, pp. 444-450, 449-450 (quoted). L. P. Ayres, *Open-Air Schools*, 1910. James F. Rogers, *Schools and Classes for Delicate Children*, U. S. Bureau of Education Bulletin, 1930, No. 22.

America has had its inception in volunteer work of the local dental association or some other private group. When the experimental stage is past, the dental inspection in schools and the remedial work in clinics are usually administered by the public-school authorities in cooperation with the dental association.[95]

Dental work in schools is a preventive plan with these objectives: "1. To insure every school child healthy, properly erupted teeth, if possible; 2. To avoid such handicaps as might arise from poor teeth or improper eruption of teeth; 3. To accomplish these ends by (a) teaching the child how to care for his teeth properly; (b) providing the child with regular examinations of his teeth to determine any treatment needed; (c) notifying parents of the existence of any defects requiring treatment; (d) assuring the child of treatment though not necessarily giving it to him."[96]

Other Aids in School Hygiene.—Other aids in school hygiene have developed as a result of the growing health supervision of children. This is seen especially in the formation of special classes of children of similar ability or similar mental or physical deficiency. Modern schools now have sight-conservation classes, classes for children with cardiac affections, special classes for the crippled, blind, deaf, and mentally defective. In many instances the beginning of such work came through the efforts of a private organization, then it was taken over and extended by the public authorities. A generalization that may be made from this experience is as follows. The function of a private organization is to experiment and demonstrate. It has the necessary freedom and flexibility. The function of a public organization is to carry the work forward on a large scale. It has means and organization.

Discussion of these devices will be deferred until later, when the social aspects of education are considered, for the special educational problems are perhaps more important than the public-health aspects.[97]

Health Education.—Health education of the children, carried on either directly with the children or indirectly through the teachers and parents, embodies the largest single contribution that has been made to the program for child hygiene as it relates to children of preschool and school age. "If all children could be taught how to live sanely and healthfully, if they could be made interested in keeping themselves sound and physically fit, if they could absorb the

---

[95] L. H. Gulick and L. P. Ayres, *Medical Inspection of Schools*, 1913, pp. 114-142.

[96] T. D. Wood and H. G. Rowell, *Health Supervision and Medical Inspection of Schools*, 1928, p. 232.

[97] *Ibid.*, pp. 290-385. S. Josephine Baker, *Child Hygiene*, 1925, pp. 450-459.

essentials necessary to achieve proper personal hygiene and themselves apply the methods whereby health may be attained, they would inevitably demand the environmental conditions that make health possible. . . . All organized health effort depends for its success upon the extent of the health education of the population at all ages. Health education of adults is a long, complicated, expensive, and only partially successful process. Health education of children is a sure, direct, easy, and economical measure in attaining the desired result.''[98]

[98] *Ibid.*, pp. 466-467.

CHAPTER XIV

THE WINNING FIGHT AGAINST DISEASE

TODAY scientists are waging the greatest warfare of all time—the battle of Man *versus* Microbe. Led by such generals as Pasteur, Koch, Smith, Bruce, Ross, Reed, Ehrlich, and many others, mankind has been emerging victorious. Devastating epidemics, formerly a constant menace, now rarely occur. Modern science has made possible the conquest of at least six major communicable diseases, *viz.*, smallpox, yellow fever, typhoid fever, cholera, typhus, and bubonic plague; that is to say, methods have been provided by science for their elimination, and the only difficulty lies in the practical application of the procedures rather than in the procedures themselves. These diseases have caused inestimable suffering and economic loss; their control has been a great boon to mankind.

Smallpox.—The first successful example of a specific immunity created to control a communicable disease was that of vaccination against smallpox, introduced by Edward Jenner a century and a quarter ago. It was in 1796 that Jenner gave us the modern practice of vaccination, which possessed all the advantages of inoculation without its dangers. His was one of the most important investigations which has ever been made by man. The practice of inoculation against smallpox, which depended on the production of immunity by inoculating the individual with the material from the pustules of a smallpox patient, had been in vogue in Asia, particularly among the Hindus and Persians, for at least three centuries before the Christian era, and was finally introduced into England in 1718 by Lady Mary Wortley Montagu, the wife of the British ambassador at Constantinople. The reaction to this treatment was often severe and sometimes fatal, and it had little effect upon the general prevalence of the disease. Jenner's discovery of the more certain method of vaccination was made in the following way.

In the rural district in which he lived many of the cattle were infected with a mild eruptive disease known as cowpox, and this disease was often contracted by the men and girls who milked the cows. There was a common belief that those who had had the cowpox were resistant against smallpox, and this theory Jenner tested out by vaccinating a boy, James Phipps, with cowpox material and then inoculating with true smallpox matter, in the fashion generally practised at the time for protection against natural small-pox. The cowpox vaccination "took"; the smallpox inoculation failed to "take," showing that the vaccination had produced in the boy an effective immunity against the smallpox germ. During the years 1799-1801 over 3000 different persons were thus vaccinated, and then inoculated, at the London Small-Pox Hospital with the demonstration of complete protection in every case. There is perhaps no other procedure in medicine which rests upon so ample and sure a basis of direct experimental evidence. Since Jenner's day it has been shown that the inoculation of human smallpox material into the cow produces cowpox, and that by exposure to the body fluids of the cow the germ of smallpox has permanently lost its power to produce smallpox. Vac-cine retains, however, the power to stimulate the human body so that it becomes immune against the virulent disease. The effect is not life-long nor absolute. It wears off with the passage of time, so that vaccination should be repeated about once in seven years.[1]

The effectiveness of smallpox prevention has been amply demon-strated.

One of the most clear cut cases is the experience of Cuba following the American occupation of the island and the enforcement of vaccination. During the eight years before the American army entered Havana, that is, before vaccination was enforced, there were 3,132 deaths from smallpox in the city; during the next eight years there were seven. "In 1905 and 1906 over three million vaccinations were performed in the Philippine Islands with the result that a toll of 40,000 deaths a year was changed to a few hundreds; the latter occurring in remote places which had not been reached with fresh and potent vaccine. In the provinces immediately adjacent to Manila there were 6,000 deaths a year from smallpox before vaccination and none after. When the health service of the Philippines was turned over to native officials in 1914, vaccination was neglected, and as soon as enough susceptible children had been added to the population the disease broke out once more. In 1918 there were again 50,000 deaths from smallpox in the Philippines, *nine-tenths* of them among the unvaccinated children."[2]

Before the practice of vaccination was effectively carried out, Japan had thousands of cases and deaths each year. Smallpox epidemics were especially severe. In 1909 a law was passed requiring vaccination of each infant within three months after birth. This measure alone apparently had the effect of greatly reducing both the incidence and mortality. There has been no serious epidemic of smallpox in Japan since vaccination was generally introduced.

[1] C.-E. A. Winslow, *Man and the Microbe*, 1924, pp. 54-55. *Cf.* Herbert H. Waite, *Disease Prevention*, 1926, pp. 2, 9-14.
[2] C.-E. A. Winslow, *Man and the Microbe*, 1924, p. 56.

There is no excuse for smallpox. Take the classic case, described by Sir William Osler in his "Practice of Medicine,"[3] of the Montreal outbreak of 1885. "For years there had been no small-pox in the city, and a large unprotected population grew up among the French-Canadians, many of whom were opposed to vaccination. On Feb. 28, a Pullman car conductor, who had travelled from Chicago, was admitted into the Hôtel-Dieu, the civic small-pox hospital being at the time closed. Isolation was not carried out, and on the 1st of April a servant in the hospital died of small-pox. Following her decease, the authorities of the hospital dismissed all patients presenting no symptoms of contagion, who could go home. The disease spread like fire in dry grass, and within nine months 3,164 persons died in the city of small-pox." As a result, vaccination became general, and there has not been an epidemic of smallpox in Montreal since that time, owing to the vigilance in enforcing the school vaccination laws. The disease has disappeared to such an extent that it is now practically unknown.

Despite the conclusiveness of these demonstrations, there is still great laxity about vaccination. Conservatism and desire for individual freedom of action are hard to overcome. In proof of the fact, England celebrated the centenary of the discovery of vaccination by having an epidemic of smallpox in the town in which Jenner was born. In England any conscientious objector is excused from vaccination if he appears before a magistrate and states his position. Many people take advantage of this exemption. There are many communities in the United States which are heading straight for an experience like that of the Philippine Islands through neglect of the safeguard of vaccination. In 1916 there were 15,450 cases of smallpox with 48 deaths; in 1920 there were 94,691 cases with 366 deaths. "We shall, no doubt, have some striking demonstration of the folly of neglect of vaccination during the next ten years; but any community which desires to do so can stamp out smallpox and keep it under control by the practice of vaccination and revaccination."[4]

Typhoid Fever.—Not long ago typhoid fever was a common cause of sickness and death throughout the United States. Even as late as 1900 the death-rate was 36 per 100,000 in the Registration Area. Epidemics raged in the large cities of the country because of polluted water-supplies and because little was done to prevent the spread of the disease through secondary infection. But, with the installation

[3] *The Principles and Practice of Medicine,* 1912, p. 316.
[4] C.-E. A. Winslow, *Man and the Microbe,* 1924, p. 57.

of excellent water systems in the larger cities of the country, the protection of food and milk supplies, and the introduction of inoculation, the typhoid-fever death-rate has sharply declined. This disease is now not far from extinction, certainly in the northern and urban sections of the country. There need never be another epidemic of typhoid fever.

The value of typhoid inoculation was proved during the World War. Inoculation by means of a simple injection of vaccine under the skin will in most cases prevent the disease. Typhoid, notoriously a disease of camps, was through sanitation and preventive inoculation practically unknown in the armies during the World War. In the Franco-Prussian War, of all deaths 60 per cent were caused by typhoid fever. During the Boer War, disease, especially dysentery and typhoid fever, was a more serious cause of loss of life and service than the casualties of fighting. In the British Army during the Boer War there were approximately 30,000 cases of typhoid fever with 5,877 deaths. During the Civil War the losses from typhoid exceeded the number of those killed in action. In the Spanish-American War, of the 107,973 men of the United States Army, 20,738 contracted typhoid fever, and of this number 1,580 died. Nearly 1 of every 5 men was infected, and of those ill the death-rate was 7.8 per cent, of the entire army 1.5 per cent. During the World War vaccination was compulsory in the American Army. There were only 488 cases of typhoid fever with 88 deaths in approximately 2,000,000 troops in France. No more conclusive evidence could be given of the efficacy of anti-typhoid vaccination.[5]

Sir Arthur Newsholme[6] says "typhoid fever is becoming so rare that some medical teachers are almost deploring the fact that they cannot find cases to use in teaching their medical students. Typhoid seems destined to follow the path of typhus fever which practically disappeared from civilized communities three decades ago."

Asiatic Cholera.—Many serious epidemics of cholera have occurred in the past. During recent years there were important epidemics in the period from 1879 to 1910. "Koch, in 1883, isolated the cause of Asiatic cholera, the *Spirillum choleræ asiaticæ*, while engaged in the study of the epidemic which broke out in Egypt in 1879. This epidemic spread over Asia and into Europe. At times cholera epidemics have been so widespread that they might be regarded as

[5] Herbert H. Waite, *Disease Prevention*, 1926, pp. 41-42. Sir Arthur Newsholme, *Evolution of Preventive Medicine*, 1927, p. 105.
[6] Milbank Memorial Fund, *Quarterly Bulletin*, July, 1928, 6:3:55.

pandemic. The epidemic which began in 1891 is said by Castellani to have had its origin in India, at the celebration of a religious festival, during which those who had gathered for the ceremonies bathed in the Ganges River and polluted it with cholera discharges. In 1892 it had spread to Europe and Africa, a violent epidemic occurring in Hamburg, Germany, from whence a few cases came to the Port of New York. In Russia 400,000 are said to have died as a result of this epidemic. It prevailed in the armies during the Balkan War in 1912, and in the World War in the Austrian Army in Galicia, and there were outbreaks in Mesopotamia, Greece and Turkey. Quarantine regulations have kept the disease out of the United States almost completely for the past fifty years."[7]

The germ causing cholera is restricted to the intestinal tract, and prevention is chiefly based on the concurrent disinfection of the bowel discharges. All things which are, or may have been, contaminated, should be disinfected, and all the measures used in preventing typhoid fever, such as the protection of the water, food, and milk supplies, are a means of combating cholera. Preventive vaccination is of value but it is less effective than anti-typhoid vaccination.

THE PREVENTION OF INSECT-BORNE DISEASES

The first definite proof and demonstration that a disease may be transmitted by insects was made by an American, Theobald Smith, in 1893. He showed that Texas cattle fever is spread among the animals by a species of tick. Within a few years of this discovery, there was shown the relation of the mosquito to malaria and yellow fever, of the rat and the flea to plague, of the tsetse-fly to African sleeping sickness, and of the louse to typhus fever. "These discoveries of insect transmission of disease were of as far-reaching importance to the world as those of Copernicus, Columbus, or of Edison. Ross, Reed, Nicolle, Kitasato, McCoy and others showed insects to be the center of a system around which revolved the great pestilences which have scourged the race from antiquity. They did not discover unknown continents, but they made it possible to create a new world within the tropics. The practical use of their researches made the Panama Canal possible, saved the South from yellow fever, reduced disease and increased progress wherever the flea, louse, or mosquito are to be found."[8]

[7] Herbert H. Waite, *Disease Prevention*, 1926, p. 134. *Cf.* Sir Arthur Newsholme, *The Story of Modern Preventive Medicine*, 1928, pp. 81-88.

[8] J. Howard Beard, "Progress of Public Health Work," *The Scientific Monthly*, Feb., 1922, 14:2:143. *Cf.* Paul de Kruif, *Microbe Hunters*, 1926, chs. VIII-XI.

The development of our knowledge of insect-borne diseases, such as malaria, yellow fever, plague, African sleeping sickness, and typhus fever, furnishes the most fascinating chapter in medical history.

Malaria.—Considering sickness and disability as well as direct mortality, the most important of these diseases from a world-wide point of view is malaria. It is held directly or indirectly responsible for more than half of all deaths. Sir William Osler has justly called it "the greatest single destroyer of the human race." "At first thought this would seem surprising in view of the fact that we have exact knowledge concerning the greater part of the life history of the parasite which causes it, the way in which it is spread, its specific treatment and means for its control and prevention. It is world-wide in its distribution but is especially prevalent in tropical and subtropical regions. It reaps its harvest of death by the millions every year and incapacitates by the hundreds of millions those whom it does not exterminate. Many of the latter are so reduced in resistance by this disease that they become easy victims to other diseases."[9]

"The secret of this mysterious malady—the bad air disease (*mal' aria*)—was revealed in 1898 when it was discovered that the infecting germ was transmitted by the bite of mosquitoes of the genus *Anopheles*, and in no other way. Its connection with night air, marshy areas, and excavated soil was at once explained by the fact that these mosquitoes breed in stagnant water, and there was placed within our grasp a simple and effective method of controlling this disease through measures directed against its insect host."[10] The most effective means of controlling and preventing this disease are the screening of houses; the destruction of the mosquitoes by draining marshes and removing all small accumulations of stagnant water; the destruction of the larvae by spreading oil on marsh lands and stocking small ponds with fish which eat the wrigglers; and the systematic use of quinine which cures those who are ill, eliminates the germs from the blood of carriers, and protects those who are well against infection. "The International Health Board has carried on a series of striking demonstrations of the value of malaria control measures in various southern States and tropical countries and has demonstrated that by the control of mosquito breeding areas, by screening, or by the systematic use of quinin, it is possible to elimi-

[9] Herbert H. Waite, *Disease Prevention*, 1926, p. 382.
[10] C.-E. A. Winslow, *Man and the Microbe*, 1924, pp. 34-36. *Cf.* Herbert H. Waite, *Disease Prevention*, 1926, pp. 399-412.

nate from four-fifths to nine-tenths of the malaria in the worst infected districts at a cost which generally amounts to between fifty cents and a dollar per inhabitant a year.''[11]

Yellow Fever.—The discovery of the cause and mode of transmission of yellow fever is one of the finest events in the annals of the United States Army. In 1900, Surgeon-General Sternberg appointed a commission to study sanitary conditions in Cuba. The Spanish-American War had just ended and sanitary conditions in Cuba were frightful. Malaria was prevalent, and the danger of yellow fever in the troops was very great. The commission was placed under the command of Major Walter Reed, Surgeon, United States Army. Associated with him were Drs. James Carroll, Aristides Agramonte, and Jesse W. Lazear. Reed's suspicions were soon directed toward the stegomyia mosquito as the cause of yellow fever, but he needed proof. Since animals will not catch yellow fever, it was necessary to call for volunteers to serve as human guinea-pigs. A member of the commission, Carroll, was the first of the volunteers to succumb to the infection. He became ill four days after having allowed an infected mosquito to bite him. He recovered from the infection, but died on March 9, 1907, of myocarditis, which had undoubtedly been brought on through the previous attack of yellow fever. On the 13th of September, Lazear, while working in the wards occupied by yellow-fever patients, noticed a mosquito on his hand. He did not remove it, and as a result became infected. After a very serious illness he died on September 25, 1900. A systematic campaign was now started. ''Camp Lazear'' was established in the country a short distance from Havana, and a call was issued for volunteers from the army of occupation as subjects of investigation. The first to respond were Private John R. Kissenger of Ohio and John J. Moran, a civilian clerk in the office of General Fitzhugh Lee. Dr. Reed pointed out the danger. They were determined. He talked of compensation. They refused. ''The one condition on which we volunteer, sir,'' said Private Kissenger and civilian clerk John J. Moran, ''is that we get no compensation for it.'' To the tip of his cap went the hand of Major Reed: ''Gentlemen, I salute you!'' Later he declared that this exhibition of moral courage had ''never been surpassed in the annals of the army.''

Experiments were now devised to show that yellow fever was transmitted by the mosquito alone. A small building was erected, all windows, doors, and every other possible opening being absolutely

[11] C.-E. A. Winslow, *Man and the Microbe*, 1924, p. 36.

mosquito-proof. A wire mosquito screen divided the room into two spaces. In one of the spaces 15 mosquitoes which had fed on yellow fever patients were liberated. A non-immune volunteer entered the room with the mosquitoes and remained there for nearly half an hour, during which time he was bitten by 7 mosquitoes. Twice after this he entered the room, remaining in it 64 minutes and receiving 15 mosquito bites. Four days later he suffered an attack of yellow fever. Two other non-immune men slept for 13 nights in the mosquito-free room without disturbance of any sort.

To show that the disease was transmitted by the mosquito and not through the excreta of yellow-fever patients or anything which had come in contact with them, another house was constructed and made mosquito-proof. For 20 days this house was occupied by 3 non-immunes after the clothing, bedding, eating utensils, and vessels, soiled with the discharges, blood, and vomitus of yellow-fever patients had been placed in it. The bed clothing which they used had been brought from the beds of patients who had died of yellow fever, without being subjected to washing or any other treatment to remove anything with which it might have been soiled. The experiment was twice repeated by other non-immune volunteers. During the entire period all the men who occupied the house were strictly quarantined and protected from mosquitoes. None of those exposed to these experiments contracted yellow fever. That they were not immune was subsequently shown, since four of them became infected either by mosquito bites or the injection of blood from yellow-fever patients.

During these investigations there were produced experimentally 14 cases of yellow fever through infected mosquito bites, 6 by blood injection, 2 by the injection of filtered blood-serum. The use of the filtered blood-serum, in 1901, demonstrated that the disease was due to a filterable virus.

The facts demonstrated by the commission may be summarized as follows: yellow fever is acquired only through the bite of the *Aëdes calopus*. The mosquito, to become infectious, must bite the yellow-fever patient during the first 5 days of his illness. An interval of at least 12 days must elapse, after the mosquito has obtained the infected blood, before it can infect man.

The importance of the results which have already accrued from these discoveries cannot be overestimated. Yellow fever has been eliminated from the United States and practically so from the West Indies, and it is only a question of time when it will be eradicated from all parts of the world. In 1925 only 3 cases were reported from the entire Western Hemisphere—and even these three were not certainly authentic. Yet before sanitary measures were introduced for the control and prevention of yellow fever, periodic epidemics occurred in tropical America, particularly in the Atlantic seaports. In times past hardly a city along the Atlantic Coast and the Gulf of Mexico was not visited with epidemics of yellow fever. All the southern states bordering on the Gulf of Mexico have from time to time been invaded. At the present time yellow fever apparently occurs only in Brazil, Colombia, and along the West Coast of Africa.

As to preventive measures, all that has been said concerning the prevention of malaria applies to yellow fever, with the exception of the use of quinine, which has no effect in this case. Yellow fever can be much more easily controlled and prevented than can malaria. "Only one species of mosquito transmits yellow fever; several species transmit malaria. The yellow fever mosquito is domestic in its habits and remains in the near vicinity of human habitations; the malaria mosquitoes are wild and are found in swamps, marshes, etc., and hence have a wider distribution. The yellow fever mosquitoes are limited to tropical and subtropical countries; the malaria mosquitoes may be found in nearly all regions and climates. The yellow fever patient is only infective to the mosquito during the first days of his illness; the malaria patient throughout the course of his disease."[12] The two most important considerations in the prevention of yellow fever are: the destruction of the mosquito and of its breeding places, and the screening of yellow-fever patients so that *Aëdes calopus* cannot obtain access to them.

Bubonic Plague.—The progress of sanitary science has similarly robbed bubonic plague of its terrors. This disease—the "Black Death" of the Middle Ages—has at times spread over the whole of the known world. In 1348 Europe was invaded by an epidemic which had its origin in China. As a result of this epidemic 13,000,000 people are said to have died in China and about 24,000,000 in the rest of the East. Hecker estimates that 25,000,000 persons, one-fourth of the population of Europe, perished in this epidemic. From the fourteenth century to the present time numerous epidemics with frightful mortality have prevailed. Although it has not been as widespread in its invasion of the whole world as it was in the fourteenth century, it has claimed a large toll, especially in certain places. De Foe's *Journal of the Plague Year* describes the devastation which occurred

[12] Herbert H. Waite, *Disease Prevention*, 1926, pp. 48-50, 414, 421 (quoted), 422-424. Paul de Kruif, *Microbe Hunters*, 1926, ch. XI.

in London in 1665, in which 70,000 persons perished. In 1871 plague again broke out in China and Eastern Siberia and passed to India, where it claimed 6 million victims in a period of 10 years. In the 20-year period ended in 1923, plague killed over 11,000,000 people in India alone. In India, China, and other parts of Asia it has been endemic for centuries. Western Europe has been almost free from plague since the middle of the eighteenth century. The plague which began in Hong Kong in 1893 would have spread over the entire world, with devastation on a very extensive scale, as in the Middle Ages, had it not been for modern sanitation.[13]

In 1894 the Japanese Kitasato and the Frenchman Yersin, working independently, discovered the cause of bubonic or black plague, the *Bacillus pestis*. This discovery by itself meant little until it was ascertained how the disease was transmitted. In ancient times it was observed that epidemics of plague were preceded by epidemics in rats, which were so fatal that many dead rats were found in the streets, buildings, and other places. This coincidence led many to believe that in some way these rats were connected with the spread of the disease. Yersin, in 1894, established the identity of the disease in man and rats. In 1914 the British Plague Commission in India proved conclusively that bubonic plague is conveyed from the rat to man through the rat flea. The experiments were carried out as follows. "The inhabitants of a plague-stricken village had abandoned it, as often happened. Guinea-pigs were then allowed to run about some of the houses. Many of them speedily died of plague and rat fleas infected with plague germs were found upon them. Other guinea-pigs were exposed in boxes covered with netting to exclude fleas and none had the disease. Others protected from fleas by tanglefoot placed around the cages remained well. Others, still, were exposed to soiled clothing in infected houses, but remained well, except in the few instances in which fleas happened to remain. The problem of plague was, after centuries of speculation, solved by a few simple experiments."[14]

Further investigations have shown that eight species of fleas are carriers of the plague bacillus and that the rat is not the only rodent which has plague. In recent years it has been demonstrated that the marmot has probably been the responsible agent in keeping the disease endemic in Tibet; in California the ground squirrel has become

[13] Herbert H. Waite, *Disease Prevention*, 1926, pp. 37-40.
[14] Charles V. Chapin, "The Science of Epidemic Diseases," *The Scientific Monthly*, June, 1928, 26:6:489.

infected, and the disease is so widely disseminated in these rodents that many years will probably be required to stamp it out. The rat, however, is the chief offender and the principal carrier.

The modern method of plague control is built chiefly upon the eradication of rats by trapping, by poisoning and, above all, by eliminating rat-breeding places, and upon a system of quarantine which includes the destruction of rats on ships coming from infected ports. One of the main reasons why in past centuries plague decimated populations was the abundant feeding of rats and their rapid multiplication which was favored by the retention of decomposing food and other organic refuse in and about houses. The most effective suppressive measure is to separate the rat from its customary food supply. The second is to eliminate the hiding places of these animals in order to restrict breeding.[15]

During the past twenty years, plague has at times spread to ports all over the world—in Australia, in England, in Brazil, in Texas, Louisiana, and California. Yet everywhere, except in India, the disease has been held in check by vigorous anti-rat campaigns wherever a human case occurs or a rodent case in the vicinity of human habitations. In no well-organized community today need there be the slightest fear of a real plague epidemic.

African Sleeping Sickness.—Sleeping sickness or trypanosomiasis is a specific communicable disease characterized by a division into two stages. In the first there is irregular fever, enlarged glands, edema, and a rash; in the second a protracted and progressive lethargy with nervous symptoms. The disease prevails in tropical Africa, especially about the head waters of the Nile, in the lake region, and in the Congo. It is gradually spreading with increasing morbidity and mortality. African trypanosomiasis is the most important and widespread disease in equatorial Africa. During the 10 years between 1896 and 1906 there were from 400,000 to 500,000 deaths among the natives of the Congo region. It is stated that in one district in Central Africa the population was reduced from 300,000 to 100,000 in the course of 7 years, from 1901 to 1908, and there are records of whole villages and islands being depopulated.

The way to the discovery of the cause of sleeping sickness was paved by David Bruce, who in 1894 not only discovered that nagana, a horse disease of Zululand, was caused by a trypanosome, but dem-

[15] United States Public Health Service, *The Rat: A Health Menace That Should Be Eradicated*, Public Health Reports, Aug. 17, 1928, 43:33:2157-2159. C.-E. A. Winslow, *Man and the Microbe*, 1924, p. 40.

onstrated that it was transmitted by the tsetse-fly. He later proved that the tsetse-fly carried sleeping sickness. In 1901 Dutton discovered the cause of sleeping sickness, *Trypanosoma gambiense*, in the blood of an Englishman in Gambia. It was found during the febrile stage of the disease and was not suspected, even after further work by Dutton and Todd, to be the cause of sleeping sickness. These two investigators recognized the trypanosome in only the first stage of the disease, which they called Gambia fever. Bruce and Navarro, in 1903, showed that the tsetse-fly, *Glossina palpalis*, is the carrier of the disease, and that Gambia fever and sleeping sickness are two stages of one and the same infection. It has since been abundantly demonstrated that the tsetse-fly transmits sleeping sickness through its bite. It is thought that the flies usually transmit the infection after the parasite has undergone development in their bodies. Man serves as a source of infection. It is quite probable that certain wild animals may furnish a reservoir. The tsetse-fly may carry a virulent organism for a period of 185 days or more, or even to the end of its life. At least two species of tsetse-flies transmit infection: *Glossina palpalis* transmits Gambian trypanosomiasis or Gambian sleeping sickness; *Glossina morsitans* transmits Rhodesian sleeping sickness. There is no evidence that either form of African sleeping sickness is ever transmitted in any other way.

One of the most important measures for the prevention of sleeping sickness is the isolation of all persons who harbor the trypanosome. A number of drugs have been prepared for treating patients, with good results in some cases. Since the tsetse-fly is the principal if not the only means of transmitting African sleeping sickness, the destruction of this fly would be the logical point of attack, but at the present time this seems an impossibility. Other means must be taken for protection. Areas where the fly has its habitat should be avoided; areas free from flies should be chosen for the location of villages, camps, and other habitations. Around these habitations there should be a cleared area extending for a distance of at least 300 yards and kept constantly cultivated. The brush should be cleared from the shores of islands and lakes for a distance of 100 yards or more. In cleared areas the soil in which the pupae burrow becomes hardened— resulting in the destruction of many of them. It is possible to suppress an epidemic by moving the inhabitants out of the infected area into another where there are no tsetse-flies. A practical application of this method was put into execution in the Protectorate of Uganda, with the result that an epidemic which had taken a death toll of approximately 200,000 was quickly terminated. Since it is probable that wild and domestic animals act as the chief sources from which the parasites are transmitted to man through the insect carriers, it will be necessary to consider them also in any campaign directed toward the control and prevention of sleeping sickness.[16]

Typhus Fever.—Typhus fever, which is usually, if not always, transmitted by the body louse, is a disease associated with unsanitary conditions and therefore prevails where overcrowding, destitution, famine, and squalor exist. In times past it frequently visited jails, prisons, almshouses, camps, ships, and armies. Hence its popular names: "camp fever," "jail fever," "ship fever." In the epidemic form it is chiefly communicated from one person to another through close and intimate contact. It has prevailed in various parts of Europe, Asia, Africa, and the Americas; in Europe especially in Great Britain, Ireland, and Russia. Important epidemics have prevailed in the United States on many occasions, notably in 1812, 1830, 1847, 1865, 1881, 1883, and 1893. Endemic foci exist today in Russia, the Balkan States, Poland, Galicia, Spain, Ireland, Northern Italy, Northern Africa, Mexico, and in some of the cooler areas in Asia.

Previous to 1850, typhus fever was frequently the scourge of armies. It decimated the troops of Napoleon in the retreat from Moscow and has constantly hung like a black cloud over the trails of armies. Since 1850 it has not prevailed, at least in epidemics, except in squalid and vermin-infested districts. With the outbreak of the Balkan Wars, typhus developed to grave epidemic proportions in Serbia. Typhus fever broke out in the Serbian army in 1914. By January, 1915, the epidemic had begun to spread, reaching its height in March and April. At this time as many as 9,000 cases were reported daily. The mortality was estimated to be from 30 to 60 per cent, and within 6 months' time 150,000 people perished from this disease. The American Red Cross Commission, assisted by smaller units from England, France, and Russia, were able in 6 months, by using delousing methods, to stamp out the disease. "Throughout the Great War typhus was kept under control—to burst out once more in gigantic conflagration with the breakdown of civilization in revolutionary Russia. In 1921, the whole world was menaced with an invasion more deadly than that of the Red Armies; but in Poland, where the principal battle line was set, the Polish Sanitary Administration, aided by the Epidemic Commission of the League of

<hr />

[16] Herbert H. Waite, *Disease Prevention*, 1926, pp. 50-52, 480-487. Paul de Kruif, *Microbe Hunters*, 1926, ch. IX.

Nations, established quarantine stations, disinfecting plants, and hospitals which were completely successful in checking the westward spread of the disease.''[17]

In 1900 it was shown by Moczutkowski that the virus of the disease is present in the blood. He acquired the disease by inoculating himself with blood from a typhus-fever patient. In 1909, Nicolle discovered that this disease was transmitted by the bite of the body louse; he infected a chimpanzee by subjecting it to a louse which had fed upon a typhus patient. In 1914, Hegler and Prowazek observed and described the small, ovoid, non-motile bacteria-like bodies which are the cause of typhus fever.

With knowledge of how the disease is conveyed, intelligent methods of control may be put into effect. The prevention of typhus fever requires the eradication of lice and the early diagnosis of the disease, with prompt and efficient isolation of infected persons. Knowledge of the habits and life history of the louse indicates lines along which measures for combating lice infestation in military and civil life may usefully be directed. Such measures comprise: (1) The detection of men who are infested with lice. (2) The disinfection of all clothing and bedding belonging to lice-infested men. (3) The cleansing of the man himself. (4) Cleansing of billets, etc.[18]

From the foregoing it is clear that hardly less than marvelous results have been accomplished in controlling the insect-borne diseases.

CONQUEST OF DISEASE BY VACCINES, ANTITOXINS, AND SERUMS

Some diseases which exhibited alarming epidemic proportions fifty years ago no longer occupy a prominent place in mortality statistics. Notable among them are scarlet fever, diphtheria, measles, and whooping cough. The reduced incidence of these diseases has been effected largely through the use of antitoxins, serums, vaccines, and other biological products. Since these products are made directly or indirectly from the germs, it is as if the germs were being set against themselves.

To Pasteur belongs the credit for demonstrating the principle that immunity can be produced by the injection of weakened or killed germs or extracts from dead germs. He opened the way for one of the most brilliant chapters in the history of public health, a chapter which is still in the course of being written.

[17] C.-E. A. Winslow, *Man and the Microbe*, 1924, p. 40.
[18] Herbert H. Waite, *Disease Prevention*, 1926, pp. 54-55, 445-457.

Natural Immunity.—The immunity to most diseases that are classed as contagious depends principally on antibodies in the blood. These are substances which protect the body against the germs of infectious diseases. Some persons have a great degree of natural immunity to certain diseases. For example, about half of all persons have diphtheria antitoxin in their blood in sufficient amount to protect them against ordinary modes of diphtheria infection. No person is entirely immune. An immune person is able to overcome the few germs that are taken into his body at one time during an ordinary exposure to infection, but any person will take a disease if a sufficiently large number of the germs of that disease enter the body at one time.[19]

Acquired Immunity.—An acquired immunity is *passive* when the antibodies are injected into the body, and *active* when the antibodies are produced by the body itself. Passive immunity is produced by the injection of antitoxins which are taken from another person or from lower animals. It lasts for only a few days or weeks, for the substances which are injected are foreign to the body and are soon expelled, and no new ones are produced. An active immunity may last for months or years, since the antibodies are native to the body and a new supply is continually formed by the cells.

An active immunity may be induced by (*a*) an attack of a disease; (*b*) the injection of the living germs of a disease; (*c*) the injection of the dead germs of a disease; (*d*) the injection of a toxin.

Inducing immunity by producing an attack of a disease was often practiced with smallpox before the discovery of vaccination. Some persons still follow this practice in the case of the milder forms of contagious diseases, such as mumps, measles, and chickenpox. They do this on the mistaken theory that every one must have the disease, the sooner the better.

A mild and harmless attack of a disease will protect the body as fully as will a virulent case. The body will be protected by the introduction of living disease germs whose virulence and power of growth have been diminished to such a degree that they are barely able to grow. Yet these weakened germs may equal an attack of the disease in stimulating the cells of the body to produce antibodies. A preparation of living germs used for injection into the body is called a virus. The two most common diseases prevented by the use of injections of living germs are smallpox and rabies.

[19] This and the following adapted from F. Overton and W. J. Denno, *The Health Officer*, 1920, ch. XIV.

Vaccines.—A virus does not act until the few germs that are introduced into the body have multiplied to millions. A danger in the use of living germs is that they may multiply too much; this is overcome by the use of killed germs to produce immunity. A preparation of killed disease germs used for an injection into the body is called a vaccine. Vaccines are used for the prevention and cure of diseases and for the preparation of serums.

In the nineties, effective vaccines were prepared for cholera and for typhoid fever. A good vaccine has been developed to combat plague. There is one which is extensively used but of somewhat problematical value for whooping cough, and there is promise of the development of vaccines for tuberculosis and pneumonia.

Vaccines are of doubtful value in curing a severe case of disease. The immunity produced by vaccines is generally more or less permanent, but requires time to become manifest. Therefore vaccines are commonly used for the prevention of disease rather than for cure. This difficulty can be overcome by the use of serums.

Serums.—The injection of bacterial vaccines into suitable animals causes the animals to produce far more antibodies than they need. A few ounces of their serum, injected into the human body, contain enough antibodies to immunize the individual.

A serum is either antitoxic or bacteriolytic. Two antitoxic serums are those of diphtheria and tetanus. They act only upon the toxins of bacteria, and do not destroy the bacteria themselves. Bacteriolytic serums act by dissolving bacteria. One of the most successful bacteriolytic serums is that used in treating epidemic cerebrospinal meningitis. Serums are also produced for the treatment of certain forms of pneumonia and of streptococcic infections. There are also serums of proved effectiveness against plague, dysentery, and yellow fever. A serum is potent only against the variety of bacteria with which it is produced, but if the variety of bacteria in the body is known, its serum may have great value.

"Even in the case of diseases which are not common to man and the lower animals the principles of serum therapy may be applied by the treatment of one human case with immune blood derived from another human case which has recently recovered from an attack. Such a procedure has been used with success in pneumonia, scarlet fever, measles, and mumps; and here, too, there is reason to hope for substantial new developments in the future."[20]

[20] C.-E. A. Winslow, *Man and the Microbe*, 1924, pp. 62-63.

Toxins and Antitoxins.—A poison which is produced by disease germs is usually called a toxin. There are very few true toxins, the most notable being those of diphtheria and tetanus. The bacteria of these two diseases are only slightly poisonous, but if the toxin of either disease is injected into the body, it produces the signs and symptoms of the disease.

When a toxin is injected into the tissues, it causes the cells to produce an antibody called an antitoxin. The antitoxin combines with the toxin, if any is present in the body, and renders it inert. The antitoxin which is produced in the body is the principal factor in bringing about recovery in diphtheria or tetanus. The antitoxins for these diseases may be produced in animals and then used for the prevention and cure of the diseases in man. This discovery was made by Behring and Kitasato in 1890, who demonstrated that the blood serum from an immunized animal not only protects against infection but also cures animals already suffering from the disease. When an animal receives an injection of toxin, it produces an antitoxin in excess of that required to neutralize the toxin. When the injection is repeated several times, increasing quantities of antitoxin are produced, and are contained in the blood. A horse is generally used for producing antitoxin because it forms a large quantity in proportion to its size, and also because the effect of its serum is seldom harmful to man.

The Case of Diphtheria.—One of the best examples of the effectiveness of these measures is seen in the case of diphtheria, formerly one of the most important causes of death among children. Before 1895, when the diphtheria antitoxin was introduced, tracheotomy—cutting open the windpipe—was a common though often fatal operation. The benefits accruing from the discovery of diphtheria antitoxin have been great. Though they cannot be accurately determined, owing to the lack of complete vital statistics, it can, however, be conservatively affirmed that diphtheria antitoxin has more than halved the diphtheria death-rate. This result has been obtained notwithstanding the fact that there are many individuals suffering from diphtheria who do not receive the antitoxin treatment, and there are many others in whom the treatment is not begun until the disease has existed several days. The earlier the antitoxin is given the better the results.

In 1913 Schick introduced a simple but very accurate and valuable clinical test to determine the susceptibility or immunity of individuals to diphtheria. The Schick reaction depends on the local irritant action of minute quantities of diphtheria toxin when injected intracutaneously. If antitoxin is absent in the individual's blood or is present only in amounts insufficient for protection from diphtheria, a positive reaction will appear in from twenty-four to ninety-six hours.

Methods have since been evolved to immunize individuals who are shown by a positive Schick reaction to be susceptible to diphtheria. Toxin-antitoxin vaccine is employed. Diphtheria toxin is so poisonous that in order to use it for the purpose of immunizing human beings or animals, the doses must be at first minute and only gradually increased in amount. This process consumes much time, and unless carried on with the utmost skill and patience is not wholly safe. Experiments with mixtures of toxin and antitoxin showed that the toxin could be neutralized to the extent of not being poisonous, and yet have the power to stimulate the development of antitoxin. This mixture of toxin and antitoxin, when injected into a person who is susceptible to diphtheria, changes him from a positive reactor to a negative reactor, or, in other words, renders him immune to the disease. The incidence and death-rate of diphtheria have been greatly reduced by this method. When the first registration figures became available in 1900, the diphtheria death-rate was 43.4 per 100,000; by 1926, it had been reduced to 7.5. Today the possibility of the complete elimination of diphtheria is considered imminent. More widespread application of known methods of prevention will completely conquer this scourge of childhood.[21]

THE DECLINE OF TUBERCULOSIS

Tuberculosis, the Great White Plague, used to be the leading cause of death in the United States, accounting for a tenth of all cases. It affects chiefly the young and those in the prime of life; hence its tremendous economic cost. This disease, perhaps more than any other, has been associated with unfavorable economic conditions; it is more prevalent among the poor than among the well-to-do. Improper food, bad housing and overcrowding, overwork and worry appear to lower resistance and thus encourage the spread of the infection.[22] It was formerly regarded as hereditary and no hope was held out for the person afflicted.

The first battle in the warfare against tuberculosis was won when Robert Koch in 1882 discovered the tuberculosis bacillus. The next significant achievement was the demonstration by Dr. Edward L.

[21] Herbert H. Waite, *Disease Prevention*, 1926, pp. 34, 184-198. Louis I. Dublin, *Health and Wealth*, 1928, p. 12.
[22] Harry H. Moore, *Public Health in the United States*, 1923, pp. 90-91.

Trudeau of the curative value of outdoor living and proper regimen. Compelled by tuberculosis to give up his medical practice in New York City, in 1873, he went to the Adirondack Mountains, where he cured himself and devoted his life to the study and prevention of the disease. In 1884 he founded the Adirondack Cottage Sanitarium at Saranac Lake, New York, for the treatment of incipient tuberculosis in working men and women, the first American institution attempting the climatic and open-air method of treatment of this disease. In 1894 he founded the Saranac Laboratory for the Study of Tuberculosis, the first research laboratory for the purpose in America. In 1903 the Henry Phipps Institute for the Study, Treatment and Prevention of Tuberculosis was established, and in 1905 the National Tuberculosis Association.

The control of the spread of tuberculosis involves two main items—the elimination of infection from bovine sources, and the checking of infection passing from one human being to another. The factor of bovine infection is now admirably cared for by the general pasteurization of the city milk supply. The control of the spread of tuberculosis from human sources involves two main considerations: the detection of cases of the disease in an incipient stage, and the systematic supervision and treatment of these cases, in the home and sanatorium, until the disease is arrested.

The death-rate from tuberculosis has shown a marked decline. In 1900, the first year for reliable statistics on tuberculosis in the United States, the death-rate was 195.2 per 100,000 of population. In 1910 the rate in the same geographic area (the ten original registration states and the District of Columbia) had dropped to 164.7, or 15.6 per cent in the ten-year period. In 1920 the rate in the same states was 112.0. This is 42.6 per cent less than the figure for 1900. In the second decade (1910 to 1920) the rate fell a little more than twice as rapidly as in the first decade. In 1925 the rate went down to the low figure of 82.9 per 100,000. Today more than 100,000 people, who under the old conditions would have succumbed to the disease, are kept alive each year.[23]

In connection with this decline of the tuberculosis death-rate there are two outstanding explanations. The first, espoused by most of the workers in the field of public health, ascribes the decline to the great improvement in the social and economic well-being of the general population. The lowered death-rate is due, they say, primarily to activities within human control. The campaign against tuberculosis

[23] Louis I. Dublin, *Health and Wealth*, 1928, pp. 12, 84.

was accordingly directed (1) toward finding the many individuals in the early stages of the disease, strengthening their resistance through good food, adequate rest, and outdoor living, and making them well again if possible, and (2) toward preventing their infecting other individuals. That meant the training of many physicians in the technique of diagnosis, the establishment of tuberculosis clinics and sanatoria for the care of early cases and other institutions for the more advanced cases, and the segregation of those individuals who might be a source of danger to others.

The second explanation minimizes the importance of the environmental factors in the control of tuberculosis. "It places great emphasis on the fact that the decline in tuberculosis antedates by many years the development of the tuberculosis campaign as at present understood, going back, in fact, to the early decades of the nineteenth century. Those who support this second view emphasize the all importance of the genetic—that is, the constitutional factors. They grant the universality of infection, but they insist that those who break down are a special group whose constitutions, in advance, have doomed them to tuberculosis disease. They insist, moreover, that the tendency to have tuberculosis is inherited like other physical characteristics, and that observation will discover a distinctly tuberculous stock or phthisical constitution, quite irrespective of the environment, mode of life, or any effort that man might make either to avoid infection or to build up individual resistance. A corollary of this explanation has been that hardly any of the decline to which we have called attention could have resulted from the tuberculosis campaign. It is not in the nature of the disease, this group says, to be amenable to the kind of treatment that has been given to environmental factors."[24]

Certainly the entire gain should not be ascribed solely to the tuberculosis movement. It is probable that increase in real wages of the working classes, improved working conditions in factories, and the improved well-being of the general population are more responsible than are the direct activities of the movement itself. "But, it is to the great credit of the tuberculosis campaign that so much of the enlightenment that now prevails in the relationship between employers and employees has resulted from the intelligent stimulation by health and social workers who have been interested in the control of tu-

[24] Louis I. Dublin, *Health and Wealth*, 1928, pp. 87 ff. (p. 89 quoted). This point of view is well expressed by Maurice Fishberg, "The Tuberculosis Game," *The American Mercury*, Feb., 1928, 13:50:129-137.

berculosis. The campaign of education has not been waged for naught. Anyone who is familiar with what has been accomplished in this country in the field of health education cannot fail to be impressed with the value of the work. The tuberculosis movement, be it through either its direct or its indirect influences, has made the body of American men, women, and children more resistant to the development of infection, keener to know the state of their health, more intelligent as to their needs when disease has developed, and more likely to obtain proper and sufficient care. The tuberculosis movement, therefore, stands clearly and outstandingly as a major force in what has been accomplished.''[25]

VENEREAL DISEASE CONTROL

''The venereal diseases,'' says Dr. Waite,[26] ''are a greater menace to the individual, the family, the community, the State, the World at large, and the coming generations than any other disease or group of diseases. It is not possible to estimate with any degree of accuracy the extent of the devastation which they have brought upon mankind in the past nor the toll which they are exacting at the present time. This is largely due to the fact that the existence of these diseases has been concealed and as a result the vast majority of those afflicted have freely mingled with their fellowmen, the latter neither knowing nor suspecting that they were coming into more or less intimate contact with individuals infected with a dangerous and destructive communicable disease.''

Of the two most important venereal diseases, gonorrhea is the more prevalent, syphilis the more serious. Dr. Rosenau[27] summarizes the case against each as follows:

Gonorrhea is the most constantly prevalent of all serious infectious diseases, except measles; affects all ages and classes of society; is responsible for from 6,000 to 10,000 cases of blindness in the United States; is the cause of 60 per cent of blindness of the newborn; is the cause of more than 10 per cent of all blindness; is the cause of from 60 to 75 per cent of surgical operations on the female generative organs; of 50 per cent of sterility; of many chronic diseases of the joints, bladder and generative organs; greatly decreases earning capacity; is the underlying cause of untold suffering and misery; and affects practically all prostitutes, public and clandestine. Notwithstanding, gonorrhea is a preventable disease.

[25] Louis I. Dublin, *Health and Wealth*, 1928, pp. 128-129, *Cf*. W. H. Welch, *Public Health in Theory and Practice*, 1925, pp. 44-45.
[26] *Disease Prevention*, 1926, p. 493.
[27] *Preventive Medicine and Hygiene*, 1927, pp. 62-63, 67.

Syphilis affects about 8 per cent of the total population, occurs at all ages and in all classes of society, is the cause of from 10 to 35 per cent of all insanity, and is one of the causes of mentally and physically deficient children. It is the cause of locomotor ataxia, paresis, and the chief cause of apoplectic strokes in early life, and is responsible for a large proportion of diseases of the heart and blood-vessels; is the cause of nearly half of abortions and miscarriages. Syphilis decreases the length of life about one-third; it also lowers the standard of health and paves the way for other diseases; it greatly decreases earning capacity; is the most serious cause of disruption of home and happiness, and causes untold suffering and misery. Withal, it is largely preventable and occasionally curable. The public health control of syphilis depends upon early diagnosis and facilities for prompt treatment.

Outstanding milestones in the history of the control of syphilis include the discovery in 1906 by Schaudinn of the germ of syphilis (*Treponema pallidum* or *Spirocheta pallida*), the discovery in 1907 by Wassermann of a blood test for syphilis, and the invention in 1910 by Ehrlich of salvarsan (a compound of arsenic now made in the United States under the name arsphenamine) for the treatment of syphilis. Many refinements in diagnosis and treatment have since occurred.[28]

Up to the time of the World War little attention was paid in the United States to the problem of venereal-disease control. The War made it necessary for the nation to face the problem. The government put into effect a program of preventive measures known internationally as the "American plan," which was so successful that "there was less venereal disease in the United States Army during the recent war than among the troops of any nation during any war of recent centuries."[29] Professor Winslow[30] says: "It is probable that since the beginning of time there has never been a cleaner group of young men than the American Expeditionary Force; and the reflex effect upon the civilian campaign against venereal disease was so great that I am convinced America has gained in this one direction more lives than it lost through the destruction wrought by German shot and shell."

Its effect upon the civilian campaign was first seen in the passage in 1918 of the Chamberlain-Kahn Act which provided for an allotment for the ensuing two years of $4,000,000 to the state boards of

[28] H. E. Kleinschmidt, "Milestones of Progress in the Control of Syphilis," *Journal of Social Hygiene*, Oct., 1923, 9:7:404-405.

[29] Harry H. Moore, *Public Health in the United States*, 1923, pp. 96-97.

[30] *Evolution and Significance of the Modern Public Health Campaign*, 1923, pp. 59-60.

health for the program of combating venereal diseases, and created the Division of Venereal Diseases in the United States Public Health Service and the United States Interdepartmental Social Hygiene Board. Soon afterwards most state boards of health established divisions of venereal disease, and a comprehensive program was put into effect under the leadership of the Public Health Service. The number of venereal-disease clinics was rapidly increased.

The program of venereal-disease control is known as social hygiene. It deals with such problems as the combating of the venereal diseases, the promotion of sex education, the reduction of commercialized prostitution, and other social problems growing out of sex. The measures recognized today as the essentials in a social-hygiene program consist of medical and public-health work, legal and protective action, education, and recreation.

The medical measures include the discovery, reporting, and isolation of cases, the improvement of treatment by practicing physicians, and the abolition of quacks and proprietary medicines advertised as cures for venereal diseases. The legal measures involve the enactment and enforcement of laws for the suppression of prostitution and the subscription by each applicant for marriage license that he is free from venereal disease. The dissemination of information through lectures, lantern slides, pamphlets, motion pictures, newspaper advertisements, and similar devices make up the educational measures. The education of the public regarding venereal diseases is conducted along two lines: first, concerning the diseases themselves, and second, regarding sex matters in general. The social measures consist in the provision of proper amusement and recreation. To the extent that prohibition is enforced, it is undoubtedly a factor in reducing the incidence of venereal disease.

As a result of these measures great progress has been made in the control of the venereal diseases. The conspiracy of silence has been broken, sex is being regarded as a matter for scientific study instead of being too dirty or too holy to discuss, more cases of venereal disease are being treated and prevented from infecting others, fewer persons are deliberately exposing themselves to infection.

HEALTH PROBLEMS OF THE FUTURE

The victories which have been won in the field of infectious diseases have thrown into relief hazards of another sort. The decline in recent years in the preventable diseases of youth and early maturity has resulted in a marked change in the proportion and number of

persons in middle life and old age. The life-conservation campaign of
the past quarter of a century has saved millions of people in the
early adult ages and has transferred them to those ages where they
are exposed to the effects of diseases characteristic of the advanced
years of life. The control over the external infections has resulted in
a greater interest in the defects of our internal organism. Today the
emphasis is shifting from the infectious diseases of youth to the
degenerative conditions of middle life, such as heart disease, the
hardening of the arteries, Bright's disease, the nervous disorders,
and cancer. There is good evidence that these conditions, taken together, are increasing.[31]

The eight diseases or groups of diseases which, in the United States
Registration Area in 1927, most often resulted in death, were, in
order of frequency:

Diseases of the heart.
Pneumonia and influenza.
Cancer.
Nephritis.
Cerebral hemorrhage and softening of the brain.
Tuberculosis.
Congenital malformations and diseases of early childhood
    (excluding diarrhea and enteritis).
Diarrhea and enteritis.

Heart Disease.—Heart disease is now first in the list of causes of
death. It is also first in the amount of damage it does through producing disability and invalidism. In the United States the deaths
of nearly 200,000 persons are ascribed to it each year. If the present
situation should continue unchecked, 1 in every 5 of the population
now living will eventually succumb to this disease. Altogether,
2,000,000 persons in the United States, or about 2 per cent of the
entire population, suffer from some form of heart trouble; many of
them cannot engage in productive activities and are, to a greater or
lesser degree, a drain on the resources of the people. At least 15 of
every 1000 school children have already acquired some definite disorder of the heart. At least 30 of every 1000 men and women of
working age must reckon with heart disease as a disability in work
or a handicap in their pleasures. Ten per cent of the total bed capacity
of our general hospitals is used year in and year out for the care
of patients with heart disease. Twenty-five per cent of all visits to

[31] Louis I. Dublin, *Health and Wealth*, 1928, pp. 63, 138-139.

city dispensaries are made by heart patients. Of all serious and ultimately fatal diseases those of the heart are of the longest duration.[32] Proper medical and nursing care of such patients is expensive. With the possible exception of certain diseases of the mind, heart diseases cause the most persistent chronic handicap to self-support. The annual reports of charitable organizations show strikingly the prominence of heart disease as a primary cause of dependence. It has more than replaced tuberculosis, which is being relegated to a position of decreasing importance. The problem is an outstanding one in contemporary medicine.

In response to the pressure from clinic and social agency for relief, there developed in 1915 the beginning of the campaign against heart disease. Facts were the first necessity. "The four main causes of heart diseases are the general infections, chiefly rheumatic fever and syphilis; poisonings by alcohol, tea, coffee and tobacco; poor bodily habits, physical indolence, obesity, occasional extreme exertion without sufficient training; and congenital defects, those errors of development in the prenatal months of the infant which leave the heart imperfect at birth. Of all heart diseases which come under systematic hospital or out-patient care either in public or private practice, from 70 to 95 per cent are due to general infections."[33] The tuberculosis campaign slogan—communicable, preventable, curable—applies also to heart disease. The commonest causes of heart disease, rheumatism and syphilis, are properly considered communicable. Many heart diseases are entirely preventable. Some are wholly curable. In heart disease as in practically every other preventable or curable disorder, success in treatment and, in large measure, in prevention depends upon the earliness of correct diagnosis—often while the patient is still unaware of evidences of disorder.

Two lines of attack are imperative in the campaign against heart disease. The first affects the individual; the second concerns the community as a whole. The campaign as it applies to the individual is largely one of personal hygiene designed to avoid heart impairments. Its principal methods are protection against infections which often leave heart disease in their wake, saner and more temperate living, and periodic health examinations. The latter is the key to the problem so far as the individual is concerned. It is a striking fact that most persons who have heart disease have discovered this in the

[32] Louis I. Dublin, *Health and Wealth*, 1928, pp. 63-64. Haven Emerson, "Heart Disease," *The Survey*, Nov. 1, 1924, 53:3:114.

[33] Haven Emerson, "Heart Disease," *The Survey*, Nov. 1, 1924, 53:3:115.

most accidental and casual fashion. Usually the cases are found as the result of a life insurance examination or through the health examination of children at school or by industrial physicians in examining applicants for employment.

The contribution the community can make is many-sided. It includes the dissemination of knowledge of right living and the inculcation of good habits of life through the agency of the schools and the other channels of public education, the provision of heart clinics with skilled examiners and adequate equipment, and the establishment of sanatoria and convalescent homes. Suitable work must also be found for cardiac patients. Only the organized agencies of the community can provide the foregoing services.[34]

Following the start made in New York in 1915 in campaigning against heart disease, associations have been established in a number of cities. In general they have a central office of information, special dispensary classes for diagnosis and home supervision of indigent or wage-earner patients, and beds for convalescent care of heart patients. There are now 140 special cardiac clinics in operation throughout the United States and Canada, 48 of them being in New York City. In 1924 the campaign assumed a national aspect through the incorporation of the American Heart Association. It is a medium for the expression of opinion in heart-disease prevention and for common interest in study and report of results, a central agency for popular education, and a force for coördinating the separate movements scattered throughout this country and Canada.[35]

Cancer.—Cancer is now one of the half dozen leading causes of death, and appears to be increasing, especially among those of advancing years. Dublin[36] believes that "the increase in the death rate from cancer can no longer be explained away on the score of improved diagnosis, or of changing age and race constitution of populations. The facts point unmistakably to a significant increase in the cancer rate."

Before science explained the true nature of tuberculosis there were a number of popular misconceptions concerning the disorder, misinformation which had to be dispelled. The same holds true today regarding cancer. Authentic information about cancer and its control was given to the public in 1926 by the International Symposium on Cancer Control. A resolution was adopted which furnished prac-

[34] Louis I. Dublin, *Health and Wealth*, 1928, pp. 77-79.
[35] Haven Emerson, "Heart Disease," *The Survey*, Nov. 1, 1924, 53:3:117.
[36] *Health and Wealth*, 1928, p. 134.

tical facts and sound working opinions to serve as the basis of the campaign against cancer. The preamble to the resolution reads: ''Although the present state of knowledge of cancer is not sufficient to permit of the formulation of such procedures for the suppression of this malady as have been successfully employed for the control of infectious diseases, there is enough well established fact and sound working opinion concerning the prevention, diagnosis, and treatment of cancer to save many lives, if this information is carried properly into effect.'' The resolution contains fifteen numbered paragraphs, of which the following are probably the most significant.[37]

The causation of cancer is not completely understood, but it may be accepted that for all practical purposes cancer is not to be looked upon as contagious or infectious.

Cancer itself is not hereditary, although a certain predisposition or susceptibility to cancer is apparently transmissible through inheritance. This does not signify that, because one's parent or parents or other members of the family have suffered from cancer, cancer will necessarily appear in other persons of the same or succeeding generations.

Persons who have cancer must apply to competent physicians at a sufficiently early stage in the disease, in order to have a fair chance of cure. This applies to all forms of cancer. In some forms early treatment affords the only possibility of cure.

The public must be taught the earliest danger signals of cancer which can be recognized by persons without a special knowledge of the subject, and induced to seek competent medical attention when any of these indications are believed to be present.

The most reliable forms of treatment, in fact, the only ones as yet justified by experience and observation, depend upon surgery, radium, and X-rays.

Efforts toward the control of cancer should be made in two principal directions: (1) the promotion of research in order to increase the existing knowledge of the subject, and (2) the practical employment of the information which is at hand. Even with our present knowledge many lives could be saved which are sacrificed by unnecessary delay.

A number of cities now have clinics for cancer; health departments and associations are urging medical examination; campaigns of educational publicity are being conducted. Much of this program has been promoted by the American Society for the Control of Cancer, founded in 1913. Up to the present, the dissemination of knowledge has been the chief occupation of the Society.[38] The campaign against

[37] American Society for the Control of Cancer, *Cancer Control*, 1927, pp. 327-329.
[38] George A. Soper, ''The Organized Movement for the Control of Cancer in America,'' in *Cancer Control*, 1927, pp. 148-154.

cancer is just beginning. "The efforts which have been made during the past ten years to deal with cancer are, in the light of our figures [of its increase] relatively puny. Where we ought to be spending millions for research, we are spending thousands; where we have a few hundred physicians trained to recognize and treat cancerous states, we need thousands. The recognized facilities for the care and treatment of hopeful cases are pitiably inadequate and unorganized. What are intelligent laymen, physicians, and surgeons going to do about the huge cancer hazard which confronts the average citizen today?"[39]

Mental Disease.—Few people realize the vast domain in medicine that is filled by mental disease. At each succeeding census since 1890 there has been a notable increase in resident patients in institutions for mental disease. A considerable part of the apparent disproportionate increase of mental disease may be accounted for by the more general use of hospitals in recent years and the increase in number and capacity of such hospitals. The transformation of asylums and other custodial institutions into hospitals for the treatment of mental disease is a factor of great importance. The confidence of the people in the efficacy of the treatment afforded has been strengthened, and much of the prejudice against institutional treatment of the insane has disappeared. The marked trend of population from country to city, where the incidence of mental disorder is higher, may account in part for the increased number of patients. The progress of public-health work in reducing the death-rate and adding to the average length of life has also been an important factor. The shifting in the age distribution of the general population from the younger to the more advanced age groups—in process during the past forty years and still obtaining—has had marked influence on the prevalence of mental disease. Since the rate of mental disease increases with advancing years, the general population of today would naturally have a higher rate of mental disease than would the younger population of former census periods.[40]

In 1923 there were 267,617 patients in hospitals for mental disease. The number of mental patients in institutions almost equals the total number of patients in all the general hospitals in the United States. In the Army and Navy, mental diseases have for many years occupied first or second place in discharges for disability. States that make full

[39] Louis I. Dublin, *Health and Wealth*, 1928, p. 148.
[40] U. S. Bureau of the Census, *Patients in Hospitals for Mental Disease*, 1923, pp. 13-14.

provision for the care of mental diseases in public institutions spend more for this purpose than they do for any other except education.[41]

A movement to improve the treatment of the insane and to prevent mental disease resulted from the publication by Clifford W. Beers, in 1907, of a remarkable autobiography, *A Mind That Found Itself.* The mental-hygiene movement was founded by Mr. Beers as a result of his own experiences in the dark territory of insanity. In 1908 he organized the Connecticut Society for Mental Hygiene, the first association for the sole purpose of combating mental disease and promoting mental health. A year later he founded the National Committee for Mental Hygiene, of which he is Secretary. He has since been active in extending the movement throughout this and other countries.

The mental-hygiene movement has opened a new era with respect to knowledge of mental disorders and to the treatment of the insane, and has presented a more accurate and practical point of view from which to regard the feeble-minded. Essentially concerned with prevention— the prevention of mental and nervous disorders and of mental deficiency—and with the promotion of mental health, it is part of the public-health movement and is destined, as Mr. Beers suggests, to take a place in the public mind as prominent as that held during recent years by the campaign against tuberculosis.

"The old idea of an asylum for the insane as a place of confinement for abnormal persons is now being replaced by the modern idea of the hospital for the insane as a curative establishment for the sick. This change has been furthered by legislation, which has required transference from country to state care, removal of the insane from prisons, and the segregation of the criminal, the incurable, and the epileptic insane and of the feeble-minded, while amelioration of the condition of the insane in hospitals has been marked by the decline of mechanical and medicinal restraint. The growing belief that mental diseases are curable and the spread of scientific conceptions concerning them have also been influential factors in bringing about improved conditions. In this work a large part has been played by the national and local mental hygiene societies through their programs of education. The ordinary layman has been informed concerning these once horrifying disorders."[42]

The fostering of mental hygiene research and the establishment of mental-hygiene clinics are among other important steps. The mental-hygiene movement, like most social movements, appears to have passed

[41] Clifford W. Beers, *A Mind That Found Itself*, 1924, p. 360.
[42] Maurice R. Davie, *Social Aspects of Mental Hygiene*, 1925, p. 2.

from the curative stage to the preventive and constructive; emphasis upon the care of those who are already sick or otherwise in need has been shifted toward precautionary measures against the recurrence of sickness and toward the positive achievement of health and happiness. Improvement in the treatment and care of the mentally ill or mentally defective has been expanded to include both the prevention of nervous and mental disorders and of mental defect and also the conservation of mental health.

THE GAIN IN AVERAGE DURATION OF LIFE

An outstanding result of the public-health movement has been the great decline in the death-rate which has occurred especially during the last 50 years. The facts for New York City are fairly typical of what has happened in other large cities of the country. In 1875, the death-rate was 28.3 per 1000; in 1925, it was 11.5, or a reduction of 59.4 per cent. A better measure of the improvement is perhaps the gain in average duration of life. In 1880, the average life-span was about 40 years in New York City; and most likely in other urban centers in the United States. It is now 55 or 56 years, a gain of about 15 years in less than a half-century. The greatest gains have been achieved recently. In 1901 a baby born in the United States Registration Area might expect to live 49.24 years; this expectation of life has now risen to 57.74 years. The present figures are not accidental but the result of a definite trend which has been fairly continuous for a whole generation, reflecting the work of a new force in the life of the people.[43]

"Your grandparents," says Dr. Emerson,[44] "if they were city dwellers, lost one child in four before it was a year old, while you and your friends maintain the silver ratio of sixteen living to one lost. Let us get on a gold basis of not less than twenty-five babies living for every one we lose before our children learn to mock us for our backwardness. . . . Those same grandparents of ours fifty years ago saw four hundred of their friends and neighbors carried off by tuberculosis where less than a hundred are lost today. . . . Within the experience of men and women still active and responsible for health services we have reduced our deaths in cities in this country to a third. A death rate of twelve per thousand is common in our cities instead of thirty-six."

It is estimated that among primitive races and among the ancients,

[43] Louis I. Dublin, *Health and Wealth*, 1928, p. 11.
[44] "The Robust City," *The Survey*, Nov. 1, 1925, 55:3:123-124.

the average duration of life was probably not more than 20 years. This does not mean that a long life was impossible for certain individuals, but rather that longevity was relatively rare. In India, at the present time, the expectation of life is not more than 25 years. The great majority of the population die either in infancy, childhood or early adult life; few reach old age. But under conditions of Western civilization, life is much more favorable and large numbers survive to old age. Even before the beginning of the public-health era, in 1840, the expectation of life was about 40 years in England and in New England. Today it is in advance of 58 years in this country. Half the population born today may expect to reach the age of 66; and one-quarter may hope to reach the age of 77. A little over a hundred years ago half the population could expect to reach only 18 years of age and a quarter 52 years.[45] A resolution of the American Public Health Association in 1922 states that there is nothing "inherently impracticable or extravagant in the proposal that within the next 50 years as much as 20 years may be added to the expectancy of life which now prevails throughout the United States."[46] "If we were but willing to utilize the knowledge which we have of preventive medicine, in the life of the American people, we should raise the expectation of life from its present point of 57 or 58 years to close to 65. The discovery of a method to control cancer and a few other obscure diseases would further increase this expectation appreciably. But, even if we discount these future discoveries and limit ourselves to the application of such knowledge as we now have and which is only waiting to be applied, an average duration of life of 65 years is an entirely possible one for the American people. The people of New Zealand are very close to such an achievement at the present time. What they can do, we with our superior resources can do likewise."[47]

THE REWARD OF PUBLIC-HEALTH WORK

In the ringing slogan of Dr. Hermann M. Biggs, whom Dr. Haven Emerson calls our first health statesman, "public health is purchasable; within certain limitations a community can determine its own death rate."[48]

In 1921 the city of Salem, Ohio, suffered an epidemic of typhoid fever which in round numbers cost the community half a million dol-

[45] Louis I. Dublin, *Health and Wealth*, 1928, pp. 149-150. Paul Popenoe, "Back to Methuselah?" *The Scientific Monthly*, Dec., 1927, 25:6:535.
[46] Harry H. Moore, *Public Health in the United States*, 1923, p. 11.
[47] Louis I. Dublin, *Health and Wealth*, 1928, p. 15.
[48] See C.-E. A. Winslow, *The Life of Hermann M. Biggs*, 1929.

lars. The epidemic resulted from an attempt of the city fathers to save $1,500 by substituting a tile pipe for an iron one in the construction of the sewer system.

For the past 15 years a business organization, the Metropolitan Life Insurance Company, has spent an average of more than a million dollars a year in its public-health campaign for industrial policyholders. This vast investment has reaped a return of 200 per cent, resulting from the lowered death-rate which the Company attributes to that campaign. In 1911 the Metropolitan instituted a program of health education and of nursing service for its millions of industrial policyholders. The Company has expended altogether over 20 million dollars in this campaign. It has increased its annual budget for welfare work in response to an ever-increasing demand for service and also to the increasingly favorable results of the work done. The death-rate among the industrial policyholders has declined fully twice as fast as it has in the general population. As a result, the expectation of life of this group of workers and their families has increased by 9 years since 1911, whereas the corresponding increase in the general population is about 5 years. Health work, when properly undertaken and adequately financed, pays by every test of a modern business organization.[49]

These two bits of evidence demonstrate "that the cost of sickness and premature death is very great; that public-health procedures are an effective means of preventing much sickness and death; and that an extension of public-health facilities will pay large dividends to any community which will organize and administer them effectively."[50]

Despite the accomplishments of the public-health movement, there is still room for improvement. Public-health work today is in its infancy in spite of its achievements and the demonstration of its power, since about one-third of the deaths which occur each year could be prevented by the proper application of present knowledge. Our death-rate from causes related to maternity is the highest of any civilized country. "Most American communities still have political health administrations, inadequately financed, inadequately manned. Less than fifty cents per capita probably represents the total expenditure of the American people for public health. The money spent for medical service is almost altogether for the care of disease and not for its prevention. The relationship were better reversed."[51]

[49] Louis I. Dublin, *Health and Wealth*, 1928, pp. 13-14.
[50] Louis I. Dublin, "Health Work Pays," *The Survey*, Nov. 1, 1925, 55:3:125.
[51] Louis I. Dublin, *Health and Wealth*, 1928, p. 16.

Conclusion.—Thus, in his war against the microbe, man has won the initial battle. He has discovered the nature and weakness of his adversary. In general he has the proper ammunition to win a more complete victory. He has enlisted his scientists, physicians, nurses, and public-health workers as the standing army; he must now draft the general public as a militia, and direct the shot and shell in a continuous barrage which will eventually work toward the eradication of this dangerous foe.

PART IV

EDUCATION

CHAPTER XV

EDUCATION IN A CHANGING CIVILIZATION

IT IS a fundamental principle of social evolution that, as the basic conditions of life change, institutions must change accordingly. The law of all life is adjustment. New life-conditions call for new methods and new types of adjustment. All social institutions are affected, although in varying degrees of directness, by the stress toward adaptation.[1] The most recent, radical changes calling forth new types of adjustment we have characterized as industrialization and urbanization. In earlier chapters illustrations have been given of the adjustments being effected in various fields—city planning, traffic control, housing, public health. Here attention will be directed to certain significant changes in public education. The fundamentally social viewpoint presented is that effective education is preparation for life. The work of the schools is to fit people for social conditions that are continually changing; hence the work of the schools must correspondingly change. "Social growth is never complete; it is especially rapid in our generation. Public education must grow and change as fast as social conditions make such changes necessary. It can never be complete, crystallized, perfected."[2] Education, however, is ultraconservative, and selective changes have come only after prolonged struggle. There is much cultural lag.[3] Yet, when viewed from the perspective of its history, American education today contrasts sharply with the situation a century or two ago.

1. ESTABLISHMENT OF THE AMERICAN PUBLIC-SCHOOL SYSTEM

Historically, the educational system in this country began with private, endowed, and parochial schools. Free, common, elementary schools and public high schools and colleges came at a much later date. "Schools, with us, as with the older European countries from which our early settlers came, arose as children of the Church. From

[1] See A. G. Keller, *Societal Evolution*, 1915, ch. VIII. A. G. Keller, *Starting-Points in Social Science*, 1923, chs. I, II.
[2] Leonard P. Ayres, *The Cleveland School Survey, Summary Volume*, 1917, p. 60.
[3] *Cf.* W. F. Ogburn, *Social Change*, 1922, pp. 200-212.

instruments of religion they have been gradually changed into instruments of the State."[4]

Colonial Attitudes toward Public Education.—The most prominent characteristic of Colonial schooling was the predominance of the religious purpose in instruction. Grammar schools and colleges existed mainly to insure a supply of learned ministers for service in church and state. Although the church motive in education and church control generally prevailed, the various colonies held different views regarding public responsibility for education. Three type attitudes toward public education arose. They later materially shaped the educational development of the different states during the early part of our national history.

1. The Compulsory-Maintenance Attitude.—This was characteristic of the New England colonies with the exception of Rhode Island. At first, the typical English educational system was established; that is, private instruction in reading and religion in the homes and by the master of apprentices, Latin grammar schools in the larger towns to prepare boys for the colony college, and an English-type college to prepare ministers for the churches. As in England, the system was voluntary and clearly subordinate to the church.

It early became evident, however, that these voluntary efforts on the part of the people and the towns would not be sufficient to insure that general education which was required by the Puritan religious theory. Accordingly, the leaders in the Puritan Church appealed to what was then their servant, the state as represented in the Colonial legislature, to assist them in compelling parents and masters to observe their obligations. The result was the famous Massachusettts Laws of 1642 and 1647, compelling the towns to establish schools and parents to send their children to school to learn to read and to receive instruction in religion.

The Law of 1642 directed the selectmen of each town to ascertain, from time to time, if parents and masters were attending to their educational duties; if all children were being trained "in learning and labor and other employments which may be profitable to the commonwealth"; and if the children were being taught "to read and understand the principles of religion and the capital laws of the country." The officers were empowered to impose fines on those who failed to give proper instruction or to report when required. This law of 1642 is remarkable in that, for the first time in the English-

---

[4] Ellwood P. Cubberley, *Public Education in the United States*, 1919, p. 13.

speaking world, a legislative body representing the state ordered that all children should be taught to read.

This law was supplemented in 1647 by further order of the General Court of Massachusetts Colony, which required every town having 50 householders to provide a schoolmaster to teach all children "as shall resort to him, to write and reade"; and which furthermore required every town of 100 families to "set up a gramar schoole, yᵉ master thereof being able to instruct youth so farr as they may be fited for yᵉ university," under a penalty of five pounds sterling for failure to do so. This was the first time among English-speaking people that the state asserted the right to require communities to establish and maintain schools.

These two Massachusetts laws sprang from the conviction that all children should be educated, and that the parent, community, and state should be jointly charged with this responsibility. They embodied the principles upon which modern compulsory education rests, and became the basis of the public-school system of Massachusetts and the prototype of similar state systems throughout the United States. They represent "the very foundation stones upon which our American public school systems have been constructed."[5] "It is important to note here," states Mr. Martin,[6] the historian of the Massachusetts public-school system, "that the idea underlying all this is neither paternal nor socialistic. The child is to be educated, not to advance his personal interests, but because the state will suffer if he is not educated. The state does not provide schools to relieve the parent, nor because it can educate better than the parent can, but because it can thereby better enforce the obligation which it imposes."

The idea that it is the duty of the state to compel all children to acquire a minimum of education was of slow growth, and little or no progress therein was made for the next two hundred years. It is only in comparatively recent times, as we shall later see, that all states have adopted laws embodying this principle.

2. *The Parochial-School Attitude.*—This was the policy of the middle colonies, where, unlike New England, no sect was in a majority. Church control by each denomination was, as a result, considered to be the most satisfactory plan, and hence no appeal to the state was made by the churches for assistance in carrying out their religious purposes. The clergymen were usually the teachers in the parochial

[5] *Ibid.*, p. 18.
[6] George H. Martin, *The Evolution of the Massachusetts Public School System*, 1894, p. 16.

schools which were established. In a few of the larger towns private pay-schools were opened. These schools, like the church services, were conducted in the language of the different immigrant groups. Girls were educated as well as boys. Emphasis was placed on reading, writing, counting, and religion, rather than upon any form of higher training. The result was the development in Pennsylvania, and to some extent in the other middle colonies as well, of a policy depending upon church and private effort for educational advantages. Education, aside from certain rudimentary and religious instruction, was left largely for those who could afford to pay for the privilege.

3. *The Pauper-School Non-State-Interference Attitude.*—In the southern colonies, the development of social classes, in contrast to the New England type of democracy, made common schools impossible, and the lack of any strong religious motive for education led to the adoption of English practices instead of the development of distinctively Colonial schools. The tutor in the home, education in small private and select pay-schools, or education in the mother country for the sons of the well-to-do planters were the prevailing methods adopted among the wealthier people, while the poorer classes were left with only such advantages as apprenticeship training and the few pauper schools established by the churches might provide. There was no state interest in the problem of education except to see that orphans and children of the very poor were properly apprenticed and trained in some useful trade. Virginia stands as the clearest example of this third type of Colonial attitude toward education.

Professor Ellwood P. Cubberley,[7] from whom much of this account is adapted, comments on these early American attitudes toward education as follows:

The seventeenth century witnessed the transplanting of European ideas as to government and religion and education to the new American colonies, and by the eighteenth century we find three clearly marked types of educational practice or conceptions as to educational responsibility established on American soil.

The first was the strong Calvinistic conception of a religious State, supporting a system of common schools, higher Latin schools, and a college, both for religious and civic ends. This type dominated New England, and is best represented by Massachusetts. From New England it spread westward, and deeply influenced the educational development of all States to which New England people migrated. It was the educational contribution of Cal-

---

[7] *Public Education in the United States,* 1919, ch. II (pp. 23-24 quoted). See also R. G. Boone, *Education in the United States,* 1889, chs. I-III.

vinism to America. Out of it, by the later separation of Church and State, our modern state school systems have been evolved.

The second was the parochial school conception of the Dutch, Moravians, Mennonites, German Lutherans, German-Reformed Church, Quakers, Presbyterians, Baptists, and Catholics. This type is best represented by Protestant Pennsylvania and Catholic Maryland. It stood for church control of all educational effort, resented state interference, was dominated only by church purposes, and in time came to be a serious obstacle in the way of state organization and control.

The third type, into which the second type tended to fuse, was the attitude of the Church of England, which conceived of public education, aside from collegiate education, as intended chiefly for orphans and the children of the poor, and as a charity which the State was under little or no obligation to assist in supporting. All children of the upper and middle classes in society attended private or church schools, or were taught by tutors in their homes, and for such instruction paid a proper tuition fee. Paupers and orphans, in limited numbers were, for a limited time, provided with some form of useful education at the expense of either the Church or the State.

These three types of attitude toward public education became fixed American types, and deeply influenced subsequent American educational development.

The Battle for Free State Schools.—The first half-century of our national life may be regarded as a period of transition from church to state control of education. The movement for state schools was furthered by the growth of cities, the rise of manufacturing, the extension of the suffrage, and other fundamental social changes which were reflected in a great educational awakening. The main battle for tax-supported, publicly controlled and directed, and non-sectarian common schools was fought during the second quarter of the nineteenth century. In 1825 such schools were the distant hope of statesmen and reformers; in 1850 they were becoming an actuality in almost every northern state. The twenty-five years intervening marked a period of public agitation and educational propaganda, of many hard legislative fights, of many bitter contests with church and private-school interests. Cubberley[8] believes that "excepting the battle for the abolition of slavery, perhaps no question has ever been before the American people for settlement which caused so much feeling or aroused such bitter antagonisms."

The two most outstanding leaders in the struggle for a state system of schools were Horace Mann and Henry Barnard. Mann in particular pointed the way to many subsequent reforms in the adminis-

[8] *Public Education in the United States,* 1919, p. 119.

tration of public education; to Barnard we owe a special debt as our first great educational scholar. The accomplishments of these conspicuous leaders during the formative period of American education are listed in the following biographical sketches.[9]

Horace Mann (1796-1859), a prominent Brown University graduate, lawyer and member of the State Senate, became professionally interested in education in 1837, when he accepted the position of Secretary of the recently established Massachusetts State Board of Education. He soon became the acknowledged leader in school organization in the United States. Everywhere he preached the doctrine of liberal taxation for public education, with the result that during the twelve years of his secretaryship the appropriations for public education were more than doubled, salaries of teachers greatly increased, and a full month added to the length of the school term. He organized the first three state normal schools in America and some of the earliest teachers' institutes. He labored continually to improve teaching methods, and worked especially for the introduction of Pestalozzian reforms and the substitution of the word-method in teaching reading for the slow and wasteful alphabet method. He edited the *Massachusetts Common School Journal*, wrote a careful report on schoolhouse hygiene, introduced school libraries throughout the State, and stimulated the development of the high school. In his hands the printed "school returns," first required by the law of 1826, became "powerful instruments in educating the public." His vigorous condemnation of the district system of school administration, to which he devoted his fourth *Report*, contributed to its ultimate abandonment. His twelve carefully written *Reports* on the condition of education in Massachusetts and elsewhere, with his intelligent discussion of the aims and purposes of public education, occupy a commanding place in the history of American education, while he will always be regarded as perhaps the greatest of the "founders" of the American system of free public schools. No one did more than he to establish in the minds of the American people the conception that education should be universal, non-sectarian, and free, and that its aim should be social efficiency, civic virtue, and character, rather than mere learning or the advancement of sectarian ends. Under his practical leadership an unorganized and heterogeneous series of community school systems was reduced to organization and welded together into a state school system, and the people of Massachusetts were effectively recalled to their ancient belief in and duty toward the education of the people.

Almost equally important, though of a somewhat different character, was the work of Henry Barnard (1811-1900) in Connecticut and Rhode Island. A graduate of Yale and, like Mann, educated for the law, Barnard turned aside to teach and became deeply interested in education. In 1839 he became

---

[9] Adapted from Ellwood P. Cubberley, *Public Education in the United States,* 1919, pp. 166-168. *Cf.* George H. Martin, *The Evolution of the Massachusetts Public School System,* 1894, pp. 160-185.

the first Secretary of the Connecticut State Board of Commissioners for Common Schools; this office he held until 1842. In 1839 he organized the first teachers' institute in America which met for more than a few days, and he used this new instrument extensively to awaken the teachers of the State to proper conceptions of their work. He established the *Connecticut Common School Journal* to disseminate his ideas. He also organized school libraries, and urged the establishment of evening schools. He strove to improve the physical condition of the schools by writing much on schoolhouse construction. He studied the "school returns," and used the statistical data to arouse interest. In 1843 he was called to Rhode Island to examine and report upon the existing schools. From 1845 to 1849 he acted as State Commissioner of Public Schools there, where he rendered a service similar to that previously performed in Connecticut. In addition he organized a series of town libraries throughout the State. From 1851 to 1855 he was again in Connecticut, as principal of the newly established state normal school and *ex-officio* Secretary of the Connecticut State Board of Education. He now rewrote the school laws, increased taxation for schools, checked the power of the districts, and laid the foundations of a state system of schools. In 1855 he began the editing of his famous *American Journal of Education*, a vast encyclopaedia of educational information which finally reached thirty-one volumes. From 1858 to 1860 he served as President of the University of Wisconsin, and from 1867 to 1870 as the first United States Commissioner of Education.

The strategic points in the struggle for common schools were the securing of tax support, the elimination of the pauper-school idea, making the schools entirely free, the establishment of state supervision in lieu of the ineffective district system, and the elimination of sectarianism. Following this victory came the successful battle to extend the system upward, to include the public high school and the state university.

The Battle to Extend the System Upward.—The common schools which had been established in the different states by 1850 supplied an elementary education to the children of the masses. Education in advance of this training was in semi-private institutions—the academies and colleges—in which a tuition fee was charged. An effort was now made to extend the public system so as to provide to pupils, free of charge, a more complete education than the common schools afforded.

The first American school of higher training was the Latin grammar school, with a limited curriculum and exclusively college-preparatory ends. It belonged to the early period of class education. It was largely displaced, during the first half of the nineteenth century, by the more American academy, with its more practical studies and open to both sexes. Many academies were founded by philanthropic bequests; many became semi-state institutions through the state aid extended to them. Not being bound up with the colleges, as the earlier Latin grammar schools had largely been, the academies became primarily independent institutions, taking pupils who had completed the common-school course and giving them an advanced education in modern languages, the sciences, mathematics, history, and the more useful subjects of the time, with a view to rounding out their studies and preparing them for business life and the rising professions. They marked a transition from the aristocratic Latin grammar school of Colonial times to the more democratic high school of today. The demand for an upward extension of the public-school system to provide academy instruction for the poor as well as the rich now made itself felt. "As the colonial Latin grammar school had represented the educational needs of a society based on classes, and the academies had represented a transition period and marked the growth of a middle class, so the rising democracy of the second quarter of the nineteenth century now demanded and obtained the democratic high school, supported by the public and equally open to all, to meet the educational needs of a new society built on the basis of a new and aggressive democracy."[10]

The first high school in the United States was established in Boston, in 1821, but the real beginning of the American high school as a distinct institution dates from the Massachusetts law of 1827, which required the establishment of a high school in every town having 500 families or over, and specified the subjects which should be taught. From Massachusetts the movement for free public high schools spread to New York and to other states in the East, though it was not until after 1865 that any marked development took place. The democratic West soon adopted the idea and established high schools as soon as cities developed and the needs of the population warranted. In the South the main high-school development dates from relatively recent times. The period of most rapid growth in high school enrollment the country over has occurred since 1905.

The crowning phase of this struggle of democracy for a system of state-supported schools was the creation of the state university. "Up to about 1870 the provision of higher education, as had been the case earlier with the provision of secondary education by the academies, had been left largely to private effort. There were, to be sure, a few state universities before 1870, though usually these were not better than the denominational colleges around them, and often they maintained a non-denominational character only by preserving a proper

[10] Ellwood P. Cubberley, *Public Education in the United States*, 1919, p. 190.

balance between the different denominations in the employment of their faculties. Speaking generally, higher education in the United States before 1870 was provided very largely in the tuitional colleges of the different religious denominations, rather than by the State. Of the 246 colleges founded by the close of the year 1860, but 17 were state institutions, and but two or three others had any state connections.'' The great period of state-university foundation came after 1860, and that of state-university expansion after 1885. The state university is today found in every new state and in some of the original states. ''For a long time small, poorly supported by the states, much like the church colleges about them in character and often inferior in quality, one by one the state universities have freed themselves alike from denominational restrictions on the one hand and political control on the other, and have set about rendering the service to the State which a state university ought to render.''[11]

College Education for Women.—Another development, thoroughly indicative of the democracy of the West, was the opening of collegiate and professional instruction to women. In 1800 women could not enter any college in the United States. In 1821 Emma Willard had opened a seminary for girls at Troy, New York, and in 1837 Mount Holyoke Seminary (later college) was opened by Mary Lyon in Massachusetts. These mark the beginnings of higher education for women. By 1840 there were but seven institutions of all kinds for the higher education of women, but by 1860 the number had increased to sixty-one. Perhaps half of these later developed into colleges for women. After the Civil War, during which so many women filled places, especially teaching positions, formerly held by men, the colleges began to open their doors somewhat generally to women students. This movement was greatly furthered by the development of state universities. Every state west of the Mississippi River, except Missouri, made its state university coëducational from its first opening, and of those east of the same river all but three soon followed the lead of Indiana (1868), Michigan, and Illinois (1870) in opening their doors freely to women students.[12]

Federal Aid to Education.—From early days, public education in the United States has been encouraged and assisted by the Federal Government. The federal educational policy has been closely related to the federal land policy. The Ordinance of the Northwest Territory (1787) was the starting-point of both. In adopting the Ordinance for

[11] *Ibid.*, chs. V-VII (pp. 204 and 207 quoted).
[12] *Ibid.*, pp. 209-210.

the government of that part of the territory lying north of the Ohio, Congress provided that "Religion, morality and knowledge, being necessary to good government and the happiness of mankind, schools and the means of education shall forever be encouraged." This provision, and the ultimate settlement of the territory largely by people of New England stock, determined the future attitude toward public education of the states eventually erected therefrom.

In addition to the federal land grants for "the support and maintenance of public schools" in all the public-land states, there have been five great types of federal aid to education.

1. The federal land grants for the founding, support, and maintenance of state universities in all the thirty-one public-land states.

2. The federal land grants for the establishment of colleges of agriculture and mechanic arts in every state (Morrill Act of 1862) and the subsequent and current grants of money for their support (Morrill Act of 1890 and the Nelson Amendment, 1907). In 1887 Congress passed the Hatch Act, which established an experiment station at each of these colleges. Additional funds for research, especially for agricultural research, have subsequently been made available through the Hatch Adams and Purnell Acts.

In none of these cases does the grant of federal money carry an obligation to the states to appropriate further funds. In the following instances of federal subsidies, the state or local community must provide an amount of money equal to the federal grant.

3. The Smith-Lever Act of 1914, designed to encourage agricultural extension.

4. The Smith-Hughes Vocational Education Act of 1917, which created the Federal Board for Vocational Education and provided for an annual appropriation (increasing to $7,000,000) to aid and encourage the states to carry forward education in agriculture, trades and industries, and home economics, and to prepare teachers of these vocational subjects.

5. The National Civilian Vocational Rehabilitation Act, approved in 1920, which provides for grants of money from the federal treasury to promote the reëducation of disabled workers.

It is the land-grant colleges and vocational education that receive the major portion of federal monies. There are today 69 land-grant colleges—52 for white students and 17 for Negroes.

As a result of this federal aid, public education has been popularized and brought favorably to the attention of the citizens and statesmen in every generation. Federal encouragement and promotion of education have not involved any effort on the part of the United States Government to control the details of educational administration. Federal aid has stimulated the states and local communities to expand and develop their own systems of public education.[13]

Compulsory School Attendance.—It is not enough to have free public education. To make public education effective and universal, attendance at school must be required by law. The first legislation embodying this principle, as we have already seen, was the Massachusetts Laws of 1642 and 1647; but these in time fell into disuse. Compulsory attendance had to wait the establishment of free public schools. The first modern compulsory-attendance law was enacted by Massachusetts in 1852. The problems of formulating effective compulsory-education laws have confronted legislators and school officials since that time to the present. The success which has crowned the efforts in this direction has been truly remarkable. America's profound faith in education is the best explanation of this advance.

The lead of Massachusetts was followed in the next four decades by the northern and western states. Most of the southern states have provided for compulsory attendance since the opening of the present century. The following table gives the date of enactment of the first compulsory attendance law in each state.

DATE OF ENACTMENT OF FIRST COMPULSORY ATTENDANCE LAW IN EACH STATE

State	Year	State	Year	State	Year
Massachusetts	1852	Illinois	1883	Maryland	1902
District of Columbia	1864	North Dakota	1883	Missouri	1905
Vermont	1867	South Dakota	1883	Tennessee	1905
New Hampshire	1871	Montana	1883	Delaware	1907
Michigan	1871	Minnesota	1885	North Carolina	1907
Washington	1871	Nebraska	1887	Oklahoma	1907
Connecticut	1872	Idaho	1887	Virginia	1908
Nevada	1873	Colorado	1889	Arkansas	1909
New York	1874	Oregon	1889	Louisiana	1910
Kansas	1874	Utah	1890	Alabama	1915
California	1874	New Mexico	1891	Florida	1915
Maine	1875	Pennsylvania	1895	South Carolina	1915
New Jersey	1875	Kentucky	1896	Texas	1915
Wyoming	1876	West Virginia	1897	Georgia	1916
Ohio	1877	Indiana	1897	Mississippi	1918
Wisconsin	1879	Arizona	1899		
Rhode Island	1883	Iowa	1902		

[13] John A. Keith, "Results of Federal Aid to Education," *Social Forces*, Dec., 1926, 5:2:305-314. Arthur J. Klein, "Education," *American Journal of Sociology*, May, 1930, 35:6:1063-1071. Walton C. John, *Agricultural and Mechanical Colleges*, U. S. Bureau of Education Bulletin, 1920, No. 8. Walter J. Greenleaf, *Land-Grant Colleges and Universities*, U. S. Bureau of Education Bulletin, 1930, No. 28. Ward W. Keesecker, *Digest of Legislation providing Federal Subsidies for Education*, U. S. Bureau of Education Bulletin, 1930, No. 8. The U. S. Bureau of Education has recently changed its name to Office of Education, but for the sake of uniformity the old title is maintained in the references given here.

This development may be summarized by decades as follows:

NUMBER OF COMPULSORY-ATTENDANCE LAWS PASSED BY
DECADES

1850–59	1	1890–99	7
1860–69	2	1900–09	9
1870–79	13	1910–19	7
1880–89	10		

The above table discloses that compulsory education took root in the seventies and eighties, and that nearly half of the state laws have been passed since 1890. This clearly shows that the idea of an education for everybody is very recent. The profound effect of the adoption of the principle of universal education will be indicated below.

The compulsory-attendance laws now in force show considerable variation.[14] The main items in their provisions may be summarized as follows, with the District of Columbia treated as a state.

The average minimum age for compulsory attendance is 7.36 years. Two states make the age of 6 the minimum; twenty-eight states the age of 7; eighteen the age of 8; one state the age of 9.

The average maximum age for compulsory regular school attendance is 16. Five states require attendance until 18; five until 17; thirty-one until 16; three until 15; five until 14.

The average number of years of regular school attendance required is 8.65. One state requires 12 years; one 11 years; eight states require 10 years; twenty-one require 9 years; twelve require 8 years; two require 7 years; and four require 6 years.

The average minimum annual school term required is 7.23 months. One state requires 38 weeks; eight states require 9 months; eighteen require 8 months; eleven require 7 months; six require 6 months; one requires 5 months; two require 4 months; one requires 3 months; and one state (Alabama) has no minimum school term.

Exemptions from compulsory school attendance are granted in certain respects. The minimum amount of education necessary to exempt from school attendance is the completion of the high-school course in 4 states, completion of the elementary school course in 39 states, while 6 states do not specify the amount necessary. The average amount of education required throughout the United States for labor permits under the present laws is equivalent to the fifth grade. Twenty-two states have provisions for exemptions, under certain conditions, on account of distance from school. Eighteen states exempt for certain poverty reasons. Fifteen states have indefinite provisions relating to exemptions (for reasons satisfactory to local school authorities, etc.).

[14] Ward W. Keesecker, *Laws Relating to Compulsory Education*, U. S. Bureau of Education Bulletin, 1928, No. 20. *Review of Educational Legislation*, 1929-1930, Bulletin, 1931, No. 20, pp. 25-26.

Eight state laws provide, subject to certain limitations, exemption from school attendance in order to attend or comply with church observances.

The compulsory attendance laws vary not only in requirements but in the degree to which they are enforced. That the administration of our educational system is not perfect is indicated by the statistics compiled in the United States Bureau of Education for the school year 1919-20. These disclose approximately 7,000,000 of the school population (5 to 17 years of age inclusive) who were not enrolled in public or private schools. This situation goes far to explain the presence of approximately 1,000,000 illiterate persons, between 10 and 25 years of age, reported by the 1920 census. Whether any improvement has occurred since then cannot be ascertained until the 1930 census returns on school attendance and illiteracy are available.

A comparison of earlier compulsory education laws with those more recently enacted discloses certain tendencies, the most important of which are the following:

To lengthen the period of compulsory education by making it effective at an earlier and to a later age. The establishment of kindergartens and compulsory attendance for part-time, continuation, or evening schools are, in part, an expression of this tendency.

To increase the annual required school attendance.

To extend the compulsory provisions to include various handicapped children; also to provide parental schools for delinquents.

To require more education for exemption and for labor permits.

To provide public relief to indigent children and subject them more completely to the attendance requirements.

To provide transportation for children not living within the usual walking distance from school.

The general effect of these tendencies has been to bring more children under the provisions of compulsory education and to subject all children to a longer period of formal schooling. The laws reflect a profound belief in universal education. Indeed, this has become one of our most deeply rooted national mores.

2. REORGANIZATION OF THE SCHOOL SYSTEM TO MEET NEW CONDITIONS

The general structure of the American educational system may be said to have taken form toward the close of the nineteenth century. Free, tax-supported, and state-controlled common schools had been generally established, and attendance at them, except in the South, had been made compulsory. Public high schools and universities had been provided. The famous American educational ladder, typifying the seemingly democratic nature of the public-school system, was completed. This was the eight-four-four system, composed of the eight-year elementary school, the four-year secondary school, and the four-year college. The way, it was held, was open to any child to obtain, at public expense, an education that began with the first grade of the elementary school and terminated with the college. This democratic organization was favorably compared with the European two-class school system. In many European countries the elementary school has generally been regarded not as a place of preparation for the secondary school, but as furnishing a distinct and measurably complete scheme of education designed especially for the children of the laboring and artisan classes. The secondary school, on the other hand, is intended for children of prosperous parents who plan to fit themselves for the professions or to enter the civil service. The origin and fundamental distinction between the two systems is a social one.

In the American school system the curriculum was essentially the same for all students, and was dictated in the last analysis by the college. The elementary school regarded its primary function to be preparation for the high school. The latter measured its success by the number of pupils it prepared for college. This was the view despite the fact, as shown by Ayres,[15] that the general tendency of American cities was to carry all their children through the fifth grade, to take half of them to the eighth grade, and 1 in 10 through high school, and, we might add, only 1 in 100 through college. Education was geared up, not for the 99, but for the 1. It was an excellent example of the tail wagging the dog. Our educational system, it was complained in the nineties, was the joint product of indiscriminate borrowings from other countries and the operation of chance influences rather than the fruit of a careful analysis of the nature of children and the needs of society. Certainly, it had grown up in a more or less haphazard way, it had not been worked out systematically.

Beginning roughly about 1890, our public-school system has been faced with increasingly serious problems. These have arisen in the main from the extraordinary growth of the school population and the changing social conditions. The first brought diversification as well as added numbers, and the great influx of children from all social classes and practically all levels of ability gave rise to innumerable problems of method, curriculum, and organization. The changing social conditions rendered the traditional curriculum maladjusted to

[15] Leonard P. Ayres, *Laggards in Our Schools*, 1909, p. 4.

the new community requirements. The importance of these two factors demands close examination.

Increasing Enrollments.—School enrollments, especially in high school and college, have increased tremendously since the nineties. The elementary schools have been less affected. For almost a generation the number of children attending elementary schools has done little more than keep pace with the growth of population. This is, of course, due to the fact that before the close of the last century the elementary school, except in the South, was already reaching practically all children of appropriate age. The development of the kindergarten and more recently of the nursery school, involving the extension of elementary education downward into what have been called the preschool years, has added many thousands to the enrollment, but the total number in the elementary schools is so great that these additional pupils constitute but a small proportion. The enrollment in secondary school and in college has increased at an unprecedented rate. In the 36 years from 1890 to 1926 the population of the continental United States increased 86 per cent; the college and university enrollment increased about 550 per cent; and the secondary-school enrollment increased almost 1,100 per cent. Although the first public high school was organized in 1821, this type of school did not enroll to exceed 10 per cent of the children of high-school age until about 1905. Within the next ten years another 10 per cent were enrolled. The 30 per cent mark was reached about 1921, and the 40 per cent mark about 1923. By 1930 more than one-half of the population of ages 15 to 18 inclusive was actually enrolled in secondary schools. High-school attendance is almost as common today as it was rare a generation ago. An expansion of the institutions of higher education, which may follow a course similar to that pursued by the secondary schools since 1890, began after the close of the World War. The number of persons attending colleges, universities, and professional schools of college grade (including normal schools and teachers' colleges) in 1890 was but 157,000. By 1900 this number had grown to 238,000; by 1910, to 356,000; by 1920, to 597,000. Four years later, in 1924, the enormous total of 911,000 was reached. This is almost precisely the secondary-school enrollment for 1910. Since then the million mark has been passed.

The latest statistics show approximately 30,000,000 persons enrolled in the educational institutions of the nation. Of this huge multitude, amounting to one-fourth of the total population, about 20 millions are attending public kindergarten and elementary schools, 5 millions are registered in public high schools, some 4½ millions in private and special schools, and 1½ millions are pursuing studies in college, university, and professional school.[16]

Changing Social Conditions.—More fundamental in its effect on education is the tremendous social change that has occurred. Within the past century the character of American society has been transformed. The change has been especially striking since the decade 1880-90, which marks a turning-point in the social and economic history of the United States. Before the eighties, we were largely a simple, homogeneous, agricultural population living in sparsely settled communities. We are now a complex, heterogeneous, urban population crowded together in a modern industrial society. Even rural life has been transformed; it has in a sense been urbanized. The more significant factors in this social change we have already discussed in the first two chapters. Among them are the expansion of industry and commerce, the growth of manufacturing, increasing use of machinery, improvement in the means of communication and transportation, increasing concentration of the population in urban centers, growing cosmopolitanism as a result of the increased volume and changed character of immigration, the increasing participation by Negroes in the life of American society, the rise of the wage-earning class, the changing position of women and their entrance into gainful occupations, changes in the organization and functions of the family, increasing complexity of the social organization, the advancement of science and the accumulation of knowledge and their applications to the affairs of men.

In short, "the obvious fact is that our social life has undergone a thorough and radical change. If our education is to have any meaning for life, it must pass through an equally complete transformation. This transformation is not something to appear suddenly, to be executed in a day by conscious purpose. It is already in progress. Those modifications of our school system which often appear (even to those most actively concerned with them, to say nothing of their spectators) to

[16] George S. Counts, "Education," *American Journal of Sociology*, July, 1928, 34:1:177-181. Frank M. Phillips, *Statistics of Public High Schools*, 1927-28, U. S. Bureau of Education Bulletin, 1929, No. 35, pp. 1-4. Carl A. Jessen, *Secondary Education*, U. S. Bureau of Education Bulletin, 1929, No. 22. *Biennial Survey of Education*, 1924-26, U. S. Bureau of Education Bulletin, 1928, No. 25. Robert and Helen Lynd, *Middletown*, 1929, ch. XIII. W. D. Bontwell, "Fourth of Nation is now in School," New York *Times*, Sept. 20, 1931. Walton C. John, *College and University Education*, U. S. Bureau of Education Bulletin, 1931, No. 20.

be mere changes of detail, mere improvement within the school mechanism, are in reality signs and evidences of evolution.''[17]

The Problem of Adjustment.—Two facts that must be held in mind when developing an adaptive educational system—two sociological tests by which an educational system must be judged—are, first, adaptation to the life background of the children and to individual differences, and second, adaptation to the future needs of the pupils and the requirements of the communities in which they will live. Both these conditions have been radically affected by the extraordinary growth of the school population and the changed social conditions, and the schools have been brought face to face with new difficulties. The school body today, especially in the secondary and higher schools, is no longer the selected unified group it once was. It is drawn from every walk of life, it is extraordinarily cosmopolitan, it shows the widest variation in attitudes and aptitudes, in abilities and interests. If we are dedicated to the proposition of educating everybody, we must at once recognize the tremendous range of individual differences and provide a highly differentiated type of training to meet the requirements of all. To the traditional eight-four-four system there must be added many new types of schools adapted to the needs of the great mass of pupils. The adult life which these pupils will lead in the modern complex industrial society calls for new types of preparation, new subject-matter of instruction, to fit them for new occupations and a changed social life. Much work of vocational content must be introduced. The traditional curriculum, which arose as an adjustment to the social and economic conditions of an earlier time, is not adapted to our changed civilization nor to a democratic society where the ideal is universal education. The freer and more complex a society becomes, the more essential is education for all classes to prepare them for their part in the life of the community.

The Work of John Dewey.—The foremost interpreter, in educational terms, of the great social and industrial changes through which we have passed, and the one who has done more, since 1895, to develop and propound an educational philosophy suited to the changed and changing conditions in our national life, is John Dewey,[18] for many years head of the School of Education at the University of Chicago, but more recently Professor of Philosophy at Columbia Uni-

---

[17] John Dewey, *The School and Society*, 1915, pp. 26-27. *Cf.* William H. Kilpatrick, *Education for a Changing Civilization*, 1927.
[18] See his *The School and Society*, 1915; *Democracy and Education*, 1920; *The Schools of Tomorrow*, 1915 (with Evelyn Dewey); and some of his essays in *Characters and Events*, 1929.

versity. "His work, both experimental and theoretical, has tended both to psychologize and socialize American education; to give to it a practical content, along scientific and industrial lines; and to interpret to the child the new social conditions of modern society by connecting the activities of the school closely with those of real life. Believing that the public school is the chief remedy for the ills of society, he has tried to change the work of the school so as to make it a miniature of society itself. Social efficiency, and not mere knowledge, he conceives to be the end, and this social efficiency is to be produced through participation in the activities of an institution of society, the school. The different parts of the school system thus become a unified institution, in which children are taught how to live amid the complexities of modern social life." For example, he writes regarding the introduction of manual-arts work:

We must conceive of work in wood and metal, of weaving, sewing, and cooking, as methods of living and learning, not as distinct studies. We must conceive of them in their social significance, as types of the processes by which society keeps itself going, as agencies for bringing home to the child some of the primal necessities of community life, and as ways in which these needs have been met by the growing insight and ingenuity of man; in short, as instrumentalities through which the school itself shall be made a genuine form of active community life, instead of a place set apart in which to learn lessons.[19]

"Education, therefore, in Dewey's conception, involves not merely learning, but play, construction, use of tools, contact with nature, expression, and activity, and the school should be a place where children are working rather than listening, learning life by living life, and becoming acquainted with social institutions and industrial processes by studying them. The work of the school is in large part to reduce the complexity of modern life to such terms as children can understand, and to introduce the child to modern life through simplified experiences. Its primary business may be said to be to train children in coöperative and mutually helpful living. The virtues of a school, as Dewey points out, are learning by doing; the use of muscles, sight and feeling, as well as hearing; and the employment of energy, originality, and initiative. The virtues of the school in the past were the colorless, negative virtues of obedience, docility, and submission. Mere obedience and the careful performance of imposed tasks he holds to be not only a poor preparation for social and industrial efficiency, but

[19] John Dewey, *The School and Society*, 1915, p. 11.

a poor preparation for democratic society and government as well. Responsibility for good government, with us, rests with all, and the school should prepare for the political life of tomorrow by training its pupils to meet responsibilities, developing initiative, awakening social insight, and causing each to shoulder a fair share of the work of government in the school."[20]

Conservatism in Education.—Education, true to its character, has been slow to adjust to the new conditions. A fundamental criticism to be leveled against current schooling is "the persistence, in the body of what is taught, of traditional material which is irrelevant to present conditions—subject-matter of instruction which though valuable in some past period is so remote from the perplexities and issues of present life that its mastery, even if fairly adequate, affords no resource for discriminating insight, no protection against being duped in facing the emergencies of to-day. From the standpoint of this criterion of education, a large portion of current material of instruction is simply aside from the mark."[21]

The colleges, being far removed from the problems of the masses, have been ultra-conservative. In the past they have to a large extent contented themselves with shaping their materials by traditional patterns. "They have not been highly sensitive to the fact when these patterns became or threatened to become obsolete. Even in the professions and technical fields of education relatively less attention has been paid to the life occupation of students than the manufacturer pays to the services that his product will render. The arts college has frequently repudiated all concern with the means by which its graduates shall earn their living. More important still, the colleges have seldom studied the society in which the student will live in order to determine the elements of knowledge and character which, in his world, will make for personal happiness, rich experience, and social usefulness. They have rested content in the faith that studies derived from the medieval period are still necessary to make life useful and happy in an age of cheap printing, swift transportation, machine production, and universal public education."[22] University leaders themselves are most emphatic in the statement of their realization of these maladjustments. Dean Hawkes, of Columbia University, for instance, sums up his critical judgment of colleges as follows: "There is no

[20] Ellwood P. Cubberley, *Public Education in the United States*, 1919, pp. 359-360.

[21] John Dewey, *Characters and Events*, 1929, II, 779.

[22] Arthur J. Klein, *Higher Education, Biennial Survey, 1926-28*, U. S. Bureau of Education Bulletin, 1929, No. 11, pp. 1-2.

doubt in my mind that the American college has failed more signally in relating the student's education to the kind of life that he is going to live than in any other direction.''

Many colleges and universities are now recognizing these facts and are taking measures to adjust their work to present conditions of living and of employment. They are also showing concern over student reaction to the curriculum. ''The content of instruction given in the colleges, as well as in the lower schools, has been largely imposed upon students without any very real reference to the student's own conception of values. This is perhaps unavoidable to a degree. On the other hand, the usefulness of much material studied is so remote and unreal that the colleges themselves have had difficulty in making out a case for it. An attempt was made at Vassar two years ago to determine why college students study. The most important factors were interest in the subject and realization of the value of the work for the future.''[23] No one doubts that understanding by the student of the economic and personal usefulness of his work would transform his attitude toward his college course. Since the colleges now wish to take advantage of this factor in the teaching process, modifications of both curricula and methods, in adjustment to the life activities of the present social order, may be expected.

Reorganization of the School System.—Although the school has lagged in adjusting to changing conditions, many modifications of the school system have taken place or are now occurring. Teaching methods have been changed, special classes introduced, old curricula revised and new ones inaugurated, the school system reorganized, and new schools created. The most marked changes have taken place in secondary education. The high-school curriculum has been altered from one almost classical in character to several curricula containing much vocational work. The regular high school has been reorganized into junior and senior levels. The junior-high-school movement is essentially a downward extension of the secondary school to include one or more years of the traditional elementary school. It also means an enrichment of the program of studies and the introduction of less formal methods into these years. Trade schools, commercial high schools, and other types of vocational schools have been introduced. Secondary education has also been expanded upward to include the first two years of the traditional college. The junior college as an in-

[23] Arthur J. Klein, *Higher Education, Biennial Survey, 1926-28,* U. S. Bureau of Education Bulletin, 1929, No. 11, pp. 3-4. *Cf.* A. B. Crawford, *Incentives to Study; a Survey of Student Opinion,* 1929, chs. VII, VIII.

dependent two-year unit has been established, and the regular college and university have been expanded by the addition of new departments, divisions, and schools. The following diagram illustrates some of the more important respects in which the traditional high school and college have been modified.[24]

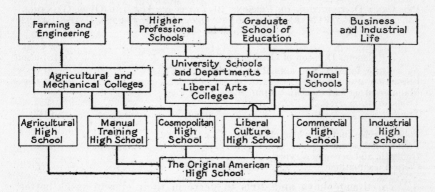

In short, the whole structure from top to bottom has been modified. Schooling suited to different tastes and abilities and offering an equal opportunity to all to prepare for their life work is being provided. American education is becoming more truly democratic. In contrast with the traditional eight-four-four system, offering only academic instruction, stands the complex and highly differentiated system of today.

3. VOCATIONAL EDUCATION

One of the most significant adaptations of the public-school system to modern social conditions is the development of a vocational-education program; that is, education for agricultural, commercial, industrial, home-making, and professional callings. It represents an effort to make the public-school system democratic in fact as well as in name —adapted to the needs of all the various groups enrolled. It also implies a fuller recognition of individual differences, which are fundamental to a consideration of the types of training that should be provided—differences not only in native intelligence and mental alertness, but also in attitudes, aptitudes, and opportunities relative to life occupational interests as they are conditioned by economic and other environmental circumstances. If the school is to be adapted to the

[24] Adapted from Ellwood P. Cubberley, *Public Education in the United States*, 1919, p. 419.

background and the future needs of its pupils, it cannot neglect to prepare them along vocational lines. What their future occupations will be is indicated by the federal census reports enumerating and classifying the occupations of those gainfully employed. The situation in 1920 was as follows:

PER CENT DISTRIBUTION OF PERSONS 10 YEARS OF AGE AND OVER GAINFULLY EMPLOYED IN EACH GENERAL DIVISION OF OCCUPATIONS, FOR THE UNITED STATES, 1920

General Division of Occupations	Per Cent Distribution
Agriculture, forestry, and animal husbandry	26.3
Extraction of minerals	2.6
Manufacturing and mechanical pursuits	30.8
Transportation	7.4
Trade	10.2
Public service (not elsewhere classified)	1.9
Professional service	5.2
Domestic and personal service	8.2
Clerical occupations	7.5

"To educate boys and girls to perform their chosen tasks better, to understand the relation of their particular work to the whole, to know what their labor is worth and demand a proper return for it, and to broaden their horizon so that both their money and their leisure time may be spent for the things that are most worth while— this is the task of vocational education."[25]

Need of Vocational Education.—Preparation for vocations is essential to individual and national efficiency and welfare. But why should the public schools undertake to give this training? They are not the traditional agency. Other agencies than the school have long been responsible for vocational education. The home was the first great instrumentality to this end. It was later supplemented by the apprenticeship system. But the home, the shop, and other means of participation in productive industry are no longer effective. The rise of industrialism, the increase of knowledge and of specialization have rendered them obsolete. The old apprenticeship system, under which boys worked in small shops for a term of years and learned a trade in an all-around way, broke down with the development of the factory system, with large-scale production, extensive use of machinery and minute subdivision of labor. Within recent years, some large manufacturing concerns have established apprenticeship schools to train their own workmen. In adaptation to modern methods of industry,

[25] *Report of the Commission on National Aid to Vocational Education,* 63d Congress, 2d Session, House of Representatives, Document No. 1004, 1914, I, 26-27. *Cf.* David Snedden, *Vocational Education,* 1920, chs. I-IV.

these schools are quite different from the old-style apprenticeship system. They are, however, few in number and affect only an insignificant percentage of the youth entering industry. The majority of young people who have taken up some mechanical pursuit have left school after satisfying the minimum requirements of the compulsory-attendance law, without having had any industrial training, and getting none later. Usually they have been placed at some simple machine operation task and kept there. They have found little opportunity to get experience in different branches, to acquire the general mechanical knowledge that is essential to advancement. This can be obtained only in school. The increasing specialization of modern industry is unfavorable to an all-around development for those who take part in it. Unless boys and girls acquire some general knowledge of industrial processes and their interrelations, before they become wage-earners, there is little chance of their ever acquiring such knowledge. The result has been that the young people have knocked about for a few years and finally settled down to some low grade of skilled or semi-skilled work far below what they would be able to do if they had had adequate training in school. This has been wasteful of human labor and promotive of industrial and social unrest. The skilled trades are relatively undersupplied with competent workmen, whereas unskilled and especially factory employments are relatively oversupplied. It is significant that a large proportion of the foremen and highly skilled workers in American industry are immigrants who have been trained in European trade schools.

The Commission on National Aid to Vocational Education, created by act of Congress, approved January 20, 1914, to investigate the problem of vocational education and to report on the desirability and feasibility of national aid for the promotion of vocational training, found that there were, in 1910, some 26,900,000 men and women engaged in agriculture and in manufacturing and mechanical pursuits alone, of whom only 1 per cent were adequately trained for the work they were doing. In this whole country there were fewer trade schools of all kinds than existed in the little German kingdom of Bavaria, with a population not much greater than that of New York City. There were more workers being trained at public expense in the city of Munich alone than in all the larger cities of the United States.[26]

The Smith-Hughes Vocational Education Act.—Pursuant to the recommendations of the Commission, Congress in 1917 passed the

[26] *Report of the Commission on National Aid to Vocational Education,* 63d Congress, 2d session, House of Representatives, Document No. 1004, 1914, I, 17.

Smith-Hughes Vocational Education Act. This law created the Federal Board for Vocational Education, charged with the administration of the act, and provided for appropriations ultimately aggregating 7 million dollars annually to be made available for coöperation with the states accepting the terms of the act, in promoting vocational training in agriculture, in trades and industries, in home economics, and in the training of teachers for these vocational subjects. Each state must match the federal money dollar for dollar. The courses must be given in public schools, must be for those over 14 years of age, must be of less than college grade, and must be primarily intended for those who are preparing to enter or have already entered a trade or useful industrial pursuit. Both full-time and part-time classes are provided for.

The Smith-Hughes Act marks a milestone in the history of vocational education in the United States. Prior to the passage of this act, only 8 of our 48 states (Massachusetts, Connecticut, New York, New Jersey, Pennsylvania, Indiana, Wisconsin, and California) had made any provision for vocational education. Only 25,000 students were in vocational industrial schools in the United States at that time—less than 0.10 per cent of the workers. For the year ending June 30, 1930, the 48 states and local communities, including the Territory of Hawaii, spent $3.04 of their own money for vocational education for every dollar spent by the Federal Government. There were 1,064,303 persons enrolled in public vocational schools and classes organized under the provisions of state plans as approved by the Federal Board for Vocational Education, at a total cost of nearly $30,000,000.[27] Had we depended upon isolated state and local action, it would have been at least a generation, and probably longer, before anything approaching a national system of vocational education would have been evolved.

Types of Vocational Schools.—A great variety of vocational schools and courses have come into existence in recent years, as the public-school system has been modified in response to the new demands. Some of the more important types are briefly described below.

1. Prevocational Schools or Courses.—These are designed to give to boys and girls between the ages of 12 and 15, during part of each day, some intensive work in manual arts and home-making subjects and some instruction along industrial and commercial lines, in an effort to discover their natural bent for vocational education, and to give

[27] *Fourteenth Annual Report of the Federal Board for Vocational Education,* 1930, pp. 3-6.

them a better foundation for vocational courses, to be taken up later, than is commonly furnished by the regular school work. Manual-arts courses include projects in a variety of activities such as wood working, metal working, painting, drawing, printing, and electricity. The girls are taught such subjects as designing, millinery, dress-making, cooking, and applied art.

Manual arts were originally introduced into American schools— first the high school, then the elementary school—in the eighties, being advocated particularly for the industrial classes. They soon came to be regarded, however, as being of advantage to all children, and as a substitute for the valuable informal training along these lines formerly obtained in the home, on the farm, and in the community. More and more manual-arts work has become recognized as a part of the general education program and not a form of special education. Such work contrasts sharply with vocational courses, which are coming to be more strictly for employment purposes, enrolling those students who should have training preparatory for entering upon employment in some specific trade. Manual training is rarely controlled by the motive of vocational training, and it rarely results in any recognizable form of vocational efficiency. It furnishes opportunities for educational development and creates additional experiences favorable for the discovery of aptitudes and interests. It is of prevocational rather than vocational value. The emphasis of instruction in manual-arts courses is shifting from that of skill in the use of tools and machinery to that of industrial intelligence and developmental experiences, and general, elementary, fundamental, manipulative abilities for general education values, including guidance. The work coming under this objective is a responsibility of the general education program.[28]

The growth of the junior-high-school movement, which dates from about the beginning of the present century, has been accompanied by a very material increase in the manual-arts work. This is due, first, to the philosophy of the junior high school, which emphasizes the need for providing for individual and group differences, for exploration and discovery of aptitudes and interests, and for an enriched curriculum of general education; and second, to the flexibility of the instructional organization which more easily permits the introduction of shop

[28] Frank M. Leavitt and Edith Brown, *Prevocational Education*, 1915. Frank M. Leavitt, *Examples of Industrial Education*, 1912, chs. X, XI. Paul Hanus, *The Beginnings in Industrial Education*, 1908. David Snedden, *The Problem of Vocational Education*, 1910, pp. 10-18, 42-46. Maris M. Proffitt, "Industrial Education," *Biennial Survey of Education, 1924-26*, U. S. Bureau of Education Bulletin, 1928, No. 25, ch. VII; *Biennial Survey of Education, 1928-30*, U. S. Bureau of Education Bulletin, 1931, No. 20, ch. IV.

courses. No vocational training as such is given in the junior high school, but large opportunities are offered for practical arts training which may help toward vocation-finding. Its work in this respect is thus prevocational.

In the commercial field, an increasing number of junior high schools are offering junior business training courses. If the present trends continue, the time is not far distant when junior business training and commercial geography will be the outstanding leaders in the junior high schools of the small communities, and junior business training, elementary office practice, and typewriting in the larger communities. In the development of the junior business training course, the administrators are seeking a general business course in harmony with the objectives of the school. The leaders in the social sciences point to the need of general business information for all. Those interested in vocational guidance consider the course as a subsidiary step in the guidance program. Those who study the drop-out tables and junior commercial occupation surveys emphasize the need of helping the pupils who leave school early. Practically all consider the course as prevocational for those who later enter the commercial training courses of the senior high school. Gradually there is developing general agreement concerning the objectives and content.

Besides motivating the school work on the vocational side, the junior high school serves many other functions. It is a partial solution to the problem of articulation between units in the educational system. It concludes elementary and initiates secondary education. Bridging the gap between the elementary and the high school, and thereby inducing pupils to remain in school a longer time, has been one of its avowed purposes. How well it is achieving this objective cannot be definitely stated, but it holds the possibility of making the path of education easier. In 1928, there were 1,403 separately organized junior high schools in the United States, enrolling 839,388 pupils, and in addition 2,429 junior-high-school departments in connection with senior high schools (the junior-senior organization), enrolling 741,941 pupils.[29]

Both the reorganized high school and the regular high school show an adaptation to changing social conditions in the expansion of the

[29] Leonard V. Koos, *The Junior High School*, 1920, ch. II. David Snedden, *Vocational Education*, 1920, pp. 339-351. W. T. Bawden, *Vocational Education*, U. S. Bureau of Education Bulletin, 1919, No. 25, pp. 16-17, 23-26. Maris M. Proffitt, *Industrial Education*, U. S. Bureau of Education Bulletin, 1929, No. 21, p. 3. J. O. Malott, *Commercial Education*, U. S. Bureau of Education Bulletin, 1929, No. 26, p. 17. Carl A. Jessen, *Secondary Education*, U. S. Bureau of Education Bulletin, 1929, No. 22, pp. 14-18.

curriculum, especially in the addition of subjects of prevocational value. Information regarding enrollment by subject in public high schools has been collected by the Bureau of Education since 1890. During that first year, 1890, data were assembled showing enrollment in nine subjects, namely, Latin, Greek, French, German, algebra, geometry, physics, chemistry, and general history, which subjects, with English, comprised almost the entire high-school curriculum at that time. The expansion of the high-school program enables high schools now to report enrollments in about 250 different subjects. Prominent among the new subjects introduced are agriculture, home economics, art and drawing, manual training, social sciences, and commercial subjects.[30] In some instances, out of these special subjects and courses in high school have evolved separate schools more definitely vocational in nature, such as the agricultural, manual-training, technical, household-arts, and commercial high schools.

2. Trade Schools.—Sharply distinguished from the courses and schools mentioned above are trade schools, which undertake to teach trades in their entirety, to turn out skilled mechanics. In the former schools the educational motive is predominant; in the latter, the bread-and-butter motive controls. The first are broadly conceived and leave the way open to higher training in agricultural and mechanical colleges, in scientific schools and technical institutes. The trade school, on the other hand, is a finishing school, and its curriculum is narrow and highly specialized.

The trade school is of long standing in Western Europe, but until recently it was little known here and for the most part was outside the public-school system. The father of trade schools in the United States was Colonel Auchmuty, who founded the New York Trade School, in 1881, to teach the building trades. The aim was the attainment of working skill in the shortest possible time. By 1900 some half dozen schools of the trade or industrial type had been established privately in different parts of the country. The first American trade school for girls was the Manhattan Trade School, started in 1902 in New York City by philanthropic effort. Its purpose was to train the youngest and poorest wage-earners to be self-supporting as soon as possible. The work of this school did much to awaken public interest in trade education. In 1910 the school was made part of the free public-school system of the city.[31]

[30] Frank M. Phillips, *Statistics of Public High Schools, 1927-28*, U. S. Bureau of Education Bulletin, 1929, No. 35, pp. 7-14.
[31] Mary S. Woolman, *The Making of a Girls Trade School*, 1909. Ellwood P. Cubberley, *Public Education in the United States*, 1919, pp. 412-415.

The majority of the trade schools in the United States have from the first been privately conducted. These schools today fall into two classes—the short-course and the long-course trade schools. The first are operated for profit. They advertise to teach a trade—almost any trade—in a few months. The long-course trade schools generally owe their existence to philanthropic endowments. They give academic as well as trade instruction, and their courses cover several years' work.

Public provision for trade instruction in the United States dates from 1906 when Massachusetts led the way by creating a state commission on industrial education, with power to superintend the creation and maintenance of industrial schools for boys and girls, and appropriated state aid therefor. In 1907 Wisconsin enacted the first trade-school law, authorizing the creation of industrial schools by the cities of the state. The Milwaukee School of Trades, established earlier by private effort, was now taken over and made a part of the city school system, and a number of trade schools were organized in other cities. In 1909 New York likewise permitted the organization of trade schools in cities. A few other states made similar provision, but the greatest stimulus to trade instruction, as to vocational education in general, came, as we have seen, with the passage of the Smith-Hughes Act of 1917. By 1930 there were 618,674 persons enrolled in federally aided trade and industrial schools.

A number of special problems have arisen with the establishment of trade training which will have to be worked out by the process of experimentation and selection. Industrial education has the task of harmonizing the work of the school with that of industry. The traditions of the school are all intellectual; that is, in the past all attention has been directed toward the solving of problems which are largely logical or bear on memory and mental habit. The traditions of the shop are those of training the worker's mind and hands in such a way as to turn out in a given unit of time the maximum product of a certain grade of quality. The school has a tendency to overvalue method, the shop to overvalue results. The education of the industrial worker must then be one that will meet first of all the requirements of the shop—speed and accuracy, which depend upon knowledge of the approved methods of shop practice, which is a constantly changing factor; and secondly, the requirements of the community, as represented in the school, that the worker understand what he is doing, why he does it, the relation of his work to that of other workers —in short, what may be called the cultural side of his work. The school has in the past stood largely for this broadness, or at least has attempted to satisfy the demand that the individual shall know more than what is necessary for mere economic survival. The worker's broader knowledge of the trade or industry is ultimately of distinct advantage to the community as a producing group. Industry itself gains by this breadth.

A serious difficulty encountered in the establishment of trade schools is that of securing satisfactory teachers. Either academic school teachers must be asked to teach trades or mechanics must be asked to teach school. The former will tend to emphasize method, the latter to stress results. The combination of a good teacher and a good mechanic is hard to find. Special training is necessary. This need has been anticipated by the Smith-Hughes Act, under the provisions of which, courses have been established in every state to prepare teachers of trade, industrial, and other vocational subjects.[32]

3. Coöperative Schools.—The coöperative system of education, involving the coöperation of school and industry, was first inaugurated in 1906 by the University of Cincinnati, through the efforts of Dean Herman Schneider, of the College of Engineering. Dean Schneider, realizing that it is impossible for a school to keep up with all the new processes and machinery of modern industry, devised a plan whereby the students could get their practical experience in the manufacturing plants of the city and have this practical work coördinate with the theoretical instruction at the University. The course he developed is so planned that the students, who are divided into two sections, spend alternate weeks at the University and in the industrial plants of the city. Each man has an alternate, so that the shopwork is continued by students of one section while those of the other section are in school. Their practical work is as carefully planned as is the theoretical work in the University. Under this arrangement, the theoretical instruction given in the regular four-year course is combined with the practical experience of a newly devised shop-apprenticeship system. The course is five years, but the graduate does not need to undergo an apprenticeship as is usually the case with graduates of the traditional course. The student is paid for his work, and a contract is signed in triplicate: by the student, the University, and the firm.

[32] Ruth M. Weeks, *The People's School; a Study in Vocational Training,* 1912, chs. IX, X, XI. Frank M. Leavitt, *Examples of Industrial Education,* 1912, ch. XIII. William T. Bawden, *Vocational Education,* U. S. Bureau of Education Bulletin, 1919, No. 25, pp. 18-20. *Fourteenth Annual Report of the Federal Board for Vocational Education,* 1930, pp. 3, 5, 9-12.

The essential features of the plan seem to be the following:

(1) A definite coöperative arrangement between the educational institution and one or more industrial plants, by which the theoretical instruction is given by the institution and the practical experience is given by the industries, and both are coördinated in a systematic and progressive educational program.

(2) Willingness on the part of the industrial plant to make such adjustments in equipment, processes, and methods as are necessary for promotion of the educational aim.

(3) Willingness on the part of the educational institution to eliminate non-essentials and to base theoretical instruction on what actually happens.

(4) Careful selection of employers, instructors, and student-workers, who are capable of being inspired with a vision of the responsibilities as well as the possibilities of the plan.

(5) Administration of the device of alternating periods in such a way as to secure continuous and progressive action on the process or job in the factory, as well as in the work of the student and the instructor in the school.

From the employer's point of view, the most important elements of the coöperative plan are: first, the selection of workers; and, second, the awakening of an enlightened interest in their work through coördinated instruction. From the standpoint of the school and the student, the most important feature of coöperative education is "the *realization* of theory through its practical applications." In a very literal sense the studies in the curriculum become "applied subjects." In the use of the word "coöperative," emphasis is placed not only on the kind of training given, but also on the relation between school and industry, and on the method of bringing them together.[33]

The coöperative plan at the University of Cincinnati has been adapted to various kinds of industries and has been extended to the field of commerce, where business houses coöperate with the University in giving the students their practical training. The School of Applied Social Sciences of Western Reserve University has applied the scheme to the training of social workers. There are other applications of the coöperative course by colleges and professional schools, the most noteworthy instance being Antioch College, which has adopted the plan for the entire undergraduate body.

The coöperative plan has also been extended to the secondary schools, notable pioneer examples being the work at Fitchburg and Beverly, Massachusetts. The Industrial Department of the Fitchburg High

[33] Clyde W. Park, *The Cooperative System of Education*, U. S. Bureau of Education Bulletin, 1916, No. 37 (p. 32 quoted).

School inaugurated the plan in 1908. The course is four years in duration. The students spend the first year wholly in school, and during the next three years they alternate weekly between shop and school. Every candidate is given a trial period of two months, at the close of the first year. If he likes the work and shows aptitude for the trade, he takes the course; otherwise he drops out and, if he chooses, takes up some other course in the high school. The students are indentured for three years and receive pay for the weeks they are at work. The coöperative plan as established at the Beverly Industrial School, in 1909, differs from the Fitchburg plan in that there is no indenture, the trustees of the school retain full control of the pupils while in the factory, and the same person instructs a particular division in both factory and school. "By this means the work is conducted in a way to contribute most effectually to the boy's progress in his trade, and not to suit the exigencies of the factory; and the instruction is imparted by a trained teacher and not left to the uncertain pedagogical ability of the ordinary foreman. Most important of all, it safeguards the pupils from exploitation and the manufacturers from unjust suspicion."[34]

In 1921 the first coöperative high school in the commercial field was opened in New York City. The coöperative plan has in recent years been extended in a number of cities in both industrial and commercial lines. Among recent developments has been the appointment of coordinators for part-time students who act in an official capacity between industry and the school relative to the employment work and the school training of the individual students, thus bringing about a unified plan of procedure for work and training. Sometimes the coordinators are men from the industries, and in some instances carry on the work of coördination without expense to the school.

The coöperative plan in the secondary schools has many advantages. It makes continuation in school possible for some boys and girls, because of the wages earned on part-time. It improves conditions of child labor through the supervision exercised by the school and the coöperation of employers. It induces many children to remain in school because the school work is thus made more interesting and practical, and the student can see a more direct relation between schooling and the promotion of his own interests. The opportunity to engage in gainful employment on half-time under suitable auspices has a definite prevocational value, assisting young people to discover

[34] A. L. Safford, "The Beverly Industrial School," quoted in Frank M. Leavitt, *Examples of Industrial Education*, 1912, p. 211.

their tastes and probable aptitudes. The plan gives the student, at the very least, a foothold in some industry or occupation, so that he does not feel lost when the time comes to leave school and take up the responsibilities of self-support. The scheme affords practice under shop conditions, yet leaves a large amount of time for school work. It does not neglect the need for general education, but insures to each individual an amount of cultural and liberalizing education sufficient to serve as a foundation for further study if he later finds it possible to continue his education. The coöperating concerns favor the plan because they are assured of an efficient labor supply and full-time operation of machines. The participation of industry in the programs of educational organizations has resulted in a better understanding by the public schools of the training needs of industry, and a better appreciation by industry of the possibilities of training in and through coöperation with the public schools, all of which is conducive to the development of a feasible vocational-education program.[35]

4. Part-Time or Continuation Schools.—These schools are designed to administer to the needs of boys and girls who have been forced into the industrial market with inadequate preparation and small appreciation of the nature of life's economic problem. By means of the continuation school, these youthful workers can still be earning money and at the same time be getting more education, especially of a vocational nature.

The continuation-school idea was first developed in Germany, and the best examples of this type of school are to be found in Munich. The first public continuation school in the United States was opened in Cincinnati in 1909. It was of the voluntary type, for the benefit of machine-shop apprentices. The idea was suggested to the board of education by some of the leading local manufacturers, who perceived the need of a practical school operating in the daytime for the education of apprentices. Under the plan as established, the apprentices attended the school one-half day or four hours a week, were paid their usual wage for attendance, and docked for absence. The work of the school was closely applied to the work of the shop. One hour was devoted to blue-print reading and free-hand and mechanical drawing, one hour to practical mathematics, one hour to shop science and

---

[35] Frank M. Leavitt, *Examples of Industrial Education*, 1912, ch. XIV. William T. Bawden, *Vocational Education*, U. S. Bureau of Education Bulletin, 1919, No. 25, pp. 21-23. Clyde W. Park, *The Cooperative System of Education*, U. S. Bureau of Education Bulletin, 1916, No. 37, pp. 32-36. Maris M. Proffitt, *Industrial Education, 1926-28*, U. S. Bureau of Education Bulletin, 1929, No. 21, pp. 5-7; 1931, No. 20, p. 16.

theory, and one hour to reading, English, spelling, commercial geography, and civics.[36]

The compulsory type of part-time continuation school was inaugurated by Wisconsin in 1911. Between 1911 and 1918 only a few other states followed Wisconsin's example, but in 1918, stimulated by the Smith-Hughes Act, some seventeen states enacted such laws. By 1930, thirty states had legislation requiring attendance upon part-time, continuation, or evening schools. The age limits for such attendance are as follows:

AGE LIMITS FOR COMPULSORY PART-TIME, CONTINUATION,
OR EVENING SCHOOL ATTENDANCE

Ages	Number of States
14–16	13
14–18	8
16–21 (for illiterates)	3
16–18	2
Under 18	2
Under 17	1
12–16	1
	30

In all states providing part-time education it appears that attendance in regular public or approved private schools for the required time is acceptable in lieu of part-time, continuation, or evening-school attendance; but where minors are employed or for some reason are not attending regular day school, and where part-time or continuation schools are provided, attendance therein is compulsory, unless excused for physical or mental disability or for educational attainments such as completion of the grammar-school or high-school course. The amount of attendance required in part-time, continuation, or evening schools in the different states varies from 4 to 8 hours per week and generally extends over the same period as that of the regular public schools. These laws, in effect, extend the age limits of compulsory education, but qualify the requirement by allowing part-time attendance after a certain age.[37]

The courses provided by part-time instruction may be trade-extension courses supplemental to the trade or industrial pursuit in which the minor is engaged; they may be preparatory for a trade

[36] Frank M. Leavitt, *Examples of Industrial Education*, 1912, pp. 224-229. Ruth M. Weeks, *The People's School*, 1912, pp. 137-143.

[37] *Monthly Labor Review*, April, 1920, X, 133-135. Ward W. Keesecker, *Laws Relating to Compulsory Education*, U. S. Bureau of Education Bulletin, 1928, No. 20, pp. 4, 8-10; *Review of Educational Legislation, 1929-30*, U. S. Bureau of Education Bulletin, 1931, No. 20, pp. 25-26.

entirely different from the one in which he is now working; or they may be of a general character suitable to the development of the civic and vocational intelligence of the young worker. The aim is to give the young people some vocational experience, to assist them in choosing their occupation or profession, and, after the choice has been made, to help them increase their proficiency, and thus make advancement more rapid.[38]

This new educational device has many advantages. It enables the school to give special training to a greater number of children at less expense than any other system. To the employer it means a more efficient class of employees who are learning to be skilled workmen; it thus helps in solving the problem of scarcity of skilled men. To the child it affords an opportunity to secure a practical education while still working. It furnishes an opportunity for vocational guidance. It keeps the child longer under the supervision of the public schools, giving him added advantages of general education, citizenship training, health supervision, and social development. The continuation school is considered by its sponsors another step forward toward a full realization of the American doctrine of an equal opportunity for all.

5. *Business Schools and Courses.*—In 1928, approximately one million pupils in the public and private high schools, private business colleges, and universities were definitely preparing to enter business occupations. The number is increasing annually, especially in the case of women, who comprise two-thirds of those enrolled in business curricula. Of the total number preparing for business occupations, two-thirds are enrolled in the public high schools, where they constitute approximately 17 per cent of the total enrollment. In addition, numerous other high-school pupils are taking one or more commercial subjects for non-vocational objectives.

In the junior high school, as mentioned above, significant developments center round the junior business training course, considered as prevocational for those who pursue the major commercial courses in the senior high schools. In the latter schools, and particularly in the special high schools of commerce, the trend of developments is toward closer coördination of the training program with initial employment opportunities. Secondary commercial education is rapidly entering an era of definite training for occupational efficiency in a wide variety of initial positions. Courses in retail selling, clerical

[38] Maris M. Proffitt, *Industrial Education, 1926-28*, U. S. Bureau of Education Bulletin, 1929, No. 21, pp. 8-11.

training, and machine operation, however, have not as yet been promoted in accordance with the needs. There is a wide variation in the stages of development of business education in the different communities. Secondary commercial education appears to be passing concurrently through the stages of introducing, lengthening, up-grading, and differentiating the curricula, and developing programs of guidance, placement, and supervision. The Smith-Hughes Act makes no provision for federal aid for commercial education. In this field the responsibility of the Federal Board for Vocational Education is limited entirely to research.

Private commercial and business schools, of widely varying standards, have existed for a long time and are very numerous. Accrediting associations have been active in endeavoring to raise the standards of these schools. Recently there has been a tendency among private business schools to seek junior-college and collegiate standing. Many of the schools have sought the privilege of granting degrees in commerce and business. "The larger and probably better-managed schools are endeavoring to attract high-school graduates rather than those who have dropped out of high school. For success over a long period these schools are very definitely dependent upon satisfactorily preparing their pupils for job proficiency and upon finding suitable employment for them. The majority of these schools realize, therefore, that high-school graduates, or those who have had from two to four years of high-school education contribute more to the reputation of their training programs than do students with less education. The endeavor on the part of a large number of these schools to obtain students of higher qualifications is in harmony with the up-grading requirements for business positions."[39]

Of the million students reported in 1928 to be preparing for business occupations, about 60,000 were majoring in business subjects in the colleges and universities. Over 80 per cent of these were men. The number of higher institutions reporting commerce and business curricula was 132. In addition, approximately 400 colleges and universities, or about half the total number, were offering some business courses, usually one or two in each of three or four subjects in this field. These institutions ordinarily permit the students to pursue a general business major. Such a curriculum provides orientation in general business but seldom prepares for proficiency in highly specialized initial opportunities. The list of higher institutions offering a

[39] J. O. Malott, *Commercial Education, 1926-28*, U. S. Bureau of Education Bulletin, 1929, No. 26, p. 20.

sufficient number of specific business courses to prepare for immediate job proficiency or a career in any specialized field is comparatively small. There are 93 collegiate schools of commerce, of which 31 have bureaus of business research. Increased attention is being devoted by these schools to the problems of training for executive levels of business occupations and to research as an essential in enriching and giving greater reality to the business courses.

In general, commercial education is faced with many difficult problems. It has been handicapped by the extremely rapid development of new and diverse industries, the equally rapid modification of older industries and business practices, the reshaping of domestic and foreign business relationships, and other recent economic changes. No other phase of secondary vocational education has so many students enrolled, is composed of so many subjects, or prepares for so vast a variety of gainful occupations. No other phase has so little supervision to give direction to research and to obtain a prompt and general application of the findings of worthy investigations. As a result, commercial education has been slower than other types of vocational education to develop a coördinated and progressive program.[40]

6. *The Junior College as a Vocational School.*—The junior college as ordinarily organized is an independent two-year unit to which pupils are admitted upon graduation from high school. Though in origin antedating by a decade or so the junior high school, it has gained headway much more slowly. In 1900 there were 8 junior colleges in the country. By 1910 the number had increased to 27; by 1920, to 207. In 1928 Whitney found 382 junior colleges operating with an enrollment of 44,372 students. Directory material tentatively prepared in the fall of 1928 by the American Association of Junior Colleges listed 408 junior colleges, with an enrollment of 50,529 students. The junior college, though widely distributed, prevails to a greater extent in the southern, mid-west, and Pacific-coast states. The public junior college is found primarily in the Middle West and in California; the private especially in Missouri and the southern states.

There are several types of junior colleges, serving different functions, only one of which concerns us here. Opinion appears to be crystallizing in favor of two general types of curricula, one preparatory to further college work, the other terminal with the end of the

[40] J. O. Malott, *Commercial Education, 1926-28,* U. S. Bureau of Education Bulletin, 1929, No. 26. Frank M. Phillips, *Statistics of Public High Schools, 1927-28,* U. S. Bureau of Education Bulletin, 1929, No. 35, pp. 13, 14, 102. *Thirteenth Annual Report of the Federal Board for Vocational Education,* 1929, pp. 18-20.

junior-college course. In the first case, the junior college has often arisen because the financial condition of many small colleges has made it impossible for them to do a high grade of work throughout the four-year course. They have therefore confined themselves to freshman and sophomore courses, for which their incomes are more adequate. Such colleges give two years of work, either preprofessional training or general cultural courses, acceptable to colleges and universities. The latter institutions, thus relieved of the first two years of work, can concentrate their efforts on the last two years and on graduate instruction. This type of junior college or curriculum allows students to remain near home for two years longer before they go away to larger institutions. It also aids somewhat in the problem of articulation between units in the educational system.

The terminal type of curriculum makes of the junior college a finishing school. It completes the formal education of students who are not going on. The terminal courses are usually designed for students who desire some specific type of vocational education. If we may, following Koos's suggestion, define trade-training as that which is concluded during the high-school period, and professional training that which requires four or more years beyond the high school, then the vocational training which is concluded during the junior-college period may be called semi-professional. The semi-professions for which the junior college offers training are to be found chiefly in the fields of commerce, industry, agriculture, home economics, and teaching in the public schools. These vocational needs are not met by other agencies. The junior college thus offers peculiar advantages to a certain group of students. Its development may be regarded as a part of the movement to democratize the public-school system.[41]

7. *Professional Schools.*—Higher education in the United States, especially in the state universities and the colleges of agriculture and mechanic arts, has shown an expansion of the curriculum and a development of vocational training and vocational schools similar to that of secondary education, in adjustment to changing social conditions. In fact, professional education was the first type of vocational education to arise. The Colonial colleges, which were religious in origin, were largely training schools for the ministry, and this long continued to be their one professional purpose. The curriculum consisted mainly of Hebrew, Latin, Greek, mathematics, ethics, theology,

[41] F. L. Whitney, *The Junior College in America,* 1928. Leonard V. Koos, *The Junior-College Movement,* 1925, pp. 11, 19-27, 49-63, 121, 145, ch. V. Carl A. Jessen, *Secondary Education,* U. S. Bureau of Education Bulletin, 1929, No. 22, pp. 6-7, 16. *School Life,* July 15, 1920.

and philosophy. No one was considered "fit to be dignified with his first degree" at Harvard until he was "found able to read the originals of the Old and New Testaments into the Latin tongue, and to resolve them logically." At Yale all students were required to take Hebrew and were drilled in theology and the Shorter Catechism. "All undergraduates," reads one of the college rules, "shall repeat sermons in the hall in their course. Scholars when in their chambers and together are forbidden to speak English, Latin being required. All undergraduates except Freshmen shall read some part of the Old Testament out of Hebrew in the morning, and shall turn some part of the New Testament out of English into Latin or Greek at evening at the time of recitation." In a pamphlet published in 1754, President Clap of Yale declared that "Colleges are *Societies of Ministers*, for training up Persons for the Work of the *Ministry*," and that "The great design of founding this school [Yale], was to Educate Ministers in our *own Way*." In the advertisement published in the New York papers announcing the opening of King's College (now Columbia University), in 1754, it was stated

The chief Thing that is aimed at in this College is to teach and engage the Children *to know God in Jesus Christ*, and to love and serve him in all *Sobriety, Godliness,* and *Richness* of Life, with a perfect Heart and a Willing Mind: and to train them up in all Virtuous Habits, and all such useful Knowledge as may render them creditable to their Families and Friends, Ornaments to their Country, and useful to the Public Weal in their generation.

During the seventeenth, eighteenth, and early nineteenth centuries, the only ministerial training was the regular college course, usually followed by reading and practice in the home of some pastor. The first separate schools of theology were established in 1812 at Princeton, in 1819 at Harvard, and in 1822 at Yale.

The first professional instruction to be added by the early universities was medicine, a medical school being established at Pennsylvania as early as 1765, at King's in 1767, Harvard in 1782, Dartmouth in 1798, and Yale in 1813. The University of Maryland department of medicine and the College of Physicians and Surgeons at New York were both established in 1807. The first permanent instruction in law to be given by a university came with the establishment of the law faculty of the University of Maryland in 1812, and the opening of a law school at Harvard in 1817, Yale in 1824, and the University of Virginia in 1826. The medical and law schools of Colonial times were the offices of practicing physicians and lawyers. The first college of dentistry was opened in Baltimore in 1839, and the second at Cincinnati in 1845. The first college of pharmacy was opened at Philadelphia in 1822. These subjects, now so common in our state universities, are all of relatively recent development.[42]

The movement toward liberalizing the college curriculum and introducing more vocational schools, as well as opening professional instruction to women on the same terms as men, was greatly accelerated by the rise of the state university and the establishment by Congress, in 1862, of an entirely new type of higher instruction in the colleges of agriculture and mechanical arts. Before 1850 the colleges usually offered but one course, based on Greek, Latin, and mathematics, known as the classical course, and leading to the B.A. degree. By 1880 the colleges were offering three or four parallel courses, much as the high schools did twenty years later. These led to different degrees— B.A., B.L., B.S., and Ph.B. Graduate instruction was also organized, and courses leading to the M.A., M.S., and Ph.D. degrees were in time provided. "With the creation of new chairs to represent new subjects of study, or subdivisions of old subjects, which became common after about 1875, the next tendency was to reorganize the colleges by departments, such as Greek, Latin, English, history, mathematics, physics, biology, etc. This became the common form of organization for the larger universities after about 1890, and still continues. With the very rapid increase in the quantity of knowledge, and the subdivision of old subjects into many new chairs, the more recent tendency has been to re-group the university into a series of colleges and schools. To-day a large state university would include most or all of the following colleges, schools, or divisions, each subdivided into a number of departments or branches of knowledge, and often leading to separate degrees.

"1. The college of liberal arts.
2. The college of engineering.
3. The college of agriculture.
4. The school of history and economics.
5. The school of pure science.
6. The school of education.
7. The school of household arts.
8. The school of fine arts.
9. The school of business administration.
10. The school of journalism.
11. The school of law.
12. The school of medicine.
13. The school of veterinary medicine.
14. The school of pharmacy.
15. The school of dentistry.

[42] Ellwood P. Cubberley, *Public Education in the United States*, 1919, pp. 201-202, 208-209. Charles F. Thwing, *A History of Higher Education in America*, 1906, chs. I-VI, XX.

16. The school of forestry.
17. The school of mining.
18. The school of architecture.

19. The university-extension division.
20. The summer-school division."[43]

This rapid development and subdivision of the university into schools and colleges indicates the assumption of new service for the welfare of the state. That the state has appreciated the service has been shown by a university development previously unknown. Since about 1885, when the state universities began to turn their attention to serving and advancing the welfare of the state, university attendance and revenues have advanced at an unprecedented rate. The larger state universities were enrolling, in 1930, ten to fifteen thousand (California, 17,242) full-time students each. Including part-time and summer-session students, enrollments in these institutions reach to twenty and thirty thousand. The states have put millions into the equipment and maintenance of these higher institutions, believing in them as creators of advanced public opinion and as training schools for the future leaders of the state. Gifts to the support of private institutions have provided examples of extraordinary generosity and have emphasized the interest of alumni in the institutions in which they obtained their training. American colleges and universities, both publicly and privately endowed, have during this period of expansion received more money than has ever been given to aid higher education in any land.[44]

Vocational Guidance.—Vocational guidance represents an attempt, first through philanthropic initiative and support and later through agencies for public education, to lessen the misdirection of energy and general loss of effectiveness at present involved in the efforts of young persons, especially in urban centers, to find suitable employment. The historic agency of vocational guidance has been the home. Under earlier conditions, in a simpler economic and social situation, the range of occupations was small, and children usually followed the occupations of their parents. At least they could be guided as to choice of occupation and to a certain extent receive vocational training in the home. In the modern urban community, the home has become less and less adapted to giving effective vocational guidance. The tremendous expansion and growing complexity of industrial

[43] Ellwood P. Cubberley, *Public Education in the United States,* 1919, pp. 432-433. Charles F. Thwing, *A History of Higher Education in America,* 1906, chs. XIII, XV, XXI.
[44] Arthur J. Klein, *Higher Education, Biennial Survey, 1926-28,* U. S. Bureau of Education Bulletin, 1929, No. 11, pp. 17-21, 37-42. Ellwood P. Cubberley, *Public Education in the United States,* 1919, pp. 433-434.

society, the minute subdivision and increasing specialization of labor, have made it impossible for parents to know the various occupations now available, the technical knowledge and skill required, the employment conditions in the various divisions, and other facts germane to the intelligent selection of a vocation. The idea underlying vocational guidance is not primarily to find jobs for young people, but rather to provide parents and pupils with information about the demands and opportunities in the different life careers, and the best means of preparing for and entering them. The real purpose is to sort out capacities and adaptabilities, to prolong preparation in school, and steer young people away from vocations for which they have no natural aptitude and from essentially blind-alley occupations. Vocational guidance includes all systematic efforts, under private or public control, and excluding the traditional activities of the home, the conscious and chief purpose of which is to secure the most economical and effective adjustment of young people to the employments which they can most advantageously follow. It is an important factor in the final satisfactory adjustment of the individual into a wage-earning life occupation.

The pioneer organization for vocational study and guidance in this country was the Vocation Bureau of Boston, established in 1908. It grew out of the work of Prof. Frank Parsons at the Civic Service House in the north end of the city. The Bureau soon became connected in its work with the public schools, business houses, and manufacturing establishments. Lectures as to careers were given to the upper classes in the elementary schools; printed matter on vocations was distributed; vocational counselors were appointed in all the schools, and pupil record-cards were made out. Boston soon became the center of the movement, and from there it has spread over the United States.

Among the means employed in the vocational guidance of youth are (1) selected readings given under the supervision of the school, with a view to conveying information concerning economic activities, the abilities demanded in the various occupations, the factors of success, etc.; (2) individual or group conferences of pupils with teachers and vocational counselors; (3) systematic study of young persons for the purpose of advising them concerning lines of employment they can most effectively enter; (4) prevocational education, for exploration and discovery of aptitudes and interests; (5) maintenance of employment agencies for young persons, and follow-up work.

In the public schools increasing emphasis is being placed upon an educational guidance procedure covering a term of years and aiming, through various forms of direct and indirect experience, to furnish opportunities for the gradual development and discovery of aptitudes and interests and for gaining reliable information about the training required for specific occupations and the employment conditions in those occupations. Indirect experience includes reading, study, and observation relative to occupations; direct experience includes manipulative work in a variety of construction materials and in various mechanical operations performed in the school shops and in employment. One means of providing indirect experience which is receiving increasing emphasis is the inclusion in the program of studies of a course in occupations, usually offered in one of the junior-high-school years or in connection with the work in continuation-school classes. In 1928, 1,694 high schools reported 41,095 boys and 36,471 girls enrolled in courses in occupations.

Among other recent trends are a growing demand that teachers in guidance work and those doing vocational counseling have specific training, the assumption by vocational schools of the responsibility for finding jobs for their students when they are ready to leave school and go to work, and increase of occupational research. Contributions to the latter end have come from studies and practices of an experimental or pioneer nature carried on by the industrial education, the guidance and placement, and the research divisions in the public schools; by the employment and personnel divisions of industrial plants; and by industrial associations interested in the training and up-grading of employees in the industries they represent. The most important contributions have included studies dealing with the following subjects:

(*a*) Occupational levels. These studies have furnished valuable information relative to the technical knowledge and skill required for employment in the different levels of a major occupational division of work.

(*b*) Job analyses made for instructional purposes. These have added materially to our knowledge of the abilities necessary to do the jobs included in a particular occupation.

(*c*) Success factors. Considerable attention has been given to the types of abilities that make for success in different occupations. In addition to the factors of skill and technical knowledge, which are essential, there are other factors of a personal character such as specific interests, temperament, emotional stability, and social adjustment which are frequently the causes of success or failure.

These various types of studies and experimental practices have set forth more clearly the feasibility of providing vocational courses and the possibilities which such courses have for vocational efficiency. They have resulted in a stimulation of vocational education in the public schools, especially in the coöperation of the schools with industry in providing practical types of training.

Notwithstanding the increase in the number of schools offering courses in occupations, and the fact that many schools have teachers who do some counseling and make some contacts with industries for the purpose of finding employment for pupils seeking wage-earning positions, only a small percentage of schools have a coördinated and centralized program covering all phases of guidance work. Fewer still have such a program under the direction of a person employed with reference to his special qualifications for the task. Although the subject of vocational guidance has been discussed for years, its inclusion in local school programs is not general, and in many instances the procedure is varied and often experimental. However, there is a growing demand for the development of guidance work. The committee on resolutions of the National Education Association recommended, in 1927, "that educational and vocational guidance be considered a primary obligation of organized education."[45]

Developments are also taking place in the institutions of higher learning. "Placement and employment services have, of course, been offered by the colleges in more or less haphazard fashion for many years. Systematic services of this kind are now developing at a precipitant rate. Such services, even though highly developed and rendering excellent aid, may be carried on without any reference to the educational program. The process may consist merely of attempting to find positions for the product as it is, without any apparent effort to modify the process or the form of the educational offering to meet the needs of the positions in which graduates are placed. It is, therefore, especially significant that, in many instances, educational and vocational guidance and placement of students are being closely related to the activities of the college curriculum. Such efforts range from the attenuated relations implied by the creation by Middlebury College of a new office which combines the functions of director of admissions and alumni secretary to the formation of bureaus similar to the bureau of educational records and guidance at the University

[45] Maris M. Proffitt, *Industrial Education, 1926-28*, U. S. Bureau of Education Bulletin, 1929, No. 21, pp. 3-4, 15-20. Committee on Vocational Education of the National Education Association, *Vocational Secondary Education*, U. S. Bureau of Education Bulletin, 1916, No. 21. Meyer Bloomfield, *The Vocational Guidance of Youth*, 1911, pp. 29-34, 72-85, 86-100; *Readings in Vocational Guidance*, 1915. John M. Brewer, *The Vocational Guidance Movement*, 1918. J. C. Wright and Charles R. Allen, *The Administration of Vocational Education*, 1926, ch. XV.

of Wisconsin. President Frank, of the University of Wisconsin, describes the purposes of this bureau as follows:

"The bureau of educational records and guidance will go beyond the mere keeping of grades to the assembling of a wide range of information respecting the life and work of the students as the background and basis for the development of an effective service of counsel and guidance to the students— an end that is not always achieved by the prevailing system of advisers.

"The bureau likewise will be the assembly point for a richly detailed fund of information regarding the nature and results of the educational processes to which the students are subjected. This will provide facilities that will make it possible for the university to keep up a continuous study of the results of its enterprises and to take its own educational pulse."[46]

This develoment is in line with that progressive thought in higher education which is keenly desirous of harmonizing the activities within college walls with the practical and social situations of the world outside.

4. OTHER ADJUSTMENTS OF THE SCHOOL SYSTEM

Work-Study-and-Play or Platoon Schools.—This is a plan of school organization under which it is possible, financially and administratively, to give to all children in a school system the opportunities for an enriched curriculum of work and study and play which the development of cities and industrialism has made it imperative to provide. The enlarged program involves additional equipment such as shops, laboratories, gymnasiums, auditoriums, playgrounds, and school gardens. The platoon plan makes it financially possible to have in every school these enriched educational facilities as well as classrooms, because it applies to the school the principle upon which all other public utilities are run, that of multiple use of facilities. It contrasts sharply with traditional methods of school administration. Up to the present time the public-school system has been running on what engineers call the "peak load" plan of operation, i.e., on the principle of reserving a school seat for the exclusive use of each child during the entire year. Under this conventional plan of school administration, a given classroom is the "home room" of one class. Each pupil has an individual seat and desk which is not used by any other pupil. When the children leave their classroom seats to go to the special activities on the playgrounds, in the shops, in the audi-

[46] Arthur J. Klein, *Higher Education, Biennial Survey, 1926-28*, U. S. Bureau of Education Bulletin, 1929, No. 11, p. 3.

torium, or in the gymnasium, the seats remain vacant. The result is that it is difficult to provide enough seats for all the children to study in, enough playgrounds for all of them to play in, or enough shops for them to work in, although large sums of money are invested in these facilities, which the children can use for only a fraction of the day.

Under the new plan, all activities in the school—classrooms, auditoriums, gymnasiums, shops, laboratories, and playgrounds—are in use every hour of the day. The children are divided into two large groups or platoons, each having the same number of classes and each containing all the grades. During the first half of the morning session one group of classes is engaged in regular work in the regular classrooms, while the second platoon is engaged in special work in special classrooms and in the auditorium, gymnasium, playground, etc. At the mid-point of the morning session the two groups change places, those who have been in the regular rooms going to the special ones and those who have been doing special work going to the regular rooms to take up regular class work. In the afternoon a similar shift is made.[47]

The implications of the plan are significant. Division of the school into platoons alternating between the classrooms and the rooms for special activities reduces by one-half the number of classrooms needed. Since the cost of a classroom at present is approximately $12,000, this means that in a 30-class school only 15 classrooms are required instead of 30, with the result that 15 times $12,000 is released for all other activities in the school. Under such circumstances it is possible to supply a school seat for every child when he needs it and also the special facilities enumerated above at no greater cost than it takes to supply classrooms only under the traditional plan.

Besides rearrangement of the daily time-schedule and of rooms and equipment, the platoon plan also involves instructional changes. A given teacher is charged with the care and instructon in regular lines of work of two groups of pupils instead of one. To offset this added burden and responsibility, the teacher is relieved of work in the special subjects, such as music and physical training, which demand for best results not only special preparation but a special form of interest. These subjects are entrusted to teachers who have this interest and training and who now find their whole school day filled with the instruction of several grades in their particular subjects.

[47] Charles L. Spain, *The Platoon School*, 1924, p. 50.

In short, the platoon plan is a readjustment in the relation of building and equipment to curriculum. It aims to secure:

1. Better instruction and improved results in special branches without increased expense and without sacrificing the regular subjects of the curriculum.

2. The filling of important gaps in the present curriculum without the increase in cost that often prohibits such additions.

3. A more constant use of the whole school building and especially increased use of facilities usually considered "extras," such as auditoriums, gymnasiums, manual-training rooms, and the like.

4. A larger enrollment within the same building.

In 1927, there were 115 cities having one or more schools on the platoon plan. Thirty-four cities with a population of almost six million have organized all their schools on the plan or have adopted it as a city-wide policy.[48]

The Gary Plan.—The most notable experiment affecting the use of building space, indeed, one of the most original pieces of constructive work ever attempted in American education, is the plan, or rather the program of innovations, instituted by Superintendent William Wirt at Gary, Indiana. "The unique conditions at Gary, which required a school system to be produced at once, without any previous local traditions to follow or to overcome, gave unusual chance for the initiative that Mr. Wirt has shown. In fact Mr. Wirt was not only unhampered by local conditions: he freed himself from the general traditions as well. His attempt to determine and meet the individual needs of many differing classes of pupils has brought a series of striking changes from the usual curriculum and the customary teaching methods. His influence on educational procedure is certainly one to be reckoned with."[49]

Mr. Wirt states that he has had only two fixed principles in establishing work-study-and-play schools: "First, that children should be busy all day long at work, study, and play under right conditions. Second: Cities can finance an adequate work-study-and-play program only when all the facilities of the entire community for the work, study, and play of children are properly coördinated with the school,

[48] S. O. Hartwell, *Overcrowded Schools and the Platoon Plan*, 1916, pp. 19-23 (21-22 quoted). Charles L. Spain, *The Platoon School*, 1924. W. S. Deffenbaugh, "Recent Movements in City School Systems," *Biennial Survey of Education, 1924-26*, U. S. Bureau of Education Bulletin, 1928, No. 25, pp. 66-67.
[49] S. O. Hartwell, *Overcrowded Schools and the Platoon Plan*, 1916, pp. 13-14.

the coördinating agent, so that all facilities supplement one another and 'peak-loads' are avoided by keeping all facilities of the school plant in use all of the time.''[50]

Briefly stated, the Gary plan is a work-study-and-play scheme of the most varied kind. The school plant carries out ''a belief in educating the whole child, physically, artistically, manually, scientifically, as well as intellectually.'' Mr. Wirt believes that, by putting in the child's way all the opportunities for varied development, the child will be able to select those activities for which he is best suited, and thus develop his capacities to their highest power. This can be done only in a school which provides, besides the ordinary classrooms, also playgrounds and gardens, gymnasiums and swimming pools, special drawing and music rooms, science laboratories, machine shops, and intimate and constant contact with supplementary community activities outside of school. In the latter case, libraries, churches, the Y.M.C.A., etc., are allied with the schools to the extent of caring for part of the children part of the time. The Wirt school is based on a fourfold unity of interests—play and exercise, intellectual study, special work in shop and laboratory, etc., and social and expressive activity in auditorium or outside community agency.

At Gary the schools run on a four-quarter plan, each quarter of twelve weeks' duration. Both the elementary-school and the high-school work are given under the same roof. Specialization in instruction and, in consequence, the departmental system run through the schools. By means of the administrative readjustments of the duplicate or platoon plan, all special rooms as well as all classrooms are used throughout the school day. The school day is eight hours long, with the school plant open also all day Saturday. Continuation schools and social and recreational centers are conducted in the same plant in the evening.

''To sum up, the Gary school forms a children's community, which aims to provide the practical natural education of the old school, shop, and home which educated our forefathers. It is a necessary evolution and reorganization of the public school to meet the changed social and industrial conditions of the modern city. The school community, by providing a fourfold activity of work, study, and play, uses the children's time and keeps them from the demoralizing influence of the streets. In the 'auditorium' it provides a public theater which may motivate all the work and study. By coöperating with all the commu-

[50] William Wirt, Introduction, *The Gary Schools,* by R. S. Bourne, 1916, pp. xvii-xviii.

nity agencies which provide wholesome activities for children, it makes them all more valuable and effective. And by making the school as far as possible a self-sustaining community, it gives meaning and purpose to all the work, trains the children for the outside world, and cultivates the social virtues."[51]

The development of the Gary system, the evolution of the platoon plan, and other features of educational administration of similar character are the results of a new philosophy of education which emphasizes the importance of an enriched curriculum of studies and activities for the pupils, together with the necessity of utilizing the school plant and equipment to a much higher degree of efficiency than heretofore.

Extended Use of School Buildings.—Recent modifications of the public-school system have led not only to a more intensive use of the school building and equipment, as in the platoon plan, but to a more extensive use as well. The schools have become community centers. The American people are no longer satisfied for their school buildings, erected usually at heavy cost, to be used only for day classes in ordinary instruction. Idleness during six-sevenths of the hours of the year is contrary to the principle of full utilization of plant, and it means waste of investment.

"In the eighties the schoolhouses of our cities were used only between nine in the morning and three or four in the afternoon, and for from 150 to 180 days in the year. The remainder of the time the school plant stood idle, and boys and girls were not allowed even about the grounds. The buildings usually contained only classrooms and an office, and were not adapted to other than day-school uses. Today, everywhere, the tendency is to change these earlier conditions, and to put the school plant to the largest possible community use. Through playgrounds, school gardens, vacation schools, and evening schools, our school grounds and school buildings in the cities and towns give much more service than formerly. As new school buildings have been erected and old ones rebuilt, they have been better fitted for use by the addition of an assembly hall, play rooms, a science room, a library room, and rooms for manual-training and household arts. Some also have workshops, baths, swimming-pools, and a gymnasium. As this more extensive and more expensive equipment has

[51] Randolph S. Bourne, *The Gary Schools*, 1916, pp. 55-56. George M. Wiley, *The Gary System and the Platoon Plan*, 1925. Abraham Flexner and Frank P. Bachman, *The Gary Schools*, 1918. S. O. Hartwell, *Overcrowded Schools and the Platoon Plan*, 1916, pp. 14-18. Ellwood P. Cubberley, *Public Education in the United States*, 1919, p. 464.

been added to the schools; as the need for new efforts to assimilate the new classes in society has become evident; and as an increased participation in the functions of government through the initiative, referendum, recall, primary, and women's suffrage has come about, along with an increasing cosmopolitanism in our people; the demand has come that the public school, as the one great, active, unifying, non-racial, non-political, non-sectarian force in our national life, should take upon itself a new service and make of itself a center for the formation and education of community sentiment. As the school plant already belongs to the people, it has also been demanded that it be put to a more constant after-school use for the benefit of the community about it.''[52]

This has been done in many cities and in rural communities as well. The movement dates from about 1900. Statistics collected by the United States Bureau of Education show that 722 cities and towns were carrying on community-center activities in their school buildings in 1923-24. These activities include lectures on all kinds of human-welfare topics, athletics, entertainments, adult society meetings, clubs for civic discussion, public meetings, dramatics, social dancing, banquets, quiet reading and study, and the like. The first quarter of the century has thus witnessed a wide extension of the use of schoolhouses for social, recreational, and community purposes. Thirty-two states have definitely provided by law for such use, and in the other states school authorities permit it under their general powers as custodians.[53] Since activities with a recreational content bulk largest in the average school-center program, this movement will be discussed more fully later, when public provisions for recreation are considered.

Public-School Provision for Handicapped Children.—In further extension of the principle of adapting the school to the needs of the child, the public schools, since 1890, have paid increasing attention to the education of handicapped children, that is, children who, by virtue of exceptional circumstances or by inherent or acquired constitution, deviate so much from the normal as to cause a special status to arise with reference to their educational and social treatment. A specialized type of education has been developed for each of the following main classes: the blind, deaf, crippled, and mentally deficient.

Historically, the care and education of these classes were first provided for in state institutions or by philanthropic organizations. They

[52] Ellwood P. Cubberley, *Public Education in the United States*, 1919, pp. 428-429.

[53] Eleanor T. Glueck, *Extended Use of School Buildings*, U. S. Bureau of Education Bulletin, 1927, No. 5, pp. 1-9.

were not considered to be a legitimate public-school problem. Until the beginning of this century, "It was assumed—it is even now sometimes argued—that the business of the schools is to teach the statutory subjects (reading, writing and arithmetic). But the principle of compulsory education in a democratic country has carried with it implications and complications which have brought about an altogether different point of view. A policy of exclusion of exceptional children would have led only to confusion and injustice. The public school in progressive communities is steadily shouldering the whole problem of defective and handicapped pupils, and one can find today examples of special tax-supported provisions for every type of exceptional school child."[54] The welfare of no less than three quarters of a million of physically and mentally handicapped children is affected by this change of policy.

This phase of the school's work is closely related to the health supervision of school children, which we have discussed above. A thorough medical examination must precede the separation of children into groups or classes for special instruction, and health supervision must be exercised while they are in attendance. The problems presented by handicapped children are obviously social problems and only educational in that the efficiency of the educational work depends upon their being properly understood and solved. The school, by the assumption of this work, becomes a social agency. Indeed, Dr. Gesell[55] holds that our vast aggregation of elementary schools ought to be regarded as our largest and, in a sense, our most legitimate child-welfare agency. "Certainly the historic sanction and strategic position of the public school system in the American commonwealth make it the most promising instrument for the further development of public policies in behalf of a very large proportion of those exceptional children who because of handicap or other circumstances need a special measure of extra parental care during the years of their education."

In addition to the provisions mentioned earlier under school hygiene, the following represent the main developments in the public-school system for the care and education of handicapped children.

1. *Special Classes for the Mentally Deficient.*—The schools have long been laboring under the heavy burden of laggard children—the

[54] Arnold L. Gesell, "Public School Provision for Exceptional Children," *Annals Amer. Acad. Polit. Soc. Sci.*, Nov., 1921, 98:187:74. *Cf.* Elise H. Martens, *Education of Exceptional Children*, U. S. Bureau of Education Bulletin, 1931, No. 20, ch. XI.
[55] *Ibid.*, p. 73.

bane of teachers and a drag on the progress of other pupils.[56] Financially, it has been estimated that 10 per cent of public-school expenditures in this country have gone into the waste motion of permitting over-age children to repeat grades. Modern psychology finally showed that many of these retarded children were not merely slow to learn, or lazy, or indifferent, but were lacking in the intellectual capacity for regular classroom work beyond perhaps the two or three most elementary grades. "Once the public schools became aware that the mentally deficient were present in large numbers in their own enrollment and that the relegation of all such cases to institutions was from many points of view out of the question, educators turned their attention to the organization of special classes or special schools for these handicapped pupils as a means of promoting the efficiency of the entire school system. This expedient, far from doing violence to educational practice, only hastened recognition of the varying capacities and differing abilities of all the children in the schools and the consequent abandonment in the more forward-looking systems of the one-for-all curriculum based on the fiction of the average child. In keeping with this modern tendency of adapting the school to the child, the special classes, at first frankly an expedient to rid the school of an overwhelming burden, are now generally recognized to have as rightful a place in the educational system and as much of an educational mission as any other classes. Thus it has come to pass that by far the largest and most important part of the whole mental deficiency program has fallen squarely upon the public schools. Although the educational authorities, even in the more progressive centers, are as yet far from having made complete special provision for all mentally deficient children of school age outside of institutions, the responsibility of the school for educating the subnormal child is now generally accepted, and appreciable progress in the formation of special classes is being made each year."[57]

These special classes, by whatever name they may be called in particular school systems, are usually reserved for those pupils with intelligence quotients under 70. Most authorities agree that about 2 per cent of the usual school enrollment are so mentally retarded as to require instruction in special classes. In addition to these definitely defective children, there are in every school system many children of borderline intelligence, between 70 and 90 I.Q. for the most part, and

[56] Leonard P. Ayres, *Laggards in Our Schools*, 1909, chs. II, IV, XI.
[57] Stanley P. Davies, *Social Control of the Mentally Deficient*, 1930, pp. 293-294.

others who appear potentially normal, but who are for the time being pedagogically or intellectually retarded. A number of school systems have found it advantageous to organize for this group a distinct series of classes half way between the regular grades and the special classes. These are frequently termed "ungraded classes." Many pupils from the ungraded classes can eventually be restored to regular grade work; a few on further observation will prove to be quite definitely deficient, and need to be transferred to special classes.

The first special class for mentally deficient children to be organized in the school systems of this country was established in Providence in 1896. Within the next few years Springfield, Chicago, Boston, New York, Philadelphia, and Los Angeles organized such classes, and thereafter in rapid sequence most of the larger cities of the country. Fifteen states have enacted statutes making mandatory or permissive the establishment of special classes for mentally handicapped children in connection with the public schools. In a number of states special classes have been established by the educational authorities without specific legislative enactment. According to the figures compiled by the United States Bureau of Education for the school year 1929-30, there were 55,154 subnormal and backward children enrolled in the special classes of 315 city day-school systems reporting from 41 states.[58] These figures presumably do not cover the total enrollment in special classes throughout the country, since many school systems doubtless having special classes failed to report.

Special-class instruction differs in kind, as well as in degree, from that of the graded classroom. Although the development of a social type of personality may be no less the ultimate objective in the education of normal children than in that of the mentally deficient, yet in striving for this objective with the latter group more stress needs to be placed upon such fundamentals as personal hygiene, physical education, habit training, motor and sense training, speech correction, emotional control, and the formation of character. Personality training is basic in all special-class work. Beyond that, it is the aim of special-class instruction to give the pupils as much of the usual type of schooling, including the three R's, as they are able to acquire, always recognizing that a limit is soon reached in these directions beyond which it is useless to make further efforts. The most

[58] Frank M. Phillips, *Schools and Classes for Feebleminded and Subnormal Children, 1926-27*, U. S. Bureau of Education Bulletin, 1928, No. 5, p. 2. Arch O. Heck, *Special Schools and Classes*, U. S. Bureau of Education Bulletin, 1930, No. 7, pp. 6-12.

conspicuous differentiating factor between the regular and special classes is doubtless the emphasis placed in the latter upon manual and trade training. Handwork of all sorts offers educational opportunities for the mentally deficient after their progress in academic work has come to a halt. In contrast with their intellectual limitations, many special-class pupils are able to develop a considerable degree of skill in fashioning materials. For the younger children, basket-weaving, clay-modeling, rug-weaving, chair-caning, and various forms of wood working do well enough as educational projects. For the later years there is need of more definite vocational training. This, however, is generally lacking. Although most school systems in the larger centers have developed well-organized trade schools, all subnormal pupils, usually even those of the borderline and dull normal type, have been rigidly excluded. The Federal Board for Vocational Education has stipulated that its funds shall not be used for mentally defective children. A number of school systems are now endeavoring to meet this problem by the establishment of shop or vocational centers to which the more promising of the special-class pupils can be sent for practical training during the last few school years.

Because of the nature of the work and the greater necessity for individual attention, it is generally recognized that the size of special classes must be appreciably smaller than that of graded classes. The general practice has been to limit the enrollment to from 15 to 18 pupils. There is a special need of following the mentally handicapped child into the home and community, and of bringing all possible forces to bear to correct conditions which tend to counteract the work which the school is doing in developing the boy or girl into a social and economic asset. Many special-class teachers give unsparingly of their own free time to home-visiting and the organization of wholesome associations for their pupils. An organized visiting-teacher service should assist with these out-of-school problems.

"From the viewpoint of the backward pupil himself, the special class is a haven. It is in the regular grades that his intellectual limitations constantly stand out in such a way as to draw the jibes of fellow pupils and make him painfully conscious of his shortcomings. In the special class he finds himself among his peers; he can keep up with his group; he may even excel. His individual aptitudes and interests are considered and he is given an opportunity for self-expression in a type of work in which he takes a natural interest, and in which he can do well. All this leads to satisfaction and contentment, and as the leaders in special class work in any city can testify, is reflected in decreased truancy and general improvement in behavior."[59]

The public school has an important rôle to play in the mental-deficiency program. It can aid greatly in the early identification of cases, in individual study and classification of all mentally deficient pupils, in selection of those for whom institutional care is needed, and in providing adequate training for the rest. It is in a unique position to do preventive and constructive work. It has the great advantage over the institution that it gets the mentally deficient young, before serious harm has been done, and while there is still every opportunity to mold character and personality in the right direction and to develop to the utmost their limited capacities.

"When the public schools shall have fully recognized that they have no right to deprive a child of educational advantages suited to his needs just because he appears on one of the lower levels of the intelligence curve, and when they shall have provided an adequate number of special classes supplemented by competent psychological, psychiatric, and visiting teacher service, then a large part of the 'problem of mental deficiency' will have been solved."[60]

2. *Classes for the Blind.*—Since 1832, when the first school for the blind (Perkins Institution in Boston) was opened in the United States, a system of education for those who must learn to see with their fingers has been gradually developing throughout the country, but only since the beginning of the present century has provision been made for teaching the blind in special classes in the public schools. The first city to take up the work was Chicago, in 1900. Other cities pioneering in establishing public-school classes for the blind were Cincinnati in 1905, Milwaukee in 1907, Cleveland and New York City in 1909, and Newark in 1910. In 1927 the United States Bureau of Education received reports from 80 schools and institutions for the blind—47 state institutions, 21 schools or classes in city school systems, 5 private institutions, 5 other private institutions supported partly by state funds, and 2 schools in the Philippine Islands and Porto Rico. The total enrollment in these schools or classes for 1927 was 6,084. During the year, 177 pupils were graduated from high-school departments.[61]

The public-school classes for the blind have advantages over the

[59] Stanley P. Davies, *Social Control of the Mentally Deficient*, 1930, pp. 306-313 (307-308 quoted).

[60] *Ibid.*, ch. XV (p. 323 quoted).

[61] Frank M. Phillips, *Schools and Classes for the Blind, 1926-27*, U. S. Bureau of Education Bulletin, 1928, No. 9, pp. 1-2.

state institutions and private boarding schools in that they preserve the home as a factor in the child's life and give him a more normal environment during the period of growth. The child is saved from institutionalization. There is also the advantage of economy. The per pupil cost of education in a public-school class for the blind is less than half of the per pupil cost in an institution.

For the instruction of the blind, special apparatus and special teachers are provided. The pupils are taught the Braille system of raised type—based on a cell of six points or dots—and the use of the Braille typewriter as well as the regular one. The Braille arithmetic slate, sand or embossed maps, and other special equipment are used. Special attention is paid to handwork and physical training. In some cities, notably Chicago and Cleveland, the blind children attend the regular classes for part of their work, such as music and recitations. This program is carried out partly to reduce the cost of education and partly to bring the child in touch with the outside world and to make the seeing pupils more sympathetic. As a result of the public-school training, an increasing number of blind children have gone on to the regular high school and college.[62]

3. Sight-Saving Classes.—For all practical purposes children having less than one-tenth vision are considered blind and are eligible for admission to a school or special class for the blind. There is, however, a large group of children who have considerably more than one-tenth vision, yet, because of eye defect or disease, cannot read ordinary print or see figures or letters written on the blackboard. There is another large group of children who can see the blackboard work and read the textbook, but only by such strain on their vision and their nervous system that any result they may accomplish is at the expense of their sight and general health. The operation of the compulsory-education laws has brought these pupils forcibly to the attention of school and health authorities.

The proportion of pupils having such visual defects varies in different places from 1 to every 500 of the school population in the smaller cities to 1 to 1000 in the larger cities. This difference is probably a result of the more adequate school medical inspection in the larger communities, where periodic examination is made of the eyes of each pupil and conditions that need rectifying are discovered sufficiently early to prevent serious outcome in many cases. Although the number of such pupils is small, it is two or three times as large as

[62] Harry Best, *The Blind*, 1919, Part III, Provision for the Education of Blind Children, ch. XV.

the number of blind children. Furthermore, neglect of this class has made it a fruitful field from which the ranks of the blind in later life have been recruited.

"Many of these pupils have had a hopeless prospect in the past. Some of them who have had the good fortune to fall in with considerate teachers and who have had wise parents have managed to get through school with few ill effects. Others have worried along, always at the foot of the class, repeating every other year, studying when their eyes would permit, bluffing when their eyes would not, idling away their time, and when their self-respect asserted itself, playing truant. Some of these pupils eventually drop out of school either with or without a doctor's certificate. Other pupils of this class sooner or later find their way into a school for the blind. In such schools they are no less misfits than they are in the regular classes in the public schools. Schools for the blind accept them, not because it is felt that they belong in such institutions, but because there seems to be no other place to send them."[63]

Beginning with Boston and Cleveland, in 1913, special classes known as conservation of vision or sight-saving classes have been started for such children. To Robert B. Irwin, Supervisor of the Department for the Blind, Cleveland Public Schools, and himself blind, belongs the credit for introducing and promoting the idea of conservation of vision classes in America. Many large cities have followed the lead of Boston and Cleveland, and seven states (Massachusetts, Ohio, Illinois, Minnesota, Wisconsin, New York, and Pennsylvania) have enacted laws providing financial assistance to cities conducting such classes. The findings of school medical inspection indicate that every city having a population of 20,000 or more is in need of a class of this kind. According to information furnished by the National Committee for the Prevention of Blindness, 96 cities located in 21 states had sight-saving classes in the public schools in 1929-30.

Sight-saving classes, according to Mr. Irwin, have three fairly definite aims: first, to instruct the pupils with a minimum of eye-strain; second, to teach them how to conserve the vision they possess; and third, to provide such vocational guidance and, if necessary, vocational training as will enable them to fill the most useful places in the community their powers will permit.

[63] R. B. Irwin, *Sight-Saving Classes in the Public Schools*, Harvard Bulletins in Education, No. VII, Nov., 1920, pp. 11-12.

The success of the class for conservation of vision depends largely upon the adequacy of the equipment. The room or building selected for these classes must have good lighting conditions; it should be a model so far as eye-hygiene is concerned. The blackboards—the most essential part of the equipment, since written work in these classes is done largely thereon—must be so placed as to eliminate glare. Pupils above the fourth grade are taught to typewrite, using the touch method. This enables them to do much of their written work without any eye-strain whatever. Large-type books and charts are provided. Instead of ordinary textbook maps or even wall maps, which contain so much detail and fine print, outline maps painted on slated cloth are used. Much emphasis is placed upon hand training. The pupils are taught to use their hands without looking closely at what they are doing. It is hoped in this way to relieve them of much habitual eye-strain in their everyday occupations. The children are given thorough instruction in eye-hygiene and the conservation of vision. This instruction is supplemented by home visits. The results justify the care and additional expense incurred in conducting these classes. Experience has demonstrated that these classes have actually conserved vision and greatly improved scholarship.

The responsibility still rests upon the school to place these children in occupations where they can attain a maximum of efficiency with a minimum of eye-strain. In most places, sight-saving-class pupils receive more or less aid in securing suitable employment after leaving school. In Cleveland a vocational-guidance worker has been added to the staff of the sight-saving-class department. Her task does not end until each pupil is placed in the position for which he is best fitted by training and natural inclination, and is thus given a chance to prove himself socially and industrially a successful member of the community.[64]

4. Classes for the Deaf.—Educational provisions for deaf children have closely paralleled those for the blind, beginning early in the nineteenth century with state institutions and private schools and ending toward the close of the century with day schools operated as part of the city school system. The same advantages noted above in the case of the blind apply to the establishment of special classes for

[64] R. B. Irwin, *Sight-Saving Classes in the Public Schools*, Harvard Bulletins in Education, No. VII, Nov., 1920. Winifred Hathaway, *Manual for Conservation of Vision Classes*, National Committee for the Prevention of Blindness, Publications No. 18, Nov., 1919. George B. Mangold, *Problems of Child Welfare*, 1924, pp. 172-175.

the deaf in the regular public schools. Special classes for the deaf have been more readily established because the deaf exceed the blind in number and can reach school without assistance. Large cities may have a sufficient number of deaf children to establish a special school building for them. This plan is superior to that of special classes in the regular school buildings, since it makes possible a system of grading, offers economies in equipment, and provides more adequate courses in industrial training.

The first method used in teaching the deaf was the manual, including sign language and the manual alphabet ("finger-spelling"). In recent years this has been largely superseded, especially in the day schools, by the oral method, in which the children are taught speech and lip-reading. In those relatively few cases where it is possible to improve hearing, the auricular method is employed. The social adjustment of the deaf is greatly promoted by the oral method, which enables them to converse with the hearing.

Intellectually the deaf suffer serious disadvantages. The blind can master a formal education more rapidly than the deaf, and their scholastic attainments are usually superior. This is because they have no difficulty in acquiring language. Speech is normally learned through a process of imitating what is heard. The child born deaf hears no sounds and therefore has nothing to imitate; he remains mute unless taught artificially to speak. The acquisition of speech is also hindered if deafness occurs before the habit of speech is fully established—usually taken as occurring by the age of eight. On the other hand, the deaf experience a much lesser problem of economic adjustment than do the blind. That eyesight is an invaluable asset for industrial efficiency is evidenced by the fact that few of the deaf receive charitable relief whereas many of the blind are so assisted.

The Horace Mann School, in Boston, established in 1869, is accredited with being the first day school for the deaf in the United States. Two others were opened before 1890; from 1891 to 1900 there were 22 started. Since then the number has increased more rapidly. In 1926-27 the United States Bureau of Education received reports from 168 schools for the deaf. Of this total number of schools, 69 were supported and controlled by the state, 83 were parts of city school systems, and 16 were private institutions. The state schools reported 13,134 pupils, the city schools 3,515, and the private schools 933—a total enrollment of 17,582. Between 6 and 7 per cent of these children were in high-school grades. Gallaudet College, Washington, D. C., is a national institution of higher education for the deaf.[65]

5. *Classes for Crippled Children.*—A great many children with slight deformities have always attended school in regular classes with children not so handicapped. Other crippled children are in such a physical condition that they need medical care in hospitals or convalescent homes. Their education must be provided for in these residential institutions. Still another group of crippled children are simply in need of special educational facilities, but are unable to attend the regular public-school classes. Until the beginning of this century this last group was mostly neglected. Children incapable of attending school unassisted have been excluded from public-school classes and excused from the compulsory-attendance law. "The various social agencies that come in contact with the untaught crippled child in his home have given impetus to the movement among the schools to establish special educational facilities for children too crippled to compete with the normal child. Since many of these children need orthopedic care, they have been considered outside the proper jurisdiction of the school board. The new view, however, demands that education be provided, that appropriate equipment be obtained by the schools, that some system of transportation be provided, and that a plan of coöperation between the department of school hygiene and the private or public philanthropies providing orthopedic care be carefully followed."[66]

Special day-school classes for cripples are also needed for the development of a social type of personality. "Every child wants to be like other children. The habit of children over 6 years of age is to go to school. Any child who is unable to do so because he is physically crippled misses a great deal more than instruction. Many crippled children have grown up to be 'queer' in an unnecessary degree because they have mingled so little with children of their own age. They have been treated in special fashion by their parents, sometimes harshly in ignorant homes, but more often with a mistaken kindness which saved the 'poor cripple' of the family all exertion and robbed him of the ambition to develop such powers of mind and body as he possessed. For such children there is no other tonic like the give-and-take of life in the schoolroom and on the playground."[67]

[65] Frank M. Phillips, *Schools for the Deaf, 1926-27,* U. S. Bureau of Education Bulletin, 1928, No. 8, pp. 1-2. Harry Best, *The Deaf,* 1914, Part II. George B. Mangold, *Problems of Child Welfare,* 1924, pp. 175-177.
[66] George B. Mangold, *Problems of Child Welfare,* 1924, p. 178.
[67] Edith Reeves Solenberger, *Public School Classes for Crippled Children,* U. S. Bureau of Education Bulletin, 1918, No. 10, p. 7.

Chicago in 1899 established the first public-school class for crippled children in the United States. It now maintains under the board of education a permanent school building for the exclusive use of crippled children. Cleveland also has a public-school building especially designed and built for crippled children, and similar day-school buildings though privately owned are to be found in Boston and New York. Most of the crippled children attending the special public-school classes for cripples are taught in rooms set aside for them in the regular school buildings. New York City inaugurated special classes for crippled children in the public schools in 1906. There are now about 50 classes, located in 16 public-school buildings, enrolling over a thousand pupils. These classes are made convenient to pupils, being usually on the first floor and close to play facilities. Special desks and seats and other needed equipment have been liberally provided. Similar provisions for crippled children may be found in Baltimore, Philadelphia, and Detroit. These cities, with Chicago, Cleveland, and New York, are the pioneers and leaders in this work. In 1930, some 85 cities had made provision for the special education of crippled children.

The children are usually admitted to a special class for cripples upon the recommendation of the department of medical supervision, and while in attendance they are under the care of an orthopedic surgeon. The board of education provides transportation facilities and in some cities a noon lunch. In other cases the special expense is met by private contributions. The per capita cost of special-class education of cripples, though considerable, is less than that for the education of the blind and deaf.

The physical condition of many crippled children makes necessary slow progress in school work. Handwork and vocational training are emphasized wherever possible and are closely adapted to the physical condition of the individual child. The same arguments which are advanced for the occupational training of healthy children apply also to crippled children. In addition there is a special mental-hygiene value in such work for the latter group. If they can feel that they are doing useful work—and especially if they are exercising some developed talent or skill—they are at once raised to a much happier plane of life, and their work acts as a tonic both to mind and body. Their attention is diverted from their ailments and incapacity, and this helps to neutralize the painful self-consciousness which often aggravates their sufferings. The cripple of wage-earning age takes great strides toward a normal point of view when he finds himself actually doing useful work.[68]

As compared with the situation of other handicapped children, educational provisions for the crippled are still meager. Whereas special provision for the deaf and blind children is made in all states and for feeble-minded and delinquent children in most of the states, few states make any special provision for the care and education of crippled children, and in only a few cities are there separate schools or classes for them, and in the schools of most cities, towns, and rural districts not even suitable seats and desks are provided for them. The National Vocational Rehabilitation Act, passed in 1920, to assist the states in providing for the vocational rehabilitation of physically disabled persons of employable age and for their return to civil employment, does not specifically provide for the promotion of local rehabilitation services in the schools. Hence there has been but little development in this direction.[69] As a class, cripples have been largely neglected, though they are more numerous than both blind and deaf. The complete and careful survey—based on a house-to-house canvass —made in Cleveland in 1916, showed that there were 6 cripples for each 1,000 inhabitants.[70] In this study a cripple was defined as one physically handicapped by defects of skeleton or skeletal muscles. Twenty-two per cent of all cases were under 15 years of age, 9 per cent were from 15 to 19 years of age. In 49 per cent of the cases the disability occurred before the age of 15. These figures emphasize the public-school importance of the crippled child. Although some crippled children need hospital care (and the public school can aid in providing for their education while there), many present mainly an educational and vocational problem, which is a task the public school could well undertake to a greater degree than is now the case.

The Visiting Teacher.—"Every teacher, every social worker, and many a parent is familiar with the problem child—the boy or girl whose school progress or whose reactions to normal requirements point toward later inefficiency, delinquency, or some other failure in

[68] Edith Reeves, *Care and Education of Crippled Children in the United States,* 1914, chs. III, IV. Edith Reeves Solenberger, *Public School Classes for Crippled Children,* U. S. Bureau of Education Bulletin, 1918, No. 10, pp. 34-45. Arch O. Heck, *Education of Crippled Children,* U. S. Bureau of Education Bulletin, 1930, No. 11.

[69] *Thirteenth Annual Report of the Federal Board for Vocational Education,* 1929, Sec. III, Vocational Rehabilitation.

[70] Lucy Wright and Amy Hamburger, *Education and Occupations of Cripples, Juvenile and Adult: A Survey of All the Cripples of Cleveland, Ohio, in 1916,* Publications of the Red Cross Institute for Crippled and Disabled Men, Series II, No. 3, 1918.

personal or social adjustment. What is the trouble with such children, and what can be done for them? How can the school obtain and utilize a knowledge of the forces that are affecting their success, and give them in fullest measure the benefits of their educational experience?"[71] An answer to these questions is being made by the visiting teacher, a specialist recently introduced into the public school system. She combines the two-fold basic training and experience of a teacher and a social case worker. She is familiar with the principles of modern psychology and psychiatry, and has special knowledge of the behavior problems of children.

The function of the visiting teacher has been well stated by Mr. Howard W. Nudd, Chairman of the National Committee on Visiting Teachers, as follows:[72]

The visiting teacher's treatment of problem children is based upon the fact that useful citizenship and right living are the normal outgrowth of sound training and wholesome behavior in childhood and that the attainment of these ends is vitally affected by environmental influences and by the child's attitude toward himself, toward others, and toward the opportunities and the obstacles he may encounter. His scholastic progress and deportment in school, his heredity, his emotional nature, his interests, ambitions, and dislikes, and the experiences which evoke the reactions that shape his character thus become the subjects of the visiting teacher's inquiry and take her into the home, the class-room, or wherever a situation exists that may help to reveal and explain the causes of his difficulties.

The school is, of course, but one of the many forces that influence the child's life and create the attitudes toward self and others which so largely determine his achievement and behavior. The child is in school scarcely 12 per cent of the time. Influences in home and neighborhood, which operate during 88 per cent of the time, must, so far as is possible, be coördinated with those of the school, if all the factors which enter into the process of development are to be understood and made to count most for the child and society. Traced back to its ultimate source the trouble with the problem child not infrequently lies in the home and particularly in the failure of the responsible adults to understand and successfully manage some of their own problems.[73] Someone is needed within the school system whose duty

---

[71] Howard W. Nudd, *The Purpose and Scope of Visiting Teacher Work*, Publications of the Joint Committee on Methods of Preventing Delinquency, Reprint Series No. 3, 1926, p. 3.

[72] *Ibid.*, p. 4.

[73] See *Three Problem Children, Narratives from the Case Records of a Child Guidance Clinic*, Joint Committee on Methods of Preventing Delinquency, Publication No. 2. Mary B. Sayles, *The Problem Child at Home, A Study in Parent-Child Relationships*, 1928.

it should be to know the conditions under which the pupils live and play, and their consequent educational needs, to become acquainted with the individual child in his home and school relations, to discover handicapping factors and to bring about the adjustment of his special difficulties through the coöperation of home, school, and social agencies.[74] This need is met by the visiting teacher.

"The visiting teacher's services are devoted primarily to the needs of those individual children who present problems of scholarship or conduct of a baffling, erratic, troublesome, or suspicious nature, or who show signs of apparent neglect or other difficulties which the regular staff of the school finds itself unable to understand or to deal with unaided. Such children include those who, for some unaccountable reason, fall below standard in scholarship, although they are not subnormal; the repeater, the restive, and the over-age who are counting the days until they may 'go to work'; the precocious and the gifted who have difficulty in finding full scope or wholesome outlet for their interests and abilities; the adolescent who appear unable, without special guidance, to avoid the pitfalls they encounter; those whose conduct gives suspicion of undesirable companionship or unwholesome interests and shows tendencies toward unsocial behavior or delinquency; the irritable, the worried, the violent-tempered and the repressed; the indescribable who are perpetually stumbling into difficulties or getting out of tune with their environment and who are always in need of counsel; and the apparently neglected, abused or overworked, whose home conditions appear so adverse that special assistance, supervision, or guidance is needed."[75]

Much of what is known today as visiting-teacher work has always been performed by the regular teaching staff, especially by those rare souls who possessed a keen understanding of child nature, an insight into personal characteristics, and a special gift for smoothing out the tangles in social relations. Changing conditions, however, both in and out of school, have made this less common and have demanded the services of a specialist. The increased size of classes, the increased amount of work, the growth of after-school activities have prevented the teacher from knowing the home and out-of-school life of her pupils and from maintaining the close personal relationships with the children that she often did in former years. The growing complexity of city life, the instability of the family, the increased cosmo-

[74] Jane F. Culbert, "The Visiting Teacher," *Annals Amer. Acad. Polit. Soc. Sci.*, Nov., 1921, 98:187:82.
[75] Howard W. Nudd, *The Purpose and Scope of Visiting Teacher Work*, Publications of the Joint Committee on Methods of Preventing Delinquency, Reprint Series No. 3, 1926, pp. 7-8.

politan character of the population, the changing economic conditions, and other aspects of social change have intensified the problems
and made them more complex. Except in extremely simple cases,
there is needed a larger experience in social work than the class
teacher can be expected to acquire while performing with full efficiency her regular duties. Furthermore, such work not only involves
visits during regular school hours to see the mother alone, or at night
to talk over with the family group the problems of the child, but requires a flexible time schedule for follow-up work and for emergency
calls to various social agencies which the exigencies of class instruction make impossible. There is thus need of a specialist to assist the
regular staff. The visiting teacher must know intimately the teachers
and principals with whom she must coöperate and through whom
much of her work is accomplished; she must work closely with all
special school officials, particularly the nurse, the psychologist, and
the attendance officer.[76]

Among the reasons given for referring children to the visiting
teachers—as indicated by a study of case records—are the following,
listed roughly in order of importance: (1) maladjustments in
scholarship, including subnormality, retardation, deficiency in lessons, precocity; (2) adverse home conditions—poverty, neglect, improper guardianship, immorality, cruelty; (3) irregular attendance;
(4) misconduct: in school, out of school, involving morals; (5) late-
ness; (6) physical condition.[77]

Many different types of treatment are employed by the visiting
teacher in an attempt to effect an adjustment. The school may modify
requirements to meet the need of the child by changing the class,
transferring the child to a special school, shifting emphasis from one
phase of school work to another, adopting a new approach to the
child, or connecting his school work more closely with his outside
interests. Frequently the desired result is effected by changing the
child's own attitude toward his problem. Many times the adjustment
of the difficulty lies in the home, but to remedy some situations, the
visiting teacher may put the child or the family in touch with a
social agency. Frequently the satisfactory outcome involves the combined help of family, school, and social agencies as well as the redirec-

---

[76] *Ibid.*, p. 26.   J. J. Oppenheimer, *The Visiting Teacher Movement*, 1925,
chs. II, III, IV.

[77] Public Education Association, *The Visiting Teacher in the United States*,
1921, p. 25; 1923, p. 23. Mabel B. Ellis, *The Visiting Teacher in Rochester*, 1925,
pp. 97-101.

tion of the child's interests and energy, as the following case clearly illustrates.[78]

William's teacher and parents made almost simultaneous complaints at the principal's office. The latter complained that the boy stayed out late at night, hanging on the street corners with "loafers," that he was disobedient, that he used the money given him to buy the baby's milk for cigarettes and for gambling; the teacher said that he was doing nothing in class but making trouble, that he "wasn't interested in a blessed thing." The parents wanted to have him "put away," and the teacher wished to have him "demoted until he learned to behave."

The visiting teacher found William a tall, overgrown, awkward boy, all arms and legs, who felt as big as a man, and had no feeling but resentment against the school for refusing to give him his working papers so that he "could go to work like a man." He was in a lower grade than most boys of his age because he had come to America only a few years before. Because he had to "stay in school with the kids," he took it out on the teacher. He neglected his lessons, bothered the other boys and was a constant drag on the class. He carried his grudge out from school and tried to do all the grown-up things he could think of, and cultivated the acquaintance of the older group of "loafers." His road was leading down-hill precipitately.

The visiting teacher explained the working paper situation to the boy, found out the kind of work he wished to go into, showed him the advantage for that trade of further education, and made him see that his recent conduct had been babyish rather than manly. The teacher, of course, gave him a new start, and the parents were made to realize that the boy needed wholesome recreation and association with older boys. Arrangements were made for him to join an athletic club at a nearby settlement where he was tried out in a position of responsibility which seemed to him worthy of his age and mettle.

William's remaining seven months of school were profitable to him and not a drawback to his classmates. When he left school, he had lost the grudge and had gained a feeling of fair play and loyalty. His relation to his parents was helpful, his friends were the kind of which they approved, and his conduct no longer a source of worry.

Many extremely interesting case records, explaining what the visiting teacher does and how she does it, have been published by the Joint Committee on Methods of Preventing Delinquency, under the auspices of the Commonwealth Fund. The following case, selected because of its brevity, is typical.[79]

---

[78] Jane F. Culbert, "The Visiting Teacher," *Annals Amer. Acad. Polit. Soc. Sci.*, Nov., 1921, 98:187:84-85.

[79] Mabel B. Ellis, *The Visiting Teacher in Rochester*, 1925, p. 120. See also Mary B. Sayles, *The Problem Child in School, Narratives from Case Records of Visiting Teachers*, 1926.

Problems Presented: Retardation; attendance. Disobedience at home; parents dead; no control by grandmother.

Fern was fifteen years old and in the fifth grade. She lived with her grandmother who had little control of her and the girl was in the habit of running away from school and spending her time on the streets. The visiting teacher found that she hated school because she could not do the work of the grade and was older than the other children who made fun of her and called her "dunce."

Fern was tested by the child study department and her mental age was found to be three years below her life age. She was transferred to a girls' vocational class with pupils of her own size, age, and mental ability. Instead of wearing the unhappy, sullen, and worried expression which characterized her at first, Fern became all smiles. She was not tardy nor absent after the transfer. She helped in the preparation of the teachers' lunch and in the afternoon took entire charge of the distribution of milk in the grades. At the suggestion of the visiting teacher the Family Welfare Society, who were already interested in the family, provided proper shoes for Fern and cloth so that the girl could make her own dresses in school.

The latest report from the grandmother was: "What have you done to Fern? She stays in nights and is so nice to me!"

The value of the visiting-teacher movement is attested by its growth. The first visiting teachers began work in the year 1906-07 in New York City, Boston, and Hartford, Connecticut. In these communities and later in other places, as has frequently happened with other educational experiments, the impulse came from outside the school system. Also like other innovations in the school organization and curriculum, such as medical inspection, mental examinations, and manual training, visiting-teacher work was first intended for the benefit of the less fortunate children in schools in the poorer sections of the city. In a similar fashion the service is being extended to benefit the normal and the more favored children of the better schools. Private organizations—in Boston, settlements and civic organizations; in New York City, settlements and the Public Education Association; in Hartford, the director of the Psychological Clinic—first saw the need and privately maintained the work until school boards became convinced of its value and incorporated it as part of the system. In other cities, like Rochester and Mt. Vernon, New York, and Cleveland, Ohio, the work was introduced directly by the school authorities themselves. Great impetus was given to the movement in 1921, when the Commonwealth Fund included the work in its Program for the Prevention of Delinquency, and, through the Public Education Association of the City of New York, organized a National Committee on Visiting Teachers to establish demonstrations in thirty communities in the United States presenting a wide variety of geographical, social, and educational situations. The directors of the Fund realized that even though much of the visiting teacher's work is concerned with scholarship, behavior, and other types of maladjustment which may not necessarily lead to delinquency, still much delinquency can be prevented if problems of behavior and personality are adequately dealt with early in the child's school life.[80] In 1926, 74 cities reported visiting teachers, many of the cities having from 15 to 20 such teachers each.[81]

Students of the field of child welfare who are turning to the school as the logical place for the detection and study of child maladjustments see great promise in the growth of visiting-teacher work. They look forward to the time "when each child shall be dealt with as an individual; when he will be properly graded, his task fitted to his capacity. They anticipate the time when all the forces at work upon the child may be harnessed to pull toward one goal. Then, as a natural outcome, it is hoped that retardation will become negligible; nervousness and mental disorders will be guarded against; juvenile delinquency will be reduced to a minimum, and industrial inefficiency will be greatly lessened, because each child will go out, not prematurely and handicapped by inadequate training or the sense and habit of failure, but equipped and able to realize his potentialities."[82]

The Socialization of Education.—The recent movements and developments in the public-school system which we have traced above have tended to transform the school into a social agency serving the broad aim of social welfare. Education has been socialized and democratized by the introduction of compulsory attendance, vocational training and guidance, part-time and continuation classes, school hygiene, education of handicapped children, prevention of truancy and non-attendance, the work of the visiting teacher, the development of the school as a community center, and educational extension. It must be clear that the socialization of education in these directions will have a large part in preventing social ills. If only

[80] J. J. Oppenheimer, *The Visiting Teacher Movement*, 1925, ch. I. Public Education Association, *The Visiting Teacher in the United States*, 1921 and 1923, ch. I. Howard W. Nudd, *The Purpose and Scope of Visiting Teacher Work*, Publications of the Joint Committee on Methods of Preventing Delinquency, Reprint Series No. 3, 1926, pp. 27-30.

[81] W. S. Deffenbaugh, "Recent Movements in City School Systems," *Biennial Survey of Education, 1924-26*, U. S. Bureau of Education Bulletin, 1928, No. 25, pp. 76-77.

[82] Jane F. Culbert, "The Visiting Teacher," *Annals Amer. Acad. Polit. Soc. Sci.*, Nov., 1921, 98:187:89.

people knew how to care for their bodies, how to choose an occupation and prepare themselves for it, and how to play their part as citizens, many of the problems of society would be greatly reduced and the general tone of social and political life improved.[83]

Herein lies the justification for the greatly increased expenditures which the growth of the work of the school and the extraordinary expansion of educational institutions have involved. In 1890 the total cost of public education was but $141,000,000. In 1900 this increased to $215,000,000, in 1910 to $426,000,000, in 1920 to $1,036,000,000, in 1930 to about $2,500,000,000. These figures need to be corrected for the changing value of the dollar, but they suggest an enormous growth in the cost of education. At that, the American people expend less for education than for luxuries. The amount spent for tobacco alone is about equal to the total public bill for education. The amount expended for passenger automobiles is several times as large. Great as are the expenditures for public education, they need to be increased. Better school buildings and more adequate equipment, especially in rural districts, better-trained and higher-paid teachers, further expansion of the curriculum and the development of a philosophy of education more adjusted to the requirements of an industrial society are among the urgent needs. Despite its conservatism, public education has made notable advances in adaptation to changing social conditions. The process must continue.

[83] Stuart A. Queen, *Social Work in the Light of History*, 1922, pp. 59-61.

CHAPTER XVI

ADULT EDUCATION

THE term "adult education" came into general use in the United States soon after the World War. It was first adopted as a substitute for the term "Americanization," which was applied to the movement, then receiving much public attention, to assimilate the foreign-born population. The War had disclosed much evidence of lack of assimilation and had given great stimulus to the demand for instruction of immigrants. Almost every large community established classes for preparing the foreign-born for American citizenship. The War also revealed a large problem of native illiteracy, and to the classes for immigrants came also native-born citizens that they might learn to read and write the English language. "Americanization" evidently did not fit, and to avoid its use the term "adult education," which has a much broader significance and was well known in Europe, came into general usage. Adult education then became a slogan for the continued education of all adults. Besides the instruction of immigrants and illiterates, numerous other activities which had long been carried on were attached to the movement, and new organizations were formed to promote various phases of education for grown men and women.[1]

Adult education is a new name for an old practice. In this country, different aspects of adult education, furthered by agencies adapted to the conditions of the time, have existed from the earliest days. It was one of the first forms of education to be set up. In later years, our grandparents supported the lyceums, and they did their reading seriously; our mothers, particularly in the smaller communities, were grouped in coteries for mutual intellectual improvement. The development of adult education, as we now understand it, however, as an organized movement, has been very recent and, since the war, very rapid.[2]

The idea of educating adults is old. Both Plato and Aristotle thought of education as an interest which as a matter of course extended into adult life. The emphasis upon the education of the adult mind, how-

[1] L. R. Alderman, *Adult Education Activities During the Biennium, 1926-28*, U. S. Bureau of Education Bulletin, 1929, No. 23, pp. 1-2.
[2] Frederick P. Keppel, "Education for Adults," *Yale Review*, April, 1926, 15:3:419.

ever, is new, and is in contrast with much modern thought on the subject of education. Modern educators are chiefly interested in the problem of educating children. Within the last century, education became more or less completely identified with schooling, and was allocated almost exclusively to the period of childhood and youth. It was not realized that people are molded by all that influences them. The institutions of daily life, home, work, politics, leisure, and religion, as well as school, all these play upon us and help to make us what we are, either positively or negatively. It was not until the War that we began to find out how imperfect, for a democracy, must be any scheme that identifies education with schooling, and that limits it to youth.[3] According to the traditional American view, when schooling is over, education is complete.

On the last day of the academic year all over our country in colleges and high-schools, orators are solemnly explaining to young people that the day which ends their schooling is called "Commencement Day" because it is the day on which they stop being educated and commence real life. And the young people before them, deadly weary of their schooling, nod their heads in heart-felt agreement with this water-tight partition between education and real life. First one and then the other, with no mixing! That's what they have been taught, by their schooling, and that is the principle on which most of them act.[4]

Adult education, on the other hand, is not concerned with entrance or exit examinations, with commencement or diploma. It stresses education as a life process. It logically calls for a reorganization of the content of the material which is presented for learning to youthful students and the spreading out of the process in accordance with some plan whereby the individual will systematically continue to study and to acquire intellectual equipment throughout life. As a social movement, it aspires to make continued education universal, instead of limited to the few. "The average mature individual is not, like the ancient Greek student, a member of the leisure class, nor may he like the mediæval scholar retreat to a cloister. He must earn his living and seek education during his leisure time. To be sure, the formal and professional education of our time has still the advantages of a certain privilege and seclusion. Adult education must necessarily proceed without these valuable aids to learning. In earlier ages it was generally believed that education could not be achieved without these advantages. Modern men insist that the spiritual values of life be real-

---

[3] Joseph K. Hart, *Adult Education*, 1927, pp. vii, 187.
[4] Dorothy Canfield Fisher, *Why Stop Learning?* 1927, p. 10.

ized not in contemplative aloofness but in the life of activity. They also demand a satisfactory existence for as many people as possible; hence all are to have opportunity to share in the cultural goods of civilization. Education is made universal and, below a certain age, compulsory. But it is obvious that unless education is to remain the privilege of a few professionally trained scholars, large numbers of people must be given the facilities for continued study after school or college days are passed."[5]

"Any one who considers for the moment the signs of the times, knows that the next battle in the campaign of democracy is going to rage around the question of the possibility and advisability of general education for the majority of grown-ups, just as the battle of the last century has been about the possibility and advisability of general schooling for all the young."[6]

The adult-education movement is partly due to the facts that adults now have more leisure than ever before and that the principles of education are better understood. Cutten, in his *Threat of Leisure*, remarks on the greatly increased leisure resulting from the Industrial Revolution, and the opportunity it affords for further education. The mind grows by use, and its ability to acquire new concepts does not stop with maturity but is in fact dependent largely upon what it has already acquired. That learning ability is tenacious is revealed most strikingly by the study made by Professor Thorndike and his colleagues, who carried on an extensive series of tests concerning changes in the amount and nature of ability to learn from about age 15 to about age 45, and especially from age 25 to 45. "In general," they concluded, "nobody under 45 should restrain himself from trying to learn anything because of a belief or fear that he is too old to be able to learn it. . . . Teachers of adults of age 25 to 45 should expect them to learn at nearly the same rate and in nearly the same manner as they would have learned the same thing at fifteen to twenty. What that rate and manner will be depends upon the general intelligence and special capacities of the individual. . . . Adult education suffers no mystical handicap because of the age of the students."[7]

The adult-education movement represents not only an adjustment to the problems of illiteracy and immigrant instruction—it is not

[5] Everett Dean Martin, *The Meaning of a Liberal Education*, 1926, p. 309. Cf. Eduard C. Lindeman, *The Meaning of Adult Education*, 1926, ch. I.
[6] Dorothy Canfield Fisher, *Why Stop Learning?* 1927, pp. 14-15.
[7] Edward L. Thorndike, Elsie O. Bregman, J. Warren Tilton, and Ella Woodyard, *Adult Learning*, 1928, pp. 177-178, 179.

necessarily for the benighted—it has also been called forth by the problems created by the unprecedented industrial and social changes, which have revolutionized industry and transformed village into city. Adults no less than youth need education for intelligent living in this changed world.

The old time village has largely disintegrated, due to the changes of modern living, but the village mind is still with us: our communities, for all their schools, and books, and radios, still develop little in most of their members but the same old village mind, with, it may be, some smatterings of phrases picked up on excursions into some alien territory. The village has merely been transferred to the city. Most city residents have come from villages, bringing their village minds with them. The Iowa farmer in a California city is an example. And almost all who have been born in cities have grown up in some local area and have come to maturity with the fragmentary sort of a mind that a fragment of a city tends to call forth. There is probably no more provincial person in the world than the native resident of New York City.[8]

The task of adult education is to make sure that eventually there will be produced generations of adults whose intellectual history from childhood on will have been that of normal progression, full development, and actual achievement of an intelligent adjustment to the changing modern world and its opportunities, its tasks, and its responsibilities.

The activities in the field of adult education are too numerous for complete mention and too diverse for all-inclusive classification. They represent an astonishing variety of effort, and afford picturesque contrasts between their respective values. Some of them suggest the "clutter of tail-tags which always float behind the rising kite of a new popular fashion."[9] In every new movement one may expect the "lunatic fringe." Limiting our attention to the more important, the more definitely organized and more responsible agencies of adult education, we may classify them roughly into the scholastic and non-scholastic types. In the first division fall the schools, both public and private, commercial and non-commercial, whose activities range from the elementary to the collegiate and professional type of education. These are the more formal agencies. Their work, as we shall see, is preponderantly vocational in character, and much of it is highly commercialized. Formal adult education may be defined as the process of learning, on the initiative of the individual, seriously and consecu-

[8] Joseph K. Hart, *Adult Education*, 1927, pp. 5 (quoted), 257.
[9] Dorothy Canfield Fisher, *Why Stop Learning?* 1927, p. 259.

tively undertaken as a supplement to some primary occupation.[10] Its outstanding characteristics are that it is carried on voluntarily and during the leisure time of a mature individual, it is somewhat continuous and is pursued under guidance. Turning to the less formal opportunities for adults, we find a great variety of agencies, such as the lyceums and chautauquas, clubs, public lecture courses and forums, libraries and museums. We must also reckon with the motion picture, the theatre, and the radio. How far the newspapers and magazines contribute to what may fairly be called adult education depends upon the quality of the periodical and its readers. Probably more people than we realize are, through them, becoming well informed. The various agencies reach millions of people annually. The whole field of adult education appears as a comprehensive though diffuse and vague new kind of education, which transcends all schools and all barriers of age.

All in all, it is certainly safe to say that education for adults has now become one of our major industries. This vast movement has grown up outside our best educational traditions and leadership, and so without the guidance and control by which it might have profited. The steps in the movement for adult education have been limited generally to those which will pay. Even within the university organization itself, this is true. All along the line, but especially in the scholastic field, the development of adult education has been controlled by this economic factor, and in the majority of cases the enterprise in this country is frankly commercial in character.[11] In the formal field of adult education the overwhelming emphasis has been on vocational courses, courses in which the student can see a quick return for his investment. This is indicative of a general demand for vocational education, due largely to the fact that until recently the public schools inadequately prepared the students for their life work. This situation has furnished an excellent opportunity for commercialization. As we study some of the agencies, such as correspondence schools, lyceums, and chautauquas, we wonder whether the general interest in adult education is evidence of a spontaneous and growing desire for knowledge, or is something promoted, worked up by interests which would "educate the masses" in order to attain certain economic ends.

1. THE SCHOOL TYPE OF AGENCY

In the field of public education of adults the chief agencies are city school systems, state departments of education, and colleges and

[10] Frederick P. Keppel, "Education for Adults," *Yale Review*, April, 1926, 15:3:418.

[11] *Ibid.*, pp. 420-421, 424.

universities. The main provisions include classes for illiterates and for foreigners, public evening schools, and the various activities coming under the head of university extension. Some of these activities are also provided by private agencies, such as the Y.M.C.A., the commercial correspondence schools, and the privately endowed institutions of higher learning.

Public-School Classes for Adults.—The first public-school provision for adult education was the evening school, which dates from the eighteen-forties. The first public evening high school was started in Cincinnati in 1856. Originally, evening schools were begun to provide education for those unable to attend during the day, and this continued to be their important function up to about 1900. Since that time, however, the evening school, both elementary and high, has been greatly expanded and materially changed in character.[12]

With the more general enforcement of compulsory education, the urgent need for providing duplicate elementary schools for children at work during the day has in large part disappeared, since such children are now required to attend day elementary schools until they reach a certain age, varying among the states from 14 to 18 years. In consequence, evening elementary schools are now chiefly useful, in states enforcing a good compulsory-education law, in providing the foreign-born with the elements of an English education and in teaching native illiterates. The World War, as was noted above, gave great stimulus to the organization of such instruction, for it revealed the fact that a very large number of men of military age were unfitted for general military assignment because of the lack of ability to read ordinary communications or to convey information by writing; it also disclosed that a large proportion of the foreign-born population was not assimilated. Many communities started classes for these groups, and a number of states passed laws to aid and promote such work. In 1928, some 26 states had enacted legislation to provide education for adult foreigners, and some 25 states (including most of the former) had made legal provision for the education of adult native illiterates. Twenty-two states include both provisions, and 21 states give financial aid to local communities for this type of adult education. These states reported 2,429 communities as holding public-school classes for such adults in the year 1927-28, with a total enrollment of 262,308.[13]

Since the beginning of the century, the evening high schools have

[12] Ellwood P. Cubberley, *Public Education in the United States*, 1919, pp. 421-423.
[13] L. R. Alderman, *Adult Education Activities During the Biennium, 1926-28*, U. S. Bureau of Education Bulletin, 1929, No. 23, pp. 4-5.

also assumed new functions and have grown vastly in importance. Though continuing to offer cultural studies for those who have completed the elementary schools and wish, while working, to continue study, they have now largely become schools for training along scientific, technical, home arts, commercial, and industrial lines. A few students use the evening high schools to prepare for entrance to college or a technical school, but the large majority attend them to attain greater efficiency in the occupations in which they are engaged. This expansion of the evening high school along vocational lines has been greatly furthered by the Smith-Hughes Act. Probably more than a million persons are enrolled in public evening schools. The typical age is 19 or 20. Most of them left day school, not because of financial pressure, but because they had lost interest. Their reason for returning is the realization that education pays.[14]

Y.M.C.A. Schools.—In addition to the provision of libraries, reading rooms, lectures, practical talks, Americanization work, and other informal types of education, the Y.M.C.A.'s in the larger cities are carrying on a regular school type of adult education. It is this phase of their work which will be considered here.

The Y.M.C.A. was one of the pioneers in the development of evening education for employed men and boys. The beginnings of its work in this field go back to 1866, when 4 associations had 60 students enrolled in evening classes. During the eighties, evening educational classes became a generally recognized part of the Y.M.C.A. program. In 1892 the educational department of the International Committee was organized, and as a result of its activity the educational work of the associations increased in extent and improved in quality. By 1900, the number of associations doing educational work was 288, and the total number of different students 24,395. The period of greatest expansion and organization has been since the beginning of the present century. Meanwhile emphasis has shifted from elementary and high-school subjects to the development of vocational training. At the present time more than 75 per cent of the Y.M.C.A. educational work is vocational in its major objectives. In 1923, when a study was made for the United States Bureau of Education, there were 365 association schools enrolling 120,205 students.[15]

The student body in the association schools ranges in age from 15

[14] Frederick P. Keppel, "Education for Adults," *Yale Review*, April, 1926, 15:3:419-420. L. R. Alderman and Ellen C. Lombard, *Adult Education*, U. S. Bureau of Education Bulletin, 1931, No. 20, pp. 7-8.
[15] William F. Hirsch, *Educational Work of the Young Men's Christian Association*, U. S. Bureau of Education Bulletin, 1923, No. 7.

years to well past 50; the average age is approximately 25 years. The persons appealed to by the association's educational program are, in the main, men who have had a number of years of experience in earning a living and who have learned the value of a more thorough educational preparation for their vocational careers. An analysis of the student enrollment by subjects shows 48.7 per cent taking commercial subjects, 17 per cent industrial, 6.7 per cent professional, 14.1 per cent academic, and 13.5 per cent socio-civic subjects. The students in the association schools pay nearly the full expense of maintaining the schools. The field in which the schools operate is that of formal part-time adult education—a field of service which is largely unoccupied. Their objectives are educational and character building.

Since 1919, a definite effort to standardize subjects and courses of study has been carried on by the United Y.M.C.A. Schools. Where the existing text material cannot readily be adapted to the needs of the course as outlined, specially written texts have been prepared. Such textbooks have already been published in salesmanship, public speaking, foremanship, business letters and reports, income tax, C.P.A. accounting, advertising, and traffic management. The process of standardization has finally led to the adoption of a national system of interchangeable credit certificates. These certificates are accepted for credit by any of the schools in the system in cases where students are obliged to transfer from one city to another. They are also accepted as credits toward collegiate degrees, which are now offered by 22 leading association schools, on authority granted by the respective state departments of education.

The schools conducted by the Y.M.C.A. are of the following types.

Schools of Commerce.—More than 50 of the association schools have adopted the standard four-year curricula of college grade work for the school of commerce. Three of these curricula, namely, accountancy, marketing, and management, lead to a degree.

Law Schools.—"Twenty of the associations have developed evening law schools, which are being conducted on the principle of meeting all of the reasonable demands for adequate legal education and proper development of character in prospective candidates for admission to the bar. All of these schools have at least a three years' course, and it is only a matter of time when all will require four years of legal studies in addition to the other preparation required by the various States of candidates for the bar examination."

Engineering Schools.—There are 12 Y.M.C.A. engineering schools, the most notable one being the Day Co-operative Engineering School of the Boston Y.M.C.A. It is the second largest coöperative engineering school in the United

States, having over 900 students enrolled. This school requires the completion of a 5 years' course, which leads to the degree of mechanical, civil, electrical, or chemical engineer.

Automotive and Machine-Shop Schools.—Before the business depression of 1921 there were 75 automotive schools among the associations, enrolling more than 15,000 students. There are now about 50 such schools in operation. They give instruction in automotive repair work, electricity, battery construction and repair, vulcanizing and acetylene welding, as well as in automotive driving. A considerable number of them also teach machine-shop work.

College Preparatory Schools.—These schools are of two kinds: the evening preparatory schools, conducted by the associations in all of the larger cities, and the day secondary schools for boys, conducted by 8. In the evening preparatory schools will be found hundreds of earnest students, many of them of mature age, who are obliged to secure their high-school experience through evening study. A few of these students are taking the work simply to secure high-school education; a larger number are preparing for entrance to college or professional school. The day secondary schools have developed because of the desire of many parents to place their boys in secondary schools which have a definite character-building program and a Christian atmosphere. The full-time day secondary schools are comparable to the higher type of academies.

Miscellaneous Schools.—There are other types of schools, such as radio, junior commercial, pharmacy, machine trades, mechanical dentistry, employed boys, etc., which space will not permit to be more than mentioned.

Thus the former plan of a collection of unrelated classes and subjects has been supplanted by the organization of real schools with standard unit courses arranged in two-, three-, and four-year curricula. The standardized and coördinated educational work of the Y.M.C.A. has demonstrated that part-time education can be made a serious undertaking, and that it can provide for the man obliged to earn his living a practical and worthwhile means for obtaining college and technical training.

Educational Work of the Y.W.C.A.—Most of the educational work of the Y.W.C.A. is of the informal type, carried on through club programs and other association projects. In some cases, however, the Y.W.C.A. has organized schools and classes. It is not the purpose of the association to duplicate existing agencies. Only if instruction in the subjects asked for cannot be found elsewhere, or if it is given under conditions that make it not available for the girl in question, does the Y.W.C.A. undertake to provide it.

About forty of the larger city associations maintain organized schools. Noteworthy among them are those in Cincinnati, Philadelphia, Germantown, Indianapolis, Dallas, San Francisco, Seattle, Brooklyn, and New York. Each has its own special field of interest, the result of the special kind of community whose needs it has tried to meet. The Ballard School, in New York, established in 1873, was the first, and it is probably the most highly developed. This school and the Harlem Branch School may serve as illustrations; they show certain characteristics common to all the schools.

During the year 1921 there were enrolled in the Ballard School, in day and evening classes, some 3,577 students in 46 different subjects. The total registration was 5,153. Two-thirds of the enrollment is in evening classes. Courses vary in length from nine months to a single lesson. Only a few of the teachers give full time. The secretarial course and the various business classes are taken during their leisure hours by many employed girls who are ambitious to fit themselves for better positions and higher salaries. English courses, elocution, dramatics, and public speaking are often chosen for a similar reason. The "trained attendants" course, conducted in coöperation with certain hospitals, and the course in tea-room management conclude the list of the more common types of work provided.

Much more than the Ballard School, the "School of Opportunity," Harlem Branch, New York, plans for girls of less than high-school education. "It has among its students employed girls who have left school early to go to work and are ambitious for more education because their work has shown them specific needs for it; younger girls whose parents send them to the Young Women's Christian Association school in the hope that its atmosphere and its intimate individual attention will get a hold on them that the public school with its larger classes has not been able to get; older girls and married women who in the late twenties, the thirties, and the early forties find themselves in need of preparation for making a living or a better living, or have grown tired of economic dependency, or turn to some sort of study or craft because they begin to find life insufficiently interesting."[16] Among the courses given are scientific treatment of hair and skin, domestic arts, costume design, interior decorating, music, and fine arts. They are usually taken for vocational purposes.

University Extension.—University extension originated in England about the middle of the nineteenth century as a method for

---

[16] Education and Research Division, National Board of Y. W. C. A., *Educational Work of the Young Women's Christian Association*, U. S. Bureau of Education Bulletin, 1923, No. 26.

extending the advantages of university instruction by means of lectures and classes at important centers. The movement first took form as a result of the pioneer work of Professor James Stuart, of Cambridge, from 1867 on, when several English universities took up his lecture method with growing success. The movement developed in response to the demand for some form of higher education, literary and scientific, applicable to the masses of the people. This demand eventually found expression in the organization of the so-called tutorial classes. Since the most striking characteristic of university extension in England is its vital relation to the labor movement, it will be discussed more fully later, when consideration is given to workers' education.

University extension came to America about 1890. Among the pioneer institutions attempting this service were Columbia, Chicago, and Wisconsin. As an organized movement, however, it dates only from 1906, when the University of Wisconsin organized its extension division with a dean and separate faculty. By 1915, when the National University Extension Association was established, 28 educational institutions had organized for extension work. In 1930, more than 400 institutions of higher education were conducting such activities. The state universities have been most active in this field, probably because their large expenditures of money taken from the taxpayers of the state can be justified only by rendering service to the whole people.

The term "general university extension" is applied to the extension activities of universities and colleges in the fields not covered by agricultural and home-economics extension. The latter, which has developed independently, is conducted by the federal land-grant colleges, under the federal subsidy acts (q.v.). The various offerings of state and federal agencies in this field reach hundreds of thousands throughout the country.

General university extension activities may be divided into *formal instruction* and *informal service*. By formal instruction is meant correspondence or home study; class instruction; study-group programs involving a definite plan of study for a period of time; short courses, institutes, and conferences given on the campus or in centers throughout the state; and radio lectures of an organized and consecutive sort. The aim of this type of instruction is systematic and consecutive teaching, resulting in the permanent acquisition of a definite portion of knowledge. A large majority of institutions place great emphasis on the formal side of extension work, which constitutes the backbone of university extension. Formal instruction may be of both credit and non-credit types. The credit type covers courses, given either by correspondence, by class work off the campus, or by means of radio, which are in all essential respects equivalent to courses given on the campus and have the same prerequisites. Non-credit courses are given by these and other means, the aim being to give the benefits of college instruction without any thought of credit in the institution. Some of the non-credit courses are of college grade; some are much below college grade.

By informal service is meant service involving flexible methods and materials. The results are often inspirational and informational, but are less permanent than those of formal instruction. A host of activities compose the offering grouped under this heading. Some of the more important items are the following: lectures, both singly and in series; lyceum courses; general radio broadcasting, including lectures and entertainment features; package library service; visual-education service, including the distribution of films, slides, art collections, exhibits and stereographs; general information service, including the answering of inquiries from various individuals and groups throughout the state; women's club work; school and community service in drama, music, debating, etc.; health service; workers' education; library extension other than package library service; government research or municipal reference bureau; play and recreation service; community institutes; assistance in community organization and improvement; community-center aids; surveys; short graduate medical courses; forestry extension service; engineering extension service; citizenship education; retail salesmanship, including short courses and institutes on business.

Eight of the activities, both formal and informal, mentioned above, comprise the major portion of the work of the various university-extension divisions. These activities, together with the number of colleges and universities reporting to the United States Bureau of Education, in 1928, as conducting them, are as follows: Correspondence instruction, given by 101 institutions; class instruction, by 181; institutes, conferences, and short courses, by 141; visual education, by 52; public lectures, school or community service, public information, and package library service, by 195 institutions. General university extension reaches millions of people annually.[17]

[17] L. R. Alderman, *College and University Extension Helps in Adult Education,* U. S. Bureau of Education Bulletin, 1928, No. 3, pp. 13, 21-22; "Public Education of Adults," *Biennial Survey of Education, 1924-26,* U. S. Bureau of Education Bulletin, 1928, No. 25, p. 296. Thomas H. Shelby, *General University Ex-*

The two kinds of extension work most in demand are correspondence instruction and work in classes held outside the institution. These are the activities usually in mind when people speak of university extension. They annually enroll about 150,000 students. The courses are largely practical or vocational, and are taken primarily for the immediate advantage which the student expects to derive from them. This motive also characterizes the work in cultural subjects, for these courses are taken most commonly by women teachers in the fields in which they are teaching. "It is fair to assume that the fact that academic credits may be obtained towards degrees or certificates, which, in turn, lead to elevation in the educational hierarchy, is a more potent influence than what we used to call the pursuit of learning."[18]

Class Instruction.—In every state of the Union there are institutions of higher learning that give class work outside their own walls. An individual desiring to take work in this way should inquire through his local public-school department or through the public library as to what courses are given in that vicinity. If no classes are provided, and he can find a group of ten or more persons who desire to study the same subject, he should then ask the college or university of his choice to organize such a class and furnish an instructor.

The more common type of extension work where regular classes are held is extension in time rather than in place: late afternoon and evening classes meeting either in or near the university buildings. These are common wherever the population is sufficient to support them. They are the specialty of the Association of Urban Universities, a group of some thirty institutions which, though offering some courses of less than college seriousness, concentrates its main effort on duplicating at night the courses which are offered by day in the undergraduate college and in certain professional schools. To such courses students are admitted who meet exactly the same entrance requirements as do day students, and they are granted their certificates, diplomas, and degrees upon completing the same course of study. These classes, in many cases, are organized in down-town centers; for example, Cleveland College of Western Reserve University has taken as its main function the education of adults.[19]

tension, U. S. Bureau of Education Bulletin, 1926, No. 5, pp. 2, 3-4, 6. L. R. Alderman and Ellen C. Lombard, *Adult Education,* U. S. Bureau of Education Bulletin, 1931, No. 20, ch. XII.

[18] Frederick P. Keppel, "Education for Adults," *Yale Review,* April, 1926, 15:3:423.

[19] L. R. Alderman, *Adult Education Activities During the Biennium, 1926-28,* U. S. Bureau of Education Bulletin, 1929, No. 23, p. 16.

Correspondence Instruction.—The idea of giving instruction by correspondence originated at the Chautauqua Institution, largely through the influence of Dr. William Rainey Harper, who came to this famous summer school in 1879 as director of its School of Languages. When the summer session was over, a number of students who wanted to continue studying languages during the winter asked Dr. Harper to outline a course of study and to help them with advice by mail. He did so. Later the work was more definitely organized, and in 1883 correspondence was formally adopted by Chautauqua as a method of instruction. When Dr. Harper became President of the University of Chicago, in 1892, he at once established a correspondence division of the department of extension. From Chicago the idea spread to other institutions, and today the greater part of the work of university extension departments is by correspondence.

The essential characteristic of correspondence study is not the fact that it is instruction by mail; that is in many cases merely incidental. The distinguishing feature is the method of study: constant, written efforts by the student and correction by the teacher. "As ordinarily applied in correspondence study, the method consists of the assignment by the instructor of definitely planned work, the writing out by the student of the results of his work, the correction and criticism by the instructor of the written lessons, and the suggestion and assistance upon points where the student needs such special help. The student is tested on the whole of every lesson. He not only recites the entire lesson, but reduces it to writing, so that any error may be detected and corrected. The criticism by the instructor is also clearly and definitely written."[20] There is no temptation to bluff or take a chance on not being called on to recite; the correspondence student recites every lesson, writing it out at his leisure, taking time for logical thinking and expression. The instructor reads the paper, considers it out of his experience, notes on it commendation or criticism, answers any questions that may have been asked, advises how to study, and acts as a private personal tutor. This is a description of what correspondence instruction should be, not what it always is. The development of correspondence study has been made possible by inexpensive methods of quickly reproducing written material in considerable quantity and by cheap and rapid mail service.

Some of the outstanding advantages of study by correspondence are these: (1) The student may advance as rapidly as his time, ability,

[20] Arthur J. Klein, *Correspondence Study in Universities and Colleges,* U. S. Bureau of Education Bulletin, 1920, No. 10, p. 8.

and industry will warrant. No time is wasted waiting for others. (2) As all lessons are written, one is sure to get good practice in written expression. (3) A much wider range of subjects is offered than through class work outside the institution, since the latter entails the necessity of finding a group of people who desire to study the same subject at the same time. On the other hand, the personal equation is absent, and the time for preparation is more elastic. Too much is left to the individual. To succeed, he must have a studious mind and a high degree of will power and persistence. The majority of persons who enroll in correspondence courses never complete them.

The courses given by colleges and universities conducting correspondence study may be high-school and college-entrance courses, those taken for college credit, or non-credit courses designed to meet practical needs without reference to the academic grade of the work. The amount of the fee charged for correspondence courses is determined by the other available resources of the institution and by the cost of this form of instruction. A common method is to reckon the fee for a course upon the basis of so much per lesson or per credit granted. This varies from $1 to $8 a credit, and from 30 cents to 70 cents per lesson in state-supported institutions. Some charge a flat rate and permit the student to carry as much work as he can do. In addition to the course fee, an enrollment fee, varying in amount from $1 to $5, is charged. Students are also required to pay a small fee for extension of time when they fail to complete their work within the limits set by the correspondence study regulations. Further, students must pay postage at least one way, and in several institutions full postage both ways on manuscripts sent in. Sometimes examination fees are also asked. The fees are made as low as possible under present conditions for residents of the state; but non-residents are charged in most cases an amount 50 per cent greater than the fee for residents.

A study made by the Division of University Extension of the Massachusetts State Department of Education from the records of 1,200 correspondence students indicates that over half of the students were seeking immediate practical aid when they began correspondence study. Their average age was 26.3 years. The same study shows that 34 per cent of the students had previous elementary education only, 49 per cent secondary education, 8 per cent collegiate, 8 per cent professional, and the balance private, vocational- or evening-school education. The experience of the extension division of the University of Wisconsin has been that about 30 per cent of the students have had elementary training only, 35 per cent have been high-school students or graduates, and about 25 per cent have had all or some part of a college course. The University of Wisconsin also found that of some 25,000 registrations made in 10 years, about 40 per cent of the courses were completed. "That such a large proportion should complete the work when study is purely voluntary and so often carried on under adverse conditions is a remarkable testimony to the correspondence method of instruction."[21]

Instruction by Radio.—Instruction by means of radio is becoming general with college and university extension divisions. This method, which usually supplements the textbook or other lesson material, involves the broadcasting by the institution of detailed information in regard to the lesson, outlining the main points, explaining the different passages. The student, after receiving the radio instruction and supplementing it by the study of textbooks or other material, writes out his lesson as in regular correspondence courses and sends it to the instructor in charge of the subject at the university. "Some of the advantages of extension work by radio are: (1) It creates more interest and probably reaches many more people than does regular correspondence instruction. (2) It saves time required otherwise for transmitting the lesson by mail to the student. (3) It enables the instructor to give whatever emphasis is needed by using the voice instead of the pen. (4) It enables the instructor to bring into his discussion more timely illustrations of the subject studied than is possible by correspondence courses alone."[22] Sixty-five institutions report the use of radio either in giving lectures or in conducting other extension work. For a small fee a student may register with the extension division of the university giving the radio correspondence course, have his assignments corrected, and receive credit for his work. In addition to those who are studying by radio, the total number of which is unknown, there are many thousands who listen in on the courses that are given.

Commercial Correspondence Schools.—The first commercial correspondence school was established in Pennsylvania in 1891. It had its birth in a desire to improve the conditions of the miners of the state. Thomas J. Foster, proprietor and editor of the *Mining Herald*, a newspaper published at Shenandoah, in the coal-mining district of

[21] Arthur J. Klein, *Correspondence Study in Universities and Colleges*, U. S. Bureau of Education Bulletin, 1920, No. 10 (p. 22 quoted).
[22] L. R. Alderman, *College and University Extension Helps in Adult Education*, U. S. Bureau of Education Bulletin, 1928, No. 3, pp. 32-34. J. J. Tigert, "Radio in the American School System," Supplement to Vol. CXLII of the *Annals Amer. Acad. Polit. Soc. Sci.*, 1929, pp. 73-75. Armstrong Perry, *Radio and Education*, U. S. Bureau of Education Bulletin, 1931, No. 20, ch. XVIII.

eastern Pennsylvania, began to study for himself the causes of the numerous mine accidents with their appalling wastage of human life. He became convinced that the principal reason was the ignorance of mine owners, superintendents, and workmen alike, and that the remedy lay in education. He determined to do his share as an editor to improve conditions. He began the publication of a column, called "Questions and Answers," dealing with mining problems. In 1891 he had a course covering the subject of coal mining in its various aspects prepared by some engineers, a course which anyone could study at home. Within six months, more than a thousand men were studying this course by mail. Requests for information on other subjects came in from machinists, draftsmen, and others employed in the mines and associated industries, and courses on these subjects were prepared. The curriculum was expanded to include other fields, and thus was established the International Correspondence Schools, with headquarters at Scranton, Pa., the largest and best-known of the correspondence schools.

Created to teach a single subject, the I.C.S. now gives instruction in more than 300 courses, mainly business training, technical, and industrial courses. More than 2,500,000 students, representing a great range of occupations and a great many countries, have been enrolled on its books. "No matter where you live," it advertises, "the I.C.S. will come to you. No matter what your handicaps or how small your means, we have a plan to meet your circumstances. No matter how limited your previous education, the simply-written, wonderfully-illustrated I.C.S. textbooks make it easy to learn. No matter what career you may choose, some one of the 300 I.C.S. courses will surely suit your needs." The school is incorporated under the laws of the State of Pennsylvania, has no endowment or bonded indebtedness, and has with slight exception paid its stockholders satisfactory dividends over a long period of years. The financial success of this initial venture into the field of technical and vocational education by correspondence has led literally hundreds of others to invade the field, only a few of them, however, having a similar success. The rate of mortality among private correspondence schools is high, the average length of life being six years.

There are today probably 350 private correspondence schools in the United States. They enroll approximately 1,500,000 new students annually, and receive about $70,000,000 in tuition fees. These students together with those enrolled the previous year and still engaged on their course make a total of at least 2,000,000 persons being instructed by such schools, a number three times as large as the enrollment in all the resident colleges, universities, and professional schools combined. More persons are affected by these schools than by any other agency of formal education excepting only the grade schools.

There is nothing inherent in correspondence as a method of instruction to disqualify it as a way to education. But the activities of the majority of the private correspondence schools are such as to discredit the field. A large proportion of the schools are not conducted as schools at all. They are commercial enterprises designed to make quick and easy profits. Many of them are in the shady zone bordering on the criminal. A large proportion of those who enroll in correspondence courses are wasting time, money, and energy, or even are being swindled. At least 80 per cent of all private correspondence schools are owned or controlled by private individuals. "The promoter of correspondence schools," writes Noffsinger,[23] who has made a first-hand investigation of the subject, "tends to be of the type that knows nothing and cares less for educational standards. He sees only the possibility of reaping a rich harvest from dupes through clever advertisements and shrewd campaigns of follow-up letters and 'extra-special' offers. Many, many schools are today being conducted by such men." Some of the schools are simply swindles. Consider, for example, the case of a school in the class known as "diploma mills." At the suggestion of Mr. Noffsinger, a letter was sent to one of these "universities" saying that the writer had had two years of college work, had taught several years in an ungraded country school and now wanted to secure the degree of doctor of philosophy. In a few days a reply was received assuring the writer that his case had been "considered before the entire faculty," which had decided that "in the event the writer had ever written a magazine article" it was very probable that he would be "entitled to receive the Ph.D. degree." If he would send the school the "name" of the article, together with $8.50, the diploma would probably be sent him. This "institution of higher learning" offers more than 800 courses and is conducted by a faculty consisting of a man and his wife, both of them government clerks, aided by their only child. "There is another class of schools even worse. These are the schools of chiropractic, naturopathy, electro-therapeutics, masso-therapy and other healing cults, which have in their charters the right to grant degrees and honors not only in their

[23] John S. Noffsinger, *Correspondence Schools, Lyceums, Chautauquas*, 1926, p. 24. Much of this section is adapted from the first nine chapters of his excellent and authoritative book.

respective professions but 'all the degrees in liberal arts and sciences.' There are between ten and twenty of such institutions chartered every year in the District of Columbia alone.'[24]

Approximately 80 per cent of all students by correspondence take vocational courses. The schools giving such courses vary from conscientious to fraudulent, and the work from adequate to useless. The courses range from Accountancy to Wrestling, with Cheese Making, Dentistry, Inventive Science, Piano Tuning, Reinforced Concrete, Soap Manufacture, Suggestotherapy, and hundreds of others making up the list. There is practically no subject that is not offered, despite the fact that some subjects can never be taught by correspondence, no matter what the school or who the teacher. An examination of a large number of courses shows the fee per course to range from $10 to $280; for the greater number it is around $40. The fee per lesson ranges from a few cents to $11.25, with $1.66 as the median— assuming that the course is completed.

Three methods are utilized to enroll students. Some schools employ one, most of them employ all. They are direct mail, salesmanship, and advertising. The first method is probably used less than either of the other two, except by those schools which offer highly specialized courses to certain vocational and professional groups. Lists of names are compiled from classified vocational registers or from directories, or they may be purchased from professional listing houses ("sucker lists"). The names are then circularized. If there is a reply, an aggressive follow-up system begins to operate.

Most of the older, conservative, and substantial correspondence schools use personal salesmen to get new enrollments. The salesmen are highly trained. In fact, the most intensive work of most correspondence schools is devoted to developing the sales force. This is by far the most highly organized and carefully conducted department of the school. At least 5,000 skilled correspondence-school salesmen are at work, subjecting young people to a terrific "selling" pressure. The salesmen are usually paid commissions on the number of enrollments they obtain. This is a dangerous practice, for it leads to the enrollment of many students in no way qualified by their previous preparation or experience to take a course. The whole emphasis on salesmanship is one of the most serious criticisms to be made against the system of correspondence instruction as it now exists. Perhaps it cannot be avoided when schools are organized for profit. The sales force and the highly cultivated art of salesmanship un-

[24] *Ibid.*, p. 29.

doubtedly result in the satisfaction of existing needs, but they also create a demand which is often artificial, and they tend to commercialize the whole field.

The commercialization of education through correspondence schools is also seen in the method of advertising. A school may well be judged by its advertisements. One that is honestly administered and has some qualifications to be classed as educational is restrained in its pronouncements or promises. Most schools are not. Their advertisements make preposterous claims and stress the money appeal in a grotesque way. Consider, for example, the following correspondence school advertisements culled from popular magazines.

STUDY LAW AT HOME.—Abe Lincoln did it! Also thousands of other great lawyers, politicians and business men. *You* too can become a lawyer through home study. . . . Legally trained men win the highest positions and biggest success in business and public life. Be independent. Greater opportunities now than ever before. Big corporations are headed by men with legal training. Law-trained men earn $5,000 to $10,000 annually.

HIGH-SCHOOL COURSE IN TWO YEARS.—You can complete this simplified High-School Course at home inside of two years. Meets all requirements for entrance to college and the leading professions.

BE A NURSE.—Learn in spare time at home. Earn $30-$35 a week.

BE A JAZZ MUSIC MASTER.—Play Piano by Ear. No tedious ding-dong daily practice—just 20 brief, entertaining lessons, easily mastered.

EVEN if you don't know a single Note of Music, choose your favorite instrument now. Learn to play any instrument right at home—in a few months through remarkable method. Easy as A. B. C. No exercises—no teacher. Entertain your friends.

LEARN HOW TO WRITE SHORT STORIES.—Recently an American writer was paid $1,800 for a single short story. By learning to tell the stories of her dreams this woman has found her way to fame and fortune. You can learn to write, too. A new practical course of instruction will give you the training right in your own home during your spare time. Endorsed by eminent writers. [Ring Lardner, by the way, maintains, "You can't make a great short-story writer out of a born drug-clerk, even by correspondence."]

OVER 70,000 high-class positions paying up to $10,000 a year are open each year in the hotels of the United States. You can have one of these high-class big-pay positions, with luxurious apartment and meals and fascinating work. No previous experience necessary. The —— Schools guarantee to give you the valuable knowledge that it has taken some of the most successful hotel men years to obtain. We train you by mail in your spare time at home.

BE AN AUTO EXPERT.—World's Biggest Business Needs You! Send for my Big Auto Book right now! Same remarkable Book showed thousands the

way to *amazingly quick* Pay Raises. From $21 a week to $300 in one week
is what it did for Joe ——.

WANTED: Men to Keep Pace with R. B. C——. When a young man can
advance in four years from a routine job to the position of Sales Manager
of one of the big wholesale houses of Chicago—without any pull except his
own initiative—there must be a reason. There *is* a reason. It's summed up in
the —— *salary-doubling plan*. What that plan has done for R. B. C—— it
can do for any man sincerely ambitious to increase his earnings.

TRAIN AT HOME FOR A FINE ELECTRICAL JOB! If you are now earning less
than $40 a week—if you want to be an *Electrical Expert*—if you want to
step quickly into the class of men earning from $60 to $250 a week—*write
me at once!*

Getting in touch with —— is nothing more or less than getting measured
for more money.

IT'S A SHAME FOR YOU NOT TO EARN $10,000 A YEAR—WHEN OTHERS DO
IT SO EASILY. When a farmhand steps from $50 to $1,000 a month—when
a fireman jumps from $60 a month to a job paying him $500 for two weeks'
work—when a former railway mail clerk at a yearly salary of $1,600 changes
his job and earns $1,000 in thirty days—and when hundreds of others quickly
jump from small pay to magnificent earnings in the same way—then it's a
shame for you not to earn *your* $10,000 a Year!

"Well—well ——" Babbitt sought for adequate expression of his
admiration [after listening to his son. Ted read some correspondence-
school advertisements]. "I'm a son of a gun! I knew this correspondence-school business had become a mighty profitable game—makes
suburban real-estate look like two cents!—but I didn't realize it'd got
to be such a reg'lar key-industry! Must rank right up with groceries
and movies. Always figured somebody'd come along with the brains to
not leave education to a lot of bookworms and impractical theorists
but make a big thing out of it."

A composite photograph, based on Noffsinger's study, pictures the
typical correspondence-school student as "a young man 26 years old,
away from formal schooling for ten years, probably married and
living in a town of less than 100,000 population in a state with
superior educational facilities. He is engaged in business or industry
or in some semi-skilled occupation and has gone far enough to appreciate the fact that the unskilled worker in every line is handicapped. In
casting about for guidance in his field of major interest he sees an
advertisement of a correspondence course in a popular magazine,
assuring him that that way lies success, if it does not promise him
fabulous fortune. In response to his letter of inquiry he is bom-
barded with high-powered sales-letters and literature sent by special

delivery and timed to arrive at his home on Sunday morning when
his wife will see it and they can discuss his future. If he is able to
withstand the special inducements thus offered provided he enrolls
within a few days, he decides to forego the golden opportunity just
in time to meet a personal representative of some other school who
is skilled in handling such cases and forthwith has his name signed
on the dotted line.''[25]

Though many enroll in correspondence courses, few survive. Data
obtained from 75 schools show that the proportion of students completing courses normally running a year is just 6 per cent. Shorter
courses have a higher percentage of completions. All told, about 19
out of 20 of the registrants in correspondence courses drop out before
the completion of the course.

There is a legitimate field for correspondence study and much
demand for it; great numbers of Americans are unprepared to earn
their livelihood. The slowness on the part of the public schools to
furnish vocational training is one reason why these schools came into
existence and flourished. A way must be found to enable students to
distinguish between *bona fide* correspondence schools and those which
are simply swindles. There are two means by which the sheep may be
separated from the goats. First, the government, both national and
state, must accept responsibility. Adequate legislation and enforcement
by strict supervision are indispensable. As matters now stand, only a
few states make any effort, never very thorough, at regulation. In
most states the correspondence school has the same status as any other
business corporation. Indeed, if it is not incorporated at all, it is
subject to no other restrictions than those imposed on all individuals
by the criminal laws. Many quack schools often get their charters here
in order to operate principally in other countries, where legal supervision is stringent and the word university carries certain connotations. They have agents throughout the world trafficking in what one
American consul calls ''damnifying degrees.'' The files of the Department of State contain hundreds of reports from American consuls in
Europe, Asia, and South America bearing on the activities of the
agents of American diploma mills. Many of the present abuses would
be corrected if each state legislature should create a supervising board
for all the colleges and universities within its borders, and give this
body power to investigate all institutions desiring to incorporate as
colleges or universities and to grant charters only if they conform to
certain standards. Further, state legislatures should amend their laws

[25] *Ibid.*, pp. 59-60.

to require persons desiring to incorporate for educational purposes to show greater financial resources. The sum of $50,000 or $100,000 would be enough to eliminate many of the present abuses. This would keep out the clerk who sets up a university with himself and wife as faculty.

Secondly, the responsibility devolves upon the reputable schools to purge their profession. It is, indeed, to their interest to do so. As the situation is now, the burden of proof rests upon all correspondence schools. Already some of the honest, intelligently run schools have formed what they call the "National Home Study Council" in the interests of better education. It was incorporated in 1926, with headquarters in Washington, D. C. The purpose, according to its charter, is the "Promoting of sound educational standards and ethical business practices within the home-study field." It aims to coöperate with other interested agencies in making effective a constructive program designed to curb, if not to eliminate, unfair exploitation of thousands of people by the many so-called correspondence schools. Joint effort by the reputable and well-established schools should not only create public confidence in the correspondence school but lay a foundation for a science of education by correspondence. Out of such effort certain standards of practice, ethical and educational, should develop, and education by correspondence may eventually be entitled to more serious consideration and to a less dubious right to inclusion within the field of adult education.[26]

Workers' Education.—This phase of adult education—slightly associated with university extension in this country, largely so in Great Britain—differs from the other types in that there is less agreement as to what it should be; the idea is mixed up with other considerations, such as the workers' economic program; and a spirit of class consciousness runs through the whole subject. In this country particularly, it is seldom considered on its own merits, it is seldom clear-headed and well-planned, the emphasis being often too much on the workers and too little on the education. Viewed from the motive back of each manifestation—what did the organizers of the different sorts of workers' education think about workers, what sort of education did they think good for workers?—there are three main types. The first branch—first in order of introduction—is based on the truism that sharp tools are better than dull ones, trained workmen better than untrained—better for the workmen, better for the employer.

[26] *Ibid.*, chs. VIII, IX. Dorothy Canfield Fisher, *Why Stop Learning?* 1927, pp. 21-43.

This is technically called "pointed education" and is limited to training workers to increased skill in the industry at which they are making their living. To a certain extent it is the modern equivalent of the apprentice system and the instruction given in guilds. Second, those who believe labor is a homogeneous class still fighting for its rights, have felt the need for special schools to teach their economic and social point of view—to train working-people more consciously to resist exploitation. This is known as "class-education." Third, a few educators believe that workers are essentially not different from other people and should have opportunities for general self-improvement, or general culture.

Among the activities in this field are courses conducted by industries and business establishments; local classes for workers organized in cities by university-extension departments, notably the University of California and the Division of University Extension of the Massachusetts State Department of Education; labor colleges like Brookwood, at Katonah, New York; and summer schools for workers, as at Bryn Mawr College, the University of Wisconsin, and Barnard College, Columbia. Frequently, in the workmen's colleges and university-extension classes, not the least potent means of the workers' education is the noisy argument of those who insist upon lecturing the lecturer. A problem experienced in many countries is to supply extension teachers who are conservative enough to please those who support the universities financially and at the same time progressive enough to suit the radical workingman. There is a charge and countercharge of a lack of open minds. In this country, workers' education classes attract about 30,000 persons.[27]

The Work in Other Countries.—The overwhelming emphasis on the vocational in our adult education, not to mention the high degree of commercialization, contrasts sharply with the situation in other countries. In England and in Denmark, for example,—the two countries which have most to teach us—the most interesting and significant work is being done in the non-vocational field.

University Extension in England.—The most striking characteristic of the English extension movement, as we have already seen, is its vital relation to the labor movement. University extension in England is actively coöperating with the workingmen's societies. The Workers' Educational Association, founded in 1903, has secured labor representatives on the governing bodies and committees of some sixty uni-

---

[27] Dorothy Canfield Fisher, *Why Stop Learning?* 1927, pp. 180-211. Joseph K. Hart, *Adult Education,* 1927, p. 183.

versities. Its aim is "to articulate the educational aspirations of labor." It consists of a federation of about 2,700 working-class and educational bodies, banded together for the purposes of stimulating the demand for higher education among working people, supplying their needs in coöperation with universities and other educational authorities, and acting as a bureau of intelligence upon all matters which affect the education of working people. The Workers' Educational Association has been called "the training school whence many of the most alert political and economic thinkers in England have sprung or been inspired." The best-known part of its work is that of the university tutorial classes. These are classes of not over thirty students who agree to study for three years, not to miss a single attendance from other than unavoidable causes, and to write twelve essays in connection with each of the three sessions of twenty-four lessons each. The classes meet once a week for two hours, one hour being devoted to lecture and one to give-and-take discussion. Competent teachers are furnished from Oxford or Cambridge or one of the municipal universities. The classes are financed coöperatively by the university, the labor organization, and the board of education. About 30,000 workers are registered. The emphasis is on cultural education. The Association aims to satisfy the intellectual, æsthetic, and spiritual needs of the workman student and thus give him a fuller life.[28]

The Folk High-Schools of Denmark.—There is almost nothing in this country for wage-earners comparable to the Danish folk schools, where the aim is purely cultural. This is an educational activity for workers where the purpose of both teacher and grown-up student is neither to make more money, nor to fight a more winning battle for recognition and power, but to develop each individual personality as harmoniously as possible. The people's high schools of Denmark are institutions of learning to which go young grown men and women of the working-classes, of their own free will, paying moderately for the privilege of living and learning there. They are set in the countryside, homes rather than schools; they are run in the plainest, simplest way, with the teachers and students doing the household and other work together. By this means the cost of the course is reduced to a sum which dare not be mentioned here because no American would

[28] W. S. Bittner, *The University Extension Movement*, U. S. Bureau of Education Bulletin, 1919, No. 84, pp. 14-37. Frederick P. Keppel, "Education for Adults," *Yale Review*, April, 1926, 15:3:425-426. *International Handbook of Adult Education*, 1929, pp. 83-92.

believe that anything worthwhile could possibly be secured for so small an amount.

The idea of these schools, which were begun in 1844, was conceived by Bishop Nicholai S. F. Grundtvig, known as "the prophet of the North." In his own words, his purpose was to found schools the aim of which was not "examinations and an assured livelihood, but education and enlightenment for its own sake." These schools seek to "awaken and develop the sense of responsibility in the young" and to "call forth the individuality of the pupil." There are now about sixty of them in active operation in Denmark. Each school holds two sessions a year: one of three months in the summer for young women, the other of five months in the winter for young men. The pupils in a school vary from 100 to 150 in number. They are between 18 and 25 years old. They study history, literature, poetry, natural sciences, mathematics, music and sometimes design. Teaching is by means of lectures. There is no discussion in the classroom, but students go individually or by groups to their teachers for long discussions and conversations. No textbooks are used. Students are stimulated to use the books in the library; but no lessons are ever assigned to them in the books. There are no entrance requirements except that of age; there are no tests or examinations. What any student gets out of the course or courses he gets for its own sake. These schools exist not to fill but to awaken the minds of the students. When the mind of an individual is awake, he can go on with his own education indefinitely. The emphasis throughout is placed on self-education.

The people's high schools have been attended by about 300,000 young men and women, or more than 30 per cent of the adults of the rural and village communities. The influence of these schools has been tremendous. The spirit of the whole nation has been literally changed by this system of non-vocational adult education. After the war of 1864 and the loss of Schleswig and Holstein, Danish morale was at a dangerously low ebb. Within two or three generations, however, the national spirit has been made over, partly through the adoption of the principle of coöperation in agriculture and marketing, but primarily through the system of folk schools which the people themselves have built up. On all hands it is agreed that Denmark's great advance along economic, social, political, and moral lines is to be credited primarily to these schools. They have laid the foundation of modern Danish civilization.[29]

[29] Joseph K. Hart, *Adult Education*, 1927, pp. 268-283. Dorothy Canfield Fisher, *Why Stop Learning?* 1927, pp. 211-214, 263-270. Frederick P. Keppel, "Educa-

2. THE NON-SCHOOL TYPE OF AGENCY

The Historical Lyceum.—"I am as ready as Carlyle," writes Dorothy Canfield Fisher,[30] "to denounce the lecture habit as a meaningless survival from days when there were not books enough to go around, sure to be discarded as soon as mankind had learned the better tool. But I lack Carlyle's vigorous assumption that my personal preference is right. . . . At any rate, the early Lyceum movement was very firmly based on the spoken word. Perhaps it began when the spoken word was the only generally available medium. Books were scarce and high-priced in the eighteen-twenties and early thirties, when Josiah Holbrook dreamed his great dream. Whatever his reason for choosing his method, it was a sound one. It had vitality. Even today when books are cheap, public libraries open to all, and magazines, subsidized by advertisers, are almost given away, it still lives vigorously in the Chautauquas, in Women's Clubs, in the organized lecture bureaus."

The lyceum was one of the first channels for the diffusion of learning in the United States. It was fundamentally an outgrowth of early American conditions, but the immediate stimulus to its founding and spread came from the enthusiasm of Josiah Holbrook, of Derby, Connecticut. For a number of years Mr. Holbrook lectured throughout Connecticut and Massachusetts on geology, mineralogy, and other natural sciences, informally encouraging small groups to band together for sustained study in the subjects in which they were interested. Then he became sponsor of formal proposals for an organization in every town to study history, art, science, and public questions with the aid of libraries and other necessary institutions and equipment. The purposes and advantages of the town lyceum, as stated by its promoters, were to improve conversation by introducing good topics into the daily intercourse of families, neighbors, and friends; to elevate the amusements of the community by making the weekly exercises of the lyceum both instructive and enjoyable; to help young people to save money by keeping them away from dancing masters, military exercises, etc., which cost more than the yearly lyceum fee of $2.00; to call into use neglected libraries and to give occasion for the establishing of new ones; to provide a seminary for teachers; to encourage and assist existing academies; to raise the

---

tion for Adults," *Yale Review*, April, 1926, 15:3:425-426. *International Handbook of Adult Education*, 1929, pp. 69-80.

[30] *Why Stop Learning?* 1927, pp. 150-151.

character of existing district schools; to compile data for town histories; to make town maps, and agricultural and geological surveys; and to begin a state collection of minerals.[31]

The first lyceum was organized in 1826 at Millbury, Massachusetts. By 1828 there were approximately 100 branches as the result of Mr. Holbrook's personal efforts while traveling about. By the end of 1834 nearly 3,000 town lyceums were scattered from Boston to Detroit, from Maine to Florida. In many parts of the country, but especially in New England, the town lyceums continued to be the focus of the intellectual life of the community. Once a week throughout the winter everyone interested met at the schoolhouse or tavern, and listened to or took part in debates or discussions on topics of general interest—the National Bank, the tariff, education, slavery, women's rights, temperance. At first local talent carried out the program. Gradually as that began to grow thin and too familiar, and as the number of lyceums which could pay for speakers increased, the practice arose and became fixed of inviting paid lecturers. There emerged a group of men who gave a part of their time to lecturing as a profession. Some of them were the most distinguished men of their time; on the early roster of lyceum speakers appear such names as Ralph Waldo Emerson, Henry D. Thoreau, James Russell Lowell, Oliver Wendell Holmes, Edward Everett Hale; and, later, Henry Ward Beecher, Louis Agassiz, Wendell Phillips, Horace Greeley, Charles A. Dana, and George William Curtis. Practically all of Emerson's essays were written for delivery on the lyceum platform. Lyceums furnished audiences for Dickens and Thackeray on their American tours. Statistics are lacking as to how the lyceums throve in all sections, but they certainly lived in New England and the North generally. The foremost lyceum in the country was the one in Boston. It was presided over for many years by Daniel Webster. Gradually the lyceums became political rather than literary in tone, but that was natural considering the temper of the times. At least they continued to reflect what their members really cared about.

The lyceum as such practically ceased to exist at the time of the Civil War. But after the war there was formed in the Middle West the Associated Literary Societies, a league of about a hundred literary societies, as some of the surviving lyceums had begun to call themselves. The main object of the new association was the coöperative

---

[31] *American Lyceum, or Society for the Improvement of Schools, and Diffusion of Useful Knowledge*, 1829, pp. 5-10. Josiah Holbrook, *Schools, Lyceums, and Lyceum Seminary*, 1829.

booking of lectures. This association later amalgamated with lecture and musical bureaus in Boston and New York. Thus the offspring of the lyceum grew and took on new form. It became prosperous. With large bureaus competing for the best speakers, fees mounted. Mark Twain was paid $300 for one lecture, then Henry Ward Beecher $500 and even $1,000. Henry M. Stanley, on his return from Africa, signed a contract for a hundred lectures for which he was paid $100,000. More often, however, lesser lights and practitioners of other arts, like music, were booked. In this wise the informal, serious-minded and spontaneous gathering of villagers at the schoolhouse or tavern has become the prosperous commercial lecture bureau of today.[32]

The Modern Lyceum.—It is a far cry from the lyceum of Josiah Holbrook and the earnest New England town to what calls itself a lyceum today. The latter is a bureau which sends out popular lecturers or musical teams to small towns several times a year for a fee which yields a profit. It is a booking agency. The lyceum has been commercialized.

The typical lyceum course consists of five numbers given in the late fall, winter, and early spring. These are usually a lecture, one mixed "entertainment," two musical numbers, and a drama. Sometimes the play is omitted and another musical number substituted. The course may be sponsored by a local church or two or more churches in co-operation, a ladies' aid society, public-school officials, a group of merchants, or a lodge. Their objects may be just the provision of entertainment for the town or the raising of funds for some special purpose or for their own respective needs. The immediate cause is the persuasiveness of a "sales-resistance-breaking" lyceum-bureau salesman. In any case, there is but a faint trace of any desire to provide educational advantages. "The old lyceum was given to solid discourse and serious debate, to concern with matters of science and politics. Now one lyceum offering in five is a lecture, the rest is entertainment. And what are these lectures? The platform that once was occupied by Emerson, Thoreau, Lowell, Agassiz and Holmes now sounds to what the lyceum profession itself calls the 'mother-home-heaven' message. A check of 3,000 lecture titles taken at random showed 53 per cent to be of the category designated as inspirational. One quarter might with charity be called informational and the rest were of a civic or educational nature, also using those adjectives

[32] John S. Noffinger, *Correspondence Schools, Lyceums, Chautauquas*, 1926, pp. 99-106. Dorothy Canfield Fisher, *Why Stop Learning?* 1927, pp. 151-155.

broadly. A small, a very, very small, proportion indicated substance; the rest, even of those called informational or civic, were patently thinned out and sweetened. . . . The ideal may be described as the Russell H. Conwell classic, 'Acres of Diamonds.' The lecturers, in the overwhelming majority, are professional speaking troupers, those who can moralize heavily without touching real moral issues, who can philosophize entertainingly, be very deep and yet amusing, who can sound the broad note and always end optimistically. Here are found the political hack, the lame duck officeholder and the misfit clergyman. They 'glad-hand' oratorically and collectively. Now and again there is an exception, a celebrity in the public eye who is a drawing card; he is sincere, but his managers see that he eliminates all but the human interest.''[33]

The modern lyceum is a village function. Its chief *raison d'être* is the lack of anything else. It flourishes in communities where there is no library, no theatre, no concert hall, not even a moving-picture theatre with regular performances; where there is no source of group amusement but the church social and perhaps the ladies' aid society and a lodge, and where there is no educational outlet at all. A conservative estimate places the total lyceum audience each year at five million. The popular lyceum, like the popular magazine, gives the public what the public wants or is conventionally supposed to want, that is, supposed by those who make a profit out of giving it just that. Its weakness as an agency of adult education is that it is a purely commercial venture.[34]

The Historical Chautauqua.—The Chautauqua, which arose from the Methodist camp meeting, is truly indigenous to American soil. It goes back to the circuit rider who ministered religiously to the frontier families which had pushed westward from the Atlantic seaboard all through the nineteenth century. The circuit rider's visits, which were infrequent and usually irregular, were made the occasion for the gathering of all the settlers in the vicinity, who tarried for days to hear the expounding of the Gospel. They brought their whole families and tents to house them. These religious gatherings came to be called camp meetings. At certain places they were held at stated times every year. One such place was at Fair Point, New York, on Chautauqua Lake, where a Methodist camp meeting of some importance was held every summer. To this camp meeting in 1873

[33] John S. Noffsinger, *Correspondence Schools, Lyceums, Chautauquas*, 1926, pp. 115-116.
[34] *Ibid.*, pp. 113-118.

came two unusual men—the Rev. John H. Vincent and Lewis Miller, the one an enthusiastic Sunday-school worker, the other a substantial manufacturer of farm machinery from Akron, Ohio, interested in education and religious work. Through their efforts, a Sunday School Institute on the camp-meeting plan was started. Later a demand arose for a broader program, and secular cultural subjects were added. In a few years the Chautauqua camp meeting had become a full-fledged summer school, the first one in America. Out of it grew, as has already been told, the correspondence-school division. The next important step was the organization of the Chautauqua Literary and Scientific Circle, composed of small local groups all over the country who read books selected by the Chautauqua directors on suggested plans and meet at intervals for discussion and analysis of their reading. The Circle began in 1878 with 7,000 enrolled. In the first twenty years of its existence, 10,000 local groups were formed in the United States and Canada, usually in small communities where other cultural or educational agencies, except for the young, were lacking. The Chautauqua Literary and Scientific Circle was their library, forum, and lyceum, all in one.

The Chautauqua prospered, and its fame spread far and wide. It became the characteristic popular-education movement of the latter third of the nineteenth century. Facilities for travel were not easy, and so chautauquas were started elsewhere. Within forty years, between two and three hundred were organized and operated for shorter or longer periods. The local independent chautauquas tended to differ from the parent institution in that the idea of study, of taking an active part in an educational effort, though not entirely lost sight of, became pretty generally overshadowed by more restful programs of lectures, music, and miscellaneous entertainment. This expansion was also accompanied by the inevitable step to "business efficiency." "To start a permanent chautauqua required initiative, vision and capital. Few communities could command all three. But in the large cities there were numerous individuals who had at least enterprise, capital and an eye for opportunities. They organized traveling or circuit chautauquas, aimed to appeal to small communities which could never hope to have their own. A program was arranged and a route drawn up, providing a stay of from three days to a week in each community, usually a county seat. And the whole company, lecturers, musicians and performers, were booked and routed like a theatrical company. In this wise the chautauqua became a national institution, although in its most frequent manifestation, as we shall see, there was little in common between the original idea and its usual form except the name."[35]

The Modern Chautauqua.—The modern chautauqua has two distinct and separate manifestations. The first is the institution on Lake Chautauqua in New York State, from which chautauquas take their name. This is the parent institution, still alive, living on among its numerous but hardly aristocratic children. A few chautauquas in the country are patterned after it; that is, they are permanent institutions, educational in character, holding their sessions annually at the same place. The second is the large number of traveling and circuit chautauquas which have preëmpted the name. Though called chautauquas, they are enterprises of an entirely different order. Their forte is "Main Street" entertainment.

(a) The Chautauqua Institution in New York is carried on along the lines which were laid down early in its history, except that in 1900 it suspended its correspondence-study department. The two main divisions of the Institution are the Summer School and the Chautauqua Literary and Scientific Circle. The summer session lasts two months, and is attended by 12,000 to 15,000 persons. The Chautauqua summer school is the oldest in the country; its early success inspired the universities to establish summer schools, just as the correspondence-study department pointed the way for university-extension departments. The number of readers in the Circle averages about 10,000 a year.

(b) The modern traveling or circuit chautauqua operates in the summer months as a circus. It has a permanent troupe, which travels from town to town on schedule. During the winter the chautauqua salesman is out selling the program to the towns. The chautauqua visits larger towns than the lyceums, because it costs more to bring it. A program costs a town from $500 to $2,000, depending on the attractions and the length of the program. About 5,000,000 persons attend these chautauquas every year.

In general, what was said of the modern lyceum programs applies equally to those of the traveling chautauquas. They consist of music, lectures, and entertainments—"superior vaudeville, calculated to amuse in conventional ways." The lectures are of the lyceum type— mother-home-heaven. "The chautauqua gives the public what it thinks the public wants, and the public takes it, which makes money for the chautauqua and thus spares the chautauqua any need of conceiving

[35] *Ibid.*, pp. 107-112 (111-112 quoted).

and carrying out a program with more specific gravity. But it is also possible that the public would also be found to want—that is, be willing to pay for—something better. Nobody knows, and certainly the chautauqua makes no effort to find out. Nevertheless, 5,000,000 persons in the United States depend on the chautauqua for mental and imaginative recreation and exercise during the summer, as they do on the lyceum during the winter. Neither can be ignored, no matter what one think of it."[36] They are the glass through which many Americans look at life apart from their immediate material concerns. They have probably saved many small towns from dullness and stagnation. But now that there are other attractions, like the radio and the moving picture, the vogue of the chautauqua and the lyceum is falling off.

Women's Clubs.—The women's club movement dates from soon after the Civil War. It reflects the changing position of women. The war itself was an important influence in this respect, for it was during and immediately after the Civil War that women first began in appreciable numbers to be nurses, librarians, and teachers, and to follow other out-of-the-home careers. Later came their entrance into industry and into wage-earning occupations generally. Meanwhile conditions in the home were radically changed by the introduction of labor-saving devices and the removal of occupations formerly performed there, so that women not gainfully employed found greatly increased leisure. "The factories did all their manufacturing for them; the schools did the education; their husbands did the thinking; and the 'hired girl' did the work; and those grown women, potentially powerful daughters of mighty pioneer parents, slowly starving and suffocating, were told to thank God for their safe, sheltered lives."[37] Instead of languishing in the home, they turned to study, seeking "to escape from the narrowness of their own personalities into the civilized impersonal world of thought." Women's clubs, with a membership composed of married women of the social class that kept one hired girl and enjoyed delicate health, sprang up. "Timidly, under a hot fire of mockery and disapproval, without a single sympathetic voice raised, such women crept out of their homes once a week or twice a month, and gathered together to read papers to each other on such carefully noncontroversial subjects as 'The History of Holland' and 'Raphael's Madonnas.' It was little enough, in the way of intellectual life, Heaven knows. But apparently it was

[36] *Ibid.*, pp. 119-130 (129-130 quoted). Joseph K. Hart, *Adult Education*, 1927, pp. 175-177. Dorothy Canfield Fisher, *Why Stop Learning?* 1927, pp. 155-163.
[37] Dorothy Canfield Fisher, *Why Stop Learning?* 1927, p. 96.

enough to keep the breath of intellectual life in the lungs of those American women.''[38]

Beginning with the nineties, women's clubs multiplied rapidly, and state and national federations were formed. Today there are two million members of the General Federation of Women's Clubs and probably a million more in other organizations of women not connected with the national organization. These clubs have grown up without any foreign examples to copy; "the Women's Club is as native to our soil as the sugar maple and the Ford car." They have also grown up without the assistance of professional educators, which may have been the salvation of the movement. Though "stumbling and fumbling their way towards education, taking the wrong paths, losing themselves in the brambles, thinking they were advancing when they were going around in a circle, not knowing where to find the right books, not having the right books available, never having heard of the right books," these women club members nevertheless evidenced a real desire for mental self-improvement.[39]

Their efforts along this line have long been centered in writing and listening to papers and speeches. Most of the women's club programs tend to oscillate somewhat from subject to subject in an effort to be as comprehensive as possible in each year's work and to follow out some of the suggestions made to them through the Federation. The program of one characteristic federated club in Middletown took up within one year "Prophets of the Bible," "Wonders of the Radio," "What Do Colleges for Women in the Orient Accomplish?" and "The Life of Paul." Another club proceeded within one winter from "Recent Religious Movements: Christian Science and New Thought," to "The Dictograph," "Mural Paintings," "The Panama Canal," "The Drama," "Hull House," and "Dress." The year's work of yet another included meetings on "Waterways," "Animals," "Our Nation," "Socialism," and "The Simple Life."[40] The original aim of women's clubs was to attain "culture," and their programs were predominantly literary and artistic. They are now tending to study seriously more practical and civic affairs. There is a trend away from the almost exclusive preoccupation with "literature" as the heart of the things worth studying toward more active interest in the life of the community. The social side of women's club life, while prominent, has not usurped the leading place. "They still expect and

[38] *Ibid.*, p. 98.
[39] *Ibid.*, p. 103.
[40] Robert and Helen Lynd, *Middletown*, 1929, pp. 285-301.

demand from their clubs intellectual stimulus and food for intellectual growth—if it is no more than 'something new to think about,' in the picturesque and significant phrase which one occasionally hears used by an American clubwoman. Whatever may be thought by professional educators about the quality of this intellectual food, the fact that they wish for it, and try for it, and get some of it, sets them apart from all women of their class in other countries, and from most other grown-ups in their own. They still wish to go on learning!"[41]

The women's clubs have in many instances furthered community service. They have coöperated with the public schools and with colleges and universities, provided classes for all sorts of study not only for themselves and their daughters but "for the daughters and granddaughters of the woman who was Mother's hired girl," conducted courses on citizenship, promoted interest in civic affairs, stimulated the visiting-teacher and other movements, aided in Americanization, and done certain philanthropic work.

Other adult education activities in which women primarily are concerned can be mentioned only in passing. The National League of Women Voters, the National Women's Party, and similar organizations are engaged in extensive programs of education, mostly in the field of politics. The National League of Girls Clubs is active in adult education. Parent-teacher associations and business and professional women's clubs are among other national agencies in this field.

Men's Clubs.—The activities of numerous men's organizations touch more or less directly upon the subject of adult education. The plans of unnumbered fraternal organizations must be passed by with a mere mention. More important in the field of self-education are the associations of lawyers, doctors, bankers, ministers, and other professional groups who meet to listen to papers on the details of their work, and who acquire thereby stimulating additions to their professional knowledge. The most characteristic expression of men's club activities today is to be found in such organizations as Rotary, Kiwanis, Civitans, Lions, etc. These are termed civic or service clubs, but more accurately speaking they are primarily business men's clubs. They are not an outgrowth of the early discussion clubs; they are bred of a different stock and nourished at the breast of the local business life. Speeches form the *pièce de résistance* of the programs, where the oratory of the speaker is nearly, if not quite, as important as the subject of his address. In Middletown, for example, "The relative

[41] Dorothy Canfield Fisher, *Why Stop Learning?* 1927, pp. 112-113.

unimportance of lecture subjects today appears in the civic clubs which are kept alive week after week by an endless succession of speeches on almost every subject from Gandhi to the manufacture of a local brand of gas burners for coffee roasters. . . . If the subject of the address is one with which the hearers are unfamiliar or upon which they have no fixed views, they frequently adopt bodily not only the speaker's opinion but its weighting of emotion. It is not uncommon to hear a final judgment on 'the Philippine problem,' 'economic fundamentals,' 'the cause of cancer,' or 'the future of the white race,' delivered with the preamble, 'Well, I heard —— say at Chautauqua (or at Rotary) two years ago . . .' Heckling is unknown; people think with the speaker; rarely do they challenge his thought.''[42]

The speeches at the meetings of the civic clubs, of which Rotary may be taken as an example, are of three kinds: '' (1) speeches from a Middletown member on his 'classification'—'Being a motion picture exhibitor,' 'Making and selling high-tension insulators,' merchandizing, advertising, the law; (2) speeches by the head of a local charity, the librarian, the director of the vocational work in the schools, or by the head of organizations such as the state bankers' association; (3) speeches by 'outside speakers' routed to Middletown through the International Rotary headquarters and speaking on 'Sound Economics,' 'R.O.T.C. in the Colleges,' 'Tax Revision,' 'The United States and World Leadership,' and similar topics. Nowhere is Middletown's predilection for a 'real good speaker' or its ready acceptance of the views of a person who pleases it more apparent.

''The civic work of these clubs with their slogans of 'service' and 'the under-privileged boy' is likewise of three kinds: (1) certain annual affairs such as inviting the honor students of the high school to one of their luncheons, holding special club chapels in the high school, attending the county poor farm in a body at Christmas time and making speeches and distributing small gifts, conducting an annual Christmas party for one hundred or so needy boys, or an annual Easter egg hunt in a local park, at which hundreds of children search among the leaves for the lucky egg drawing prizes of merchandise and money; each of the clubs does four or five of these civic things a year; (2) the sporadic good turn to meet some local need—giving a radio to the Orphans' Home, or agreeing to take turns week after week in bringing a crippled boy to high school in their automobiles; (3) considerably less common activities of the more

[42] Robert and Helen Lynd, *Middletown*, 1929, pp. 227-228.

ambitious sort, e.g., one club secured a summer camp for the local Y.W.C.A. The Dynamo Club of young business men, affiliated with the Chamber of Commerce and differing from the other civic clubs in that its membership is open to any member of the Chamber, secured a municipal golf course for the city and organized a local drive to utilize school yards as playgrounds.

"The lack of coherence in the subjects of the speeches to which each of these clubs listens week after week and in the noncontroversial charity which constitutes their civic work suggests that, as in the women's study clubs, the reason for their dominance lies in neither of these activities but in the instrumental and symbolic character of their organization. Not only are they a business asset, but by their use of first names, sending of flowers on birthdays, and similar devices, they tend to re-create in part an informal social intercourse becoming increasingly rare in this wary urban civilization."[43]

Educational Work of Settlements.—Education has from the start been one of the main activities of the social settlement. In some respects the settlement has been a pioneer in educational methods and devices. It pointed the way to manual training and domestic science before the public schools undertook such work. It served as an experiment station for trying out projects such as the visiting kindergartner, summer nursery, and playground kindergartens. Story-telling as a means for encouraging good reading on the part of children originated with the settlement. It was one of the first agencies to take up Americanization work. Hull House and Denison House anticipated the work of university extension in their cities.

Among the organized educational activities of settlements are circulating libraries, reading rooms, and branches of the public library; classes for those who desire business and industrial training, for those whose education has been neglected, for foreigners to learn English and prepare for citizenship; classes for the study of literature, history, and economics; lectures on all sorts of subjects; dramatic activities; exhibits and museum classes; music and art instruction. In general, the settlement undertakes to supplement the home and the school; it tends to socialize education.[44]

Newspapers and Magazines.—If education is broadly conceived to comprehend all that disciplines and enlightens the understanding, cultivates the taste, and forms the manners and habits, then there

---

[43] *Ibid.*, pp. 302-304.
[44] Robert A. Woods and Albert J. Kennedy, *The Settlement Horizon*, 1922, chs. XII-XIV. Arthur C. Holden, *The Settlement Idea*, 1922, ch. XI.

are a thousand and one aspects of modern social life which have an immeasurable influence along educational lines. Chief, perhaps, among such instrumentalities are the movies and theatre, the radio, magazines, and newspapers. Their influence is all-pervasive. To a large extent they are engaged in making the adult mind or at least in confirming the views already held. We have already noted some of the influence of the radio along educational lines; we will have occasion to refer to it again. The motion picture and the legitimate theatre will be discussed later under recreation. The newspaper, which plays so characteristic a part in modern American life, will be treated more fully in the next chapter. Here we may simply note the great increase of periodical reading, especially among the working classes, and the marked increase in the number and circulation of magazines.

The *Saturday Evening Post*, which is regarded by Hart[45] as probably our most influential single instrument of adult education today, circulates more than two million copies and is read by probably five million people weekly. ''Those who read it regularly take it literally. Rooted in our more conservative political, industrial and social folkway attitudes, it defends those attitudes against practically all change. It may be counted as a consistent educator of millions of adult minds to the sacredness of the *status quo*. In the face of the need of re-thinking practically all the structures of our social and intellectual worlds, here is a block of persons most of whom can be definitely counted either as inert or as belonging to the opposition. The *American Magazine* performs a similar function in the realm of business education. The individualistic formula of the pioneer age—'look out for yourself and you'll make the grand smash, sooner or later'—is held to be the supreme law and the true morality for our present age. The supplies of stories of poor boys and some poor girls who have become millionaires through early rising and shrewd use of their wits seem unlimited. That the formula is fallacious beyond a certain point does not deter either the editor or the reader. . . . There are plenty of other magazines which—each in its own way—help to mold the mind of America. In fact, that is what each of the newspapers, magazines and picture journals exists for. The moral is plain: if America wants any different sort of adult mind than she now has, she will have to find some way of providing a different sort of food for that mind.''

In Middletown it was found that approximately one in each five of the homes in the city receives the *American Magazine* and one in

[45] Joseph K. Hart, *Adult Education*, 1927, pp. 188-189.

each six the *Saturday Evening Post*. Each of the following goes regularly into from one in each five to one in each ten of the homes: *Delineator, Ladies' Home Journal, McCall's, Physical Culture, True Story, Woman's Home Companion*. "Middletown appears to read magazines primarily for the vicarious living in fictional form they contain."[46]

The Modern Public Library.—A revolution was produced in library administration when the fact was appreciated that readers are as necessary to a properly functioning library as are books themselves. Acceptance of this idea has transformed the library from a storehouse into a community reading-club.

The oldest libraries were storehouses, first and foremost. In the kind of library that was common in the Middle Ages, the preservation of the physical substance of the book was the important thing. It is so today only in the great book museums. In the public library, it is so no longer. The quicker the physical book wears out in legitimate service, the better. For the modern library conceives its function to be the encouragement of reading. The library is now required to be an active, not merely a passive force; it not only guards and preserves its books, but it makes them accessible to those who want them and it tries to see that those who need them realize that need and act accordingly. It conceives of its duties as extending to the entire community, instead of being limited, as in the old library, to those who voluntarily entered its doors. "Books without readers, in the modern view, are no more worthy to be called a library than are readers without books. To make readers of non-readers, to create and stimulate the desire for good reading, to bring book and reader together and to offer every facility for finding and using books with ease and in comfort— these are conspicuous among the worthy aims of the public library as we see it today."[47]

This emphasis on the reader as well as on the book—this recognition of persons as well as things, as part of the material to be dealt with by the library—may be described as a process of socialization. The modern public library has become, or is becoming, socialized. This is the meaning of the great multiplication of facilities in the modern library, some of which will be described below—the lending of books for home use, free access to shelves, cheerful and homelike library buildings, rooms for children, coöperation with schools, inter-

[46] Robert and Helen Lynd, *Middletown*, 1929, pp. 231, 239-242 (241 quoted).
[47] Arthur E. Bostwick, *The Public Library in the United States*, 1929, pp. 6-7. Most of this section is adapted from this and his other excellent and authoritative books on the modern library.

library loans, longer hours of opening, more useful catalogues and lists, the extension of branch-library systems and of traveling and home libraries, coördination of work through lectures and exhibits—the thousand and one activities that distinguish the modern library from its more passive predecessor.[48]

This broadening of the library idea and the consequent ramification of the functions of the library in so many different directions has not taken place without opposition, nor is it accepted today, even by all librarians. It has found its greatest exemplification in the United States, partly because we are little hampered by tradition and more readily try experiments, also because of our attempt at universal education. Important also have been the influence of Andrew Carnegie with his gifts of over $40,000,000 for the establishment of public libraries and the emphasis they have laid on circulation.[49] The library has always been definitely an educational institution. Its service to scholars has been incalculable. Yet in the Middle Ages, when 100 per cent of its users were of this class, they would have laughed at the idea that it would ever become an instrument of popular education. But universal education has come, and the library has an important part to play in the movement. The modern library realizes that it has an educative mission, akin to that of the school but carried out in a way of its own. This realization was first given practical expression in the case of the child. Special book service to children has been rendered by public libraries since the nineties. "It now includes a special staff of assistants, trained in knowledge of children's literature, its selection and use in special cases, a separate room or rooms in every main and branch library, devoted entirely to the children and their reading, and generally a special department in the library under a chief who directs the activities of all the children's rooms in the system, with their staffs."[50] Special service has also been extended to adults, the libraries employing "readers' advisers" to whom puzzled readers may apply for aid in any matter concerned with the use of books. The increased activity of the public library has also been in adjustment to changing living conditions. The smallness of city apartments and the frequency of moving tend to diminish book-buying and to increase the demand on free libraries for books. "The ordinary private residence is no more the place for a compre-

[48] These points are covered fully in Bostwick's *The American Public Library*, 1923, especially chs. V-IX, XIII, XVIII, XIX, XXII-XXIV.

[49] Dorothy Canfield Fisher, *Why Stop Learning?* 1927, pp. 44-78. Matthew Paxton, "Free Books," *The American Mercury*, Jan., 1931, 22:85:38-39, 45.

[50] Arthur E. Bostwick, *The Public Library in the United States*, 1929, pp. 48-49.

hensive library than it is the place for the loom, the butter churn, or the cobbler's bench. As well keep a spool of every shade of sewing silk, lest once in twenty years it be needed, or a barrel of molasses, as thousands of books for a possible emergency. The public library must become the central depot for the mass of books used by any community."[51]

The Open Shelf and Home Use.—The two prime necessities of the reader are to have access to books in bulk and to be able to enjoy them in the privacy of his own home. "The old libraries had books by the thousand. But at first it was impossible, or at least difficult, to get access to them at all; later they were available one at a time, upon formal application and after long waiting; and having been obtained they must be used in the library building. All this has been changed. 'Free access,' or the 'open shelf,' by which is meant the opportunity to see and examine at least a large part of the book collection with as much freedom as in one's own private library, has removed some of these limitations. The others have vanished with the wide spread of 'home use'—the privilege of removing one or more books to the reader's home and keeping them there for a stated period."[52]

The open shelf and home use constitute the magna carta of the public library. They have pulled down the barrier between book and reader, which was erected by ancient tradition and fostered by conditions that long ago ceased to exist, and they have made possible the new freedom of the book to its fullest extent. To facilitate and give expression to this freedom has necessitated a re-adaptation of the library that has so modified the appearance and arrangement of library buildings, outside and inside, the character of the apparatus used in the service, the organization, training, and spirit of the personnel, as to have revolutionized the character of the institution itself.

Interior Arrangements.—Opening the shelves and allowing home use necessitated immediate expansion of facilities. There must be ample and comfortable reading space for a large public. Books must be so shelved that this public may examine and select at ease, without interfering with each other's comfort. In the earliest modern libraries the tendency was to shelve all the books together in order of subjects in a storage space called a "stack room." In such order they were of

[51] Lucy Elliot Keeler, "Cobwebs on the Family Library," *The Bookman*, Feb., 1920, 50:6:575.
[52] Arthur E. Bostwick, *The Public Library in the United States*, 1929, pp. 7-8.

course easier to find, and it was easier to see at a glance what the library contained on any one subject. But as the "open shelf" gained ground, it became inconvenient to admit the general public to such a storage space. Thus books came more and more to be kept on wall shelves in reading rooms, and often one subject, such as art, history or economics, occupied an entire room. This is called the "departmental system." Most libraries now keep some books in a stack room and others on open shelves, partly by departments.

The new arrangement also demanded that the books be so classified and catalogued as to make search and selection possible with a minimum of time and labor. "The catalog must be made, not for the scholar alone, but also for the man in the street. Assistants must be on hand to give advice, aid and direction. Clearly worded signs and labels must abound. Heat and light must be adapted to the comfort of readers and the library must be open for long hours to accommodate all classes. There must be also a system for recording the books that are taken home and for receipting for them when they are returned. Persons qualified to borrow must be identified and registered. Books retained unduly must be followed up and secured. . . . Books must so far as possible be prepared for rough handling, and having received it they must be mended or rebound before they go irrevocably to pieces. Departments for mending and binding are thus larger and more essential in the new library."[53]

Expansion of Service.—Long before it had reached this point, the American public library found that a single center in a town was not enough for complete service. In the process of bringing book and reader together, the reader cannot be required to do all the traveling; the book must be brought to him, at least part way. Thus we have a phase of what is called "library extension"—the building and operation of systems of branch libraries, the placing of books in public schools, and of deposits in factories, stores, churches, settlements, and other places, the establishment of traveling libraries and of stations where books may be ordered for delivery on the following day. Unlike the other extension devices, the branch library is a complete library in itself, having its separate quarters, its own permanent stock of books, generally its own catalogue, and sometimes its own separate list of registered borrowers. Some of the branch libraries are especially adapted to local neighborhood needs, as in Cleveland, for example, where foreign-language collections are centralized in the various branches according to the grouping of the foreign-born population.

[53] *Ibid.*, pp. 12-13, 16, 21-23.

The headquarters for all this activity must be in the central building, and sufficient space, properly located, must be provided to carry it on. A system of transportation is needed, and automobiles, sometimes a whole fleet of them, must form part of the library's plant.

Library extension has even been pushed far into the rural districts, and the county instead of the city or town has been made the unit of administration and service. Most states now allow counties to establish and operate public libraries, and an increasing advantage is taken of this privilege. In California, practically the whole state is covered in this way, and every citizen, no matter in how lonely a region, has access to books, either through an adjacent county library station or through the visits of a well-stocked book wagon.

As further evidence of expanded service, the modern public library building contains many facilities unknown to older libraries—rooms for art exhibits, collections of post cards or textile fabrics; indexes to current lectures, exhibitions and concerts; a free writing room, with writing materials; a library training school, perhaps; assembly and club rooms for the use of neighborhood organizations for social, educational, civic, and other purposes; a photographic plant, with copying machines; lunch rooms and rest rooms for the staff; an extensive telephone switchboard, etc. All these things are reflected in the size and interior arrangement of the building.

The modern library has also developed special service for various groups of readers. Thus it serves the school, the social or study club, the church, the technical or scientific association, industrial and commercial organizations, and other groups bound together by special interests. Some libraries have organized business departments or branches for the special use of business men. Some conduct an information service. A number have special collections of books for the blind.

Library Publicity.—A necessary activity in accordance with the new concept of the library is to keep the public informed. Well-considered publicity is as essential to the public library as to a commercial firm. The public must be apprised of its existence, of the varied service that it renders, and of its necessary limitations. "Every library now directs much time and thought toward this, the press lends its powerful aid, and even such agencies as the moving picture and the radio are enlisted. 'Library publicity,' in fact, has become a special branch of the art. Books are written about it, and the American Library Association devotes to it part of the attention of its expert staff, sending out press bulletins of interesting and important library news to all parts of the country. This is what the advertisers call 'general publicity,' like the advertisements on billboards urging us to eat more oranges or drink more milk, without mentioning any special distributor. In addition, specific libraries see that their own local news is made public in whatever way seems to the librarian to be most convenient and effective."[54]

By these and other means the attempt has successfully been made to bring the library to the people. The American public library, the country over, has made for itself a place in education which is unique in the history of the world.

The Modern Museum.—Museums were originally asylums for things no longer of use, or at best they were simply storehouses. They are now changing their functions and promise to become, as they have already become in many places, active centers of scientific work and important agents of public instruction.

In the old-time museum, the specimens were all-important, and they must have scientific labels whether the average visitor to the museum understood them or not. The visitor was of no consequence in the determination of museum policy, unless the idea was to make him aware of his ignorance. The museum was a storehouse, used more to please and educate the curators than to entertain and instruct the public. As an evidence of the original spirit towards the "general public," consider the following quotation from the regulations of the British Museum as it was in 1761, when it was formally "open to the public".[55]

Fifteen persons are allowed to view it in one Company, the Time allotted is two Hours; and when any number not exceeding fifteen are inclined to see it, they must send a list of their Christian and Sirnames, Additions and Places of Abode to the Porter's Lodge, in order to their being entered in the Book; in a few Days the respective Tickets will be made out, specifying the Day and Hour in which they are to come, which on being sent for, are delivered. If by any Accident, some of the Parties are prevented from coming, it is proper they send their ticket back to the lodge as nobody can be admitted with it but themselves. *It is to be remarked that the fewer Names* there are in a List, the sooner they are likely to be admitted to see it.

Museums began to live only from the moment when it was generally recognized that an essential part of public life is good provision for free, general, visual education. In this they followed the course of the libraries, which burst into new life when detached from their exclu-

[54] *Ibid.*, pp. 40-42. Matthew Paxton, "Free Books," *The American Mercury*, Jan., 1931, 22:85:42-43.
[55] Quoted by Dorothy Canfield Fisher, *Why Stop Learning?* 1927, pp. 223-224.

sive connection with institutions of learning or with small groups of literati. The movement in this country dates mainly from the beginning of the twentieth century.

As in the case of modern libraries, where effort was directed to making the use of books easy for an immensely larger number than had ever used books before, so with museums the ingenuity of the directors has been employed to invent new means for connecting intelligently the inexpert eyes of the general public with the exhibits on display. They began with labels, which are now printed in plain, untechnical English. Then came modern, complete catalogues. Then, again as in the case of books, the matter of arranging the exhibits was seen to be a vital part of the abandonment of the old scorn of the inexpert visitor. Specimens were prepared and arranged so as to be more realistic and instructive. The very buildings in which museums were housed began to change, as library buildings had changed. "Men with creative imaginations began to see an ideal of scientific lighting and of rooms small enough not to oppress the imagination on entering, yet large enough to keep together exhibits with an inner natural unity . . . in other words an ideal of a museum arranged around the idea of the public, not of the exhibits. The benumbing museum of our youth, at the very sight of which we fainted with fatigue, was, so the best minds in the new profession decreed, to become as forgotten a mistake of the past as the libraries where our grandfathers read, which regularly required a day or two days to produce any given volume. The ideal now becomes to induce visitors to love things of beauty, to view them with pleasure, and to depart with a sense of exhilaration."[56]

The art, historical, industrial, natural history, and other museums of a number of cities, chief among them Boston, New York, Chicago, Cleveland, Cincinnati, Toledo, Detroit, Milwaukee, Minneapolis, St. Louis, Newark, Philadelphia, and Baltimore, have developed into genuine educational institutions. They coöperate with the public schools, send out exhibits to libraries and other institutions, provide qualified persons to conduct groups of visitors through the museum and discuss the treasures intelligently and interestingly, give public lecture courses and concerts, provide assembly halls and club rooms, distribute attractive reading material, hold classes, show educational films, and in other ways undertake to serve and instruct the public.

An important part of the educational work of museums is effected through their coöperation with the public schools and higher institu-

[56] *Ibid.*, p. 251.

tions of learning. Many museums in the larger cities, such as the National Museum in Washington, the Field Museum of Chicago, the Philadelphia Commercial Museum, the Cleveland Art Museum, and others, supply the schools with illustrative material. Teachers are invited to bring their classes to the museum, where they are aided by a wealth of interesting articles placed at their command. A number of children's museums, excellent institutions like those in Brooklyn and Boston, give valuable opportunities for visual education to school children. A unique provision in this field is the Educational Museum of the St. Louis Public Schools, which supplies all the schools of the city with objects and pictures for the illustration of all phases of school work. This museum is an integral part of the school system. It is a traveling museum, a museum on wheels. The material, arranged in 12,000 groups and collections, is sent to the schools by large automobile trucks in the service of the museum. The schools are divided into five sections, each of which has a delivery once a week.[57]

Among the other examples of museums carrying on an active educational work, especially with the public schools, is the Philadelphia Commercial Museum, organized in 1894. It is a public institution, supported by appropriations from the city of Philadelphia for its general work, from the State of Pennsylvania for its special educational work, and by subscriptions from manufacturers and merchants in the United States for special service along commercial lines. The department of exhibits has charge of the museum. Its collections illustrate the important commercial products of the world and the present conditions of life and industry in all countries. The exhibits are of great value to schools for illustrating geography, commerce, industries, and economics. A very active and important educational work is carried on. The free educational activities are briefly as follows:

Study of the exhibits, under the guidance of competent museum assistants.

Daily lectures to visiting classes, on subjects chosen by the teachers.

Special lectures to teachers and others.

Loan lectures, which consist of lantern slides and appropriate reading matter for the use of schools outside of Philadelphia. Lanterns and screens go with these lectures.

School collections or miniature museums, which are given free of cost to schools for classroom use.

[57] Carl G. Rathmann, *Visual Education and the St. Louis School Museum*, U. S. Bureau of Education Bulletin, 1924, No. 39.

The work of the educational department has grown until it now covers the entire state. Its primary aim is to teach fundamental facts in regard to the commerce, industries, and products of the world.[58]

A type of museum new to America is the technical museum. Outstanding examples are the New York Museum of the Peaceful Arts, the Chicago Museum of Science and Industry, and the technical museum of Philadelphia, which is part of the Franklin Institute. These new institutions are frankly patterned after the Deutsches Museum of Munich, which is the most remarkable institution of its kind in the world, a convincing demonstration of what can be done to bring the fundamentals of science, engineering, and industry to the people. The Chicago Museum, in addition, plans to interpret the social phases and cultural aspects of science and technology.[59]

As a result of letting the public into the museum and adapting the museum to the needs of the masses, all attendance records have been broken. The Cleveland Museum of Art, organized along these modern lines, has an attendance of about 300,000 a year. The annual attendance at both the Metropolitan Museum of Art of New York and the Chicago Art Institute runs into the hundreds of thousands each year. Similar institutions in other cities are patronized at least as persistently.

European museums started about twenty years earlier than our own along the new path which leads to a wide popular use of exhibits as a part of mass education. In the matter of history museums, folk-art and industrial-art museums, they have gone ahead without much loss of energy from inner dissensions; but in the matter of art museums there has been, in spite of Ruskin's example, a long battle about accepting the principle at the base of the whole conception of the "new museum."

"Would you not degrade art by trying to bring it down to the level of the people?"

"But on the other hand, could you not bring up the level of the people by opening before them the same doors which have led others to artistic appreciation?"

"Would you not breed a new and loathly class, who would think themselves cultivated when they were nothing but pretentious fools?"

"But might you not, on the contrary, slowly bring into being that general

[58] Charles R. Toothaker, *Educational Work of the Commercial Museum of Philadelphia*, U. S. Bureau of Education Bulletin, 1920, No. 13.
[59] Waldemar Kaempffert, "The Great Museum of the Machine Age," *The New York Times Magazine*, Oct. 26, 1930, pp. 4, 5, 16.

acceptance of the importance of art and culture in human life which has in the past always proved the best, indeed the only spring-board from which born artists can leap to their great exploits?"

These are some of the questions which have been flying thick about this new development in mass education.[60]

[60] Dorothy Canfield Fisher, *Why Stop Learning?* 1927, pp. 248-249.

CHAPTER XVII

THE AMERICAN NEWSPAPER

IN MODERN society the greatest power for disseminating information is the newspaper. It brings news from everywhere and is within reach of everyone. "The newspaper overshadows every other educational agency. The lecture-room, the pulpit, the public meeting, the pamphlet, the book are relatively unimportant, for whereas these reach but a small minority of the people during irregular intervals, the daily paper comes constantly in touch with the great masses who read it and depend upon it for their information and recreation."[1] Its closest rival is the radio. As an entertainer, the radio stands head and shoulders above it, but as an agency of mass education, the radio is inferior to it. Upon the newspaper more than any other agency, the great mass of the people depend for their knowledge of their own and other societies. For a few cents they obtain a quantity of reading matter equal to the contents of a thick book and often produced at an expense a hundredfold greater than that of a book. Probably millions of people read nothing but the newspaper. Certainly there is no other publication that most people read every day. "Now the power to determine each day what shall seem important and what shall be neglected is a power unlike any that has been exercised since the Pope lost his hold on the secular mind."[2]

The power of the press and its service to society are both far-reaching. The press asserts for itself a great position as the Fourth Estate. Its freedom is sanctioned by the Constitution. It claims the right to act as censor of the government and defender of the people's liberties; it enjoys a special classification in the mails and other privileges. To journalism democracy owes in large part not only its strength but also its important victories. Journalism, in turn, owes to democracy its enjoyment of enormous privileges, its practical admission into the government. Though strange instruments have appeared in the course of this development, the growth of democracy has meant increase of the power of journalism. In the everyday life of society the press is an indispensable agent. Without it, the people

[1] James Edward Rogers, *The American Newspaper*, 1909, p. 104.
[2] Walter Lippmann, *Liberty and the News*, 1920, p. 48.

511

would be deprived of information about their own community and the world at large, business would suffer, health officers could not go far in combating epidemics and in carrying on their other activities, alleviation of suffering during great disasters would be tremendously handicapped, campaigns for civic betterment and drives for educational, religious, and charitable causes would be curtailed, the machinery of government could not properly function. During the general strike in England the government was practically suspended, because the newspapers were unable to publish.

Thus the press occupies a peculiar position in society and has great potential power as an instrument of social welfare. Its powers and privileges carry with them great responsibilities, for it can lead or mislead the public. "It is a great educational force for good or evil, and those who conduct the press, while they exercise its power, should recognize their responsibility."[3]

The Press an Urban Institution.—Newspapers are read everywhere in America, but the most persistent readers are found in the larger cities. Here a newspaper is a daily necessity. Even the newly arrived immigrant cannot wait until he learns to read English, but must have a daily journal printed in his native tongue. On Sunday the newspaper reading goes on with unusual energy. Knowing that their patrons will have plenty of time on their hands, the publishers enlarge their papers for this day to four or five times the ordinary size, and having done this, print about twice the usual number of copies. No other country has anything like the American Sunday newspaper. There are plenty of persons who do little else on Sundays than pore over newspapers.

The daily newspaper is an urban institution. Reading, which was a luxury in the country, has become a necessity in the city. "This is true, in part," thinks Prof. Robert E. Park,[4] "because city people—who live in tenements or in apartment houses or in hotels—have, generally speaking, no neighbors. In such a world it is almost as necessary to be able to read a newspaper as it is to speak the language. How else can one know what is going on in this vastly complicated life of the city? Newspapers and newspaper circulation have inevitably grown with the growth of cities. For that reason newspapers circulate more widely in cities, and particularly in great cities, than they do in small towns and in rural communities. In Chicago,

[3] Moorfield Storey, "The Daily Press," *The Atlantic Monthly*, Jan., 1922, CXXIX, 41.

[4] "The Yellow Press," *Sociology and Social Research*, Sept.-Oct., 1927, 12:1:3-4.

for example, there are 91 papers published and circulated every day for every one hundred of the population. Outside of the city, the proportion is 19 newspapers circulated for every one hundred of the population.''

As in the case of other commonplace necessities, dependence on the newspaper is only fully realized when the object is missing. A sort of paralysis crept over New York City in the fall of 1923, when, owing to a press-room strike, the city found itself shorn for a few days of its customary news, entertainment, and advertising. ''What had been taken quite as a matter of course became, in its absence, of vital importance. Merchants lost millions of dollars in those few days; sales fell off alarmingly. Commuters stared stonily at flying landscapes, and Wall Street had to content itself with a thin dribble of news from the ticker. What was happening at the City Hall, in Chicago, London, Charleston, Samoa? Millions of confused and angry readers found themselves cut off at a single stroke from the outside world, even from the tidings of their own vast community. And millions of admirers of the Gumps, and thirsters for advice to the lovelorn, were bereft of their daily pabulum. Where were the japes of the columnists, where the soporific of the bedtime story? The good that newspapers did was not interrèd during that hiatus, but leaped out of nothing into life, and the evil they had been accused of doing was forgot.''[5]

The American newspaper is an urban institution in another sense: the papers of large cities control and dominate the field. According to Mr. John L. Given,[6] formerly of the New York *Evening Sun*, about 175 papers, printed in cities having over 100,000 inhabitants, constitute the press of the country for general news. They are the key papers which collect the news dealing with great events, and even the people who do not read any one of them depend ultimately upon them for news of the outer world. For they make up the great press associations which coöperate in the exchange of news. Each is, therefore, not only the informant of its own readers, but it is the local reporter for the newspapers of other cities and for the rural press and the special press as well. Some of these key papers are very much richer than others, so that for international news, in the main, the whole press of the nation may depend upon the reports of the press associations and the special services of a few metropolitan dailies.

[5] Silas Bent, *Ballyhoo, The Voice of the Press*, 1927, p. 170.
[6] *Making a Newspaper*, 1912, p. 13.

Ten centers dominate the feature field. Not only is the run of news syndicated to papers large and small, but so are illustrations, fiction, comic strips, even editorials. Syndicated matter has come more and more to be the daily bread of the small-town newspaper. Practically the only news gathered by the small paper is the strictly local reading matter. The metropolitan press sets the tempo and determines the character of the other dailies in this country.[7]

Increased Circulation.—Freedom of the press, universal education, and cheapness in price have given the American newspaper one of its special characteristics, namely, its enormous circulation. In the year 1850 a newspaper of 50,000 subscribers living within a radius of 30 miles was considered a large journal. Contrast this with any one of the modern New York dailies with a circulation of half a million or more, distributed even to points 500 or more miles away. The increase has occurred mainly since the eighties. In 1880, the total circulation of newspapers in the United States was about 3½ millions. In 1930, the average daily circulation of the morning and evening newspapers of the United States was 39,589,172 copies. On Sunday an average of 26,413,047 copies were regularly distributed among the people. There were 388 morning, 1,554 evening, and 521 Sunday newspapers. An official estimate places the number of dwellings in the United States at approximately 20 million. On this basis, there was thus an average of nearly two daily newspapers for each dwelling, and on Sunday a newspaper for every dwelling, with more than 6 million copies to spare. Nowhere else in the world do people consume newspapers in such volume. It is the outstanding fact of American journalism.[8]

This vast increase in newspaper circulation has been made possible by inventions and improvements in the art of printing and in mechanical equipment, progress in the manufacture of paper and reduction in its cost, the increased facility of gathering news, and the economy of time and labor which these advances have entailed. The newspaper has also been affected by economic changes and discoveries in other fields. "The invention of telephone and telegraph, of electricity, the increase in the facilities of transportation, the lowering of the stamp rate, have all been vital factors that have played important parts toward increasing the size and circulation of the daily

[7] Silas Bent, *Ballyhoo*, 1927, pp. xv-xvi. Walter Lippmann, *Public Opinion*, 1922, p. 325.

[8] *Editor and Publisher*, "International Year Book Number for 1931," Jan. 31, 1931, 63:37:17, 120. *Cf.* N. W. Ayer and Son's *Directory of Newspapers and Periodicals*, 1931.

paper. Without these inventions modern journalism would not be what it is today.''[9]

The Newspaper as a Mirror of the Times.—The various stages through which the newspaper has passed reflect the social conditions of the different periods. The small, local, conservative newspaper before 1880 was the product of an agricultural society. It dealt little with the great outside world. It expressed and typified the habits and temperament of the American people at that stage of development. Then came a period of transition, about 1880, when this country began to forge ahead as an industrial and urbanized nation. As a result, American journalism became liberal, progressive, and national. Between 1880 and the Spanish-American War, as we shall see later, the newspaper underwent a radical change. From this stage sprang the present-day paper, catering to the masses and changing its standards as conditions changed. Today we have a sensational, commercial, and international newspaper whose character is shaped by the industrial development and the rapid growth of cities. The modern press is characteristic of the machine age. It is a development of our cities, and it reflects the nervousness, rush, excitability, superficiality, and over-stimulation of city life. Thus journalism is a mirror of the times. It is a mirror of the people in general, and the individual paper is a mirror of its subscribers.

Old-Style Versus New-Style Newspaper.—Before 1880 it was considered a luxury to subscribe to a newspaper. The only classes that habitually read daily papers were business and professional men interested in the more serious affairs of life. As a result of this, the newspaper was dignified and excluded all traces of sensationalism. It was a publication intended to appeal to grown men only, and men of staid habits, at that. It printed the news, but it made no pretense of providing light or easy reading. It ignored one-half of the adult population entirely—the women—in bidding for readers, and took no account whatever of the children.

The new-style newspaper is conducted on a different plan. It strives to please by offering something to everybody. The solid news is given as in the old-style papers, but the stories are written so that they are entertaining. Many new features have been added. There is a continued story; a whole page or more of sporting news is presented; musical comment and art notes are included; the chess-lover gets a

---

[9] James Edward Rogers, *The American Newspaper*, 1909, p. 191. *Cf.* James L. Given, *Making a Newspaper*, 1912, pp. 15-18.

column; the man who likes town talk is considered; the fisherman is
told where the fish are biting; pictures are provided for those who
like them; in short, all tastes are remembered. And a particular effort
is made to please the women. Every bit of current news in which it
is thought they will be interested is exploited at length, and this is
supplemented by the talk of women's clubs, fashion notes, beauty
hints, recipes, and dress patterns. Even the advertising is mainly
directed toward women. Women spend all of a man's money, so
Dorothy Dix says, except what he spends on his vices. To the children
an appeal little less insistent is made. For them there are funny pictures, jokes, puzzles, descriptions of games, and frequently—this with
the Sunday edition—coupons entitling them to dolls, boxes of paints,
and other articles that might be expected to appeal to juvenile hearts.
The change is most marked in the Sunday paper, the chief support
of the hundred syndicates which make possible its marvelous bulk
and variety. Samuel K. Ratcliffe, the English journalist, calls the
American Sunday newspaper "an astonishing organization for the
prevention of reading." In short, the new-style newspaper, when it
does what its editors strive to make it do, delivers a universal appeal,
and once gaining access to a home, becomes a household necessity. To
a certain extent it becomes the daily instructor and entertainer for
the whole family.[10]

The old-style newspaper represented certain classes; the new-style
paper exists for the masses, and this fact determines its character and
policy. Modern newspapers are largely what the masses of the people
make them.

Classification of American Newspapers.—Newspapers lend themselves to manifold classification. From the viewpoint of different
readers, they appear as molders of public opinion, as recorders of
current events, or as scandal-mongering busybodies. When American
newspapers are classified on the basis of the manner of presentation
of news and the relative stress laid on the various classes of material
that make up the contents of the paper, three types appear: the
conservative, the sensational, and the yellow. The conservative paper,
following the old school, is found primarily in the small town and
country. Sensational and yellow newspapers are more characteristic
of the city. But one type blends into the other, and the standard of
judgment varies with time. Newspapers which were earlier regarded
as sensational would be considered conservative today. The classifica-

[10] John L. Given, *Making a Newspaper*, 1912, pp. 3-4.

tion is largely subjective and relative. A careful critic of the press briefly describes each type as follows.[11]

1. The conservative paper gives the daily news sanely, and as far as possible presents the truth unvarnished and without much comment. Its chief attention is given to politics and business. It has few photographs, its editorials are straightforward and unbiased, its news columns give no undue balance to the unusual, the morbid, or the vulgar. It aims to be an unprejudiced agent for reporting the events of the day.

2. The sensational journals not only give the news as they find it, but they color it, or as the newspaper slang goes, they "doctor" it. Whereas the conservative paper writes *for* its readers, the sensational journal writes *to* them. Under this policy, the paper becomes spectacular, excited, changeable, declamatory, and often argumentative. It gives greater space to crime, sports, and society news. Big headlines and a greater number of photographs are interspersed among the news. The editorials begin to swing more and more with the shifting of public opinion or at the dictation of the owners of the paper. One becomes conscious of a definite editorial policy which follows rather than leads, of an eye to expediency and a frank hunt for subscribers. This is the most distinctive type of American paper, characteristic of our cities.

3. The essential characteristic of the yellow journal is that it creates news. Another of its methods is to select news from what is available with a view to attract supporters to its own opinions and to cajole readers to its ends. It aims to fix prejudices, to arouse feeling, and for its own purposes to prey upon the lower passions of the great mass of mankind. It devotes the greatest proportionate amount of its space to reports of crime and vice. In regard to format, yellow newspapers are usually distinguished by a flaring make-up, that is, striking headlines in glaring type and many illustrations to give as vivid a description as possible of crime, sport, divorce, and, in general, the dramatics of life. "Every item of news is worked up into a story told with a rush and a dash, the aim of which is to excite the reader. Every avenue of suggestion is used for sensational purposes. Editors manufacture news; men with vivid imaginations and clever pens are paid large salaries to compose fictitious 'writeups.' Other men are paid big sums to make 'scare headlines' in large red or black letters." An editor once defined the most successful newspaperman as

[11] James Edward Rogers, *The American Newspaper*, 1909, pp. 32-33, 51-60 (55 quoted).

"he who best knew where hell was going to break out next and had a reporter on the spot." On this basis, what is especially distinctive of yellow journalism is that when hell is quiet and there is no sign of an eruption, a reporter is immediately sent to make one at any cost.

As a final example, we may note how newspapermen themselves classify newspapers. They generally say that without making fine distinctions there are three kinds of journalism in America.[12]

First, there is the kind which merely records—the common or garden variety. "This brand recites what occurs in plain sight, but on dull days, when fires and accidents are few and the local politicians are quiet, it fills its columns with material which can be procured in profusion through the expenditure of no greater effort than the wielding of a pair of shears. Against this kind of journalism not much can be said. But there is nothing to say for it." It flourishes best in small towns, and is not often found in large cities. Most of the papers which represent this type are nothing more than bread-winners, looked upon by their owners and editors as mediums through which a living is to be gained. "And as good livings are rarely gained through them, they are seldom regarded with affection."

The second kind of journalism—the ideal type from the point of view of newspapermen—endeavors to present a picture of the world's progress. It records the everyday occurrences about which everyone wants to know, but, not content with this, acts as a disseminator of general information and deals with causes and effects as well as events. "It does what most individuals cannot do because of a lack of time or opportunity—keeps watch on the men who serve the public, guards the public purse, and restrains those who would infringe on the public rights—tells of public improvements that are under way and suggests others, and heralds, in words that everyone can understand, great inventions and wonderful discoveries. Where it can it tells what is going to occur. It tells what the scientists, the educators, the law-makers, the artists, and the writers are doing, and contrasts the past with the present. Continually it makes known that which is useful and instructive, as well as that which is only entertaining. In brief, it presents a picture of the world's progress." This kind of journalism is an ideal rather than a reality. A few papers come very close to it; many which aim to attain it fall far short. But it may be called the standard type.

The third kind of journalism is the familiar yellow variety, about

[12] John L. Given, *Making a Newspaper*, 1912, pp. 6-11 (6-7 quoted).

which there has been so much discussion and criticism. Its origin and development have been briefly as follows.

Yellow Journalism.—What we know as yellow journalism was baptized and christened at the altar of the Sunday newspaper. It got its name in 1897, when the leading exponent of the school was exploiting with much ostentation a series of colored pictures in which the foremost character wore a yellow dress and was known, on account of his attire and youth, as the Yellow Kid. A rival journal started a similar series in its comic supplement. One of the long-established papers coined the term "yellow journalism," using the word yellow in its slang interpretation, which is, cowardly, mean, contemptible. When less opprobriously employed, the term refers to the unusual and the ultra-sensational in journalism.[13]

The beginnings of yellow journalism go back to an earlier period. Its foundation was laid in 1835, when the elder James Gordon Bennett started to publish the New York *Herald*. Previous to that time the editors of the country thought more of molding public opinion than they did of presenting the news, and their highest ambition apparently was to become involved in editorial controversies. The *Herald* from the start was run on a different principle. It aimed first to give the news, and the editor did not wait for the news to be brought to him; he went out and got it, and when it became necessary he went pretty far. That he had the right idea as to what the people wanted was quickly shown. Starting with a capital of less than $500, he had his paper firmly established within a few years, and in the early forties he was well on the highway of success.[14] Bennett was the first to sense the value of police court items, Wall Street deals, and personal intimacies; and he "set the pattern for modern journalism in making the daily paper not only a budget of information but a form of entertainment and a vehicle of 'escape' literature. Fashionable folk were outraged at his reports of their doings. The reports were printed not for the fashionables but for kitchen maids."[15] Villard[16] regards James Gordon Bennett, and his son who succeeded him, as the most remarkable news men this country has ever produced. The father revolutionized the whole science of news-getting, and the son outdid him by creating exclusive news. The

[13] Don C. Seitz, *Joseph Pulitzer, His Life and Letters*, 1924, pp. 231-232.
[14] James Melvin Lee, *History of American Journalism*, 1917, pp. 193-200. George Henry Payne, *History of Journalism in the United States*, 1920, ch. XV.
[15] Silas Bent, *Ballyhoo*, 1927, p. 48.
[16] Oswald Garrison Villard, *Some Newspapers and Newspaper-men*, 1923, ch. XVI.

father began his career as a rank sensationalist, a muckraker, a purveyor of scandal; but gradually what we should today call the yellow-
ness of the *Herald* began to fade away. The paper was mild compared
to later journals, and it was a remarkably accurate news sheet. In
1920 it was merged with the New York *Tribune*.

The next important stage in the development of yellow journalism
came in 1883, when Joseph Pulitzer purchased the New York *World*,
and set out to build up a large circulation by appealing to the laboring or semi-educated classes. At the start, this paper under its new
ownership touched much lower depths of journalism than had the
Herald under the elder Bennett. In 1896 William Randolph Hearst
entered the New York field by purchasing the New York *Journal*,
which he separated into a morning edition called the New York
American, and an evening edition retaining the old name. Then began
the rivalry between Hearst and Pulitzer for the field, and the development of still more sensational methods. It was at this time that yellow
journalism was christened. As Pulitzer had outdone Bennett in yel-
lowness, so Hearst outdid Pulitzer. Villard[17] says of Hearst, "He
has done more to degrade the entire American press than any one
else in its history—more than Pulitzer and both the Bennetts combined." Financially, he has been the most successful. "Pulitzer's
principal contribution to yellow journalism was muckraking, Hearst's
was mainly 'jazz.' The newspaper had been conducted up to this time
upon the theory that its business was to instruct. Hearst rejected that
conception. His appeal was frankly not to the intellect but to the
heart. The newspaper was for him first and last a form of entertainment."[18] The Hearst papers have remained the same, whereas the
World until its recent demise grew more conservative with time. It
became a great liberal daily, "one of the few remaining assets in the
field of journalism in which Americans with ideals can take pride."[19]
In 1931 the morning *World* came to an end and the evening edition was combined with the *Telegram*.

The yellow press, in the sense that the term was used in the nineties,
no longer exists. It has passed into history. "Not that the press has
not retained all, or most all of the characteristics which it acquired
in that dazzling period of newspaper enterprise and innovation, but
these innovations no longer dazzle nor bewilder us. . . . Looking
back upon it now, we can see that whatever else it was responsible

[17] *Ibid.*, p. 15.
[18] Robert E. Park and Ernest W. Burgess, *The City*, 1925, p. 96.
[19] Oswald Garrison Villard, *Some Newspapers and Newspaper-men*, 1923, pp.
43, 62.

for, the yellow press did make reading easy and popular. It did bring within the circle of a single public a larger number of people and a wider range of interests and intelligence than any other type of newspaper had ever done before. The circulation of newspapers between 1880 and 1890, when the yellow press was in its first bloom, increased 135.2 per cent.''[20]

Originated through a desire to gain readers and advertisers, yellow journalism has produced results. Its original disciples have readers by the hundred thousand (the Sunday edition of the New York *American* is over a million) and they have about all the advertising that they can well handle. More than this, they are not afraid of losing either readers or advertisers. They know that they can hold the advertisers as long as they have readers, and the readers they hold in a tight embrace. ''The yellow journals stole their early patrons from no other publications. Instead, they offered something attractive to persons not in the habit of reading, and thus created a demand where none had existed. And even now the bulk of the yellow journals go either into the hands of those persons upon whom matter-of-fact stories and subdued headlines make no impression, or those who, while depending upon other papers for information which can be accepted as true, elect to look at pictures, read sensations, and acquire mild doses of philosophy in the form of out-of-the-ordinary editorials, as a kind of relaxation. To please persons in either class is by no means an easy task; they demand thrills every day and they will not tolerate dullness or pedantry. Because of this the yellow journals have room for none other than particularly active journalists. . . . The editors do not like everything about yellow journalism—the red, yellow, and green inks, the double reading headlines, the exaggeration, and the bombast—but they do not consider it a subject for raillery; at least they do not so acknowledge. Their contention is that they go to extremes to attract readers, but that in doing this they gain wide followings, and are thus enabled to right wrongs, protect the weak, and strive with effect for the public good. That the yellow journals really do some of these things cannot be denied. . . . Toned down, yellow journalism is more fallacious than vicious, and its most prominent earmarks are impudence and impertinence. And even at its worst yellow journalism was not as bad as it was pictured. . . . Adhering to facts, instances where yellow journalism has done worse

[20] Robert E. Park, ''The Yellow Press,'' *Sociology and Social Research*, Sept.-Oct., 1927, 12:1:11.

than exaggerate and offend by exposing things that might better have been hid from view are hard to find.''[21]

The Tabloids.—A new development of yellow journalism has been brought by the tabloid picture papers of the present, with their insatiable prying into human privacies. They are called tabloids because of their smaller size—they are as long as the ordinary newspaper is broad and have five columns to the page instead of eight—and picture papers because nearly all of the first page and a good part of the other pages are occupied by illustrations. But the word tabloid has come to have other connotations as a new outcropping of sensationalism. Charles A. Dana—''the god of all American newspapermen''—who in his long service as editor of the New York *Sun* had made of journalism an art, once defined news as the biting of a dog by a man. [''If a dog bites a man, it is not news. But if a man bites a dog, it is news.''] As a symbol of the newspaper editor's belief that news fell within hard, clear lines, easy to mark off, it took on the authority and sanctity of a litany. The tabloids broke loose from the old news tradition, and won readers, advertising and profit by ''measuring news solely on the basis of its interest for large numbers of adult infants.''[22]

Lord Northcliffe, proprietor of the sensational type of newspaper in England, was the inventor of the modern tabloid. Of him it has been said that ''he got out a paper for people who couldn't think, and it was a great success; then he got out a paper for people who couldn't read, and it was an even greater success.'' The story is told of a reporter for a tabloid newspaper who approached a prominent person and asked for an interview. ''Interview?'' exclaimed the latter in surprise. ''Why, yes,'' was the reply, ''some of our subscribers can read.'' Certain it is, anyway, that no small number of the new tabloid readers were recruits who had never read newspapers before. Like the yellow journals of the nineties, the tabloids have dipped down into subcirculation strata.

The first successful tabloid paper of the present vintage in America was a child of the Chicago *Tribune*, and was established in New York City on June 26, 1919. It was called the daily *News*. In an extraordinarily brief period it achieved the largest daily and Sunday circulation in the United States. In less than eight years it had passed the million mark. In June, 1924, the Hearst forces issued a competitor,

[21] John L. Given, *Making a Newspaper*, 1912, pp. 10-11.
[22] Oliver H. P. Garrett, ''The Gods Confused,'' *The American Mercury*, Nov., 1927, 12:47:327.

called the daily *Mirror*, and in the fall of 1924 Bernarr MacFadden founded the (so-called porno-) *Graphic*. It was not long before the three of them claimed two out of every five daily-paper readers in Manhattan.[23] The *Editor and Publisher Year Book for 1931* gives the morning circulation of the *News* as 1,312,457, its Sunday circulation as 1,616,106; the daily circulation of the *Mirror* as 501,201; and that of the evening *Graphic* as 280,239.

The phenomenal growth of the tabloids was greatly promoted by their lurid and salacious treatment of several notorious trials—the Browning separation suit and the Hall-Mills and Snyder-Gray murder cases. The tabloids, however, differ from other sensational papers only in the matter of degree. There is nothing new in their methods, nor in their selection of news for emphasis, nor in their use of pictures and headlines. The only innovation may be said to be their "discovery that the exhibitionist who enjoys the public exploitation of his private affairs is the most fecund of all news subjects—a generic mother of news stories, capable of infinite creations without a still birth in the lot of them."[24] Though regarded as outside of respectable newspaper circles, the tabloids have forced the other newspapers, through competition, to adopt some of their methods, such as bigger and bigger headlines, more and more pictures, and fuller and fuller reporting of "legalized lewdness." They may also bring about general acceptance of the smaller format. "The one thing the tabloids are doing is to train the public to read small-sized newspapers, which are infinitely handier and easier to read than the larger papers. The small pages also force economy in news-writing. Eventually a more substantial news content will develop, probably in the *News*, and out of the pioneer of tabloid muck-raking will come a legitimate, convenient, improved type of newspaper."[25]

The history of the cheapening of the press, which we have briefly sketched, may be summarized as follows. The elder Bennett was, in a sense, the father of yellow journalism, although his offspring was not christened until the Hearst-Pulitzer war gave it new vitality, just as it has received a new lease of life since the advent of the tabloids. The genealogy may be traced thus: Bennett begat sensationalism; sensationalism begat yellow journalism; yellow journalism begat the tabloids.

---

[23] Silas Bent, *Ballyhoo*, 1927, ch. VII.

[24] Oliver H. P. Garrett, "The Gods Confused," *The American Mercury*, Nov., 1927, 12:47:328.

[25] Hugh Kent, "The New York Dailies," *The American Mercury*, Nov., 1926, 9:35:318.

Commercialization of the Press.—During the last two decades of the nineteenth century, the larger daily newspapers underwent a financial readjustment which brought profound changes in American journalism. It became impersonal and commercial. Formerly the editor was practically supreme in control. Power now passed into the hands of the business interests. Many factors contributed to bring about this result. "The telegraph and the cable made news a most perishable commodity because of the rapidity with which it could be placed before the public. Shop-worn goods the merchant can sell at a special sale to bring at least the cost of production, but stale news the publisher cannot market at any price. The franchise in a press association became harder to get and at the same time carried with it a constantly increasing charge for better service. Presses jumped from hundreds to tens of thousands in cost of manufacture. . . . Typographical unions kept pushing the wages of printers and pressmen higher and higher up the scale. Competition reduced the selling price, but increased the cost of distribution. . . . Additions to the editorial staff increased the number of employees while 'bids' from rivals raised the salaries of other members. More and more the revenue came from advertising and less and less from circulation. Such conditions demanded a business pilot at the wheel to steer the newspaper craft sailing over seas uncharted by editors of previous periods."[26]

The increasingly large amount of capital required to run a city newspaper and the increasing proportion of revenue received from advertising have been the two most fundamental factors in this development. The metropolitan daily represents too heavy a financial investment to be organized on any save a sound business basis. The investment in some of the New York dailies amounts to millions. There was a time when the subscriber paid his money primarily to see what his favorite editor had to say, or because the journal was strongly of his own political persuasion. The basis of the newspaper's revenue was sales and subscriptions. This sort of personal and political journalism began to disappear when the newspapers found that the rewards of selling advertising space and of merchandizing news are far greater than those afforded by the rivalrous journalism of the old tradition. So the newspapers became a vehicle of advertising, as well as a purveyor of the news of the day. Today more than half the space of the newspaper is given to advertisements, and the advertiser contributes three-fourths of the revenue of the press. A metropolitan daily which sells for two

[26] James Melvin Lee, *History of American Journalism*, 1917, p. 353.

cents may cost as much as fourteen. By and large the advertiser pays the difference, plus the profit to the publisher. Circulation has become merely the means to an end. It is an asset only when it can be sold to the advertiser, who buys it with the revenues secured through indirect taxation of the reader. Thus the newspaper has been placed on a business basis. It has become essentially a commercial enterprise, involving a large capital investment, while the metropolitan press has entered the ranks of "Big Business." With a total income of over a billion dollars a year, the American newspaper is now, in fact, a major industry.

A significant manifestation of this development has been the marked tendency toward group-ownership and merger. In 1930, there were 57 chains or groups of newspapers, controlling over 300 newspapers, published in 40 states. The largest was the Scripps-Howard group, with 25 dailies. The W. R. Hearst group was a close second, with 24 newspapers. The Hearst papers, however, have about twice the circulation of the Scripps-Howard group. The combined circulation of the newspaper chains is about 40 per cent of the total circulation of the country.[27] Mergers, which are a twin phenomenon with chains, have been making heavy inroads, especially since the World War. The following table, covering the period from 1921 to 1930, discloses that although the total circulations of all classes of newspapers have increased, the number of newspapers has declined.[28]

	Number of newspapers		Total circulations	
	1921	1930	1921	1930
Morning papers..........	427	388	10,144,260	14,434,257
Evening papers..........	1,601	1,554	18,279,480	25,154,915
Sunday papers..........	545	521	19,041,413	26,413,047

Some newspapers have been entirely eliminated; others have been merged. The morning papers have been most affected. They are more susceptible than evening papers to outside competition, and because of their smaller circulation and the time of issue they are less

[27] *Editor and Publisher*, "International Year Book Number for 1931," Jan. 31, 1931, 63:37:126-128. The character of British journalism has undergone a similar change. Today it is in the hands of a small group of press magnates, each controlling numerous and varied types of publications. S. K. Ratcliffe, "The Revolution in Fleet Street," *Nineteenth Century*, July, 1930, 108:15-24.
[28] *Ibid.*, p. 120.

effective advertising media. In large cities there has been a marked tendency toward reduction of the number of morning newspapers to one strong publication. Even cities of 500,000 or more population, cities like Detroit, Cleveland, Baltimore, Pittsburgh, Buffalo, and Milwaukee, have but one morning newspaper. In fact, of the 93 cities of 100,000 or more inhabitants each, 59 have only one morning paper, and in 30 of these cases it is combined with another edition. Seventeen cities of this population class have no morning paper. Thus 76 of the 93 largest cities in the United States have either one morning newspaper or none at all.[29]

Despite their reduced number, morning papers in large cities have experienced an increased aggregate circulation. Much of this circulation expansion has taken place in the dense suburban fringe that has developed around the large city. Moreover, improved means of transportation (the New York *Times*, for one, uses the airplane) and extension of rural mail delivery system have tended to widen their area of circulation beyond the metropolitan district. The metropolitan dailies have thus come into direct news competition with small-town newspapers, and the latter have suffered. This situation, coupled with the growing competition among the local papers for local advertising, has led to a reduction of their number. The consolidation process noted above in the case of large cities has been pushed still farther in cities of less than 50,000 population. It has led to the complete elimination of the morning paper in favor of a strong evening paper. A corollary development has been the suspension of the Sunday supplement of the former morning issue.

William Preston Beazell,[30] an experienced newspaperman, believes that newspaper circulation has now reached the saturation point and that this condition will bring about a marked increase in consolidations and a still more persistent growth of newspaper chains.

The capitalistic organization of the newspaper, together with increasing costs of production and competition for advertising, are the chief explanation of the consolidation movement. The late Frank A. Munsey, most prominent among the dealers in dailies, was wont to say: "The same law of economics applies to the newspaper business that operates in all other important businesses to-day; small units in any line are no longer competitive factors."[31] The part played by ad-

[29] Data compiled from the list of United States daily newspapers given in *Editor and Publisher*, "International Year Book Number for 1931," Jan. 31, 1931, 63:37:18-110.
[30] "To-Morrow's Newspaper," *The Atlantic Monthly*, July, 1930, CXLVI, 25.
[31] Quoted by Silas Bent, *Ballyhoo*, 1927, p. 261.

vertising has been great, for newspaper consolidations have been most marked since the World War, which brought a flood of advertising. The advertiser does not want to spend money for overlapping circulation. He would prefer but one paper in every morning and afternoon field, if that could be arranged. In many instances he has exerted economic pressure to bring about mergers, and in others he has prevented the establishment of new papers. "Few negotiations toward merger, or even toward the advent of chain ownership, have been carried beyond the preliminary stages without consultation with the principal advertisers of the community. On the whole the change has been to the satisfaction of the advertiser. It is not always that he finds himself spending less money, but he is getting better returns."[32] The new function of the newspaper as a modern vehicle of advertising coincides with this view.

The Effect on Editorial Policy.—The chain systems and the mergers have contributed to the stabilizing of the industry. They have permitted newspapers to reap more of the rewards that come from selling space for advertising. They have been a factor in the organization and standardization of news-gathering. But the consolidation movement has also reduced or eliminated editorial competition, which is essential to the usefulness of the daily press. Standardization has invaded the editorial department; even editorials are syndicated. Daily journals of pronounced opinion and of strong political allegiance are disappearing. There are several two-paper towns in which the morning and the evening paper, of different political affiliation, have come under one business management, with the editors free to conduct the papers along their old political allegiances, though the same hand signs the pay checks of both editors. The latest development, however, appears to be the elimination of political ties and the elimination of the economically weak. In cities with but one morning newspaper there is no possibility of differing views being presented to the morning newspaper-reading public.

All this means a trend away from journalism of opinion to journalism of commerce. The editor, once supreme, is now subordinate. "The cry of today that the period of the great editors is gone is directly connected with the commercialization of the press and its domination by the owners for whom the editors are but hired men. Greeley, Garrison, Bowen, Godkin, Bowles, and others, the journalists who have profoundly stirred the conscience of America, either owned their

---

[32] William Preston Beazell, "To-Morrow's Newspaper," *The Atlantic Monthly*, July, 1930, CXLVI, 27.

journals or were given a complete freedom of expression. That they were also profoundly engrossed in moral causes helps to explain their power."[33] The newspaper is no longer a product of individual endeavor, but a business concern, even a corporation issuing stocks and bonds.

With this changed character of the newspaper has come a less positive influence on public opinion. The smaller, older papers, which were ably edited, had a tremendous influence on people who formulated opinion, an influence much greater than that exercised by the present newspapers of huge circulation. Big newspapers go to so many readers, representing so many different views, that the tendency is to express no opinion except on matters in which the majority are in agreement. An opinion or policy for all is no opinion or policy at all. With less attention being paid to controversial news and editorials, the field for public instruction is limited. The commercial newspaper tends to follow, not lead, public opinion. The editorial writer of an important newspaper expresses his "growing suspicion that the men who direct the policies of most American newspapers have not the least desire to mold public opinion. Their loftiest aspiration is to guess, twenty-four hours in advance, which way public opinion is going to swing, so as to be able to jump to that side."[34]

An attempt to study quantitatively the question of the direct influence of newspapers on public opinion in the case of certain specific public issues was made in Seattle in 1926. Nearly a thousand residents of the city were selected at random and interviewed regarding their position on four questions of public interest which had been prominently before the electorate within the last eight months preceding the investigation. There was discovered no significant relationship between the attitude of the newspaper and the attitude of the reader on the questions investigated. "The results, as far as this study is concerned, indicate unmistakably (1) that a modern commercial newspaper has little direct influence on the opinions of its readers on public questions. It probably seeks to discover and reflect that opinion rather than to make it. (2) The stand of a newspaper on public questions is a negligible factor in the reader's estimation in selecting his newspaper. (3) Only when a paper is the organ of some homogeneous group [e.g., organized labor] does a slight correspondence between the attitudes of the newspaper and its readers appear. (4) Newspaper opinions are perhaps themselves the products of the various forces which make

[33] Oswald Garrison Villard, *Some Newspapers and Newspaper-men*, 1923, pp. 313-314.

[34] Gerald W. Johnson, "Why Men Work for Newspapers," *The American Mercury*, May, 1929, 17:65:87.

opinion in a community. Of these, the newspaper is undoubtedly one, but its influence as such has perhaps been grossly overestimated or at least the nature of this influence has been misunderstood.''[35]

The late Arthur Twining Hadley,[36] sometime President of Yale University, pointed out that ''one of the great difficulties which beset the newspaper editor when he tries to discuss public questions is the fact that most of his readers have a strong pecuniary or personal interest in having them decided in some particular way. . . . If an editor wishes to make his paper popular with a certain class, he lays stress on the arguments which that class likes and feeds them with the facts which they want to believe. His readers gradually get into a position where their prepossessions have been strengthened until they become prejudices, and where misinformation has been added to prejudice until it becomes almost irremovable.'' Writing from the point of view of adult education, Joseph K. Hart[37] says: ''Most newspapers are important as repeaters of particular legends. 'I'll believe anything,' said Mr. Dooley, 'if ye'll only tell it to me often enough!' Under the guise of telling the news, 'newspapers' repeat the legends of their group, or their sect, or their class, or their party. They do not 'edit' the news. They merely *select* the news that tends to support their favorite legends. The people who like any special legend of wealth, or party, or sect, or government read the paper that upholds that legend. Papers do not so much make mind, therefore; they mostly merely hold ready-made minds in line. Hence we may say that the characteristic of this type of adult education is that it plays upon passive and docile minds and keeps them passive and docile.''

On the other hand, it is a real question whether there can be any effective public opinion, if by public opinion we mean mass opinion. Walter Lippmann, as we saw in an earlier chapter where the consequences of city growth were discussed, pointed out that it is impossible for the citizen to know what is going on and to have an opinion worth expressing on every question which confronts a self-governing community. Each of us cannot acquire a competent opinion about all public affairs. Nor can the press help us. The press deals with a society in which the governing forces are exceedingly complex and are imperfectly recorded. ''The theory that the press can itself record those forces is false. It can normally record only what has been recorded for it by the working of institutions. Everything else is

[35] George A. Lundberg, ''The Newspaper and Public Opinion,'' *Social Forces*, June, 1926, 4:4:712-713.
[36] *Standards of Public Morality*, 1907, pp. 15-16.
[37] *Adult Education*, 1927, p. 248.

argument and opinion, and fluctuates with the vicissitudes, the self-consciousness, and the courage of the human mind."[38] Lippmann concludes that the newspapers necessarily and inevitably reflect, and therefore, in greater or lesser measure, intensify the defective organization of public opinion.

We shall return to this point later. Here we may simply note that whatever may be the function of the press, as a leader or follower of public opinion, a great responsibility rests upon it to give the facts without bias. "The news columns are common carriers. When those who control them arrogate to themselves the right to determine by their own consciences what shall be reported and for what purpose, democracy is unworkable. Public opinion is blockaded. For when a people can no longer confidently repair 'to the best fountains for their information,' then anyone's guess and anyone's rumor, each man's hope and each man's whim becomes the basis of government. All that the sharpest critics of democracy have alleged is true, if there is no steady supply of trustworthy and relevant news."[39]

Suppression and Distortion of News.—The charge has been made that because of the paramount importance of advertising, newspapers are bound to come under the influence of big business, and that this affects both the news and editorial columns. It has even been claimed that news is suppressed at the behest of commercial patrons. Such cases have occurred, but they are extremely rare and are fraught with much danger to the press. Readers will not stand any interference on the part of the advertiser in an attempt to control editorial policies. Newspapers are bound to respect the point of view of the buying public, for without this support they cannot live. The newspaper publisher can much better afford to alienate an individual advertiser than risk losing circulation by being caught accommodating him.

In a long experience, reportorial and editorial, dating back to the beginning of this century, Silas Bent[40] has known but two stories to be suppressed. In his *History of American Journalism* James Melvin Lee[41] cites evidence to disprove the charge that advertisers dictate the policy of newspapers, and points out that the advertisers, especially the department stores which are the largest users of advertising space, simply cannot get along without the newspapers. They are dependent on newspaper advertising for their business. "The object of every

[38] Walter Lippmann, *Public Opinion*, 1922, p. 361.
[39] Walter Lippmann, *Liberty and the News*, 1920, p. 11.
[40] *Ballyhoo*, 1927, p. 22.
[41] Pp. 430-440.

publisher," says Walter Lippmann,[42] "is to turn his circulation from a medley of catch-as-catch-can news stand buyers into a devoted band of constant readers. A newspaper that can really depend upon the loyalty of its readers is as independent as a newspaper can be, given the economics of modern journalism. A body of readers who stay by it through thick and thin is a power greater than any which the individual advertiser can wield, and a power great enough to break up a combination of advertisers."

Labor has insisted that its side is not fairly presented by the capitalistic press. There is some truth to this assertion. Newspapers often given biased reports of strikes and other industrial conflicts. The Colorado coal miners' strike was clearly misrepresented at the source, and through the Associated Press the misrepresentation was spread all over the country. The newspapers of Pittsburgh in particular, and of the nation in general, persistently misrepresented the steel strike of 1919. There was very definite selection of news and garbling of reports.[43] But to charge, as Upton Sinclair[44] does in his indictment of the press, that there is a conspiracy among newspaper men to withhold the truth from the public, is very far-fetched. The reason these things happen is that the press is first of all a human and therefore fallible institution, and secondly it requires much capital; it tends to represent business interests and to be on the side of the established order.

"The whole process of corrupting the news, where corruption today exists, is less often the deliberate work of men bent on falsehood than a process of drifting before the winds of circumstance, timidity, and self-interest."[45] Furthermore, as Lippmann[46] points out, in order to tell the truth about the steel worker in the Pittsburgh district, there was needed a staff of investigators, a great deal of time, and several fat volumes of print. "It is impossible to suppose that any daily newspaper could normally regard the making of Pittsburgh Surveys, or even Interchurch Steel Reports, as one of its tasks. News which requires so much trouble as that to obtain is beyond the resources of a daily press." He adds that "if you are going to blame 'capitalism' for the faults of the press, you are compelled to prove that those faults do not exist except where capitalism controls. That Mr. Sinclair cannot

[42] *Public Opinion*, 1922, pp. 326-327.
[43] Charles Grant Miller, "Pittsburgh's Prostituted Press,"*The Nation*, Jan. 5, 1921, CXII, 8-11. Interchurch World Movement, Commission on Inquiry, *Public Opinion and the Steel Strike*, 1921, pp. 87-162.
[44] *The Brass Check*, 1919.
[45] Frederick L. Allen, "Newspapers and the Truth," *The Atlantic Monthly*, Jan., 1922, CXXIX, 50, 52.
[46] *Public Opinion*, 1922, pp. 336-337, 347.

do this, is shown by the fact that while in his diagnosis he traces everything to capitalism, in his prescription he ignores both capitalism and
anti-capitalism.''

The fundamental influence of capitalism on newspapers is to be
found in the commercial standard of selecting news. It is this which
gives the modern newspaper its main characteristics. This subject is
so important that it needs to be examined in some detail.

Selection of News.—It is essential at once to realize that no newspaper prints all the news. No newspaper is able to gather all the news.
No newspaper today is able to print all the news that it gathers. It
must select the news to be printed. It must also decide what emphasis
each item shall receive, whether it shall be carried in an obscure corner
on page 17 or under a three-column spread on the front page. From
these tasks there is no escape, and with them goes a great responsibility.

The way in which selection and emphasis are made determines the
character of the newspaper. News can be played down or played up,
and in the distinction between the two lies the whole range between
the radical and the Bourbon in the newspaper world, between the New
York *Times* and the tabloids.

What event shall be selected for the leading story? In the ordinary
grist of the day's news there is no one event of such tremendous importance that it overshadows everything else. Usually there are a
number of events upon any one of which the best talent and the best
space that the newspaper can provide might be expended. The selection
of the lead story is therefore absolutely a matter left to the editor's
judgment. Take two newspapers published in the same city on the
same morning. The headline of one reads: "Britain pledges aid to
Berlin against French aggression; France openly backs Poles.'' The
headline of the second is "Mrs. Stillman's Other Love.'' "Which you
prefer is a matter of taste, but not entirely a matter of the editor's
taste. It is a matter of his judgment as to what will absorb the half
hour's attention a certain set of readers will give to his newspaper.''[47]
"If day after day among half a dozen stories available the indecent
one is always the one played up, the newspaper is indecent. And it
is indecent because the editors choose to have it so.''[48]

The newspaper is free to select most of the news that it prints, and
it is free to invade any field, from gross obscenity to the most abstruse
philosophy, knowing that news may be garnered there. The restrictions
that lie upon it are almost entirely restrictions of manner, not of

[47] Walter Lippmann, *Public Opinion*, 1922, p. 354.
[48] Gerald W. Johnson, *What is News?* 1926, pp. 16-17.

matter. The criteria usually set up by newspapermen for good news stories are timeliness, significance, and, overriding both of these, interest. In this view the reading public concurs. The positive influence of the public on the news amounts to a demand that it shall be written interestingly and that it shall not fail to take into account whatever events have power to move great numbers of men.[49] Also, readers wish to read about themselves. The function of becoming, as Mr. Lee[50] puts it, "the printed diary of the home town," is one that every newspaper no matter where it is published must in some measure fill. Negatively, and broadly, the public mores control: news cannot be printed which offends the mores of the group.

With these qualifications, news is what newspapers choose to make it. The newspapers are in effect keepers of the people's conscience and do determine what the people shall and shall not read. The total impression of what they print, and its validity as a basis of public opinion, is a resultant of editorial selection and the editorial viewpoint.[51]

The Commercial Standard.—As a result of the economics of modern journalism, the selection and emphasis of news are dictated by the commercial standard, which is, to select and emphasize that which will gain most readers. It is the standard imposed upon the staff by the head of the business, rather than set up by the workers of their own volition. "The newspaper editor," writes the former editor of the New York *World*,[52] "occupies a strange position. His enterprises depend upon indirect taxation levied by his advertisers upon his readers; the patronage of the advertisers depends upon the editor's skill in holding together an effective group of customers. These customers deliver judgment according to their private experiences and their stereotyped expectations, for in the nature of things they have no independent knowledge of most news they read. If the judgment is not unfavorable, the editor is at least within range of a circulation that pays. But in order to secure that circulation, he cannot rely wholly upon news of the greater environment. He handles that as interestingly as he can, of course, but the quality of the general news, especially about public affairs, is not in itself sufficient to cause very large numbers of readers to discriminate among the dailies. . . . In order to differentiate themselves and collect a steady public most papers have to go outside the field of general news. They go to the dazzling levels of society, to scandal and crime, to sports, pictures, actresses, advice

[49] *Ibid.*, pp. 14, 16, 43.
[50] James Melvin Lee, *History of American Journalism*, 1917, p. 406.
[51] Gerald W. Johnson, *What is News?* 1926, p. 18.
[52] Walter Lippmann, *Public Opinion*, 1922, p. 333.

to the lovelorn, highschool notes, women's pages, buyer's pages, cooking receipts, chess, whist, gardening, comic strips, thundering partisanship, not because publishers and editors are interested in everything but news, but because they have to find some way of holding on to that alleged host of passionately interested readers, who are supposed by some critics of the press to be clamoring for the truth and nothing but the truth."

To gain financial success, a newspaper must secure a large circulation, and the easiest means to attain that end is the selection of news that will excite the interest and pique the curiosity of the greatest possible number of readers. People of good education and superior intelligence are comparatively rare, so that for the purpose of building circulation quickly it is hardly worth while to attempt to interest them. It is necessary to work on lower levels of intelligence to touch great numbers. Hence the sensationalism that is commercially profitable is invariably the type that appeals to low mentality.[53]

Joseph Pulitzer once dictated a memorandum on the kind of news he thought a metropolitan daily should seek: "What is original, distinctive, dramatic, romantic, thrilling, unique, curious, quaint, humorous, odd, apt to be talked about, without shocking good taste or lowering the general tone, good tone, and above all without impairing the confidence of the people in the truth of the stories or the character of the paper for reliability and scrupulous cleanness."[54] That was not all Pulitzer thought a newspaper should print—he was a great crusader—but so far as routine news is concerned, this was his view. It is significant that "nowhere in this memorandum did Pulitzer designate social importance or economic or historical magnitude as a factor. The paper which follows his prescription, and most of them do, need not instruct nor inform us."[55]

The question, "What is news?" is answered by George C. Bastian in *Editing the Day's News* as follows:

1 ordinary man + 1 ordinary life = 0.
1 ordinary man + 1 extraordinary adventure = News.
1 ordinary husband + 1 ordinary wife = 0.
1 husband + 3 wives = News.
1 bank cashier + 1 wife + 7 children = 0.
1 bank cashier — $10,000 = News.
1 chorus girl + 1 bank president — $100,000 = News.

[53] Gerald W. Johnson, *What is News?* 1926, pp. 52-53. William Graham Sumner, *Folkways*, 1906, pp. 50-51.
[54] Don C. Seitz, *Joseph Pulitzer, His Life and Letters*, 1924, p. 416.
[55] Silas Bent, *Ballyhoo*, 1927, p. 26.

1 man + 1 auto + 1 gun + 1 quart = News.
1 man + 1 wife + 1 row + 1 lawsuit = News.
1 man + 1 achievement = News.
1 woman + 1 adventure or achievement = News.
1 ordinary man + 1 ordinary life of 79 years = 0.
1 ordinary man + 1 ordinary life of 100 years = News.

One of the great American news agencies, with correspondents all over the world, instructed its reporters by cable: "Think Stuff Unwanted." They were also advised, in one sentence, as to the most desirable subjects for mail articles: "Women, liquor, wealth, religion, science, and immorality." What was wanted in the scientific field was not an interview with Einstein but a sensational statement by some quack to the effect that he had discovered a cure for cancer, established an air route between the earth and the moon, or transformed the sun's rays into a source of motor energy.[56]

The principles of Hearst journalism, as set forth in a memorandum for the reporters of the Washington *Times*, are as follows:[57]

The Washington *Times* should be full of bright, snappy, interesting local stories.

We have a natural tendency to place emphasis on matters which are ponderous, dull and uninteresting. We must resist this tendency.

We must consider that the *composite* newspaper reader does not care a hang about tax rates, budgets, insurance, disarmament, naval appropriations, public utilities policies, municipal improvements, or scores of other subjects which may appear to be important.

Newspaper readers are most interested in stories which contain the elements most dominant in the primitive emotions of themselves, namely:

1. Self-preservation.
2. Love, or Reproduction.
3. Ambition.

Stories containing one of these elements are good; those which contain two of the elements are better; those which contain all three elements form first-class newspaper material.

The newspaper that goes in for entertainment at all costs is bound to distort the news, because it leaves out much that is important but not entertaining, and puts in much that is entertaining but not important. "A newspaper devoted mainly to trivialities is at best a comic sheet and at worst the admiration and delight of half-wits."[58]

[56] Horace J. Hubbell, "Think Stuff Unwanted," *The American Mercury*, March, 1927, 10:39:263.
[57] "Americana," *The American Mercury*, Dec., 1927, 12:48:417.
[58] Gerald W. Johnson, *What is News?* 1926, p. 93.

Yet entertainment, distraction, and excitement are quite demon-strably the qualities that sell a big circulation; the journals whose function is mainly the forming of opinion are almost without excep-tion subsidized, and not daily. Sex, religion, conflict and death, sus-pense, violence, and money—these have been shown to be the great circulation-building themes. Here are to be found the primary sources of news which will be certain to interest all the public.[59]

Ballyhoo.—Emphasis on news of this sort has given the press of today its distinguishing characteristic. Silas Bent terms it "ballyhoo." The newspaperman is its victim as well as its impresario. Ballyhoo had its real beginnings in the last decade of the nineteenth century. "We may trace its trend by glancing at the results of two surveys, one made in 1899, the other in 1923. In each there was set down the space allotted by sixty-three leading American newspapers to various types of news. During this twenty-four-year period, there was a decline of seventy-seven per cent in editorials, a decline of eighty-four per cent in letters to the editor, and a decline of sixty-six per cent in society items. Let us look now at the figures for certain categories of news, for advertising and illustrations. General and political news, each increased one per cent—no ballyhoo there; business news in-creased four per cent; foreign, nine; sports, forty-seven; crime, fifty-eight! Meanwhile advertising was increasing forty-seven per cent, and illustrations eighty-four per cent."[60] This statement is itself partially ballyhoo, inasmuch as these figures do not tell the whole story; they do not indicate the amount of space given to each item. About 60 per cent of the newspaper today is devoted to advertising, about 25 per cent to news, 10 per cent to features, and less than 5 per cent to opinion.

Crime News.—The question of crime news is one that has espe-cially engaged the attention of the critics of the press. It looms large in the change of sensationalism. The complaint, if discriminating, con-verges on the treatment of crime news rather than its amount. A recent study of one hundred newspapers reveals that the amount of space devoted to news of crime, divorce, and scandal is not excessive. This study, made by the University of Oregon School of Journalism, dis-closes that the modern newspaper devotes only 1.4 per cent of its total space, or 3.5 per cent of its news space, to crime, divorce, and scandal. Though the amount of space devoted to these subjects is not

[59] Richard Owen Boyer, "The Trade of the Journalist," *The American Mer-cury*, Jan., 1929, 16:61:22.
[60] Silas Bent, *Ballyhoo*, 1927, p. 42.

great, the emphasis given to them is. There has been a definite tendency, noted by this study, for crime and scandal news to gravitate toward a conspicuous position on the front page and to big headlines. Furthermore, when a really big crime story "breaks," it is played up tremendously. A survey of thirty-six additional papers found that 16.2 per cent of the front pages were devoted to crime, divorce and scandal, although the percentage of the entire space had proved to be only 1.4 per cent.[61] Virtue is not as good copy for newspapers as is vice.

Crime stories unquestionably have a place in newspapers simply because in this imperfect world crime is part of the show. "The newspaper that fails to give any account whatever of the crimes and follies of the day is giving to its readers a biased and misleading account of the human spectacle. Insofar as it covers up discreditable happenings, it deprives the world of the prophylactic effect of sunlight in shadowed places."[62] Furthermore, contrary to generally accepted opinion, newspapers, even the most sensational, suppress much more than they print in the matter of criminal news.[63]

Although crime news must be printed, many newspapers give it disproportionate emphasis. "Crime waves" are mainly a figment of the newspapers' own creation. Newspapers hinder more than they help the administration of criminal justice. They often prejudice a case before and during trial.[64] Yellow sheets and tabloids assume extralegal authority. "During my nineteenth year," writes a reporter,[65] "with no more sense than most in that year, I had a man and his wife arrested for murder, two brothers arrested for a second murder, went into a number of private homes and questioned their owners as to their sex life, charged a society matron with being a thief, and in every instance I was wrong. But I worked for a powerful yellow, and my victims knew the consequences of doing me bodily harm." Individual criminals who catch the newspaperman's fancy are played up grotesquely. The New York State Crime Commission says that Chapman was glorified by the newspapers:[66]

[61] New York *Times*, July 1, 1928.
[62] Gerald W. Johnson, *What Is News?* 1926, p. 60.
[63] James Melvin Lee, *History of American Journalism*, 1917, p. 442.
[64] W. K. Wisehart, "Newspapers and Criminal Justice," *Criminal Justice in Cleveland*, 1923, Part VII. Joseph L. Holmes, *Crime and the Press*, Reprinted from the *Journal of Criminal Law and Criminology*, Vol. XX, Nos. 1 and 2, May and August, 1929.
[65] Richard Owen Boyer, "The Trade of a Journalist," *The American Mercury*, Jan., 1929, 16:61:23.
[66] *New York State Crime Commission Report*, Legislative Document (1927) No. 94, p. 309.

The impression was created by the newspapers that Gerald Chapman was a sort of super-bandit and that he possessed an intelligence greatly superior to that of the average person. The fact was, however, that he had spent most of his life, since becoming a criminal, in custody; that he had been caught many times rather easily, and that he ought really to be classified as a rather blundering and incompetent member of his class. This did not prevent, however, a whole flood of newspaper publicity in connection with him, including romantic accounts of his life and publication by one of the tabloids of his complete life and letters.

Newspaper work is not evangelism, and to assert that the newspaper-man's duty is to write nothing save what will edify and enlighten is nonsense. But the public would ask that newspapermen have some sense of proportion and decency.

Is the Newspaper Simply a Business Venture?—The commercial character of modern journalism is the fundamental reason for the strictures against the press today. It is also the basis of the news-paperman's answer to the criticism. When the view that the press is bound to lay before its readers only the truth, that it should print only the news which is fit to print, and that it should be a great educational force for good, when this view is presented to editors, they are apt to remind the critic that a newspaper is a commercial enterprise; that it must secure adequate circulation, or die; that, to gain circulation, it must publish what its readers wish to see; and that it cannot take a higher stand than its readers permit. "In adopting this rule, the editor, of course, abandons to a great extent his position as leader. His readers lead him, not he his readers. . . . The press must either lead or follow; and, if it follows by catering to a depraved public taste or a popular prejudice, it is largely responsible for the taste or prejudice, for both grow by what feeds them. To every editor is presented the question: 'Shall I seek money through increased circulation and advertisements, or shall I try to create a sound public opinion and make my journal a power for good?' "[67]

The newspaperman may reply that his position is not a cure of souls, any more than is the position of a grocer. "One obligation, and only one, rests upon newspapermen and grocers alike, and that is to see that the goods they dispense are not adulterated, especially with poisonous matter."[68] But the press is more than a business. It is a social service fundamental to the national life and exerting profound influence upon it. If the press be a corporation, it is a public-

[67] Moorfield Storey, "The Daily Press," *The Atlantic Monthly*, Jan., 1922, CXXIX, 41.
[68] Gerald W. Johnson, *What Is News?* 1926, p. 59.

service corporation with all the social responsibility that this implies. It has thus been regarded by the people. The tradition of the press is that of censor of the state and palladium of the people's liberties. It is not a business pure and simple, because the community applies one ethical measure to the press and another to trade or manufacture. The critics of the press are merely voicing the moral standards of the community, when they expect it to live on the same plane as that on which the school, the church, and the disinterested professions are supposed to live.[69] If newspapers are in reality pure business ventures conducted for the purpose of making money, or if they wish to be so regarded, they should renounce their special rights and privileges.

News of Informational Value.—James Melvin Lee, Director of the Department of Journalism, New York University, thinks news of genuinely instructive and informative character, instead of concentration on sports, scandal and crime, the trivial, thrilling and entertaining, could be made to pay. "Crowded as is the New York field," he writes,[70] "it would, in my opinion, support a newspaper which adopted as its motto, 'All the news that's important.' The experiment of producing a paper living up to that motto has never been made in the United States. Some of the foreign newspapers which feature not 'what's interesting,' but 'what's important,' more than break even from their sales."

At least two newspapers in the United States—the New York *Times* and the *Christian Science Monitor*—have pointed the way toward that ideal. The New York *Times*, under the ownership of Adolph S. Ochs since 1896, has demonstrated that there is profit in news, of which it gives an extraordinarily large amount. It has been unusually successful financially, though it has not stooped to comic supplements, a Red Magic section, serial fiction, advice to the lovelorn, and other circulation-building devices. The greatest *news*paper in the world, it is the world's richest newspaper. "Its annual profits run around four millions. When Ochs gained control he capitalized it at one million, but has since increased the common stock tenfold, and has retired all the bonds. His property has none of the fine frenzy of the crusading press. It has no mission to save the people from themselves or from their overlords. It shares the mystical faith which William Allen White attributes to Mr. Coolidge, that prosperity is godliness, or at least godly. It never 'makes' news, unless the Hundred Neediest Cases [and its feature articles dealing with airplanes] can be called

[69] Walter Lippmann, *Public Opinion*, 1922, pp. 321-322.
[70] Quoted by Silas Bent, *Ballyhoo*, 1927, p. 45.

that. It never campaigns to expose corruption or industrial ills. Its editorial premise is America-as-it-is."[71]

The *Times* under Mr. Ochs's leadership has been clean and enterprising, able and shrewd. Not that it has invariably lived up to the suggestion in its motto of printing only the news fit for publication —it has engaged in some ballyhoo—nor has it always given an unbiased account. It has been charged, for instance, with misrepresenting Russian news, with relating "within a comparatively brief period that Petrograd had fallen six times, been on the verge of capture three times more, been burned to the ground twice, been in absolute panic twice and in revolt against the Bolsheviks on six different occasions—all without the slightest foundation in fact."[72] This treatment of Russian news has been set forth both by *The Nation* and *The New Republic* without any refutation. The *Times* has tended to purvey the news which especially interested its owners and editors and which supported its editorial viewpoint. But it has rendered a genuine public service in increasing the volume of news and especially of foreign news. "Mr. Ochs's greatest contribution to our journalism has been his faith in news as a sales asset. . . . Mr. Ochs's increase of the volume of his news and the number of his news departments (notably in the commercial field) has had a beneficial influence upon the entire press of the country. It has led many thousands to read the *Times* to whom its opinions were anathema. Particularly worth while and public-spirited has been the cabling of important speeches and documents in full."[73] Its special signed articles on questions of public importance and the unusually large amount of attention it gives to subjects of social, economic, and historical significance are among its other valuable features. Full credit must also be given to the *Times* for keeping its advertising columns clean (tens of thousands of lines of announcements are excluded monthly because they do not meet the *Times* standards of acceptance) and for the excellence of its auxiliary publications—*Mid-week Pictorial, Current History Magazine,* and *Annalist.* More than most American newspapers, it instructs and informs.

Founded in 1908 "to injure no man but to bless all mankind," the *Christian Science Monitor* presents a striking contrast to commercialized journalism of today. It is utterly free from ballyhoo. It has the

[71] Silas Bent, *Ballyhoo*, 1927, p. 168.
[72] Oswald Garrison Villard, *Some Newspapers and Newspaper-men,* 1923, pp. 8-9. Walter Lippmann and Charles Merz, *A Test of the News,* Supplement to *The New Republic,* Aug., 1920.
[73] *Ibid.,* pp. 5-6.

highest technical and ethical standards. Instead of being a mirror for reflecting destructive agencies, it aims to be a journal to record achievements in every useful field of human endeavor. It is international in scope. It has the admiration of most newspapermen for the ability with which its news is edited and its editorial page conducted, but they attribute its high standards to the fact that it operates under a subsidy and is therefore not amenable to the full influence of the economic forces which play upon its competitors; its existence is not entirely dependent on advertising and circulation.[74]

In accordance with certain tenets of the Church of Christ, Scientist, of which the paper is an organ, the *Monitor* maintains a frank policy of suppression in regard to news of crime, violence and death, of scandal, misery, and vice. It even suppresses tidings about tea, coffee, and tobacco, medical or hygienic articles, and life, accident, and health insurance. These and other things may not be advertised through its columns. "As for the rest, all the tests applied by the most conservative dailies are also in force in the *Monitor* office. No 'blue sky' advertising is possible, no suggestion of 'sacrifice' or 'fire' sales and no 'catch-line' sensationalism; its columns are the cleanest of the clean and its business announcements about as strictly limited to the bare facts as those of the New York dailies in 1805.'"[75]

Aside from these inhibitions, it seeks in its news columns to present accurately and fairly the things it is permitted to report. From the start it has been more international in scope than most rivals in the secular field, and it enjoys a remarkable national and international circulation. Unlike so many of its contemporaries, it seeks to place its foreign correspondence on the level of that of the best English newspapers, and to give an intelligent survey of what is happening in all parts of the world. It keeps its news standards up and calls upon its readers to rise to them. Nor does it cast a Christian Science hue over all that it writes. It attempts to proselytize extraordinarily little. Its religious propaganda is limited to a daily article on one of the back pages. Art and education are given prominent positions in the paper; there is excellent business news, with special attention paid to commercial conditions in foreign lands; the sporting news is without the usual ballyhoo. The *Monitor* never buys or sells syndicated matter. It is handsomely illustrated and dignified in appearance. A leading historian of American journalism writes: "It is but justice

[74] Silas Bent, *Ballyhoo*, 1927, pp. 202, 203.
[75] Oswald Garrison Villard, *Some Newspapers and Newspaper-men*, 1923, p. 121.

to the *Monitor* to say that no paper has a higher standard of ethics. Its circulation has not been confined by any means to members of the Christian Science Church. Even a distinguished Chicago journalist once remarked, 'I haven't any more use for Christian Science than Hetty Green had for a poorhouse, but I consider *The Christian Science Monitor* one of the greatest dailies in America and I read it religiously, not for its propaganda, but for its secular news.' "[76]

In his provocative survey of American newspapers, Oswald Garrison Villard,[77] editor of *The Nation*, says: "As it is, the *Monitor* today offers the best example of a journal owned by a group which we have yet seen in this country. But for all its high technical standards and its ideals it is far from being the perfect newspaper. Nor can it become that while it is so hopelessly enmeshed in its Christian Science inhibitions which prevent it from giving all the news and make it colour a good deal of that which it prints. But because it is the organ of a society established upon an ethical basis; because it has such ready-made bases of support; because it is entirely without the profit-motive and beyond the lure of dividends; and because it has conceived its mission to be international, it is one of the most interesting and vital of contemporary journalistic experiments. . . . Even with the disadvantages of its church ownership, the *Monitor* stands far above the usual American daily in both manners and morals."

The Importance of Newspaper Accuracy.—A cardinal rule of newspaper ethics is that what the press presents as fact shall be fact, given correctly and without bias. Its significance, as Walter Lippmann has ably argued in his book *Liberty and the News*, lies in the fact that access to accurate accounts of what is going on about us is one of the indispensable conditions of freedom. It is vital that the individual shall be able to form his opinion upon the facts. If these facts are withheld from him or misrepresented to him, his opinion is as valueless as that of a judge who has heard incomplete or false evidence in a case. "The war, however, with its censorship, its development of the art of propaganda, and the improvement which it brought about in methods of swaying masses of men by controlling or doctoring the news, has made us realize that the problem of newspaper conduct is larger and more fundamental than we had supposed it to be. We now see that it is immensely important that the press shall give us the facts straight; and not merely the facts relating to de-

[76] James Melvin Lee, *History of American Journalism*, 1917, p. 414.
[77] *Some Newspapers and Newspaper-men*, 1923, pp. 129-130.

partment stores and other large business concerns, but the entire mass of facts about the world in which we live—political, economic, religious, scientific, social, and industrial.''[78]

Sources of Newspaper Inaccuracy.—This basic principle of newspaper ethics—that what is presented as sheer fact should be accurate and without bias—is easy to state. It is harder to live up to than anybody who has not faced the newspaperman's problem for himself can imagine.

1. The Personal Equation.—In the first place, it is hard for a reporter, just as for any other person, to give an absolutely accurate account of any event, even when he has seen it with his own eyes. The fallibility of even first-hand evidence from eye-witnesses is well known; no one can read a book like the late Professor Münsterberg's *On The Witness Stand* without appreciating what the reporter is up against. Furthermore, it is exceedingly difficult to write an account of any event without coloring it with one's own opinions. ''Though the reporter has every intention of stating only the clear facts, he may give them bias simply through his choice of language. Suppose one senator denounces another in a speech. Shall the reporter write, 'Senator A—sternly rebuked Senator B—,' or shall he use the words 'vigorously attacked,' or 'sharply attacked,' or 'fiercely attacked'? If he decides upon 'sternly rebuked,' he seems to favor Senator A—, who uttered the rebuke; if he says 'fiercely attacked,' he gives no such favorable impression, and the reader tends instinctively to side with the senator who was attacked.''[79]

2. Speed.—An added element of difficulty is caused by the speed with which newspapermen have to work. ''Laymen are much impressed by the speed with which newspapers are written. They are constantly expressing amazement over the fact that newspapermen can turn out anything intelligible within the short space of time allotted to them. The pressure of time is a handicap, to be sure. It bars from the business some men who might otherwise be well qualified for it. It presents a constant temptation to do slip-shod work, and is an excuse, if not a reason, for endless inaccuracies.''[80]

An associated difficulty is the circumstance that much of the color of a story is necessarily given it in the newspaper office by men who

[78] Frederick L. Allen, ''Newspapers and the Truth,'' *The Atlantic Monthly*, Jan., 1922, CXXIX, 44. *Cf.* Everett Dean Martin, *The Meaning of a Liberal Education*, 1926, p. 45.

[79] Frederick L. Allen, ''Newspapers and the Truth,'' *The Atlantic Monthly*, Jan., 1922, CXXIX, 46.

[80] Gerald W. Johnson, *What Is News?* 1926, p. 67.

lack a first-hand acquaintance with the facts. "There is no opportunity to wait a few hours for a chance to check facts: they are usually worthless unless given to the public instantly. City reporters telephone much of their news to the office, where their statements are taken down hurriedly in a telephone booth, and then thrown into shape by a member of the office staff. Always the headlines are written by the office staff; they have to be, because the reporter cannot tell what size and style of headline is needed, and because the writing of headlines requires a special training. The man who concocts them must read each news-story rapidly and write his 'head' promptly. He cannot waste time upon niceties of emphasis; the all-important thing for him is that the head shall have exactly the right number of letters to fill its space, and that it shall be original and dramatic enough to catch the reader's attention. Like the reporter, he finds that bias insists on creeping into his presentation of the gist of the news."[81]

3. *Inadequately Trained Reporters.*—The reporter not only needs training in the tests of credibility and rigorous discipline in the use of words, he also needs to be highly educated. The newspaperman's contribution to the advancement of knowledge lies in his ability to clarify and make assimilable by the masses the results of the researches of scholars, in a word, popularization. The importance of this contribution is immense in a democratic country, where the weight of majority opinion is felt in every department of life. "Genuine popularization is principally clarification. Its difficulty lies in the fact that no man is capable of clarifying a subject until he understands it himself. Then the ability to clarify many subjects means a pretty thorough understanding of many subjects, which is learning." But "genuine popularization is rare—as rare as first-rate newspapermen. What often passes for popularization is the muddle-headed work of incompetent journalists which, so far from clarifying an obscure subject, renders it unrecognizable even to the expert."[82] Another source of trouble is the desire to make a good story out of the event reported. Frederick L. Allen,[83] in charge of the publicity work of Harvard University, cites an example:

"Here, for instance, are the headlines and the first two paragraphs of an item which appeared lately in a Boston paper:—

[81] Frederick L. Allen, "Newspapers and the Truth," *The Atlantic Monthly*, Jan., 1922, CXXIX, 47.
[82] Gerald W. Johnson, *What Is News?* 1926, pp. 30, 31.
[83] "Newspapers and the Truth," *The Atlantic Monthly*, Jan., 1922, CXXIX, 48-49.

DISCOVERS NEW NEBULAR MASS

Prof. Sliphe of Harvard Finds it Going at Record Speed

Prof. V. M. Sliphe of Harvard, stationed at the Flagstaff, Ariz., observatory, peered through his telescope a few nights ago, according to a dispatch received at the Cambridge observatory, and much to his surprise saw a faint, cloud-like, self-luminous mass of attenuated matter situated far outside the solar system, traveling at the rate of 200 kilometres per second. This rate of speed is twice as great as the fastest nebula yet discovered and 100 times greater than the average speed of the lowly star. In fact, it is the greatest velocity known to astronomy.

The telescope at Flagstaff is situated on San Francisco peak at an altitude of 13,000 feet. Harvard astronomers are manifesting much interest in the matter because of its supposed great distance from the stars ordinarily seen in the heavens and because of the tremendous speed at which it is traveling.

Now, the facts of the case were that the discoverer's name was not Sliphe, but Slipher; that he was not connected with Harvard, but with the Lowell Observatory; that he did not discover the nebula, which had been known for a long time, but only ascertained its speed; that the telescope at Flagstaff is not at an altitude of thirteen thousand feet, but of about seven thousand; and that it is not situated on San Francisco Peak, but merely in the neighborhood. It would be difficult for ignorance and carelessness to bring about more errors in the space of two paragraphs. What happened was that the Lowell Observatory reported its discovery to the Harvard Observatory, which made a brief announcement to the press; and the news-writer took this announcement, and tried, as he would have put it, to 'make a good story out of it.' 'Make a good story.' That is the cause of infinite newspaper inaccuracy.''

''Newspapers try to develop special abilities in their reporters and, so far as possible, to keep men assigned to the subjects which they know about; but the field of news is so immense that much of it has to be covered by inexpert men. Besides, many reporters have only a limited education; they know so little that they have no idea how their ignorance handicaps them. And they generally tend to be careless. Their immediate object is usually to get the most newsy and sensational story they can.'' The fault here lies largely with the newspaper policy, for it is by writing such stories that reporters on many papers hold their jobs and gain promotion. If the reporter turns in a story that is too heavy, the editor will brighten it up. For example, a Boston newspaper printed an interview with a Harvard

physician on the importance of using the feet properly in standing
and walking, as shown in the physical examination of Harvard freshmen. It was an interesting interview, carefully prepared by an intelligent and competent reporter. But the editor to whom the interview
was submitted decided that it needed to be "jazzed." So he headed it—

WHY BE SAD? FEET ARE THE SOURCE OF ALL JOY
Harvard Expert Tells How to Drive Clouds Away in Six Short Weeks

And the editor surrounded the illustration—a photograph of the physician—with a border of "Joys" and "Glooms," after the fashion of
the comic cartoons. No wonder scientific men shudder at interviews,
when they see what is done to them in type. Mr. Allen holds that most
newspaper inaccuracy is not the result so much of the inherent difficulty of properly collecting and presenting the facts, as of the ignorance, carelessness, and thoughtless indifference to truth of a considerable proportion of newspaper men.[84]

Judged by the importance of the calling, newspapers ought to attract a high type of personnel. This they do not appear to do. One of
the things which deter many men of ability and character from entering newspaper work is the prospect of low pay and difficult hours.
Most newspapermen do not get a Sunday holiday; their day of rest
may come at any time in the week. Men on morning newspapers must
work all night. Their wives must paddle their own canoes, socially,
and raise the children single-handed. Most newspaper offices—those
of the New York *Times* and the *Christian Science Monitor* are conspicuous exceptions—are ugly, crowded, and grimy—far less agreeable
places to work in than business offices. These circumstances tend to
make journalism an unattractive calling.[85]

Moreover, there appears to be but little professional standard in
journalism. Most reporters speak of newspaper work as "the game."
Perhaps they have not been permitted to learn it in such a way that
they can think of it as a profession.[86] "Reporting, which theoretically
constitutes the foundation of the whole institution, is the most poorly
paid branch of newspaper work, and is the least regarded. By and
large, able men go into it only by necessity or for experience, and
with the definite intention of being graduated as soon as possible.
For straight reporting is not a career that offers many great rewards.

---

[84] *Ibid.*, p. 48.
[85] *Ibid.*, p. 49; Gerald W. Johnson, "Why Men Work for Newspapers," *The
American Mercury*, May, 1929, 17:65:85-86.
[86] Silas Bent, *Ballyhoo*, 1927, p. 67.

The rewards in journalism go to specialty work, to signed correspondence which has editorial quality, to executives, and to men with a knack and flavor of their own. This is due, no doubt, to what economists call the rent of ability. But this economic principle operates with such peculiar violence in journalism that newsgathering does not attract to itself anything like the number of trained and able men which its public importance would seem to demand. The fact that the able men take up 'straight reporting' with the intention of leaving it as soon as possible is, I think, the chief reason why it has never developed in sufficient measure those corporate traditions that give to a profession prestige and a jealous self-respect. For it is these corporate traditions which engender the pride of craft, which tend to raise the standards of admission, punish breaches of the code, and give men the strength to insist upon their status in society.''[87]

4. *The Nature of News.*—A very direct relationship exists between the certainty of news and the system of record. Wherever there is a good machinery of record, the modern news service works with great precision. Wherever such machinery is lacking, the news is bound to be biased and subjective. In what fields does a machinery of knowledge exist? What provision has society made for the accurate recording of events? What kind of news is objective, what kind is subject to choice and opinion? An answer to these questions is suggested by the means employed by newspapers to uncover the news.

Newspapers do not try to keep an eye on all mankind, nor even to watch the city and its people. They devote most of their attention to a comparatively small number of places where it is made known when the life of anyone departs from ordinary paths, or when events worth telling about occur. The most obvious place to uncover the run of news is where people's affairs touch public authority. It is here that marriages, births, deaths, contracts, failures, arrivals, departures, lawsuits, disorders, epidemics, and calamities are made known. For example,

John Smith, let it be supposed, becomes a broker. For ten years he pursues the even tenor of his way and except for his customers and his friends no one gives him a thought. To the newspapers he is as if he were not. But in the eleventh year he suffers heavy losses and, at last, his resources all gone, summons his lawyer and arranges for the making of an assignment. The lawyer posts off to the County Clerk's office, and a clerk there makes the necessary entries in the office docket. Herein step the newspapers. While the clerk is writing Smith's business obituary a reporter glances over his

[87] Walter Lippmann, *Public Opinion*, 1922, p. 334.

shoulder, and a few minutes later the newspapers know Smith's troubles and are as well informed concerning his business status [*i.e.*, the bald facts which are recorded in the County Clerk's office] as they would be had they kept a reporter at his door every day for over ten years. Had Smith dropped dead instead of merely making an assignment his name would have reached the newspapers by way of the Coroners' office instead of the County Clerk's office, and in fact, while Smith did not know it, the newspapers were prepared and ready for him no matter what he did. They even had representatives waiting for him at the Morgue. He was safe only when he walked the straight and narrow path and kept quiet.[88]

Thus, an overt act "uncovers" the news about Smith. Whether the news will be followed up or not is another matter. The point is that before a series of events become news they have usually to make themselves noticeable in some more or less overt, generally crudely overt, act. In the first instance, therefore, the news is not a mirror of social conditions, but the report of an aspect that has obtruded itself. The news does not tell you how the seed is germinating in the ground, but it may tell you when the first sprout breaks through the surface.[89]

The chief place for uncovering the news is police headquarters. The police, with their manifold duties and their first-hand information regarding fire, accidents, suicides, crime, etc., are the most important newsgatherers and the newspapers' dearest friends; they save them from the expense of employing reporters to patrol the streets. Police headquarters is so important a news center that newspapers maintain branch offices nearby which are connected by telephone with the editorial rooms. "The press bureau at Police Headquarters, where the news which there is no occasion for keeping secret is made public, never closes, and night and day, year in and year out, the newspapers, through the eyes of their reporters, watch its bulletins. Never is the watch half-hearted, either, for any moment may see displayed a bulletin which will lead to whole pages of newspaper writing."[90]

Next to police headquarters, the police courts are important as news centers, and are kept under close observation by newspapers. Other places which are watched constantly are the coroner's office, the county courts, the stock exchange, city hall, and the county clerk's office. Newspapers watch carefully, but not continually, other courts, the district attorney's office, post office, United States commissioner's office, ship news where incoming and outgoing vessels are reported, barge office where immigrants land, surrogate's office where wills are

[88] John L. Given, *Making a Newspaper*, 1912, p. 57.
[89] Walter Lippmann, *Public Opinion*, 1922, pp. 340-341.
[90] John L. Given, *Making a Newspaper*, 1912, chs. V, VI, VII (p. 78 quoted).

filed and testimony concerning wills in litigation is heard, and political headquarters during campaigns. Reporters visit at least once a day police stations, city courts, headquarters of the board of health, fire department, park department, building department, city and county jail, public hospitals, leading hotels, the morgue, county sheriff's office, and the offices of city officials. It is only for the news which escapes all these watchers that the newspapers trust to luck. The reporters who do the watching are called "department men," and each one of them guards the same place day after day. There are in New York reporters who have not changed their station in over fifteen years.

Now, unless an event is capable of being named, measured, given shape, made specific, it either fails to take on the character of news, or it is subject to the accidents and prejudices of observation. The body of exact knowledge, which it requires no outstanding ability or training to deal with, is very small. The rest is in the journalist's own discretion. "Once he departs from the region where it is definitely recorded at the County Clerk's office that John Smith has gone into bankruptcy, all fixed standards disappear. The story of why John Smith failed, his human frailties, the analysis of the economic conditions on which he was shipwrecked, all of this can be told in a hundred different ways. There is no discipline in applied psychology, as there is a discipline in medicine, engineering, or even law, which has authority to direct the journalist's mind when he passes from the news to the vague realm of truth. . . . Where there is no objective test, his own opinion is in some vital measure constructed out of his own stereotypes, according to his own code, and by the urgency of his own interest. He knows that he is seeing the world through subjective lenses."[91]

Lippmann argues that news and truth are not the same thing, and must be clearly distinguished. "The function of news is to signalize an event, the function of truth is to bring to light the hidden facts, to set them into relation with each other, and make a picture of reality on which men can act. Only at those points, where social conditions take recognizable and measurable shape, do the body of truth and the body of news coincide. That is a comparatively small part of the whole field of human interest. In this sector, and only in this sector, the tests of the news are sufficiently exact to make the charges of perversion or suppression more than a partisan judgment. There is no defense, no extenuation, no excuse whatever, for stating six

[91] Walter Lippmann, *Public Opinion*, 1922, pp. 359-360.

times that Lenin is dead, when the only information the paper possesses is a report that he is dead from a source repeatedly shown to be
unreliable. The news, in that instance, is not 'Lenin Dead' but
'Helsingfors Says Lenin is Dead.' And a newspaper can be asked
to take the responsibility of not making Lenin more dead than the
source of the news is reliable; if there is one subject on which editors
are most responsible it is in their judgment of the reliability of the
source.''[92]

The topics which form the principal indictment by reformers
against the press are subjects which must be left to the discretion
of newspapers because no good machinery of record exists. ''All news
about states of mind is of this character: so are all descriptions of
personalities, of sincerity, aspiration, motive, intention, of mass feeling, of national feeling, of public opinion, the policies of foreign
governments. So is much news about what is going to happen. So are
questions turning on private profit, private income, wages, working
conditions, the efficiency of labor, educational opportunity, unemployment, monotony, health, discrimination, unfairness, restraint of trade,
waste, 'backward peoples,' conservatism, imperialism, radicalism,
liberty, honor, righteousness. All involve data that are at best
spasmodically recorded. The data may be hidden because of a censorship or a tradition of privacy, they may not exist because nobody
thinks record important, because he thinks it red tape, or because nobody has yet invented an objective system of measurement. Then the
news on these subjects is bound to be debatable, when it is not wholly
neglected. The events which are not scored are reported either as personal and conventional opinion, or they are not news. They do not
take shape until somebody protests, or somebody investigates, or somebody publicly, in the etymological meaning of the word, makes an
issue of them.''[93]

5. *News of Interested Origin.*—The above-mentioned situation is
the underlying reason for the existence of the publicity agent. The
enormous discretion as to what facts and what impressions shall be
reported is steadily convincing every organized group of people that,
whether it wishes to secure publicity or to avoid it, the exercise of discretion cannot be left to the reporter. It is safer to hire a publicity
agent to stand between the group and the newspapers and serve as
the medium through which the news comes. ''Were reporting the
simple recovery of obvious facts, the press agent would be little more

[92] *Ibid.*, pp. 358-359.
[93] *Ibid.*, pp. 343-344.

than a clerk. But since, in respect to most of the big topics of news, the facts are not simple, and not at all obvious, but subject to choice and opinion, it is natural that everyone should wish to make his own choice of facts for the newspapers to print. The publicity man does that. And in doing it, he certainly saves the reporter much trouble, by presenting him a clear picture of a situation out of which he might otherwise make neither head nor tail. But it follows that the picture which the publicity man makes for the reporter is the one he wishes the public to see. He is censor and propagandist, responsible only to his employers, and to the whole truth responsible only as it accords with the employer's conception of his own interests.''[94]

Silas Bent[95] classifies publicity agents as follows: (1) the press agents—theatrical, sports, personal, and so on through a long category; (2) publicity directors, who serve a useful function as reportorial auxiliaries; and (3) the counsel in public relations, who is essentially a special pleader before the court of public opinion. Between the three classes as practitioners there is no sharp line of demarkation. The counsel in public relations may be a press agent. The term ''publicity director'' is used arbitrarily to mean one who disseminates news of general interest and authentic value. It is estimated that there are five thousand publicity agencies and persons, including the three types, in New York City alone, and that in Washington there are two thousand. The great corporations, banks, railroads, all the organizations of business and of social and political activity have them. Even statesmen have them. Thus many of the direct channels to news have been closed, and the information for the public is first filtered through these agents. It is estimated that more than half of the ''reading matter'' in metropolitan newspapers is of interested origin, arising from and on occasion being created by agencies which have a special stake in its presentation. Yet it is presented as though it were an impartial and colorless statement of fact, on which the reader may with security base an opinion. Sometimes it is mere trivia, and does no more harm than to intrude worthless material into the field of thought. Sometimes it is important and legitimate news, which takes the form of the publicity hand-out because the press is too indolent or too niggardly to gather such news for itself. Sometimes it is propaganda of the sinister sort.

A competent publicity director can be of great service to the popularization of knowledge when he acts as intermediary between the

[94] *Ibid.*, pp. 344-345.
[95] *Ballyhoo*, 1927, ch. V.

press and the scientist. Much work of educational value is done by
the publicity directors of universities, libraries, churches, governmental agencies, civic and commercial chambers. But a large part of
publicity material is sheer propaganda and as such is opposed to
genuine education. As Everett Dean Martin[96] remarks, ''The propagandist is interested in *what* people think; the educator in *how* they
think. The propagandist has a definite aim. He strives to convert, to
sell, to secure assent, to prove a case, to support one side of an issue.
He is striving for an effect. He wishes people to come to a conclusion;
to accept his case and close their minds and act. The educator strives
for the open mind. He has no case to prove, which may not later be
reversed. He is willing to reconsider, to be experimental, to hold his
conclusions tentatively. The result for which he strives is a type of
student who will not jump at the propagandist's hasty conclusions
or be taken in by his catch-words. . . . Even in the service of a good
cause, propaganda makes for superficiality in both him who gives
and him who receives it.''

6. *The Fault of the Reader.*—Just as the newspaper cannot print
all the news, not even all the news it gathers, so the reader cannot
read all the newspaper, nor has he the interest to do so. He reads
what catches his fancy and skims the rest. To a large extent he is
a headline reader. But headlines are often misleading; the caption
writers, as we have seen, are among the worst offenders in the matter
of inaccuracy. ''Headlines are not summaries of the paragraphs that
follow. They are not the most important part of the news. They are
often entirely insignificant. They often distort or exaggerate the
more detailed account below. They are the paper's advertisement of
its news. They constitute the most sensational and supposedly the
most enticing bit of the article which they advertise. Sometimes this
may serve to give the reader some idea of daily happenings, but
ordinarily he receives an incomplete and inaccurate impression.''[97]
The inevitable result of headline reading is a biased and inaccurate
impression of the reported events.

The speed with which the average person reads the newspaper is
also a source of error. Lippmann[98] quotes the results of three studies
of the habits of the newspaper-reading public, which show that the
majority of those who replied to the inquiries thought that they spent

[96] *The Meaning of a Liberal Education*, 1926, ch. III (p. 45 quoted).
[97] Hayes Baker-Crothers and Ruth Allison Hudnut, *Problems of Citizenship*,
1924, p. 51. *Cf.* George C. Bastian, *Editing the Day's News*, 1929, ch. X, on
the art of headline writing.
[98] *Public Opinion*, 1922, ch. IV.

a quarter of an hour a day reading newspapers. He warns that the figures are not to be accepted too literally, since very few people have an accurate idea of fifteen minutes, but even so, it is evident that the time given by the average person to reading the news of the world amounts to relatively little. We have already seen that the speed with which newspapers are written is a serious handicap upon the news-writer. So is the speed with which they are read. The whole newspaper commands its readers' attention only for a few minutes. Within those few minutes the individual news-writer must seize the reader's attention despite the competition of all the other news-writers. "It follows as a matter of course that in the attempt to catch the reader's attention the subject is often maltreated. Whatever point seems likely to attract the reader is dragged prominently to the fore, although it may be relatively trivial, with the result that the wandering mind of the reader is given a false and often ludicrous conception of the whole article. It was by this process that Dr. William Osler, a great scientist and an eminently sane man, was indelibly branded by public opinion as the doctor who advocated chloroforming men at forty. Dr. Osler in the course of his address did say something like that in a facetious aside, but some reporter, incapable of making the speaker's real argument of sufficient dramatic interest to insure the reader's attention, seized upon the side remark and played it up as if it had been the main thesis."[99]

The slovenly way in which most of us are accustomed to read the papers is an enemy of truth. "For every report that we read through thoroughly and weigh for ourselves, checking the generalizations and summaries in headline and leading paragraph by the details which follow, there are ten that we only glance at. Usually we carry away nothing but the dim impression that Mr. X has done something disastrous, or that Governor Y has made another fine speech; we retain the bias, and little else. If you doubt that you yourself skim the paper in this way, try handing it to somebody else after you have finished, and making him examine you on the contents of an important article. You will probably soon realize how vaguely most of your news-reading is done, and understand how easily the twist of a phrase in headline or leading paragraph, by giving a biased impression, may cause thousands of readers to form opinions based, not on the facts, but on somebody else's view of the facts."[100]

[99] Gerald W. Johnson, *What is News?* 1926, pp. 68-69.
[100] Frederick L. Allen, "Newspapers and the Truth," *The Atlantic Monthly*, Jan., 1922, CXXIX, 45-46.

Much would be gained if newspaper readers knew enough about newspaper organization and methods to be better judges of the credibility of the news. Lectures on "How to Read the Newspapers" could profitably be given in colleges, schools, and elsewhere. There are three general things that the reader should remember as a guide to intelligent newspaper reading: his own and his paper's liability to partisanship, the mistake of reading only headlines, the necessity of applying certain tests to the news.[101] "It is as essential for the citizen of this day to be able to read the morning paper with a discriminating eye—to be able to distinguish the A.P. dispatch from the special correspondent's forecast of conditions, and the fact story from the rumor story, and to be able to take into account the probable bias of the paper and make allowance for it—as it is for a lawyer to learn to assess the value of evidence. Only as we are able to estimate the relative amount of credence to be given to conflicting reports, and to judge for ourselves the reliability of the sources of the news, do we come somewhere near seeing that true picture of the world about us which we must see if we are to play our part in it intelligently and independently."[102]

It has been said that an educated man is one who can read a modern newspaper without being humbugged; one who has the knowledge which frees his mind from the domination of conventions and the contagion of catch-words. Professor Sumner[103] once said, "Suggestion is a legitimate device, if it is honestly used, for inculcating knowledge or principles of conduct; that is, for education in the broadest sense of the word. Criticism is the operation by which suggestion is limited and corrected. It is by criticism that the person is protected against credulity, emotion, and fallacy. The power of criticism is the one which education should chiefly train. . . . An educated man ought to be beyond the reach of suggestions from advertisements, newspapers, speeches, and stories. If he is wise, just when a crowd is filled with enthusiasm and emotion, he will leave it and will go off by himself to form his judgment. In short, individuality and personality of character are the opposites of suggestibility."

In a broader sense, the reading public is in large part responsible for the present state of journalism, in that newspapers are what their audiences make them. Whitelaw Reid, when editor of the New York

<hr />

[101] Hayes Baker-Crothers and Ruth Allison Hudnut, *Problems of Citizenship*, 1924, ch. IV, an excellent discussion of this point.

[102] Frederick L. Allen, "Newspapers and the Truth," *The Atlantic Monthly*, Jan., 1922, CXXIX, 54.

[103] *Folkways*, 1906, p. 24.

Tribune, said: "The newspaper cannot uniformly resist the popular sentiment any more than the stream can flow above its fountain. To say that the newspapers are getting worse is to say that the people are getting worse."[104] A more accurate statement would be that if newspapers are getting worse, it is because they are reaching down to classes of lower and lower levels of intelligence and discrimination. Attention has already been called to the fact that journalism is a mirror of the times, a mirror of the people in general, and the individual paper a mirror of its subscribers. The late President Hadley[105] expressed this view and showed its relation to inaccurate and irresponsible opinions as follows:

If we are to have responsible newspapers, the reform must begin with the readers themselves. Most of the men who edit newspapers will give the people the kind of newspapers they want. There will, of course, be exceptionally good editors who will make their papers better than their readers demand, and try to educate the people up to a higher level; just as there will be exceptionally bad editors, who will make papers worse than the readers want, and be the instruments, whether they try to or not, of educating the public down to a lower level.

But the average editor will work for the average reader. He cannot be any more independent of the man who buys his goods than the manufacturer or merchant can be. A manufacturer who refuses to produce things that the people want, because he thinks they ought to want something better, will be driven out of business, and so will a newspaper editor. People sometimes talk of "yellow journalism" as if the editors of the yellow journals were solely responsible for their existence. They are responsible to some degree; but to a still larger degree the responsibility lies with the public that will buy and read their news. . . .

If the public cares more for sensations than it does for facts, more for excitement than it does for evidence, it is obvious that its opinions will be based on wrong data and often on dangerous ones, and that its conclusions will be unwise and irresponsible. And as long as public opinion is unwise or irresponsible, the government of the country will be bad.

Advancing Standards.—Along with the development of the press as a business organization, and particularly with the growth of chain papers, there have come a more economical harvesting of the daily news-crop, its more economical distribution, the standardization of its form, and a tendency toward elimination of bias. The principal news-gathering agencies are the Associated Press, a coöperative organ-

[104] Quoted by James Melvin Lee, *History of Modern Journalism,* 1917, p. 429.
[105] Arthur Twining Hadley, "The Public Duty of Newspaper Readers," *Youth's Companion,* Nov. 5, 1908, LXXXII, 555.

ization, the United Press, owned by the Scripps-Howard group, and the International News, a Hearst property. The Scripps-Howard newspapers preferred not to join the Associated Press but to set up their own agency. The United Press differs from the Associated Press in that its services are available not merely to the members but to any newspaper which can pay the necessary charges for a leased wire, etc. Hearst has his own service because he can seldom get an Associated Press franchise; he sells it to papers other than his own.[106]

The Associated Press has done more than any other agency to bring colorless reporting to American newspapers. According to one of its statements, "The service is intended to be limited to the reporting of events without bias. . . . It is the theory of the organization that, in a self-governing country like ours, the citizens, if given the facts, must be able to form their own opinions concerning them." Although it is difficult to distinguish sharply between fact and opinion—and both alike are frequently news—the official policy of the Associated Press is sound, and this great news-disseminating service is about as thoroughly imbued with the spirit of impartiality as any organization of its size and extent could well be. Its reports from Washington are models of fairness as between Republicans and Democrats. The principle of a separation of functions as between the gathering of news and its interpretation is a necessary foundation of the whole system of accurate news reporting. "The policy of the Associated Press is in this respect not merely sound, but absolutely vital, and the organization, in so far as it realizes that policy, is in fact a public service of much greater importance than some branches of government."[107]

Lippmann[108] believes that it is possible to go much farther than we have ever gone in fixing personal responsibility for the truthfulness of news. "We ought to know the names of the whole staff of every periodical. While it is not necessary, or even desirable, that each article should be signed, each article should be documented, and false documentation should be illegal. An item of news should always state whether it is received from one of the great news-agencies, or from a reporter, or from a press bureau. Particular emphasis should be put on marking news supplied by press bureaus, whether they are labeled 'Geneva,' or 'Stockholm,' or 'El Paso.' " Furthermore, the accountability of publishers should be increased. "For somehow the commu-

[106] James Melvin Lee, *History of American Journalism*, 1917, pp. 383-385, 415-416. Silas Bent, *Ballyhoo*, 1927, pp. 229, 255-256, 269.
[107] William Orton, "News and Opinion," *American Journal of Sociology*, July, 1927, 33:1:90.
[108] *Liberty and the News*, 1920, pp. 72-73, 76.

nity must find a way of making the men who publish news accept responsibility for an honest effort not to misrepresent the facts."

Newspapers today are making a more deliberate effort to secure men of education and discrimination for reporters. Schools of journalism are proving valuable to this end, both on account of the preparation they give and of the added prestige they lend to the profession. The idea of a professional school of journalism was first conceived and given support by Joseph Pulitzer, who was keenly aware of the responsibility that is placed on newspapermen and their need for professional training.[109] In his will, dated April 16, 1904, he provided for the endowment of such a school at Columbia University, as evidence of his "desire to assist in attracting to this profession young men of character and ability, also to help those already engaged in the profession to acquire the highest moral and intellectual training." The school opened in 1912. The *Editor and Publisher International Year Book for 1930* lists 134 institutions as having schools, departments or courses in journalism, the latter given under the direction of the English department. Only the schools, of which there were 16, and the departments, 50 in number, can be considered as giving any professional training. The degree of bachelor of journalism or an equivalent degree is granted to several hundred students each year.

This remarkable growth has presented many problems of grave difficulty to the teacher of journalism. As one of them remarks, "He has had to prove that journalism is a profession, that it can be taught, and that he has found ways of teaching it. He has had to convert the practicing editor to the value of the work, and find out what this editor wanted taught to the incoming generation. He has had to establish standards, map out a curriculum, invent laboratory disciplines, and write his textbooks. He was in the midst of a revolution; everything he did was an innovation; and so at the moment he is rather more interested in stabilizing his judgments, and appraising the results of his first endeavors than in introducing more novel methods. In his endeavors, the teacher is receiving honest criticism and willing aid from the newspaper profession."[110] The teaching of journalism as a profession is still experimental, but the transition of

[109] Don C. Seitz, *Joseph Pulitzer, His Life and Letters*, 1924, pp. 435-462. George Henry Payne, History of Journalism in the United States, 1920, pp. 367, 368, 371.
[110] Leon Whipple, "Journalism," *The Survey*, June 1, 1928, 60:2:29-2. Stanley Walker, city editor of the New York *Herald Tribune*, contends that schools of journalism are costly and unnecessary, and that a high proportion of their graduates go into propaganda work. "A City Editor's Testament," *The American Mercury*, Sept., 1931, 24:93:28-30.

journalism from an occupation to a profession is clearly indicated. With advancing training of the journalist, the existing news-structure may be made more serviceable to democracy.

Another hopeful sign is the growing public interest in the press. In recent years there has been a great increase in the number of articles about the press which have appeared in magazines, and in the frequency with which the press has been a subject of discussion at forums, clubs, etc. Journalism will be greatly aided by the development of a critical sense on the part of newspaper patrons. This will be promoted by greater knowledge of newspaper organization and methods. Some newspapers have recently adopted the "open shop policy" for visitors and have provided official guides to take guests through the plant and explain how a newspaper is edited and made. Delegations from the public schools are invited. The Baltimore *Sun*, which has been a leader in this respect, presents to each visitor a very instructive booklet, "The Making of a Newspaper." Other newspapers have printed booklets in the interests of readers; an especially noteworthy example is the one put out by the New York *Times* and entitled "How to Read a Newspaper."[111]

Frederick L. Allen[112] believes that "The newspaper profession is steadily advancing, not only in the effectiveness of its news-gathering machinery, but also in its standing in the community and in its ethical standards." James Melvin Lee[113] designates the period from 1900 on as one of social readjustment, with advancing ethics. "Practically every newspaper before 1900 had been, as Mr. Watterson [late editor of the Louisville *Courier-Journal*] asserted, a law unto itself, without standards of either work or duty: its code of ethics, not yet codified like those of medicine and of law, had been, like its stylebook, individualistic in character. The most important change to leave its mark upon the journalism of the period was not in the gathering of news, not in the speed with which it could be placed before the public, not in the ownership and control of the journal from the individual to the incorporated company, but in the ethical advance made in all departments of the newspaper. New standards of ethics were established, not only for the editorial, but also for the advertising and circulation departments. Yet the press but reflected again the trend of the times, for it was an era of moral awakening."

[111] James Melvin Lee, "Journalism," *The American Year Book*, 1926, pp. 993-994.

[112] "Newspapers and the Truth," *The Atlantic Monthly*, Jan., 1922, CXXIX, 52.

[113] *History of American Journalism*, 1917, pp. 388, 443.

He further states as his opinion that "the ethics of journalism today [1917] are higher than those of any other profession. What the press does is known and read by all men. It does not print one edition for one class of subscribers and another for another. Every reader knows exactly where the paper stands. It may be on the wrong side but it is publicly labeled so that no one is deceived. What other profession can say as much?" In other words, the newspaper itself suffers pitiless publicity, and "the wages of sin is publicity." Gerald W. Johnson[114] points out that honesty is the best *policy* for the newspaper, because "the newspaper that lies will inevitably be caught lying, and while lying may be a venial sin, getting caught at it is disastrous to prestige."

On the other hand, there are many signs that disillusionment about the press is increasing. The public is experiencing "a growing sense of being baffled and misled; and wise publishers will not pooh-pooh these omens."[115] There has been an increasing flood of literature on the newspapers, most of it in outspoken criticism. Much dissatisfaction over the present state of affairs is being expressed by newspapermen themselves. The peculiar privileges of the press are being threatened. The position of the press as an institution is being questioned.

The Press as an Institution.—The position of the newspaper as an institution is a peculiar one. "The press is the one institution whose freedom Congress is specifically forbidden to touch. It has a special classification in the mails. Certain of its communications are privileged. The right of its representatives to be present at all discussions of public affairs is usually unquestioned by courts and legislatures. The second President of the United States was the last one who attempted to exercise any sort of regulatory power over the newspapers, in time of peace, and his attempt resulted in the destruction, not only of his own political career, but also of his political party."[116]

The special position accorded to the press, its charter of freedom, was granted to it in its capacity as a public utility. Freedom of the press was and is a privilege, and not an inalienable right. It was granted because the grantors expected to derive certain benefits from it; and in theory, if the benefits should fail, the grant might in perfect justice be withdrawn. It is based upon two propositions: first, that the press shall act as a censor of government and a surrogate of popu-

[114] *What is News?* 1926, pp. 94-95.
[115] Walter Lippmann, *Liberty and the News*, 1920, pp. 75-76.
[116] Gerald W. Johnson, *What is News?* 1926, p. 73.

lar liberties; and second, that it shall afford a prompt, accurate and unbiased supply of information—the raw material of mass opinion. Neither of these functions, on which the first amendment to the Constitution rests, bears any direct relation to the enterprise of filling a newspaper's coffers or advancing personal political ends. Each is charged with a public use. "Much more distinctly than transportation, water power, or communication by post, telegraph, telephone and radio—all of which are under strict governmental supervision and regulation—the press is burdened with responsibility for general well-being, public morality and the harmonious operation of democratic government. The extent to which it is conscious of its responsibility and acknowledges the bases of its privileges must finally determine whether it shall continue in the enjoyment of them. There is no question that it is subject to the same regulation and inspection as any other public utility, and if the Government chooses to get down to Constitutional brass tacks there is little hope of protection under the first amendment."[117]

The press has gradually been losing ground. The restrictions of the post-office department have grown more and more rigid. "The second-class mailing privilege has come to be of so little value that periodicals of large national circulation have partially abandoned it, and daily newspapers have entirely abandoned it insofar as their circulation within a radius of fifty to a hundred miles of the office of publication is concerned. The disposition of Congress to pass regulatory laws increases. The Postmaster-General has assumed the right of absolute censorship, a position more autocratic than that of the Russian censorship under the czars, and the assumption goes unchallenged. It is the nature of government to extend its authority constantly unless it is frequently and sharply checked; so the encroachment of officialdom upon the freedom of the press is a natural phenomenon. The significant fact is that this encroachment has suffered no check from public opinion recently, and seems unlikely to suffer one. . . . It is fairly clear that the prestige of the press with the people is crumbling."[118]

If this conclusion is correct, it may be explained by the growing doubt on the part of the people that they are deriving from a free press the benefits they are entitled to expect from it. "The voter has not reasoned it out in detail. He merely observes that the newspapers he knows are too often full of scandal, murder, sudden death, and advertisements for him to regard them as priceless bulwarks of his

[117] Silas Bent, *Ballyhoo*, 1927, pp. 371-372.
[118] Gerald W. Johnson, *What is News?* 1926, pp. 76-77.

own liberties. The proportion of advertising matter is the basis of the new postal legislation. Members of Congress have specifically disavowed any obligation to grant newspapers special mailing privileges in order that they may make money; and since the stinging implication is that most of them are now frankly out solely to make money, therefore the low postal rates were withdrawn. If it is right to withdraw low postal rates on that ground, it is right to withdraw any other privileges on the same ground. If a newspaper is purely a commercial institution, why should it have the right, for instance, to criticise the government with impunity? Why should its representatives be granted special privileges in the houses of Congress and in the courts? Why should they receive any more consideration from the government than is accorded to clerks in a dry-goods store? Obviously, the purely commercial standard is not a safe one for the press to adopt if it has any regard for its own future."[119]

The impression that the newspapers, if they really have a high function in the state, are not discharging it conspicuously well, persists and perhaps increases. The old respect for the press as "the sentinel on the watch-tower" and "the palladium of the people's liberties" appears to be declining. This may be true, even though circulation is increasing. A newspaper's influence is measured by the number of people who read it *and believe in it*. "The public will read any sort of news story, provided it is well enough written; that is to say, provided it conforms, not only with literary standards, but also with the specific requirements of the newspaper-reading public. It will buy a paper containing any sort of well-written news, thereby assuring the paper's financial success. But it will not necessarily respect the paper that it buys and reads. It will respect only the paper whose news policy is pertinent to the public's own larger interests, the paper that obviously is striving to present news that affects other than its own fortunes, and news that bears other than a trivial and passing interest. But public respect is essential to the newspaper in the long run, and for two reasons. First, public respect for the press is the only guaranty that the privileged position of the press will be maintained. Second, public respect is the outward, visible symbol of the power that lends to the advertising space of an influential newspaper a large part of its value."[120]

We have seen that newspaper workers themselves define an ideal newspaper as an institution devoted to the business of giving its

[119] *Ibid.*, pp. 77-78.
[120] *Ibid.*, pp. 83-84.

patrons an adequate conception of the world as it exists. How do the papers today measure up to this standard? A newspaperman answers the question as follows:[121]

The world as it exists is not populated exclusively, or largely, by murderers, burglars, roués, and lunatics; not by heavyweights, middleweights, welterweights, lightweights, featherweights, and bantamweights; not by jockeys, major and minor leaguers, backfield and line men, professional and amateur golfers, and Bill Tilden; not by vaudeville actors, Rotarians, and clergymen. So a newspaper that confines its news largely to the doings of any of these classes is only part of a newspaper. These people are in and of the world, and are therefore entitled to a place in any adequate picture of the whole company. But none of them dominates the scene.

The newspaper that gives its readers an adequate conception of the world as it exists must not confine itself to the obvious and spectacular. It must consider every detail and bring to light those that are significant, but obscure. It must cause the casual and inattentive spectator to understand much that is not immediately apparent. But this is just what has been described as the keenest intellectual delight of good newspapermen. A newspaper that gives its readers an adequate conception of the world as it exists is therefore an ideal newspaper from the standpoint of the craftsman.

The newspaper that follows this course must subordinate its own financial interest, must become more than solely a business venture. Sometimes, indeed, it must do things that are likely to be detrimental to its immediate financial interest. But this develops public respect. One sees occasionally in the New York *Times* an announcement something like this: "The TIMES regrets that owing to pressure of news it has been compelled to omit eight columns of advertising today." That is very impressive. The subordination of its immediate economic concern to its larger purpose maintains and strengthens the newspaper as an institution. It lends to newspaper proprietorship a value over and above the financial return—a civic and social value, which is imponderable and incalculable, but which most men prize. It gives to the proprietor a position of power and dignity. Moreover, the continuance of such a policy insures a cumulative increase of those intangible values which are eventually translated, at least in part, into the economic value of goodwill. So in the long run it works out that the news which is of ideal value to the individual worker is also of value to the newspaper as an institution.

[121] *Ibid.,* pp. 84-86.

Part V

RECREATION

CHAPTER XVIII

RECREATION IN THE MACHINE AGE

THE term recreation covers many things—play, change from drudgery, rest for mind and body, excitement, complete oblivion, sport, amusement. It includes all the ways in which people spend their spare time or leisure moments, and since interests and appeals differ widely, the field is extraordinarily diversified.

One is tempted, says L. P. Jacks,[1] the Principal of Manchester College, Oxford, to define leisure simply as the opposite of labor. "But this clearly will not do, for the obvious reason that what is a leisure occupation to one man is a labor occupation to another; climbing the Matterhorn, for example, which is a leisure occupation for the tourist in Switzerland, but a labor occupation, and a pretty strenuous one too, for the guide. . . . I propose therefore to define leisure as that part of a man's (or a woman's) life when he is not engaged in earning his living or in preparing for doing so." Leisure is a time of enjoyment, of play, though these concepts are not necessarily the opposite of employment and work. Employment may be the very essence of enjoyment, and the best kinds of work and play may be almost indistinguishable. The word leisure originally meant "an opportunity to do something." The present popular definition seems to be "a chance to do nothing."[2]

The Increased Amount of Leisure.—A striking characteristic of modern society is the enormous amount of spare time it enjoys as compared with its predecessors. Once a privilege of the few, leisure has now become a possession of the many. Though still unevenly distributed—some having more than they know what to do with, others far less than they desire, and some none at all save a few hours for eating and sleeping—the total amount of leisure available is unprecedented. This is due to a variety of causes, all of which are more or less intimately connected one with another and refer to the Industrial Revolution as a source. First, there has occurred a general rise in the standard of living which demands, among other things, more time at

[1] "Leisure: A New and Perplexing Problem," *The New York Times Magazine*, July 5, 1931.
[2] George B. Cutten, *The Threat of Leisure*, 1926, p. 3.

liberty for the pursuit of pleasure. Increasing wages have brought the means of diversion within the reach of larger numbers. Hours of labor have been shortened through legislation and trades' union activity; pension and insurance systems have enabled workers in all ranks to "retire" at a certain age; and, more important, scientific machinery has been substituted for human labor and has permitted the necessary work of the world to be done in a shorter period of time. Even within the space of a generation, the standard working week has been shortened by nearly 20 per cent. In 1890 the workday in industrially advanced countries was close to ten hours. Today it is close to eight hours. Many millions of laboring men and women have won, since the year 1890, two additional hours of daily respite from toil, and more leisure time will undoubtedly be added in the future. The lessening of the number of hours spent daily in getting a living and in home-making, the almost universal habit of the Saturday half-holiday, and the increasing prevalence of summer vacations have transformed leisure from a concern of the "idle rich" and a sporadic, semi-occasional event for the masses into an everyday phenomenon of wide social significance.[3]

Passive Recreation.—How do we as a people actually pass our hours of recreation and relaxation? Professor Patrick[4] answers the question as follows: "Well, some of us read, say newspapers or magazines or books of fiction, some of us smoke or even drink, some make social calls or just lounge and chatter, some simply sit, some talk or fuss or gossip, some play pool or billiards. A very large number go to the movies. Some play bridge. Some play poker or shoot craps. Some bet on baseball, football, or horse-racing. Many ride in motor cars. Occasionally one or two ride horseback. A few walk. A very few swim or exhibit themselves in scanty costumes with the ostensible purpose of swimming. Once in a while one may go to the gymnasium. Some play golf or tennis. A large number dance. A few go fishing or hunting or camping. A certain number actually participate in baseball, football or basketball. This is not intended as a complete list of our recreational activities, but may afford a basis for the present study."

The characteristic leisure-time pursuits, especially in the city, are largely passive, that is, looking at or listening to something or talking or playing cards or riding in an auto. In Middletown it was found

[3] George B. Cutten, *The Threat of Leisure*, 1926, ch. II. Robert and Helen Lynd, *Middletown*, 1929, p. 225.
[4] "The Play of a Nation," *Scientific Monthly*, Oct., 1921, XIII, 351.

that the leisure of virtually all women and of most of the men over thirty is mainly spent sitting down.[5] This tendency to take recreation second-hand through watching, listening, riding, rather than through active participation, is less true of the foreigners in our cities, who, until they are Americanized, display considerable ingenuity and organization in self-amusement. To them music, art, drama, and similar leisure-time activities are things of creative enjoyment rather than of passive knowledge. Americans depend almost wholly upon others for their diversions. The question is not "What shall I do tonight?" or "What can we do to amuse ourselves?" but "What's doing tonight?" that is, what is being done that will divert us without requiring much exertion on our part? So we have theatres, movies, amusement parks, commercialized sports, and a host of other things to entertain those who can pay for their fun. The national sport of America is said to be baseball; more accurately speaking, it is watching baseball. City amusements have always been essentially spectacles, and the recent extensive growth of urban population has greatly increased the spectator habit.

Specialists in the field of recreation are of the opinion that participating forms of recreation, such as mountain climbing, camping and outdoor sports generally, gardening, naturalizing, amateur acting, and good books are superior in recreational value to those of second- and third-hand participation—what Stuart Chase[6] terms "clicking turnstiles, Roman stadia, burning up the roads, Hollywood, jazz, gin, Coney Island, dollar-a-hole golf, comic strips, wood-pulp confession magazines and books—bad books." According to this view, the normal outlet of excitement is muscular action. To enjoy the excitement constantly and not have the corresponding action is to lead an incomplete and unhygienic life. What all recreation-lovers wish to promote is freer self-activity and fuller physical expression.[7] Professor Patrick[8] believes that golf, tennis, baseball, football, and basketball stand out preëminently as really recreative sports. Hunting and fishing, swimming and camping constitute a group of sports which rank high in his list of valuable recreations. The recreations, however, which attract the greatest number of people, such as the dance, the movies, and the auto, he ranks low in recreational value, while one of them he

[5] Robert and Helen Lynd, *Middletown*, 1929, p. 226.
[6] Address before the annual convention of the American Library Association, reported in the New York *Times*, June 28, 1931.
[7] Clarence A. Perry, "Is Commercial Recreation an Octopus?" *The Playground*, Feb., 1928, 21:11:604-606.
[8] "The Play of a Nation," *The Scientific Monthly*, Oct., 1921, XIII, 352 ff.

thinks has a doubtful social value, and one a widespread pernicious influence.

Leisure-time Inventions.—Since the nineties a number of new inventions, of which the automobile, the movies, and the radio are outstanding examples, have swept through the country and revolutionized its leisure. With an estimated participation of 50,000,000 listeners a night, 100,000,000 movie admissions a week, and a pleasure motoring bill of $5,000,000,000 a year, the new recreational means rank highest in respect to the numbers affected.

1. The Automobile.—More than any other development since the nineties, the automobile has made leisure-time enjoyment a regularly expected part of every day and week rather than an occasional event. It has multiplied many-fold the readily available leisure-time options of even the wage-earning class. Picnics in a park or a nearby wood or at the shore can be a matter of a moment's decision on a hot afternoon. It has also been influential in spreading the vacation habit. "The automobile is extending the radius of those who are allowed vacations with pay and is putting short trips within the reach of some for whom such vacations are still 'not in the dictionary.' "[9] Touring has become a widespread practice, it being estimated that at least forty million persons in ten million cars take to the road annually as tourists.[10] This, as we shall see, has been a great incentive to the development of state and national parks. The increase in surfaced roads and in closed cars is rapidly making the automobile a year-round tool for leisure-time activities. Walking for pleasure threatens to become extinct. Ownership of a car has now reached the point of being an accepted essential of normal living.

The advent of the automobile created a new situation with reference to play space. Until the coming of the high-speed motor vehicle, streets and highways were much used for walking, for riding on horses and bicycles, and for children's play. When traffic moved slowly there was little objection raised to the use of streets for recreative purposes by the inhabitants of the houses fronting upon them. Except in crowded areas with much through-traffic, little danger arose from this use. When, however, the horse vehicle was replaced by the motor car, the speed of the latter created an entirely new situation. The automobile soon became the predominant user of street surface, and every other use had to give way to it. Today it is forgotten that streets and

[9] Robert and Helen Lynd, *Middletown*, 1929, pp. 254-256, 260, 262-263 (quoted).
[10] *The Survey*, July 1, 1931, 66:7:350.

highways were once footways and play-spaces as much as traffic ways. The only adjustment to the situation is the provision of new space for play off the street. While the automobile has greatly increased the need for more playgrounds and neighborhood parks in central areas, it has, as already observed, facilitated travel to suburban parks, open country districts and seaside resorts. Instead, therefore, of being a wholly destructive agent in regard to recreation, it has modified the character and location of the facilities that are needed and has increased the demand for special kinds of recreation spaces. It has made the distant places more accessible, perhaps, to the majority. On the whole, this may mean that most adults are as well off in regard to open-air recreation as ever they were, motor-riding having been substituted for walking or cycling and the distant park or beach for the local park.[11]

The cheap automobile, coming into popular favor as the saloon went out, has provided a way to spend time which formerly was consumed in the saloon, and in many cases this time is spent now in company with the other members of the family, in rides at the end of the day, on half-holidays, and on Sundays. Although the automobile has tended thus to establish domestic solidarity and family happiness,[12] it has upset the equilibrium of habits formed under earlier conditions. Antagonism arises from the belief that "when auto riding tends to replace the traditional call in the family parlor as a way of approach between the unmarried, 'the home is endangered,' and all-day Sunday motor trips are a 'threat against the church'; it is in the activities concerned with the home and religion that the automobile occasions the greatest emotional conflicts."[13] The Lynds found in Middletown that use of the automobile ranked high among the sources of disagreement between children and their parents. "The extensive use of this new tool by the young has enormously extended their mobility and the range of alternatives before them; joining a crowd motoring over to dance in a town twenty miles away may be a matter of a moment's decision, with no one's permission asked. . . . In 1890 a 'well-brought-up' boy and girl were commonly forbidden to sit together in the dark; but motion pictures and the automobile have lifted this taboo, and, once lifted, it is easy for the practice to become widely extended. Buggy-riding in 1890 allowed only a narrow range of mo-

[11] Lee F. Hanmer, *Public Recreation*, Regional Survey of New York and its Environs, 1928, V, 30-32.

[12] George B. Cutten, *The Threat of Leisure*, 1926, pp. 78-79.

[13] Robert and Helen Lynd, *Middletown*, 1929, pp. 137-138, 254.

bility; three to eight were generally accepted hours for riding, and being out after eight-thirty without a chaperon was largely forbidden. In an auto, however, a party may go to a city halfway across the state in an afternoon or evening, and unchaperoned automobile parties as late as midnight, while subject to criticism, are not exceptional.''

The widespread use of automobiles has led to the development of roadhouses and has complicated the problem of city dance-hall regulation. The Cleveland Recreation Survey reports that ''auto parties which are the result of pick-up acquaintances at dances are growing to constitute one of a modern city's most serious social problems. Only alert and wise chaperones and capable policing of the floor, the building and even the sidewalks and streets near the building can keep this undesirable practice at a minimum.''[14] The judge of a juvenile court avers that ''the automobile has become a house of prostitution on wheels.''[15]

2. The Movies.—Like the automobile, the motion picture is more than simply a new way of doing an old thing; it has added new dimensions to the city's leisure. It is the one totally new art form or amusement which modern civilization has produced.[16] No other type of commercialized recreation is comparable to it in appeal, as measured by attendance figures, and none has been more influential in increasing the spectacle-watching habit.

It is difficult to appreciate the fact that in 1900 the movies were commercially unknown. In 1930 it was estimated that there were some 22,000 motion-picture houses in the United States, seating 11,300,000 and with a daily attendance of 15,000,000.[17] In large centers the total weekly attendance at motion-picture shows is a number equal to the entire population of the city. The American public pays in at the box office each year well over $500,000,000 to see motion pictures. The movie industry is said to employ upwards of 300,000 persons in all its branches, and the investment in the motion-picture field is stated to approximate $2,000,000,000. More than $125,000,000 is spent annually in production.[18] Here, certainly, is an example of Big Business.

The movies have become the most popular entertainment of the country, nay, of the world, and their influence is one of the strongest social energies of our time. What are the causes of this movement

---

[14] Raymond Moley, *Commercial Recreation*, 1920, p. 87. See ch. XIX, below.
[15] Robert and Helen Lynd, *Middletown*, 1929, p. 114.
[16] Ida Craven, ''Amusements, Public,'' *Encyclopaedia of the Social Sciences*, 1930, II, 42.
[17] *United States Daily*, May 3, 1930.
[18] Will Hays, *See and Hear*, 1929, p. 35.

which was undreamed of only a short time ago? Wherein lies the appeal of the movies? The low price of admission accounts in part for the crowding of picture houses, yet the rush has been increasing while the prices have climbed. Even those who are drawn by the cheapness of the performance would hardly push their money under the little window so often if they did not enjoy the plays and were not stirred by a pleasure which holds them for hours. There must be inner values which make the photoplay so extremely attractive. To a certain degree the mere technical cleverness of the pictures even today holds the interest spellbound as in those early days when nothing but this technical skill could claim the attention. Moreover, we are captivated by the undeniable beauty of many settings. An intellectual interest, too, finds its satisfaction. Yet a stronger power of the photoplay lies in its own dramatic qualities. The plot is usually based on the fundamental emotions which are common to all and which are understood by everybody. Love and hate, gratitude and envy, hope and fear, pity and jealousy, repentance and sinfulness, and all the similar crude emotions have been sufficient for the construction of most scenarios.[19] Other explanations of the popularity of the motion picture refer to it as a wish-fulfilment, a vicarious experience, an escape from reality. It enables the spectators to live vicariously the more brilliant, interesting, adventurous, romantic, successful, or comic lives of the shadow figures before them on the screen. It brings a glimpse of fairyland into some lives that are drab and prosy. To those who have no beauty in their daily surroundings, beauty is brought in many forms upon the screen. In the industrial city the theatre is the one source of mystery and romance. It is an antidote to the monotony and strain of industry. "The luxury of the contemporary moving picture theatre, the sense of richness in all the trappings of the show, the sanctuary the movie presents from all burdensome worries, have made it a real crowd-centre; it is the urban counterpart of the church sociable, the town or mass meeting, the county fair."[20] More than any other form of popular art or entertainment it represents the spirit of the twentieth century.

It is generally agreed by the historians of the motion picture that Thomas A. Edison laid the technological foundation of the art.[21] In

[19] Hugo Münsterberg, *The Photoplay*, 1916, pp. 215-221. Terry Ramsaye, *A Million and One Nights*, 1926, p. xi.

[20] Gilbert Seldes, *An Hour with the Movies and the Talkies*, 1929, pp. 14, 113-114 (quoted). Jane Addams, *The Spirit of Youth and the City Streets*, 1923, ch. IV. Joseph P. Kennedy, ed., *The Story of the Films*, 1927, pp. 189-191.

[21] Among the excellent histories of the movies are the following: Terry Ramsaye, *A Million and One Nights*, 1926, 2 vols. L'Estrange Fawcett, *Films: Facts and Forecasts*, 1927. Paul Rotha, *The Film Till Now*, 1930.

1887, having perfected the phonograph, he undertook to supplement the sound images with another mechanical device which would present visual images alongside those of sound. It is interesting to observe that this ambition of Edison, which brought the film into being, is precisely the opposite of the aim of the present-day producer, who attempts to supplement the visual images with their recorded sounds. In 1889 Edison, utilizing the film strips which had been evolved by Eastman in place of the photographic plate, produced the kinetoscope, the original cinema machine. The kinetoscope was a penny-in-the-slot peep-show, into which one could look and see something like a modern film passing across his line of vision. Exhibited at the Chicago Exposition in 1893 and presented commercially to the New York public in 1894, the kinetoscope soon became a means for popular amusement and entertainment in this and in other countries, and the appetite of commercialism was whetted. At once efforts to improve on the Edison machine were started in many places. The difficulty with the kinetoscope was that only one person at a time could see the pictures. This limitation gave rise to a demand for a machine like the magic lantern, which would project the pictures on to a screen so that they could be seen by a whole roomful of people. Edison, however, disliked the proposal, believing that collective showings would rapidly exhaust the market, and he omitted even to patent his device in foreign countries. Success in devising a machine to project the films upon a large screen came almost at the same time to Auguste and Louis Lumière in Paris and to Robert W. Paul in London. Other projectors were invented by other people, but it is generally conceded that the English engineer was the first actually to project satisfactorily a moving picture on the screen. That was in 1895, and being a man of foresight, Paul quickly turned the discovery to commercial advantage. The moving-picture theatre, strictly speaking, thus began in England, though it has found its greatest development in the United States.

By 1903 the mechanism was perfected, and the transition between peep-shows in penny arcades and the screen was effected. Then began the second phase of the film's development—the evolution of the film-story. In the early days the producer was content to photograph topical events, horse-races, boxing-matches, and so on. No one attempted to stage a film-play, though Paul as early as 1896 produced at the Alhambra Theatre a semi-fictional film entitled *The Soldier's Courtship*, 40 feet in length. Few films were longer than that. The era of the film-play is usually said to have opened with the production in 1903 of *The Great Train Robbery* by Edison employes. It was 800 feet long, took ten to twelve minutes to show, and created a furore in America. It inaugurated the era of the popular one-reeler, which meant that the average length of a film had been increased from 40 to 1,000 feet, and the one-reeler ruled supreme for eight or nine years before anyone thought seriously of producing a film which, by taking an hour or more to show, would compete with the length of a play. The one-reeler corresponded roughly to a music-hall turn, and could be easily incorporated in a vaudeville program. This was the movie's original place, a part of a vaudeville show; it was even used as a "chaser" to empty the house. But it went on to call for establishments of its own, where it would be the principal attraction. In Europe for many years the film continued to be shown in music-halls, but in America its popularity gave rise to that peculiar institutions, the "nickelodeon," or the little picture-theatre, for which the admission charged was a nickel, and to which attention was directed by a screeching phonograph. By 1907, there were about 5,000 nickelodeons in the United States. Any old room sufficed, but gradually the penny arcades, where once the peep-shows had reigned, were turned over to the new-fangled pictures. Many of the present heads of the motion-picture industry in America ran and made money out of the nickelodeon. As the motion picture increasingly discovered that it had a vast public, larger and finer houses were built, and in less than twenty-five years there were more than 20,000 motion-picture theatres in this country.

The rise of the motion-picture theatres created a demand for story pictures, which reacted with revolutionary effect on the art of the films. The mere ability to crank a camera and develop films was no longer sufficient. Now the motion picture had to reach out for players and stories and directors. A whole creative craftsmanship had to be evolved. Outstanding among the pioneer directors was David W. Griffith, whose film *The Birth of a Nation*, produced in 1915, was the first great achievement of the American screen. Most notable among the actors for their meteoric success and world-wide popularity were Mary Pickford and Charlie Chaplin. Gradually films began to be known by the names of the people who made them or appeared in them, and the star-system was born. This ushered in the next period in the film's development, the era of names. Since then the history of the motion picture is sufficiently vivid in memory. In 1914, the year of Chaplin's first picture, Mary Pickford received a contract for $2,000 a week; two years later Chaplin was getting $10,000 a week and a bonus and Miss Pickford was asking a million dollars a year. As Gilbert Seldes[22] remarks, "We are in the familiar range of the movie at last."

For many years the motion picture was merely a photographic reproduction of the theatre; stage people used stage material for the movies. Then the film, developing attributes and properties peculiar to itself, succeeded in breaking away from the hampering traditions of the theatre, and established itself as an independent form of expression. Though the early movie was inferior to the theatre in that the color was lacking, the real depth of the objective stage was missing, and above all the spoken word had been silenced, yet it had certain superiorities over the stage, and development along these lines hastened the trend away from the theatre. Among these advantages were the handling of crowds and pageantry on a larger scale, the use of natural backgrounds, the rapid change of scenes, the intertwining of the actions in different scenes, the passing through physically impossible experiences, the realization of supernatural effects, the gigantic enlargement of small details, and the use of technical tricks— the flash-back, parallel actions, the projection of a scene or person as seen from different angles, the dissolves, and so on—all of which are impossible on the stage. The art of the photoplay has developed so many new features of its own, features which have not even any similarity to the technique of the stage, that it should be recognized as a new art acknowledged in its own æsthetic independence, an art as different from that of the theatre as the painter's art is different from that of the sculptor.[23] Leading critics believe that every good thing in the movies has been accomplished either in profound indifference to the stage or against the experience of the stage. They therefore look with dismay upon the development of the talking picture, which is bringing the film once again into close relation to the theatre.[24]

The advent of the sound and dialogue film marks the opening of the next great cycle in the history of the cinema. On August 7, 1926, Vitaphone made its début at Warner's Theatre on Broadway and gave the world the first practical demonstration of the new era in motion-picture entertainment that sound was to presage. Shortly thereafter, William Fox brought out the Movietone, and within a few years talking pictures had swept the field. The revolution created by the intro-

[22] *An Hour with the Movies and the Talkies*, 1929, p. 32.
[23] Hugo Münsterberg, *The Photoplay*, 1916, pp. 27-38.
[24] Gilbert Seldes, *An Hour with the Movies and the Talkies*, 1929, pp. 54-56. Paul Rotha, *The Film Till Now*, 1930, p. 311.

duction of sound is best exemplified by the fact that not more than a bare half dozen original silent features were produced in 1930 by major producing companies in Hollywood.[25] The immediate effect of sound was to increase attendance at motion-picture theatres. Early in 1926, motion pictures had reached what appeared to be a peak in popularity and were even declining. By 1930, owing to the great attraction of the audible screen, attendance at picture showings in the United States had increased fifteen million weekly. With the same familiarity with which the public received motion pictures under its own affectionate title of "movies," it now accepted the new device under the name of "talkies." Development in the technique of sound pictures will undoubtedly continue, and the new art of the talking picture will be established.[26] Other innovations are in the offing, notably the stereoscopic screen (a large stage screen with three-dimensional effect) and the color film. Indeed, experts say that the day is just around the corner when people will see a motion picture flashed on the screen as large as the ordinary stage, the figures moving in perspective, speaking naturally, all in the vivid colors of life. A still more revolutionary effect may be produced when television or an outgrowth from it becomes commercially developed.

The thirty-odd years of the movie's existence do not constitute a past in the sense that the arts of fiction and painting, for instance, have a past. Yet in that short period of time a tremendous development has taken place, and a genuine art—"the first great proletarian art"—has flowered.[27] Starting as a one-reel comedy of fights, fallings, and a chase or two, the film has come to challenge competition with the drama and the novel in the field of fiction, with the newspaper and the magazine in the field of news and art, and with books and lectures in school work. Through the medium of motion pictures, world news is disseminated, social and historic events are pictured, and the wonders of nature unveiled. In many respects the motion picture is the most nearly perfect substitute for immediate observation. As an instrument of education, however, it is still held back by the prejudice against making the schoolroom interesting and exciting.[28] Perhaps the greatest mission which the photoplay may have is that of æsthetic

[25] The Film Daily Year Book, 1930, p. I.
[26] Will Hays, See and Hear, 1929, p. 61. John Scotland, The Talkies, 1930.
[27] Terry Ramsaye, A Million and One Nights, 1926, p. xi.
[28] Gilbert Seldes, An Hour with the Movies and the Talkies, 1929, p. 111. Emanuel Cohen, "The Business of International News by Motion Pictures," Annals Amer. Acad. Polit. Soc. Sci., Nov., 1926, CXXVIII, 74-78. Ernest L. Crandall, "Possibilities of the Cinema in Education," ibid., 109-115. J. R. Rutland, State Censorship of Motion Pictures, 1923, p. 177.

cultivation. No art reaches a larger audience daily, no æsthetic influence finds spectators in a more receptive frame of mind. "On the other hand, no training demands a more persistent and planful arousing of the mind than the æsthetic training, and never is progress more difficult than when the teacher adjusts himself to the mere liking of the pupils. . . . The moving picture audience could only by slow steps be brought from the tasteless and vulgar eccentricities of the first period to the best plays of today, and the best plays of today can be nothing but the beginning of the great upward movement which we hope for in the photoplay."[29] The weakness of the movie is its transiency. Where nothing stands still, nothing endures. "The careers of the motion picture actors are generally brief; those of the majority of the plays almost ephemeral. The circulation of a popular picture is immediate and world-wide. Twenty million people may witness it in a year. But this vast diffusion is paid for by a corresponding brevity. The scenario writer and the director see their finest work flash upon the screen and fade away, perhaps into oblivion; whereas some book, of which a bare handful of copies was sold while the author lived, may be read and treasured a thousand years afterward."[30]

The power of the moving picture to supplement the schoolroom, the newspaper and the library by spreading information and knowledge is, after all, secondary to its general task, to bring entertainment and amusement to the masses. How it performs this task is a matter of social importance. No other form of commercialized recreation has attracted so much critical attention, and in no other case has so much public concern been shown over the possible effects of a recreational device. The problems occasioned by the movies and the attempts at regulation will be discussed in the following chapter.

3. *The Radio.*—From beginnings embedded in the pursuit of mathematical and physical sciences, radio communication has evolved to one of the most far-reaching and sociologically significant of modern inventions. It has become a means of communication which is employed for almost every conceivable purpose from the business affairs of the financier to the amusement of children. As an industry it now gives employment in the United States alone to about 200,000 persons, and as a service it counts among its direct daily beneficiaries perhaps a third of our population.[31] Of its many and extraordinarily valuable

[29] Hugo Münsterberg, *The Photoplay*, 1916, pp. 228-229.
[30] Joseph P. Kennedy, *The Story of the Films*, 1927, pp. vi-vii.
[31] Laurens E. Whittemore, "The Development of Radio," *Supplement to Volume CXLII, Annals Amer. Acad. Polit. Soc. Sci.*, March, 1929, p. 1. General J. G. Harbord, "The Commercial Uses of Radio," *ibid.*, p. 61.

uses and adaptations, we are concerned here solely with broadcasting, the most conspicuous and popular phase of the radio art. Organized broadcasting made its début in the United States on November 2, 1920, when Westinghouse station KDKA transmitted bulletins on the result of the presidential election of that year. The federal census of 1930 enumerated over 12,500,000 radio sets among the people. One need only look about him to witness the radio's present widespread appeal.

Not the least remarkable feature of this new invention is its accessibility, which accounts in part for its tremendous appeal and phenomenal growth. "Here skill and ingenuity can in part offset money as an open sesame to swift sharing of the enjoyments of the wealthy. With but little equipment one can call the life of the rest of the world from the air, and this equipment can be purchased piecemeal at the ten-cent store."[32] The growth of the radio was at first viewed with alarm by certain well-established institutions and enterprises. "The church, grand opera, the motion picture, commercial sports, such as the prize fight, baseball and football, and especially the newspaper were all concerned. The fears have not been realized. Except, perhaps, in the case of prize fights radio broadcasting has, probably in the main, increased the visible attendance as well as created a great invisible audience. In fact, certain churches have tended to organize their service with chief reference to the microphone. In no case but that of the newspaper, however, have we accurate statistics, and these show no decline in the rate of increase of the daily paper. . . . In fact, the newspaper and the radio have become closely interrelated. The radio fan of necessity has to depend in large part upon the report of radio programs in the daily paper."[33]

As has been so generally the case, particularly in America, this new device has been commercialized. The chief feature of broadcasting is the "sponsored program" paid for by manufacturing concerns which have found in it a means of appealing to the purchasing power represented by the listening audience. "Apart from the 'offerings' of the advertisers, air time is filled out with the 'sustaining' or 'unsponsored' programmes offered by the stations themselves. These vary all the way from the playing of victrola records to musical and news events of a very high order. . . . Despite recent improvements in the quality of the advertising programmes, it is the sustaining programmes that

[32] Robert and Helen Lynd, *Middletown*, 1929, p. 269.
[33] Ernest W. Burgess, "Communication," *American Journal of Sociology*, May, 1930, 35:6:998.

furnish practically all material of genuine cultural or educational value. And the question naturally arises whether the growth of advertising will not eventually crowd out the sustaining programme altogether.''[34] Dr. Lee DeForest, pioneer radio inventor, has decried ''the use of broadcast for direct and blatant advertising.'' He fears that it will curtail the usefulness and beneficence of radio, in the home and in the school, as a means of entertainment, of education, and of uplift generally.[35] In other countries, government control prevents the too extensive use of broadcasting for advertising; in the United States the government has control of nothing but wave lengths, and that only since 1927. Though conceding the danger of active governmental supervision of broadcasting, Professor William Orton[36] believes that present conditions are so bad that the chance is worth taking. He thinks that commercial programs will never give us the enlightenment, the artistic entertainment and the intellectual stimulus prophesied by everyone only a few years ago.

Analysis of radio programs discloses that they are chiefly for entertainment.[37] According to a survey of some four thousand broadcast hours of seventy-five stations by the White House Conference on Child Health and Protection, jazz rules the ether by occupying more time on the air than any other radio entertainment. In no other country is this popular form of music rated so importantly on radio programs. Of the total of 52.9 per cent of time devoted to music, which ranks first in broadcasting, 33.9 per cent is devoted to jazz, the report reveals. An analysis of twenty-four European stations, serving twelve countries, discloses that jazz occupies only 7 per cent of the radio time, although 58.5 per cent is given to music.[38] On the other hand, no less an authority than Walter Damrosch maintains that radio has democratized art and is educating the entire nation to a true appreciation of the best in music.[39]

Mechanical inventions such as the phonograph and radio are unquestionably bringing to the people more contacts with more kinds of music than ever before. Prior to the nineties, diffusion of musical knowledge was entirely in the handicraft stage; today it has entered

[34] William Orton, ''The Level of Thirteen-Year-Olds,'' *The Atlantic Monthly*, Jan., 1931, CXLVII, 3.
[35] Quoted in Associated Press dispatch, Aug. 18, 1930.
[36] ''The Level of Thirteen-Year-Olds,'' *The Atlantic Monthly*, Jan., 1931, CXLVII, 1-10.
[37] George A. Lundberg, ''The Content of Radio Programs,'' *Social Forces*, Sept., 1928, 7:1:58-60.
[38] New York *Times*, Nov. 16, 1930.
[39] New York *Times*, Dec. 11, 1930.

a machine stage. An inevitable accompaniment of this mechanization has been the change from active participation to passive enjoyment. Music is becoming more and more a matter of listening to others.[40]

As to the place of radio in relation to other leisure habits, the situation is too recent and fluctuating to offer much prediction. But it seems not unlikely that, while furnishing a new means of diversified enjoyment, radio will at the same time operate, with national advertising, syndicated newspapers, and other means of large-scale diffusion, as yet another means of standardizing habits.[41] Amusements have always been a unifying force in society; their very strength lies in the standardization of tastes which they can effect.[42]

The Effect of Social Change.—The growth of cities has profoundly affected recreation, both directly and through its influence on other institutions, notably the family. The multiplication of interests outside the family group, as observed in work, education, and other respects, applies also to recreation. The home in the modern city can no longer be the center of life in leisure hours. Housing conditions, for one thing, militate against it. The majority of city families live in multiple dwellings, which means little room and many neighbors. There is little chance for peaceful domesticity: the streets are noisy; some of the neighbors keep unseasonable hours and have vociferous pets; others are amateur musicians; there are also player-pianos, Victrolas, and radios. Rest and recuperation are not to be found at home. Vacations must be spent away from it, and Sundays and holidays must be spent in an automobile or on a trolley car. All must go away when in search of pleasure and recreation.[43] Moreover, in the city are found many people living apart from family life—the rooming and lodging-house population. These people must of necessity find their diversions in public places of amusement; they are among the chief patrons of commercialized recreation. Under these conditions, the home-made entertainments that enlivened the more spontaneous parties of the nineties have tended to narrow in scope and even to disappear.

At the same time that the family is declining as a unit of leisure-time pursuits, the basis of other associations is shifting. The neighborhood and the church have both declined as places of most constant association of friends. Other types of association, such as the club, have been

[40] Robert and Helen Lynd, *Middletown*, 1929, pp. 244-245.

[41] *Ibid.*, p. 271.

[42] Ida Craven, "Amusements, Public," *Encyclopaedia of the Social Sciences*, 1930, II, 44.

[43] James E. Cutler, "Durable Monogamous Wedlock," *American Journal of Sociology*, Sept., 1916, 22:2:228-229.

substituted. Whole-family parties have disappeared before the specialized parties for each age group. City-wide recreational agencies, both philanthropic and publicly supported, have multiplied, and organized sports have greatly increased.[44]

Another reason for the declining importance of the home in recreation is that home-made entertainments are not exciting enough; people today feel that they must get out with the crowd and see what's doing. The psychological effect of city life upon the majority of city-dwellers has already been noted to be one of constant stimulation and nervous excitement. In this jazz age, ''leisure'' has become mainly a restless search for excitement. Much of the new spirit is evidenced in the following advertisement of the New Masses Workers' and Peasants' Costume Ball in New York City:[45]

> Jazz, Sing, Riot, Hell, Fun, Dance—If you like to Blow Off Steam—If you need something Red-hot to make you forget prohibition—If you're tired of being good—If you're sick of your job—If you want to meet pretty girls, Bohemians, Red Devils, Anarchists, Nuts, Writers, Roughnecks, Wage Slaves, Cops, Esthetes, and Heywood Broun—*Come! Come! Come!*

Moreover, much of our recreation is taken in crowds, and the participants are open to suggestion from crowd influences. Each is likely to do what the crowd does, whatever that may be. Changing fashions are closely followed. Each new fad has its votaries, wildly enthusiastic over it—until a new fad comes along. This tendency, combined with the spectator attitude, explains why in recent years marathon dancing, Channel swimming, pole-sitting, plane-flying, eating and fasting, talking or playing to make an endurance record, have been prominent forms of diversion. Record breaking is not a new phenomenon—Plutarch protested against the false emphasis upon it in his time—but never has it been so prevalent as today.[46]

Industrialization, too, is having its effect on recreation. Perhaps it is not excitement that we seek in play as much as release from those forms of mental activity which are fatigued in our daily life of grind. The present work-a-day world involves concentration, sustained effort, and controlled association, and the exigencies of our social life demand the constant checking or inhibition of a vast number of natural im-

---

[44] For an excellent discussion of this trend, see Robert and Helen Lynd, *Middletown*, 1929, ch. XIX.

[45] Quoted in the *Saturday Review of Literature*, Dec. 25, 1926.

[46] L. H. Robbins, ''Strange 'Immortals' who Have Their Pantheon,'' *The New York Times Magazine*, Nov. 4, 1928. Ida Craven, ''Amusements, Public,'' *Encyclopaedia of the Social Sciences*, 1930, II, 44.

pulses and appetites.[47] Some release is demanded. Especially does youth seem to be affected by industrial conditions. The speeding-up process, the nervous strain, the monotony, the lack of emotional incentive to work, and the impossibility of finding self-expression in one's job have combined to produce the revolt of youth against the factory system. It tries to compensate for this deficiency by finding self-expression and adventure in leisure-time pursuits. If unguided and untrained, its imagination becomes misdirected and the spirit of adventure goes wrong.[48]

The Control of Leisure.—Recreation has become a matter of public concern, and has received both official and unofficial attention. Public regulation is one of the social consequences of the concentration of population in urban centers. The increased complexity of social relations and the closer interdependence of the individuals of the community have necessitated a restriction on personal liberty. In the city, personal conduct becomes a matter of social importance. The activity of each individual affects the welfare of others. A different standard of individual liberty is required from that which was necessary under rural conditions. Certain activities, as playing ball on the street, must be curtailed.

Regulation has also come about because of the demoralizing factor which has often been present in recreation. Commercialized recreation in particular has been associated with vice and immorality, with delinquency and crime. "History shows that amusements are a pitfall in which good mores may be lost and evil ones produced. They require conventional control and good judgment to guide them. This requirement cannot be set aside. Amusements always present a necessity for moral education and moral will. This fact has impressed itself on men in all ages, and all religions have produced Puritan and ascetic sects who sought welfare, not in satisfying but in counteracting the desire for amusement and pleasure. Their efforts have proved that there is no solution in that direction. There must be an educated judgment at work all the time, and it must form correct judgments to be made real by a cultivated will, or the whole societal interest may be lost without the evil tendency being perceived."[49]

The recent transition from rural to urban life for a large part of the population has enhanced the problem. Our accepted traditions and rules of conduct were established under rural conditions: the new

[47] G. T. W. Patrick, "The Play of a Nation," *Scientific Monthly*, Oct., 1921, XIII, 351-352.
[48] Jane Addams, *The Spirit of Youth and the City Streets*, 1923, chs. I-III, V.
[49] William G. Sumner, *Folkways*, 1906, pp. 603-604.

environment tends constantly to break them down. The growth of cities has, as we have seen, been accompanied by a certain breaking away from home ties, from church affiliations, from moral obligations. New rules of conduct adapted to the city will, of course, in time be developed, but meanwhile during the period of transition a certain amount of demoralization is inevitable. The impersonality and anonymity of city life tend to promote it. There is lack of parental supervision and of the control of neighborhood opinion. Under earlier conditions, ''what the neighbors might think'' seriously conditioned one's life. Watchful eyes observed one in everything he did. This is largely lacking in the city. Plato says somewhere in the *Republic* that none of us would be very trustworthy if we were invisible. The person in a strange city is in that condition. So far as people who count for him are concerned, he is invisible. Consequently country people do things in the city they never think of doing at home; and our good citizens who go away to Paris do not always behave so well there as here. When vacationing, some people tend to take a vacation from their morals as well as from their work.[50]

It has been said that the hours of leisure are the hours of danger. They are also the hours with the greatest opportunity for cultural advancement. Civilization owes much of its development to leisure. In his working time man rarely does what he likes most to do. It is in his spare time—the time which he has at his own disposal—that he does those things which build his character, develop his personality, and broaden his intelligence. How leisure hours are spent is fraught with significance. ''The use of a nation's leisure is the test of its civilization.''[51] The amount of leisure, as we have seen, has been greatly increased through the reduction in working hours, and more will unquestionably be added. More leisure for what? For rest, recreation, and education, or for dissipation, excitement, and demoralization? The additional leisure may be a curse or a blessing; it depends upon how it is used. Some students hold that the greater part of modern recreation should be called de-creation rather than re-creation, in that it does not build up the spirit lost by virtue of mechanized work, but, on the contrary, compounds the difficulties through mechanizing leisure time. They believe that men are now threatened with more leisure than their education has fitted them for dealing with, more than nature intended them to have, more than they are, as yet, capable of enjoying or mak-

[50] Henry S. Curtis, ''The Relation of Public Recreation to Problems of Sex,'' *Journal of Social Hygiene*, April, 1924, 10:4:207.
[51] Percy Mackaye, *The Civic Theatre*, 1912, p. 30.

ing use of. Leisure, to be used to best advantage, should be spent in doing something pleasant, diverting, cultural, useful; it should be mentally satisfying. Communities should organize to provide desirable means of recreation, and individuals should be taught to spent their leisure in a satisfying manner. Education should train for leisure as well as for work.[52]

Classification of Recreational Agencies.—The agencies through which people spend their spare time fall into three main groups: First, the commercialized, or those agencies which are owned and operated for profit; second, those which are supported by private funds; and third, those which are public in the sense of being maintained through taxation. Of these three types of recreational agencies, those which are commercial are in the number attending and in capital invested much more important than the others. In a recreation study in Chicago, for example, it was found that out of 3,164 centers, 263 were public or municipal, 881 were privately supported, and 2,020 were commercial. The yearly attendance at the public recreation centers was about 44,000,000, at the private 15,000,000, and at the commercial 171,-000,000.[53] The total cost of all leisure-time activities in the United States has been estimated to run to over twenty billions, or about one-quarter of the national income. Much of this is expended for commercialized forms. It is claimed that "more money is spent in this country on commercialized leisure than on anything else except food, and more invested in this enterprise than in anything except land. There are more than twenty million daily admissions to the moving picture exhibitions. Last year thirty million dollars were spent in admissions to circuses in this country; one large circus was seen by three and one-half million people, and more than one hundred million paid admissions to sporting events. . . . It has been estimated that this country pays over one hundred million dollars a year to jazz orchestras. The gate receipts of the Carpentier-Dempsey prize fight were $1,-600,000, and of last year's baseball world's series over one million dollars. . . . These give some indication as to the methods and forms of commercialized amusement, and the advantage which business has taken of the unattached leisure of the people."[54] It is estimated that over one hundred million dollars are spent annually on commercialized

[52] George B. Cutten, *The Threat of Leisure*, 1926, chs. VI-VIII. L. P. Jacks, "Leisure: A New and Perplexing Problem," *New York Times Magazine*, July 5, 1931.

[53] Jessie F. Binford, "Community Responsibility for Delinquency," *Proceedings of the National Probation Association*, 1928, p. 128.

[54] George B. Cutten, *The Threat of Leisure*, 1926, pp. 70-71.

recreation in New York City alone. Some of the more important forms
of commercialized recreation, the problems which they present, and the
attempts to regulate them will be discussed in the next chapter. The
following two chapters will consider the constructive action that is
being taken at private and public expense to provide opportunities for
meeting the recreational needs of the people.

CHAPTER XIX

COMMERCIALIZED RECREATION

COMMERCIALIZED recreation has a large and legitimate place in the recreational life of the modern city; it performs a very definite service in increasing recreational opportunities. A particular facility tends to become commercialized when the demand for it is from a sufficiently large portion of the public, and when it is so far capable of standardization in quality and cost price as to meet the requirements of taste and spending power of enough average individuals. There are certain types of recreation which, if they were not furnished by business interests, would not be furnished at all. Commercial agencies may appeal to groups which demand a particular type of entertainment not sufficiently widespread in its interests to justify public operation, as for example, certain kinds of musical entertainments, which appeal to only small parts of the population and which could not in justice be supported by public taxation. For many people in cities, skating would never be possible but for the commercially run skating rink. The same is true of dancing, billiards, and other wholesome amusements. It is quite obvious that the organized government cannot furnish more than a very small proportion of the recreation needed by the people of a city. If it could supply the quantity necessary, it certainly could not meet the fine distinctions in taste which a large population constantly reveals. A large number of commercial enterprises gives citizens the opportunity to get the kinds of recreation they like more nearly than the most intelligent and sympathetic paternalism could devise. Moreover, the methods which have been elaborated under the pressure of business competition oftentimes show an improvement in technique which might very well be emulated by the directors of community recreation.[1]

On the other hand, commercialized recreation has been decried because it emphasizes the place of the spectator and minimizes that of the participant. A more serious objection is that it has a demoralizing influence and is frequently associated with vice, crime, and immoral-

---

[1] Raymond Moley, *Commercial Recreation*, 1920, pp. 11-13. Clarence A. Perry, "Is Commercial Recreation an Octopus?" *The Playground*, Feb., 1928, 21:11:604-606.

ity. This has given rise to a demand for its regulation in the public interest.

Methods of Control.—Various methods of dealing with the problem have been tried. These may be designated: suppression, public regulation, trade control, and control through organized public opinion.

Of these, the least effective is the attempt at suppression. This has taken two forms: first, an endeavor to abolish Sunday amusements, and second, an attempt to make certain forms of recreation illegal at all times. The leading organization working for the "closed" Sunday is the Lord's Day Alliance, a Protestant association founded in 1898. It has sponsored measures in numerous state legislatures which would outlaw Sunday baseball, movies, concerts, newspapers, delicatessen and confectionery stores, athletics including golf, and all labor except works of necessity or charity. Sunday should be religiously observed, and all acts which are "serious interruptions of the repose and religious liberty of the community and endanger the peace and good order of society" should be prohibited. The following comment by Bertrand Russell[2] is of interest in this connection: "Sometimes the Divine commands have been curiously interpreted. For example, we are told not to work on Saturdays, and Protestants take this to mean that we are not to play on Sundays. But the same sublime authority is attributed to the new prohibition as to the old."

The movement represents an attempt to restore the Puritan Sabbath, and in a number of eastern and southern states it has been found that new laws need not be enacted for this purpose, since the old "blue laws," which had not been repealed but had become dead letters, may be revived to accomplish the same end. In New Jersey, for example, the "blue law" of 1789, which forbade the performance, on Sunday, of "any worldly business or employment, or of any interludes, plays for gain, dancing, singing, fiddling, or other music for the sake of merriment," was invoked to put an end to Sunday amusements, particularly motion pictures. The attempt, however, resulted in a boomerang to the reformers, for the authorities, at the insistence of the moving-picture exhibitors whose theatres were closed, ordered that the law be enforced to the letter, with the consequence that so many thousands of violators were found that they could not all be arrested, let alone indicted and tried. The repeated attempts to enforce the Sunday law have merely demonstrated its utter unenforce-

---

[2] *What I Believe*, 1915, p. 48.

ability.[3] The "blue Sunday" movement brings into sharp relief the conflict between rural and urban mores, a conflict that has political aspects in a number of states by reason of the "rotten borough" system which gives control of the legislature to representatives from rural districts.

Equally futile have been the attempts to suppress certain types of popular amusements. Despite all efforts, in every city, profitable and popular, though illegal, amusements continue to flourish. Such a situation is as old as organized government. Indeed, "no government has ever succeeded in suppressing or curbing really popular amusements. Gambling was forbidden in India as early as the second century B.C. by the Code of Manu, but it was never stamped out; the mime flourished in the latter days of Rome despite the prohibitions of church and emperor; the London corporation drove the theaters and bear dens outside the city limits in the eighteenth century but did not thereby control them; prize fighting occurs in New York City in spite of its illegality; those forms of amusement which are connected with organized vice are driven underground rather than eradicated."[4]

The numerous laws directed against gambling, the sale of liquor, and prostitution, though aimed at the control of morals, seem to have accomplished little but the demoralization of the police. These laws are not enacted by the city but by the state or the Federal Government; they are uniform as to all cities, irrespective of their size or population, and are usually out of harmony with the public opinion and conditions which they aim to correct. Local officers are tempted to permit evasions of a state law which they are sworn to enforce and in whose wisdom or justice a large part of the community does not believe. Violation of the law thus becomes a special illegal privilege in which the patrolman and the political boss are able to barter with protected vice. Now and again a vice society or other citizen group discovers that the laws are not being enforced, and a reform movement is inaugurated. These reform movements come to the surface more or less regularly in most of our cities, and then as regularly subside. Little or nothing is accomplished because, for one thing, the method employed is wrong; administration rather than legislation is the proper method of dealing with these problems. "Were the city free to control them by administrative acts, as the health of the com-

[3] Waldo Walker, " 'Blue Laws' Remain to Frighten Us," New York *Times*, June 24, 1928. Elsie McCormick, "Watch-Dog of the Blue Laws," *American Mercury*, May, 1928, 14:53:91-98.

[4] Ida Craven, "Amusements, Public," *Encyclopaedia of the Social Sciences*, 1930, II, 45.

munity is now protected, and were it able to adjust its ordinances or official decrees to conditions as they arise, then it would be possible to work out by experiment solutions which would harmonize prevailing opinion with the laws and at the same time enable public opinion to hold the mayor and council to responsibility for the morals of the city, which is not now possible when many of the laws have no such support or are impossible of enforcement. This would not involve an open town. Public opinion has reached a point that would not tolerate that. It would, however, lead to the enactment of such orders as would free the police from constant temptation and would enable the city to solve the problem in an intelligent way."[5]

As applied to the whole field of commercialized recreation, this is the method of public regulation which, operating mainly through the license system, provides for inspection and supervision of recreational agencies. The police power provides all the legal authority necessary to regulate conduct that may be harmful to group welfare. What action the public officials take in any given instance will depend on the character of the effective public opinion of the community.

Another possibility of effective regulation is that provided through the control exercised by the establishments themselves which furnish a given type of recreation. This is trade control, or self-regulation, which aims to establish standards and maintain conditions that meet with public approval. It takes two forms: (1) the association of proprietors or producers, e.g., a local or national billiards association, a theatrical producers association; and (2) the appointment by the trade of an arbiter or dictator, the so-called "Czar system," e.g., Judge Landis for baseball, Will Hays for the movies. Trade control attempts to eliminate that competition which leads to debasement and other abuses, and to safeguard the financial interests at stake, interests which become jeopardized when the game is not kept "on the level" and when public disapproval threatens with censorship or suppressive laws.

Social control, or the influence of public opinion, is in the last analysis the most decisive factor, for no form of commercialized recreation can survive without public support. Receipts directly feel its influence. Though of all methods of control the most pervasive, it is not very discriminating. To be effective, it must be organized and guided. This is attempted by various associations which see great possibilities in certain types of commercialized recreation and seek through

[5] Frederic C. Howe, *The Modern City and its Problems*, 1915, pp. 238-240, 242 (quoted).

constructive coöperation to improve their artistic, moral, and social quality.

The various methods of control are illustrated in the following discussion of the more important commercialized agencies of recreation.

The Old-Fashioned Saloon.—The sale of intoxicating liquor has long been associated with various forms of commercialized leisure, and it is still so associated despite all efforts at suppression. The ubiquitous saloon, which was the chief vending place, is a thing of the past. It needs to be considered, however, because of the large part it has played in the realm of recreation. What is to take its place? How important the saloon has been in the leisure hours of the workingman is indicated, for example, by the findings of the recreation survey in Cleveland, where it is stated that the abolition of the saloon caused the greatest single change in the spare-time amusement life of the city.

The old-fashioned saloon was more than a mere drinking place. As the Committee of Fifty, which conducted the most intelligent social investigation of the liquor problem, discovered, the saloon performed a double office, it satisfied a twofold thirst: it met the physical craving for intoxicating liquor, but it also gratified the longing for fellowship, for amusement, and for recreation. It had practically a monopoly of the social life of the majority of American wage-earners.[6] "In it millions of American men spent a sixth of their time and almost as much of their wages. It had more influence on more men than all the colleges from Harvard to Stanford. It affected profoundly politics, religion, the lives of families, the destiny of the nation—and it has been gone only eleven years."[7]

Like the ancient tavern, the saloon offered to its patrons a social rendezvous. It provided them at a minimum of cost with a sure stimulus to sociability, and its atmosphere was one of social freedom. Besides the provision of liquor it afforded other attractions and opportunities: tables and cards and sometimes card rooms; daily papers; headquarters for athletic information; centers of political activity; labor bureaus; rooms where labor unions and lodges might meet; sometimes a free lunch; warmth; in some cases lodgings; toilet facilities which the community neglected or refused to furnish; a friend in the bartender who would cash a check or change a bill; relief from henpecking ("a henpecked man is a friend of the bar"); and to the stranger in the city entertainment and information. Especially in

[6] *The Liquor Problem, a summary of investigations conducted by the Committee of Fifty*, 1905, ch. VI. Raymond Calkins, *Substitutes for the Saloon*, 1901, ch. I.
[7] Travis Hoke, "Corner Saloon," *American Mercury*, March, 1931, 22:87:311.

immigrant communities did it function as a workingman's club. It was equipped to cater to most of the needs of the colony. "There one could not only drown one's sorrows and meet one's fellows; one could also buy steamship tickets and money-orders for folks in the old country, play poker, eat, neck a girl, subscribe to newspapers, pay one's lodge and club dues, and—if the saloonkeeper was on friendly terms with the priest, which was not unusual—even one's church dues."[8] Here was a man's place. "Drinking was a man's sport. And women not only loathed the saloon for its intrinsic evils but, quite naturally, because men often sought each others' company there and excluded women. Safe in his saloon, a man boasted of marital independence, complained of marital injustice, gained strength to defy the dominant sex. There he could play at being devil-may-care and independent and generous and brave and debonair, at being manly—and there no woman dared invade him with drab truths. The saloon was for men only. It was their last stronghold in a world of women, and for that reason if no other, outlaw and wicked."[9]

On the other hand, many saloons were nothing but drink shops, and the prevalence of the treating habit led to wasteful extravagance. The open saloon was "a standing invitation to intemperance." It did a vast amount of mischief. It had to go, is gone, and but few want to bring it back. Yet it must be recognized that its collateral services were of great significance, and the passing of the saloon presented a problem of finding other ways of furnishing them.

Substitutes for the Saloon.—It is no secret that it is still possible to get liquor. In many communities speakeasies today outnumber the saloons of the past. In New York, for example, in the pre-Volstead era, when saloons had multiplied far beyond the requirements of public convenience, there were some 10,000 in the city. It is conceded that there are now three times as many illegal speakeasies. But Whiting Williams[10] maintains, from his intimate knowledge of the life of American workingmen, that though speakeasies outnumber saloons, they do not dispense as much liquor and in no way do they serve as a workingman's club:

The reason is plain. The present-day workers' speakeasy—I don't refer, of course, to the near-Fifth Avenue institutions patronized by our friends of the New York intelligentsia—lacks almost completely the well-known "come-hither"—the ancient lure—of the old saloon. The bright lights, the warmth,

[8] Louis Adamic, "The Bohunks," *American Mercury*, July, 1928, 14:55:323.
[9] Travis Hoke, "Corner Saloon," *American Mercury*, March, 1931, 22:87:315.
[10] "Workers' Speakeasy," *The Survey*, Feb. 1, 1931, 65:9:494.

the good cheer and fellowship, the companionable chromos of well-built femininity—all these are missing. Instead, the speakeasy is likely to offer only the grime and darkness of a sloppy kitchen, plus the furtiveness which makes everyone glance up quickly every time the door is opened to make sure that no "law" has entered. Not by any stretch of the imagination can such a place be called "the workingman's club." Because, further, the proprietor is anxious to keep an eye on all his customers and their doings, he is likely even to frown upon the comradeship of treating. Still further—and quite important—the establishment is much less likely to possess the saloon's insinuating closeness to the daily runways of the worker. Instead, the chances are that a trip, with malice or thirst aforethought, is much more likely to be required. Altogether it is plain that such a remote and uninviting establishment serves an-entirely different and decidedly lower clientele among the workers than did its legalized predecessor.

Among immigrants, especially those from southeastern Europe, the coffee house seems able to offer to the former patrons of the saloon the companionship and recreation to which they were accustomed. This distinctly European recreational institution, which the foreign-born have introduced into many of our cities, is essentially a man's institution comparable in a number of respects to the old-fashioned American saloon. Coffee houses are places where the foreign-born workingmen can sit and chat, play cards, have refreshments, listen to music, dance, and in other ways find companionship and diversion —all at a surprisingly low cost. The only problem presented which has demanded public regulation is that of casual prostitution, which has been associated with some coffee houses whose proprietors have seen in it a chance to make additional profits. The great preponderance of men over women in certain immigrant communities has been an important factor in this situation. The problem of coffee-house immorality can be met by increased police vigilance and by a system of licensing which will afford to proprietors of high standards and ability public protection against the competition by the unscrupulous and vicious. Properly conducted and regulated, the coffee house can go far in supplying a wholesome substitute for the saloon. For thousands of foreign-born workmen in many cities it furnishes the only suitable spare-time diversion within reach.[11]

Various other substitutes for the saloon as a social center have been suggested, such as the social settlement, the institutional church, the community center, and men's club-houses provided by industrial concerns or by the municipality.[12] All these may contribute, but it is not

[11] Raymond Moley, *Commercial Recreation*, 1920, pp. 96-108.
[12] *Cf.* Raymond Calkins, *Substitutes for the Saloon*, rev. ed., 1919.

likely that the interest which so many found in the saloon can be
arbitrarily directed into other channels. Nothing short of a general
community effort to increase the capacity and attractiveness of all
recreational agencies will be sufficient to meet the need.

Night Clubs.—The old-fashioned saloon is a memory and likewise
the saloon "back room." In their places, under the influence of the
prohibition laws, has come an entirely new machinery for those who
seek more or less questionable amusement after dark. This device is
known under the general title of the night club. The term is very
loose and inaccurate. It is used popularly to cover many varieties of
enterprises, some of which may not even operate at night. It does not
accurately describe the place which is open from 11 A.M. to 6 P.M.
only; nor can it be correctly applied to the public cabaret whose
patrons are not required to be members, even though many such places
incorporate the word "club" in their names. Whereas all the clandestine "clubs" are speakeasies, not all speakeasies are clubs.

The fact that all clubs have "hostesses" still further increases the
confusion. Many respectable places, which are not clubs in the strict
sense of the word, as well as the ordinary clandestine clubs, employ
hostesses. Going still further down the scale, one finds speakeasy
houses of prostitution which now call their inmates "hostesses." The
hostess of the night club and speakeasy is the American counterpart
of the geisha girl. She is employed for the main purpose of increasing the sales of food, liquor and other drinks; incidentally she is to
provide aesthetic, social, and sexual entertainment for the men
customers.[13]

"The clubs, accurately speaking, require some form of membership. A prospective patron is introduced by a 'club member,' or by a
taxi driver, or by a tout or runner, the three latter receiving a percentage of the expenditures of each new prospect on his first visit.
Frequently strangers are admitted with no introduction at all, if
they have something to identify them as ordinary citizens. The only
persons who are prima facie ineligible to membership are those who
are known to be [unfriendly] federal revenue officers or policemen.
Every person not recognized as an officer of the law who enters the
place is given a 'membership card' and thenceforth is a full-fledged
member with all the rights and privileges thereunto appertaining.
Registration of name and address in a registry book is sometimes
required. In reality membership has no technical significance. The so-

[13] The Committee of Fourteen, New York City, *Annual Report for 1928,* p. 13.

called 'members' are persons believed to be bona-fide customers.
Patronage is stimulated by circularizing selected lists, such as the
Social Register, social clubs, and the like, and enclosing an application
for a 'membership card.' . . . Of course it is obvious that these places
are, in reality, not clubs at all. They are places which were originated
to thwart the prohibition act and are still popularly considered only
as violators of that law. It is difficult to place them under one general
classification, because they shade up into the realm of the respectable
cabaret and they shade down to the prostitution dive, with many on
the border-line.''[14] ''A night club may be anything from a place to
which refined parents may safely take their débutante daughters to
one that not even a strong man should enter unless he is provided with
a steel vest, a copper-lined digestive tract, and a sawed-off shotgun.''[15]

A classification of the ''night clubs'' of New York distinguishes
five types, ranging from the respectable to the disreputable. As the
scale descends, emphasis shifts from entertainment to liquor to sex.[16]

(1) The ''respectable'' night clubs are, as a rule, the better-known
ones. They are thoroughly genteel resorts from the point of view of
almost anyone except members of the Anti-Saloon League. They are
habitually frequented by the smart society of the metropolis, with a
fair sprinkling of visitors who hit the trail of the white lights because
they believe they are in this way seeing Life with a capital letter.
They are places where débutantes in opera cloaks derive a wicked
thrill from sipping cocktails and throwing confetti. ''Their entertainment is up to the Broadway standard, whatever that may be at a
given moment, their liquor is not immediately fatal to life, or health,
and with one or two exceptions they observe the 3 o'clock closing
hour. These are really cabarets, although the word has fallen out of
use.'' According to one investigation of 373 night clubs and speakeasies, 52 were believed to be ''respectable.'' According to another,
6 out of 157 were so classified.

(2) On the fringe of the ''respectable'' night clubs are those in
which the entertainment is of a more vulgar sort. There is more
boisterousness and drunkenness, and hostesses are on hand to stimulate
the sale of drinks to unaccompanied men. If prostitution is a problem
in connection with these clubs, it is so only incidentally. Their profits

[14] George E. Worthington, ''The Night Clubs of New York,'' *The Survey*,
Jan. 1, 1929, 61:7:413-414.
[15] R. L. Duffus, ''Now the Night Clubs Are Under Fire,'' New York *Times*,
July 15, 1928.
[16] The following is adapted from the article by R. L. Duffus, supplemented by
the annual reports of the Committee of Fourteen, New York City.

come from the sale of drinks and food, for which they charge exorbitantly.

(3) As the night club starts to go down in the scale, the first symptom is usually a liberality, to put it mildly, in the nature of its revues. Between numbers the entertainers circulate among the tables and make friends with unaccompanied men. "If these men are gentlemen, according to the standards laid down by Lorelei Lee [see *Gentlemen Prefer Blondes*], they buy drinks for the entertainers. These drinks may be no more than water colored with licorice, but they are paid for as if they were whisky, and the entertainer receives a share of the profits. But persons with a nose for scandal should not assume that all such entertainers are ladies with elastic notions of personal conduct. Many of them—perhaps most of them—could be classified under the more charitable head of gold-diggers. They flourish because gold-digging can be made pleasant for the men subjected to it."

(4) Below the type of night club just described come the clubs of the lower depths, most of which are clandestine in their mode of operation. These are known along Broadway as "sucker dives" or "gyp joints"—terms which well describe their aim in life. They have their regular patrons, but they rejoice above all in capturing an easy mark who is out to taste life in a great city. Their victims are picked up by personal solicitation by street touts or by information furnished by bell boys and taxi drivers. The best business-getter for the clandestine club is undoubtedly the taxi driver. If one accepts the invitation, as the investigators of the Committee of Fourteen did, he will find himself in a more or less gaudily decorated interior, where drinks are for sale freely and girls are on hand to see that the customers buy liberally. They are also on hand for other purposes, according to the reports of the investigators. In general, however, the hostesses in the "gyp joints" are expected to be gold-diggers rather than prostitutes. The hostess must do her best to get the customer to spend money. She is never to drink liquor which he has brought in, but only the club's own. When a man offers her a cigarette she must inquire the brand and tell him she does not smoke that kind, then order a different brand from the cigarette girl at the customer's expense. The hostess must always appear to be hungry and order sandwiches or Chinese food from time to time. She must try to get the customer to buy her flowers or souvenirs which are brought to the table. While remembering her own tips, she must not forget that the musicians and entertainers want something too, and the customer must under-

stand that he is the contributor. Before he has finished, the patron may find himself anywhere from $30 to $300 out of pocket. Once he is within the toils, every man's hand is against him. The taxi driver who has brought him to the address and whom he has probably tipped handsomely may receive as high as 40 per cent of everything he spends at the club. Sometimes more sinister eyes are upon him. The night clubs of the lower sort are much frequented by gangsters. If a customer departs with enough money on his person to make it worth while, he is likely to be followed and robbed.

(5) At the bottom of the list are the clubs or speakeasies in which the illicit sale of liquor is only a blind; that is to say, their proprietors pretend to be violating a federal law against liquor while in reality they are making it their business to violate the state laws against prostitution.

In the opinion of the Committee of Fourteen of New York City, the development of night clubs and speakeasies has greatly increased the problem of commercialized prostitution. A total of 392 night clubs and speakeasies were investigated by them more than once in 1928. Of this number, 380 were found to be definitely identified with prostitution.[17] Such clubs, they hold, present a situation as serious as that of the Raines-law hotels of evil fame a quarter of a century earlier.

The Raines law was passed in 1896 through the efforts of State Senator John Raines, the son of an up-state Methodist minister, as an amendment to the excise law, for the purpose of decreasing the sale of liquor. Unwittingly it served to accomplish the promotion of prostitution. This law provided that hotels alone could serve drinks on Sunday, the most profitable day in the week. A hotel, according to the statute, was a place with ten or more bedrooms, a kitchen, and provisions for furnishing sandwiches (one for each table was enough for an entire day, since the law did not require its consumption). Within a few years hotels of this type sprang up in all parts of New York, eventually becoming so numerous that competition was keener than it had ever been in the past. No legitimate demand existed for the rooms which the law required, and to meet the overhead the proprietors sought and found a source of profit in the rooms through prostitution.[18] It was to end this condition that the Committee of Fourteen was organized in 1905. In that year it investigated 1,200

[17] The Committee of Fourteen, New York City, *Annual Report for 1928*, pp. 9-11.

[18] H. F. Pringle, "Vice and the Volstead Act," *Harper's Monthly Magazine*, Nov., 1928, No. 942, pp. 765-766.

Manhattan hotels and declared that at least 700 were "places of evil resort."

The development of speakeasy clubs has again united the sale of liquor and the traffic in women. Immorality, according to trained investigators, has attached itself to the speakeasy and to the disreputable sort of night club because the proprietors found that they could not make a living solely by the sale of liquor. It has become so simple to buy a drink in New York that the mere lure of bootleg liquor is not sufficient to keep the night clubs going. Being already outside the law by selling liquor, the night clubs find it natural and logical to step a little farther outside in order to add to their profits. New York City has attempted to deal with the problem by the passage of a new ordinance on June 30, 1931. This law requires a license for all dance halls, cabarets and night clubs, the licensing power residing in the Police Department. Hotels, to be exempt from the limitations of this law, must have a minimum of 200 rooms. The "curfew hour" for such places of entertainment is set at 3 A.M. A license may be revoked for any violation of the law or upon the ground that disorderly, obscene, or immoral conduct is permitted on the licensed premises. To the extent that the law is enforced, it will improve conditions in the licensed places, but there still remains the problem of the clandestine establishments which are the worst offenders against public morality. Only the utmost police vigilance, backed by organized public opinion, can ferret out these places and suppress them.

The Business of Dancing.—A public dance hall is a place or space open to the public where dancing may be engaged in upon the payment of a fee. There are three main types of public dance halls in American cities: the rented hall, where the activities of the management are limited to leasing the hall for dances arranged by outside social or commercial organizations; the dance palace, and the closed hall, where the management itself provides the entertainment. It is to the latter types that the attention of reformers and the press has been especially directed.

1. Rented Halls.—As a rule, rented halls were originally the ballrooms of various social, fraternal, or union organizations, whose headquarters were equipped for recreational activities. But the majority of them are now run by commercial organizations. This change has occurred especially since the passage of the Volstead Act, which made operation under social auspices difficult, because previously a large part of the upkeep had been defrayed by the sale of beer and light wines. In New York City, only 16 rented halls out of a total of 103 are still owned by social organizations.

Several types of dances are held in the rented halls. "One-night" dances are occasionally given by one or more persons, usually young men, as business ventures. The expenses of the dance are paid by the entrepreneurs, who seek to make a profit from the attendance which is secured partly by advertising, partly by personal solicitation. In addition, social club dances are given at regular intervals, and family parties are frequently held in small rented halls. The latter are extremely popular in foreign sections. Both types of dances are generally small, and the persons attending are usually acquainted; in some halls, family groups form the majority. These dances, by and large, have a wholesome social atmosphere. On the other hand, adequate supervision is almost impossible in many cities owing to the small number of supervisors available. Some commissioners of recreation report that the rented halls give the most trouble, especially in the foreign districts, where drinking and fighting are often uncontrolled.[19]

2. Closed Halls.—The term "closed hall" originated in the Far West, where it was used to designate the type of dance hall, intimately associated with vice, that flourished on the old "Barbary Coast" of San Francisco. The closed hall caters only to male patronage, for the most part to men who are strangers in the city or who are not welcomed elsewhere because of their dress, nationality, or color. It is peculiar to areas of homeless men, particularly those of foreign birth. In Chicago, one closed hall is frequented altogether by Greeks, and another by Filipinos and Chinese.[20] Closed halls are usually converted stores on second or third floors of office buildings and require a relatively small investment.

In the closed hall the commercialization of the dance has been carried to the extreme. Girls are hired on a commission basis to dance with men patrons, and couples are usually not admitted. In New York, the admission charge includes six or eight dances. Thereafter, each dance must be paid for at the rate of ten cents or, in some instances, two for a quarter. Dances are short, averaging from 40 to 60 seconds in length. Both the patrons and the young women dance partners are exploited. Patrons must spend several dollars for any reasonable number of dances. "The girls are paid four cents a dance, or five if they are on duty on both Saturday and Sunday nights. In order

[19] Ella Gardner, *Public Dance Halls*, Children's Bureau Publication No. 189, 1929, p. 33.

[20] Harvey W. Zorbaugh, *The Gold Coast and the Slum*, 1929, p. 121.

9 See Cressey. The Taxi Dance Hall

to make a fair living, say $20.00 per week, a girl must dance four hundred dances a week or about seventy dances an evening. These are crowded into four hours or one dance every three minutes. It is strenuous physical work and the girls admit that the wear of the work is considerable. A large proportion of the girls dance only two or three evenings per week and have other positions during the day."[21] One such dancing partner, who entered the work because she liked to dance, relates:[22]

> I have been doing this now for a couple of years. But dancing is no longer a pleasure to me. It is hard work. Sometimes when I get through I am so exhausted that I can scarcely drag one foot above the other. If I do not dance until the hall closes the manager complains and says he will have to supplant me with a girl with a little more pep. And if I don't dance most of the night, I do not make enough money to gratify my tastes and pay my expenses. I have found good and bad proprietors of dance halls. Some of them have a real interest in the girls and will not stand for their being insulted. There are others, however, who expect a girl to swallow all sorts of insults.

Investigations disclose that many of the men and boys attending the closed halls do not dance but seem to be there merely to pick up acquaintance with a girl, and that some of the dancing partners are occasional or professional prostitutes. The closed hall is generally considered objectionable, although some officials hold that in ports and other cities with a large floating population the closed hall has its place if closely supervised, such supervision to include rigid exclusion of young girls as paid dancing partners.

A situation comparable to the employment of girl dancing partners is the custom, found in another type of dance hall, of providing young men, popularly known as "gigolos," to dance with unattended women. These male dancing partners have long been familiar figures at Paris dancing clubs and night resorts, and recently they have appeared in some American cities. Gigolos exist because husbands and friends are usually engaged in business, and dancing partners are therefore scarce. Many women are no longer young, but their feet are still youthful and to them dancing is a passion. In the gigolos they find attractive young men who are willing partners and who dance divinely. Some women have learned, however, that such acquaintances

[21] Leroy E. Bowman and Maria Ward Lambin, "Evidences of Social Relations as Seen in Types of New York City Dance Halls," *Social Forces*, Jan., 1925, 3:2:287.
[22] New York *Times*, Oct. 2, 1928.

may prove embarrassing and expensive. The Paris police recently began a drive on gigolos who have been preying on women, stealing from them and blackmailing fashionable ladies who have been indiscreet.[23]

3. *Dance Palaces.*—In contrast to the closed halls, the dance palaces or academies solicit general patronage. They are usually large places, with handsome appointments, attended by huge crowds. Some of them can accommodate several thousand patrons at a time. The music is good. Dances vary in length from three to six minutes, and intermissions are about as long. The admission price usually entitles a patron to from three to six dances; thereafter an extra charge of five cents per dance is made. Much of the space is set aside for lounging and not more than half of the patrons dance at any one time. For the most part the patrons are young and unacquainted. The majority find their partners after they arrive, and this seems to be one of the chief attractions of the halls. It is becoming increasingly the practice for the management to employ so-called "hostesses" or "instructresses" who act as dancing partners for male patrons.

Dance palaces are located as a rule in the central, down-town sections where neighborhood acquaintance, with the restraining influence which it exerts, is almost wholly lacking. Nevertheless, the managers of these halls appreciate the importance from a business standpoint of preventing trouble. Many of them have found that offending the community standards of respectability does not pay, and hence they regard the reputation of the hall as a valuable business asset. In most cities the managers of the big ballrooms are coöperative, for business reasons, in attempts to improve public dancing standards.[24] The chief problems presented are the control of the type of dancing and the exclusion of young persons.

Dance-Hall Regulation.—Until recent years the public dance hall was unregulated and was regarded by many persons as being impossible of successful regulation. In small towns as well as in large industrial centers it had a bad reputation. The stories of crime and debauchery which newspapers reported from time to time as having their origin in dance halls or academies revealed the fact that many of them were connected with saloons and so-called hotels which encouraged immorality on the part of the dance-hall patrons and tolerated the presence of criminals. Police attended these dances not as inspectors or supervisors but in order to be at hand to interfere in

[23] New York *Times*, Feb. 5, 1928; Oct. 9, 1928; Associated Press dispatch under Chicago date-line, Aug. 3, 1931.

[24] Ella Gardner, *Public Dance Halls*, Children's Bureau Publication No. 189, 1929, pp. 33-34.

case of brawls or too flagrant disorder of any kind. "With the development of the community recreation movement studies were made of commercialized recreation, and with the facts as to the conditions in the dance halls made public, attempts were made at public control or regulation. The investigations revealed that the public dance halls offered almost the only opportunity for this form of social recreation to many farm boys and girls who came to the towns for their amusements, to large numbers of young people who were working in industrial centers away from their parents and childhood friends, and to many city boys and girls whose parents through poverty or ignorance made no provision for the social needs of their children. The movement for the regulation of commercialized recreation and the provision of community dance halls and other forms of recreation for young people developed almost simultaneously as a result. The investigations did not reveal uniformly bad conditions in the public dance halls, and this fact furnished the best argument for successful regulation."[25]

Thirty-one states in 1928 had laws specifically regulating the operation of public dance halls. Some of these laws affect all public dances and dance halls within the state or all not regulated by city ordinances, whereas others apply only to dances held outside the limits of municipal corporations. Practically every state has authorized its cities and towns to prohibit or to regulate and license public amusements, including public dances; and a number make the license or permit compulsory, designating in the law the officer who shall have the power to issue it. In addition to the specific state laws, some 240 cities of 15,000 or more population each reported to the United States Children's Bureau in 1928 that they had ordinances regulating public dance halls. Even in cities in which no dance-hall regulations have been adopted, the general powers of the police would include supervision at public dance places. There has been a steady increase in dance-hall legislation since 1910; about 75 per cent of the more complete ordinances have been enacted since 1918. "This increase may be attributed to the fuller recognition of the social factors involved in this type of amusement and the consequent need for regulation and supervision, or, as suggested by some city officers, it may be the direct result of conditions arising out of the demand for excitement and the consequent increase in the number of dance halls following the war years."[26]

[25] *Ibid.*, p. 1.
[26] *Ibid.*, p. 9.

The laws regulating public dance halls relate to the following sub-jects: licensing, as a prerequisite to which there must be an investiga-tion to determine the suitability of the place in which the dance is to be held, and the taking of affidavits as to the character of the appli-cants; minimum age of participants; hours of closing; Sunday pro-hibitions; lighting of premises; conduct of dancers; types of dances; and supervision by police officers or specially qualified matrons. It is rapidly becoming the practice to delegate the official supervision of dance halls, as well as other places of public recreation, to police-women, a practice which has the advantage of centralized control and more regular enforcement.[27]

Where there is a law there is a way to get around it, and in a few cities dance-hall operators have taken advantage of the wording of the ordinance to defeat its purpose. If only the hour when dancing must stop is set, dances are stopped at that time for ten or fifteen minutes—and then continued. If the ordinance, however, prohibits dancing and keeping dance halls open after a certain hour, evasion seems impossible. Another method of evading the dance regulations is illustrated by a large dance pavilion in an amusement park within the limits of a certain city. The management obtained a state charter for a club and ran the dance hall as a "boating club," although there was no water anywhere near it. Membership dues were the ad-mission price to the dancing. Chartered as a club, the hall was not regulated by the city ordinance, and the state law that required all public amusement places to be closed on Sunday did not apply to it.[28]

A source of disorder in public dance halls results from the practice of patrons leaving the hall and anterooms at frequent intervals throughout the evening, during which absences drinking and other offenses are often committed. To control this practice, forty cities have ordinances that prohibit the issuance of pass-out checks and re-quire that the regular admission fee be demanded for each entrance to the dance hall. The chief problems of present-day dance-hall super-vision are: supervision of music, dancing, and general conduct in the halls; provision for and protection of minors; and control of the after-the-dance rendezvous. Much has been accomplished under good supervision in improving the conduct of dances and in keeping out those who attend for purposes of soliciting prostitution. The most troublesome problem is that presented by the after-the-dance rendez-

[27] Helen D. Pigeon, "Policewomen and Public Recreation," *The American City*, Oct., 1927, XXXVII, 448-450.
[28] Ella Gardner, *Public Dance Halls*, Children's Bureau Publication No. 189, 1929, pp. 16, 30.

vous. It is relatively easy to regulate decorum in the dance hall, but it is almost impossible to control the conduct of the patrons after they leave.

Roadhouses.—The problem of dance-hall regulation has been greatly enhanced by the development of out-of-town dance halls and roadhouses, which, following the advent of good roads and the almost universal use of the automobile, have sprung up all over the country-side. As recreational centers and even as restaurants, roadhouses are in a class apart, for, even though they may be licensed by the village or county where located, they draw their patronage from outside the licensing area and are more or less a law unto themselves because of their isolation. They are most difficult to investigate and supervise; they openly offer what has been legislated against and condemned in the majority of the cities. In some instances the city dance halls serve merely as a recruiting place for the roadhouses, young girls going to them with the idea of meeting men who will take them to the country places. The local authorities are either bullied into issuing licenses and shut their eyes to conditions, or they are tempted by the large license fees. Federal, state, and county law-enforcing officials do not have the personnel even if they have the desire adequately to regulate and supervise these places.

The Juvenile Protective Association of Chicago in coöperation with the American Social Hygiene Association recently investigated the roadhouses in Cook County. The survey revealed that some of the roadhouses were legitimately conducted, but the majority were nothing more than speakeasies which served in some instances as gathering places and even regular hang-outs for a lawless and criminal element. The sale of apparent intoxicants and the indecent dancing constituted only a portion of the serious indictment to be drawn against the majority of Cook County roadhouses.[29]

A few states, of which Wisconsin may serve as an example, have undertaken to regulate roadhouses. The Wisconsin Legislature of 1923 passed an act enabling county boards of supervisors to enact ordinances for the licensing and regulation of dance halls and other places of amusement, and to appoint inspectors with the powers of deputy sheriffs. The ordinances that have been passed provide for annual licenses of public dance halls, some of them requiring also permits for each public dance. The regulations as to the conduct of dances include requirements that they be closed by a certain hour, usually

[29] Jessie F. Binford, ''Cook County (Illinois) Roadhouses,'' *Journal of Social Hygiene*, May, 1930, 16:5:257-264.

1 A.M.; that minors under 16 years of age shall be excluded unless accompanied by parents or guardians; that dance halls be well lighted; that the use or possession of intoxicating liquor by persons attending dances be forbidden; that intoxicated persons, idlers, and loiterers shall be excluded; in a few counties that dancers shall not be allowed to leave the hall except during regular intermissions or by permission of the inspector; that no disorderly or vulgar conduct shall be permitted; that dance halls shall be kept in a healthful and sanitary condition; and sundry other provisions. The annual licenses of dance halls may be revoked by the board of supervisors for violation of the rules. Conditions are reported to have been improved, especially as to closing hours and conduct on the dance floors, yet the ordinances are still inadequately enforced.[30]

Regulation of dance halls is necessary, but community interest in the problem should not stop there. It is just as necessary, and more constructive, to develop counter-attractions and to increase the opportunities for wholesome recreation under private and municipal management. Many private agencies, such as settlements and the Christian Associations, have undertaken to provide substitutes for the commercial halls, and a number of cities have established municipal dance halls in public parks and in community centers where dancing may be enjoyed at less cost and under more wholesome conditions.

Amusement Parks.—A typically American development is the amusement park, often located beyond the city limits and consequently outside the control of the municipal police. Games of chance, somewhat lurid exhibitions and attractions made exhilarating by the suggestion of danger, and various contrivances for giving people psychological shocks, are the predominant features of many of these parks. The appeal to the senses is direct, the shock to the nervous system is great. Such places do not get the people away from the artificial life of the city or from the influence of mercenary motives. There is scarcely anything in city life more artificial than this type of park. People even pay to get artificial bumps.[31]

That commercial amusement parks can offer entertainment of high standard and be successful financially is proved by the experience of a number of them, of which Euclid Beach Park in Cleveland is a

[30] Francis H. Hiller, "The Working of County Dance Hall Ordinances in Wisconsin," *Journal of Social Hygiene*, Jan., 1927, 13:1:1-11.

[31] Bruce Bliven, "Coney Island for Battered Souls," *The New Republic*, Nov. 23, 1921, 28:364:372-374. Some vivid descriptions of Coney Island as O. Henry knew it may be found in his short stories, *e.g.*, *Brickdust Row, A Lickpenny Lover*, and *The Greater Coney*.

noteworthy example. This park is under single management, no concessions being allowed. It is clean morally and physically. Attractions which are of the nature of an exhibition are omitted, with the exception of a motion-picture show. Beyond the roller coasters and a few other similar attractions, which are intended chiefly for children, every amusement gives patrons the opportunity to amuse themselves. The most important of these are the dance hall (where a high standard of decorum has been rigidly maintained), the athletic field, the roller rink, and the benches and tables for family parties. The history of this park has clearly demonstrated that active participation in their own recreation is actually sought by large numbers of people.[32]

Before the use of automobiles became so general, amusement parks were frequently conducted by traction companies. When trolley patronage declined, most of these parks were closed. Shore properties in many states have survived, however, under municipal control. Playland, at Rye on Long Island Sound, operated by the Westchester County Park Commission, is a notable example of success in this line.[33]

Some psychologists maintain that the stimulating and exhilarating type of amusement park fills a real need in the lives of industrial workers. Modern industry so influences its workers that they require a more violent form of recreation than do those whose work is not so arduous. It takes something more stimulating than most public parks furnish to satisfy the recreational needs of bodies and brains worn with long hours of hard labor. "The shows which are the most popular are those that give the sharpest excitement, the most immediate nervous stimulation. And it is interesting to see that since industry has forced the habit of association on a larger and larger scale, people are unable to get satisfaction for the play impulse except in a crowd. The nervous organism comes to be pitched to such a high key that none of its tendencies manifest themselves without the stimulus of a large group present and indulging in the same satisfactions. It is a grave question, in this situation, how much further strain we can impose on our physical equipment without a break. If the necessary reaction from modern industry is the greater elaboration of our amusement park technique of thrills and horrors, modern industry must plead guilty to a charge of fundamental importance. The play of the husking bee, charades, dancing at home among friends, outdoor

[32] Raymond Moley, *Commercial Recreation*, 1920, pp. 112-123.
[33] Harry C. Stone, "Commercial Recreation," *Social Work Year Book*, 1929, p. 92.

picnics, and the other homely enjoyments is not to be sighed for simply because it is attached to a simple manner of life. Its loss is to be lamented because apparently it was the more normal psychological form of play in a generation when all the claims of life on the nervous system were less wearing and exacting than is the case today."[34]

Pool and Billiard Rooms.—From a recreational standpoint, pool and billiards are among the most attractive indoor games ever devised. They induce the participants to develop skill and to enter actively into their own amusement. The game of billiards, for example, requires not only a high degree of muscular control but invites the use of considerable mental calculation. Played well, it exercises mental and physical functions to a remarkable degree. The well-known sports authority, Grantland Rice, says of billiards: "A game that builds sportsmanship, that provides wholesome relaxation, recreation and exercise—when played under proper conditions." In both pool and billiards there is the added zest of some element of chance, which, however, is reduced to a minimum by long experience and added skill. When the habit of playing pool or billiards is acquired early in life, it may furnish a life-long spare-time activity. However, the surroundings of the commercial billiard rooms have been such that young boys are often prohibited from learning, because their parents fear that bad habits may be developed as a consequence of visiting such places. Investigations have given grounds for this fear, for many billiard rooms are of a questionable character, patronized by young men of irregular habits. In some instances they are the favorite loafing places for criminal and vicious characters.[35]

The chief problem of the billiard room is the loafer. He is a hindrance to the proprietor who seeks legitimate profit and is the main factor in making the billiard room a "trouble spot" for the police. Frequently there are more persons not playing than playing. One way of eliminating the loafing problem is to reduce the number of onlookers to a minimum, a process which may be assisted by removing all chairs and benches from the rooms except those which are used by the players. But if the whole problem of recreation is kept in mind, the solution is not as easy as this. Viewed objectively and with perspective, loafing appears as a natural phenomenon and to have, as it were, its legitimate as well as its illegitimate aspects. The

[34] Ordway Tead, *Instincts in Industry; a study of working-class psychology,* 1918, pp. 173-174.
[35] John J. Phelan, *Pool, Billiards and Bowling Alleys as a Phase of Commercialized Amusements in Toledo, Ohio,* 1919. Raymond Moley, *Commercial Recreation,* 1920, pp. 54 ff.

community loafing place has been a part of every civilization and seems to satisfy a human need. In Colonial days and long afterwards the taverns were the chief gathering places of Americans and the chief news exchanges. The general store was the forum of the country-side. The drug store, the post office, the barber shop, the blacksmith shop, the livery stable have been important centers of community life, gratifying the desire for companionship and gossip and serving as forums where the affairs of the world could be settled.[36] What institution in the city is to fill this need, now that the old centers, along with the saloon, have largely disappeared, and loafing on the street corner has been made a police offense? The billiard room seems to be one answer. It has, in addition to the qualifications of warmth, light, and companionship which are met by these other and earlier loafing places, the interest which attaches to watching a game involving skill and chance. In fact, a game of billiards or pool is well worth watching, and under proper conditions is a wholesome method of spending spare time. Pool and billiards as a trade depend upon the very kind of interest that is developed by watching the game played. It would, therefore, be very poor business for the proprietor to eliminate all except those who are playing. There is also the fact that a young man will play a part of an evening and watch others the rest of the time. To play pool or billiards all evening is too expensive for boys and men who are working for ordinary wages. The billiard room, in short, may well serve as a "legitimate" loafing place—a rendezvous for friends and a source of human companionship. This cannot be accomplished, however, without regulation, especially that which will exclude undesirable characters. Probably the problem can be met in some measure by reducing the number of onlookers as much as possible through wise action of the proprietor himself and some assistance by public authorities.[37]

From the standpoint of police regulation, gambling in billiard rooms is more difficult to regulate than loafing. The Cleveland Recreation Survey discovered that gambling was common in at least two-thirds of the pool and billiard rooms of that city. The profits accruing to the proprietor from gambling are secured through an arrangement whereby a certain fixed percentage of every bet goes to the "house." In this way very large profits are made by some of the more unscrupulous managers. "To those who are familiar with the psychology

[36] L. H. Robbins, "Yet Another of Our Old Forums Passes: The Drug Store Now Joins the Centres Whence Debate Has Fled," *The New York Times Magazine*, Aug. 2, 1931, pp. 14, 22.

[37] Raymond Moley, *Commercial Recreation*, 1920, pp. 61-63.

of gambling and the difficulty attending the keeping it out of all wholesome games, the problem of regulation is not as easy as it seems to some. There are those who would decry all attempts at regulation and who assert that the gambling instinct is developed by certain inherent factors in our competitive economic system. To these all attempts at regulation are doomed to fail. There are others who believe that added policing with good, courageous administration of the law and a firm fastening down of eighteenth century systems of morality would produce a 'clean' town. Those who are struggling with an actual situation and are attempting to adjust conditions to suit this day and generation, must, with an eye to practical results, seek an adjustment somewhere between these two extremes. Any business in which gambling is largely involved loses in prestige and influence. Because of this fact, pool and billiards have suffered very greatly in popular esteem because of the certainty with which gambling has been attached to them. In order to save these games as means of wholesome recreation for large numbers of people, there must be more effective public regulation. . . . However, no amount of inspection could adequately prevent gambling, when a public policy permits a business to be carried on which can not exist without illegitimate profits. The chief fault is in the great number of rooms and in the economic conditions upon which they depend.''[38]

The economics of the billiard-room situation, as suggested in the above quotation, is a factor of the greatest practical importance in any attempt at regulation. No billiard room with less than five or six tables can furnish a living income to its proprietor, if he restricts himself to purely legitimate profits. The great proportion of billiard rooms are as small as this, and most of them are not conducted as a regular business but are rather an adjunct to another business, such as a cigar store or barber shop, or they serve as a means of supplementing the income of persons whose primary interests are elsewhere. This situation is an extremely bad thing for the trade. It means that men who are making the management of billiard rooms their main interest in life and who perhaps have a considerable investment involved, are compelled to lower their standards in order to compete with places which do not and cannot earn more than a small profit in a legitimate way. ''When we consider that most of these small rooms are nevertheless yielding high illegitimate profits, it will be seen that the pressure upon the regular professional billiard room proprietor to lower his

[38] *Ibid.*, pp. 67-68.

standards is almost irresistible. From the standpoint of public policy, we must either make gambling legitimate in all places or protect the proprietor who is attempting to provide a wholesome place where clean sport may be purchased.''[39]

In view of these facts, the Cleveland Recreation Survey recommended a drastic reduction in the number of billiard rooms as the first step in any effective movement for improved public regulation. The number of billiard rooms, it urged, should be definitely limited to 1 for each 5,000 people. The license fee should be raised to a figure high enough to make the keeping of a three-table room practically impossible. This could be done by fixing a very large fee for the first table, with a small additional charge for all tables over one. With a limited number of licenses, great care should be exercised in granting them to applicants. Among the advantages to be gained by concentrating the playing of pool and billiards in fewer places are these: public authorities would find the process of inspection greatly facilitated; the proprietors of these large rooms, which represent a considerable investment, would be much more careful not to endanger their license by permitting unlawful acts on the premises; the trade association of billiard-room proprietors, which is a potent factor in improving the standards of the game, would find its authority extended and its professional spirit strengthened.

Trade control is an important device and should be encouraged through a wise public policy. In many cities a noticeable effort is being made by the owners of billiard rooms to raise standards and leave the term ''pool room'' for race-track use; the National Billiard Association of America is working toward the same end. All establishments affiliated with the N.B.A. pledge themselves to uphold the policies of the Association, which are directed toward maintaining proper conditions in billiard rooms throughout the country and improving the game by providing amateur and professional tournaments. It urges the public to play billiards in rooms that have the N.B.A. franchise.

To supplement the policy of public regulation and trade control, all public and private agencies for furnishing recreation should recognize the value of pool and billiards as a spare-time occupation. Community centers, settlements, churches, and similar agencies are peculiarly fitted to provide such opportunities for youths, especially those below the legal age limit for commercial establishments. These provisions could be made upon a strictly self-supporting basis. A

[39] *Ibid.*, p. 58.

game with the recreational virtue possessed by billiards should be placed within the easy reach of all.

Motion Pictures.—No other form of commercialized recreation has been so severely criticized as motion pictures, the history of which as a form of art and amusement we have already traced. Welfare organizations, religious bodies, and educators express much concern about them, especially because of their possible effect on children. Although film stories and their treatment are primarily for adult audiences, most of the discussions concerning them are with the child audience in mind. This makes at once for widely divergent views. While friends of the cinema point out the immense educational and artistic value of many films, the stimulation of ambition and widening of horizons by the revelation of other and better modes of life, and the richer compensations of vicarious experience, its opponents hurl the charges of overemphasis of false values, exaggeration and caricature of life, destruction of taste and morality, incitement to crime, and downright and utter banality.[40] Some investigators maintain that at least a fifth of the motion-picture plays tend to have some demoralizing effect on those who see them.[41] If this is true, then, in view of the huge attendance at movies, coupled with the persuasiveness of the screen, the total effect must be enormous.

The effect of the movies on conduct is a subject on which there is as yet no body of scientific knowledge. It may be that the relation is impossible to determine. It is extraordinarily subtle and complex, and there is the further complicating factor of wide individual differences; people who visit the movies are already conditioned, and a given photoplay will convey different impressions and suggestions to different individuals. Certainly there is no agreement as to the relation of the movie to specific conduct. In the matter of incitement to delinquency and crime, for example, some detectives, judges, and others place much blame on the movies; they see a connection between the number of criminal cases and the type of motion picture exhibited. On the other hand, two of the leading authorities in the field of juvenile delinquency, on the basis of their study of 4,000 juvenile delinquents in Chicago and Boston, state: "Starting with ideas somewhat to the contrary, we have been surprised to find that moving picture shows seem to have very little effect in the production of delinquent

[40] Leonard D. White, in Foreword to *Children and Movies* by Alice Miller Mitchell, 1929, p. xii. Lee F. Hanmer, "Motion Pictures," *Social Work Year Book, 1929*, p. 280.

[41] Donald R. Young, *Motion Pictures*, 1922, p. 64.

tendencies; we could discover no reason to attribute more than 1% of the cases to this cause."[42]

The movie producers maintain that most crime pictures show the criminal under arrest and being punished, being killed by his own gang, or making such restitution as to entitle him to return to a place in society on a newer and better basis. In the course of an hour and a half of the play, crime is committed and punishment is meted out; cause is followed by effect and the lesson is plain enough. In fact, justice follows more swiftly in the photoplay than in actual life, where the delay in criminal justice is notorious.[43] But, as a noted psychologist, the late Professor Münsterberg, long ago pointed out, it is not enough to have the villain punished in the last few pictures of the reel. The true moral influence must come from the positive spirit of the play itself. "If scenes of vice or crime are shown with all their lure and glamour the moral devastation of such a suggestive show is not undone by the appended social reaction. The misguided boys or girls feel sure that they would be successful enough not to be trapped. The mind through a mechanism which has been understood better and better by the psychologists in recent years suppresses the ideas which are contrary to the secret wishes and makes those ideas flourish by which those 'subconscious' impulses are fulfilled. . . . Those may have been exceptional cases only when grave crimes have been traced directly back to the impulses from unwholesome photoplays, but no psychologist can determine exactly how much the general spirit of righteousness, of honesty, of sexual cleanliness and modesty, may be weakened by the unbridled influence of plays of low moral standard. All countries seem to have been awakened to this social danger."[44]

Children and the Movies.—An important factor in the problem, and one denied by no one, is that motion pictures have been made for adults only, yet they are viewed by millions of children. "The motion picture is the only art that attempts to appeal to all ages by the same standard of intelligence. Books, plays, pictures, and even music are created especially for children. The movie is administered to juveniles in adult doses. . . . So far motion pictures for juveniles are not being produced. Of course there are some films that are quite appropriate for children, but in the sense that books are being written

[42] William Healy and Augusta F. Bronner, *Delinquents and Criminals*, 1926, p. 181.

[43] *The Motion Picture Monthly*, Jan., 1931, 7:1:2-3.

[44] Hugo Münsterberg, *The Photoplay*, 1916, pp. 222, 227.

and published primarily for the juvenile public movies are not."[45] An inevitable result is that children are constantly being thrown into contact with types of behavior which they do not ordinarily experience from reading or conversation outside. This fact may be important in the growing sophistication of children and youth today. It is claimed that "in place of simple living, wholesome play, well chosen stories, reasonable hours of going to bed, the movies give the children sophistication, emotional stimulation, false ideals of living, nervous excitement and late hours, together with initiation into adult indulgences of crime and passion."[46] In the investigation conducted by the Chicago Motion Picture Commission the consensus of opinion was that the children became precocious about sex matters, that there was a general demoralizing effect on modesty and purity, that a disregard of marriage ties was fostered, and that the authority of teachers and parents was materially lessened. "There are three hundred and ten public schools in Chicago and three hundred and fifty theatres. . . . Is the school or the movie going to be the more potent educational influence on the lives of Chicago children?"[47]

Perhaps the most extensive study of children and movies is that made by Mrs. Mitchell. Although it gives no evidence on which to base a psychological analysis of conduct as affected by frequency of attendance or by the kinds of pictures seen, it is excellent in revealing the surface facts of the time and the intensity of the stimuli.[48] The material for this study was furnished by 10,052 Chicago children representing three groups: average public-school children, juvenile delinquents, and a specific group of children who have a certain degree of organized leadership in their lives, as the Boy Scouts and the Girl Scouts. Data were gathered for the most part from children by means of written quizzes which were given in the classroom as regular school routine and under the supervision of the teacher. Further information was obtained through personal interviews in selected cases. Only 1.7 per cent of the children studied reported that they did not go to the movies at all. The majority of these exceptional cases gave religious restrictions as the reason. Of the total number of children, 90.6 per cent attend the movies at regular intervals, the attendance varying from once a month to seven times a week. The

[45] Alice Miller Mitchell, *Children and Movies*, 1929, pp. 36-37.
[46] F. Zeta Youmans, "Opportunity Night," *The Survey*, Sept. 1, 1927, 58:11:488.
[47] *Ibid.*, p. 485.
[48] Alice Miller Mitchell, *Children and Movies*, 1929. *Cf.* review by Kimball Young, in *American Journal of Sociology*, Sept., 1930, 3:7:307-308.

majority of the children go to the movies on an average of once or twice a week. "Left to themselves the children apparently turn to the movies for entertainment. With some guidance toward other outlets such as is offered by the Boy Scouts and similar organizations, interests are placed elsewhere and attendance at the movies is lowered."[49] Delinquent boys attend the movies more frequently than do Boy Scouts. The latter go to the movies less frequently but more regularly than do other children. The investigation reveals that children attend movies more frequently at night than in the afternoon. The majority of children are not accompanied by their parents or older relatives, but attend with companions of their own age. As to the kind of picture preferred, boys like best the western, adventure, comedy, and mystery types, whereas romance, comedy, and western are the most popular with the girls.

Among the suggestions for meeting the problem of children and the movies is that of limiting them to special matinées. One of the main difficulties in the way of special children's shows is the continuous-performance principle. Most cinemas begin showing about midday, and give a non-stop succession of films until about eleven at night. Another difficulty is that special children's performances would not usually pay except at certain theatres, or on Saturday afternoons and during holiday periods. Moreover, if a performance or a picture is labeled "for children," the young folk usually avoid it—which is an evidence of good taste on their part, in the light of the type of pictures commonly selected. The main reason for the failure of the children's matinée is that it does not accomplish the purpose for which it is planned, namely, to give children children's pictures. Such pictures are not yet being made, though *Tom Sawyer, Huckleberry Finn, Skippy,* and *Daddy Long Legs* are steps in that direction. A more successful plan than the production of special pictures for children is the present tendency toward the selection of family programs in which the child finds a place. The pictures are selected from lists prepared by private organizations engaged in previewing films and grading them according to family entertainment standards.

Another method of dealing with the problem is through legislation which regulates or prohibits the attendance of minors at motion-picture performances. In the United States a few cities prohibit the attendance of children under certain ages at moving-picture shows during school hours and unless accompanied by adults at other times. In other countries such regulations are much more common, and are

[49] Alice Miller Mitchell, *Children and Movies,* 1929, p. 25.

part of a general censorship plan, as when children under a certain age are not permitted in theatres unless the films have been accepted by censors.[50] The regulations vary considerably. The story is told of a Dutch pedagogue who took his sixteen-year-old son on a northern-European tour. In Oslo, the father, having some business appointment, told the boy to visit a theatre where a French dramatic film was showing. The son asked: ''Who'll take me?''

''Nobody,'' said the pedagogue. ''It's only at home and in Germany that you have to be eighteen to go alone. Here the rule is sixteen.''

''But this is the film they wouldn't let even you take me to in Brussels.''

''That was because of a Belgian ruling.''

''Well, why is it wrong for me to go alone to any film in Holland, when it isn't wrong for me to go alone in Norway to a film that it's wrong for me to go to, even with you, in Belgium?''

The father's explanation is unrecorded. The anecdote indicates, however, how different are the government cinema-standards—and how irreconcilable.[51]

A remedy which stands out more prominently than the others is the responsibility of the parent. Opponents of censorship maintain that the ultimate responsibility rests with the parents to see that their children do not attend exhibitions of pictures which are not suitable for juvenile minds, and at the same time to educate them in morals and taste so that they reject or become immune to the gross matter. The parent should know before his child leaves home for the picture show what kind of pictures that child is going to see. ''He should know either because he himself has seen the picture, because it has been recommended by some one in whom he has confidence, or because it is listed as proper for the juvenile mind in the bulletin of a reputable club or society organized for the purpose of reviewing and passing judgment on pictures. It ought not to be necessary for the state to assume the duties of a parent.—No parent allows his child to read books or go to plays indiscriminately. Why should he change this policy with reference to motion pictures?''[52] On the other hand, although the parent will admit his duty to censor his child's contacts with adult matter and guide his taste to right

[50] *Film Daily Year Book*, 1930, pp. 1007 ff. William M. Seabury, *Motion Picture Problems*, 1929, pp. 291-306.

[51] Reginald W. Kaufman, ''The International Child Versus the International Censor,'' *The Motion Picture Monthly*, Feb., 1931, 7:2:2.

[52] Report of the Municipal Committee of the Cleveland, Ohio, Chamber of Commerce, ''Shall the Movies be Censored?'' May 24, 1922.

standards, he will confess that it is a difficult task when the movies and similar influences are practically all-pervasive, and when training in standards is complicated by the constant chances to have these standards lowered by the easily accessible cheap and vulgar. The very things he is educating against are also doing some of the educating. It is natural for him to desire some control over the child's environment so that his task will be made easier. Why not a censorship? The same argument can be used for the general public. "How are you going to teach average people selective standards of taste and morals when their standards are constantly being formed by the very things they are supposed to have standards about? The dilemma is obvious."[53]

Censorship by Law.—Those interested in public welfare are particularly concerned in obtaining pictures that are better in a moral, educational, cultural, and ethical sense. By what means can this desirable result be achieved? There are two schools of thought on this subject. One encourages the production of films of higher dramatic, artistic, and moral values; the other seeks to prevent the showing of those that fall below certain prescribed standards. The first is constructive coöperation, which will be discussed later. The second is censorship, to which attention is now turned.

Motion-picture censorship prevails all over the world—in Canada, Australia, India, Japan, North and South Africa, most countries of Europe and South America. In the United States it is the exception rather than the rule, and it is the only example of an admitted previous censorship in "the land of the free." "The American," comment Ernst and Seagle,[54] "who has revolted against every other licensing of the arts has tolerated this. The Supreme Court of the United States in 1915 upheld the regulation, against the invocation of the First Amendment, holding that the moving picture was not essentially a medium for the communication of ideas, and not so much an art as an industry. It may well have been influenced by the general spirit of repression and censorship which prevailed in wartime. It did not even take the precaution to exempt news or educational films, and the printed matter in others." These authors believe that the youthfulness of the movies and the assumed low character of the mass of movie patrons account for the censorship.

Censorship laws in the United States are either municipal, state, or federal. The first direct censorship legislation addressed to the

[53] Leon Whipple, "Plans and Censors," *The Survey*, Aug. 1, 1931, 66:9:447.
[54] Morris L. Ernst and William Seagle, *To the Pure*, 1928, p. 28.

motion picture occurred in Chicago in 1907, when a city ordinance was passed, entrusting the issuance of picture permits to the chief of police. Many cities followed the example of Chicago in enacting censorship ordinances.[55] There are just two federal laws touching the subject. First, immoral pictures are classed for purposes of federal regulation with immoral books, pictures, and other indecent matter, and a penalty is imposed for bringing them into the country or for transporting them from one state to another. The only statute definition of what constitutes an immoral film is the phrase ''obscene, lewd, or lascivious, or any filthy . . . motion picture,'' which has been considered by the courts to be an adequate definition for legal purposes. This federal legislation is little more than an obsolete blue law. There is little probability that in its present form it will ever be anything but a dead letter law. The terms used in it are subject to various interpretations; specific scenes and subjects may or may not be in violation of them, depending on who is doing the deciding.[56] The other federal statute designed to protect the public morals from possible undesirable motion-picture films is the Sims law, enacted by Congress in 1912, which makes interstate traffic in fight films unlawful. In view of the facts that it is perfectly legal to hold pugilistic contests in many states, entirely legal to report their full details in the newspapers and relate them over the radio, wholly legal to print any number of ''still pictures'' of the fight, but a crime to send a complete film of their action across a state line, the law appears to be illogical and absurd. It has been easy to violate, and once the pictures are across the state line and in the hands of exhibitors, their showing is entirely legal, so far as the federal law is concerned.

Censorship laws have thus far been passed by seven American states, the dates of enactment being as follows: Pennsylvania, 1911; Ohio and Kansas, 1913; Maryland, 1916; New York and Florida, 1921; and Virginia, 1922. The Florida situation is peculiar in that the law establishes no censorship board of its own, but prohibits the exhibition of any film not passed by the National Board of Review, a private organization, or by the Motion Picture Commission of the State of New York. Three of the states—Kansas, Pennsylvania, and New York—have since repealed that part of the law affecting news reels and educational subjects. These state censorship laws usually provide that no new pictures may be exhibited until they have been reviewed and approved. They characterize as objectionable a film that is ob-

[55] Terry Ramsaye, *A Million and One Nights*, 1926, p. 476.
[56] Donald R. Young, *Motion Pictures*, 1922, pp. 55, 57.

scene, indecent, immoral, inhuman, sacrilegious, or is of such a character that its exhibition would tend to corrupt morals or incite to crime. The examiners may take one of three actions: approve without change, approve subject to specific eliminations, or condemn *in toto*. It should be noted that in every city and state in the Union, irrespective of whether a censorship act is in force, the police officials have full power to regulate performances that may be injurious to public welfare. The only thing new about the censorship act is that it provides a separate body of officials to deal with a specific problem of conduct, instead of leaving the entire field to the already existing authorities. Advocates of censorship argue that the ordinary police authorities are unable to exercise a suitable care over the motion-picture house and that they have neither the time nor the knowledge to deal adequately with the problem. Why not, then, specially delegated officers to view, certificate, and license films?[57]

The Work of the Censors.—The whole subject of censorship is admittedly a matter of taste, opinion, and judgment. What do the specially appointed guardians of the public morals disapprove of? What are their standards of judging objectionable material? An answer may be found by examining their work.

The practices of the sundry state and local censors are as various as the individual and community complexes they represent. As elsewhere in the social organization of life, sin in this field is largely a matter of place and time. Pennsylvania is worried most about sex and more especially about childbirth. Chicago, with its municipal censorship, hates gun scenes. Ohio is bitterly opposed to seduction and its technique. The Maryland Free State is sensitive about shootings. New York censors are particularly opposed to scenes showing corrupt politics and gangsters in cahoots with politicians and police officials. Kansas is bent on eliminating drinking scenes and is opposed, as a state without capital punishment, to hanging even on the screen. Censors differ among themselves. *Carmen*, for example, was rejected in three states for three different reasons. In general, however, they follow certain common rules. Censors generally feel that people who love each other must be married. Kipling's story, *Without Benefit of Clergy*, was, the censors felt, too shocking to be shown to the world, so they quickly made it safe by having the couple married in the first place. The title, *Without Benefit of Clergy*, however, remained, so the whole picture as it appeared was nonsensical. Approaching maternity

[57] Ellis P. Oberholtzer, ''Censor and the 'Movie Menace,' '' *North American Review*, Nov., 1920, 212:641-7. Donald R. Young, *Motion Pictures*, 1922, pp. 17-18.

may not be even subtly indicated. In most censorship states, every baby must have a full and legal set of parents. In certain Massachusetts towns, operating under local censorship, illegitimate children may be shown on the screen on weekdays but not on Sundays. Great stress is laid on the fact that children must be protected from all knowledge of "evil." In *Brother Officers* the Kansas censors cut out scenes showing baby clothes designed for a baby yet to be born and gave as the official reason: "The average child believes a stork brings the baby. We can't disillusion the child."

The Maryland board, in six months, ordered the elimination of over one hundred scenes in which a man was kissing a woman on her neck. Kansas censors do not object to neck-kissing, but are rabid on the subject of nose-thumbing. One of the orders of the latter board is: "Eliminate close view of hairpin." Ohio censors forbade this joke: "Bootlegging must be good business." "Aw, it ain't the coin that counts so much wit' me, lady. It's the people youse meet." Reason: "It would incite to crime." Also as a crime incentive, the following was ordered eliminated from a Mack Sennett comedy: "Will you drink your hair tonic here or take it home?" The following ante-diluvian joke came under the ban: An uncle was spanking two children. He said, "This hurts me more than it does you." "Yes," was the reply, "but not in the same place." It was blotted out as inde-cent. In the course of *Dame Chance* appeared a letter reading: "I will lease and furnish an apartment, provide you with servants and open accounts for you in the shops." The Ohio censors added the line: ". . . and I will always treat you with respect." This board forbade the exhibition of the Willard-Dempsey fight films, yet in the same week when these pictures were rejected a film was being shown in the state which included a scene in which one man was knocked down in a physical combat five times—exactly the number of times that Champion Willard fell during the first round—the only difference being that Mr. Willard was much better prepared for this indignity than the actor in the approved drama.

The motion-picture censor board of Portland, Oregon, decided that *guts* is a vulgar word and must be eliminated in pictures. The matter came about through an appeal to the board from the viewers, who were divided in their opinions. "He ain't got enough guts to shoot" was the sub-title under fire. Some of the viewers wanted it cut out, declaring it was vulgar. One viewer said it was "expressive" and gave the idea, and that she had seen the word *guts* used in "strong" editorials in the Portland daily papers. Another objected to the use of *ain't* as strongly as to the other word. The secretary of the board suggested that *intestinal stamina* might be used in place of the offensive word *guts*, but that did not seem to meet the situation. Then the president of the board spoke for that body and declared that the word objected to is, indeed, offensive and is avoided in polite conversation, and that she believed the board would hold with the viewers protesting against it.

The Pennsylvania Board of Censors is the chief bugaboo of the moving-picture producers. It has a list of about thirty standards which guide it in its work. Among the things objected to are the following: prenatal or childbed scenes; pictures including themes and incidents having to do with eugenics, birth control, and race suicide; pictures showing men and women living together without marriage; "views of women smoking will not be disapproved as such, but when women are smoking in suggestive postures or their manner of smoking is suggestive or degrading, such scenes will be disapproved." In one scene in the picture *The Four Horsemen of the Apocalypse,* a nurse appears and announces: "It's a boy!" To the Pennsylvania censors that phrase implied that somewhere, even if off-stage, there had been a scene of childbirth. So it was eliminated by the substitution of a title reading: "The boy is better." This led a film critic to remark that it was the first case of pre-natal screen colic he had ever heard of. In *Way Down East* the Pennsylvania State Board of Censors allowed the baby in the picture to die, but would not let it be born. Among other eliminations in this same picture are the following:

Reel 2—Eliminate subtitle: "Anna's delicate beauty a whip to Sanderson's jaded appetite!" and substitute: "The susceptible Sanderson obsessed by a new desire."

Reel 4—Eliminate subtitle: "Sanderson belongs to a class which, if it cannot get what it wants in one way, will go any length to get it in another," and substitute: "Sanderson, not to be turned aside from his evil intentions, goes on in his own way."

Reel 6—In subtitle: "For all we know she might be some loose woman, wanderin' around. I won't take her into my hum," substitute the word "adventuress" for "loose woman."

Sometimes the changes ordered show more subtlety on the censors' part than on that of the scenario writer's, as, for example, the order to eliminate "Do you think the bed is big enough for two?" and substitute "Another pillow?" In one picture the Pennsylvania Board ordered: "Insert newspaper notice of marriage before showing bedroom scene." The same board prevented the showing of a farcical scene in which a man burns a letter from his wife, because (forsooth) it showed contempt of the marital relation. Shows banned in Philadelphia are often presented across the river in Camden, New Jersey, with the fact that they were forbidden by the Pennsylvania State Board of Censors featured in the advertisements.

The above examples of the action taken by the official censors, culled from various sources,[58] are presented as a fair sampling of their work. Donald Young,[59] himself in favor of censorship, has stated of censors that "at best, they can eliminate only the crudest violations of our moral code. When they attempt more, they become ridiculous." Many plays, it is claimed, have been ruined by the slashing of the censors, with an attendant loss to the producers. Much of the slashing has been of doubtful value.

Foreign experience has been similar. The action of the censors is inconsistent, different rulings being laid down by different countries, and the artistic value of the film is often spoiled. Consider the case of *The Joyless Street*, a German production ten thousand feet in length, about the same as *Ben-Hur* or *The Big Parade*. "France accepted the film, deleting two thousand feet and every shot of the 'street' itself. Vienna extracted all sequences in which Werner Krauss appeared as the butcher. Russia turned the American lieutenant into a doctor and made the butcher the murderer instead of the girl. After having run a year in Germany, an attempt was made to censor it. In America it was not shown at all, and in England once, at a private performance of the Film Society. That is the history of a creative work which contained less harmful matter than *Our Dancing Daughters* or *Hot for Paris*, and it gives some idea of the censorship's power to destroy the qualities of any film."[60]

Sex and Censorship.—It is claimed by some opponents of censorship that, through fear of the censors, producers and directors are making poor pictures and are trying to insert sex appeal into films without exactly saying so—to include intimations of salaciousness that cannot be immediately recognized by the censors. It is thus that they explain the scenes of prolonged amorousness (between engaged

[58] Morris L. Ernst and Pare Lorentz, *Censored: The Private Life of the Movies*, 1930, pp. 19-69. James R. Quirk, "The Wowsers Tackle the Movies," *American Mercury*, July, 1927, 11:43:349-356. "Americana," *ibid.*, Sept., 1927, 12:45:50. Brenda Ueland, "Censoring the Movies," *Liberty*, March 20, 1926. Raymond Moley, *Commercial Recreation*, 1920, p. 39.
[59] "Social Standards and the Motion Picture," *Annals Amer. Acad. Polit. Soc. Sci.*, Nov., 1926, CXXVIII, 148.
[60] Paul Rotha, *The Film Till Now*, 1930, p. 37.

couples), the pictures of husbands assaulting their wedded wives, and the roadhouse scenes with fade-ins to the orgies of declining Rome.[61] Attention is also drawn to what happens, under censorship, to the titles of plays taken over by the movies: *The Admirable Crichton* becomes *Male and Female*; *The Bachelor* becomes *The Virtuous Vamp*; *The Jewels of the Madonna* becomes *Sin*; *The Queen's Husband* becomes *The Royal Bed*; *Children of the Street* becomes *Ladies for Hire*; *Olympia* becomes *His Glorious Night*; *Jenny Lind* becomes *A Lady's Morals*; *The Command to Love* becomes *The Boudoir Diplomat*; *The Second Man* becomes *He Knew Women*. Titles such as the following abound: *Manhandled, Womanhandled, Altars of Desire, Hot Sheiks, Flaming Passion, Her Man, Oh For a Man, She's My Weakness, Indiscreet, The Forbidden Woman, Tarnished Lady, Free Love, Woman Hungry, One Mad Kiss, One Romantic Night, A Night of Love, Right to Love, Virtuous Sin, Sin Takes a Holiday, Young Sinners,* and *Laughing Sinners*.

Like the misleading and suggestive title, the various forms of advertising suggest, often falsely, immorality in the film. Striking scenes are selected from the film and lithographed for posters. Selected because of their ability to attract attention, and often presenting isolated scenes which represent immorality or violence, they are generally grossly misleading. The movie industry seems to believe that people want or need to be shocked into going to see their product. And there are film advertisements such as these: *The Truth About Youth* . . . How Far Must a Girl Go—To Hold the Man She Loves—When She Sees Him Stolen by a Sex-Flaunting Siren? Should She Fight Fire with Fire? *A Night at Susie's* . . . And Although I Lost Everything a Woman Holds Dear—I Won the Man I Loved. *The Lottery Bride* . . . She Was Made For Love—Young—Beautiful—Loved by the Man She Loved—His Kisses on Her Lips—She Gambled Away Her Beauty to a Stranger. *Dancing Sweeties* . . . They Met at 9— Danced at 10—Kissed at 11—And Married at Midnight.[62] The whole public injury does not come from pictures which are so gross as to be obscene. A much more insidious danger of debasement comes from those which are immoral in their teachings. It is difficult for censorship to reach that, just as it cannot touch poor taste, vulgarity, inanity, crudity, misrepresentation, etc., which do not present fundamental moral questions.

[61] Brenda Ueland, "Censoring the Movies," *Liberty*, March 20, 1926.
[62] *The Theatre Guild Magazine*, April, 1931.

The noted critic George Jean Nathan[63] maintains that the contention that absurd censorship is responsible for the childish quality of the movies and their concentration on sex is sheer buncombe. "I have investigated carefully the deletions that have been ordered by the various censorship bodies over a period of years and in not a single case would any one of the pictures have been perceptibly better had it been allowed to remain intact. The censors are idiotic, true enough; some of their recommendations are unbelievably asinine. But the pictures would have been just as bad if they had not meddled with them. The censors are the movie people's alibi. . . . All that the movie censors usually do is to change a few subtitles, awful garbage in the first place, cut out exaggerated gum-suckings and brassière-squeezings that any artistically intelligent director would never have put into the film, and object to elaborations of incidents that every writer with an ounce of dramatic ability would himself recognize at once as utterly nonsensical and entirely needless. The movie ignoramuses are simply up to their old trick of passing the buck. The only ones to blame for the abysmal stupidity of the movies are themselves. The circumstance that the censors have stolen some small coins out of their purse can't conceal the fact that that purse betrays an unmistakable resemblance to a sow's ear."

The Question of Artistic Quality.—Many critics agree that the real curse of the movies is not censorship but mediocrity, for the great money-making pictures as well as the artistic triumphs have generally been censor-proof. "Not more than one out of every fifty pictures made is worth seeing."[64] Professor Münsterberg[65] long ago complained of the "trivializing influence of a steady contact with things which are not worth knowing. The larger part of the film literature of today is certainly harmful in this sense. The intellectual background of most photoplays is insipid. . . . This lack of originality and inspiration is not necessary; it does not lie in the art form." An English critic states: "Hollywood movies are slick, facile, and well-finished. At the same time, they display an absence of good taste, of intelligence, and, if the term is allowable, of culture."[66] The following parody illustrates this view:[67]

[63] "Notes on the Movies," *American Mercury*, Sept., 1927, 12:45:117-118.

[64] Welford Beaton, "Mad Movie Money," *The American Mercury*, Sept., 1927, 12:45:31. *Cf.* James R. Quirk, "The Wowsers Tackle the Movies," *ibid.*, July, 1927, 11:43:352.

[65] *The Photoplay*, 1916, p. 225.

[66] Paul Rotha, *The Film Till Now*, 1930, p. 80.

[67] E. B. W., in *Life*, February, 1927.

How to Write a Movie

First think of a title. Some name like "The Doll's House" or "Martin Chuzzlewit" will do.

Once you have the title, the battle is half over. The plot concerns a girl named Sue, daughter of a middle-class family. The first scene shows the living-room of Sue's papa's house in Glendale. The room is three hundred feet long and two hundred feet wide, and has porphyry stairs and a butler in a striped waistcoat.

Sue's papa is mad because Sue doesn't marry Harold Dingrath, apprentice to the local taxidermist. He expresses this anger by taking a cigar out of his mouth and dashing it to the floor. The butler picks it up and finishes it. (That's your comic touch.)

That night Harold arrives at Sue's in an eight-cylinder car, which he evidently earned by stuffing birds in his spare time. Sue's mamma, who is also promoting the match, makes a very crude remark, such as, "Harold, did you know my Sue is a hell of a good cook?" This bothers Sue, who has delicacy, and when Harold proposes she tells him she doesn't love him—which the audience knows is an out-and-out fib. When Harold leaves, she runs to the door and presses her lips against it. Harold is doing exactly the same thing on the other side. (That's your pathos.)

Now is the time to let Another Woman enter Harold's life. The looser she is the better. A good way of introducing her is by showing first a close-up of a cigarette in a long ivory holder, then the sinuous hand, then the sinuous arm, finally the Other Woman's face. (There's your sex appeal.)

Next run the sub-title, "Years roll by and Spring has come to southern France." Show apple blossoms. Sue has drifted there and has married a nobleman, who won her on a bet, but she is his wife *in name only*. Keep the audience straight on this point by showing how the nobleman rolls up in a blanket and sleeps on the mantelpiece all night long. (That's your imagination.)

In the last reel Sue and Harold meet by accident in Australia, where Harold has gone to get away from the Other Woman. The audience will have to guess why Sue is there. Anyway, there she is. (That's your dénouement.)

Change the title from "Martin Chuzzlewit" to "Sex" and send it to any good producer. There's nothing to it.

The influence of motion pictures upon the races of the Far East and upon the illiterate peoples of the world is by many regarded as harmful and as a menace to the prestige of white civilization. If this is so, then American producers must shoulder most of the blame, for fully 90 per cent of the pictures shown throughout the world are American made. At the very least, the movies give an utterly distorted basis for any sane judgment of American civilization. The following comment is much to the point.[68]

People who see American pictures abroad will learn that in the United States all wealthy girls live in modernistic houses, are continually drinking cocktails, and after a harrowing experience fall in love with the right man and give up the fast life to become devoted, respectable mothers; that gangmen are as common as bond salesmen, and that they engage in open street battles with the handsome dicks that are fighting to save their own brothers who are invariably members of the gang; that all American Negroes have epileptic fits at the slightest suggestion of the supernatural; that all actors are good guys despite some fatal weakness, and that they receive the news of the death of a member of their family before each performance; that all wealthy Americans keep mistresses, live in pent houses, and wear a tail coat every night for dinner.

The foreigner is given an exceptionally good opportunity to see just what the American college is like. The students all wear sweaters, dilapidated hats, and corduroy trousers. Every collegian is an expert on the ukelele, in fact no other instrument has ever been seen on the campus, with the possible exception of the saxophone. The athletic hero always has a misunderstanding with his girl friend the day before the big game. He gets drunk at one of those fast collegiate roadhouses and is brought home by his ever-faithful roomie. In the game he plays very badly until he picks his girl out of the thirty thousand spectators and learns from her eyes that she is all for him. In a flash he is a bounding ball of energy and with perfect ease he makes an eighty yard dash for a touchdown. It's a grand sport this American football! College must be such a lark over in the States!

Numerous reasons are ascribed for the inartistic character of many movies. One is that the business end of the industry is too closely tied up with the actual producing end. The movie magnates have unquestionably much business acumen, but they do not qualify as judges of dramatic literature, as producers and artists. Before entering the movie business they were running tent shows, furrier stores, haberdasheries, peep-shows, pants-pressing shops and loan offices. In such hands, it is claimed, the film could hardly have been expected to rise above the lowest form of entertainment. Moreover, the primary aim of film producers is to make the maximum of financial return in the shortest possible time, a method hardly congenial to so intricate an art as the cinema. Yet when the critics cry that no good can come of the film now, because the wrong men are running it, the answer

[68] Arouet, "With Sound," *Yale Daily News*, March 11, 1930.

may be made that someone had to run it. The men of taste pooh-poohed it, and the men of money embraced it.[69]

Another condition bearing on the point is the ownership of chains of key theatres by the large producing companies. This assures the producer a definite outlet for his product, but it has the effect of making the producer's success depend not so much upon the merit of his product as upon his control of theatres. Like the monopoly of first-run theatres, block-booking or wholesale selling of films is said to discourage the production of artistic and meritorious pictures. By this method the large companies, which produce along with a few desirable and really excellent pictures many undesirable ones, are able to force upon large numbers of exhibitors a quantity of pictures which the exhibitor does not want.[70] On the other hand, the producers maintain that block-booking makes possible the production and exhibition of high-class, artistic pictures, which are often box-office failures, by selling them in the same lot with box-office successes. Thus, Clara Bow pictures carried the artistically important but financially unsuccessful film, *Old Ironsides*.[71]

The movies are handicapped by the circumstance that they must all be fashioned with a universal audience in mind. There are no different circuits of movie houses, as there are of theatres—though the little theatre movement is beginning to spread to the movie field—and hence a single picture must be made to appeal to all kinds and conditions of movie-goers in the mass. "A movie must be manufactured to meet the ten-cent and two-dollar trade on common ground. It succeeds in meeting the former."[72] It has been said that the public gets the kind of play and film it demands. Entertainment caters to the public taste; it does not create it, for it is too commercialized an undertaking. "The film-man will make a picture based on a warehouse catalogue, or on 'Problems in Electro-therapeutics,' or on Gray's 'Anatomy,' if enough people will buy it. Educate children to appreciate good films, and they will not ask for bad. . . . If they are wrongly brought up, you should blame, not the film-man, but their educational system. What place in modern education does the cultivation of the

[69] George Jean Nathan, "Notes on the Movies," *American Mercury*, Sept., 1927, 12:45:118. Paul Rotha, *The Film Till Now*, 1930, p. 38. Terry Ramsaye, *A Million and One Nights*, 1926, p. 414. L'Estrange Fawcett, *Films: Facts and Forecasts*, 1927, pp. 251-252.

[70] William M. Seabury, *The Public and the Motion Picture Industry*, 1926, pp. 30, 45, 59-60. Block-booking was declared illegal in 1930.

[71] *Motion Picture Monthly*, Dec., 1930, 6:12:9-11.

[72] George Jean Nathan, "Notes on the Movies," *American Mercury*, Sept., 1927, 12:45:122.

artistic senses occupy? . . . Even as things are today children like the best films best; they dislike the ugly, horrible films."[73] The history of Educational Pictures, Inc., is significant. It was organized in 1915 with the sole idea of producing strictly educational pictures. It did not take the company long to find out that the demand did not exist and that it could not survive by doing that alone. So it undertook to supply the theatres of the country with a line of comedies, which, with the Kinogram news weekly, at present constitutes its releases.[74] That explains the incongruity of labeling these pictures "educational."

An English critic maintains that women must bear the responsibility to a large extent for the cinema fare, good and bad, provided. It is for them that films generally are created, for they form the backbone of the audiences.[75]

The average film is made for women to enjoy. It deals with the primitive instincts—love, hate, envy, revenge—which are always more quickly aroused in woman than in man, and it is played in an atmosphere of smartness. Women are largely responsible for the smartness of the American film, the highly and not always artistically ornate setting, the pretty-pretty design. They demand the "baronial hall," and the cabaret scene, and extravagance generally, because by nature they enjoy seeing money scattered about. Male critics are always condemning the wanton expenditure shown in American film-production, but they do not realise why it continues, and they do not study the psychology of the audience as the American production committees do.

As long as woman obtains a pleasurable sensation, she will pardon stupid films, banal films, impossible films. Technique, photography, acting conventions mean little to her. Primarily she demands a love-story in a smart setting with a happy ending, because she likes to imagine herself as the heroine. She always wants to wear fine clothes, and to be beautiful and admired; therefore, the heroine is always pretty and attractive, superbly gowned and coiffured (even in the Antarctic!) Woman always wants to marry; therefore, the heroine always falls on the hero's neck in the last hundred feet. She is always willing to love and be loved; therefore, 90 per cent. of films are love-stories. She considers sympathy and self-sacrifice, however selfish she is herself, to be predominant female virtues; therefore, 80 per cent. of films give the heroine such attributes, and very few heroines come to bad ends.

One thing only does the woman demand in the film—a moral conclusion—partly because it is usually more pleasurable than an unsatisfactory finish.

[73] L'Estrange Fawcett, *Films: Facts and Forecasts*, 1927, pp. 233, 236.
[74] Earle W. Hammons, "Short Reels and Educational Subjects," in *The Story of the Films*, Joseph P. Kennedy, editor, 1927, ch. VII.
[75] L'Estrange Fawcett, *Films: Facts and Forecasts*, 1927, pp. 239-241

Virtue and steadfastness rewarded and vice and crime punished; not a new doctrine—in fact, just about as old as the world. But it suits woman, for she maintains her position in society by professed adhesion to the moral code, the Ten Commandments, and law and order.

The same critic has pointed out that while there are thousands of awful films, there are also thousands of awful plays and pictures and much bad music. What we should judge the film by is its aspirations and the best examples of its art. It is the one good film in a hundred, and not the ninety-and-nine pot-boilers, that is worth attention and encouragement. "Do we take the theatre and the film too seriously?" he also asks. "Live and let live as a principle in entertainment purveying has some ground for consideration, and the perpetual lament that the state of the theatre and the cinema is deplorable becomes wearisome. Every age has heard the same complaints, and there are several people in this country who would seriously like to see amusement reduced to a penance. No doubt the Puritans in Queen Elizabeth's reign, who had their noses slit for their political and religious beliefs, bemoaned the elevation of Shakespeare to the position of a court dramatist, because he got Anne Hathaway into trouble before he wed her. And when he joked in loose strains to tickle the groundlings, how the good folk must have squirmed in their seats! And it is doubtful if the Puritans of Athens enjoyed some of Aristophanes' humour compared with the staider drama of Sophocles. They sighed for the good old days, and said the Greek stage was going to the frogs."[76]

Opposition to State Censorship.—Among the leading opponents of legal censorship are naturally the producers themselves. They object to censorship because of its hampering influence, because it ruins the plays, and because of the cost involved when changes are ordered or the picture is entirely condemned. They point out, with some logic, that if there must be legal censorship it should be done by the federal government, for otherwise changes would have to be made to suit the varying views of boards in forty-eight different states.

Others are opposed to censorship of the movies for the same reasons that they object to censorship of art and literature. Censorship is fatal to the growth and development of any art form. "The motion picture is a new art, and it should enjoy the same freedom of expression as the other arts. What would our literature, our sculpture, our painting be today if every book before publication had been submitted to a censor with absolute powers of approval, rejection and elimination?

[76] *Ibid.*, pp. 255, 270.

Or if only such statues and canvases were permitted to live in our galleries as had pleased a politically appointed board from the rural districts?''[77]

Censorship, it is further asserted, is futile. It is impossible for any legally constituted body of officials properly to decide what should and what should not be shown on the screen. Opinions vary, especially in different parts of the country; they even vary as between members of the same board. Censorship where tried out has not been successful. Censorship laws and agitations have probably exerted less influence upon the pictures than their own automatic improvement. Pictures in censorship states are not better than those in other states. You cannot legislate better films, any more than you can legislate better books, better magazines, better works of art, better thoughts, better impulses.

One of the favorite objections to censorship is that it is likely to become an instrument for the attainment of political purposes; that it will be used to suppress that freedom of expression so necessary to democratic government. The censor privilege has been perverted for political reason in a few instances. The Negro vote in Ohio and other states prevented the showing of *The Birth of a Nation*. The Ohio and Pennsylvania censorship boards eliminated pictures of the coal strike in 1919, the latter at the request of the governor. Ohio censors in 1930 barred *The Big House*, a powerful argument for prison reform, which was released shortly after the Ohio prison tragedy and during a political campaign.

Another argument that deserves more consideration is that it is impossible for any small group of individuals to determine a standard of morality which will be adequate for the protection of a vast number of people. The patrons of moving-picture shows are of all ages, all economic conditions, and all nationalities. A board is likely to enforce certain ideas of what is proper which represent only the caprice of a small minority. Such a possibility is repugnant to every person who in any sense values his liberty to decide for himself what what he shall do and see. A further danger in censorship is that while it begins with the elimination of certain types of exhibits, it may end with a direct influence upon the type of picture shown. A board of censors might become such a positive force that the producers themselves would be influenced to make the kind of pictures which the board would prefer.

[77] National Board of Review of Motion Pictures, *The Question of Motion Picture Censorship*, 1914.

State censorship, furthermore, is declared to be unnecessary because whatever censoring is required can be done more efficiently by the producers themselves at the source or by public opinion which in the long run is the final arbiter.[78]

Supervision from Within.—In 1922, after a series of scandals in Hollywood, public objection to motion pictures became widespread and active. To counteract this opposition and to save the industry, the leading producers formed an association and appointed Mr. Will Hays, then a member of the Harding Cabinet, as director or "Czar." Gilbert Seldes[79] remarks: "As in organized baseball, where the dictator arrived after revelations of shocking dishonesty, the appointment of a Czar is a confession of internal weakness. The motor car industry has faced depressions and inflations and has managed without a dictator; the stage has had dozens of scandals as shocking as those of Hollywood, and has not needed to place a front of respectability as its façade. The metropolitan night clubs, vaudeville, burlesque, the circus have not escaped criticism and have weathered their little storms. The movies alone rushed to cover. They had to hide not their immorality, but their lack of solid substance, of entertainment value, of intelligence."

The purposes of the Motion Picture Producers and Distributors of America, Inc., which was organized in March, 1922, were chiefly "to foster the common interests of those engaged in the motion picture industry by establishing and maintaining the highest possible moral and artistic standards of motion picture production, by developing the educational as well as the entertainment value and the general usefulness of the motion picture, and by reforming abuses relative to the industry."[80] In carrying out these objects the Association adopted a formula with reference to the selection and rejection of certain story material for picturization. The members agreed to exclude certain things from pictures which they produced and to exercise special care in the manner in which they treated certain other subjects, to the end that good taste may be emphasized. Mr. Hays explains the procedure as follows: "When any member company is offered the screen rights to a book or play of a probably questionable nature, its representatives immediately inform the offices

[78] J. R. Rutland, *State Censorship of Motion Pictures*, 1923. National Board of Review of Motion Pictures, *The Question of Motion Picture Censorship*, 1914. Donald R. Young, *Motion Pictures*, 1922, pp. 71 ff. Terry Ramsaye, *A Million and One Nights*, 1926, p. 484. Raymond Moley, *Commercial Recreation*, 1920, pp. 38, 40.

[79] *An Hour with the Movies and the Talkies*, 1929, p. 98.

[80] Will Hays, *See and Hear*, 1929, p. 26.

of our Association, representing about eighty-five per cent of the producing elements. If the judgment of the member company to the effect that the picturization of the subject matter is inadvisable is confirmed, a notice is sent to all the other member companies, giving the name of the objectionable book or play. Such company members, thus having their attention directed to the subject in question, have the opportunity of avoiding the picturization of the novel or play."[81] It is stated that more than a hundred and fifty books and plays, including some of the best sellers and stage successes, have thus been kept from the screen. In 1931 a similar "production code" was adopted for talking pictures. The Association maintains that the standards there set up have resulted in productions which are not merely good entertainment but have either social or educational value or at least are unusual in their artistic and dramatic worth.[82]

To assure support for the better pictures, the Motion Picture Producers and Distributors of America, Inc., invited great national organizations with millions of members interested in social service, education, religion, and civic affairs, to become associated with it. The result was the organization of a Public Relations Committee. In 1925 this committee, finding that the work it had sponsored had become a permanent part of the organized industry, asked that the committee be dissolved and a Department of Public Relations be established within the Association. This was done. A small active committee remained, and the advice and assistance of the larger group are still gladly received.[83]

As opposed to the adverse criticism of motion pictures mentioned above, some students of the cinema note continuous improvements, not merely in technical matters, where the advance has admittedly been astonishing, but also in the treatment of values. In the picture of realism there is less false sentiment and more truth to life. In the picture of illusion there is more imagination in interpretation. So considerable has the improvement been that "dramas" of ten or fifteen years ago make excellent comedies today. The movie magnates have recently steadfastly endeavored to improve the quality of their productions by employing accredited authors, directors, actors, and designers, and urging these artists to exert their ingenuity to give the public something appreciably better than what

[81] Will Hays, "Supervision From Within," in *The Story of the Films*, edited by Joseph P. Kennedy, 1927, p. 48. *Cf. The Motion Picture Monthly*, Nov. 1, 1927, 3:11:5.
[82] *The Motion Picture Monthly*, June-July, 1929, 7:5:8-9.
[83] Will Hays, *See and Hear*, 1929, pp. 29-30.

the public seems to want. The film appears to be winning consideration and respect. "A dozen years ago no reputable actor would be seen on it, or, if he did appear, he used a different name. Now you can scarcely keep the best actors in every country out of the studio. Gradually, it is beginning to be perceived that men of the highest intelligence can use the film as a means of expressing themselves. The tremendous technical advance made in the last two or three years is alone capable of attracting intelligent attention. Continually, one hears of scientists anxious to express their theories of life by means of a film-story."[84]

It is significant that legal censorship is not spreading. Since 1922, not one state censorship bill has become law, though more than forty have been introduced. It is claimed that this has been due in large measure to the campaigns waged by the Hays organization, which polices the business from within and bars from the screen such material as would invite restrictive legislation. It is also due to its effective lobbying. Trade control has undoubtedly had some influence in preventing the spread of state censorship. Part of the explanation is also to be found in social control.

Social Control.—Official censorship, it has been stated, is unnecessary because control may be exercised through the operation of public opinion. No practice or institution can prosper long which is repugnant to the standard of propriety held by most of the people. The public has the power of deciding whether a given picture is to be a "flop" or a box-office success. It is the final arbiter in determining the standards of production, and it seems to prefer the better type of films. The best paying pictures have in general been worthwhile pictures. "The biggest money-makers the screen has ever known are Harold Lloyd and Tom Mix. And I am prepared to bet that these two men have never appeared in a suggestive scene. That, I imagine, is sufficient answer to the screen's strongest critics. From the moral standpoint Chaplin pictures tell the same story. The 'Gold Rush' made immense sums of money. So did the early comedies, and they go on making money today, though they are now outmoded and archaic in technique. But Chaplin's sex film, 'A Woman of Paris,' was far less lucrative. . . . It alienated the very young and was too cynical for those who wanted to be rejuvenated. It remains, however, one of the cinematograph's triumphs of direction, technique, and timing."[85]

[84] L'Estrange Fawcett, *Films: Facts and Forecasts*, 1927, p. 269.
[85] *Ibid.*, pp. 247-248.

More important than the mere expression of approval or disapproval, however influential that may be on the box office, is the attempt to coöperate in a constructive way. It is much easier to call attention to the evils than to arouse public interest in the advantages of the movies; yet the latter must be done, and the best pictures supported, in order to insure improvements in production. Public opinion, to be effective, must be organized; it must also be positive and constructive. Constructive public opinion of this sort has taken form in the National Board of Review of Motion Pictures, its affiliated National Committee for Better Films and its Exceptional Photoplays Committee; the National Indorsers of Photoplays; the Film Bureau; National Motion Pictures League; and the motion-picture reviewing and reporting committees of the following social, civic, religious, and patriotic societies: the General Federation of Women's Clubs, National Congress of Parents and Teachers, Daughters of the American Revolution, International Federation of Catholic Alumnae, National Catholic Welfare Conference, National League of American Pen Women, American Association of University Women, Young Men's Christian Association, American Library Association, Association of Junior Leagues of America, and the Boy Scouts of America. Through their efforts, public support for the better pictures is organized. Annotated lists of recent productions are prepared and classified as to their suitability for different kinds of audiences. Special attention is given to pictures suitable for use in children's programs which many local "better films" committees are providing. The coöperation of the motion-picture exhibitors is usually secured in arranging Saturday morning programs for children and "family programs" at other times during the week. There is an increasing demand for more of these special occasions.[86]

"Selection Not Censorship."—The most important of the above organizations is the National Board of Review of Motion Pictures. It was organized in March, 1909, by the People's Institute at the request of the motion-picture exhibitors of New York City, in an attempt to forestall municipal regulation. The scope of the work became national in June of the same year at the request of the manufacturers of motion pictures, who agreed to submit all their product to it for pre-publicity criticism. The Board is a volunteer disinterested citizen organization, composed of upward of three hundred

[86] Lee F. Hanmer, "Motion Pictures," *Social Work Year Book*, 1929, p. 280. Symposium, "Raising the Standards of Demand," *The Motion Picture Monthly*, Feb., 1931, 7:2:10-12.

people reviewing films in New York City before they are released for general exhibition to the public, with associate, advisory members and affiliated citizen groups in many localities throughout the country. It reviews 98 to 100 per cent of all entertainment films, that is, everything except news reels, strictly scenic and educational subjects and industrial films, distributed to the public in the United States. "Passed by the National Board of Review" does not necessarily mean that the Board approves or recommends the picture upon which the legend appears. "In all cases it means that in the opinion of the reviewing committee the picture will not have a morally subversive effect upon large numbers of persons in different sections of the country. It further means that the review committee in so passing a film has detected in it, judged in a common sense way by its probable net moral effect on an audience in a motion picture theatre, nothing that violates in part or in whole what amounts to the common law against the publication of the immoral, obscene or anything detrimental to public morality."[87]

The Board has no legal power to enforce its decisions upon producers and exhibitors, but relies on public opinion. It is opposed to legal censorship and in favor of the constructive method of selecting the better pictures, publishing classified lists of them, and building up audiences and support for them. The latter service is regarded as more important than censoring. Advocates of official censorship regard the National Board of Review as insufficient, and offer as arguments the fact that its decisions are not binding, the suggestion that it may be or can easily become a tool of the producers, who contribute to its support, and the opinion that a New York City board cannot represent satisfactorily all parts of the United States. Supporters of its work maintain that the Board is impartial and efficient. Its members receive no salaries; its work is supported not only by taxes on films reviewed but also by sale of its services and by subscriptions from persons and organizations interested in the production of good pictures. It directly serves large cities in nearly forty states through bulletins and other means, and it assists churches and educational organizations in finding suitable pictures.[88] The fact should not be lost sight of that, despite differences in methods and views, the advocates of official censorship and those of constructive

[87] Wilton A. Barrett, "The Work of the National Board of Review," *Annals Amer. Acad. Polit. Soc. Sci.*, Nov., 1926, CXXVIII, 181.
[88] Donald R. Young, *Motion Pictures*, 1922, pp. 43, 44, 51. J. R. Rutland, *State Censorship of Motion Pictures*, 1923, pp. 5, 15.

coöperation are working for the same objective—the improvement of motion pictures.

Censorship of the Drama.—The demand for censorship has also affected the legitimate stage, though in this case, because of the restricted appeal of the theatrical performance as contrasted with the movies, the agitation has been more localized. It has been focused chiefly in New York City, the theatrical center of America. The question of censorship arose because of the appearance of a number of allegedly salacious plays, and the failure of other methods of dealing with the problem. Official censorship is held to be necessary because the theatre is for the most part in the hands of mere business men who are not remotely interested in it from the artistic point of view, and because many people seem to be tempted into the theatres, of which there are said to be too many, by nastiness, sensation, and nudity. Actors and authors have generally put the blame for immoral plays upon the producers, who in turn have shifted the responsibility upon the public taste.

The citizens' play jury plan has been tried and found wanting. This plan was founded in 1924 on a suggestion by Owen Davis, playwright, to avert censorship. It provided for a voluntary board of four hundred, including men and women of intelligence, character, and taste, from which twelve persons could be summoned for service. The twelve were to meet, discuss the piece in question, and render judgment. A vote of eight might drive the piece from the boards or require amendments. Their decisions were to be backed up with the power of a contract between the Actors' Equity Association and the producing managers. Any play that fell under an adverse vote of the jury was to be closed by withdrawing the cast. Much was expected from the play jury. In three years it condemned one play, modified two others, and failed to take action upon four more. In two instances the vote stood six to six. The jury, when sought, has been hard to assemble. Upon one occasion the directing committee exhausted almost a hundred names before locating twelve of the four hundred jurors who were ready to serve.[89]

Legal methods of dealing with the situation have been faced with even greater difficulties. The Wales law, popularly known as the theatre padlock law, provides that there must be a trial in a court of record and a conviction before the licensing authority can even consider the question as to whether or not the theatrical license should be revoked. If a conviction takes place, the licensing authority

[89] James C. Young, ''Censorship of the Stage,'' New York *Times*, Feb., 6, 1927.

may, in its discretion, revoke the license for any period from one day up to one year. Delay usually occurs between the arrest, indictment, and trial, and the publicity given to the event results in a jam at the box office. When at last the trial does take place, an unanimous vote by twelve jurors becomes necessary to convict. That unanimity is almost unknown in cases involving so big a factor of personal taste and personal definitions of morality. In the thirty-year period ending in 1927, there were only two convictions.[90] In 1927 the law was amended so as to condemn not only any indecent and obscene play, but any indecent or obscene part of any play or exhibition. It was also made a misdemeanor to present any play dealing with sex degeneracy or sex perversion. A further amendment in 1931 removed actors, stage-hands and musicians from prosecution in connection with obscene plays and placed responsibility solely upon authors and producers.[91] Out of the five police raids conducted under the new Wales law up to 1930, not one has resulted in a conviction.[92]

Threatened by state censorship in 1927, the theatrical producers formed a committee, headed by Winthrop Ames, to clean house. When a bill providing for official censorship was again introduced in the legislature, in 1931, another effort toward self-censorship was made. A board composed of representatives of the League of New York Theatres, the Dramatists' Guild, actors, and the public, and headed by Dr. Henry Moskowitz, was formed. Its purpose is not so much to censor offensive plays or performances as to prevent the necessity for censorship. "Probably not every obscene play can be caught before it reaches Broadway. But the board members will be in a position to stop or modify shows which are frankly offered with the belief that dirt brings money into the box office. They will know what plays are being produced in near-by towns preparatory to a New York opening, and if they anticipate general objection on grounds of lewdness they will warn the producer that police aid will be invoked. In the case of those objectionable skits used by some producers in revues, it will be even easier to utter a few firm words. The fact that the machinery for preventing public obscene performances already exists need not be stressed, for producers will know well enough what a warning means."[93] Whether the new

[90] *Ibid.*

[91] New York *Times*, April 24, 1931.

[92] James G. Wallace, ''Theatre Padlock Law Fills a Long-Felt Want,'' New York *Times*, April 7, 1927.

[93] Editorial in the New York *Times*, Feb., 20, 1931.

scheme will function adequately and succeed in warding off official censorship remains to be seen.

Philadelphia has a plan of censorship of dramatic performances which is based upon the theory that the mayor is the final authority in this respect. If he thinks that a production or any part of it violates the statutes of Pennsylvania, he has the privilege of ordering it closed or modified. The mayor appoints as his agent the Philadelphia Board of Theatre Control, composed of six members, one of whom is a paid worker. This board, which came into existence in 1923 during the régime of General Smedley D. Butler as Director of Public Safety, is not financed by the city; its funds are subscribed by the theatres themselves. It submits all its findings to the mayor, who has invariably accepted its verdict. It has no statutory existence, but it seems to work satisfactorily. In the last analysis the Board is merely a group of citizens having no official powers, and it is within the province of each succeeding mayor to recognize it or not.[94]

In Boston, the mayor grants licenses for the theatrical season, but a board consisting of the mayor, the police commissioner, and the chief justice of the municipal court may by a majority vote suspend a license at their pleasure. "The story goes that a former Boston mayor used to go regularly to New York to see plays which were under suspicion there, and then as a result of his researches banned them before they so much as reached Boston."[95]

England has had a censor throughout almost the whole of its theatrical history. He is the Lord Chamberlain, in whom resides the licensing power. The Lord Chamberlain grants licenses only if he is satisfied that, broadly speaking, the plays to be produced will not "corrupt public morals." Should his ruling be infringed, he takes action through the Home Office. From time to time complaint is made that his view of obscenity is too lax or too narrow, but on the whole his position is one of those curious English arrangements that are not founded on any logical principle yet work, in practice, with a minimum of friction.[96] It is interesting to note that the play *The Green Pastures*, winner of the Pulitzer award in 1930 and gold-starred by religious leaders in New York, was forbidden in London as sacrilegious.

[94] George H. Eckhardt, "Censorship in Philadelphia," New York *Times*, August 11, 1929. Lawrence Davies, "Censorship Change for Philadelphia," New York *Times*, Aug. 4, 1929.
[95] Morris L. Ernst and William Seagle, *To the Pure*, 1928, p. 23.
[96] Wickham Steed, "Watchdogs and Morals," *Outlook and Independent*, May 7, 1930, 155:1:4-5.

There are certain limitations to the Lord Chamberlain's authority. Even though he refuses a license to a play, it may still be given at so-called private subscription performances, over which he has no control. "As these usually take place on Sunday, which is the only day a theatre is to be had, the obscenity is for the Lord's Day. But more!—The fact that the Lord Chamberlain has refused a license for a play to be performed does not at all prevent its publication. The play has also a separate existence as a book, and upon this career it now enters and spreads its poison. What may not be had in the theatre is to be had in the bookshop. Of examples of English banned plays which have been made available in book form Shaw's *Mrs. Warren's Profession* is, perhaps, best known; but one may also mention such comparatively recent works as Zangwill's *The Next Religion*, Christopher St. John's *The Coronation*, and most recently, Dr. Marie Stopes' *Vestia*, which the Lord Chamberlain considered a little too ardent a defense of a woman's right to love."[97]

Citizen Coöperation.—As in the case of the movies, there are concerted efforts on the part of citizens for the improvement of the commercial theatre. The most conspicuous organization in this field has been the Drama League of America, established in 1910 "to encourage the recognition of the drama as a high form of art and to support such plays as were deemed worthy, to disseminate information concerning the drama and its literature, to coördinate the amateur efforts of the country, to crowd out vicious plays by attending the good and building up audiences for them through drama study, reading circles and lectures." As a part of this program over 120 local Drama League Centers, representing every state in the country, have been organized.

In 1929 the Drama League united with two other organizations having a similar purpose—the American Theater Association and the Church and Drama Association of New York—to form the Church and Drama League of America. "In addition to carrying forward the activities of its constituent bodies, the new agency aims to stimulate a widespread and intelligent interest in the drama as a social force and an educational influence. It maintains a reviewing service of plays on the professional stage, recommends desirable plays in a weekly bulletin, and is planning the organization of local constituencies which will be informed through the League's publications and lectures, and will guarantee audiences to support selected plays on

[97] Morris L. Ernst and William Seagle, *To the Pure*, 1928, p. 26.

tour. This is known as a system of 'organized audiences.' "[98] Other agencies active in this field, though not specializing in it, include the General Federation of Women's Clubs and the National Congress of Parents and Teachers. They have contributed to the encouragement of wholesome drama through lectures, studies, articles, and occasional bulletins.

[98] Sue Ann Wilson, "The Theatre," *Social Work Year Book*, 1929, p. 449.

CHAPTER XX

THE SPHERE OF PRIVATE AGENCIES

PRIVATE recreational agencies are those that are privately managed and supported. They fall into two classes, the philanthropic and the coöperative, the first serving a wide constituency and conducting a social program, the second limited to its own members and their particular interests. Our attention will be given solely to the first division, which is the more significant. Examples of the second type, which may be mentioned in passing, are the choral, dancing, dramatic, and social clubs and other self-initiated activities of foreign-born groups, often meeting at the headquarters of a foreign society or in a recreation hall owned by the particular immigrant group; secondly, the various fraternal, athletic, country, and sports clubs and the musical, art, literary, and dramatic societies of English-speaking groups; and finally, the provision for the recreation of industrial workers through employes' clubhouses, athletic grounds, and other facilities for outdoor sports, outings and picnics, company teams, entertainments, and clubs of various sorts. With partial exception of industrial recreation, which is frequently a phase of industrial welfare work, these activities are organized and supported by the participants themselves. Organizations of this type are very numerous, though hardly any city knows exactly how many exist or how large a part they play in its recreational life. The only problem of the city with regard to this type of activity is to provide for its citizens in the event that these organizations are lacking or are inadequately developed. The work of the philanthropic agencies, on the other hand, is well known. These organizations are supported wholly or largely by contributions of others than those receiving the benefits conferred. Frequently they are endowed, but more generally the income is derived from private gifts for current expenses, in many cities through the medium of the community chest. To a certain extent, revenue is also obtained from fees paid by the members or other participants.

Private agencies of recreation occupy the great middle field between the public or tax-supported and the commercial or revenue-producing agencies. Unlike commercialized recreation, which is always faced with the necessity of making money, and public recreation, which is limited by the fact that it is paid for out of public funds and is politically controlled, private recreation has a great deal of liberty; it can plan programs and carry them out to a large extent at will. It has the field of experimentation practically all to itself. It can pioneer with special groups. Its function, like that of private agencies in general, is to experiment and demonstrate and to raise standards. Private recreation is also distinguished by its provision of intimate, particular leadership through volunteers and paid workers. Most of the organizations set requirements for leaders and provide some sort of training. There are also special professional training schools for recreation or group-work leaders.[1] The work of the private agencies is also more educational, many of the activities falling in the field of adult education. It is more specifically character-training and character-building. On the other hand, the private agencies lack the resources and the extensive organization of the public and commercialized agencies and the direct check-up on quality of work that arises from the public character of the former and the self-supporting nature of the latter. Private agencies show the greatest variation in standards and technique. In its liberty, private recreation finds its weakness as well as its strength. It has been permitted to wander about in its activities without locating a goal and pointing everything in that direction. It has failed to cover all its field because the various organizations have not pulled together. It has displayed much lack of coördination. It is likely to be divided along sectarian and other special-interest lines.

Private recreational agencies may be classified according to the type of service rendered and the age or sex groups dealt with. Thus there are special agencies working with boys and girls, either together or separately, like the Boy Scouts, the Camp Fire Girls, and related organizations. Other agencies, like the Christian Associations, are concerned primarily with young men and women. The church and the social settlement, on the other hand, though they may have specialized work with different age or sex groups, deal primarily with the family as a unit. Historically the agencies working with young men and women preceded those specializing with boys and girls. In a striking number of instances these organizations first appeared in England. They represent adaptations to the changed conditions produced by the growth of cities and of industry. England experienced

[1] Margaretta Williamson, *The Social Worker in Group Work*, 1929. James E. Cutler and Maurice R. Davie, *A Study in Professional Education*, 1930.

this change earlier than did the United States, and efforts were first made there to meet the problems presented. The successful types of organization have survived, and in many cases have spread throughout the world.

The Y.M.C.A.—In 1841 a young man by the name of George Williams (1821-1905) moved from a country town in Devonshire to the city of London, where he became a clerk in a drapery establishment. His place of employment, Hitchcock & Rogers, was of the "living-in" type common at that time, with dormitories on the top floor for assistants and apprentices. These young fellows worked off what spirits were left after their day of fourteen to seventeen hours behind the counter, in a way that left much to be desired. Williams, who was an earnest, active, Christian young man, soon manifested a solicitude for the religious and moral welfare of his fellow clerks, and resolved to do what he could to turn their lives in an upward direction. He invited a small group to meet in his room for prayer and Bible study. Soon others joined the group; a number were converted; and larger rooms were used. Then he interested the head of the firm, who provided a chaplain to conduct daily prayers. Life at Hitchcock & Rogers was changed. Young men in other shops also put these ideas into operation. Finally, or to speak more accurately, as the official beginning of the story, on June 6, 1844, Williams, with eleven other young men, formed an organization which they called the Young Men's Christian Association, and engaged a salaried organizing secretary and missionary to administer and extend the work. Reading and social rooms, library, and lectures were provided, but the chief emphasis was given to the religious work by prayer meeting and Bible class. The object of the Association, as stated in the constitution, was "the improvement of the spiritual condition of young men in the drapery and other trades." Thus the Y.M.C.A. began, as "a work for young men by young men, improving their environment, giving them victory over their temptations, and above all and in all, transforming their character and life through allegiance to Jesus Christ as their Lord and Saviour."[2]

From this modest beginning, the Y.M.C.A., with a modified purpose and extended program, has spread all over the world, and in recognition of his long-continued services Williams was knighted in 1894. The latest available figures giving totals for the world show 9,735 Associations, with 1,561,365 members, and net property and

---

[2] Richard C. Morse, *History of the North American Young Men's Christian Associations*, 1919, ch. I (p. 5 quoted).

funds of $226,119,560.[3] The movement has received its greatest development in the United States. The first two organizations in North America bearing the Association name were formed in 1851, quite independently of one another, in Montreal and in Boston. The constitution of the latter turned out to be the model followed by the majority of Associations in both Canada and the United States. It established what has since been known as "the evangelical church test of active membership," and thus began the close association of the Y.M.C.A. with the church. By this ruling, active membership has been restricted to members of "evangelical" churches, which has been interpreted to mean "trinitarian." Any young man of good moral character, however, may be admitted to associate membership, with all privileges except that of voting. Associate members have long constituted the majority. In 1922 the rules of the organization were made a little more liberal by permitting 10 per cent of the governing board of an Association to be composed of persons not identified with evangelical churches.

In regard to activities, experience has shown that much more is necessary than the simple direct religious appeal, and consequently the work has expanded in a number of respects. The New York Association took the lead in this movement, which came to a head during the period 1865-1870, by amending its constitution to read: "The object of this Association shall be the improvement of the spiritual, mental, social and physical condition of young men." It was the first Association to formulate what has since been adopted throughout the Associations and is known as the fourfold division of the work. The triangle "Spirit, Mind, Body" is symbolic of this broadened conception. The rapid growth in membership dates from this time. The work came to be extended to special groups, and has been organized into state committees and a National Council for the United States. At the beginning of the year 1930, there were 1,370 Associations in the United States, organized as follows:

    722 City Associations.
    193 Railroad Associations.
     51 Colored Men's Associations.
      3 Associations for Indians.
     31 Army and Navy Associations.
    264 Associations in Colleges and Universities.
    106 Town and Country Associations.

[3] *Year Book of the Young Men's Christian Associations of Canada and the United States,* 1927, p. 280.

The total membership was 951,964, classified as follows: men twenty-five years old and over, 457,503; men eighteen to twenty-four, 236,589; boys twelve to seventeen, 257,872.[4]

The special types of work carried on in some or all Young Men's Christian Associations include the following: educational activities, comprising day and night classes in vocational and cultural subjects for boys and young men, which we have discussed in an earlier chapter; the maintenance of reading rooms in nearly every Association, and libraries in a few; employment agencies and vocation service; socials, motion-picture shows, and other entertainments; physical work, including gymnasium classes and competitive sports; dormitories for young men; restaurants and cafeterias. The work with boys has been steadily growing in importance. Among its distinctive features are the summer camp, boys' conferences, the Hi-Y groups, the Employed Boys' Brotherhood, father-and-son activities, the pentathlon and hexathlon system for all-round athletics, the point system of character development, and other programs.

A study of the clientele of the Y.M.C.A. shows that it is predominantly Protestant in affiliation although all young men are welcome to the privileges of the Association; it is predominantly drawn from the English-speaking section of the city's population, although special work is done for those of foreign birth or parentage; it is predominantly for those over 18 years of age, though the proportion of boy membership is increasing; it is predominantly from the "white-collar" class, although the Railroad Y.M.C.A. and some special programs reach selected groups of industrial workers. The groups using the buildings are largely those who seek physical exercise.[5] Though there appears to be some conflict between its religious ideals and social needs, the history of the Y.M.C.A. clearly indicates that the work has developed along lines that represent an adjustment to modern urban conditions.

The Y.W.C.A.—As young women followed the young men in the drift to the cities, seeking new occupations, there arose the same need for an organization to safeguard and help them, and the Young Women's Christian Association was formed. Again, the beginnings took place in England. "Prayer meetings were the atmosphere in which the Young Women's Christian Associations were born and

[4] Jay A. Urice, "Young Men's Christian Associations," *Social Work Year Book for 1929*, pp. 486-487.

[5] Cleveland Recreation Survey, *The Sphere of Private Agencies*, 1920, ch. II; *A Community Recreation Program*, 1920, pp. 42-43.

grew into usefulness.''[6] Two sources of the movement may be traced. The first came from the efforts of Emma Robarts, who in 1855 started prayer meetings for young women. In 1859 a Prayer Union was established, and the title Young Women's Christian Association was assumed, though the local units were called Branches. The second source arose from the work of Lady Kinnaird, who founded the Home and Institute Branch, in 1855, by enlarging the scope of a nurses' home in London to include social features, religious activities, an employment bureau, and other departments. This expanded program was emphasized in 1858 by organizing a Young Women's Christian Improvement Association in the Home. Prayer Unions increased, and Homes and Institutes sprang up all over England; in 1877 the two associations united, to form the Y.W.C.A. as we know it today.

The first Y.W.C.A. in America was organized in Boston in 1866. By the end of 1929, there were 459 local Associations, affiliated in a national organization, with 550 student Associations in addition. The former group included 263 City Associations in cities of 25,000 or more population, 143 Town Associations in communities of 10,000 to 25,000 population, and 53 Rural Communities Associations and District Associations in small communities with the surrounding country, with 9 new ones in process of organization. The total individual membership numbered 691,418.[7] Any woman 18 years of age and over is eligible to general membership, and where the new form of constitution, sanctioned by the Convention in 1926, has been adopted, is also eligible to vote and to be appointed or elected to office, provided only she be in sympathy with the purposes of the organization.

Outstanding subdivisions of the work of the Y.W.C.A. include branches for work among colored people, International Institute branches for foreign communities, and Associations among the American Indians, chiefly in government schools. Cross-cutting these variants in community organization, extensive club and educational programs are carried on among certain age, occupation, and professional-interest groups. The regular Industrial Clubs enrolled during 1929 nearly 40,000 members, and an additional 30,000 industrial workers were reached through other activities. Approximately 65,000 individuals were enrolled in the 1,000 clubs of business and professional

[6] Elizabeth Wilson, *Fifty Years of Association Work Among Young Women*, 1916, chs. II, III (p. 66 quoted).
[7] Edith T. Bremer and Elizabeth Wilson, ''Young Women's Christian Associations,'' *Social Work Year Book for 1929*, p. 488.

women, with 25,000 more participating in other ways. Group work for young girls, ages 12 to 18, operates under the title of Girl Reserves, and is carried on in colored, Indian, and International Institute branches as well as in the regular Associations. In 1929 it enrolled 250,000 members. Other activities include employment and vocation service, social case work, housing service through the residence buildings and the rooms registry departments, and recreation camps and vacation houses.[8] The general statements made above with reference to the clientele of the Y.M.C.A. apply also to that of the Y.W.C.A.

Other Youth Service Associations.—Besides the Christian Associations a number of other organizations provide a recreational, educational, and religious program for young people. The following are typical examples.

1. Girls' Friendly Society.—The Girls' Friendly Society was organized in England in 1875 under the Anglican Church for the purpose of reaching groups of young women who were then beginning to leave their homes for places in the new industrial life. The first society in this country was established in Lowell, Massachusetts, in 1877. "In both England and America the purpose was to organize a society which should uphold the highest standards of Christian character, and in which every member should find friendly companionship, a strong religious influence, and adult leadership. In both countries, also, the membership was at that time composed chiefly of girls in industry and domestic service. Volunteer leaders were readily obtained and in many instances their attitude was that of Lady Bountiful—giving help to the underprivileged. As the result of changed educational philosophy, the place of the adult has at present become that of adviser and counsellor who encourages girl initiative."[9]

The membership of the society is now non-sectarian and includes girls of every race, interest, and occupation. Candidates for membership are girls between 6 and 12 years of age, and members are from 12 years old upward. At the end of 1929, the total membership in the United States was approximately 46,000 individuals, organized in 1,115 branches in 57 dioceses. The local units, varying in size and interest, are organized in connection with Episcopal churches. Each unit has a volunteer leader who must be a communicant of the Episcopal Church. Local branches do not own clubrooms, but usually meet in the parish houses of the churches with which they are connected. An analysis of the membership shows that about 50 per cent are in school or college, 20 per cent in offices, 16 per cent at home and not gain-

---

[8] *Ibid.*, pp. 487-490.
[9] Florence L. Newbold, "Girls' Friendly Society of the United States of America," *Social Work Year Book for 1929*, p. 482. *Cf.* Helen J. Ferris, *Girls' Clubs*, 1918, pp. 150, 200, 205.

fully employed, 8 per cent in business or the professions, and 6 per cent in industry.

2. Knights of Columbus.—This is the largest organization of Catholic men in America. Applicants must be practicing Catholic men of 18 years or older, and must subscribe to being opposed to socialism as an economic system. The order was founded in Connecticut and chartered in 1882. In 1930 it enrolled 614,784 members, organized in 2,548 local councils in the United States, Canada, and other countries. Of the two classes of members—insured and associate—the latter is more numerous. The social program of the organization, which is all that concerns us here, consists in promoting and conducting educational, charitable, religious, and social welfare work, boys' clubs, Boy Scout troops, playgrounds, and summer camps. The activities of the order were greatly expanded during the World War, when it was the recognized agency for service to Catholic enlisted men. After the war the society entered actively into work for boys. A division of the movement is the society for older boys known as Columbian Squires. This is a junior order for boys from 14 to 18 years of age. It has a five-fold program of activities with extensive religious, cultural, educational, and social-civic features. Columbian Squire units have been organized in 25 states, with Knights of Columbus men as leaders.[10]

3. Jewish Community Centers.—This term is applied not only to organizations of that name but also to the Young Men's and Young Women's Hebrew Associations. With very few exceptions, all these organizations function as general community centers, providing leisure-time activities equally for Jewish men and women, boys and girls. Jewish Community Centers date back to 1874, when the Young Men's Hebrew Association of New York City was organized. The first association for girls and women, the Young Women's Hebrew Association of New York City, was established in 1902. In 1917 the National Council of Young Men's Hebrew and Kindred Associations was merged with the Jewish Welfare Board, and under the terms of the merger the local affiliated organizations became constituent societies of the national body, the Jewish Welfare Board. Member societies are organized into state and regional federations, all located in the East. The local societies include 61 Y. M. H. A.'s, 44 Y. W. H. A.'s, 54 combined Y. M. and Y. W. H. A.'s, and 102 Jewish Community Centers. The total membership in 1929 was approximately 280,000, of whom about 80,000 were boys and girls under 16 years of age, 160,000 were young men and women from 16 to 25, and 40,000 were adults over 25 years of age. Sixty-five per cent of the total number were men and boys.

The local societies provide for their membership a program of health activities, including gymnasium and swimming classes; socials, games, dances, and entertainments; also a variety of cultural and educational activities, including dramatics, music, art, discussion groups, unit courses, lectures,

[10] John J. Contway, "Knights of Columbus," *Social Work Year Book for 1929*, pp. 485-486.

concerts, forums, and lyceums. Clubs with trained leaders are provided for boys and girls of elementary and high-school age. Jewish interests are specifically encouraged, and wherever feasible Jewish elements are introduced into the general program, particularly in the cultural, educational, and social activities.[11]

The Boy Scouts.—The most distinctive and important of modern organizations for boys is the Boy Scouts. The founder of the movement was General Sir Robert Baden-Powell, though he says that he borrowed liberally from the organized activities for boys then being conducted in America by such men as Dan Beard and Ernest Thompson Seton. The movement grew up more or less spontaneously, and it is hard to fix any exact date for its beginning. Generally the year 1907 is accepted as the official date. During the summer of 1907 Baden-Powell organized a small group of boys, whom he called Boy Scouts, at a camp in Dorset, where he tried out his theories of scouting. It was the first Boy Scout troop. In 1908 he published a handbook, *Scouting for Boys*. In 1910 the movement had grown to such dimension—there were 124,000 Scouts in the United Kingdom—that Baden-Powell felt it incumbent on him to leave the Army and devote his time to its organization and development. In 1912 a Royal charter was granted as official recognition. From England the movement spread all over the world. On its twenty-first birthday the Boy Scout movement could boast of nearly 2,000,000 members. In 1929 a world Jamboree was held in England, in which 60,000 boys from more than 70 lands participated. The greatest expansion of the organization has taken place in the United States, where the Boy Scouts of America was chartered in 1910. At the close of 1929, Boy Scouts in the United States numbered 615,047, organized in 27,769 troops under 634 local councils. There were 227,501 volunteer leaders and about 1,000 full-time salaried officials. All told, over 4,000,000 boys have held membership in the Boy Scouts of America. The movement is firmly established in every state in the Union.[12]

The Boy Scout idea is a movement rather than an organization. It makes no claim to supersede the work of home, school, or church; on the contrary, it aims to supplement these institutions by engag-

[11] Harry L. Glucksman, "Jewish Community Centers," *Social Work Year Book for 1929*, pp. 483-485.

[12] E. K. Wade, *Twenty-One Years of Scouting, The Official History of the Boy Scout Movement from its Inception*, 1929. Sir Robert Baden-Powell, *Scouting and Youth Movements*, 1929, ch. II. *Twentieth Annual Report of the Boy Scouts of America*, 1929. James E. West, "Boy Scouts of America," *Social Work Year Book for 1929*, p. 399.

ing the boys' leisure energies in outdoor games and activities of cultural and practical value. Its fundamental principle is the close association of a small group of boys with an adult volunteer leader or scoutmaster who gives his time, thought, and influence to the troop for which he is responsible. Boys become eligible for membership at the age of 12. Scout troops number from 8 to 32 boys, and are sponsored by a troop committee of at least 3 adult citizens. Troops do not set up buildings of their own, but use instead the facilities of churches, schools, service clubs, granges, or similar institutions with which they are affiliated. About 50 per cent of the troops are organized in connection with churches. Several thousand are connected with public and private schools, and thousands of school teachers serve as scoutmasters.[13]

Fundamental also to the movement is the series of merit badges or ranks reached through attainment in specified lines of effort. This provides a progressive training. The boy is first admitted as a tenderfoot scout. As he becomes more proficient in the outdoor arts required, he may become a second-class and finally a first-class scout. Then there are merit badges that may be won by gaining proficiency and passing an examination in any of the common trades and crafts or in feats of skill and prowess. Scout craft includes instruction in first aid, life-saving, tracking, signaling, cycling, nature study, seamanship, camp craft, woodcraft, chivalry, and all the handicrafts. It also gives fundamental training in courage, truthfulness, friendship, kindness, democracy, and thrift.[14] The program is excellently adapted to boys of a certain age. Though the movement applies the principles of military organization, it is non-military in character. The military virtues of obedience, neatness, order, endurance, erect bearing, and the like, have been made Scout virtues. The military ideal has remained in the form of organization, the patrol and the troop, in the uniform and the occasional drills, in the marching and signaling, but it has disappeared almost entirely from the order itself. The Scouts are really citizens in uniform. The spirit and purpose of the Boy Scout movement can best be described in the words of the Scout Oath: "On my honor I will do my best: (1) to do my duty to God and my country and to obey the Scout Law; (2) to help other people at all times; (3) to keep myself physically strong, mentally awake, and morally straight."

[13] Norman E. Richardson and Ormond E. Loomis, *The Boy Scout Movement Applied by the Church*, 1915. Lorne W. Barclay, *Educational Work of the Boy Scouts*, U. S. Bureau of Education Bulletin, 1921, No. 41.
[14] Henry S. Curtis, *The Play Movement and its Significance*, 1917, ch. X.

Sir Robert Baden-Powell[15] says that the virtues and possibilities of the educative side of Scouting may be summed up in the idea that we have here one medium at any rate by which boys can be trained in character, health, skill, and sense of service to the community, and to become healthy, happy, and efficient citizens. Dean Russell, of Teachers College, Columbia University, says that the Boy Scout movement is the most significant educational contribution of our time. "The naturalist may praise it for its success in putting the boy close to nature's heart; the moralist, for its splendid code of ethics; the hygienist, for its methods of physical training; the parent, for its ability to keep his boy out of mischief; but from the standpoint of the educator, it has marvelous potency for converting the restless, irresponsible, self-centered boy into the straightforward, dependable, helpful young citizen. To the boy who will give himself to it, there is plenty of work that looks like play, standards of excellence which he can appreciate, rules of conduct which he must obey, positions of responsibility which he must occupy as soon as he qualifies himself— in a word, a program that appeals to a boy's instincts, and a method adapted to a boy's nature."[16]

The Girl Scouts.—A sister movement to the Boy Scouts is that known in England as the Girl Guides and in America as the Girl Scouts. The Girl Guides as such were "founded" by Sir Robert Baden-Powell in 1910; but their growth like that of the Boy Scouts was spontaneous, and no actual date can be given for the first appearance of girls in the movement. Sir Robert says: "The Girl Guide Movement has the distinguished feature that it started itself. Girls took up Scouting with their brothers, and we subsequently adapted it to their needs and organised it as a separate movement."[17] With the aid of his sister, Agnes, he adapted from *Scouting for Boys* a handbook for girls, called *How Girls Can Help to Build the Empire*. The title was changed in 1918 to *Girl Guiding*. From 1912 on, the movement was greatly aided by Lady Baden-Powell, who was made Chief Guide in 1918. The movement was chartered in 1915, when it had a membership of 38,000. In 1929 it had a larger enrolment than did the Boy Scouts in Great Britain.[18]

The Girl Scout organization was founded in Savannah, Georgia, in 1912 by Mrs. Juliette Low, a friend of Sir Robert Baden-Powell,

---

[15] *Scouting and Youth Movements*, 1929, pp. 15, 27.

[16] James E. Russell, "Scouting Education," *Teachers College Record*, Jan., 1917, 18:1:6-7.

[17] Sir Robert Baden-Powell, *Scouting and Youth Movements*, 1929, p. 17.

[18] E. K. Wade, *Twenty-One Years of Scouting*, 1929, ch. VIII.

who encouraged and inspired the undertaking. As a national movement it was incorporated in 1915 as the National Council of Girl Scouts, with local councils and community committees throughout the country. Both movements are united in the Girl Guides and Girl Scouts, World Bureau, organized in 1919, with 33 constituent national organizations, in 28 countries. The purpose of the Girl Scouts, as stated in its constitution, is "to help girls to realize the ideals of womanhood as a preparation for their responsibilities in the home and for service to the community. Emphasis is placed on methods of training to develop initiative, self-control, resourcefulness, and service to others, and in general the qualities of character of most value in adult life. The organization favors no creed, party, or sect; but cheerfully coöperates with any organization seeking to extend the influence for good which may be exercised by women in the home, and in religious, social, and civic affairs." In 1929 there were 10,375 local groups, organized in 3,127 communities, with a total active membership of 205,834, representing all states and territories. Of the total membership, 179,736 were Girl Scouts and 26,098 were volunteer leaders. A study made in 1928 of some 8,000 Girl Scout troops showed that 26 per cent were affiliated with churches, 20 per cent with schools, 6 per cent with clubs and associations, and 4 per cent with community houses, settlements, libraries, and other agencies. The other 44 per cent were independent or unreported.[19]

Related Organizations.—A brief statement concerning the history, aims, activities, and membership of the more important organizations related to scouting is given below.

1. Boy Rangers of America.—This organization, established in 1913, admits boys from 8 to 12 years of age; that is, from the age at which they begin to exercise initiative up to the age which makes them eligible for membership in the Boy Scouts. The Ranger program is based on Indian lore and upon records of pioneer days. Judicious selections are made from Indian habits, customs, games, and codes. The "great laws" of the organization contain the cardinal principles of character, expressed in language intelligible to younger boys. These principles in no way conflict with the religious affiliation of the boy, but are designed to supplement and strengthen his religious faith. Ranger lodges are organized in every state of the Union except Delaware. In 1929, there were over 860 lodges, with an approximate membership of 20,000 boys. Leaders, known as "guide rangers," are usually volunteers.

[19] Juliette Low, *Girl Scouts as an Educational Force*, U. S. Bureau of Education Bulletin, 1919, No. 33. Anne Hyde Choate and Helen Ferris, *Juliette Low and the Girl Scouts*, 1928. *Girl Scout Handbook*, rev. ed., 1929. Elizabeth K. Adams, "Girl Scouts," *Social Work Year Book for 1929*, p. 401.

Although most lodges have been organized in churches, many are sponsored by service clubs, Masonic lodges, Catholic or Jewish organizations, and Boy Scout councils, about 25 groups in all sponsoring the local organizations.[20]

2. *Camp Fire Girls.*—The national body was organized in 1911, with Dr. Luther H. Gulick as the first president. It was formed to provide a program of leisure-time activities for girls which should parallel but not copy the program of the Boy Scouts. The purpose of the organization is to conserve the ideals of the home, to further healthful and character-building activities, and to contribute to the social life of organized social groups in the community through the promotion of pageants, civic celebrations, amateur dramatics and music, social center activities, organized vacations, and tramping. Activities carried on by the Camp Fire Girls are grouped under the so-called "seven crafts": home, health, hand, nature, camp, business, and citizenship. Each year the largest proportion of honors is awarded in home craft. The promotion of summer camping is a major activity. In 1929 there were 7,150 Camp Fire groups and 900 Blue Bird or junior groups, organized in 2,941 communities, with 173,111 girls enrolled as members. There were 214 salaried local officials, and 10,851 volunteer group leaders. Of these groups, 40 per cent were organized under the auspices of schools, 20 per cent under the auspices of churches, and 40 per cent were organized independently.[21]

Dr. Curtis holds that the Camp Fire Girls have certain advantages over the Boy Scouts. "The scouts are seeking to promote a form of activity and of virtue that corresponds to a certain stage of human development, but which at the present belongs to history. It is a most wholesome ideal, but it is an ideal that history has left behind on account of changed conditions. It is not so with the Camp Fire Girls or better the Fireside Girls, which would really be a better name. It is no less appropriate to the present than it would have been to any time in history. It is seeking to add romance and adventure to the ordinary affairs of woman's life, and to add to her training the sense of service. The boy scouts are very much limited in their activities by living in cities. Not so the Camp Fire Girls; they can pursue their work and win their honors nearly as well in a modern city as anywhere. Their field is as wide as the home and human relationship."[22]

3. *Junior Achievement.*—Junior Achievement was founded by Theodore N. Vail, late head of the American Telephone and Telegraph Company, Senator Murray Crane, Horace A. Moses, and others, in order that boys and girls in urban centers might have service and training similar to that offered to country children by the agricultural clubs organized under the auspices of the United States Department of Agriculture. The movement was started in

[20] Emerson Brooks, "Boy Rangers of America," *Social Work Year Book for 1929*, p. 398.

[21] *The Book of the Camp Fire Girls*, 1929 edition. Lester F. Scott, "Camp Fire Girls," *Social Work Year Book for 1929*, p. 401.

[22] Henry S. Curtis, *The Play Movement and its Significance*, 1917, ch. XI (pp. 270-71 quoted).

1919 as a bureau of the Eastern States Agricultural and Industrial League, and was separately incorporated under its present name in 1926.

Junior Achievement furnishes leadership and direction to children associated in small groups or clubs for the purpose of simple hand manufacturing. The articles made are useful and artistic, and in their manufacture boys and girls gain experience in business procedure. The varieties of work undertaken are called "enterprises." Six have to do with reeds, 6 with needlecraft, 7 with textiles, 1 with food, 3 with home improvement, 10 with hammered metal, 10 with leather, 40 with woodwork, 11 with wrought iron, and 11 with electrical appliances. Great stress is laid upon business organization and sales production. At the end of 1929, approximately 1,100 clubs were in operation in 80 cities and towns, with over 10,000 boys and girls enrolled. Nearly a thousand leaders were engaged, three-fourths of whom were volunteers. The clubs are conducted under the auspices of local branches of the Y. M. C. A., Y. W. C. A., boys' clubs, girls' clubs, churches, community centers, settlements, and schools.[23]

4. Pioneer Youth of America.—This organization was started in 1924 by a group of labor leaders and educators in order to provide camp and club activities of a creative character, primarily for the children of wage-earners. It should not be confused with the Pioneers, under the auspices of the Y. M. C. A., or the Young Pioneers, a communist children's organization. Pioneer Youth aims "to build strong, healthy, and well-balanced bodies and minds; to cultivate, through creative activity, the power to think clearly and freely and to act courageously; to engender a love and understanding of nature; to acquaint children and youth with the social and economic problems that face the world; and to develop in them a sense of social responsibility and justice."

The activities carried on follow no set rules, but vary according to individual and group interests and purposes. The program includes handicrafts; hikes and trips; exercise in gymnasium and pool; dramatics, music, and games; and group organization, discussion, and investigations. During 1929 there were 207 boys and girls enrolled in two camps, and 315 children in 28 city groups or clubs in New York City, Philadelphia, and Baltimore.[24]

Neva R. Deardorff[25] says the story of Pioneer Youth as an organization deserves a prominent place in the archives of the struggle of workers' groups to secure a richer cultural life. "Like other experimental educationalists, Pioneer Youth seeks for the means by which a child may be helped to discover the powers within him and to develop them to their best social uses. More acutely perhaps than some other segments of society, these people from the ranks of labor feel the compelling need for finding ways of developing the

[23] Morris E. Alling, ''Junior Achievement,'' *Social Work Year Book for 1929,* pp. 402-403.
[24] W. Walter Ludwig, ''Pioneer Youth of America,'' *Social Work Year Book for 1929,* pp. 403-404.
[25] ''Pioneer Youth in Camp,'' *The Survey,* Oct. 15, 1929, 63:2:78.

inner resources of their boys and girls. For in all probability their children will grow up in a world in which the drift will be increasingly toward mechanization and regimentation in industry and trade and in which the problems of the mental adjustment of ordinary men and women will be new and difficult. Character education in the modern world, puzzling enough for all groups, is immensely complex for those who avowedly look forward to a new and different order. What qualities of personality will be necessary to make such a new order workable? Certainly not merely the obstructionist negativism of many who protest the present order. Whatever else may be required, it seems clear to these people that poise, reasonableness, and the capacity to work effectively in organized groups will be essential. Leadership must be both diffused and organized. Each person must learn to be both leader and follower."

5. *Woodcraft League of America.*—Believing that woodcraft was an interest to be particularly cultivated in childhood, Ernest Thompson Seton in 1902 founded the Woodcraft Indians and used the ideal red man as its model. In 1916 this organization was incorporated as the Woodcraft League of America, Inc., with Mr. Seton as chief and with field councils for local activities. Its purpose is to teach the outdoor life for its worth in building character, and to educate through recreation and activities that are simple and fundamental—camping, pioneering, home crafts, and Indian lore. "The Woodcraft League aims to set before youth an ideal figure, physically strong, dignified, courteous, self-controlled, happy in helping, equipped for emergencies, wise in the ways of the woods, in touch with men of affairs, of such all-round development that he can quickly be made a specialist in any needy place, and filled with the religion that consists not of mere observances, but of a spirit which makes one desired and helpful here today. The Woodcraft embodies the Four Fold Way of Life, that is, development along the pathways of the body, mind, spirit, and service; it takes as its basis the primitive of each country, refined and adapted for present-day use; it works primarily with recreation and teaches fun not bought with money."[26] The organization takes in both sexes and all ages, with a special program for children under 12, for grown-ups over 18, and for the family as a unit. The movement is said to be worldwide, with functioning groups in Europe, Asia, and Africa, but no figures of membership or local organizations are given.

Boys' Clubs.—As distinguished from boys' clubs conducted by settlements, the Y.M.C.A., the Knights of Columbus, the Jewish Community Centers, and similar organizations, are boys' clubs that are separately organized and have their own buildings or quarters. The history of the boys' club movement in America dates back to the period immediately following the Civil War. The basic purpose of the

[26] Ernest Thompson Seton, "Woodcraft League of America," *Social Work Year Book for 1929*, p. 404.

clubs established then was to provide within a congested area of the city a place to which boys might resort in their leisure time and find warmth, hospitality, companionship, and activities which would be interesting to them. The ideal from the beginning has been to avoid a standardized program and to allow the largest possible freedom for the inauguration of activities that would be the expression of the boys' own desires. In 1916 the Boys' Club Federation of America was founded, and it has since been the central clearing-house for the interests and activities of local clubs. Similar federations may be found in Canada and the British Isles, and local organizations in Australia, New Zealand, and Holland, all of which have been organized into an international committee with headquarters in London.

In 1930 there were 253 boys' clubs affiliated with the Boys' Club Federation of America. Only clubs that are non-sectarian in character are eligible for membership. These clubs were located in 131 cities, in 33 states, and had a membership of 238,497 boys, an average of 942 per club. Almost without exception these boys pay a modest membership fee ranging from 25 cents to $3.00 a year. There were 3,970 paid and volunteer workers. By far the greater proportion of the membership is between the ages of 8 and 16; some clubs have featured service to older boys in so-called senior divisions. The activities include athletics and gymnasium classes, bands and orchestras, camping, the program of the Boy Scouts and similar organizations mentioned above, vocational classes, entertainments, games, and other programs.[27]

Girls' Clubs.—The girls' clubs that are organized separately represent an older age group than the boys' clubs, the membership consisting almost entirely of girls and young women who are gainfully employed. The first working-women's club in the United States of which there is any record was started in 1881 by a few women employed in garment factories in New York City, who were drawn together by a common desire for recreation and self-improvement. They asked a wealthy woman of education and culture, who was their Sunday-school teacher, to direct it. It grew rapidly, soon reaching a membership of 150. A dress-making class was started and a circulating library of 500 volumes collected—at a time when trade schools and public libraries were non-existent. With the exception of gifts received for the original furnishing of the clubroom, the club was self-supporting. By 1885, eight clubs of this sort had been formed among industrial workers in New York City. They were federated

[27] *1931 Year Book of the Boys' Club Federation of America.* R. K. Atkinson, "Boys' Clubs," *Social Work Year Book for 1929*, pp. 46-48.

in the New York Association of Working Girls' Societies, now called the New York League of Girls' Clubs, whose stated purpose was "to promote the physical, intellectual and moral advancement of women workers and to afford them opportunities for friendly association and intelligent coöperation." Similar clubs and state federations were formed in Massachusetts, Connecticut, and Pennsylvania. The growth of clubs followed the path of the woman worker, and was concentrated on the Atlantic seaboard.

The attention of these early groups was focused on the problems of the employed woman—her working and living conditions and her opportunities for recreation and education. The New York organization promoted the Manhattan Trade School for Girls, the first school to provide vocational training for women. It also conceived the idea of a working-girls' hotel which should be self-supporting and have no rules or regulations except such as govern any hotel. This finally found expression in the Virginia Hotel in 1911, followed later by the Irvin, and in 1930 by the Sutton. The inexpensive summer vacation was stressed in all states, and practically every state organization had its vacation house at the seashore or in the mountains.

In 1921 the total membership in girls' clubs was 18,000, federated in 6 state associations and a national organization—the National League of Girls' Clubs. From 1922 to 1928, when it was disbanded, the National League contributed to the movement for adult education and did pioneer experiments in that field. These activities are now carried on by the state leagues through their special education departments, with paid trained secretaries.[28]

The Social Settlement.—The origin of the social settlement is commonly ascribed to a group of men who were at Oxford University, England, about 1870, and who were very much interested in social problems and deeply in sympathy with the aims and hopes of workingmen. This interest and intellectual sympathy first found expression in the University-extension movement, which was inaugurated in 1867, when James Stuart, then a fellow of Trinity College, Cambridge, began the extension of university teaching by giving courses of lectures in manufacturing towns. In 1873 he was able to secure the adoption of the plan by Cambridge University; and within a short time this service had so clearly proved its value that extension lectures were undertaken by Oxford and London universities as well. A channel

[28] Doris Maddow, "Girls' Clubs," *Social Work Year Book for 1929*, pp. 173-176.

was thus opened for an entirely novel form of contact between representatives of the centers of culture and communities of working people.

From Oxford, the movement across class lines assumed a more personal and more objective form in the work of the first actual settlement pioneer, Edward Denison (1840-1870). Denison, coming deeply under the influence of John Ruskin and his social philosophy, decided that he must have some measure of personal acquaintance with the life of toil and poverty, and accordingly he became an agent of the Society for the Relief of Distress in the district of Stepney. He soon recognized the unsatisfactory results of doling out relief; he believed there must be a better way. He resolved to study the situation more closely and thoroughly, so in 1867 he took lodgings in the district, and became what we now call a settlement worker. He soon came to see that men could best be helped by being provided with means of self-help. "Build schoolhouses," he wrote, "pay teachers, give prizes, frame workmen's clubs, help them to help themselves, lend them your brains; but give them no money, except what you sink in such undertakings as above." During the time that he was in residence, he built and endowed a school in which he himself taught Bible classes and gave lectures to workingmen. In this work he was joined by the local vicar, John Richard Green, who later became the noted historian. Aided by Green and Ruskin, Denison formed a plan whereby other young men should join him and form a colony. Only the failure of Denison's health and his untimely death prevented the establishment of such a definite organization.

The credit for making the first constructive step toward the founding of the settlement belongs to Samuel A. Barnett (1844-1913), an Oxford graduate and clergyman, who deliberately sought one of the neediest parishes in London because of his interest in working-people. In 1872 he accepted the vicarage of St. Jude's, Whitechapel, and at once undertook the reorganization of poor relief and the extension of educational work in the district. He took up, almost where Denison had left it, the enlisting of young laymen from the universities. He visited Oxford at frequent intervals for the sake of putting details of life in East London before young collegians and of engaging their active interest. It was on one of these excursions that Barnett first met Arnold Toynbee, who more than any other came to inspire the little group at Oxford to take an active interest in the struggles of the poor.

Toynbee (1852-1883), who matriculated at Balliol College, Oxford, in 1873, was an ardent disciple of Thomas Hill Green, professor of philosophy, who taught that philosophy and religion were inseparable from active philanthropy. Toynbee accepted this as a fundamental truth, and it became the chief desire of his life to assist in the betterment of living and working conditions among wage-earners. In 1875 he took lodgings near St. Jude's vicarage, participated in the club and guild work of the parish, and acted as a visitor for the Charity Organization Society. He joined a workingmen's club, organized a class of workmen, and gave a series of university-extension lectures on economic subjects, particularly the Industrial Revolution. As in the case of Denison, his activities came to an untimely end; he died, when only thirty-one, from overwork and too great mental strain on a frail body. Canon Barnett and others of his friends sought a suitable memorial for him. They decided to build a house in East London where university men might live for longer or shorter periods and study the life and problems of an industrial neighborhood, and thus gain "that close personal acquaintance with individuals which must precede any wise public action for meeting working-class needs." A building was erected in 1884 and called Toynbee Hall. It was the first social settlement. Barnett became the first head-resident, or warden, as he was called after the university manner. Toynbee Hall is still a flourishing settlement. It has furnished the model for hundreds of other settlements scattered over the world. In particular, it inspired the founders of the first American settlements, all of whom visited it and received inspiration and guidance from Mr. Barnett.[29]

The first settlement in the United States was the Neighborhood Guild, now known as University Settlement, established by Dr. Stanton Coit, a graduate of Amherst College, on the east side of New York City in 1886. The second and third American settlements were founded, both in 1889, by college women: College Settlement on the east side of New York, by Dr. Jane E. Robbins and Jean Fine, both Smith College alumnae; and Hull House in Chicago, by Jane Addams and Ellen Gates Starr, classmates at Rockford College. The fourth settlement, East Side House, in the founding of which Everett P. Wheeler, attorney and publicist, took the initiative, opened its doors in New York in 1891. Northwestern University Settlement in Chicago was established in 1891 by Charles Zueblin, a graduate of that uni-

[29] Robert A. Woods and Albert J. Kennedy, *The Settlement Horizon*, 1922, ch. II. Arthur C. Holden, *The Settlement Idea*, 1922, ch. II. For biographies of the English settlement pioneers, see F. C. Montague, *Arnold Toynbee*, Baltimore, 1889; Alfred Milner, *Arnold Toynbee, a reminiscence*, London, 1901; Baldyn Leighton, editor, *Letters and Other Writings of the Late Edward Denison*, London, 1875; Mrs. H. O. Barnett, *Canon Barnett, his life, work, and friends*, London, 1918.

versity. The sixth pioneer was Andover House in Boston, now called the South End House, organized in 1891, the first director of which was Robert A. Woods, a graduate of Andover Theological Seminary. From that time on to the beginning of the World War the number of houses doubled every five years. In 1930 there were about 500 settlements in the United States. Many of these, however, were not typical settlements, which are non-sectarian, but were conducted under the auspices of a denominational organization. The number of typical settlements does not exceed 150, and with a few exceptions all are affiliated with the National Federation of Settlements, which was organized in 1911. In 1930 the Federation embraced 160 constituent organizations, with 1,500 staff members and 7,500 volunteers.[30]

Since the founding of the movement, settlements have always purposely located in the neediest sections of cities, where the process of social disintegration was rapidly taking place owing to the rapidity of urban growth, the mobility of the population, and the influx of the foreign-born. The settlements undertook the work of reconstruction, endeavoring to promote social organization and build up neighborhood life. To accomplish this, it was necessary for them to become a component part of the life of the neighborhood, to develop local institutional resources, and to evoke local coöperation. The basis for this work lay in acquaintance, an acquaintance predicated on respect for every form of faith and every race. "The range and intensity of the personal relations between the people of the neighborhood and the staff have always been held to be the most important indications of the quality of the work of a settlement. The early residents lived in the neighborhood because they wished to identify themselves in every possible way with the people of the community. It has never been a matter of policy that residents must live in the building in which the work of the settlement is carried on. The purpose of residence is not an administrative convenience, but ease of knowing those to be served

[30] Robert A. Woods and Albert J. Kennedy, *The Settlement Horizon*, 1922, ch. IV. For comments by these and other American settlement pioneers and for biographical data, see Stanton Coit, *Neighbourhood Guilds; an instrument of social reform*, 1891; Jane E. Robbins, "First Years at the College Settlement," *The Survey*, Feb. 24, 1912, XXVII, 1800-1802; Jane Addams, *Twenty Years at Hull House*, 1910, *The Second Twenty Years at Hull House*, 1930; Charles Zueblin, "Settlements and the New Civic Spirit," *Chautauquan*, Sept., 1903, XXXVIII, 55-59; Robert A. Woods, editor, *The City Wilderness; a settlement study by residents and associates of the South End House, Boston*, 1898; *Americans in Process*, a similar study, 1902; Robert A. Woods, *Neighborhood in Nation Building*, 1922; Eleanor H. Woods, *Robert A. Woods, Champion of Democracy*, 1929; Howard E. Wilson, *Mary McDowell, Neighbor*, 1928; Graham Taylor, *Pioneering on Social Frontiers*, 1930.

equally, intimately, and humanly."[31] In view of these facts, the term "neighborhood house" is a better designation than "settlement."

The forms of work carried on in a settlement at any one time are those considered by the head worker to be specifically adapted to the needs of the local community. The program, by definition, therefore, is changing and evolutionary.[32] Settlements differ greatly among themselves; there is no uniform method characteristic of all. Each one has its own methods very largely, which have been worked out by experience in accordance with the special circumstances of the particular place. In general, however, the aims and activities are similar. From the point of view of its activities, a settlement may be defined as a neighborhood center for social, physical, civic, educational, and moral instruction and improvement. The types of activity commonly found include clubrooms for lodges and groups of all sorts; dancing facilities and classes; dramatics; community entertainments; orchestras; gymnasium classes and other athletic activity; playgrounds and summer camps; clinics, medical examinations and health education; reading rooms, library branches, lectures, kindergartens, day nurseries, vocational classes, and classes in English and in citizenship. The club is probably the sole activity which is common to all settlements. The settlements early took the boy gangs in the neighborhood and turned them into settlement clubs, building on the factors of loyalty, responsibility, and leadership. Clubs for both sexes and all age groups abound.[33] In general, the settlement has tried to offer a counter-attraction to the various forms of commercialized recreation and to reach the whole family. It has not specialized in work for any age group or either sex; any one can become a member of the settlement and find a suitable activity.

The settlement has been termed a laboratory in social science whose function is to discover ways of raising the general level of civilization, particularly among the less well-to-do elements in the community.[34] Being right on the ground and having a first-hand knowledge of actual conditions, the settlement is well fitted to serve in this capacity, and settlements have done a great deal of pioneering, experimental work, and have demonstrated the usefulness of new social devices and types of organization. The settlements developed the play-

[31] Albert J. Kennedy, "Social Settlements," *Social Work Year Book for 1929*, p. 427.
[32] *Ibid.*, pp. 424-425.
[33] Arthur C. Holden, *The Settlement Idea*, 1922, ch. VI. Robert A. Woods and Albert J. Kennedy, *The Settlement Horizon*, 1922, chs. VII, VIII.
[34] Albert J. Kennedy, "Social Settlements," *Social Work Year Book for 1929*, p. 425.

ground and the idea of directed play; they used the kindergarten classes as experiment stations for trying out projects such as the visiting kindergartner, summer nursery, and playground kindergartens. Story-telling, as an encouragement of good reading on the part of children, was in the beginning almost a specialty of settlements. The first experiment in vocational guidance was conducted by Prof. Frank Parsons at Civic Service House, in Boston, a settlement working with young men and women in a foreign section. Settlements established vocational classes and demonstrated the desirability of including such provision in the curriculum of the public schools; they started the ungraded class for subnormal children. Branch libraries, evening classes, Americanization classes, music schools for working people were first started or promoted by them. The settlements were pioneers in the little theatre movement in the United States, the Hull House players antedating all others. The Henry Street nursing settlement in New York City conducted the first experiment in school nursing, did pioneer preventive work with tuberculosis patients, started milk stations, began the nursing of industrial policyholders, established the first demonstration center for teaching housekeeping, and its head resident, Lillian D. Wald, originated the idea of a children's bureau in the Federal Government. Settlement workers gathered the facts regarding industrial and living conditions and agitated for corrective social legislation. They were among the pioneers in the movements to reform conditions affecting child labor, sweat shops, women in industry, industrial accidents, and unemployment. They were among the early agitators for tenement-house reform, and they helped in the movement to improve municipal government and administration.[35]

Many of the activities originated or promoted by the settlements have since been taken over and extended by the public-health authorities, the public schools, public departments of recreation, and various other official agencies. This situation, along with restriction of immigration, a general improvement in the condition of the masses, and other social changes, has greatly altered the work of settlements in recent years. Some settlements have even found their neighborhoods completely wiped out through the encroachment of industry and the migration of the people. This has happened particularly in New York and Boston, and an increasing number of settlements in the more thickly settled portions of these cities is bound to be affected. In gen-

[35] Robert A. Woods and Albert J. Kennedy, *The Settlement Horizon*, 1922, *seriatim*. Lillian D. Wald, *The House on Henry Street*, 1915, *seriatim*.

eral, as the result of these changes, settlements have abandoned or greatly reduced the emphasis on certain activities and redirected their efforts along other lines. Support of labor legislation, interpretation of the labor-union position in strikes, and promotion of studies of working and living conditions among wage-earners were important motives of the first twenty-five years of settlement work. These activities are now carried on so much more capably by the unions themselves that the assistance of the settlement is not welcomed by labor leaders, and such work has diminished. Less attention than formerly is paid at the present time to local, state, and national politics. Few houses make direct onslaught against party machines. There is still, however, a good deal of supervision of the work done by city departments of housing, health, sanitation, and recreation. Coöperation with the public schools continues, but in a reduced amount. Settlements here and there, however, give space for public kindergartens and crafts classes which supplement the work of the school, and take part in the vacation school programs. Practically all houses find that although formal training in cooking, sewing, and the domestic arts has been developed by the public schools, the desire to engage in these activities is by no means satisfied by class instruction, and there is still a demand for the informal opportunities offered by the settlement. At the present time, settlements are best supplementing the work of the public educational authorities by building up strong departments in the arts. Since 1920 important work has been done in providing such instruction as a means of personal development and recreation for children and young people. Many new departments of pottery, modeling, drawing, and embroidery have been established. The settlement needlecraft shops remain the chief and most important means in the country for encouraging foreign-born women to preserve skill learned abroad in the use of the needle. The most thoroughly developed artistic interest is music. The first settlement music department was established at Hull House in 1892. Since 1910 the work has grown rapidly, until now there are 15 music schools, which are in the nature of conservatories, and in addition 50 music departments in which a more limited range of instruction is offered. Settlement music schools and departments are today the most outstanding educational institutions for the musical training of working-class children to be found anywhere. As community resources for curative work have increased, settlements have naturally reduced their clinics in favor of educational enterprises in personal hygiene. Athletics still holds its well-established place as the chief interest among boys and men. It is now a matter of universal policy for settlements to have an adequate gymnasium, showers, and, in a growing number of instances, swimming pools. Many settlement workers regard the camp as the most important single activity. The settlement camps were pioneers in the "back to nature" movement among tenement-dwellers. They had as their motive the all-round development, physical, social and educational, of children and youth. There are now very few houses which do not carry one or more camps for children and young people, and in some instances special camps for mothers with small children are conducted. Nearly all these camps operate on a maintenance or semi-maintenance basis. In short, as the activities of the settlements have been taken over by public departments, and as social conditions have changed, the settlements have modified their work mainly toward the development of an educational program.[36]

The settlement has thus given an outstanding illustration of the principle that it is the function of a private agency to experiment and demonstrate.

The Salvation Army.—A special type of organization, which arose in response to conditions of degradation and misery in the large city, is the Salvation Army, founded in London by William Booth (1829-1912), a former Methodist minister. In 1865 Booth established in East London the Christian Mission, which, with the aid of his wife and a number of converts, he made into a flourishing institution. This was accomplished despite the opposition of the churches and in the face of bitter attacks upon him as a bombastic clown or as a raving fanatic bent upon setting up a new sect. In 1878 he organized the work on a military basis and changed the name to the Salvation Army.[37] It has since become an international religious organization patterned after an army in its discipline, terminology, and administrative details. The movement appeared in the United States in 1880. It was first incorporated in this country in New York State in 1889. The work in the United States is now organized in three territories with headquarters in New York City, Chicago, and San Francisco. The Salvation Army finds its chief field of activity in great cities, where it deals with a class of people notoriously estranged from the churches—the homeless, the poverty-stricken, the vicious,

[36] Albert J. Kennedy, "Social Settlements," *Social Work Year Book for 1929*, pp. 428-431. Jane Addams, *The Second Twenty Years at Hull House*, 1930, chs. XI, XII.

[37] Harold Begbie, *The Life of General Booth, the Founder of the Salvation Army*, 1920, Vol. I, chs. XXII, XXIV, XXVII.

the criminal, the unfortunate—the so-called submerged tenth. It works with people who are beyond the reach of the ordinary church, the Christian Association, the settlement, and similar organizations.

General Booth was an autocrat, conscious of power and achievement, and the organization of the Salvation Army bears the stamp of his personality. "Despotic by temperament and by habit and by conviction, he was nevertheless a simple man at heart, hallowed by a love which sweetened his tumultuous mind, and held to his course by a dogmatic faith which was the very breath of his existence."[38] His was a spirit which could touch the human heart in many lands and in almost all the varied circumstances of life. The three qualities most characteristic of him were sympathy, earnestness, and masterfulness. The work of the organization which he founded is extremely centralized and highly standardized. The supreme command of the Army throughout the world rests with the General at International Headquarters in London. The official "Orders and Regulations for Staff Officers" of the Salvation Army includes this statement: "The authority of the Salvation Army government is based upon the conviction that God has Himself created the Army and therefore arranged for its particular form of government." In the handbook the principle of discipline receives an overwhelming emphasis.

During its history of over half a century, the Salvation Army has spread to about 80 countries, and has "preached salvation," to use its own phrase, in over 50 languages. "It has weathered a long experience of vituperation and ridicule amounting almost to persecution, and has steadily grown in the respect of outside people. It has maintained its original form of organization without modification, and it exhibits throughout its personnel an altogether remarkable unity of purpose. If this record be considered in connection with these facts: that through practically all of its history its uniformed officers have been for the most part men and women of limited education, limited experience in life, limited culture, that the government of the Army, not only with reference to its official work but with reference to the private lives of its personnel, is one of the absolute authority of a military system, that its soldier membership has been recruited in the main from the least privileged groups in the community, that the officer of highest rank, a colonel, receives only $29.50 a week, that to be an officer means the forswearing forever of intoxicating liquor, drugs, tobacco, profanity, impurity, and the common forms of or-

[38] *Ibid.*, Vol. I, p. 356; *cf.* Vol. II, ch. XI.

ganized recreation, it becomes evident that the Army must have within itself a cohesive force of remarkable quality.''[39]

The extraordinary discipline and unity of the Salvation Army are frequently explained as being due to its complete military organization. There are two other factors which have been even more potent influences. First is its magnification under all circumstances of its one great purpose, the evangelization of men. This doctrine has been maintained consistently from the beginning without being obscured by the intricacies of theology. As presented by the Army it is simple, intelligible, and capable of awakening an unlimited amount of emotional drive. It means practically the same thing to all Salvationists. The second most important factor in the solidarity of the Army is its achievement of a completely sufficient life within the organization itself. Salvationists live in a Salvation Army world. Having eschewed all interest in worldly affairs, they must perforce turn to the Army for satisfaction of cravings for fellowship, diversion, inspiration, and achievement.[40]

To the ordinary outsider the Salvation Army is a combination of a uniform, a tambourine, and a street meeting. As a factor in the life of society, the Army is an organization in most respects analogous to a church. Its methods may not be traditional and acceptable church methods, but essentially the Army is an ecclesiastical institution. The characteristic methods of its religious work appear most noticeably at the indoor meetings. ''Like the traditional service of religious worship, the Army meetings include music, spiritual readings, prayer, and preaching. So far they are orthodox. This music, however, is usually provided by a band, and the tunes are as likely to be reminiscent of popular dances as of traditional church music. Applause for platform sentiments approved by the congregation is spontaneous and vigorous. Intercourse between the leader and the congregation may be as formal as that of the ordinary pulpit, or as informal as conversation. . . . Many features of Salvation Army worship have been profoundly distasteful to religionists of other schools and have been the basis of no small amount of bitter criticism. A brass band playing music which suggests the dance, applause within a religious service, complete informality of discussions including spontaneous and impromptu participation by the congregation, expression of extreme emotional response to highly charged religious stimuli, spec-

[39] Porter R. Lee and Walter W. Pettit, *Social Salvage, A Study of the Central Organization and Administration of the Salvation Army*, 1924, pp. 15-16.
[40] *Ibid.*, pp. 16-17.

tacular street meetings, have all been condemned as cheap and theatrical devices to awaken an emotional response in the people who would not otherwise be interested in religious matters, and whose interest must necessarily be transitory."[41] But if obvious satisfaction upon the part of the participants is a test of the success of a religious meeting, it must be admitted that the Salvation Army meetings have been successful; and reverence is not entirely lacking in "salvation with jazz." The Army methods appear to be adapted to the type of personality it strives to reach; traditional church methods would be totally ineffectual.

Starting as a religious organization pure and simple, the Army came to develop under the leadership of General Booth extensive enterprises of a charitable and social nature. The philosophy behind these enterprises and the original conception of their scope are the theme of General Booth's book, published in 1890, entitled "In Darkest England and the Way Out." The development of the social work has become so extensive that in the public mind it overshadows the religious work. By Army leaders, however, it has never been regarded as distinct from the religious work, but only as one other medium through which its religious work could be carried on. The Salvation Army's one aim is spiritual regeneration, the salvation of souls. All else is incidental; all activities are merely a means to this end. If a soul can be saved by ministry to the body, very well. One and the same formula expresses religion and social work.[42] The purpose of the Army, as officially stated, is "to promote the spiritual, moral, and physical reformation of all who need it."

To the ordinary American citizen the most familiar evidences of the Army's program of social work are the uniformed workers on the sidewalks at Christmas time collecting money for Christmas dinners, and the increasingly familiar wagons and automobiles which travel about town collecting waste materials and other things discarded by households. The range of the Army's social work, however, includes many other and more important activities, of which the following are the most typical:

Industrial homes, which provide homeless men with employment in sorting and packing waste paper, refinishing and repairing furniture, clothing, etc., for which they are paid in meals and lodgings and, if the amount of work done warrants it, in wages as well.

[41] *Ibid.*, p. 21.
[42] *The Survey*, Nov. 15, 1924, 53:4:195-198.

Women's homes and hospitals, which exist primarily for the reclamation of poor and unfortunate girls, particularly unmarried mothers.

"Eventide Homes" for men who have grown too feeble to work. These are usually on farms, where the men can be comfortably located and do such work as they are able around the garden or the barns.

Hotels for transient men, and residences for working-girls, which were noted in an earlier chapter.

Settlements, which stress poor relief in the "slums." They usually maintain day nurseries, which are a means of bringing the worker into touch with poor families, and sometimes they conduct classes of a religious and recreational nature for the people of the neighborhood.

Hospitals and dispensaries, which are primarily organized for patients who do not want charity and cannot pay the expensive rates which many hospitals require.

Summer camps and club activities for boys and girls.

Prisoner aid work, including supervision of men who are paroled to Army officers, the visiting of prisons and other institutions, and assistance rendered to prisoners' families.

Relief work through which food and other supplies are distributed to families in need. This is carried on by the corps officers as one of their regular duties, except when the work is of sufficient magnitude to justify the full-time employment of one or more persons.

The social work of the Salvation Army has been criticized as being emotionally prompted, indiscriminate, with little attention paid to the causes of social inadequacy, and incompletely recorded. Its institutional work is of higher standard than its relief or family welfare work, which is said to be on the whole sporadic, inadequate for its own purpose, and uncorrelated with similar efforts in the communities in which the Army operates. However, it is probably not much more inefficient than that of the majority of American churches attempting general relief work and of no small number of other private and public agencies for relief. "The Army has been most successful in those enterprises where organization solidarity, personal interest and devotion count for most and are most easily and informally expressed. They have been weakest perhaps in judgment as to the value of new enterprises and in absorbing as rapidly as has been done elsewhere those lessons of experience and those discoveries of modern science and organization which have during recent years contributed to the progressive raising of standards in many fields of work."[43]

[43] Porter R. Lee and Walter W. Pettit, *Social Salvage*, 1924, ch. II, p. 30 quoted.

"The Church in the Changing City."—The great changes consequent upon the growth of cities and of industry have seriously affected
the American church, with its background and traditions of rural
Protestantism. The mobility of the city population and its cosmopolitan character, the disintegration of neighborhoods, the changing housing conditions, and the rapid social change generally, have presented
a great problem of adaptation, and the conservative church has lagged
behind. Protestantism is now a smaller fraction of the total than it
once was, because the growth of American cities has been largely
from non-Protestant sources. The old-time family constituency has
rapidly diminished. The family tends to be broken up religiously—
the boy may go to the club at the Y.M.C.A., the girl to the Y.W.C.A.,
the young people to the popular downtown preaching, while the old
people stick to the neighborhood church. The death-rate of the urban
Protestant church is high. There is a great leakage in membership,
the number of old members leaving is nearly as great as the number
of new members joining. The majority of those within the church are
but loosely attached to it.[44]

"The city church, generally speaking, has no stable constituency.
The pastor preaches to a procession of nomads. Not only is there a
continuous 'turnover' of membership, but the attitude of mind that
prevails in the city is migratory, lacking a 'homing instinct,' and
possessing no permanent store of interests or susceptibilities. It is an
over-stimulated mind—sophisticated, often blasé. Since the traditional Protestant appeal is the pulpit appeal, building up and maintaining a city congregation easily degenerates into a sort of competitive platform stunt. The Saturday newspaper church announcements
are highly instructive in this respect. Our city churches have often
more in common with the theater or lyceum than with their religious
prototypes of the days when the interest in theology was greater and
when there was a readier response to evangelistic appeal."[45]

Another of the major handicaps of urban Protestant Christianity
is the conviction widely held among organized industrial workers and
their supporters that most prosperous city churches tend to be
capitalistic in their sympathies. The charge is made that Protestantism
has isolated itself from a large part of the population because of its
views regarding property. "The Protestant church has inherited certain traditions about the sanctity of private property, and the ethics
emphasized by Protestantism are property ethics. It is the church of

[44] H. Paul Douglass, *The City's Church*, 1929, chs. II, VI.
[45] F. Ernest Johnson, editor, *The Social Work of the Churches*, 1930, p. 33.

the business man and represents his point of view. There is abundant reason for this. From the old pioneer days on, it has been a sign of almost moral inferiority in this country for a man to be without some property. The thrifty man, who denied himself present satisfactions, in the earnest expectation of larger accumulations later on, was commendable. Private property has long been regarded as the test of a man's willingness to work hard, and to conserve his earnings by frugal living and the denial of frivolous desires. Possession was a mark of strength of character. Conversely, not to possess, however condoned, in reality meant shiftless and weak character. People holding these views have too often dominated the Protestant church, and their opinions persist. Given the rural economic conditions of the pioneer period, few would dispute this doctrine. But in the complex conditions of modern industry, it is by no means evident that possession is a token of moral superiority. . . . The results of this point of view are two-fold: an undue adulation of the wealthy, and a frequent contempt and unconcern for the disinherited and outcast of our industrial system—the masses, the industrial workers who own no property."[46]

The Protestant church appears to be most solicitous for the people of wealth. It sets itself to win and to hold those who represent property. The average minister is attracted to the church where people of means congregate, and both the ministry and the church as a whole seem to hold the wealthy congregation in high honor. There appears to be no place in the councils of the Protestant church for the leaders of the laboring groups in this country. To the working classes, the church appears as the apologist for the existing industrial order. The church has little or nothing to say regarding many of the vital issues of the day. Its attempt to conduct forums frequently ends when the influential members of the congregation object to the discussion of labor vs. capital. Pressure brought by the Board of Trade in Detroit caused churches to cancel previous arrangements made with the American Federation of Labor for delegates to its annual convention in that city to speak in local churches and the Y.M.C.A., though a few preachers of all faiths joined in a rebuke to the business men for their "affront to the church."[47] The Interchurch World movement failed partly because of internal discord but also because of the publication of its findings in the steel strike of 1919. On the other hand, there are indications that the church is concerning itself with the

[46] James J. Coale, "Protestantism and the Masses," *Yale Review*, Oct., 1921, XI, 82.
[47] "The Detroit Churches' Ban on Labor," *Literary Digest*, Oct. 23, 1926.

problems of the masses. It has issued various pronouncements on social issues. The most widely endorsed of the various statements is the "Social Ideals of the Churches," commonly called the "Social Creed." Originally formulated by the Methodist Episcopal Church in 1908, it was adopted by the Federal Council of the Churches of Christ in America the same year, reaffirmed in 1919, and ordered revised for the meeting in 1932. It has much to say on the rights of labor, the protection of the worker, and the equitable division of the product of industry.[48] But, broadly speaking, it can hardly be said that the church is an influential factor in the lives of the working classes as a whole.

The handicaps that challenge the city church are presented in an acute form in the case of those churches which find themselves, owing to urban change, stranded in the downtown sections. They are located in what were once good residential districts but are now deteriorated areas surrounding the central business sections. Most of the former residents have moved away, and a new group of people, primarily wage-earners and immigrants, has moved in. For a while there may be a small constituency, now widely scattered, which has only vitality enough to preserve a sentimental attachment for an institution that was once vital and flourishing, but sooner or later the church must adopt some way of meeting the problem. The most radical, and at the same time the easiest and most frequent means of avoiding the consequences of adverse environmental change is for the church to run away from the old neighborhood and its problems, and find a more congenial location. As a result there has occurred, *pari passu* with the growth of cities, a migration of churches from the older, more central locations toward the better residential sections and suburbs. This phenomenon is especially characteristic of Protestant churches, partly because they are older and more numerous, and also because the new influx into the downtown sections has been predominantly non-Protestant. The greater concern of the church for people of wealth is also a factor. The Catholic church, with its variety of services for different classes of people and its centralized administration, is more adaptable. Catholic churches are generally established and kept where they are needed. Yet some Catholic and Jewish churches have abandoned the central sections, though not to the same extent as Protestant churches.

Another possibility for the downtown church which is forced by environmental changes to make radical adjustments is to retain the

[48] F. Ernest Johnson, editor, *The Social Work of the Churches*, 1930, pp. 29, 39, 122 ff.

old property but to build its program on the basis of an appeal to select elements in its community or to certain portions of its geographical parish. This is possible because the constituency of a church, even the largest, is but a small fraction of the people, and contrasts in social fortunes may be found within a short distance. "Very wealthy people, for example, may inhabit little patches of territory, like islands in a sea of less favored society. Mixed areas do not go entirely bad, nor do bad areas go bad all at once. Hence, in many cases, at least for a time, a church can get along fairly well in its original location in spite of extreme environmental change, if it confines itself to its own kind of people and avoids the particular areas of extremest disadvantage where its own kind is not present."[49] As another adjustment by avoidance, the church may make its appeal to the city as a whole, draw a constituency of fairly uniform type from great distances, and become virtually independent of its immediate environment. Such a church has little or no parish in the traditional sense.

A further method of meeting the situation is that of compromise. The church may go a step or two in the direction of adaptation to the local situation, while continuing to work selectively along old lines and developing distant constituencies which urban mobility and the prestige of central locations make available. Such churches also add to the old program distinct though generally limited ministries designed expressly to meet the needs of the dominant populations now living in the vicinity. The compromise may be through building up different constituencies which use the same plant and staff, but have relatively little to do with each other. This situation is illustrated by a church that now finds itself in a rooming-house section with a foreign district a little to one side. Its constituencies are composed of (1) old families long connected with the church who come now from other parts of the city and suburbs; (2) children from the side streets and a few young people from the rooming houses near by; and (3) footloose young people from all over the city who flock to the church's recently built community house. The community house is alive daily with clubs and athletic activities, which are for the new people; the old members never enter it.[50] In final compromise, the church often divides into institutions, the original work being maintained in the old location for a select constituency drawn from a distance, while a

[49] H. Paul Douglass, *The Church in the Changing City*, 1927, pp. xvii-xviii.
[50] H. Paul Douglass, *The City's Church*, 1929, pp. 107-108.

near-by branch church—mission or chapel—serves the newer elements in the neighborhood.

Finally, the church may make a conscious effort to adapt itself completely to the changed environment. Professor Douglass[51] uses the word "readaptation" to denote a remaking of the church's policy and program in response to the demands of the environment. Readaptation may mean "institutionalizing" in greater or less degree the church's plant, equipment, and program in order to meet the social and educational needs of its immediate environment. It may mean, on the other hand, the elaborate development of activities involved in the ministry of a "family church" to a stable constituency. The most pronounced example of the readapted church is the so-called socialized or institutional church. Such a church seeks to become a real factor, not only in the religious life of the community, but in its social, physical, recreational, and educational life as well. Josiah Strong[52] says: "A distinguishing characteristic of the socialized church is that it adapts itself to the needs of the local environment. In the tenement-house district, it finds that the people living around it have in their homes no opportunity to take a bath; it therefore furnishes bathing facilities. It sees that the people have little or no healthful social life; it accordingly opens attractive social rooms, and organizes clubs for men, women, boys, and girls. The people know little of legitimate amusement; the church therefore provides it. They are ignorant of household economy; the church establishes its cooking-schools, its sewing-classes, and the like. In their homes the people have few books and papers; in the church they find a free reading-room and library. The homes afford no opportunity for intellectual cultivation; the church opens evening schools and provides lecture courses. As in the human organism, when one organ fails, its functions are often undertaken and more or less imperfectly performed by some other organ; so in the great social organism of the city, when the home fails, the church sometimes undertakes its functions." A church of this sort is really taking on some of the characteristics and functions of the social settlement. It is essentially an agency of social welfare, a community center rather than a church. In the course of time the traditional church characteristics tend to become so secondary and so overlaid with other activities that the question naturally arises, "Why call it a church at all?" Some institutional churches do indeed call themselves Christian centers or institutes.

[51] *Ibid.*, pp. 112-122; *The Church in the Changing City*, 1927, pp. xx-xxii.
[52] *The Challenge of the City*, 1908, pp. 209-210.

"The fortunes of the institutional church, long ago defined as a church which attempts to 'save all men, and all the man, by all possible means,' have been varied. It seems safe to say that the institutional ideal is less accepted than a few years ago, presumably because (1) the community is more and more able to provide its own services of a material and educational sort; (2) the institutional church tends to become more of an institution and less of a church; (3) the Protestant churches often find themselves carrying on a heavy 'activities' program in a Catholic neighborhood, and making little distinctively religious impression, save as proselytizing agents; (4) the net result of such activities when not integrated with a continuing, progressive program of religious education appears to be small. Those city churches which have the necessary resources now tend toward the ideal of a parish house equipped for educational and parish activities, not on a broad institutional basis but as part of an educational program for a stable constituency. The change would appear to be of vital significance."[53]

Aside from these large city churches with ample parish-house facilities for recreation and athletic events, most church recreational activities are mainly social, and include parties, banquets, outings, and sometimes dramatics. Very few directors of recreation are employed by individual churches, and as a rule leadership in that activity is an incidental function of the director of religious education.[54]

The church is no exception to the rule that all social institutions must adapt to changing conditions. Because of its natural conservatism the church has lagged behind, and many city churches still follow rural traditions and rural methods. Dr. Douglass[55] found in his study of 1,044 churches in cities having 100,000 or more population that more than half of them must be regarded as in the city rather than of it. "The city church on the whole has not yet shaken the dust of the country from its feet." Though the churches have made little conscious attempt to adapt themselves to urban requirements, a certain amount of automatic adjustment has taken place. Forces outside the church are tending to change its character. A noticeable differentiation has occurred, showing a range from the rural type to the church that is more or less completely urbanized. Following Douglass's classification, there are five types of urban churches: (1) the typical group; (2) the underdeveloped or less than average group; (3) the elaborated

[53] F. Ernest Johnson, editor, *The Social Work of the Churches*, 1930, p. 37.
[54] Lynn Rohrbough, "Church Recreation," *Social Work Year Book for 1929*, p. 81.
[55] *1000 City Churches*, 1926 (p. 86 quoted).

or more than average group; (4) the socially adapted group showing the extreme of high development; and (5) the erratic group. "Nine out of every ten urban churches belong to these types. Perhaps as many as a fourth may fairly be called elaborated, a possible tenth socially adapted. The rest are just average or less."[56]

1. The Average Church.—The typical urban Protestant church is an exceedingly modest institution in view of the bigness of the city. Most frequently it consists of a group of not more than 200 people and a poorly paid minister, carrying on the thought and pattern of the rural church. Its characteristic size is from 100 to 200 members, its budget is from $2,000 to $3,000, its minister's salary from $1,000 to $2,000. "It is a middle-aged institution which used to be farther downtown and which in more than half the number of cases has occupied its present location less than twenty-five years. With respect to leadership, it is a one-man enterprise, managed by a single paid minister, a man with a college and theological education and some twenty years' experience in the ministry, whom it keeps from two to five years before exchanging for another like him." The average church is only partially urbanized and adapted.

2. The Less Than Average Church.—This group of underdeveloped churches includes the typical churches of Negroes, rural immigrants, and the emotional sects; also stranded churches which have seen better days; certain racially clannish, theologically narrow churches whose alien traits or rigid characteristics prevent their falling into step with the majority; finally, young churches which are only fragments of what they soon hope to be, "though it is doubtful whether the standard denominations should or need allow such premature enterprises to be born within their households." In the main, the less than average churches represent religion imported into the city by incoming populations who have yet to be urbanized and, frequently, to be Americanized as well. In this stage the church is neither naturalized nor adapted.

3. The More Than Average Church.—Such churches have been termed "elaborated" because although their program and range of activities are pronouncedly more inclusive and more novel than those of the average church, they are arrived at rather by the elaboration of principles already implicit than by the adoption of exceptional or revolutionary principles. More than average wealth coupled with progressive ideas is likely to cause evolution along these lines. Also adverse pressure, pronounced but not extreme, may force a church into elaboration of program, especially when it is under the necessity of drawing and holding a distant constituency. In some cases the development has come through the consolidation of little churches into a strong community church, which aims to change the basis of organization from that of the denominational group and its traditions to

[56] H. Paul Douglass, *The City's Church*, 1929, ch. V (p. 141 quoted).

that of the community and its needs. The community-church movement, however, has been more characteristic of the small town and open country than of the city.[57]

Elaborated churches have a membership of from 500 to 1,000, a budget of $5,000 to $10,000, and a staff of paid workers averaging 3. Most new churches of this type are provided with departmental rooms for educational work, offices which are open daily, a large social room, club rooms for boys and girls, often a large assembly hall, dining hall, and kitchen. Several thousand churches have gymnasiums, and a great many have swimming pools with showers and lockers, and a few have bowling alleys. The large church with a well-equipped building and a staff of specialists is becoming more common. Many churches now have on their staffs a competent secretary, a director of religious education, a visitor, frequently a social case worker, and part-time directors for boys' and girls' work.[58] This is a case of specialization with which the city is familiar, in contrast to the simple and less-differentiated program and methods of the traditional church.

The constituency of the elaborated church is composed primarily of people who are in comfortable circumstances but who must economize on housing space. They tend to use their church, with its many activities, departments, enlarged staff and plant, as they do hotels, restaurants, and theatres. "Here they exercise the genuine but casual religiousness of city nomads, often with very slight contact with other departments of the institution, and with little sense of responsibility for its life as a whole. Separate constituencies, it may be, are grouped within the same church administration, under the same roof. For the one constituency, church life is conventional. The church is, to all intents, a mere average church. For the other constituency, church life affords an all-around program for this or that age or sex group. The two are identified only through the staff. The church is a community clubhouse, or a less specialized Y. M. and Y. W. C. A. combined. Such distinctly urban tendencies, sometimes accompanied by a definite effort of the pulpit to interpret urban life constructively, mark the elaborated church as an advanced example of adaptation. Usually, however, it exists for normally prosperous and adjusted populations, not for the exceptionally handicapped and maladjusted."[59]

Some students hold that the elaborated type of church is most suited to the situation found in the suburb or outlying residential district. "Here the primary fact is domicile. Civic and business interests are remote and activities center about residence. Communities tend to be homogeneous, and fellowship is more easily cultivated. Families tend to be large, and religious education is at a premium. Remoteness from the city creates a demand for social activities within the community, and the church is often able to meet this demand as the city church seldom can. . . . The dangers of suburban

[57] David R. Piper, *Community Churches*, 1928, p. 8.
[58] F. Ernest Johnson, editor, *The Social Work of the Churches*, 1930, p. 37.
[59] H. Paul Douglass, *The City's Church*, 1929, pp. 143-144.

churches are obvious—they tend to become comfortable family affairs with an unnaturally restricted fellowship; they foster a 'respectable,' non-militant, non-missionary, often anti-social, type of religion. The crusading spirit of Christianity as a prophetic religion does not seem to thrive, either in pulpit or in pew, in the typical suburban church."[60]

4. *The Socially Adapted Church.*—This type is institutionally the most highly developed of all. It departs most radically from tradition. It exists as a definite response to the social needs of the unassimilated or handicapped populations of the city, and expresses a definite purpose to adapt an ecclesiastical agency and program to the meeting of these needs. Membership averages over 1,000, and may be over 2,000. The budget is from $25,000 to $50,000, in a few cases as much as $75,000. The staff varies from 2 to 20 or 30 workers, with an average of 6 or 7. The institutional church, as we have already seen, has added to the traditional core, consisting of worship, religious education and recreation, many of the phases of service ordinarily associated with schools and social agencies. All the lines of service go on all the time. "The socially adapted church bears its explanation on its face. It deliberately sets itself to match the city on the side of the city's greatest need, and so far as possible to afford leadership and opportunity for the most alien and unprivileged of its populations, with whom its best successes are likely to be one-sided. It is not necessary to assume that the organization of community service in parochial form through the so-called institutional church reflects the best method of meeting urban social need in its extremes. Very likely it is often better to undertake the same forms of service through other philanthropic agencies or the publicly supported welfare departments of municipalities. The socially adapted church does constitute, however, one of the valid alternatives which definitely reflect the influences of the city upon forms of ecclesiastical organization."[61]

5. *Erratic Churches.*—Douglass uses this term to apply to "a few wandering stars discharged here and there into the religious firmament at a tangent to the major lines of development." Some are churches for foreign-speaking people whose newness to America and to Protestantism alike exaggerates the foreign group's special need of economic adjustment. Sometimes such churches have worked out very exceptional combinations of programs and emphases. Churches of migrant Negroes occasionally show the same traits. Also included in the group are churches that are ultra-traditional and, on the other hand, those that exhibit original experimentation in ritual. Perhaps there may also be included the more radical "community churches," the "labor" churches, and those which propagate Christian socialist teachings, all of which are propagandist centers rather than churches in the strict sense of the word.[62]

[60] F. Ernest Johnson, editor, *The Social Work of the Churches*, 1930, p. 38.
[61] H. Paul Douglass, *The City's Church*, 1929, pp. 144-145.
[62] *Ibid.*, p. 138; F. Ernest Johnson, editor, *The Social Work of the Churches*, 1930, p. 38.

Cutting across this classification is the emphasis on preaching, which in some churches is far and away the dominant interest and the distinguishing feature. ''Although preaching has not the vogue it once had, gifted preachers give a distinctive character to their churches which makes them independent of immediate environmental limitations. With the coming of the radio the possibilities of the 'pulpit church' become unpredictably great. It would seem that with pulpits able to assemble people from great distances, either physically or on the radio, and thus to create an intellectual and spiritual community that is independent of the physical community, the 'pulpit' church must be recognized as representing a distinct norm of church life and activity. The obvious danger is that mere uniqueness or sensationalism may create a spurious evidence of success. Many a church has capitalized an uncommon form of sensationalism or an eccentricity which, owing to the large territory upon which it may draw, brings large audiences, and this fact is advertised as an evidence of spiritual power.''[63]

In summary, ''the average church is a distinctly inconspicuous institution; the underdeveloped, a feeble flickering light. The elaborated church, in its outline and structure, is merely a reasonable enlargement to match urban conditions, while the socially adapted church would seem to be a wholly commendable effort to meet urban needs in specific ways.''[64]

[63] F. Ernest Johnson, editor, *The Social Work of the Churches*, 1930, p. 39.
[64] H. Paul Douglass, *The City's Church*, 1929, p. 140.

Chapter XXI

PUBLIC PROVISIONS FOR RECREATION

THERE is a growing tendency on the part of city, state, and national governments to regard the spending of public moneys for recreation purposes as a legitimate and necessary use for such funds. This official interest in the field of recreation is a comparatively recent phenomenon. With two exceptions, no states in 1915 had enacted legislation empowering municipalities to create recreation departments as integral elements of the city government. In 1927, twenty-one states had such laws. As recently as 1921, only twenty states had taken steps toward the establishment of state parks; in 1927 forty-three of the forty-eight states had either acquired areas for parks or had taken the necessary steps to their acquisition.[1] The utilization of federal lands for recreational purposes began in the latter part of the nineteenth century, but its main development has come since the creation of the National Park Service by act of Congress in 1916. The expenditures of American cities for recreation have been appreciable only since the turn of the century. The latest report of the Bureau of the Census, covering the 1928 expenditures of 250 cities having a population of 30,000 or over, indicates that these cities paid $73,018,422 for outlays for recreation and $62,871,118 for operation and maintenance, making a total expenditure for recreation in 1928 of $135,889,540. Per capita expenditures for operation and maintenance of municipal recreation departments increased from 35 cents in 1903, the year of earliest report, to $1.45 in 1928. These figures cover all types of municipal recreation, viz., playgrounds, parks and trees, open spaces, museums, art galleries, swimming and bathing places, athletics, music, entertainments, and celebrations.[2]

The development of municipal recreation may be illustrated in the case of New York City. In 1792 the city of Manhattan set aside what is now Battery Park for "a public promenade ground," entrusting its administration to three men appointed by the Governor. This was New York's first public provision for recreation. During the nine-

[1] Andrew G. Truxal, *Outdoor Recreation Legislation and its Effectiveness*, 1929, pp. 8, 99.
[2] U. S. Bureau of the Census, *Financial Statistics of Cities Having a Population of over 30,000*, 1928, pp. 332, 372.

teenth century a few other parks and recreation grounds were acquired, often in the face of adverse public opinion. Since 1900, however, the increase in park area and in recreation facilities has been noteworthy. In 1930, New York City had over 10,000 acres of parks, 737 playgrounds under leadership, 13 recreation buildings, 152 indoor community centers, 42 athletic fields, 152 baseball diamonds, 8 bathing beaches, 1 nine-hole and 5 eighteen-hole golf courses, 18 indoor and 4 outdoor swimming pools, and 558 tennis courts, all under municipal management. The city expended during the year for the playgrounds and other facilities $3,290,095.85, a per capita expenditure of 47 cents. Although the total amount spent by New York City for public recreation activities is the greatest of any American city, its per capita expenditure is fifteenth.[3]

The Field of Public Recreation.—Public provision for recreation has developed because the concentration of large populations in small areas, together with the absorption of natural recreation spaces by commerce and industry, has given rise to problems concerning the physical safety and health of children and the opportunities for wholesome exercise and recreation for young people and adults. As contrasted with other agencies, the scope of public recreation is to furnish that kind of recreation which is too urgently needed to permit the city to allow it to go uncared for, and that kind which can be done in a fairly wholesale way. Playgrounds for children of school age are an illustration. As a part of the education and development of a city's future citizens, play is an absolute essential. The playground is as important as the school building. The selection of areas for play, the planning of playgrounds and parks, the control of their surroundings, and the expert guidance of play are all of due importance in the city plan. Furthermore, playgrounds, athletic fields, parks, and the like require much more space than the average philanthropic or profit-seeking enterprise can secure. No private or commercial agency can plan adequately for the future needs of such spaces, needs which must be met before real estate values become prohibitive. Furthermore, the city already owns some facilities used for other purposes, such as schools, libraries, and museums, which are adapted to recreational use. In short, public recreation is that part of the recreational system which alone can be done adequately by public funds. Condi-

---

[3] Lee F. Hanmer, *Public Recreation*, Regional Survey of New York and its Environs, 1928, V, ch. II. *Recreation*, Year Book Number, June, 1931, pp. 170-171.

tions of city life make it necessary to supplement very widely other provisions for recreation, especially in regard to recreation areas.[4] The modern point of view in regard to recreation is to emphasize the preventive and constructive side; that is, by furnishing adequate public recreation facilities, by stimulating the private agencies, and by regulating the commercialized, a good deal of disease, demoralization, vice, delinquency and crime may be prevented, and normal, healthy, efficient citizens may be produced.

Value of Play.—In the common literature of play, the words play and recreation are often used interchangeably, but in origin, of course, recreation means re-creation, and is used to describe the rebuilding process which follows toil. There are various theories of play. It has been explained as a safety-valve for overflowing motor energy and high spirits, as a method of education or preparation for life activities, as a recapitulation of the earlier activities of the race that have survived in modified form in the play of the child, as pleasurable emotion, which is enhanced by crowds, and as recreation.[5] Play has been defined as a mode of human behavior, either individual or collective, involving pleasurable activity of any kind not undertaken for the sake of a reward beyond itself and performed during any age period of the individual.[6]

Whatever its explanation, play is a biological and social necessity for children. It is the most fundamental thing about a child. Playtime is most significant time for the child, who in the course of a year has more hours for play than for school or sleep or anything else. The value of play is manifold. It increases the physical fitness of the young; it develops coöperation, a sense of mutual rights, sportsmanship, obedience, loyalty, friendliness, democracy and other qualities; it is an antidote for anti-social tendencies; it affords mental development and acts as a mental stimulus. It is in his play that the child gains control of his body, that he acquires accuracy and precision in motion, and in judging distance, sights, and sounds. It is the way by which the child, particularly the young child, learns of life—the way he learns, as Chesterton puts it, such fundamental things as the hardness of wood and the wetness of water. Play for the child is one of the most serious facts of its life; it is a form of work for the young and the basis of all natural education. For the adult it is also highly

[4] Rowland Haynes and Stanley P. Davies, *Public Provision for Recreation,* 1920, ch. I.

[5] Henry S. Curtis, *Education through Play,* 1920, ch. I.

[6] Clarence E. Rainwater, *The Play Movement in the United States,* 1922, p. 8.

desirable and essential.[7] Looked at from these points of view, play is a matter of public concern, and the community should not only have ample space for play but should see that proper consideration is given to the environment of the places in which play is carried on.

Play Space in Cities.—The rapid growth of cities reacted very unfavorably to the play of children. In the absence of city planning, no foresight was exercised, no adequate provisions were made for play space, and as cities grew, open areas diminished before the encroachment of commerce, industry, and housing. Nearly always, in the history of American cities, industrial and commercial expansion, with its resultant concentration of population, has deprived the children of play spaces and the people generally of breathing and recreation areas. Desirable natural features such as waterfronts have usually been absorbed by such expansion, to be redeemed only by a great expenditure of money and effort. New York City, for example, has 191 miles of waterfront and utilizes only about 25 miles for park purposes. Its public bathing-beach facilities are confined to 4.5 miles, with an additional 2.5 miles under construction. In the central parts of the city there are densely populated districts within easy reach of the waterfront but deprived of its recreational advantages because the land uses have not been well planned and controlled, and because the method of disposal of sewage and other refuse is such as to make the water unsanitary and in some places offensive. Industrial structures, ranging all the way from docks and warehouses to heavy, smoke-belching industries and offensive slaughter houses, have had first claim on the waterfront.[8] The *laissez-faire* attitude of the public toward child play, the restrictions placed upon space in which to play as urbanization increased, and the differences between the languages and the games of the children of many nationalities mingled in the cities, resulted in a rapid disorganization of child play in urban communities.[9]

With the growth of cities and the disappearance of the traditional play spaces, the streets became almost the sole playgrounds. With the coming of the automobile even the streets were taken away from the children. The play of the streets is illegal, dangerous, interrupted, unregulated, unordered. Often it results in breaking the law, and the child who had nothing more serious in mind than playing gets a

[7] Henry S. Curtis, *Education Through Play*, 1920, chs. II-IV. Joseph Lee, *Play in Education*, 1915, chs. I-VI.

[8] Lee F. Hanmer, *Public Recreation*, Regional Survey of New York and its Environs, 1928, V, 113-114.

[9] Clarence E. Rainwater, *The Play Movement in the United States*, 1922, p. 9.

court record. The harmful things which children do on the streets outnumber the good things they may do and know how to do if only they have proper and sufficient playgrounds.

The playground movement, as we shall soon see, arose as an answer to the problem and undertook to provide safe and adequate places in which to play. But in the congested sections of old and large cities, like New York, Chicago, Philadelphia, Baltimore, and Boston, there are too many children and land is too expensive to provide playgrounds. A number of adjustments have been made to this situation.

1. Closing Streets for Play.—Certain streets which are but little needed as thoroughfares are closed to traffic during the hours when the children are not in school. In this way a safe if not attractive playground can be furnished, which is accessible to every child. In some instances, play leaders have been provided and a directed playground with simple apparatus and games conducted. As a makeshift it is not bad, but it has many obvious disadvantages.

2. Interior Courts as Playgrounds.—Because of the lack of other facilities for children's play, and because the streets are becoming increasingly dangerous, resort is being made to the backyards and roofs in some parts of New York City. An organization known as "Home Playyards, Inc.," has been experimenting for several years in the use of interior courts of tenement-house blocks as playgrounds and in providing play leaders through the coöperation of other agencies. This organization has succeeded in 22 different places in persuading property owners to remove backyard fences and pool their backyard space, or most of it, for play uses. This space has been laid out and equipped for active play under play leaders, both volunteers and paid workers.

3. Roof Playgrounds.—There are over 150 instances in New York City in which roofs of buildings are used for recreational purposes. Schools, libraries, settlements, tenements, apartment houses, office buildings, and industrial plants are found in this group. Roof playgrounds are most numerous on school buildings, there being 120 buildings thus equipped. These roofs are used as outdoor gymnasiums for physical-training classes during the day, and in some cases are made available for after-school use in the afternoon and evening. They provide play space with abundance of sunshine and fresh air and are away from the noise and danger of the streets. The roofs of libraries and settlements are utilized in a number of instances as play spaces, and also for fresh-air classes for tubercular and crippled children.

Roof play spaces on tenement and apartment houses are limited to the children living in the buildings, and serve as places of free play without supervision other than that provided by parents. With proper physical safeguards, such roofs serve a very useful purpose. Various problems arise in the creation of roof play spaces on tenements which have to be considered. Usually the roofs are of such light construction that they need to be reinforced to stand the strain of vigorous play and to deaden the noise in the rooms below. In modern, well-built tenements the roofs have been designed for play purposes and are of such construction that they are practically sound-proof. To be fully equipped, the roof should be completely enclosed by a wire cage, such as is found on the school roof play spaces, although this is quite expensive. The caging prevents balls and other objects from being thrown off into the street.

The use of roofs for recreation in business buildings is perhaps more general than in tenement buildings. Nearly all the large department stores utilize at least portions of their great roofs for this purpose. Industrial plants and factories also are beginning to set aside roof space on their buildings for the use of their employees.

4. Recreation Piers.—A recreation pier is usually a second story added to an ordinary pier. It has the advantage of economy of site, as contrasted with an equal area of land, the combination of recreational and commercial utility, and the enhancement of the attractiveness of the waterfronts. Its function is chiefly that of providing play space for children by day and promenades and "cool spots" for adults at night. Sometimes band concerts are given and dances held. Although not so large as some playgrounds, recreation piers have the advantage of being completely covered, making them particularly useful on rainy days. Being over the water they give in a few thousand feet of space a sense of separation from buildings and traffic, such as a large park affords. In New York City some of the most congested areas are by or near the waterfront. Recreation piers may thus serve a large and needy population. Whereas eight recreation piers were operating in Manhattan and one in Brooklyn several years ago, now only three of the Manhattan piers and the one in Brooklyn are in use. A new one is being built in the latter borough. At present these piers are open to the public only in June, July, August, and part of September. If they were enclosed, they could be used twelve months in the year instead of only three months as at present. Baltimore has, in the heart of its congested section, a recreation pier which is a twelve-month recreation plant, functioning day and night. The municipal pier of Chicago extends into the lake three-quarters of a mile and terminates in a magnificent auditorium seating five thousand and dedicated to amateur dramatic and musical expression. Vast promenades, restaurants, and observatories are among other facilities provided.[10]

Importance of Play Leaders.—A place to play in does not solve the problem of the play needs of city children. There must be supervision and direction by play leaders. The decisive factor in the success of the playground is always the teacher or director. He is no less necessary than the teacher to the school. He may be the determining factor in forming the social ideals of the children. It is not necessary to teach children to play; but it is necessary to teach them games, which are a highly organized form of play. The city child lacks the opportunities and advantages provided by the environment in the country. A number of studies have been made by taking a census of the activities of children, whether on streets or playgrounds, who are undirected in their play. These studies have invariably shown that fully half of the children were not engaging in either organized or unorganized play, but were walking or standing around or "doing nothing." Experience has further shown that, if children are without supervision or play leadership, not all the children will have a fair chance for play. It is often a case of the survival of the toughest when the crowd is left to its own devices. Supervision is necessary also to see that property is not damaged or other offenses committed. In small towns and rural districts it is possible for parents to exercise some supervision over the play activities of children. In the city, owing to housing conditions and the lack of backyards and other near-by play spaces, such supervision is out of the question. Playground supervisors are needed to furnish the leadership which parents are not giving or cannot give and which the children greatly need. Some recreation experts are so convinced of the necessity and desirability of directed play that they urge that play be put into the curriculum of the schools, as has been done at Gary, Indiana. This system affords a solution of the play problem not only with reference to leadership but also in regard to the fullest and most uniform use of playgrounds and equipment. It furnishes trained experts to direct play; adequate and regular time for play; adequate play space, which is required

[10] Henry S. Curtis, *The Play Movement and its Significance*, 1917, ch. VI. Lee F. Hanmer, *Public Recreation*, Regional Survey of New York and its Environs, 1928, V, pp. 71, 106-108, 111, 129-130.

by a modern school on this basis; and economical, because all-day, use of play space.[11]

Before 1900, no schools gave any special attention to the training of recreation workers. Now about 140 educational institutions offer courses for the training of playground leaders, and there is one national graduate school for the training of recreation executives.[12]

The Playground and Recreation Movement.—The movement which led to the establishment and operation of public playgrounds was initiated by private individuals and agencies who first perceived the need for such provision, and who worked out the methods and technique. The work was later taken over and extended by the public authorities, with finances derived from public taxation. The most important of these private organizations was the Playground Association of America, organized in 1906 mainly through the efforts of Dr. Luther H. Gulick, who became its first president, and Dr. Henry S. Curtis, its first secretary. Joseph Lee, who succeeded Dr. Gulick as president in 1910, was the first man in America to write a book on playgrounds and was one of the early promoters of the movement in Boston. He has always been the main philosopher and spokesman of the movement. If there is any one man who may claim to be the father of the American playground movement, it is undoubtedly Joseph Lee.[13]

In 1911, the Playground Association, because of the enlarged scope of the movement, changed its name to the Playground and Recreation Association of America. In 1930 it became the National Recreation Association. It publishes the most important journal in the field, a monthly magazine now called *Recreation*, which has changed its name as the title of the organization has changed. It employs field workers to assist cities in their recreation program; helps to find qualified workers for recreation positions; gives training at recreation institutes which it holds; administers national contests in recreational activities; conducts research projects and publishes and distributes handbooks, pamphlets, and other material.

In Germany the play movement was a physical-culture movement,

[11] Henry S. Curtis, *Education Through Play*, 1920, chs. IX, X. Lee F. Hanmer, *Public Recreation*, Regional Survey of New York and its Environs, 1928, V, 105, 175.

[12] Henry S. Curtis, *Education Through Play*, 1920, ch. XVI. *Park Recreation Areas in the United States*, U. S. Bureau of Labor Statistics Bulletin, 1928, No. 462, p. 4.

[13] Henry S. Curtis, *The Play Movement and its Significance*, 1917, pp. 18-19. Joseph Lee, *Constructive and Preventive Philanthropy*, 1902; *Play in Education*, 1915.

with emphasis on health and physical development. In England it was largely the spontaneous expression of a people who enjoy play for its own sake. In the United States the play movement from the start has been primarily a social movement. Its leaders have not been thinking so much of health or physical development as they have of the social environment. The effort has been made to keep the children away from temptations and from the physically and socially dangerous streets. Later other social motives were added.

The play movement in this country has gone through various stages. It is said to date from 1885 when, following a suggestion received from Germany, a private society opened some sand gardens in Boston, with trained supervisors in charge. These were the first modern playgrounds in America. They fulfilled the conditions of play space, equipment, organization, and leadership. From Boston the movement spread to other cities, and for about a decade the sand garden was the ruling type of playground. The provision consisted of a sand heap or sand box with or without other apparatus such as swings and see-saws. The sand garden was located out-of-doors, in settlement yards, tenement courts, school yards, or parks, and was designed for the use of children under 12 years of age.[14]

During the following decade, 1895-1905, the movement was expanded in several directions. Many private organizations were established to promote playgrounds, not only for little children but for youth as well. The movement was centered chiefly in the large cities where the crowded population made playgrounds a necessity. In some cities, as New York, it was part of the movement for tenement-house reform. Much experimentation was carried on, especially in New York, Philadelphia, Boston, Providence, and Chicago, to discover what equipment, space, supervision, and activities were appropriate. These efforts marked this period as the "model playground" stage. The movement also influenced the park system and led in a number of cities to playgrounds of the small-park type. The "small parks" or squares were adaptations of park service to the changed social situation in urban communities at the close of the nineteenth century, which demanded that parks be useful as well as ornamental. The park playgrounds varied in area from 3 to 10 acres, were equipped with

[14] This section is adapted from Joseph Lee, *Constructive and Preventive Philanthropy*, 1902, chs. VIII-XIII; Henry S. Curtis, *The Play Movement and its Significance*, 1917; an article on "A Brief History of the Playground Movement in America," in *The Playground*, April, 1915, 9:1:2-11, 39-45; and more particularly from Clarence E. Rainwater, *The Play Movement in the United States*, 1922.

outdoor gymnastic apparatus, athletic fields, comfort stations, and occasionally pavilions, and were beautified by trees, shrubbery, and lawns after the manner of the municipal parks of the time. During this period of the movement five conclusions were reached: that play has an educational value as well as a recreational or amusement benefit to the participant; that facilities for youths as well as children should be provided on the same site; that provision for play should be made throughout the year although the concept of indoor equipment was not yet developed; that a place to play in does not *per se* constitute a playground—play leaders are essential; that provision for play must be made by public, not philanthropic, resources.

The concept of public provision for play received emphasis about 1900, but it was a decade before one-half of the cities maintaining facilities did so either wholly or in part by public funds and management; in 1915 the extent of public provision had reached only 57 per cent. Since then it has become the dominant feature. When the public authorities began to take over the work, the question arose as to which department of the municipality should manage the playgrounds. Various answers were made in various cities, but generally the task fell to the park department or the board of education, chiefly the latter. The school appeared as the logical place for locating the neighborhood playground because of its accessibility. There are also many economies in making the neighborhood playground a part of the school plant, since the accommodations of the school building can be arranged to serve the playground as well as the school and thus avoid duplication of equipment. School boards have come to accept as a part of their responsibility the provision of play leaders and the keeping open of the school playgrounds after school hours and on Saturdays and holidays. The vacation playground is already a fixed institution in most cities.

About 1905 the playground movement began to develop into a larger-reaching recreation movement, with social aims directed to the welfare of young and old alike. To the manual play of the sand gardens and the physical and manual activities of the model playgrounds were added three other types: (1) the sociable, including parties, dances, and clubs; (2) the aesthetic, including story telling, dramatics, choral and instrumental musical societies and programs; and (3) the civic, comprising health exhibits, forums, and lectures on public questions. Following this development, the course of the movement took two channels, terminating for the one in the erection of schools equipped to serve as social centers, and for the other in the construction of a system of recreation centers independent of the schools and provided mainly in the public parks. This is known as the "recreation center" or "community center" stage of development. It blossomed in the period of 1905 to 1912. It constituted the first attempt in the evolution of the play movement to make provision for all age groups, throughout the year, in indoor as well as outdoor activities. Incidentally, it involved provision for more varied forms of play for children than was made in any preceding stage.

Recreation centers in public parks and social centers in schools were the first community centers other than the privately conducted settlements. The first type of provision developed the field house; the second, the wider use of the school plant. Chicago stands at the summit of achievement in the first respect. Here the small-park system has produced the most complete recreation centers or field houses in the country. These recreation centers consist of playgrounds, parks, and social centers all in one. The so-called field house denotes a building devoted to the needs of social recreation rather than merely one incidental to out-of-door athletic play. It is equipped with a men's and a women's indoor gymnasium with locker rooms and shower baths, a swimming pool, an assembly hall or auditorium, clubrooms, play rooms, a branch of the public library, a refectory and other provisions. Gary, Indiana, stands for the best example of the school as a social center. This is much the more common type of community center. It has developed into a separate movement, which will be considered in more detail later on.

All the stages up to this point were directed primarily toward the provision of specific facilities for play in the more congested districts of cities, and secondarily toward the organization of play activities on these sites. The recreation center represents the highest development to date of physical provisions for play and recreation upon a given locality. Developments since then have been social rather than physical, involving the organization of activities on the one hand, and the method of supervision on the other.

This change became marked with the incorporation in the movement of attempts to regulate or organize play "outside the playgrounds." These efforts were flanked on the one hand by municipal regulation of commercialized amusement, and on the other by state recreational legislation, both permissive and mandatory, for the provision of facilities and activities. They occurred with great frequency during the years between 1911 and 1915, and involved both a general utilization of the dramatic, musical, and dancing arts, and an injection of social-welfare propaganda sufficiently to modify the concept of the function of the play movement so as to constitute a distinct epoch in its history. At this point the play movement became conscious of a wider field of action than any heretofore perceived. It became aware that it must not only provide playgrounds, but that it must raise the standards of popular amusements by the use of both restrictive and constructive measures. The former comprised efforts to regulate existing recreations, principally commercialized amusements; the latter, to provide "municipal music," "municipal theatres," "municipal dances," and "community dramatics, festivals, and pageantry." This is known as the "civic art and welfare" stage.

The city-wide method of control and provision of recreational activities came far from yielding all that was expected of it. Attainments were disappointing on both restrictive and constructive sides. The groups involved were too large and the events too infrequent. Gradually the inadequacy of the scheme was discerned and a decentralized plan of organization conceived. This plan was regional as well as functional. Its keynote was the idea of locality; and the neighborhood in place of the city, as in the former stage, was chosen as the unit of population and area upon which effort should be centered. In the "neighborhood organization" stage of the play movement there were added to the concept of the recreation centers a new meaning and a new method of operation. While making use of the same physical plant, the small-park field house, or the public school building, it utilized the principle of participation by all the residents of the locality in the support and control of the center as a "single, all-inclusive, organized society" for deliberation and action upon all questions relative to their common life, including play and recreation. It proved, however, to be exceedingly difficult, if not impossible, so to organize neighborhood life.

With the coming of the World War, new problems arose, and in 1918 War Camp Community Service was organized, at the suggestion of the Playground and Recreation Association of America, for service in making an adjustment to the social situation in the communities adjacent to army cantonments and training stations and in those industrial centers where war supplies were being produced on an extensive scale. Its method of procedure was essentially that of the "neighborhood organization" stage of the play movement, but through the war-time intensity of emotion that medium was raised to a high power of efficiency. Before the signing of the armistice, War Camp Community Service had organized the social and recreational resources of

604 communities near the cantonments for the benefit of the military and naval forces of the nation, and about 50 districts in which war industries were being carried on. Besides utilizing the types of play previously developed, it introduced many new games and stunts arranged to enable large numbers to participate at one time, as well as a number of occupations for convalescents in hospitals. Among the distinctive types of activities were community singing, pageants, dances, block parties, athletic meets, artist recitals, game rooms, and home hospitality. The Service was continued during the reconstruction period and a program developed for peace time as well as war, for small towns and rural districts as well as large cities. In 1919 it was succeeded by "Community Service, Inc.," also an outgrowth of the Playground and Recreation Association of America and with the same officers as the latter organization. Like the preceding stage, "community service" works through the neighborhood as the essential social unit. It attempts to organize the community for recreation and to promote all types of activity. It has sought to enlarge the scope of public provision for recreation and to encourage increased public appropriations for play facilities.

The main developments in the play and recreation movement which have been sketched above may be summarized as follows.[15] The transitions have been from provision for little children to that for all age groups; from facilities operated only during the summer to those maintained throughout the year; from outdoor equipment and activities to both outdoor and indoor facilities and events; from congested urban districts to both urban and rural communities; from philanthropic to municipal support and control; from "free" play and miscellaneous events to "directed" play with organized activities and correlated schedules; from a simple to a complex field of activities, including manual, physical, aesthetic, social, and civic projects; from the provision of facilities to the definition of standards for the use of leisure time; from "individual" interests to "group" and community activities.

The extent of community recreation in 1930 is indicated by the following figures given in the year book of the National Recreation Association.[16] The data cover solely the community recreation activities conducted under leadership and the facilities used chiefly for active recreation. In 1930, play leadership and supervised facilities were

[15] Cf. Clarence E. Rainwater, The Play Movement in the United States, 1922, ch. IV.
[16] Recreation, Year Book Number, June, 1931, 25:3.

reported by 980 cities. These cities conducted 13,354 separate play areas and centers, under the leadership of 24,949 paid and 8,216 volunteer recreation leaders. The total number of play areas and special facilities was as follows:

Athletic fields	1,843	Outdoor playgrounds	7,677
Baseball diamonds	4,322	Recreation buildings	642
Bathing beaches	457	Ski jumps	59
Golf courses	312	Stadiums	90
Ice skating areas	1,806	Summer camps	134
Indoor recreation centers	2,066	Swimming pools	1,042
Miniature golf courses	184	Tennis courts	8,422
	Toboggan slides	221	

Complete attendance figures do not exist, but all estimates place the number at many millions. The total expenditures during the year were $38,518,194.88, the source of support being municipal funds, combined in a few cities with private subscriptions. A number of facilities produced a revenue. The average cost of operation was less than the income received from bathing beaches, golf courses, and outdoor swimming pools. The managing authority was either park departments, schools, playground commissions, or other municipal departments, or in a few cases playground associations or other private organizations. The records during the quarter of a century preceding show that to an increasing degree local play and recreation service is being provided by municipal rather than private enterprise.

The Wider Use of the School.—Community centers, as we have already seen, whether they be recreation centers in public parks or social centers in public schools, are places where neighbors may gather for civic, social, recreational, cultural, or other purposes regardless of race or nationality, political persuasion, or religious affiliation. The commonest variety is the public-school center in which the auditorium, gymnasium, or other rooms of the building are used. The movement for a fuller use of the public-school plant and for public-school extension developed since the beginning of the present century, particularly during the years 1905 to 1912. Prior to that time the public schoolhouses in American cities and towns were available only for the regular school work and for children of legal school age. For this purpose they were open from 5 to 7 hours a day for from 150 to 190 days in the year, a total of not more than 1,400 hours a year, and were closed to all use through the remaining 7,360 hours of the year. The only exceptions were the evening classes found here and there and the occasional use of schoolrooms for public debates and for meetings of literary societies composed chiefly of older boys and girls of the school. This situation clearly involved an uneconomic use of expensive plant and equipment and a neglect of the fullest opportunities for service. The schoolhouse is specially fitted for use as a social center. It is centrally located in the neighborhood; it is non-sectarian and non-partisan; the property of no individual, group, or clique, but the common property of all; the one place in every community in which all have equal rights and all are equally at home. Why not utilize this special equipment during the margin of time left by the regular day-school work for general community activities rather than build new and expensive recreation centers in parks?

Pioneering work in the wider use of the school plant was done in New York City by the People's Institute, but the demonstration that attracted nation-wide attention was performed in Rochester, New York, during 1907 to 1909, under the direction of Edward J. Ward. Here the idea of the school center as the nucleus of district democracy was born and developed. According to the Rochester idea, the schoolhouse should be the social center of the community, where all the people can come together in a friendly way on terms of democratic equality, learn to know each other, and extend and enrich the community sympathies. The schools should be used as voting places, as community forums for the discussion of public questions, and for other civic uses, as branch libraries, and as music, art, and recreation centers. The attempt was made to organize the citizens of a precinct or district as a neighborhood civic club using the school building as headquarters for its activities. The slogan of this plan, as later fostered by the United States Bureau of Education, was ''Every Schoolhouse a Community Capitol and Every Community a little Democracy.''[17]

Other types of school centers were promoted by private organizations formed for the purpose in various cities, and the movement received an impetus under war stimulus. Gradually and increasingly the plan was adopted by the public authorities. ''Although there has been a steady increase in the number of cities in which schools have been used for centers, and in the number of centers conducted, the prophecies of the early protagonists have not been fulfilled in any great measure since the centers have not proved powerful influences of

[17] Edward J. Ward, *The Social Center*, 1913. Henry R. Jackson, *A Community Center*, 1918. Clarence A. Perry, *Wider Use of the School Plant*, 1913, pp. 270-276. Eleanor T. Glueck, *The Community Use of Schools*, 1927, pp. 18-26, 31-36.

neighborhood life. The idea has spread, however, municipalities are extending the publicly conducted centers, and various private organizations are fostering them. The development has shown several different stages. From centers for entertainment only, the centers became the seat of cultural activities; then neighborhood organization became a fad and almost a religion; war work for its period took the center of the stage, and latterly there has been a very diversified growth and a striking tendency to study the neighborhood and build programs on the basis of local need.''[18]

The current utilization of public-school buildings for community purposes may be divided into four broad classes, of which any two or more may occur simultaneously in the same building.[19]

(1) The use of the school building by individual groups, at whatever time they desire it, for other than the regular educational purposes (within legal limitations and when not interfering with regular school activities), upon permit from school authorities or other public bodies having the custody of school property.

(2) Activities initiated and supervised by the school authorities or other public bodies. In some of the larger cities (*e.g.*, New York, Boston, Washington, and Chicago) there are special bureaus within the department of education or municipal commission which are specifically charged with the conduct of all "extended use" activities. In some cases, notably Pittsburgh and Milwaukee, the same body is also responsible for the supervision of night schools.

(3) The use of the school building in the evenings for the extra-curricular activities of day-school pupils, usually under the supervision of members of the school faculty.

(4) The utilization of the building as a "center" of certain kinds of neighborhood life. Such enterprises are usually initiated by a local group, a civic society, a woman's club, or a parent-teacher association. They are sometimes also stimulated by a certain city-wide organization, such as the People's Institute of Brooklyn or Community Service of Cincinnati. The term "center" may be preceded by "community," "civic," "social," "recreation," "neighborhood," or "school." Sometimes, but not always, the name indicates the character of the dominant activity. In the organization of these activities there is usually some degree of self-support and self-government.

In 1927, 32 states had definitely provided by law for the use of schoolhouses for social, recreational, and community purposes, and in the other states school authorities permitted it under their general

[18] Leroy E. Bowman, ''Community Centers,'' *Social Work Year Book for 1929*, pp. 93-94.
[19] Eleanor T. Glueck, *Extended Use of School Buildings*, U. S. Bureau of Education Bulletin, 1927, No. 5, p. 1.

power as custodians. In a study made by the United States Bureau of
Education and published in 1927, 722 towns and cities reported 1,569
school centers. The definition adopted for a school center was any
school which is used regularly at least one evening a week for two
or more activities—or twice a week for one—not counting night
schools. The types of activities in these centers, listed in the order of
the frequency with which they were found, were as follows:

Type of Activity	Per Cent of Cases
Athletics	70
Clubs and groups	50
Entertainments	45
Society meetings	44
Lectures	27
Social occasions	27
Civic occasions	23
Dancing	21
Night schools	18
Coöperative activities	13
Rooms for quiet games and study	12
Public-library branches	10

Activities with a recreational content obviously bulk largest in the
average school-center program. Civic and educational features are
also distinctly present, but their proportion cannot be fixed with any
precision because so many activities exhibit more than one aspect. This
is especially true of many group affairs. A club may have a debate on
one evening and a dance on another, yet both are entered on the records as "club meetings." A much larger part of school-center activity
than is indicated by the above table is in reality group enterprise. The
school building is increasingly being used as the meeting place for all
sorts of local associations. Community-center work consists very
largely in organizing and developing group activities. This is accomplished in the several ways of giving accommodations to groups which
already have leaders, of finding leaders for groups which have none,
and of bringing people into group relations who are not already enjoying them. The activity is the cement which holds the individuals
together in the group unit.[20]

The Bureau of Education study shows that a little under one-half
of the school centers are supported wholly by taxation, one-third by

[20] *Ibid.*, pp. 8-9. Clarence A. Perry, *Community Center Activities*, 1916, p. 11;
The Extension of Public Education, U. S. Bureau of Education Bulletin, 1915,
No. 28.

a combination of public and private funds, and one-fifth entirely
from private sources. No replies on support were received from 283 of
the 1,569 centers. The largest proportion of control and management
is in the hands of boards of education. A distinct trend is noted toward control by boards of education or other municipal authorities,
and corresponding decreases both in partial and total control by private groups. This survey leads to the following generalizations:[21]

1. The school-center movement is enjoying a gradual growth.
2. In a majority of cases the school-center season is six or more months
in length.
3. Twice a week is the most common number of nights a center is open,
one and five evenings being next in frequency.
4. Practically two-thirds of the centers are under the management of school
authorities, and the trend is toward an increase of their control.
5. The support of school centers is predominantly by public taxation.
6. Not quite half of the school centers have a paid staff.
7. The activities of school centers show a high recreational content and
are participated in by many local groups.

"The oldest, most extensive, and one of the most constructive
sources of stimulation toward wider use of the school is the university
extension course. Through such courses the state universities specially
furnish organizing service and supply lecturers, experts, and pamphlet material on almost any community or household problems. . . . In
one or two instances the community center aspect of extension work
has become the dominating factor, and has resulted in a bureau of
community organization or service. In almost every state in the Union
the state department of education is assisting localities to establish
school centers. The service rendered is similar to that of state universities, but there is not the number of specialists to call upon. Several organizations, such as the National Recreation Association and
the National Congress of Parents and Teachers, are stimulating the
development."[22] The National Community Center Association, formed
in 1913, though not specifically devoted to furthering the school-center
movement, has aided it while carrying out its own primary purpose
to "secure and make available knowledge of community organization
by means of conferences, studies and publications."

[21] Eleanor T. Glueck, *Extended Use of School Buildings*, U. S. Bureau of
Education Bulletin, 1927, No. 5, p. 11; *cf. The Community Use of Schools*,
1927, ch. IV.
[22] Leroy E. Bowman, "Community Centers," *Social Work Year Book for
1929*, p. 94. Eleanor T. Glueck, *The Community Use of Schools*, 1927, ch. III.

The Development of Municipal Parks.—There was not a single municipal park, as such, in the United States up to 1852, and not a single park commission or municipal department that had been specifically created to handle parks and recreation. There were no legal measures enabling the people to provide parks and other recreation spaces for themselves. The first real park in the modern sense, established by the people of a democracy as a public recreation ground for their own use and enjoyment, was Central Park in New York City, which was laid out in 1853 under authority of an act of the state legislature. The earlier origin of village greens or commons is conceded, but these were usually crown grants in a more primitive state of society for use as common grazing grounds for cattle and for military drills. Their recreational use by the youths for team games and by the village folk for various gatherings on holidays was secondary. "In Europe the great public parks usually originated in crown ownership, subsequently passing in the slow processes of the growth of liberty, to the public uses and enjoyment of the people. The term park in its original meaning was defined under English law as enclosed ground stocked with beasts of the chase, held by prescription or the king's grant. London's celebrated Hyde Park of 400 acres originally belonged to the Abbey of Westminster and it became crown property on the dissolution of the monasteries in the reign of Henry VIII. History is not clear as to when the public began to have free admission to Hyde Park, but its privileges have passed irrevocably to the people for all time."[23] In America, up to the laying out of Central Park, there were no public parks with the exception of Boston Common, acquired in 1634, which belonged to the class of public or common lands.

In 1877, not over 20 American cities had municipal parks. In 1892, only 100 cities had made such provision; by 1902, 796 cities had made a beginning toward providing parks. The latest figures, given in 1928, show that approximately 1,680 cities had provided nearly 250,000 acres of municipally owned parks. The capital investment represented in the property that had been set aside for the recreation of the people prior to 1850 probably did not exceed a few hundred thousand dollars. In 1928 the capital investment in public parks and recreation spaces of American cities was estimated to be considerably over a billion dollars, and the current operation and maintenance expense

[23] V. Everit Macy, "Parks in the Modern Manner," *The Survey*, July 1, 1930, 64:7:301.

ran over a hundred million dollars annually.[24] Donations played an important part in building up municipal park systems. As nearly as can be determined, from one-fourth to one-third of the total acreage in municipal parks in American communities has been acquired through gift. A number of cities have obtained all their parks through this means, and many cities would be woefully lacking in open areas available for the leisure-time use of the people without these gifts. Donations have also been an important factor in the development of county and state parks.[25]

The park movement which began in the two decades following the Civil War, like the playground movement which arose in the next decade, failed to gain much momentum until after the close of the century. The reasons were as follows. The size of the country and the amount of open space were so great than even in rapidly growing cities no urgent need was felt for reserving space for the present or future requirements of the inhabitants. The prevalence of rural ideas and ideals under urban conditions, accentuated by rural control of state legislatures, was also of importance. The old philosophy that work was the supreme virtue and leisure potentially evil still held sway. The rapid progress of urbanization at the close of the century, however, coupled with the rising movement of city planning, convinced large numbers of people that parks and other open spaces are an urban necessity. Deprived of his natural outdoor environment in the industrial centers into which commerce and industry have forced him, man is compelled to find in parks and other open spaces the sunlight, fresh air, repose, rest, and relaxation so important to health, happiness, and joy in living. Parks have been likened unto the lungs of the city. A city is unhealthful if it is overcrowded with buildings. Parks not only promote health and efficiency; they render a great service in the creation and preservation of beauty, they stimulate the acquisition of knowledge by providing direct contact with nature, they increase neighborliness, they promote safety by taking the children off the streets, they help to prevent delinquency, and they aid in the promotion of good citizenship.[26]

Changing Conception of Parks.—The pioneer park builders and planners of America defined the park as a place where urban inhabi-

[24] *Park Recreation Areas in the United States*, U. S. Bureau of Labor Statistics Bulletin, 1928, No. 462, pp. 4-5, 11, 18.

[25] The Playground and Recreation Association of America, *Donated Parks and Play Areas in the United States*, 1920.

[26] *National Conference on Outdoor Recreation*, Senate Document No. 158, 1928, pp. 6-7.

tants could obtain the recreation coming from the peaceful enjoyment of its rural, sylvan, and natural scenery and character. Although it was recognized that the supreme functional use of parks was for the recreation of the people, the type of recreation advocated was of a passive or semi-active kind, the dominant ideal being peaceful enjoyment amid beautiful surroundings. There can be no doubt that this conception was fundamentally sound, especially as applied to city-dwelling people, and it is of even greater importance today when cities have grown larger and the stress of living has become greater. It so happens, however, that the physical and recreational needs of people are far wider than those comprehended in the early conception; active forms of recreation must also be included.

The use of parks for active recreation is perhaps the most significant trend in municipal park development in the last twenty-five years. We have moved away from the old ideal of the park as something to be seen and have come to regard it more and more as something to be used. There is not a feature of the park that does not lend itself to recreation, nor do recreational activities necessarily destroy its beauty. The free play on the park lawns has not, as a rule, injured them, and, as Joseph Lee has said, "After all, the children are fully as important as the grass" when it comes to a question of blighting one or the other.[27] The playground movement, as we have seen, exerted a profound effect on the pioneer conception of parks and their recreational functions. It initiated the new movement for many forms of active recreation, which has changed the functional uses of many existing park properties and added to the services of park-administration agencies a series of complex and difficult social problems involved in organizing for the people a wide range of recreational activities of a physical, cultural, social, and civic nature.

Among the recreation facilities in parks most frequently reported in a survey made in 1928 were areas for baseball, football, soccer, playground ball, horseshoe pitching, basket ball, field hockey, track, field events, volley ball, hand ball, and croquet. Ninety-eight cities reported golf courses in parks. Among the other sports for which facilities were provided were bowling, roque, polo, archery, and shooting. Wading and swimming pools, bathing beaches, and boating facilities were commonly found, and in the northern part of the country toboggan slides, ski jumps, skating rinks, and coasting places. Three hundred and nine cities reported 4,819 children's playgrounds in a

[27] Joseph Lee, *Constructive and Preventive Philanthropy*, 1902, p. 143.

park system. The extent to which parks are serving as community centers is shown by the large number of clubhouses, gymnasiums, and field houses reported; and the art galleries, museums, outdoor theatres, band stands, and conservatories found in many cities are indicative of the ways in which parks are an increasing factor in the cultural and educational life of the people. Thus, at the end of nearly three-quarters of a century of park development in the United States, the term "park" has come to mean any area of land or water set aside for purposes of outdoor recreation, whether it be of a passive or an active nature or of any of the degrees between those two extremes, and with the expectation that the recreation is to come in part at least from beauty of appearance.[28]

The movement for the full recreational use of parks has also brought into existence a number of new types, such as areas devoted more or less exclusively to playgrounds, athletic fields, stadiums, neighborhood recreation parks, swimming and boating centers, golf courses, and boulevards and parkways. It has emphasized the idea that the value of parks depends quite as much upon their variety, number, and distribution as upon their size. Parks to be useful must be accessible to the majority of the people. In most cities, parks are very unevenly distributed; they are peculiarly inaccessible to those who live in the most congested districts. This is because the growth of the cities was not guided by a comprehensive city plan. Take New York City as an example. In 1925 there were 10,173 acres of park within the city limits. The park area was 5.3 per cent of the total area, and provided 1 acre of park to every 577 people. On the basis of park space per capita of population, New York City ranks tenth among the 10 largest cities of the United States. Its rank is fifth on the basis of percentage

DISTRIBUTION OF PARK AREA IN NEW YORK CITY BY BOROUGHS, 1925

Borough	Per cent of park area to total area	Population per acre of park
Manhattan	12.3	1,130
The Bronx	15.5	212
Brooklyn	5.8	864
Queens	2.1	504
Richmond	1.0	369
All Five Boroughs	5.3	577

[28] *Park Recreation Areas in the United States*, U. S. Bureau of Labor Statistics Bulletin, 1928, No. 462, pp. 3, 10.

of park space area to total area. When smaller units within the city are taken into consideration, the situation appears less favorable.[29] There is a great variation in the number of people a given park area serves. Furthermore, a borough unit which shows a fairly good percentage of its total area in parks and a reasonable amount of park space with reference to population may be inadequately served because of improper distribution of its parks. Accessibility to the various areas of population is highly important. This is particularly true of the small parks and playgrounds. That end can be attained only by intelligent planning on a city-wide basis, or even a regional basis. Even Minneapolis, which leads all cities of more than 100,000 population in the percentage of park acreage to the total city acreage (14 per cent, with a provision of 1 acre of park to 80 people), shows an unequal distribution of park area per population. It needs additional neighborhood playfield parks. These are most difficult to obtain after land has once been built up; if they are to be secured in sufficient numbers and area, steps should be taken as far as possible ahead of residential development just as the streets are set aside.

Park Planning.—A well-planned park system should show a balanced relationship among the several fundamental types of properties, such as the following.

1. *Children's Playgrounds.*—These areas should include separate provision for children of kindergarten age and under and for children from 5 to 14 years of age.

2. *Neighborhood Playfield Parks.*—The primary function of this type of area is to provide opportunity for older boys and girls, young men and women and other adults to engage in all kinds of outdoor games and sports.

3. *Areas in Which Landscaping is a Predominant Characteristic.*—These include neighborhood parks or "intown" park areas, large parks, and reservations or forest parks.

4. *Boulevards and Parkways.*

5. *Miscellaneous Park Areas.*—Some are devoted to active recreation (*e.g.,* bathing beaches, golf courses, athletic fields and stadiums, municipal camp sites), some to a specific educational-recreational purpose (*e.g.,* botanical gardens, arboretums, and zoos), and some to community houses, museums of different types, and to utilitarian structures and uses.

In such a system, children's playgrounds would be the most numerous, with neighborhood playfield parks and neighborhood parks next, the two latter types being about equal in number. It is found in prac-

[29] Lee F. Hanmer, *Public Recreation*, Regional Survey of New York and its Environs, 1928, V, 39.

tice that the maximum range of effectiveness of most city parks is not over one mile, and the smaller the park the shorter its radius of usefulness. There would be fewer large parks and reservations, connected by boulevards and parkways, but they would greatly exceed in acreage the smaller types of park areas. Few park systems in the United States present this balanced relationship, the greater percentage of them being deficient in playground and neighborhood playfield areas. No general rule can be laid down as to how much play space of that sort a city needs. In any attempt to arrive at standards for play areas, especially in regard to children, a number of factors must be taken into account: the density of the population; the number of children who will play and their distribution in age groups; the distance which children of different ages will travel to a play area; and the number of children who will use the play area at any one time—the "light" load and the "peak" load.[30]

An increasing number of cities, as noted in an earlier chapter, have in recent years adopted comprehensive city plans, including provisions for parks and other open spaces. Many of the large cities also have regional park plans, either actually drawn up or in process of formation. It is coming to be more generally realized that effective planning must take in the metropolitan area, and there has been an increasing number of metropolitan park systems. Another recent development has been the acquisition by cities of park properties outside their regular limits. This extension of the park system into the open country has developed as a result of the widespread use of automobiles, especially since the War. It is now possible for a city recreation system to be extended as much as 50 miles, and in some places as much as 100 miles, into the country and still be used by large groups of city people. Approximately 100 cities have acquired parks outside the city limits. The largest of these parks is owned by Phoenix, Arizona, and comprises 15,080 acres in one property. Denver owns more than 10,000 acres in mountain parks outside the city. Seven other cities each own more than 2,000 acres in outlying parks. These park lands vary as to their accessibility; some of them are easily reached by street car, whereas others are readily accessible only by automobile. The purchase of park areas outside the city limits is a wise municipal procedure because of the probability of the great need for such areas as the city expands. Such lands are, of course, much cheaper than those

[30] *National Conference on Outdoor Recreation,* Senate Document, 1928, No. 158, pp. 8-10. Andrew G. Truxal, *Outdoor Recreation Legislation and its Effectiveness,* 1928, pp. 31 ff.

within the city limits, and it is good economic policy to acquire them before the city expands and the market value rises. There is a place in the well-balanced park system for both easily accessible and more remote areas. The wisdom of acquiring comparatively remote areas has been demonstrated by the experience of many cities.[31]

Park Finances.—Parks and playfields not only increase values to the community by promoting health, efficiency, and good citizenship; they also increase land values and they produce revenues from recreational uses and concessions. A strong practical argument is thus added to the social and aesthetic reasons for their establishment.

Revenues from the operation of certain types of recreation facilities may arise either in a lump sum from concessions or from the operation of the facilities directly by the park governing authority. The practice of charging fees for the use of certain types of recreational facilities arose partly because of the constantly rising tax rate, and partly because of the growing feeling that it was only just that the patrons of a given facility should pay for the operation and maintenance, where the general public had provided the capital outlay. Furthermore, people appear to have a much more direct feeling of responsibility for and an interest in a given facility or activity if they contribute something of monetary value than they do if the facility or activity is open to their free use. Among the facilities for the use of which fees are charged are boats and canoes, tennis, winter sports, theatres, art museums, zoölogical gardens, golf, camps, swimming pools, and dancing pavilions. A great step forward in the development of the fee system in connection with the operation and maintenance of recreation facilities would be the universal adoption of specific authority for the park and recreation governing boards to retain the revenues derived therefrom in the park and recreation fund.[32]

Real estate developers have come to realize that playgrounds and open spaces are assets, and that the increase in the value of their adjacent property more than compensates for the value of the property devoted to a public use. Convenience and accessibility to sports and recreation centers are strong contributing factors to the making of a successful suburban community. That parks tend to raise the value of land in their vicinity and to fix permanently a desirable character of surroundings is unquestioned. It has been demonstrated by a special

---

[31] *Park Recreation Areas in the United States,* U. S. Bureau of Labor Statistics Bulletin, 1928, No. 462, pp. 3-4, 9.

[32] *Ibid.,* pp. 12-13.

study of the Essex County park system in New Jersey, which revealed increases of from 200 to 600 per cent in the assessed valuations of the environs of some of its parks in 11 years.[33] The story of the park development in Westchester County, New York, and its effect upon land values furnishes an even more illuminating instance of the way in which public open spaces create values. In 1923, the year which witnessed the beginning of Westchester's park system, the total assessed valuation of taxable property was $788,029,496. In 1926 the assessed valuation had grown to $1,143,871,106. In 1929, the figure was $1,644,114,324. The Westchester County Park Commission is able to claim that a large proportion of this increase is due to the park program, because the greatest enhancement of land values has taken place along the edges of parks, and many areas have been made ripe for development for which there was no previous demand. This County also furnishes one of the best examples of the financial benefit which a community derives from developing parkways. A recent investigation of the values of land situated within 500 feet of the Bronx River Parkway showed the extraordinary average increase of 800 per cent in 15 years.[34]

The Westchester County park program is in a number of respects one of the most significant in the history of public-park development. It is a system of both land and water parks and connecting parkways, reflecting the present-day need of diversified recreation and the enormous development of the automobile. Preserving the undisturbed natural beauty of field and woodland with a minimum of formal treatment, and taking full advantage of all modern resources of invention, materials, and methods, it has attempted to provide the widest possible range of recreational opportunities for the greatest numbers. The system includes three waterfront parks along the Hudson River and two with salt-water beaches on the Long Island Sound shore. One of the latter, Playland at Rye Beach, is a seaside amusement park. In the intervening region of diversified topography between the Hudson River and the Sound, there are many reservations and forest preserve areas tied together by a comprehensive system of connecting parkways. As now established, the park system embraces more than 17,000 acres of land, and about 160 miles of parkways with 36 miles of paved motor driveways completed. The various waterfront parks have a total of 9 miles of beaches and shore lines.

[33] *National Conference on Outdoor Recreation*, Senate Document, 1928, No. 158, p. 43.
[34] Lee F. Hanmer, *Public Recreation*, Regional Survey of New York and its Environs, 1928, V, 45.

The Westchester program is not wholly idealistic but is based on sound economic principles, resting fundamentally on the relation of parks to land values. This relationship is seen in two respects: first, the utilization for park purposes of the cheapest classes of land, such as rough woodlands and rocky hillsides difficult to utilize for residential or business uses, and marsh lands which may be developed with water features; second, the influence of parks and parkways in enhancing land values not only along the immediate frontages but throughout adjoining zones of considerable depth and area. As already mentioned, the park system has created very substantial tax revenues as an offset to the appropriations for land and improvements. Beyond the enhanced property values and the resultant increase in tax revenue, the Westchester County Park Commission has developed direct income from recreational features and services, which now fully balances the operating and maintenance charges that otherwise would become a tax burden. During 1929 the total operating and maintenance budget, exclusive of bond interest and amortization charges, was $1,544,208. The income from concessions and recreational features was $1,583,632, affording a surplus of $39,424, applicable against bond interest and amortization. The governing principle adopted by the Commission is that natural park lands involving little outlay beyond the cost of land should be entirely free; but that there should be moderate charges for special services such as bath houses, swimming pools, amusement-park features and golf courses. The Commission's experience is that people are not only willing to pay for their play—they prefer to.[35]

In acquiring areas for park purposes, the authorities exercise the right of eminent domain, which justifies the taking of private property for public uses. For the values taken compensation must be paid. If the authorities could go further and condemn more land than they intend or need to use for the park development and profit by the enhanced value of the surplus, park financing would be even more economical. The principle of excess condemnation, however, has not been widely used by park authorities, partly because in many sections of the country legal power is lacking, and because elsewhere sufficient public sentiment has not been developed to support public authorities in its use. Yet if this principle could be applied by park authorities, it would go far toward solving the question of how to

[35] V. Everit Macy, ''Parks in the Modern Manner,'' *The Survey*, July 1, 1930, 64:7:301-304, 333, 336.

finance the acquisition of land for several different types of park properties, especially in newer sections of cities.[36]

County Parks.—Until nearly the close of the last century the county courthouse site and the county fair grounds were almost the only county properties that functioned in any way as parks, and their use for this purpose was purely incidental to other primary functions. The courthouse site in county-seat municipalities, however, has always served as a kind of "intown" park for the people of the local community and the surrounding country, especially in rural districts. In many communities the county fair ground is being used for athletics, civic celebrations, and other forms of community recreation, and not a few of them have been transformed into genuine community parks.

In 1895, Essex County, New Jersey, undertook the pioneering effort of establishing a county park system. The idea was not of rural origin, but grew out of the metropolitan park needs of cities in this area, and was no doubt inspired in part by the example of the Boston Metropolitan Park District, established a few years earlier. Although the plan was eminently successful, it was adopted elsewhere very slowly. Prior to 1920 very few counties had acquired parks, but since that time a number of county park systems have been established in various sections of the country. Thirty-three out of approximately 3,050 counties in the United States were reported in 1928 as having one or more county parks, with a total area of some 67,000 acres. Of this amount, 47,600 acres, or over 70 per cent, were owned by Cook County, Illinois, and Westchester County, New York. While county parks are useful as units for handling metropolitan park problems, and while they could be important links between park provisions made by cities on the one hand and by states and the national government on the other, their greatest field of usefulness will be in providing recreational opportunities for the rural districts and the people in the thousands of small towns throughout the country. The limited number of communities under 2,500 population reporting parks is an index of the lack of play facilities in numerous villages and rural districts. Millions of small-town people have no park or playground space. Open fields and vacant lots they have, to be sure, but anyone who knows village life appreciates how inadequate these are for recreation without proper equipment and competent

[36] *Park Recreation Areas in the United States*, U. S. Bureau of Labor Statistics Bulletin, 1928, No. 462, p. 11.

leadership. Some form of county recreational plan will probably be the answer to the needs in villages and country places.[37]

State Parks and Highways.—Recent years have also witnessed a rapid development of state parks. The report of the survey of state parks and forests by the National Conference on State Parks, as of the spring of 1926, listed 578 state parks, with a total area of 2,613,271 acres; 156 state forests, with 1,699,900 acres, and 2,472,934 acres of other state lands, unorganized for but capable of recreational use; a total of 6,785,105 acres. Additions reported since that survey will bring the grand total to over 7,000,000 acres.[38]

By reason of the widespread ownership of passenger cars, highways are now being extensively used for pleasure. This is leading to efforts to preserve and enhance the scenic value of public roads and to tie the state road system up with the state parks. As an example of this new development, the Connecticut State Highway Department has established a landscape division. This recognizes the fact that modern road improvement is concerned directly and drastically with landscape architecture; that is to say, with the improvement of the scenery. The activities of this division include cleaning the roadside of excess brush and weeds; grading raw slopes and planting with shrubbery, vines and grass; removal of thousands of illegal signs; preservation of native flora; creation of "highway gardens" (strips of land left between the old and the new highways when curves are straightened out); provision of parking spaces at points of special interest; and the development of picnic grounds—activities designed to make motoring in Connecticut more agreeable. One hundred and thirty-six miles of state highways in Connecticut pass through state forests and 106 miles border these areas, as well as several hundred miles of town roads. The Connecticut State Park and Forest Commission advocates the maintenance for all time of belts of natural wild country between the rapidly growing cities. It also urges the acquisition of more land on public highways so as to control the scenic values.[39] The suggestion to add to the public highways the adjacent and appertaining scenery has already been carried out in New Hampshire and Oregon, which have passed laws empowering the state to acquire title, by gift or purchase, to lands along the state highway whenever such premises may have scenic value, and to pro-

[37] *Ibid.*, pp. 10, 15, 50.

[38] *National Conference on Outdoor Recreation*, Senate Document, 1928, No. 158, p. 45.

[39] *Report of the Connecticut State Park and Forest Commission*, Public Document No. 60, 1930, pp. 36-64.

tect and administer them as a part of the road property. A number of roadside reservations have been made in these states, a practice which verges on the state park system. Indeed, the state highway and the state park systems are vitally connected with one another.

All this awakening is having its repercussions in other fields. "The minute that people understand that the roads exist for pleasure even more than for business and that that pleasure feeds mainly on the beauty of the countryside, then it becomes plain that whatever besmirches the beauty of the roadside is a palpable offense against society. The billboards get the first impact of this discovery. They are so obvious a blot on the landscape, so clear an invasion of common rights, so abominable an expression of private gain and public loss, that no long impeachment is necessary. The only defense is that they are business—legitimate business. But when someone begins to figure that the tourist trade is business too, with a wider spread and a grander total (a recent estimate has placed the sum at $3,300,000,000 per annum) it looks silly to maintain the billboards any longer against their manifest threat to the goose of the golden eggs."[40]

The campaign against improperly placed billboards has taken several forms. From the legal standpoint, billboards can be controlled only by the police power, which is defined as the power to enact laws to promote the order, safety, health, morals, and general welfare of the community. To the extent that billboards destroy the safety of highways, they can readily be reached by law. Intersections, curves, and underpasses are favorite places for billboards because here the careful driver slows down. But these billboards often obscure the dangers lurking around the corner, hide the official warning signs, and distract the motorist's attention just when it is most needed for safe driving. It is simple to regulate the placing of these advertising signs in the interest of public safety. The chief campaign against billboards, however, has been waged on aesthetic grounds; they destroy the assets of natural beauty. "Behind the Alps lies Italy, and lest we forget, behind the billboards lies America."[41] One tourist complains:[42]

I am absolutely sure she wears them.

I am confident that no metal can touch me.

I do not doubt that it is good to the last drop.

[40] Frank A. Waugh, "Country Roads—Modern Style," *The Survey*, July 1, 1931, 66:7:352.
[41] *Judge*, May 14, 1927.
[42] Lawson Paynter, "That Is All I Ask," *Life*, August 19, 1926.

I am certain that a few cents make a whale of a difference.   ·

I am willing to bet my last dollar that it floats.

I am thoroughly convinced that it is time to retire.

I realize the necessity of keeping that schoolgirl complexion.

But I am now near the end of my auto trip and I *would* like to see a little scenery.

So far, the courts have usually been unwilling to include aesthetics in the term "general welfare," though the courts in New York and Massachusetts have formally recognized the aesthetic principle of regulating billboards. Massachusetts in 1918 adopted an amendment to its constitution which established the competency of the police power to regulate unsightly advertising on private property. Under this amendment the legislature has passed billboard laws and regulations giving to the division of highways general jurisdiction over advertising signs throughout the state. There is some indication that the courts in other states are moving away from the doctrine that billboard legislation must be based solely upon considerations of safety, health, and morals, and seem likely to recognize legislation based upon aesthetics alone as part of the "general welfare" of the community. This tendency will be greatly advanced by the development of public opinion on the subject.

Public opinion against improperly placed billboards is being organized by the National Council for the Protection of Roadside Beauty, the American Civic Association, which has long waged a fight against this nuisance, and other civic improvement associations. There is evidence that the campaign is having effect. There appears to be a growing recognition by advertisers that advertising that is offensive in itself does not pay, but actually creates a prejudice against the goods it aims to market. The Standard Oil Company of California voluntarily destroyed more than $100,000 worth of its signboards along the highways of the Pacific Coast. The public reaction was so favorable that officials of the company consider the loss of these signs one of the best business moves they have made. It is significant to find one of the great national corporations, itself lately an extensive billboard advertiser, sponsoring an effective campaign of its own to the same end. Its slogan is, "Shall we have scenic or sign-ic highways?" Of significance also is the action taken in 1925 by the Outdoor Advertising Association of America in adopting the following "Standards of Practice" as a five-year program:

1. No structures to be erected which will constitute hazards to traffic.

2. No structures to be erected which will mar or impair scenic beauty.

3. No structures to be erected within the limits of state or municipal highways (public right of way).

4. Structures to be erected only upon land owned or leased by the member companies.

5. No copy to offend the moral sense of the public or to suggest violation of the law.

6. No tacking, tying, pasting or placing cards, panels, or signs of any description, other than standard structures.

"This reads like a half dozen of really good resolutions; but it should be noted that all this is to be 'Progress Through Self-Regulation.' In other words, the billboard people themselves are to be the judges of what is good and what is not, both in the boards and their location. It seems quite clear that the outdoor advertising people already have a lively sense of the public indignation at the billboard excesses, and are trying to set their house in some sort of order so as to stave off as long as possible the inevitable regulation of billboards by the police power."[43]

Billboards are not the only nuisances which may destroy the beauty of a scenic route. "There are the hot-dog stands. The places where they sell barbecues, chewing gum, postcards, temperance drinks and sometimes drinks which are not so temperance. The 'farm' stands where they offer wormy apples. . . . The 'amusement parks' with their chained bear cubs, their merry-go-rounds, their dance halls, their rural dives. As one disgusted motorist said, 'All the main thoroughfares have become linear slums.' "[44] Westchester County has solved the problem on a large scale by adopting the expedient of buying the roadside along with the roadway, including both in the road system. These parkways, for that is actually what they are, may be 300 or 400 feet wide, varying according to topography and property lines, and thus include the whole area customarily defiled. The result is salutary. Whereas the ordinary state road in suburban regions tends to depress land values, the Westchester County boulevards provide delightful sites for residences, apartment houses, hotels, and other solid and legitimate business. The appreciation of adjoining real estate is sometimes sufficient to pay for the whole improvement.

Along with the state parks, roadside parks, and scenic reserves,

[43] Harold A. Caparn, "Milestones in the Progress of Outdoor Advertising Regulation," *City Planning*, July, 1926, 2:3:164-174 (173 quoted). Horace M. Albright, "Scenic Reserves," *The Saturday Evening Post*, Sept. 14, 1929, p. 45. *The Survey*, Jan. 15, 1931, 65:8:445.

[44] Frank A. Waugh, "Country Roads—Modern Style," *The Survey*, July 1, 1931, 66:7:352.

already described, have come other improvements to make the road more engaging to the public taste, as, for example, historical monuments and reservations. "Several of the houses where Lafayette slept and George Washington had his headquarters have been preserved, sometimes restored, marked and made accessible to respectable visitors. Perhaps the most notable example in this category should be Mr. Ford's restoration of the Wayside Inn in Sudbury, Massachusetts, but there are many, many others. The D.A.R.'s and the historical societies have been busy, titles have been placed giving information, caretakers have been put in charge to see that strangers are welcomed. Doesn't that make the motor trip more interesting?"[45]

Recreation Resources of Federal Lands.—The nation's enormous holdings of federal land, even now more than 585,000 square miles in combined area, were acquired originally with no idea of use for recreation, and today the greater part of these lands are held or administered for purposes directly or indirectly economic. Up to the World War only national parks, national military parks (now proposed as national historical parks), and national monuments were administered for non-economic uses. The public domain, greatest of all in area, and approximately one-half of the entire federal lands, was held for parceling in free gift, lease, or sale among those willing to acquire and use the land; the national forests, nearly as great in area, were administered chiefly for forest conservation, watershed protection and grazing; and a score of other kinds of federal lands performed as many other kinds of service, all ultimately contributing to the nation's material welfare.

Into this establishment, since the World War, a new and great force has been injected, creating a new order. The prosperity following the close of the War put the country on a motorized basis and tremendously increased the interest in outdoor recreation. Motor-born recreation became a popular institution which permeated the federal land fabric. It secured recognition as an additional use for lands in economic classifications, a use which in most cases does not seriously interfere with original economic uses. Today it is realized that many of the federal lands, besides serving an economic interest, embrace unique opportunities for recreation, education and inspiration, and that they complement in essential degree the opportunities for the enjoyment, knowledge, and appreciation of the land, water, forest, plant, scenic and wild life resources of the nation as a whole.[46] The

[45] *Ibid.*
[46] National Conference on Outdoor Recreation, *Recreation Resources of Federal Lands,* 1928, pp. 7-13.

reservation and administration of public lands for outdoor recreation, aesthetic enjoyment, historic or scientific appreciation, along with economic use, has now become an established federal policy.

1. *National Parks.*—The creation of Yellowstone National Park, in 1872, "as a public park or pleasuring ground" marked the genesis of the national park system, although no new parks were created until 1890. From 1872 to 1916, when the National Park Service was established, a total of 14 national parks had been created. During this period the parks were valued principally for the majesty of their scenery. People visited them with serious purpose, often at great expense of time and effort, in much the same spirit in which some of them also crossed the ocean to see the Alps, the Italian lakes, the fjords of Norway or the Himalayas. The national parks were neither popularly conceived nor officially presented as recreational. The development of the national parks as a great recreational asset came with the creation of the National Park Service in the Department of the Interior and the work of its first director, Stephen T. Mather, who more than anyone else was the founder or maker of our present national park system. Under the National Park Service, the parks became a correlated system, the number was increased, and their use by the people was advanced. From 1916 to 1929, when Mr. Mather retired, the number of parks had increased from 14 to 20, the number of national monuments under the Service from 18 to 32, the appropriations for maintenance and development from $253,646 to $4,754,015, revenues from $119,433 to $808,355, and the annual number of visitors from 334,799 to 3,024,844. In 1930 there were 21 national parks and 34 national monuments in the system, with a total area of 15,846 square miles, or about the size of Massachusetts, Connecticut, and Rhode Island. "They contain the finest and most distinctive scenery on the face of the earth and the most unusual and spectacular natural phenomena known to science. Many contain wilderness areas where there will be kept forever bits of original America in its primeval state, including some preserves for wild life. Nearly all are important for the opportunity they afford to keep intact native flora and landscape. They embrace historic and prehistoric structures and landmarks of outstanding national importance. Their educational and inspirational value to our people for all time to come in incalculable."[47]

[47] Horace M. Albright, "Mather, Maker of National Parks," *The Survey*, July 1, 1930, 64:7:293-296, 333, 336 (293 quoted).

Though recreation is a major use of the national parks—and the accessible areas are being provided with every necessary facility for enjoyment by the ever-increasing throng of visitors, and camping, hiking, fishing, motoring, and other outdoor sports are in every way encouraged—their chief value is similar to that of a great museum. The primary purpose of national parks is preservation of areas of extraordinary majesty and beauty in a condition of unmodified nature. Playground use must be coördinated as secondary to these primary principles and objectives. For a while, under the influence of the idea of national parks as the "people's playgrounds," there was little appreciation on the part of the many thousands of sightseers of this basic point of view, and the distinctive features of the park system were threatened by the injection of the spirit of commercialism. Park concessioners competed with hotel keepers, cafeteria proprietors and scenery vendors for the patronage of the new millions awheel, and amusements foreign to national-park custom were introduced. "Jazz" entered national parks about 1918 to help concessioners draw and hold crowds for the increase of their profits. The government permitted it because at that time concessioners with capital were hard to find and had to be encouraged. Not all the parks were profitable then as they are today. Then came the period of education and national appreciation, with a clearer analysis and definition of national park uses and usefulness. Education and inspiration are today seen as the highest uses of the system. The official educational establishment, begun in 1921, has a chief park naturalist with headquarters at Berkeley, California, and a park naturalist for nearly every park. Some parks have one or more permanent educational assistants and extra summer staffs. This is known as the Nature Guide Service. At each park is a more or less useful museum collection indifferently housed. Plans for educational and inspirational usefulness go far beyond these. The National Parks Association, which was organized in 1919 to promote educational and inspirational uses of the system, conceives it as a group of universities, or, collectively, as a Super-University of Nature in which each park may be considered a special school. Education and inspiration are very definitely seen as the highest uses of the system.[48]

2. *National Monuments.*—A forward step in the protection of historic landmarks, historic and prehistoric structures, and other objects of historic or scientific interest or national importance was taken in

[48] National Conference on Outdoor Recreation, *Recreation Resources of Federal Lands,* 1928, pp. 53-55.

1906 by the passage of the American Antiquities Act authorizing the President permanently to protect such objects as national monuments when situated upon lands owned or controlled by the United States. Under the provisions of this act, up to 1928, 58 national monuments have been established. Of these, 54, aggregating in area over 500,000 acres, are located in 19 states, and 4, aggregating over 2,000,000 acres, are located in Alaska. Some of the national monuments, such as the Muir Woods in California or the Petrified Forest in Arizona, are administered by the National Park Service; some, such as the Gila Cliff Dwellings in New Mexico or the Bryce Canyon in Utah, are administered by the Department of Agriculture; and some, such as Mound City in Ohio and Fort Niagara in New York, are administered by the War Department. In 1930 Congress turned over to the National Park Service Wakefield, the birthplace of President Washington. The creation of this monument definitely marks the entrance of the National Park Service into the field of preservation of historic shrines most cherished by the nation. There is every indication that the number of such monuments will be increased.

In the national monuments system one finds five classes of exhibits: (a) remains of prehistoric civilization, (b) historic relics, (c) geologic examples, (d) botanic reservations, and (e) one wild animal reservation. All are classed as scientific. Although many monuments are visited by pleasure-seeking motorists, the purpose for which they were created is preservation for scientific and educational use; they are recreational only in the broadest sense of the word.[49]

3. National Forests.—The national parks and the national monuments together comprise something more than 10 million acres of public lands. Far surpassing them in size are the national forests, 159 in number, aggregating about 160 million acres, or nearly 7 per cent of the total land area of the country. They are located in 30 states, chiefly in the West, as well as in Alaska and Porto Rico.

The present system of national forests dates from 1891 when Congress created the Yellowstone Park Timberland Reserve as a measure for conserving natural resources for their economic values. Although the forests have been devoted to economic purposes, their recreational use has always been recognized. "Americans turn naturally to the mountains and the woods for their outdoor recreation. If the woods and mountains are close to well populated districts it is inevitable that the citizens of the neighborhood will use them as camping grounds

[49] *Ibid.*, pp. 64 ff. Horace M. Albright, "Mather, Maker of National Parks," *The Survey*, July 1, 1930, 64:7:294.

and for hunting, fishing, tramping and other forms of life in the open for which they offer opportunities. It is for this reason that the national forests have been used for recreation in addition to the main purposes of timber production and watershed protection. Before the national forests were thought of, the people of the surrounding country used these areas, so far as conditions permitted, for recreation; after the establishment of the forests they simply continued this use and expanded it with the growth of population and the increased accessibility of the areas. The Forest Service did not create the idea of recreational use of the national forests; rather the public came in of its own accord, each year in increasing numbers, and the Forest Service recognizing that recreation was a resource, like timber and water, used its best efforts to see that it was so handled as to make the greatest returns to the national welfare consistent with the chief purposes for which the forests were established. The national forests embrace parts of every mountain system and almost every forest region in the United States; they form the natural outlets of large populations, to which they are the logical, near-by, economically enjoyed fields for outdoor sport and recreation. To millions of people the national forests are the natural and sometimes the only available playgrounds, other than their city parks. It is most vital to them that these areas should remain open for recreational purposes; but in this day of motors and good roads even the citizens of regions remote from the national forests have a direct personal interest in recreation grounds where they can feel free to camp and enjoy themselves in their own way, so long as they obey the rules of good citizenship and good sportsmanship while in the woods."[50]

The factor which in recent years has done most to increase the use of the national forests for outdoor recreation is the extension of the public highway system under the various acts of Congress. Through this instrumentality, the national forest areas, which previously had stood as partial barriers to free trans-state movement, have been made much more accessible to the motorist. As recreational use has increased in volume, the Forest Service has initiated certain activities not so much to promote recreation as to protect public property and public health. These facilities include water-supply, garbage pits, fireplaces, tables, benches, and shelters. At the close of 1930 there were approximately 1,700 camp grounds wholly or partially improved, 1,200 hotels,

[50] National Conference on Outdoor Recreation, *Recreation Resources of Federal Lands*, 1928, ch. VI, pp. 74-75 quoted.

resorts and summer camps, and 10,770 private summer homes operating under permit. Roads and well-marked trails are being extended to make the forests easily accessible, and there are countless spots along the banks of streams and lakes where the camper may pitch his tent, free of charge, although in some forests it is necessary to secure a campfire permit. During the year the forests were visited by over 30 million vacationists, including picnickers, motorists, hikers, campers, fishermen, hunters, hotel and resort visitors, and summer residents.[51]

The use of the national forests for recreational purposes creates a fire hazard, but at the same time it should operate to enlist greater public interest in fire prevention. "The aesthete justly inveighs against the Coney Islandization of the wilderness, but such vulgarism is a pin-prick measured against the progressively mounting acreage of forest lands devastated and blackened by fire and frequently robbed of economic and social values for years to come. The primary responsibility for this condition rests with the public. The larger number of forest fires are man caused, due to carelessness; a serious number are caused by lightning in the West."[52]

The primary thought in the promotion of recreation in federal forests is wilderness recreation. The term wilderness, as here used, means a region more or less forested and of considerable extent where primitive nature is modified in the least possible degree by human influence. It is a roadless area where primitive modes of travel and outdoor life may be enjoyed. Camping and exploration by pack train or canoe are the most familiar examples. Such regions are now very few and are practically confined to the national forests and national parks of the West and one of the national forests of the Lake States. While these areas have been getting scarcer, an increasing proportion of the people have become city-dwellers engaged in indoor occupations, and good roads and modern improvements and conveniences have become the regular order of things. Under these conditions, areas where virgin nature still reigns supreme become novel, interesting, and valuable.[53]

Recreational use is a public service compatible with the laws under which the forests are administered and with sound principles of land economy and public welfare. In the public and private forests of other countries, with long-established systems of forest management, public

[51] *Recreation*, Aug., 1931, 25:5:292-293.
[52] National Conference on Outdoor Recreation, *Recreation Resources of Federal Lands*, 1928, pp. 104, 105.
[53] *Ibid.*, pp. 86, 107, 109.

use for recreation is thoroughly recognized as an important form of land service. In this country, as population grows, urbanization increases, and economic and industrial development become more intensive, there will be an increasing need for opportunities for refreshment of body and spirit which the out-of-doors alone can give.

INDEX

A

Academies, 401-402

Accidents, industrial, 310, 316; traffic, 73-76

Adjustment, problem of, 3, 11, 411, 415-416, 671; law of, 395; science as an instrument of, 70, 71, 209-210, 220, 352

Adult education, 463-510; classification of agencies of, 466-467; commercialization of, 467, 480-485; defined, 466-467; the non-school type of, 489-510; the school type of, 467-488; vocational character of, 466, 467

Adulteration, 289-290

Advertising, billboard, 705-706; correspondence school, 482-484; motion picture, 620; newspaper, 521, 524-525, 526-527, 530-531, 560-561, 562; of nostrums, 296-300, 302; radio, 577-578

Akron, Ohio, 84, 493

American Antiquities Act, 711

American Civic Association, 706

American Heart Association, 384

American Library Association, 505, 631

American Magazine, 500

American Medical Association, 294, 295, 296, 297, 298, 299, 301, 302, 332

American Red Cross, 340, 371

Americanization, 463, 469, 497, 499, 658, 659

Ames, Winthrop, 634

Amusement parks, 603-605

Anonymity in city life, 137-138, 142-143, 582

Antioch College, 424

Antitoxin, 373, 375

Apartment hotels, 102, 140

Apprenticeship system, 416-417

Arcading, 78-79

Ashes, disposal of, 268-269, 270, 272, 274

Associated Literary Societies, 490-491

Associated Press, 555-556

Association for Improving the Condition of the Poor, 113, 117, 145

Association of Urban Universities, 475

Athens, Greece, 236, 289

Atlanta, Georgia, 79

Atlantic City, New Jersey, 28

Auchmuty, Colonel, 421

Australia, 190, 347, 653

Austria, 190, 191, 347

Automobile accidents, 73-76

Automobiles, 13, 44, 57, 80, 83; and highway development, 704; and park development, 699, 704, 708; and roadhouses, 570, 602; and street play, 679, 680; increase of, 71-72; recreational advantages of, 568-570

B

Babylonia, 217

Bacteria, 221, 241, 259, 260, 261, 262, 263, 284-285, 287; *see also* Disease germs

Bacteriology, 220-223, 224, 235-236, 242

"Bad housekeeping," 122

Baden-Powell, Sir Robert, 646, 648

Ballard School, 472

Ballyhoo, 536

Baltimore, Maryland, 35, 36, 270, 433, 454, 507, 526, 681

Baltimore *Sun*, 558

Barnard, Henry, 399, 400-401

Barnard College, 486

Barnett, Samuel A., 655-656; Mrs. Samuel A., 171

"Barrel-houses," 132

Battery Park, New York City, 104, 676

Bavaria, Germany, 417

715